D1571737

The New International Commentary
on the
New Testament

General Editors

Ned B. Stonehouse
(1946–1962)

F. F. Bruce
(1962–1990)

Gordon D. Fee
(1990–   )

The Letter of
JAMES

SCOT McKNIGHT

WILLIAM B. EERDMANS PUBLISHING COMPANY
GRAND RAPIDS, MICHIGAN / CAMBRIDGE, U.K.

Wm. B. Eerdmans Publishing Co.

2140 Oak Industrial Drive N.E., Grand Rapids, Michigan 49505 /

P.O. Box 163, Cambridge CB3 9PU U.K.

www.eerdmans.com

Printed in the United States of America

17 16 15 14 13 12 11   7 6 5 4 3 2 1

Library of Congress Cataloging-in-Publication Data

McKnight, Scot.

The letter of James / Scot McKnight.

p.   cm.   — (The new international commentary on the New Testament)

Includes bibliographical references and indexes.

ISBN 978-0-8028-2627-5 (alk. paper)

1. Bible. N.T. James — Commentaries.   I. Title.

BS2785.53.M37   2011

227'.91077 — dc22

2010040751

For
Aksel

Grant, O God, that, following the example of your servant James, the brother of our Lord, your Church may give itself continually to prayer and to the reconciliation of all who are at variance and enmity; through Jesus Christ our Lord, who lives and reigns with you and the Holy Spirit, one God, now and for ever. Amen.†

The Book of Common Prayer

For the LORD your God is God of gods and Lord of lords, the great God, mighty and awesome, who is not partial and takes no bribe, who executes justice for the orphan and the widow, and who loves the strangers, providing them food and clothing.

Deuteronomy 10:17-18

A disciple is not above the teacher, but everyone who is fully qualified will be like the teacher.

Luke 6:40

At the Council of Jerusalem, the Jewish Christians asked themselves whether Christians from among the Gentiles could be saved if they were not willing to be circumcised and to observe the Mosaic law. A century later, it was the pagan Christians who were asking themselves whether a Christian who observed the law of Moses could obtain his salvation.

Pierre-Antoine Bernheim, *James, the Brother of Jesus*

Der Jakobus brief ist rehabilitiert.

Walther Bindemann, "Weisheit versus Weisheit"

The critical question is not the one we put to the text but the one that the text puts to us.

Luke Timothy Johnson, "Reading Wisdom Wisely"

CONTENTS

Editor's Preface   x

Author's Preface   xi

Abbreviations   xiii

Bibliography   xix

INTRODUCTION   **1**

JAMES IN THE STORY   4

JAMES: WHO WROTE THE LETTER?   13

    James, Brother of Jesus, in the New Testament   16

    James, Brother of Jesus, outside the New Testament   20

    James, Brother of Jesus, and the Letter   23

    James, Brother of Jesus, and the Greek Style of James   28

    James, Brother of Jesus, and Theology   34

WHAT ARE THE CENTRAL THEMES OF JAMES?   39

    God   42

    Ethics   43

WHAT IS THE STRUCTURE OF JAMES?   47

COMMENTARY   **59**

1. SALUTATION (1:1)   59

2. THE CHRISTIAN AND TRIALS (1:2-18)   68

2.1. The Purpose of Testing (1:2-4)   69

2.2. The Need for Wisdom during Testing (1:5-8)   83

2.3. Poverty and Wealth as a Test (1:9-11)   93

2.4. God, Trials, and Testing (1:12-18)   104

    Excursus: Macarisms in Context   106

3. GENERAL EXHORTATIONS (1:19-27)   133

3.1. An Exhortation on Speech (1:19-21)   134

3.2. An Exhortation on Hearing and Doing (1:22-25)   145

3.3. An Exhortation on Pure Religion (1:26-27)   162

4. THE CHRISTIAN AND PARTIALITY (2:1-13)   173

4.1. Inconsistency (2:1-4)   174

4.2. Interrogation (2:5-7)   190

4.3. Instruction (2:8-13)   203

5. THE CHRISTIAN AND WORKS (2:14-26)   224

5.1. Interrogation (2:14-17)   226

5.2. Challenge and Responses (2:18-26)   233

    Brief Excursus: James and Paul   259

6. GENERAL EXHORTATIONS FOR TEACHERS (3:1–4:12)   264

6.1. Teachers and the Tongue (3:1-12)   264

6.2. Teachers and Wisdom (3:13-18)   297

6.3. Teachers and Dissensions (4:1-10)   318

6.4. Teachers, the Community and the Tongue (4:11-12)   358

7. THE MESSIANIC COMMUNITY AND THE WEALTHY (4:13–5:11)   366

7.1. The Sin of Presumption (4:13-17)   366

7.2. The Sin of Oppression (5:1-6)   379

7.3. The Messianic Community's Response to the Wealthy (5:7-11)   400

8. CONCLUDING EXHORTATIONS (5:12-20)   423

8.1. Oaths (5:12)   423

8.2. Prayer and Healing in the Community (5:13-18)   430

8.3. Three Ecclesial Conditions and Three Responses (5:13-14)   432

8.4. The Need for the Prayer of Faith (5:15a)   440

8.5. The Promise of Forgiveness (5:15b)   442

8.6. The Exhortation to Confession (5:16a)   445

8.7. The Need for Righteous Persons to Pray (5:16b-18)   448

8.8. Communal Restoration (5:19-20)   452

INDEXES

Authors   462

Subjects   471

Scripture References   473

Extrabiblical Ancient Literature   492

EDITOR'S PREFACE

It has now been thirty-five years since the original commentary on the Epistle of James, written by James Adamson, appeared in this series (in 1976). Since the publication of that commentary, which served its generation well, there has been a considerable proliferation of interest and scholarly literature on this Epistle — long overdue in Protestant circles who had labored far too long under Luther's damning pronouncement that it was "a right strawy epistle." The present commentary has been written by one who has played a significant role in bringing about this much-needed corrective.

At the turn of the present century a replacement commentary on this Epistle had been assigned to Donald J. Verseput of Bethel Seminary. But his untimely death in 2004 at the age of 51 also brought momentary closure to that chapter for this commentary series. So it was a moment of considerable delight when a couple of years later Scot McKnight consented to pick up this task. Those who use/read this commentary will quickly recognize what a fortunate decision that has turned out to be.

Here is a commentary that is accessible to a broad readership, at once full of insight and of (that all-too-often missing) good sense and wit in commentary writing that make for both good reading and an especially helpful source for consultation as to what James is about. I therefore take special pleasure in introducing it to the larger community of pastors and scholars, who will find much help here.

GORDON D. FEE

AUTHOR'S PREFACE

I first began teaching James in the mid 1980s. My classes were mostly seminary students and we dug into the Greek text and read the standard commentaries. This commentary began in and reflects that setting. Along with digging into the Greek text, I cut my teeth by reading a few commentaries, including those by F. J. A. Hort, J. B. Mayor, M. Dibelius, C. L. Mitton, P. Davids, S. Laws, R. P. Martin, and the predecessor in this series, J. B. Adamson, and Adamson's lengthy volume on the theology of James. At that time my colleague Doug Moo was writing a small commentary on James and we had many conversations in passing about James. I cannot forget the original flush of discoveries I had with my students and the above-mentioned commentaries. A bonus for me has been that Doug Moo wrote a second commentary on James and part of the final preparation of this commentary was reading his second work. I consider it a privilege to have been his student and colleague, and even more to be a friend. A former colleague at North Park University, a classicist, David Nystrom, also wrote a commentary on James, and I recall a number of conversations with him about James as he was writing what I think is the most useful commentary on James for preachers. His facility in the ancient sources of Rome and Greece gives his commentary a special edge.

But this is not a commentary on commentaries or the ins and outs of scholarly suggestions on every point that can be raised about this most vexing of early Christian letters. In fact, every time I left a passage to begin a new one I sensed I had ignored scholars who deserved more interaction, and I apologize now to those I have neglected and to those from whom I have learned and whose names might not appear in the footnotes. Hence, this commentary will be my own interaction with the text of James. It is shaped from beginning to end for pastors, preachers, and teachers — in other words, it is an *ecclesial* commentary that attempts to expound the meaning of the text. I hope it is as much *sapientia* as it is *scientia,* wisdom as science. I do not have a pet theory about James to argue. Some find the theme of wisdom in every verse while others find poverty everywhere and yet others find ideological rhetoric everywhere. I have learned from such technical studies, but my interests are less on shedding fresh light and more on providing for preachers and teachers a commentary shaped for those who want to explain James and his significance to congregations and classes.

Throughout this commentary I have compared the NRSV with the TNIV as my two preferred translations. After I had competed the commentary it was announced that Zondervan was going to quit publishing the TNIV. My use of it in this commentary will now serve as a memorial to a useful translation.

When I was a professor at Trinity Evangelical Divinity School, my graduate assistant, John Raymond, amassed an excellent bibliography on James that has stood the test of time for me. Chris Ridgeway, my assistant now at North Park University, has generously done bibliographic tasks that, had they been left to me, would certainly delayed the completion of this commentary, and I am grateful for his assistance. Elaine Halama at North Park University's Brandel Library deserves thanksgiving beyond words for her uncommon diligence and skill. Several of my former students, now professors themselves, have read portions or all of this manuscript and I wish here to express my appreciation to them: Sam Lamerson, Doug Huffman, Matt Williams, Jon Lunde, and Steve Bryan. My colleague Joel Willitts and I have enjoyed more than a few discussions of James.

I am grateful to the Eerdmans family, not the least of my reasons being that as a college student I "hung out" at The Bookstore, became friends with Casey Lambregste, and dreamed that someday I would write a commentary in this series. I express my gratitude to Bill and Anita Eerdmans and to Sam, whom I met when he was a high-schooler and tending The Bookstore. For years I have had conversations about the Cubs with Reinder Van Til and Jann Myers. Gordon Fee invited me to write James after I finked out on Matthew, and I thank him for his grace. I also want to thank John Simpson for his patience and care in editing and Drew Strait for his help with the indexes.

This book is dedicated to our grandson, Aksel Donovan Nelson McKnight, a gift to our family from our son Lukas and his wonderful wife Annika.

*　　*　　*

A moment of silence. James readers already miss Don Verseput, a peaceful, wise James scholar whose untimely passing makes us consciously aware of not only the fragility of life but also our fellowship around this letter. Don's singular contributions were building toward larger contributions.

καρπὸς δὲ δικαιοσύνης
ἐν εἰρήνῃ σπείρεται τοῖς ποιοῦσιν εἰρήνην.

ABBREVIATIONS

AB	Anchor Bible
ABC	*African Bible Commentary* (ed. T. Adeyemo et al.; Grand Rapids: Zondervan, 2006)
ABD	*Anchor Bible Dictionary*
ABR	*Australian Biblical Review*
ABRL	Anchor Bible Reference Library
ACC: James	*James, 1-2 Peter, 1-3 John, Jude* (Ancient Christian Commentary, ed. G. Bray; Downers Grove: InterVarsity, 2000)
ANF	Ante-Nicene Fathers
ANRW	*Aufstieg und Niedergang der römischen Welt*
Ant	Josephus, *Antiquitates Judaicae (The Jewish Antiquities)*
2 Apoc. Jas.	*Second Apocalypse of James*
ATJ	*Ashland Theological Journal*
ATR	*Anglican Theological Review*
b	Babylonian Talmud
BBR	*Bulletin for Biblical Research*
BDAG	W. Bauer, W. F. Arndt, F. W. Gingrich, and F. W. Danker, *A Greek-English Lexicon of the New Testament and Other Early Christian Literature* (3d ed.; Chicago: University of Chicago Press, 2000)
BDB	F. Brown, S. R. Driver, and C. A. Briggs, *A Hebrew and English Lexicon of the Old Testament* (Oxford: Clarendon, 1907)
BDF	F. Blass, A. Debrunner, and R. W. Funk, *A Greek Grammar of the New Testament and Other Early Christian Literature* (Chicago: University of Chicago Press, 1961); all references are to paragraph number. I have checked this in every instance against the German

	edition of F. Rehkopf, *Grammatik des neutestamentlichen Griechisch* (15th ed.; Göttingen: Vandenhoeck und Ruprecht, 1979).
BETL	Bibliotheca ephemeridum theologicarum lovaniensium
BHT	Beiträge zur historischen Theologie
Biblical Social Values	*Biblical Social Values and Their Meaning: A Handbook* (ed. J. J. Pilch, B. J. Malina; Peabody: Hendrickson, 1993)
BibSac	*Bibliotheca Sacra*
BIS	Biblical Interpretation Series
B.J.	Josephus, *Bellum Judaicum (The Jewish War)*
BNTC	Black's New Testament Commentaries
BTB	*Biblical Theology Bulletin*
BWANT	Beiträge zur Wissenschaft vom Alten und Neuen Testament
BZ	*Biblische Zeitschrift*
BZNW	Beihefte zur Zeitschrift für die neutestamentliche Wissenschaft
CBQ	*Catholic Biblical Quarterly*
CBR	*Currents in Biblical Research*
CHJ	*Cambridge History of Judaism,* vol. 3 (ed. W. D. Davies and L. Finkelstein; Cambridge: Cambridge University Press, 1999)
CNT	Commentaire de Nouveau Testament
CNTOT	*Commentary on the New Testament Use of the Old Testament* (ed. G. K. Beale and D. A. Carson; Grand Rapids: Baker, 2007)
CRBS	*Currents in Research: Biblical Studies*
DBSJ	*Detroit Baptist Seminary Journal*
Did	*Didache*
DJG	*Dictionary of Jesus and the Gospels* (ed. J. B. Green, S. McKnight, and I. H. Marshall; Downers Grove: InterVarsity, 1992)
DLNTD	*Dictionary of the Later New Testament and Its Developments* (ed. R. P. Martin and P. H. Davids; Downers Grove: InterVarsity, 1997)
DMT	*Dictionary of Mission Theology* (ed. J. M. Corrie; Downers Grove: InterVarsity, 2007)
DNTB	*Dictionary of New Testament Background* (ed. C. A. Evans and S. E. Porter; Downers Grove: InterVarsity, 2000).
DOTHB	*Dictionary of the Old Testament: Historical Books* (ed.

	B. T. Arnold and H. G. M. Williamson; Downers Grove: InterVarsity, 2005)
DOTP	*Dictionary of the Old Testament: Pentateuch* (ed. T. D. Alexander and D. W. Baker; Downers Grove: InterVarsity, 2003)
DOTWPW	*Dictionary of the Old Testament: Wisdom, Poetry, and Writings* (ed. T. Longman and P. Enns; Downers Grove: InterVarsity, 2008)
DPL	*Dictionary of Paul and His Letters* (ed. G. F. Hawthorne and R. P. Martin; Downers Grove: InterVarsity, 1993)
DTIB	*Dictionary for Theological Interpretation of the Bible* (ed. K. J. Vanhoozer et al.; Grand Rapids: Baker, 2005)
ÉBib	Études bibliques
Eccl Hist	Eusebius, *Ecclesiastical History*
ECM	*Editio Critica Maior, Novum Testamentum Graecum* (4.1-2, ed. B. Aland, K. Aland, G. Mink, K. Wachtel; Stuttgart: Deutsche Bibelgesellschaft, 1997)
EDNT	*Exegetical Dictionary of the New Testament* (3 vols., ed. H. Balz and G. Schneider; Grand Rapids: Eerdmans, 1990-93)
EH	Europäischen Hochschulschriften
EJ	*The Encyclopedia of Judaism* (3 vols., ed. J. Neusner et al.; New York: Continuum, 1999).
EQ	*Evangelical Quarterly*
ÉTR	*Études Théologiques et Religieuses*
FF	Foundations and Facets
FRLANT	Forschungen zur Religion und Literatur des Alten und Neuen Testaments
FzB	Forschungen zur Bibel
GBWW	Great Books of the Western World
GEL	*Greek-English Lexicon of the New Testament: Based on Semantic Domains* (2 vols., ed. J. P. Louw and E. A. Nida; 2d ed.; New York: United Bible Societies, 1989).
HNT	Handbuch zum Neuen Testament
HTKNT	Herders theologischer Kommentar zum Neuen Testament
HTR	*Harvard Theological Review*
HvTSt	*Hervormde teologiese studies*
IBS	*Irish Biblical Studies*
ICC	International Critical Commentary
Int	*Interpretation*
ISBE	*International Standard Bible Encyclopedia* (4 vols., ed. G. Bromiley et al.; Grand Rapids: Eerdmans, 1979-88)

IVPWBC	*The IVP Women's Bible Commentary* (ed. C. C. Kroeger and M. J. Evans; Downers Grove: InterVarsity, 2002)
JBL	*Journal of Biblical Literature*
JJS	*Journal of Jewish Studies*
JPB	E. P. Sanders, *Judaism: Practice and Belief 63* BCE–66 CE (Philadelphia: Trinity, 1992)
JPFC	See Safrai below.
JPT	*Journal of Pentecostal Theology*
JPTSS	Journal of Pentecostal Theology, Supplement Series
JSNT	*Journal for the Study of the New Testament*
JSNTSup	Journal for the Study of the New Testament, Supplements
JSS	*Journal of Semitic Studies*
JSSR	*Journal for the Scientific Study of Religion*
JTS	*Journal of Theological Studies*
LB	*Linguistica Biblica*
LCL	Loeb Classical Library
LEC	Library of Early Christianity
LNTS	Library of New Testament Studies
LS	*Louvain Studies*
LSJ	*A Greek-English Lexicon* (ed. H. G. Liddell, R. Scott, H. S. Jones, and R. McKenzie; New York: Oxford University Press, 1968)
m	Mishnah
MHT	J. H. Moulton, W. F. Howard, and N. Turner, *A Grammar of New Testament Greek* (4 vols.; Edinburgh: Clark, 1906-76)
M-M	J. H. Moulton and G. Milligan, *The Vocabulary of the Greek Testament Illustrated from the Papyri and Other Non-Literary Sources* (1914-15; reprint, Grand Rapids: Eerdmans, 1972)
NCBC	New Century Bible Commentary
NDBT	*New Dictionary of Biblical Theology* (ed. T. D. Alexander and B. S. Rosner; Downers Grove: InterVarsity, 2000)
Nestle-Aland[27]	K. Aland et al., *Novum Testamentum Graece* (27th ed.; Stuttgart: Deutsche Bibelstiftung, 1993)
New Docs	*New Documents Illustrating Early Christianity* (ed. G. H. R. Horsley and S. R. Llewelyn; North Ryde: Ancient History Documentary Research Centre, Macquarie University, 1981-; Grand Rapids: Eerdmans, 1998-; cited by year and page)
NICNT	New International Commentary on the New Testament
NIDNTT	*New International Dictionary of New Testament Theology*

	(3 vols., ed. L. Coenen, E. Beyreuther, H. Bietenhard, and C. Brown; Grand Rapids: Zondervan, 1975-78)
NIGTC	New International Greek Testament Commentary
NovT	*Novum Testamentum*
NovTSup	Novum Testamentum Supplements
NRSV	New Revised Standard Version
NRTh	*La nouvelle revue théologique*
NTD	Neue Testament Deutsch
NTS	*New Testament Studies*
OCD	*Oxford Classical Dictionary* (3d ed., ed. S. Hornblower and A. Spawforth; New York: Oxford University Press, 1996)
Omanson	R. L. Omanson, *A Textual Guide to the Greek New Testament: An Adaptation of Bruce M. Metzger's* Textual Commentary *for the Needs of Translators* (Stuttgart: Deutsche Bibelgesellschaft, 2006)
ÖTK	Ökumenischer Taschenbusch-Kommentar zum Neuen Testament
OTP	*Old Testament Pseudepigrapha* (2 vols., ed. J. H. Charlesworth; New York: Doubleday, 1983)
PBM	Paternoster Biblical Monographs
PIBA	*Proceedings of the Irish Biblical Association*
PPJ	E. P. Sanders, *Paul and Palestinian Judaism* (Philadelphia: Fortress, 1977)
Pss Sol	*Psalms of Solomon*
RB	*Revue Biblique*
RevExp	*Review and Expositor*
RHPR	*Revue d'histoire et de philosophie religieuses*
Safrai, *JPFC*	S. Safrai, M. Stern, et al., *The Jewish People in the First Century* (2 vols.; Philadelphia: Fortress, 1974-76)
SB	Sources Bibliques
SBLDS	SBL Dissertation Series
SBLSBS	SBL Sources for Biblical Study
SBLSS	SBL Symposium Series
SBTS	Sources for Biblical and Theological Study
Schürer	E. Schürer, *The History of the Jewish People in the Age of Jesus Christ (175 B.C.–A.D. 135)* (4 vols.; rev. ed., ed. G. Vermes et al.; Edinburgh: Clark, 1973-87)
SNTSMS	Society for New Testament Studies Monograph Series
SNTW	Studies of the New Testament and Its World
Spicq	C. Spicq, *Theological Lexicon of the New Testament* (3 vols., trans. J. D. Ernest; Peabody: Hendrickson, 1994)

ST	*Studia Theologica*
STK	*Svensk teologisk kvartalskrift*
Str-B	H. Strack and P. Billerbeck, *Kommentar zum Neuen Testament aus Talmud und Midrasch* (6 vols. in 7; Munich: Beck, 1922-61)
SUNT	Studien zur Umwelt des Neuen Testaments
TDNT	*Theological Dictionary of the New Testament* (ed. G. Kittel and G. Friedrich, trans. G. Bromiley; Grand Rapids: Eerdmans, 1964-76)
TDOT	*Theological Dictionary of the Old Testament* (ed. by G. J. Botterweck and H. Ringgren; Grand Rapids: Eerdmans, 1974-)
THKNT	Theologischer Handkommentar zum Neuen Testament
TLOT	*Theological Lexicon of the Old Testament* (3 vols., ed. E. Jenni and C. Westermann; Peabody: Hendrickson, 1997)
TLZ	*Theologische Literaturzeitung*
TNIV	Today's New International Version
TNTC	Tyndale New Testament Commentary
TrinJ	*Trinity Journal*
TRu	*Theologische Rundschau*
TynBul	*Tyndale Bulletin*
TZ	*Theologische Zeitschrift*
WBC	Word Biblical Commentary
WiS	*Women in Scripture: A Dictionary of Named and Unnamed Women in the Hebrew Bible, the Apocryphal/ Deuterocanonical Books, and the New Testament* (ed. C. Meyers et al.; Boston: Houghton Mifflin, 2000; Grand Rapids: Eerdmans, 2001)
WTJ	*Westminster Theological Journal*
WUNT	Wissenschaftliche Untersuchungen zum Neuen Testament
ZKT	*Zeitschrift für katholische Theologie*
ZNW	*Zeitschrift für die neutestamentliche Wissenschaft*
ZTK	*Zeitschrift für Theologie und Kirche*

BIBLIOGRAPHY

I have made no attempt to provide a complete bibliography for James. For a now only slightly dated but more complete bibliography, see the commentary by W. Popkes, xviii-xxxviii.

COMMENTARIES ON JAMES

These commentaries are referred to by the author's last name.

Adamson, J. B. *The Epistle of James* (NICNT; Grand Rapids: Eerdmans, 1976).
Andria, Solomon. "James," *ABC*, 1509-16.
Bauckham, R. A. *James* (London: Routledge, 1999).
Blomberg, C. L., and M. J. Kamell. *James* (Zondervan Exegetical Commentary on the New Testament; Grand Rapids: Zondervan, 2008).
Brosend, W. F., II. *James and Jude* (New Cambridge Bible Commentary; Cambridge: Cambridge University Press, 2004).
Burchard, C. *Der Jakobusbrief* (HNT 15/1; Tübingen: Mohr, 2000).
Byron, G. L. "James" in *True to Our Native Land: An African American New Testament Commentary* (ed. B. K. Blount, et al.; Minneapolis: Fortress, 2007), 461-75.
Calvin, John. *Commentaries on the Catholic Epistles* (trans. and ed. J. Owen; reprint, Grand Rapids: Baker, 1999).
Cantinat, J. *Les Épîtres de Saint Jacques et de Saint Jude* (SB; Paris: Gabalda, 1973).
Chaine, J. *Les Épître de Saint Jacques* (ÉBib; Paris: Gabalda, 1927).
Davids, P. H. *The Epistle of James: A Commentary on the Greek Text* (NIGTC; Grand Rapids: Eerdmans, 1982).
Dibelius, M. *James: A Commentary on the Epistle of James* (Hermeneia; trans. M. A. Williams, ed. H. Koester; Philadelphia: Fortress, 1976).
Doriani, D. M. *James* (Reformed Expository Commentary; Phillipsburg: Presbyterian and Reformed, 2007).
Evans, M. J. "James," *IVPWBC*.

Frankemölle, H. *Der Brief des Jakobus* (2 vols.; ÖTK 17.1, 2; Gütersloh: Gütersloher Verlagshaus, 1994).

Grünzweig, F. *Der Brief des Jakobus* (5th ed.; Wuppertaler Studienbibel; Wuppertal: Brockhaus, 1982).

Guthrie, G. H. *James* (Expositor's Bible Commentary 13; rev. ed.; Grand Rapids: Zondervan, 2006).

Hartin, P. J. *James* (Sacra Pagina 14; Collegeville: Liturgical, 2003).

Hoppe, R. *Jakobusbrief* (Stuttgarter Kleiner Kommentar Neues Testament 15; Stuttgart: Katholisches Bibelwerk, 1989).

Hort, F. J. A. *The Epistle of James: The Greek Text with Introduction, Commentary as far as Chapter IV, Verse 7, and Additional Notes* (London: Macmillan, 1909).

Isaacs, M. E. *Reading Hebrews and James* (Macon: Smyth and Helwys, 2002).

Johnson, L. T. *The Letter of James* (AB 37A; New York: Doubleday, 1995).

Johnstone, R. *Lectures Exegetical and Practical on The Epistle of James* (Grand Rapids: Baker, 1954).

Laws, S. *A Commentary on the Epistle of James* (BNTC; London: Black, 1980).

Martin, R. P. *James* (WBC 48; Waco: Word, 1988).

Mayor, J. B. *The Epistle of St. James* (Grand Rapids: Zondervan, 1954 [1913]).

Mitton, C. L. *The Epistle of James* (Grand Rapids: Eerdmans, 1966).

Moo, D. J. *The Letter of James* (Pillar New Testament Commentary; Grand Rapids: Eerdmans, 2000).

Mussner, F. *Der Jakobusbrief* (HTKNT 13/1; 5th ed.; Freiburg: Herder, 1987).

Nystrom, D. P. *James* (NIV Application Commentary; Grand Rapids: Zondervan, 1997).

Perkins, P. *First and Second Peter, James and Jude* (Interpretation: A Bible Commentary for Teaching and Preaching; Louisville: John Knox, 1995).

Plummer, A. *The General Epistles of St. James and St. Jude* (New York: Armstrong, 1903).

Popkes, W. *Der Brief des Jakobus* (THKNT 14; Leipzig: Evangelische Verlagsanstalt, 2001).

Reicke, B. I. *The Epistles of James, Peter, and Jude* (AB 37; Garden City: Doubleday, 1964).

Robertson, A. T. *Studies in the Epistle of James* (New York: Doran, 1915).

Ropes, J. H. *A Critical and Exegetical Commentary on the Epistle of St. James* (ICC; Edinburgh: Clark, 1916).

Schrage, W., and H. R. Balz. *Die katholischen Briefe* (NTD 10; 14th ed., 4th rev.; Göttingen: Vandenhoeck und Ruprecht, 1993).

Sidebottom, E. M. *James, Jude, 2 Peter* (NCBC; Grand Rapids: Eerdmans, 1967).

Sleeper, C. F. *James* (Abingdon New Testament Commentary: Nashville: Abingdon, 1998).

Tamez, E. *The Scandalous Message of James: Faith without Works Is Dead* (rev. ed.; New York: Crossroad, 2002).

Tasker, R. V. G. *The General Epistle of James* (TNTC; Grand Rapids: Eerdmans, 1957).

Vouga, F. *L'Épître de Saint Jacques* (CNT 2d series 13a; Geneva: Labor et Fides, 1984).

Wall, R. W. *Community of the Wise: The Letter of James* (The New Testament in Context; Valley Forge: Trinity, 1997).

Witherington, B., III. *Letters and Homilies for Jewish Christians: A Socio-Rhetorical Commentary on Hebrews, James and Jude* (Downers Grove: InterVarsity, 2007).

STANDARD TEXTS AND TRANSLATIONS

In quotations of ancient texts I have generally followed, in addition to *ECM* and *OTP*, the following published texts and translations.

Epstein, I., ed., *The Babylonian Talmud* (18 vols.; London: Soncino, 1978).

García Martínez, F. *The Dead Sea Scrolls Translated: The Qumran Texts Translated* (2d ed., trans. W. G. E. Watson; Grand Rapids: Eerdmans, 1996).

Hennecke, E., and W. Schneemelcher, eds. *New Testament Apocrypha* (2 vols.; rev. ed., ed. W. Schneemelcher, trans. R. M. Wilson; Louisville: Westminster John Knox, 1991-92).

Neusner, J. *The Mishnah: A New Translation* (New Haven: Yale University Press, 1988).

Wise, M., M. Abegg, and E. Cook. *The Dead Sea Scrolls: A New Translation* (San Francisco: HarperSanFrancisco, 1996).

I have also made use of translations in the Loeb Classical Library, The Ante-Nicene Fathers, and The Nicene and Post-Nicene Fathers.

OTHER LITERATURE

Adamson, J. B. *James: The Man and His Message* (Grand Rapids: Eerdmans, 1989).

Allison, D. C., Jr. *The End of the Ages Has Come: An Early Interpretation of the Passion and Resurrection of Jesus* (Philadelphia: Fortress, 1985).

———. "Exegetical Amnesia in James," *ETL* 76 (2000) 162-66.

———. *Studies in Matthew* (Grand Rapids: Baker, 2005).

Aymer, M. P. *First Pure, Then Peaceable: Frederick Douglass, Darkness and the Epistle of James* (LNTS 379; London: Clark, 2007).

Baker, W. R. "Christology in the Epistle of James," *EQ* 74 (2002) 47-57.

———. *Personal Speech-Ethics in the Epistle of James* (WUNT 2.68; Tübingen: Mohr, 1995).

Baltzer, K. *Deutero-Isaiah: A Commentary on Isaiah 40–55* (Hermeneia; trans. M. Kohl; Minneapolis: Fortress, 2001).

Banks, R. *Paul's Idea of Community* (rev. ed.; Peabody: Hendrickson, 1994).

Batten, A. "God in the Letter of James: Patron or Benefactor?" *NTS* 50 (2004) 257-72.

Bauckham, R. "James and the Gentiles (Acts 15.13-21)," in *History, Literature, and Society in the Book of Acts* (ed. B. Witherington, III; Cambridge: Cambridge University Press, 1996), 154-84.

———. "James and the Jerusalem Church," in *The Book of Acts in Its Palestinian Setting* (The Book of Acts in Its First Century Setting 4, ed. R. Bauckham; Grand Rapids: Eerdmans, 1995), 415-80.

———. "James, 1 and 2 Peter, Jude," in Carson and Williamson, eds., *It Is Written,* 303-17.

———. *James: Wisdom of James, Disciple of Jesus the Sage* (London: Routledge, 1999).

———. *Jude and the Relatives of Jesus in the Early Church* (Edinburgh: Clark, 1990).

———. "Peter, James and the Gentiles," in Chilton and Evans, eds., *Missions,* 91-142.

Becker, J. *Christian Beginnings: Word and Community from Jesus to Post-Apostolic Times* (trans. A. S. Kidder and R. Krauss; Louisville: Westminster John Knox, 1993).

Bernheim, P.-A. *James, Brother of Jesus* (trans. J. Bowden; London: SCM, 1997).

Bindemann, W. "Weisheit versus Weisheit: Der Jakobusbrief als innerkirchlichen Diskurs," *ZNW* 86 (1995) 189-217.

Blenkinsopp, J. *Sage, Priest, Prophet: Religious and Intellectual Leadership in Ancient Israel* (Louisville: Westminster John Knox, 1995).

Bockmuehl, M. "Antioch and James the Just," in Chilton and Evans, eds., *James the Just,* 155-98; rev. ed. in Bockmuehl, *Jewish Law,* 49-83, as "James, Israel and Antioch."

———. *Jewish Law in Gentile Churches: Halakhah and the Beginning of Christian Public Ethics* (Edinburgh: Clark, 2000).

———. "The Noachide Commandments and New Testament Ethics: With Special Reference to Acts 15 and Pauline Halakhah," *RB* 102 (1995) 72-101; rev. ed. in Bockmuehl, *Jewish Law,* 145-73, as "The Noachide Commandments and New Testament Ethics."

Boyarin, D. *Border Lines: The Partition of Judaeo-Christianity* (Philadelphia: University of Pennsylvania Press, 2004).

Brown, R. E. *The Birth of the Messiah: A Commentary on the Infancy Narratives in the Gospels of Matthew and Luke* (ABRL; rev. ed.; New York: Doubleday, 1993).

———. *New Testament Essays* (Garden City: Doubleday, 1968).

Brown, W. P. *Character in Crisis: A Fresh Approach to the Wisdom Literature of the Old Testament* (Grand Rapids: Eerdmans, 1996).

———, ed. *Character and Scripture: Moral Formation, Community, and Biblical Interpretation* (Grand Rapids: Eerdmans, 2002).

Bruce, F. F. *New Testament History* (3d ed.; London: Pickering and Inglis, 1980).

Burchard, C. "Gemeinde in der strohernen Epistel: Mutmaßungen über Jakobus," in

Kirche: Festschrift für Günther Bornkamm zum 75. Geburtstag (ed. D. Lührmann and G. Strecker; Tübingen: Mohr, 1980), 315-28.

Caird, G. B. *The Language and Imagery of the Bible* (Philadelphia: Westminster, 1980).

Cargal, T. B. *Restoring the Diaspora: Discursive Structure and Purpose in the Epistle of James* (SBLDS 144; Atlanta: Scholars, 1993).

Carson, D. A., and H. G. W. Williamson, eds. *It Is Written: Scripture Citing Scripture: Essays in Honour of Barnabas Lindars, SSF* (Cambridge: Cambridge University Press, 1988).

Cheung, L. L. *The Genre, Composition and Hermeneutics of the Epistle of James* (PBM; Milton Keynes: Paternoster, 2003).

Chilton, B., and C. A. Evans, eds. *James the Just and Christian Origins* (NovTSup 98; Leiden: Brill, 1999).

Chilton, B., and C. A. Evans, eds. *The Missions of James, Peter, and Paul: Tensions in Early Christianity* (NovTSup 115; Leiden: Brill, 2005).

Chilton, B., and J. Neusner, eds. *The Brother of Jesus: James the Just and His Mission* (Louisville: Westminster John Knox, 2001).

Chilton, B., and J. Neusner, eds. *Judaism in the New Testament: Practices and Beliefs* (New York: Routledge, 1995).

Cohen, S. J. D. *The Beginnings of Jewishness: Boundaries, Varieties, Uncertainties* (Berkeley: University of California Press, 1999).

Crossan, J. D. *The Birth of Christianity: Discovering What Happened in the Years Immediately after the Execution of Jesus* (San Francisco: HarperSanFrancisco, 1998).

Davies, W. D. *Paul and Rabbinic Judaism: Some Rabbinic Elements in Pauline Theology* (Philadelphia: Fortress, 1980).

Davies, W. D., and D. C. Allison, Jr. *The Gospel According to Saint Matthew* (3 vols.; ICC; Edinburgh: Clark, 1988-97; cited as Davies-Allison).

Deissmann, A. *Bible Studies* (trans. A. Grieve; reprint Winona Lake: Alpha, 1979).

Dodd, C. H. *According to the Scriptures: The Sub-Structure of New Testament Theology* (London: Nisbet, 1952).

————. *More New Testament Studies* (Grand Rapids: Eerdmans, 1968).

Dunn, J. D. G. "The Incident at Antioch (Gal. ii.11-18)," in his *Jesus, Paul and the Law: Studies in Mark and Galatians* (Louisville: Westminster John Knox, 1990), 129-82.

————. *Jesus and the Spirit* (Philadelphia: Westminster, 1975).

————. *Jesus Remembered* (Christianity in the Making 1; Grand Rapids: Eerdmans, 2003).

————. *The Partings of the Ways between Christianity and Judaism and Their Significance for the Character of Christianity* (Philadelphia: Trinity, 1991).

————. *The Theology of Paul the Apostle* (Grand Rapids: Eerdmans, 1998).

————. *Unity and Diversity in the New Testament: An Inquiry into the Character of Earliest Christianity* (3d ed.; London: SCM, 2006).

————, ed. *Jews and Christians: The Parting of the Ways* A.D. *70 to 135* (Grand Rapids: Eerdmans, 1999).

Dyrness, W. "Mercy Triumphs over Justice: James 2:13 and the Theology of Faith and Works," *Themelios* 6 (1981) 11-16.

Edgar, D. H. *Has God Not Chosen the Poor? The Social Setting of the Epistle of James* (JSNTSup 206; Sheffield: Sheffield Academic, 2001).

————. "The Use of the Love-Command and the *Shema'* in the Epistle of James," *PIBA* 23 (2000) 9-22.

Elliott, J. H. "The Epistle of James in Rhetorical and Social Scientific Perspective: Holiness-Wholeness and Patterns of Replication," *BTB* 23 (1993) 71-81 (= "Holiness-Wholeness").

————. *A Home for the Homeless: A Social-Scientific Criticism of 1 Peter, Its Situation and Strategy* (Minneapolis: Fortress, 1990).

Elliott, J. K. "Five New Papyri of the New Testament," *NovT* 41 (1999) 209-13.

Ellis, E. E. *The Old Testament in Early Christianity: Canon and Interpretation in the Light of Modern Research* (Grand Rapids: Baker, 1992).

Evans, C. A. "Jesus and James: Martyrs of the Temple," in Chilton and Evans, eds., *James the Just,* 233-49.

Fanning, B. *Verbal Aspect in New Testament Greek* (Oxford Theological Monographs; New York: Oxford University Press, 1990).

Fishbane, M. *Biblical Interpretation in Ancient Israel* (Oxford: Clarendon, 1985).

Francis, F. O. "The Form and Function of the Opening and Closing Paragraphs of James and 1 John," *ZNW* 61 (1960) 110-26.

Frend, W. H. C. *Martyrdom and Persecution in the Early Church: A Study of a Conflict from the Maccabees to Donatus* (Grand Rapids: Baker, 1981).

Goldingay, J. *Old Testament Theology* vol. 1: *Israel's Gospel,* vol. 2: *Israel's Faith* (Downers Grove: InterVarsity, 2003, 2006).

Goppelt, L. *Typos: The Typological Interpretation of the Old Testament in the New* (trans. D. H. Madvig; Grand Rapids: Eerdmans, 1982 [= 1939]).

Gregory of Nyssa. *The Life of Saint Macrina* (trans. K. Corrigan; Toronto: Peregrina, 2001).

Grenz, S. *Renewing the Center: Evangelical Theology in a Post-Theological Era* (Grand Rapids: Baker, 2000).

————. *The Social God and the Relational Self: A Trinitarian Theology of the* Imago Dei (Louisville: Westminster John Knox, 2001).

Gruen, E. S. *Heritage and Hellenism: The Reinvention of Jewish Tradition* (Berkeley: University of California Press, 1998).

Gundry Volf, J. M. *Paul and Perseverance: Staying In and Falling Away* (Louisville: Westminster John Knox, 1990).

Hagner, D. A. *Matthew* (WBC 33A, 33B; Dallas: Word, 1993).

Hahn, F., and P. Miller. "Der Jakobusbrief," *TRu* 63 (1998) 1-73.

Harland, P. A. *Associations, Synagogues, and Congregations: Claiming a Place in Ancient Mediterranean Society* (Minneapolis: Fortress, 2003).

Hartin, P. J. *James and the "Q" Sayings of Jesus* (JSNTSup 47; Sheffield: Sheffield Academic, 1991).

———. *James of Jerusalem: Heir to Jesus of Nazareth* (Collegeville: Liturgical, 2004).

———. "The Religious Context of the Letter of James," in M. Jackson-McCabe, ed., *Jewish Christianity Reconsidered* (Minneapolis: Fortress, 2007), 203-31.

———. *A Spirituality of Perfection: Faith in Action in the Letter of James* (Collegeville: Liturgical, 1999).

Hengel, M. *Acts and the History of Earliest Christianity* (trans. J. Bowden; London: SCM, 1979).

———. *Between Jesus and Paul: Studies in the Earliest History of Christianity* (trans. J. Bowden; Philadelphia: Fortress, 1983).

———. "Der Jakobusbrief als antipaulinische Polemik," in *Tradition and Interpretation in the New Testament* (ed. G. F. Hawthorne and O. Betz; Grand Rapids: Eerdmans, 1987), 248-78.

———. *The "Hellenization" of Judaea in the First Century after Christ* (with C. Markschies; trans. J. Bowden; Philadelpia: Trinity, 1989).

———. *Jews, Greeks and Barbarians: Aspects of the Hellenization of Judaism in the Pre-Christian Period* (trans. J. Bowden; Philadelphia: Fortress, 1980).

———. *Judaism and Hellenism: Studies in Their Encounter in Palestine during the Early Hellenistic Period* (trans. J. Bowden; Philadelphia: Fortress, 1974).

———. *The Zealots: Investigations into the Jewish Freedom Movement in the Period from Herod I until 70 A.D.* (trans. D. Smith; Edinburgh: Clark, 1989).

Hennecke, E., and W. Schneemelcher, eds. *New Testament Apocrypha* (2 vols.; rev. ed., ed. W. Schneemelcher, trans. R. M. Wilson; Louisville: Westminster John Knox, 1991-92).

Hoffman, L. A. *The Sh'ma and Its Blessings* (My People's Prayer Book 1; Woodstock: Jewish Lights, 1997).

Hoppe, R. *Der theologische Hintergrund des Jakobusbriefes* (FzB 28; Würzburg: Echter, 1977).

Hurtado, L. W. *At the Origins of Christian Worship: The Context and Character of Earliest Christian Devotion* (Grand Rapids: Eerdmans, 1999).

———. "The Jerusalem Collection and the Book of Galatians," *JSNT* 5 (1979) 46-62.

———. *Lord Jesus Christ: Devotion to Jesus in Earliest Christianity* (Grand Rapids: Eerdmans, 2003).

———. *One God, One Lord: Early Christian Devotion and Ancient Jewish Monotheism* (Philadelphia: Fortress, 1988).

Jackson-McCabe, M. *Logos and Law in the Letter of James: The Law of Nature, the Law of Moses, and the Law of Freedom* (Leiden: Brill, 2001).

———. "The Messiah Jesus in the Mythic World of James," *JBL* 122 (2003) 701-30.

Jeremias, J. *Jerusalem in the Time of Jesus* (trans. F. H. and C. H. Cave; Philadelphia: Fortress, 1975).

Johnson, L. T. *Brother of Jesus, Friend of God: Studies in the Letter of James* (Grand

Rapids: Eerdmans, 2004). This volume re-issues articles and publishes lectures of Johnson on James.

———. "Reading Wisdom Wisely," *LS* 28 (2003) 99-112.

———. "The Use of Leviticus 19 in the Letter of James," *JBL* 101 (1982) 391-401.

Juel, D. *Messianic Exegesis: Christological Interpretation of the Old Testament in Early Christianity* (Philadelphia: Fortress, 1988).

Klein, M. *"Ein vollkommenes Werk." Vollkommenheit, Gesetz und Gericht als theologische Themen des Jakobusbriefes* (BWANT 139; Stuttgart/Berlin: Kohlhammer, 1995).

Klijn, A. F. J., and G. J. Reinink. *Patristic Evidence for Jewish-Christian Sects* (NovTSup 36; Leiden: Brill, 1973).

Kloppenborg Verbin, J. S. "Patronage Avoidance in James," *HvTSt* 55 (1999) 755-94.

Konradt, M. *Christliche Existenz nach dem Jakobusbrief. Eine Studie zu seiner soteriologischen und ethischen Konzeption* (SUNT 22; Göttingen: Vandenhoeck und Ruprecht, 1998.

Kugel, J. *The Idea of Biblical Poetry: Parallelism and Its History* (New Haven: Yale University Press, 1981).

Ladd, G. E., *A Theology of the New Testament* (rev. D. A. Hagner; Grand Rapids: Eerdmans, 1993).

Lieu, J. M. *Christian Identity in the Jewish and Graeco-Roman World* (Oxford: Oxford University Press, 2004).

———. *Image and Reality: The Jews in the World of the Christians in the Second Century* (Edinburgh: Clark, 1996).

Lindars, B. *New Testament Apologetic: The Doctrinal Significance of the Old Testament Quotations* (London: SCM, 1961).

Lockett, D. *Purity and Worldview in the Epistle of James* (LNTS 366; New York: Clark, 2008).

———. "The Spectrum of Wisdom and Eschatology in the Epistle of James and 4QInstruction," *TynBul* 56 (2005) 131-48.

Longenecker, R. *Biblical Exegesis in the Apostolic Period* (Grand Rapids: Eerdmans, 1975).

———. *The Christology of Early Jewish Christianity* (London: SCM, 1970).

Ludwig, M. *Wort als Gesetz. Eine Untersuchung zum Verständnis von 'Wort' und 'Gesetz' in israelitisch-frühjüdischen und neutestamentlichen Schriften. Gleichzeitig ein Beitrag zur Theologie des Jakobusbriefes* (EH 23/502; Frankfurt: Lang, 1994).

Malina, B. J. *The New Testament World: Insights from Cultural Anthropology* (3d ed.; Louisville: Westminster John Knox, 2001).

Marshall, I. H. *Kept by the Power of God: A Study of Perseverance and Falling Away* (Minneapolis: Bethany, 1969).

Maynard-Reid, P. U. *Poverty and Wealth in James* (Maryknoll: Orbis, 1987).

McKay, K. L. *A New Syntax of the Verb in New Testament Greek: An Aspectual Approach* (Studies in Biblical Greek; New York: Lang, 1994).

McKnight, S. "Collection for the Saints," *DPL,* 143-147.

————. *A Community Called Atonement* (Nashville: Abingdon, 2007).

————. "Covenant and Spirit: The Origins of the New Covenant Hermeneutic," in *The Holy Spirit and Christian Origins: Essays in Honor of James D. G. Dunn* (ed. G. N. Stanton, B. W. Longenecker, and S. C. Barton; Grand Rapids: Eerdmans, 2004), 41-54.

————. *Embracing Grace: A Gospel for All of Us* (Brewster: Paraclete, 2005).

————. "James 2:18a: The Unidentifiable Interlocutor," *WTJ* 52 (1990) 355-64.

————. *Jesus and His Death: Historiography, the Historical Jesus, and Atonement Theory* (Waco: Baylor University Press, 2005).

————. "Jesus and the Twelve," *BBR* 11 (2001) 203-31.

————. *The Jesus Creed: Loving God, Loving Others* (Brewster: Paraclete, 2004).

————. *A New Vision for Israel: The Teachings of Jesus in National Context* (Grand Rapids: Eerdmans, 1999).

————. "A Parting within the Way: Jesus and James on Israel and Purity," in Chilton and Evans, eds., *James the Just*, 83-129.

————. *Turning to Jesus: The Sociology of Conversion in the Gospels* (Louisville: Westminster John Knox, 2002).

————. "The Warning Passages of Hebrews: A Formal Analysis and Theological Conclusions," *TrinJ* 13 (1992) 21-59.

Metzger, B. M. *A Textual Commentary on the Greek New Testament* (New York: United Bible Societies, 1971).

Miller, P. D. *They Cried to the Lord: The Form and Theology of Biblical Prayer* (Minneapolis: Fortress, 1994).

Mohrlang, R. *Matthew and Paul: A Comparison of Ethical Perspectives* (SNTSMS 48; Cambridge: Cambridge University Press, 1984).

Montefiore, H. "Thou Shalt Love Thy Neighbour as Thyself," *NovT* 5 (1962) 157-70.

Moo, Douglas J. *The Epistle to the Romans* (NICNT; Grand Rapids: Eerdmans, 1996).

Morris, L. L. *Testaments of Love: A Study of Love in the Bible* (Grand Rapids: Eerdmans, 1981).

Moule, C. F. D. *An Idiom Book of New Testament Greek* (2d ed.; Cambridge: Cambridge University Press, 1963).

Mounce, William D. *Mounce's Complete Dictionary of Old and New Testament Words* (Grand Rapids: Zondervan, 2006).

Myllykoski, M. "James the Just in History and Tradition: Perspectives of Past and Present Scholarship," *CBR* 5 (2006) 73-122, 6 (2007) 11-98.

Ng, Esther Yue L. "Father-God Language and Old Testament Allusions in James," *TynBul* 54 (2003) 41-54.

Ó Fearghail, F. "On the Literary Structure of the Letter of James," *PIBA* 19 (1996) 66-83.

Ollenburger, B. C., E. A. Martens, and G. F. Hasel. *The Flowering of Old Testament Theology: A Reader in Twentieth-Century Old Testament Theology, 1930-1990* (SBTS 1; Winona Lake: Eisenbraun, 1992).

Painter, J. "James and Peter: Models of Leadership and Mission," in Chilton and Evans, eds., *Missions,* 143-209.

————. "James as the First Catholic Epistle," *Int* 60 (2006) 245-59.

————. *Just James: The Brother of Jesus in History and Tradition* (Columbia: University of South Carolina Press, 1997).

Patzia, A. G. *The Emergence of the Church: Context, Growth, Leadership and Worship* (Downers Grove: InterVarsity, 2001).

Penner, T. C. *The Epistle of James and Eschatology: Re-Reading an Ancient Christian Letter* (JSNTSup 121; Sheffield: Sheffield Academic, 1996).

————. "The Epistle of James in Current Research," *CRBS* 7 (1999) 257-308.

Perdue, L. "Paraenesis and the Epistle of James," *ZNW* 71 (1981) 241-56.

Plantinga, C., Jr. *Not the Way It's Supposed to Be: A Breviary of Sin* (Grand Rapids: Eerdmans, 1995).

Porter, S. E. *Idioms of the Greek New Testament* (Biblical Languages: Greek 2; Sheffield: Sheffield Academic, 1992).

————. *Verbal Aspect in the Greek of the New Testament, with Reference to Tense and Mood* (Studies in Biblical Greek 1; New York: Lang, 1989).

Pratscher, W. *Der Herrenbruder Jakobus und die Jakobustraditionen* (FRLANT 139; Göttingen: Vandenhoeck und Ruprecht, 1987).

Pritz, R. A. *Nazarene Jewish Christianity: From the End of the New Testament Period until Its Disappearance in the Fourth Century* (Jerusalem: Magnes, 1992).

Przybylski, B. *Righteousness in Matthew and His World of Thought* (SNTSMS 41; Cambridge: Cambridge University Press, 1980).

Reiser, M. *Jesus and Judgment: The Eschatological Proclamation in Its Jewish Context* (trans. L. M. Maloney; Minneapolis: Fortress, 1997).

Reumann, J. "Christology of James," in *Who Do You Say That I Am? Essays on Christology* (ed. M. A. Powell and D. R. Bauer; Louisville: Westminster John Knox, 1999), 128-39.

————. *Righteousness in the New Testament* (with responses by J. A. Fitzmyer and J. D. Quinn; Philadelphia: Fortress, 1982).

Robbins, V. K. "Making Christian Culture in the Epistle of James," *Scriptura* 59 (1996) 341-51.

Rolland, P. "La date de l'épître de Jacques," *NRTh* 118 (1996) 839-51.

Sanders, E. P. "Jesus and the First Table of the Jewish Law," in *Jews and Christians Speak of Jesus* (ed. A. E. Zannoni; Minneapolis: Fortress, 1994), 55-73.

Setzer, C. *Jewish Responses to Early Christians: History and Polemics, 30-150 C.E.* (Minneapolis: Fortress, 1994).

Sigal, P. "The Halakhah of James," in *Intergerini Parietis Septum (Eph. 2:14): Essays Presented to Markus Barth on His Sixty-fifth Birthday* (ed. D. Y. Hadidian; Pittsburgh: Pickwick, 1981), 337-53.

Siker, J. S. *Disinheriting the Jews: Abraham in Early Christian Controversy* (Louisville: Westminster John Knox, 1991).

Skarsaune, O. *In the Shadow of the Temple: Jewish Influences on Early Christianity* (Downers Grove: InterVarsity, 2002).

Skarsaune, O. and R. Hvalvik, eds., *Jewish Believers in Jesus: The Early Centuries* (Peabody: Hendrickson, 2007).

Stegemann, E. W., and W. Stegemann. *The Jesus Movement: A Social History of Its First Century* (trans. O. C. Dean, Jr.; Minneapolis: Fortress, 1998).

Stowers, S. K. *Letter Writing in Greco-Roman Antiquity* (LEC; Philadelphia: Westminster, 1986).

Strecker, G. *Theology of the New Testament* (trans. M. E. Boring; Louisville: Westminster John Knox, 2000).

Tamez, Elsa. *The Scandalous Message of James: Faith without Works Is Dead* (New York: Crossroad, 2002).

Taylor, M. E. "Recent Scholarship on the Structure of James," *CBR* 3 (2004) 86-115.

———. *A Text-Linguistic Investigation into the Discourse Structure of James* (LNTS 311; London: Clark, 2006).

Thurén, L. "Risky Rhetoric in James," *NovT* 37 (1995) 262-84.

Tiller, P. A. "The Rich and Poor in James: An Apocalyptic Proclamation," in *Society of Biblical Literature 1998 Seminar Papers* (Atlanta: Scholars, 1998), 2.909-20.

Turner, N. *Christian Words* (Edinburgh: Clark, 1980).

Urbach, E. E. *The Sages: Their Concepts and Beliefs* (2 vols.; Jerusalem: Magnes, 1979).

Verseput, D. J. "Genre and Story: The Community Setting of the Epistle of James," *CBQ* 62 (2000) 96-110.

———. "Reworking the Puzzle of Faith and Deeds in James 2.14-26," *NTS* 43 (1997) 97-115.

———. "Wisdom, 4Q185, and the Epistle of James," *JBL* 117 (1998) 691-707.

Volf, M. *Exclusion and Embrace: A Theological Exploration of Identity, Otherness, and Reconciliation* (Nashville: Abingdon, 1996).

Wachob, W. H. "The Apocalyptic Intertexture of the Epistle of James," in *The Intertexture of Apocalyptic Discourse in the New Testament* (ed. D. F. Watson; SBLSS 14; Atlanta: Society of Biblical Literature, 2002), 165-85.

———. *The Voice of Jesus in the Social Rhetoric of James* (SNTSMS 106; Cambridge: Cambridge University Press, 2000).

Ward, R. B. "Partiality in the Assembly: James 2:2-4," *HTR* 62 (1969) 87-97.

Webb, R. L., and J. S. Kloppenborg, eds. *Reading James with New Eyes: Methodological Reassessments of the Letter of James* (LNTS 342; London: Clark, 2007).

Welzen, H. "The Way of Perfection: Spirituality in the Letter of James," *Studies in Spirituality* 13 (2003) 81-98.

Wesley, J. *Plain Account of Christian Perfection* (Chicago: Christian Witness, n.d.).

White, J. L. *Light from Ancient Letters* (FF; Philadelphia: Fortress, 1986).

Wise, M., M. Abegg, and E. Cook. *The Dead Sea Scrolls: A New Translation* (San Francisco: HarperSanFrancisco, 1996).

Witherington, Ben, III. *The Acts of the Apostles: A Socio-Rhetorical Commentary* (Grand Rapids: Eerdmans, 1997).

Wright, C. J. H. *The Mission of God* (Downers Grove: InterVarsity, 2006).

Wright, N. T. *Jesus and the Victory of God* (Minneapolis: Fortress, 1996).

————. *What Saint Paul Really Said: Was Paul of Tarsus the Real Founder of Christianity?* (Grand Rapids: Eerdmans, 1997).

Zerwick, M. *Biblical Greek, Illustrated by Examples* (Rome: Scripta Pontificii Instituti Biblici, 1963).

Zimmerli, W. "Die Seligpreisungen der Bergpredigt und das Alte Testament," in *Donum Gentilicium: New Testament Studies in Honour of David Daube* (ed. E. Bammel, C. K. Barrett, and W. D. Davies; Oxford: Clarendon, 1978), 8-26.

INTRODUCTION

In teaching the letter of James, one should walk to the front of the room and write these words in big letters on a chalkboard:

Read James!

Under that the person then needs to write:

First, read James in light of James!

Scholars today are obsessed by the "historical James" and his place in Jewish Christianity, obsessed by Jewish and Roman and Greek parallels, and impressed by those who find the most parallels or parallels no one has noticed before. Indeed, reading James in comparison with his contemporaries and sources and — not to be forgotten — the earliest Christian documents, aids the interpreter, sometimes dramatically. Sometimes, however, reading James in light of another text leads the reader to see James in light of that text and to conclude that they are related . . . which is, of course, what we call circular reasoning. "Indeed," the one at the front of the room might say, "it's fine to compare James with others *as long as you read James in light of James first.*" Which is just what we intend to do in this commentary because thus we will discover the particular messianic profile James gives to anything he has acquired from his cultural environments. In this way the historical work gives way to exegesis, or perhaps it is better to say that exegesis sheds light on historical work. Having set a stake now in the ground, I stand next to Margaret Mitchell's sagacious warning: Yes, she argues, read James on his own terms, but if Paul happens to be one of the terms in James's world, then read James in interaction with Paul.[1] We ought not, in other words, pretend that James

---

1. M. M. Mitchell, "The Letter of James as a Document of Paulinism?" in Webb

lived alone in his world. In what follows we will cite parallels throughout to texts connected in some way to James. But we do need to learn to read James on his own terms in that world — in that order — and to learn that studying this letter is not simply reconstructing the "historical James" or "Jewish Christianity."

James is a one-of-a-kind document. At the literary level, there is no real parallel among ancient letters, essays, and homilies. At the historical level, there is nothing quite like it among the early Christian documents, even if its connections and origins are deeply disputed.[2] James is, at least in a traditional sense, the earliest Christian document we have and in many ways anticipates or precedes theological developments. We suggest, but cannot prove, that James is in part a response to early reports of Paul's missionary work in Asia Minor, perhaps even Antioch (see Acts 11:19-30; Gal 2:11-14). That is our ballpark speculation on the Jewish Christian context of James. In fact, many today see the shape of the Christian faith in this letter as a form of Judaism.[3] And yet, it needs to be observed that James fails to mention so many central ideas and institutions of Judaism, such as "Israel," Temple, and Sabbath.[4] Within Judaism this letter fits with texts like Sirach, it also shows some remarkable correspondences to the Greco-Roman rhetorical and liter-

---

and Kloppenborg, *Reading James,* 75-98. The intentional avoidance of the historical questions, ranging from Jewish and Greco-Roman contexts to the redactional layering of the text of James, is unwise but has become methodologically defensible for some. A dated but useful sketch of these issues is Cargal, *Restoring the Diaspora,* 1-8; see also Penner's tight sketch in "The Epistle of James," 280-87.

2. See the complexity of this issue in Konradt, *Christliche Existenz,* 317-38. For a masterful sketch of the scholarship on James (I can think of no better place for serious students to begin) see Penner, "The Epistle of James." Also, see Hahn and Miller, "Der Jakobusbrief"; Myllykoski, "James the Just"; Klein, *"Ein vollkommenes Werk,"* 15-32; B. D. Chilton, "James, Jesus' Brother," in *The Face of New Testament Studies* (ed. S. McKnight and G. R. Osborne; Grand Rapids: Baker, 2004), 251-62.

3. F. Mussner, "Rückbesinnung der Kirchen auf das Jüdische. Impulse aus dem Jakobusbrief," *Catholica* 52 (1998) 67-78; J. Neusner, "Introduction: What Is a Judaism?" in Chilton and Neusner, *The Brother of Jesus,* 1-9. Neusner's criteria for discovering "a Judaism": "a religious system put forth by a group that regards itself as 'Israel,' meaning, as the embodiment in the here and now of that community to which the Hebrew Scriptures of ancient Israel make reference: (1) the way of life, and (2) the worldview of (3) and 'Israel'" (p. 3). The singular problem for many in investigating such a proposal is the momentum of thinking that Judaism was a single, unitary set of beliefs and practices. See also C. A. Evans, "Comparing Judaisms," in Chilton and Neusner, *The Brother of Jesus,* 161-83; Penner, *The Epistle of James and Eschatology,* 75-103; P. H. Davids, "Palestinian Traditions in the Epistle of James," in Chilton and Evans, *James the Just and Christian Origins,* 33-57; and Chilton's introductory essay in the same volume, 3-15.

4. On this, see W. Popkes, "The Mission of James," in Chilton and Neusner, *The Brother of Jesus,* 90.

ary world, and it surprises at times in its connections to Paul, Peter, and John and to texts like *Didache* and *Barnabas,* the *Sentences of Sextus* and the *Teachings of Silvanus,* but especially *1 Clement* and the *Shepherd* of Hermas and the much terser *Sentences of Pseudo-Phocylides.* But it is the substance of James, combining as it does Torah observance in a new key with both wisdom and eschatology in a Jewish-Christian milieu, that forms its special character.[5]

James strikes in many directions at once: historians, theologians, pastors and Christians discover challenges. As a document emerging from an author who is somehow embedded in one community and ostensibly directed at another community or set of communities, James remains an enigma: in spite of the best efforts of many scholars, its *Sitz im Leben* remains elusive. While it seems most likely that James emerges from Jerusalem or at least a Judean-based setting, the audience might be at any number of locations across the disaspora.[6] When we move into the church world today, James pushes back against Christians who are too Reformed. In fact, this commentary will hope to demonstrate that the more uncomfortable Christians are with James in a Luther-like way,[7] the less they really understand Paul! At the pastoral level, James offers both wisdom and potent, harsh rhetoric. The wisdom dimension of James attracts modern and postmodern readers; the rhetoric makes many today wary, and yet others are duly impressed by the skill of this writer.

Anabaptist scholar Ronald Sider tells the story that in the happy days of hippies Upton Sinclair once read James 5:1-5 aloud to a group of ministers and attributed the words to Emma Goldman. That Sinclair had socialist leanings and that Goldman was an anarchist explains why the ministers immediately called for Goldman's deportation. What is not clear is why a group of ministers would not have recognized the memorable, if unsettling, prose of James 5![8] Elsa Tamez might provide the answer to pastoral ignorance. She opens her prophet-like study of James with these words: "If the Letter of James were sent to the Christian communities of certain countries that suffer from violence and exploitation, it would very possibly be intercepted by government security agencies. The document would be branded as subversive."[9]

---

5. Penner, *The Epistle of James and Eschatology,* 214-56, shows rare insight into the deeper level of these connections and where James "fits" in the larger spectrum. See also Cheung, *Genre, Composition,* 240-71.

6. See Bauckham, *Wisdom of James,* 185-87.

7. On which see Mussner, 42-47; and Calvin, 276-77 ("The Argument"), who also thinks James is "the son of Alphaeus."

8. R. A. Sider, *Rich Christians in an Age of Hunger* (5th ed.; Nashville: W, 1997), 133.

9. Tamez, *Scandalous Message,* 1. A. Batten, in her study "Ideological Strategies in the Letter of James," in Webb and Kloppenborg, *Reading James,* 7, repeats the dust

Which leads to this: even if we cannot reconstruct the historical context with confidence, the voice of James has some potent words about economic injustice and even public policy, and it makes many of us feel uncomfortable in our comforts.[10] That voice falls uncomfortably silent among many who are empowered. But that same voice of James delights the ears and transfigures the hopes of the unempowered.[11] To ape the famous words of Mark Twain, it is not the lack of clarity of context of James that bothers me; it is the words in the text that bother me.[12]

JAMES IN THE STORY

Many today advocate reading the Bible as Story, as a macroscopic plot that puts the whole Bible together and that, with proper nuances and differences, animated the ideas of each biblical author. In so putting the Bible together as Story, the Hebrew Bible or Tanakh becomes the "Old Testament." There is no reason to enter into the technical discussion here,[13] except to point out the

---

jacket comments on Tamez's book by J. M. Bonino that half of the congregation in a wealthy Chilean church left when James was read publicly there. See also Maynard-Reid, *Poverty and Wealth in James.*

10. See D. Warden, "The Rich and Poor in James: Implications for Institutionalized Partiality," *Journal of the Evangelical Theological Society* 43 (2000) 247-57; see also C. L. Blomberg, *Neither Poverty Nor Riches* (Grand Rapids: Eerdmans, 1999). For an attempt to relate James to our world after sketching how James functions socially in its world, see R. Crotty, "Identifying the Poor in the Letter of James," *Colloquium* 27 (1995) 11-21.

11. The question is where to begin with further reading. For the big picture of one such voice, the African American voice, and the issue of racism, see J. Kameron Carter, *Race: A Theological Account* (New York: Oxford University Press, 2008); B. Blount, *Then the Whisper Put On Flesh: New Testament Ethics in an African American Context* (Nashville: Abingdon, 2001); L. L. Enis, "Biblical Interpretation among African-American New Testament Scholars," *CBR* 4 (2005) 57-82. For James in particular, see M. P. Aymer, *First Pure, Then Peaceable: Frederick Douglass Reads James* (LNTS 379; London: Clark, 2007); and Byron.

12. A good place to begin here is the excursus in Wall, 234-47.

13. See A. C. Thiselton, *New Horizons in Hermeneutics* (Grand Rapids: Zondervan, 1992), 471-514; *Thiselton on Hermeneutics* (Grand Rapids: Eerdmans, 2006); *The Hermeneutics of Doctrine* (Grand Rapids: Eerdmans, 2007), 62-80, 541-81; N. T. Wright, *The New Testament and the People of God* (Minneapolis: Fortress, 1992), 47-80, 215-79, 371-443; *The Last Word* (San Francisco: HarperSanFrancisco, 2005); *Simply Christian* (San Francisco: HarperSanFrancisco, 2006); K. Vanhoozer, *The Drama of Doctrine* (Louisville: Westminster John Knox, 2005); *Is There a Meaning in This Text?* (Grand Rapids: Zondervan, 1998). In wider scope, the following also represent important

"chapters" of this plot. There are (in our scheme) five: creation of Eikons[14] (Gen 1–2), cracking of the Eikons (Gen 3), the covenanted community of Eikons (Gen 12; 17; 22; Exod 19–24; Jer 31; Mark 14:12-26; Acts 2; 1 Cor 11:17-34), the redemption through the perfect Eikon, Christ (Matt 1–2; John 1; Rom 8:29; 1 Cor 15:49; 2 Cor 3:18; 4:4; Col 1:15), and the consummation of the union of Eikons with the triune God (Rev 21–22).[15] It is wise to see this plot from the angle of mission, and to see that mission as the *missio Dei*.[16]

James's letter understands God's Story as the Story of Israel. In fact, each book of the Bible tells this single Story, even if each author configures that Story in its own way. James knows the breach by God's covenanted community and he finds the breach mended or fulfilled in the "twelve tribes in the Dispersion" (1:1). James reads the Bible (intertextually)[17] as Story with a plot that comes to a new chapter in Jesus Christ. Yet, James's reading of the Story is not one of replacement so much as of fulfillment: his letter summons the twelve tribes to live out the Mosaic Torah as God's enduring

---

trends: G. Loughlin, *Telling God's Story* (Cambridge: Cambridge University Press, 1996); W. A. Kort, *Story, Text, and Scripture* (University Park: Pennsylvania State University Press, 1988); T. Work, *Living and Active* (Grand Rapids: Eerdmans, 2002).

The Old Testament itself reveals inter- and intra-textual and cultural reflections: see Goldingay, *Israel's Gospel;* P. Enns, *Inspiration and Incarnation* (Grand Rapids: Baker, 2005). Jewish scholars revealing how Tanakh is read today include J. L. Kugel, *How to Read the Bible* (New York: Free, 2007); M. Z. Brettler, *How to Read the Jewish Bible* (New York: Oxford University Press, 2007).

On how the early church read the Bible, the literature is enormous. One original text that should be read early and often is Irenaeus, *On the Apostolic Preaching.* A good sketch of early Christian readings of Scripture, where narrative is seen as the heart of what went on, see R. E. Heine, *Reading the Old Testament with the Ancient Church* (Grand Rapids: Baker, 2007).

14. I use the word *eikon* instead of *imago Dei,* "image of God," since the latter has become dog-eared and overly disputed. See my *A Community Called Atonement,* 17-22.

15. See Wall, especially 23-34, 275-306, for a canonical and complementary approach to James as Story. Here James is examined within its ecclesial, canonical context, not the least of which is how James works within the second (non-Pauline) letters of the New Testament. See also the observations of Painter, "James as the First Catholic Epistle," 245-47. Many early orderings of the books of the New Testament had the "catholic" epistles after Acts and before Paul, and this put James first.

16. See C. J. H. Wright, *The Mission of God;* L. Pachuau, "Missio Dei," in *DMT* 232-34.

17. See a recent view in W. Popkes, "James and Scripture: An Exercise in Intertexuality," *NTS* 45 (1999) 213-29. A classic study at the bottom of reading the Bible this way is M. Fishbane, *Biblical Interpretation in Ancient Israel* (Oxford: Clarendon, 1988). A good example of this from a slightly different angle with respect to James is Bauckham, 29-111.

will.[18] But even here James has touched the Story with singular impact: James reads and renders the Torah *in the way Jesus taught it,* namely through the combination of loving God (1:12) and loving others (1:25; 2:8-11). In other words, when it comes to ethics James reads and interprets and applies the Torah through the lens of the *Shema* (Deut 6:4-9) and the command to love our neighbor as ourselves (Lev 19:18).[19] That James interprets ethics in the key of *Shema* is telling for how to comprehend his relationship to Judaism and for how we are to read his Story. From a different angle, but one that nonetheless complements our point about James and Shema, Jacob Neusner has demonstrated that the typical Jewish/rabbinic pattern of sin, repentance, atonement, judgment, and eternal life emerges in James naturally so that his theology emerges from within the world of Judaism.[20]

James tells this one true Story of God's redemption in moral, wisdom,[21]

18. See Ludwig, *Wort als Gesetz;* R. Wall, "Law and Gospel, Church and Canon," *Wesleyan Theological Journal* 22 (1987) 53-55.

19. See Edgar, "Love-Command," for one of the only studies that sees the significance of the *Shema* in James. I did not see Edgar's study until I had worked up my own conclusions in this regard. See also Johnson, who finds allusions to Lev 19 in a manner similar to *The Sentences of Pseudo-Phocylides* 9-21, in a number of places in James; see his *Brother of Jesus, Friend of God,* 123-35. Johnson, in my judgment, stretches the evidence at times, but the overall thesis that James is rooted in Lev 19 holds up to scrutiny. Here are the basics:

(1) Jas 2:8 quotes the LXX of Lev 19:18b.
(2) This citation is framed by "partiality" (Jas 2:1, 8, 9), which is also found in Lev 19:15.
(3) Jas 5:4 alludes to Lev 19:13, but Johnson finds the allusion because of the cumulative effect of (1) and (2) above.
(4) Jas 4:11; 5:12; and 5:20 allude to Lev 19:12-18.

Thus, Johnson finds allusions or citations to Lev 19:12, 13, 15, 16, 17b, 18a, and 18b.

20. J. Neusner, "Sin, Repentance, Atonement and Resurrection: The Perspective of Rabbinic Theology on the Views of James 1–2 and Paul in Romans 3–4," in Chilton and Evans, *Missions,* 409-34.

21. See, e.g., Hoppe, *Der theologische Hintergrund;* Frankemölle, 2.561-71; Burchard, 155-58; Hartin's many studies listed in the Bibliography above; Verseput, "Wisdom"; B. Chilton, "Wisdom and Grace," in Chilton and Evans, *Missions,* 307-22; Johnson, "Reading Wisdom Wisely"; E. Borghi, "La sagesse de la vie selon l'épître de Jacques. Lignes de Lecture," *NTS* 52 (2006) 123-41, who shows that the life of wisdom according to James is love for others. See also P. Perkins, "James 3:16–4:3," *Int* 36 (1982) 283-87. A sketch of the evidence in James can be found in the clear and comprehensive study of R. F. Chaffin, Jr., "The Theme of Wisdom in the Epistle of James," *ATJ* 29 (1997) 23-49.

At times the term "wisdom," since it has now become a cliché in James studies, is used without definition. While there are clearly wisdom themes in James, some of the more important central themes in wisdom — namely, the "fear of the Lord," the handing on of wisdom to one's sons, and the insight induced from creation and observation of life and prophetic keys[22] rather than in the more didactic, soteriological keys one finds in Paul, Peter and Hebrews.[23] Hence, James's eschatology appears to focus on the act of God's judgment, whether on the plane of history as in the Babylonian captivity and the destruction of Jerusalem or at the final judgment (4:11-12; 5:7-11).[24] What drives James then is an ecclesial, eschatological ethics of wisdom[25] and not what many have taken to be the "normal" early Christian method, namely that of (Pauline) soteriology. And his focus on ethics is on doing good, speaking the right way, and expressing the gospel in the socioeconomic ways of compassion and mercy. Hence, he targets prophetic barbs at the (compassion-less) rich, at the unloving work-less, at the unmerciful abuse of power, and at teachers who unlovingly divide and murder. There is nothing in this letter that surprises with regard to what we know of the early churches or the behaviors of early Christians.[26] Those who compare James to other writers in the New Testament end up somehow spending most of their energies on the relationship of faith and works in James in comparison with Paul, and frequently enough James comes up short to the evaluators. Ulrich Luck cleverly speaks of James, mistakenly we believe, as having "eine Sprachkompetenz ohne Sachkompetenz," a competency with language but not with substance.[27] Our conclusion is that James fits into the early churches in ways other than this soteriologically-driven manner. It is fashionable to plot James at one end of the

---

with its cause and effect, not to mention the essential skill of knowing how to live in this world by wisdom — are not present, and this cautions the zealous interpreter from finding too much wisdom in this text. I agree with Verseput: "In short, while James's epistle is certainly a hortatory text and for that reason not dissimilar to the genre of wisdom instruction at the micro level, it does not present itself to the reader on the whole as a product of wisdom reflection" ("Wisdom," 706). Verseput says wisdom is a "marginal motif" in a letter that is wisdom "only in the local sense of familiarly sapiential forms or an occasional hint of a sapiential mood" (p. 706).

22. Penner, *The Epistle of James and Eschatology*. Darian Lockett argues that the combination of wisdom, prophecy, and eschatology is not unique to James in the Jewish world; see his "The Spectrum of Wisdom." This popular Dead Sea Scrolls text is found in at least six different manuscripts, 1Q26 and 4Q415-18, 423.

23. James does, however, have a soteriology; see Konradt, *Christliche Existenz*. On the relationship of these themes, see the sketch in Penner, "Epistle of James," 275-80; also J. E. Botha, "Soteriology under Construction: The Case of James," *Acta Patristica et Byzantia* 17 (2006) 100-118.

24. See especially M. Klein, *"Ein vollkommenes Werk";* see also Wachob, "Apocalyptic Intertexture."

25. See Hartin, *James and the "Q" Sayings of Jesus*, 35-115, 199-217.

26. See Hengel, *Between Jesus and Paul;* C. Setzer, *Jewish Responses to Early Christians* (Minneapolis: Fortress, 1994); Stegemann and Stegemann, *The Jesus Movement;* E. Schnabel, *Early Christian Mission* (2 vols.; Downers Grove: InterVarsity, 2004); A. Patzia, *The Emergence of the Church* (Downers Grove: InterVarsity, 2001).

27. See U. Luck, "Die Theologie des Jakobusbriefes," *ZTK* 81 (1984) 11.

spectrum — at the rightist end — and put Paul at the leftist end, but more careful analysis reveals that James was a mediating influence in the larger picture of the first churches.[28] In fact, one common typology of the earliest Jewish messianic communities had a spectrum from full observance — with circumcision or without circumcision — to observance of the Ten Commandments and festivals to a cutting of ties with the Jewish laws more or less completely. In this typology, James belongs to the observance-without-circumcision group, and Peter is with him but leaning to a more minimal observance group with Paul, who was most likely more conservative than the Hellenists.[29] All such typologies never fit the rugged realities but they at least remind us of the varieties of earliest messianic faith.

Which is to say that James tells the Story in a context where other (Story) options were available and clawing for the same attention.[30] It would be easy to list those options — Sadducees, Pharisees, Essenes, Zealots, and proto-rabbinism come to mind. But one needs also to factor in *varieties of each dimension of Judaism,* not ignoring distinctions like Galilean Judaism or Judean Judaism, and to consider the *varieties of the earliest forms of messianic Judaism or Jewish Christianity.*[31] Many today would press in another direction and contend that James must be read in a Roman or Greek context, which gives the letter yet other resonances. All agree that the "story" James tells is to be read in context. James, in effect, is fashioning a wiki-version of the Story of Jesus as Messiah and the Twelve Tribes as a voice in conversation with other Jewish (and early Christian, Roman, Greek) voices. The voices in this conversation, we perhaps need to remind ourselves, are personal and not just intellectual views and theological positions. Theology, in the thrashing about and surfacing of ideas in the emerging shape of earliest Christianity, was far more connected to powerful leaders — apostolic, prophetic, and pastoral — than to intellectual,

28. See especially G. Boccaccini, *Middle Judaism: Jewish Thought 300 B.C.E. to 200 C.E.* (Minneapolis: Fortress, 1991), 213-28; Martin, xxxiii-xli; see below, the excursus at the end of the comments on 2:14-26; Penner, *The Epistle of James and Eschatology,* 15-32, for some of the methodological questions.

29. See R. E. Brown and J. P. Meier, *Antioch and Rome: New Testament Cradles of Catholic Christianity* (New York: Paulist, 1983). For another view of where James might be located in such a spectrum, see Pratscher, *Der Herrenbruder Jakobus,* who pushes hard for a mediating role for James during his life that was then exaggerated into anti-Paulinism later. Still, James played a role for later Christians as various groups fashioned their own views of James.

30. See especially Hartin, *James of Jerusalem.*

31. An older and still very useful sketch of this is Dunn, *Unity and Diversity.* See also the magisterial *Cambridge History of Judaism,* vol. 3: *The Early Roman Period* (ed. W. Horbury, W. D. Davies, and J. Sturdy; Cambridge: Cambridge University Press, 1999). In this context, see now Skarsaune and Hvalvik, *Jewish Believers in Jesus;* Bindemann, "Weisheit versus Weisheit."

theological, or philosophical options. Hence, the voice of James as he tells his version of the Story is a voice that blended with and stood out from other voices — like Peter's and Paul's and Barnabas's and Stephen's.[32] The authorship of this letter is disputed, but few doubt that the "James" of this letter is either the real or pseudonymous brother of Jesus, and this raises the question of how significant it was to be a "brother" or "sister" or "mother" of Jesus in the emerging leadership of Jerusalem-based and Galilean-based messianism. If one concludes that James, brother of Jesus, was responsible for this letter, then the questions are worthy of historical consideration.[33]

Yet, we have an irony when it comes to James: he has become the ignored leader. We will say more than once in this commentary that James was a "towering figure in the earliest church" and "the first bishop of the leading (mother) church of the growing Christian movement."[34] Many forget and have now forgotten James; in fact, he is sometimes said to be part of the "junk mail" of the New Testament.[35] Famously, Dibelius, in that old Teutonic style, simply announced that James had no theology, and Rudolf Bultmann, fascinated as he was with Lutheran and Pauline theology, completely ignored James in his *Theology of the New Testament*.[36] John Domi-

---

32. This observation sets us firmly in the camp of those who explore the diversity (and unity) of earliest Christianity; one can begin this discussion with Dunn, *Unity and Diversity*. On the relationship of James to Peter and Paul, see especially Chilton and Evans, *Missions*.

33. The best study I have seen of this is R. Bauckham, *Jude and the Relatives of Jesus* (Edinburgh: Clark, 1990), 5-133; see also J. W. Wenham, "The Relatives of Jesus," *Evangelical Quarterly* 47 (1975) 6-15.

This raises the issue of James as one element of what Christians call the "New Testament canon." On this see especially the introductory material in Wall, 1-38. Canon and creed are not disconnected; for that reason, the recent rise of a "theological interpretation of Scripture" surrounding the work of Francis Watson, Kevin Vanhoozer, Stephen Fowl, Daniel Treier, and others appears in this context. For a sketch that reveals the struggle of this approach, see D. Treier, *Introducing Theological Interpretation of Scripture* (Grand Rapids: Baker, 2008).

34. Painter, *Just James*, 1, 4.

35. See Johnson's excellent essay "The Importance of James for Theology" in his *Brother of Jesus, Friend of God*, 235-59. One reference to "junk mail" among others is in Painter, "James as the First Catholic Epistle," 245.

36. Dibelius, 21; R. Bultmann, *Theology of the New Testament* (trans. K. Grobel; New York: Scribner, 1951, 1955). Bultmann did make an observation about James: "Every shred of understanding for the Christian's situation as that of 'between-ness' is lacking here. The moralism of the synagogue-tradition has made its entry" (2.163). The same essential view is seen in P. Stuhlmacher, *Gerechtigkeit Gottes bei Paulus* (2d ed.; FRLANT 87; Göttingen: Vandenhoeck und Ruprecht, 1966), 191-94, who says James is much more anthropologically naïve and, theologically, has fallen back into Judaism (see p. 194).

nic Crossan, hardly a friend of Christian orthodoxy or Reformation theology, skips James in his recent study of the contours of earliest Christianity.[37] David Aune barely stops to consider James in his examination of early Christian letters,[38] and a couple recent New Testament theologies relegate James's letter to last place and shape his "theology" mostly as it relates to Paul.[39] For others James's voice is only rarely heard or seen as untheological or even anti-theological.[40] The man and the letter have suffered the same fate: oblivion or close to it. The reason seems obvious to many: as Jewish messianic communities faded so also did the theology connected to them, including what we now find in James.[41] James has become the one significant leader of the earliest churches who is now mostly ignored. I make this observation knowing full well that there is a serious resurgence, if not a renaissance, of scholarship on James. But like James in the history of the church, this resurgent scholarship is mostly ignored when it comes to Christian theology and gospel preaching.

We might lift our heads in the hope of seeing another day by returning to the place James had in the beginning.[42] We can begin with Eusebius, who provides a list of the bishops of the first-century church of Jerusalem that begins with James:

37. *The Birth of Christianity: Discovering What Happened in the Years Immediately after the Execution of Jesus* (San Francisco: HarperCollins, 1998).

38. *The New Testament in Its Literary Environment* (LEC; Philadelphia: Westminster, 1987).

39. See J. Gnilka, *Theologie des Neuen Testaments* (HTKNT Supplement 5; Freiburg: Herder, 1994); Strecker, *Theology of the New Testament*. Klaus Berger, on the other hand, places James early in his discussion of the theological history of earliest Christianity; see his *Theologiegeschichte des Urchristentums. Theologie des Neuen Testaments* (2d ed.; Tübingen: Francke, 1995), 179-95, especially 186-95. But Berger reveals his orientation with this statement: "James did not have a part in the important developments of early Christian theology" (p. 187). Thus, Christianity is for James (according to Berger) not a "Christological redemption teaching [keine christologische Erlösungslehre]" but a "method, a 'way'" (p. 197).

40. G. B. Caird and L. D. Hurst, *New Testament Theology* (Oxford: Clarendon, 1994), leave very little place at the table for James. I lament the untimely passing of my friend Lincoln Hurst and honor him once again for his devotion to completing Caird's theology. See also Andrew Chester and R. P. Martin, *The Theology of the Letters of James, Peter, and Jude* (New York: Cambridge University Press, 1994), 45.

41. Two books by Dunn initiate readers into the discussion: *Unity and Diversity* and *The Partings of the Ways;* see also Skarsaune and Hvalvik, *Jewish Believers in Jesus;* M. Jackson-McCabe, ed., *Jewish Christianity Reconsidered* (Minneapolis: Fortress, 2007).

42. A sketch can be found in W. R. Baker, "James, Book of," in *DTIB,* 347-51; the commentary below will provide more than enough positive reevaluations of James's theology.

> The first then was *James* who was called the Lord's brother, and after him Simeon was the second. The third was Justus, Zacchaeus was the fourth, Tobias the fifth, the sixth Benjamin, the seventh John, the eighth Matthias, the ninth Philip, the tenth Seneca, the eleventh Justus, the twelfth Levi, the thirteenth Ephres, the fourteenth Joseph, and last of all the fifteenth Judas (*Church History* 4.5.3; cf. 7.19.1).

Those of us in the Reformed, Lutheran, or evangelical traditions perhaps need to be warned that James may have had a louder voice than Paul's at times and that his letter is not a relic from that quaint era before theologians got everything figured out. The famous episode of Paul, Peter, and the "men from James" in Galatians 2:11-14 illustrates our point. Even if the "James" in the "men from James" reflects not an authentic message from that James but a borrowed, exaggerated authority assumed by a factional group, one cannot dispute that for some there was a *perception* of difference among the apostles James, Peter, and Paul with James exercising enough clout to push Peter away from Paul. Still, within a generation or two James disappeared from influence for many of the orthodox, and it is all too well known how mightily the Reformation struggled with the theology of James. Only by digging back to the earliest days will we see clearly enough to rescue James from behind the scenes of orthodoxy's theological focal points and discover, as if all over again, the inner vibrations of the earliest tellings of the Christian Story. At the heart of that Story was Torah.

But there is another story at work behind James which seems implicit in nearly every line of the letter and breaks forth from the water in the opening lines of the letter when James writes to people who are not in the Land. This is the Story of the Land of Israel. At the center of the biblical promises to Abraham, David, and the prophets, and a center that still has not moved from observant Jews, is God's word that they will have a place, the sacred Land of Israel, as their inheritance. Though even many today think Jesus transferred this land promise into new creation, the fact remains that many Jews and many Christians continued to rely on the Land promise. It lurks behind the promise that the meek would inherit the Land (Matt 5:5) and is possibly at work in the salt of the *Land* ("earth") in contrast to the light to the *world* (the Gentile mission, Matt 5:13-16).[43] Whether one agrees with these suggestions, the fact remains that the Jews like James believed God was faithful to his Land promise. Jerusalem was at the center of that promise; as Jerusalem went, so went the Land.[44] Judg-

---

43. I owe the suggestion of Matt 5:13-16 to my colleague Joel Willitts. See here K. J. Wenell, *Jesus and Land: Sacred and Social Space in Second Temple Judaism* (LNTS 334; London: Clark, 2007); R. L. Wilken, *The Land Called Holy: Palestine in Christian History and Thought* (New Haven: Yale University Press, 1992).

44. See P. W. L. Walker, *Jesus and the Holy City: New Testament Perspectives on Jerusalem* (Grand Rapids: Eerdmans, 1996).

ment on Jerusalem was judgment on the Land and on God's people. Early Jewish Christians did not immediately say, "The promise has changed. Forget the Land. Let's take over the Roman Empire and then the world!" No, they saw the Land as sacred.

The messianic community that formed in Jerusalem saw itself, then, as more than just one of the many churches of Jesus followers. They saw themselves at the epicenter of God's work in the world, as the church of churches, the mother church. James was the heralded leader of the Jerusalem messianic community, to whom even Paul gave his reports. He is the first listed among the "pillars" in Galatians 2:9, the one who speaks the final, discerning words in Acts 15, and the first one Paul meets when he arrives in Jerusalem for the last time (Acts 21:18). I am a Protestant and not in direct fellowship with the See of Rome, but if asked who was the "first pope," I would choose James.[45] He was at the center of the church, the whole church, because the whole church had its start in Jerusalem. What was said in Jerusalem mattered everywhere. Until 70 AD. But that gets ahead of our Story, a Story that involves the Land and Jerusalem and James as the center at the center.

Like every other book in the Bible, James crafts his chapter in this Story in the crucible of a concrete context. That context, in part, was competing versions of the Story of Israel. Sadducees, Pharisees, Essenes, and Zealots — to name the four big versions of the Story — each told their own version of the Story. Each also drew up what Thomas Holmén called "covenant path markers," particular practices that were vested with symbolic significance as what best represented faithfulness to the covenant.[46] Pharisees, for instance, vested significance in purity and food laws.[47] Just how James fit into those competing circles is not entirely clear, but a good start is offered in Craig Evans's synoptic comparison:

> In sum, we could say that if we drew three circles to represent the Judaisms of Qumran, the Rabbis, and James, the circles would overlap. *But the centers of these circles, centers which represent the essence of the respective Judaisms, would not. . . .* The Judaism of Qumran is focused on the renewal of the covenant, with great emphasis on cultic reform. The Judaism of the Rabbis is focused on studying and obeying the Torah, the key to life in this world and in the world to

45. See the suggestive sketch by P.-A. Bernheim in *James, Brother of Jesus,* 191-222.

46. T. Holmén, *Jesus and Jewish Covenant Thinking* (Biblical Interpretation Series 55; Leiden: Brill, 2001), 37-87.

47. Demonstrated long ago in J. Neusner, *The Rabbinic Traditions about the Pharisees before 70* (3 vols.; Atlanta: Scholars, 1999).

come. The Judaism of James is focused on faith and piety centered on Messiah Jesus.[48]

Finally, the letter of James is not the kind of speculative theology that one will find later in Athanasius, Augustine, or Aquinas. James writes paraenesis,[49] in fact a "paraenetic encyclical,"[50] to the twelve tribes in the Dispersion about concrete problems like testing, faith, wisdom, anger, compassion, the poor, envy, the rich, and praying for the sick. Letters, even if not close to James in tone or style or substance, are not uncommon in Judaism.[51] Breathing in and out of this context is James's gospel and theology, which give rise to his sharp answers.[52] But what can we make of James's historical situation?[53]

JAMES: WHO WROTE THE LETTER?

The first word of our letter creates a problem: "*James, a servant of God and of the Lord Jesus Christ*" (1:1). Who is this James? He assumed that his readers would know who he was and recognize his authority,[54] and

48. C. A. Evans, "Comparing Judaisms," in Chilton and Neusner, *The Brother of Jesus,* 161-83, quoting from p. 182 (italics added). See Evans's essay for more complete comparisons.

49. See especially L. Perdue, "Paraenesis and the Epistle of James," who helpfully explores the social significance of paraenesis in light of the sociological theories of Peter Berger and Thomas Luckmann.

50. Bauckham, 13; W. Popkes, "The Mission of James," in Chilton and Neusner, *The Brother of Jesus,* 89. See also M. Tsuji, *Glaube zwischen Vollkommenheit und Verweltlichung. Eine Untersuchung zur literarischen Gestalt und zur inhaltlichen Kohärenz des Jakobusbriefes* (WUNT 2.93; Tübingen: Mohr, 1997); K.-W. Niebuhr, "Der Jakobusbrief im Licht frühjüdischer Diasporabriefe," *NTS* 44 (1998) 420-43; Verseput, "Genre and Story," who then extends the letter tradition as one directed toward ancient voluntary associations. Dibelius emphasized the disunity of the letter, while these more recent studies emphasize the unity in function — the function of a letter bringing unity of identity to people under stress.

51. See Jer 29 (LXX 36); Ep Jer [= 6:1-73]; *2 Baruch* 78–87; *4 Baruch* 6:19-25; 2 Macc 1:1-9 and 1:10–2:18. See the later evidence at *b Sanhedrin* 11b.

52. See here Wall, 27-34; Strecker, *Theology of the New Testament,* 654-82; Tamez, *Scandalous Message.*

53. This is a commentary and not a monograph on all the historical issues. The intense scholarship on what could be called introductory matters — context, historical connections, authorship, life of James, date, and connections to other early Christian texts — could easily consume a long monograph. Footnotes will point interested readers to such discussions.

54. This raises the question of James's rhetoric, since it is the rhetoric that leads

13

perhaps even the term "servant" as specially characteristic of him. What are our options?[55]

Someone named "James"[56] is mentioned more than forty times in the New Testament. It is useful then to trot out the presumably separable Jameses[57] and evidence for each, and we will present them in an ascending order of probabilities, leaving the last two as the only real possibilities.

First, *James the father of Judas* (Luke 6:16; Acts 1:13).[58]
Second, *James the Less or Younger, son of Mary wife of Cleopas* (Mark 15:40; Matt 27:56; Mark 16:1; Luke 24:10).
Third, *James the son of Alphaeus, one of the Twelve* (Mark 3:18; Matt 10:3; Luke 6:15; Acts 1:13).[59]
Fourth, *James the son of Zebedee and brother of the apostle John and*

---

us to the conviction that he expected his readers to do what he said. On this, see, e.g., Wachob, *Voice of Jesus,* 1-58, where he shows that "paraenesis" is not a genre but a positive mode of rhetoric.

55. I wish to call attention to a few introductions that are pieces of scholarship in their own right: Martin, xxxi-cix; Pratscher, *Der Herrenbruder Jakobus;* Johnson, 1-164; Johnson, *Brother of Jesus, Friend of God,* 1-122; Painter, *Just James;* Bernheim, *James, Brother of Jesus;* Frankemölle, 1.39-120; Popkes, 1-69; Popkes, "The Mission of James," in Chilton and Neusner, *The Brother of Jesus,* 88-99; Penner, *The Epistle of James and Eschatology;* R. Wall, in *DLNTD,* 545-61; Bauckham. Also Chilton and Neusner, *The Brother of Jesus,* especially the chapter by J. Painter, "Who Was James?" 10-65. Hartin, "The Religious Context of the Letter of James," puts together Hartin's many writings on James in a succinct manner.

56. On the English name "James" we have the following history: Hebrew *Yakov* ("Jacob"), through the Greek form *Yakobos,* became early Latin *Jacobus* and was softened in later Latin to *Jacomus* and then Old French *Gemmes/Jaimes,* Spanish *Jaime,* Catalonian *Jaume,* and Italian *Giacomo.* Hence, the use of "Jacobite" as the adjective for James in scholarship on this letter; some suggest we should use the name "Jacob" instead of "James." See Johnson, 93, for the history of the name.

57. Some, of course, equate two or more of these Jameses. For instance, one traditional view equates (2), (3), and (5). Bernheim stretches the same references to seven possible Jameses (*James, Brother of Jesus,* 21).

58. Luke 6:16: "and Judas son of James, and Judas Iscariot, who became a traitor." Luke thus distinguishes Judas *ben Yakov* from Judas Iscariot. Both Mark 3:18 and Matt 10:4 have "Simon the Cananaean" where Luke has Judas son of James. The lists of the apostles vary. In the fourth group Matthew and Mark have James son of Alphaeus, Thaddaeus, Simon the Cananaean, and Judas Iscariot; Luke-Acts has James son of Alphaeus, Simon *the Zealot,* Judas son of James, and Judas Iscariot (the last omitted in Acts).

59. Some identify James son of Alphaeus with James son of Mary, the wife of Cleopas, who is identified with Alphaeus. A few have made this James the author of James.

also one of the Twelve (Mark 1:19; 3:17; Luke 6:14; Acts 1:13). This
James, according to Acts 12:2, was beheaded by Herod Agrippa I.
Fifth, *James the brother of Jesus, son of Mary* (Mark 6:3; Matt 13:55;
Gal 1:19; 2:9, 12; Acts 12:17; 15:13; 21:18; Jude 1; John 7:3-5;
1 Cor 9:5).[60]

Because of his premature death and a total lack of early Christian connection
to the letter, nearly everyone agrees that James the son of Zebedee, brother of
apostle John, did not write this letter. The evidence for one of the other
Jameses being the author is nonexistent. There are really only three possibilities for "James" the author of this book:

(1) the brother of Jesus wrote this letter;[61]
(2) the brother of Jesus, though the letter was written by someone else in
his name;[62]
(3) someone else whom we do not know about.

What we can do at this point is sketch the evidence we do have to see what
the brother of Jesus looks like and then ask if this person could be the author.[63] If not, then the second or third option would claim our conclusion.

---

60. Some identify this James with the son of Alphaeus and therefore also possibly
with James the father of Judas.

61. A variant on this view is a two-stage (or more) process: James spoke and
someone later edited or anthologized his speeches, leading to the theory that one might
detect two contexts — one in Jerusalem and the other later in Syrian Antioch. Thus
Davids; Martin, lxxiii, lxxvi. At times the evidence might suggest such a process, but it is
never clear enough to lead to any kind of confidence that we can prove the editorial process. This will come up now and then in the commentary.

62. Pseudonymity is not as volatile an issue as it once was. Compare J. D. G.
Dunn, "Pseudepigraphy," in *DLNTD,* 977-84 with D. A. Carson, "Pseudonymity and
Pseudepiraphy," in *DNTB,* 857-64.

63. Many studies today are devoted to developing a critical portrait of James,
brother of Jesus, including the eccentric and deservedly ignored theories of R. H.
Eisenman, *James the Brother of Jesus: The Key to Unlocking the Secrets of Early Chris-
tianity and the Dead Sea Scrolls* (New York: Viking, 1996). See the sounder treatments in
Pratscher, *Der Herrenbruder Jakobus;* Bernheim, *James, Brother of Jesus;* Painter, *Just
James;* Hartin, *James of Jerusalem.* A study worthy of note here also is M. Hengel,
"Jakobus der Herrenbruder — der erste 'Papst'?" in *Glaube und Eschatologie: Festschrift
für Werner Georg Kümmel zum 80. Geburtstag* (ed. E. Grässer and O. Merk; Tübingen:
Mohr, 1985), 71-104. For a critique of the Eisenman theories, see P. R. Davies, "James in
the Qumran Scrolls," in Chilton and Evans, *James the Just and Christian Origins,* 17-31.
For a complete survey of the discussion, see Myllykoski, "James the Just."

The so-called James Ossuary has been examined by C. A. Evans, "A Fishing

JAMES, BROTHER OF JESUS, IN THE NEW TESTAMENT

James the brother of Jesus belonged to a *large pious (Torah-observant) family under stress.* Whether one takes the Helvidian, Hieronymian, or Epiphanian view,[64] the "brother" of Jesus would have been part of a large family. According to Mark 6:3, the male children of the family included, and here I give rough transliterations of the Hebrew names: *"Yakov* and *Yosef* and *Yehuda* and *Simeon."* Add to this *"Yeshua"* and there are five boys with traditional names. Mark also mentions "sisters," though he gives them no names. That means there were at least seven children. If there is any truth to the tradition that Joseph died and left Mary a widow, James would have been part of a family in stress, and that might help explain why James sees pure religion as caring for the poor and widows (James 1:26-27).

Second, *James perhaps came to faith only after Jesus' death and as a result of the resurrection.*[65] The Gospel of John seemingly observes that the brothers of Jesus did not believe in him during his lifetime, and alternative explanations fail to convince (cf. John 7:3-5). It is often argued that, because at the crucifixion Jesus hands his mother over to the apostle John (19:25-27) and not to one of his brothers, the brothers had not yet come to faith in Jesus.

Boat, a House, and an Ossuary: What Can We Learn from the Artifacts?" in Chilton and Evans, *Missions,* 211-31; J. Magness, "Ossuaries and the Burials of Jesus and James," *JBL* 124 (2005) 121-54. Most today now think the ossuary is inauthentic. Ben Witherington, who has a dog in this fight, hangs on to the authenticity: see H. Shanks and B. Witherington III, *The Brother of Jesus: The Dramatic Story and Meaning of the First Archaeological Link to Jesus and His Family* (San Francisco: HarperSanFrancisco, 2003).

64. J. P. Meier, *A Marginal Jew: Rethinking the Historical Jesus* (ABRL; New York: Doubleday, 1991), 1.316-32; "The Brothers and Sisters of Jesus in Ecumenical Perspective," *CBQ* 54 (1992) 1-28; R. Bauckham, "The Brothers and Sisters of Jesus: An Epiphanian Response to John P. Meier," *CBQ* 56 (1994) 686-700; J. Painter, "Who Was James?" in Chilton and Neusner, *The Brother of Jesus,* 12-24; Hartin, *James of Jerusalem,* 24-35. If James is the son of a different mother, as Epiphanius argued, then he was most likely the oldest son and therefore responsible for the family. I agree with Helvidius, whom Jerome ridiculed in his *The Perpetual Virginity of the Blessed Mary,* and I think Mary had other children with Joseph. In this view, James may have been the son following Jesus in birth order.

65. J. Painter represents those who think James and the other brothers were actually believers but had a different "messianic" vision; see Painter, *Just James,* 11-41; "Who Was Jesus?" in Chilton and Neusner, *The Brother of Jesus,* 24-31; also R. Bauckham, "James and Jesus," in Chilton and Neusner, *The Brother of Jesus,* 106-9; Hartin, *James of Jerusalem,* 9-24; Bernheim, *James, Brother of Jesus,* 76-100. In essence, I see Painter's points to be a distinction without a significant difference. Furthermore, a deeper dipping of this issue into conversion theory would aid the discussion. See McKnight, *Turning to Jesus.* For other views, see Pratscher, *Der Herrenbruder Jakobus,* 13-27, who speaks of a distance between Jesus and his family during his lifetime.

But by the Day of Pentecost the brothers are in the middle of the inner circle of disciples (Acts 1:13-14; cf. Jude 1). The shift from John 19 to Acts 1, that is, from apparent unbelief at the cross to faith by Pentecost, is sudden, but neither should one discount the historical value of 1 Corinthians 15:7 as evidence that the resurrected Jesus appeared to James.[66] The evidence is not completely clear, but it leans in the direction of James having become a believer after the death of Jesus and perhaps as a result of encountering the resurrected Jesus.

We know neither whether Peter's departure from Jerusalem (Acts 12:17) reflected tensions within the Jerusalem community over the Law and the Hellenists nor whether it led to a deeper conservatism there.[67] Nonetheless, another remembered feature of James emerges: *he was a peace-seeking*[68] *leader of the church in Jerusalem.*[69] Sometime around the early to mid-40s, probably after the early dispersion of the apostolic leaders from Jerusalem, James became a mediating leader of the church in Jerusalem[70] and was called — scholarly nuances aside — an "apostle" (Gal 1:19;[71] 2:9, 12;

---

66. See Pratscher, *Der Herrenbruder Jakobus,* 29-48; McKnight, "A Parting within the Way," 98-102.

67. A good place to begin here is M. Hengel, *Between Jesus and Paul,* 1-29. Many point to a dynastic principle at work here, though much of this is wildly speculative: see, e.g., S. G. F. Brandon, "The Death of James the Just," in *Mysticism and Religion, Presented to Gershom G. Scholem* (ed. E. E. Urbach et al.; Jerusalem: Magnes, 1967), 57-69; J. D. Tabor, *The Jesus Dynasty* (New York: Simon and Schuster, 2006). A good study focusing more on charisma than on succession is D. Lambers-Petry, "Verwandte Jesu als Referenzpersonen für das Judenchristentum," in *The Image of Judaeo-Christians in Ancient Jewish and Christian Literature* (ed. P. J. Tomson and D. Lambers-Petry; WUNT 158: Tübingen: Mohr, 2003), 32-51.

68. Many speak of James as a reconciler; see Pratscher, *Der Herrenbruder Jakobus,* 49-102. But see Painter, *Just James,* 42-57, who concludes that Luke has covered up some of the tensions between James and Paul. The mediating position of James in Acts 15 is explained as Lukan *Tendenz* rather than reliable information (see Painter, *Just James,* 52). See also Hartin, *James of Jerusalem,* 45-86.

69. At this point it is worth noting that speculation from James's rhetoric to his education has led to many discussions with no consensus. D. F. Watson, whose expertise in rhetoric lends credibility to his conclusions, suggests that James received a rhetorical education approximating the secondary level but "within a Jewish context with strong Hellenistic influence." See Watson, "An Assessment of the Rhetoric," in Webb and Kloppenborg, *Reading James,* 113-14, here quoting p. 113.

70. See here Bernheim, *James, Brother of Jesus,* 149-222, for a wide-ranging sketch of the rise of James as a leader.

71. See L. P. Trudinger, "ἕτερον δὲ τῶν ἀποστόλων οὐκ εἶδον, εἰ μὴ Ἰάκωβον: A Note on Galatians i.19," *NovT* 17 (1975) 200-202; and the response by G. Howard, "Was James an Apostle? A Reflection on a New Proposal for Gal. i.19," *NovT* 19 (1977) 63-64.

1 Cor 15:7; Acts 12:17; 15:2; 21:18). Most notably, he was the peacemaker of the controversy — precipitated by the missional visions[72] of various leaders — over whether or not Gentile converts ought to be circumcised, and it brought him into direct contact with the apostle Paul.[73] This may shed light on James 3:18, where wisdom and peacemaking are connected. According to Acts 15, James argues for peace on the basis of the eschatological restoration of the house of David; and this could be behind his "twelve tribes of Israel" statement in 1:1. That restored house includes a vision for Gentiles (Acts 15, especially vv. 13-21; cf. Amos 9:11-12).

But James's theory of peace comes at a (perhaps minimal?) cost for Gentiles: he advocated in his ruling and letter that they, perhaps classified legally now as resident aliens, show respect for some Mosaic *mitzvot* (cf. Acts 15:19-21 with Lev 17–18). Some see here only major concerns with Gentile temples.[74] James argued this on the basis of the universal knowledge of the Mosaic Torah: "For in every city, for generations past, Moses has had those who proclaim him, for he has been read aloud every Sabbath in the synagogues" (Acts 15:21).[75] This James, then, is a Torah-observant Jew who expects Gentile

---

72. I cannot agree with all the details in the six factions in two missions as presented by Painter, *Just James,* 73-78, but one must acknowledge diversity. He sees missions framed to the circumcised by (1) Pharisaic believers, (2) James, and (3) Peter and to the uncircumcised by (4) Barnabas, (5) Paul, and (6) unnamed leaders mentioned in 1 Corinthians.

73. See W. R. Farmer, "James the Lord's Brother, According to Paul," in Chilton and Evans, *James the Just and Christian Origins,* 133-53. A fascinating "conversation" occurred in 404 AD between Jerome and Augustine; see Jerome, *Letters* 112.4-18; Augustine, *Letters,* 75. A recent study of this issue is P. Fredriksen, *Paul and the Jews: A Christian Defense of Jews and Judaism* (New York: Doubleday, 2008).

74. See T. Callan, "The Background of the Apostolic Decree (Acts 15:20, 29; 21:25)," *CBQ* 55 (1993) 284-97; M. Bockmuehl, "The Noachide Commands and New Testament Ethics with Special Reference to Acts 15 and Pauline Halakhah," *RB* 102 (1995) 72-101; also in Bockmuehl, *Jewish Law,* 145-72; J. Wehnert, *Die Reinheit des "christlichen Gottesvolkes" aus Juden und Heiden. Studien zum historischen und theologischen Hintergrund des sogenannten Aposteldekrets* (FRLANT 173; Göttingen: Vandenhoeck und Ruprecht, 1997); Bauckham, "James and the Gentiles"; "James and the Jerusalem Church," 452-67; "Peter, James and the Gentiles," 91-142; J. Taylor, "The Jerusalem Decrees (Acts 15.20, 29 and 21.25) and the Incident at Antioch (Gal 2.11-14)," *NTS* 47 (2001) 372-80; McKnight, "A Parting within the Way," 106-9. The exegesis found in Acts 15:13-35 involves Amos 9:11-12 as framed by Hos 3:5; Jer 12:15; and Isa 45:21 and results in a mixing of the building of the eschatological Temple with the conversion of Gentiles — leading in several instances back to Lev 17–18. Not all agree that the stipulations of Acts 15 are rooted in Lev 17–18; see, e.g., S. G. Wilson, *Luke and the Law* (SNTSMS 23; Cambridge: Cambridge University Press, 1983), 85-87; A. J. M. Wedderburn, "The 'Apostolic Decree': Tradition and Redaction," *NovT* 35 (1993) 362-89.

75. On this text, cf. Bauckham, "James and the Jerusalem Church." On Gentile

converts to observe the Torah at a minimal level and Jewish believers to continue to observe Torah. We would observe also that when Paul arrives in Jerusalem for the last time he meets with James (21:18), who exhorts him to make visibly clear (in a vow) his commitment to Torah observance (21:20-26).[76] Clearly, James is a Torah-observant leading presence in Jerusalem. One can infer, for the moment, that James wrote this letter from Jerusalem, a point that has been exploited in the careful work of Richard Bauckham.[77]

James's leadership was potent, perhaps leading to the misuse of his name. It is very difficult to know his precise contribution to the table fellowship problems in Antioch, but Galatians 2:12 puts it this way: "for until certain people came from James, [Peter] used to eat with the Gentiles. But after they came, he drew back and kept himself separate for fear of the circumcision faction." We need not resolve the issues here, whether they concern eating too frequently with Gentile Christians or eating with them at all or actual dispensing with dietary rules and just what role "Antioch" played in the discussions.[78] What matters for us is that James is connected, whether accu-

---

converts, see my *A Light among the Gentiles: Jewish Missionary Activity in the Second Temple Period* (Minneapolis: Fortress, 1991), 78-89; M. Goodman, *Mission and Conversion* (Oxford: Clarendon, 1994); L. Feldman, *Jew and Gentile in the Ancient World* (Princeton: Princeton University Press, 1993); J. C. Paget, "Jewish Proselytism at the Time of Christian Origins: Chimera or Reality?" *JSNT* 62 (1996) 65-103; I. Levinskaya, *The Book of Acts in Its Diaspora Setting* (The Book of Acts in Its First Century Setting 5; Grand Rapids: Eerdmans, 1996), 19-126.

76. See B. D. Chilton, "James in Relation to Peter, Paul, and the Remembrance of Jesus," in Chilton and Neusner, *The Brother of Jesus,* 138-59; J. Neusner, "Vow-Taking, the Nazirites, and the Law: Does James' Advice to Paul accord with Halakhah?" in Chilton and Evans, *James the Just and Christian Origins,* 59-82; R. Bauckham, "Peter, James and the Gentiles," in Chilton and Evans, *Missions,* 91-142. For a sketch of the discussions, see Myllykoski, "James the Just," part two, 11-23.

77. E.g., Bauckham, 16-23, who points to the customary power of letters stemming from Jerusalem. E.g., 2 Macc 1:1-10; Acts 15:23-29. See also P. H. Davids, "Palestinian Traditions in the Epistle of James," in Chilton and Evans, *James the Just and Christian Origins,* 33-57.

78. On this see M. Bockmuehl, "Antioch and James the Just," in Chilton and Evans, *James the Just and Christian Origins,* 155-98 (and in Bockmuehl, *Jewish Law,* 49-83), who proposes a geographical inclusion of Antioch in the Holy Land. Ezek 47:15-17; 48:1, though, refer to a more traditional mapping of the northernmost regions of the Holy Land, probably from the coast eastward to the Lake of Homs. One should not, however, discount the maximizing of the extent of the Land — to the Taurus Mountains — for some Jews, including later rabbinic evidence (e.g., *m Hullin* 4:7-8). The gravity of Bockmuehl's theory is that "many first-century Palestinian Jews regarded Antioch as the gateway from the Exile to the Holy Land" (p. 179). Therefore, the concern of the men from James and/or the circumcision party could have been with the purity of the Land and not with the Diaspora. The men from James, then, could be genuine emissaries from James and concerned

rately by the "men from James" or the "circumcision faction" or not, to Torah observance and at least its minimal observance by Gentile converts.[79]

JAMES, BROTHER OF JESUS, OUTSIDE THE NEW TESTAMENT

This view of James as a Torah-observant leader of some stature in the Jerusalem church also comes up outside the New Testament. In fact, his leadership was a growing legend.[80] Josephus tells us that the younger, rash Ananus (Annas II) was a follower of the "heartless" Sadducees and convened the Sanhedrin to try "James, the brother of Jesus who was called the Christ, and certain others." Ananus tried to take advantage of the interregnum between Festus and Albinus, but Albinus was made aware of the situation by the Pharisees, who took the opportunity to score points against the Sadducees. Ananus nonetheless accused James and the others of "having transgressed the law and delivered them up to be stoned" (*Ant* 20.199-200).

The details of the stoning of James in 62 AD were clarified, or elaborated if you will, by Clement of Alexandria and Hegesippus, whose accounts are embedded in Eusebius and, alongside these texts, one must also consider the *Second Apocalypse of James* and the Pseudo-Clementines, though their value diminishes for detecting reliable information.[81] Clement wrote, "Now there were two Jameses, one James the Just [brother of Jesus], who was thrown down from the pinnacle of the temple and beaten to death with a fuller's club, and the other [son of Zebedee] he who was beheaded" (Eusebius, *Eccl Hist* 2.1.5). Eusebius's account of Hegesippus is more complete and fascinating (2.23) while the account in the *2 Apoc. Jas.* imagines (in

---

with Jewish Christians but not with food laws; they are not to be equated with the agitators (Gal 5:10, 12). The Jacobean mission was in part political, shaped by the praxis of Jesus, and the differences between Paul and James were halakhic.

79. See J. L. Martyn, *Galatians* (AB 33A; New York: Doubleday, 1997), 228-45; Dunn, "Incident at Antioch"; W. R. Farmer, "James the Lord's Brother, According to Paul," in Chilton and Evans, *James the Just and Christian Origins,* 145-49. For a sketch of scholarship, see Myllykoski, "James the Just," part one, 108-12.

80. See Painter, *Just James,* 105-223; Martin, xlvii-lxi; Pratscher, *Der Herrenbruder Jakobus,* 102-260; Hartin, *James of Jerusalem,* 115-40, for sketches of the data. See Myllykoski, "James the Just," part two, 23-83. An analogous study designed to uncover a figure can be found in J. L. Price, "The Quest for the Historical Bibfeldt," in *The Unrelieved Paradox: Studies in the Theology of Franz Bibfeldt* (ed. M. E. Marty and J. C. Brauer; Grand Rapids: Eerdmans, 1994), 26-34.

81. See Hennecke and Schneemelcher, *New Testament Apocrypha,* 1.333-41; J. M. Robinson, *The Nag Hammadi Library in English* (3d ed.; San Francisco: Harper and Row, 1988), 269-76; Painter, *Just James,* 159-223, for more complete discussion.

Gnostic tone) what James said to those gathered around. In Eusebius we "learn" more about the precise setting of James's martryrdom: "When Paul appealed to Caesar and was sent over to Rome by Festus, the Jews were disappointed of the hope in which they had laid their plot against him and turned against James, the brother of the Lord, to whom the throne of the bishopric in Jerusalem had been allotted by the Apostles" (2.23.1). The specifics of the cause against him are also clarified: "They brought him into the midst and demanded a denial of the faith in Christ before all the people" (2.23.2). And James's response: "With a loud voice and with more courage than they had expected, [he] confessed before all the people that our Lord and Savior Jesus Christ is the son of God" (2.23.2). The Jewish mob was enraged: "They could no longer endure his testimony, since he was by all men believed to be most righteous [*dikaiotaton*] because of the height which he had reached in a life of philosophy and religion [*ton bion philosophias te kai theosebeias*]" (2.23.2). So they killed him at an opportune moment, "using anarchy as an opportunity for power since at that moment Festus had died in Judea, leaving the district without government or procurator" (2.23.2). *2 Apoc. Jas.* adds also that the crowd did not respond positively to his claims (61).

Eusebius uses some critical judgment in comparing Clement's account with Hegesippus's. To begin with, Hegesippus "belongs to the generation after the Apostles" (2.23.3) and gives the most accurate account. He informs us that James was charged to look after the church. He was holy from his mother's womb.

> He drank no wine or strong drink, nor did he eat flesh; no razor went upon his head; he did not anoint himself with oil, and he did not go to the baths. He alone was allowed to enter into the sanctuary, for he did not wear wool but linen, and he used to enter alone into the temple and be found kneeling and praying for forgiveness for the people, so that his knees grew hard like a camel's because of his constant worship of God, kneeling and asking forgiveness for the people. So from his excessive righteousness[82] he was called the Just and Oblias, that is in Greek, "*Rampart* of the people and righteousness," as the prophets declare concerning him (2.23.6-7).

Behind the word "Oblias" we are to see the vision of the eschatological Zion and the Temple in Isaiah 54:11-12:[83]

> O afflicted one, storm-tossed, and not comforted,
>   I am about to set your stones in antimony,

---

82. διά γέ τοι τὴν ὑπερβολὴν τῆς δικαιοσύνης αὐτοῦ.
83. See Bauckham, "James and the Jerusalem Church," 448-50.

> and lay your foundations with sapphires.
> I will make your pinnacles of rubies,
>   your gates of jewels,
>   and all your *wall* of precious stones.

Along with texts like Isaiah 3:10 and Psalm 118,[84] James himself was found in Scripture along with his role as the wall — protective, plumb line, rampart — which God used to build the eschatological temple. With such a prominent role in the Jerusalem church, the leaders of Judaism — Hegisippus calls them "Jews and the Scribes and the Pharisees" (2.23.10) — attempted to persuade James to reroute the people's belief in Jesus as Messiah toward safer ground (2.23.10-11). So, they got him to mount the "battlement" of the Temple at Passover to persuade the crowds.[85]

"What is the gate of Jesus?" they asked James to answer publicly, to set him up for a safe confession (2.23.12). His answer reverses their wishes: "Why do you ask me concerning the Son of Man? He is sitting in heaven on the right hand of the great power, and he will come on the clouds of heaven" (2.23.13). We are told that many responded to James in faith and that this led the offended and worried leaders to mount the same battlement, toss him down, and, in accordance with sacred texts (Wis 2:10; Isa 3:10), stone him (2.23.14-16; see *2 Apoc. Jas.* 61-62). James then prayed nearly the same prayer Jesus did for his persecutors: "forgive them, for they know not what they do" (2.23.16). The *2 Apoc. Jas.* expands the prayer (62-63). He died, according to Eusebius, from a blow to the head by a club (2.23.18) and was buried on the spot.

Luke Timothy Johnson observes, without argument and with robust assertion: "The fictionalizing tendency in such accounts is patent."[86] Perhaps, but where does one draw the line? Richard Bauckham, hardly a gullible historian, finds "Oblias" to be a *bona fide* scrap of historical information.[87] Hagiographical details creep into such accounts, especially when it comes to details of piety, but they can be seen as ornamental decoration of an otherwise credible account, and I find the same here. In general, we have a James who is pious, with a focus on the word "just" or "righteous." I find that credible, consistent with messianic Judaism, and coherent with the letter itself. We also have a James who is a leader in Jerusalem, a development that seems to have followed the dispersion of the apostles in the early forties for which we find evidence in Acts 12, 15, and 21. This, too, makes sense of the evidence. What remains are two facts: that James was martyred and how he was mar-

---

84. On which see especially C. A. Evans, "Jesus and James: Martyrs of the Temple," in Chilton and Evans, *James the Just and Christian Origins,* 233-49.

85. ἐπὶ τὸ πτερύγιον τοῦ ἱεροῦ.

86. Johnson, 100.

87. Bauckham, "James and the Jerusalem Church," 448-50.

tyred. I suspect the latter, along with clarification of the cause against him,[88] grew in detail, though the differences between Clement and Hegesippus are not as great as one might suggest. I see no reason to doubt the stubborn tradition that James, brother of Jesus, was a martyr. I doubt we will ever know if he was pushed off an embattlement, but death by stoning or from the wound of a club is not farfetched.[89]

JAMES, BROTHER OF JESUS, AND THE LETTER

The evidence suggests that the "James" of James 1:1 is the brother of Jesus, whether the writer was he or someone writing in his name.[90] One way of saying this can be found in W. H. Wachob's question: "Is it possible that the text is here setting up James of Jerusalem as the broker for God and Jesus, and the benefits they espoused (wisdom, justice, social status, self-status)?"[91] We probe deeper now into this James of Jerusalem question by considering connections between what we know of an obviously very *Jewish* James and the letter itself.

Few dispute the Jewishness of this letter, though we perhaps still need to remind ourselves that "Judaism" is not separate from "Hellenism."[92] It appeals to the Tanakh often (1:11; 2:8-10, 23; 4:6; 5:4, 5), alludes to it constantly (e.g., 1:13-15, 27; 2:20-26; 3:9; 4:7-10, 11-12; 5:10-11, 17), and breathes throughout the spirit of biblical Judaism as it came to expression in diverse ways by the first century AD. The author chooses to call his audience something thoroughly biblical — "the twelve tribes in the Dispersion" (1:1) — and he calls God "the Lord of hosts" (5:4). He frames theology at times in

88. On which see the detailed analysis by R. Bauckham, "For What Offence Was James Put to Death?" in Chilton and Evans, *James the Just and Christian Origins,* 199-232. The two primary considerations are blasphemy and leading the people to worship other gods (e.g., Deut 13; *2 Apoc Jas* 62:7), which Bauckham thinks more likely.

89. We trade here in historiographical method. See my *Jesus and His Death,* 3-46; D. C. Allison, Jr., *The Historical Christ and the Theological Jesus* (Grand Rapids: Eerdmans, 2009).

90. A point made clearly by B. S. Childs, *The New Testament as Canon: An Introduction* (Philadelphia: Fortress, 1985), 435-36, who also argues from canonical location to the inevitability of reading James in a post-Pauline context. The issue here, of course, is that not all placed James in the same canonical location. Reading biblical texts in light of canonical location, as if the "canon-iclers'" own theological decisions are determinative for meaning, involves questionable (do we know the theology of the canonizers?) and indemonstrable speculation at times.

91. Wachob, *Voice of Jesus,* 198.

92. The ground-breaking research here was by Hengel, *Judaism and Hellenism; Jews, Greeks and Barbarians; Between Jesus and Paul; "Hellenization."*

nomistic categories (2:8-10; 4:11-12) and clearly reveals a penchant for the *Shema* in the form taught by Jesus (cf. 1:12; 2:5, 8-11; Mark 12:28-32).[93] It is this Jewish James we seek, and the simplest search is to ask if the brother of Jesus fits the evidence of the letter.

Some detect *similarities between the James of Acts 15 (and his letter there) and the James of the letter.* Whether or not one thinks the letter is pseudonymous, the following parallels are worthy of attention and require a reasonable explanation:[94]

1. The letters have similar beginnings:
   - James 1:1-2: James, a servant of God and of the Lord Jesus Christ, to the twelve tribes in the Dispersion: *Greetings.* My *brothers* [and sisters] . . .
   - Acts 15:23: The *brothers,* both the apostles and the elders, to the believers of Gentile origin in Antioch and Syria and Cilicia, *greetings.*
   - See also James 1:16, 19, 25; Acts 15:25 on the word "brothers."
2. The letters each express the need to "keep" oneself from sins:
   - James 1:27: to care for orphans and widows in their distress, and to keep oneself unstained by the world.
   - Acts 15:29: that you abstain from what has been sacrificed to idols and from blood and from what is strangled and from fornication. If you keep yourselves from these, you will do well.
3. The letters each connect "listen" to "brothers":
   - James 2:5: Listen, my beloved brothers [and sisters].
   - Acts 15:13: My brothers, listen to me.
4. The letters each use the name invoked upon the believers:
   - James 2:7: Is it not they who blaspheme the excellent name that was invoked over you?
   - Acts 15:17: so that all other peoples may seek the Lord — even all the Gentiles over whom my name has been called.
5. The letters use some distinctive vocabulary:
   - "Care for" pastorally (James 1:27; Acts 15:14), "turning" as conversion (James 5:19-20; Acts 15:19).

93. See Montefiore, "Thou Shalt Love," who unfortunately misses the echoes of the *Shema* throughout James; better is Edgar, "Love-Command."

94. At work in Acts 15:14-21 are the emerging exegetical and hermeneutical beliefs of James and the earliest Christians. For this, see R. Bauckham, "James and the Gentiles (Acts 15.13-21)," in *History, Literature and Society in the Book of Acts* (ed. B. Witherington III; Cambridge: Cambridge University Press, 1996), 154-84; J. Ådna, "James' Position at the Summit Meeting of the Apostles and Elders in Jerusalem (Acts 15)," in *The Mission of the Early Church to Jews and Gentiles* (ed. J. Ådna and H. Kvalbein; WUNT 127; Tübingen: Mohr, 2000), 125-61.

An honest analysis admits these connections do not represent the most important terms in James, that some vary both in substance and form, and that each can be explained in other ways. But it must also be admitted that in a letter the length of Acts 15:23-29 the parallels to James are noteworthy if not remarkable.[95] At the minimum, these interesting coincidences cannot be forgotten in this discussion.

Even more significant is *the substantive relation of James to the Jesus traditions and teachings of Jesus,* who in a traditional explanation was the "brother" of our letter's author. Scholars have produced and reproduced such lists many times and in many ways, but at least the following deserve consideration:[96]

> The theme of joy in trial/testing is found in 1:2 and Matthew 5:10-12 par. Luke 6:22-23.
> The word "perfection" in 1:4 finds an important parallel in Matthew 5:48 (contrast Luke 6:36) and 19:21 (contrast Luke 18:21).
> The generosity of God for those in need is found in 1:5 and Matthew 7:7-9 par. Luke 11:9-11.
> The call to suspend anger in 1:20 connects to Matthew 5:22.
> The important theme of being a doer of the word, not just hearing the word, as seen in 1:22-25 reminds one of Matthew 7:24-27 par. Luke 6:47-49.
> The demand to do all the Law in 2:10 is matched in part by a similar demand in Matthew 5:19.
> The paramount significance of mercy in 2:13 finds something similar in Matthew 5:7.
> The call to peace in 3:18 is also matched by a Beatitude in Matthew 5:9.
> James's concern with the either-or of love/friendship with God or the world finds something similar in Matthew 6:24 par. Luke 16:13.
> The connection of humility and eschatological exaltation in 4:10 finds a substantive connection with yet another Beatitude in Matthew 5:5.

95. Mayor, iii-iv; J. A. T. Robinson, *Redating the New Testament* (Philadelphia: Westminster, 1976), 130-31.

96. See Adamson, *James: The Man and His Message,* 169-94; J. S. Kloppenborg, "The Reception of the Jesus Tradition in James," in *The Catholic Epistles and the Tradition* (ed. J. Schlosser; BETL 176; Leuven: Peeters, 2004), 91-139, and "The Emulation of the Jesus Tradition in the Letter of James," in Webb and Kloppenborg, *Reading James,* 121-50; Hartin, *James and the "Q" Sayings of Jesus;* "James and the Q Sermon on the Mount/Plain," in *Society of Biblical Literature 1989 Seminar Papers* (ed. D. J. Lull; Atlanta: Scholars, 1989), 440-57; Wachob, *Voice of Jesus.* For a brief sketch of views see Penner, "Epistle of James," 287-88.

The theme of not judging in 4:11-12, which in many ways brings to completion what has been said in 3:1–4:10, not to mention other subtle connections in other parts of James, is also important to the Jesus traditions, as seen in Matthew 7:1-5 par. Luke 6:37-38, 41-42.

The hostile reaction to rich oppressors in 5:2-6 finds close associations with Matthew 6:24, 25-34 par. Luke 16:13; 12:22-31.

The patience of the prophets in 5:10 matches Matthew 5:12 par. Luke 6:23.

Most notably, the statement about oaths in 5:12 must be connected to Matthew 5:33-37.[97]

The debate over the precise form of the Jesus traditions to which James is connected does not erase the reality of that connection because the connections are more remarkable even than those to the letter in Acts 15. As Hartin has concluded, "There is nothing in the Letter of James that does not conform to the vision, teaching, and mission of Jesus."[98] One needs to factor such a conclusion into not only the "christology" but also the theology and rhetoric of James. The letter is comprehensively Christian. It is especially connected to the Sermon on the Mount,[99] Q (material found in Matthew and Luke but not in Mark),[100] and Matthew apart from Luke, even where our present Matthew's version is not identical to what we see in James. Therefore, it is safer to conclude that James is more connected to Matthew[101] than to Q, or perhaps to a pre-Matthean form of Q or to the community tradition connected to Matthew's Gospel. Some would drop further back and suggest that what we can discern with plausibility is that James is somehow connected to the Synoptic tradition.[102] We hasten to observe that explicit citation by James is rare, and we stand on sure footings when we conclude that James

97. Other parallels will be discussed in the commentary, but at least these can also be mentioned: Jas 1:6 (Mark 11:22; Matt 21:21); Jas 2:8 (Mark 12:31; Matt 22:39; Luke 10:27); Jas 3:1 (Matt 23:8-12); Jas 3:2-3 (Matt 12:36-37); Jas 5:9 (Mark 13:29; Matt 24:33; Luke 21:31).

98. Hartin, "Religious Context," 229. See Penner's response in *The Epistle of James and Eschatology,* 116-20.

99. See V. V. Porter, Jr., "The Sermon on the Mount in the Book of James," *BibSac* 162 (2005) 344-60, 470-82, who musters the evidence and concludes that the parallels to the Sermon on the Mount suggest authorship of the letter by James, brother of Jesus.

100. See n. 94 above.

101. See M. Shepherd, "The Epistle of James and the Gospel of Matthew," *JBL* 75 (1956) 40-51, who famously argued that James was pervaded by Matthean parallels.

102. Konradt, *Christliche Existenz,* 320-28; Strecker, *Theology of the New Testament,* 659-63.

has made Jesus' teachings his own. It is entirely appropriate to describe these observations with the words that James is "emulating" Jesus' words.[103]

The point needs to be underlined. The more common form of connection between most early Christian texts and their predecessors, and this has been frequently observed for the early church up to the middle or late second century, is one of *allusion* (or even "emulation") rather than *explicit citation*.[104] One of the notable features of the earliest Christians was not only their use of traditions before them but even more was that the mode of use was to recapture, allude to, and carry on what had been said before.[105] This mode chafes against the all-too-common drive by contemporary historians and tradition critics to search exclusively for explicit quotations as a sign of dependence. Perhaps the analogy of "wiki" modes in current open source media will enable us to re-appreciate this mode. That is, as modern online dictionaries recapture and carry on, with new additions, subtractions, and modifications, sometimes with little or no trace of citation, so James may be said to have given his own "wiki" version of various sayings of Jesus. This is not plagiarism because there was no such thing as word property; it was instead the ultimate compliment and a way of carrying on the sacredness of the earlier tradition.[106]

103. Bauckham, *Wisdom of James,* 35-56, sketches formal parallels in aphorisms (beatitudes, "whoever" and "the one who is" sayings, conditional sayings, synonymous couplets, antitheses and paradoxes, wisdom admonitions with motive clauses, aphoristic sentences, statements of reciprocity, and debate sayings) and similitudes/parables (nine different forms). On James's reformulation of wisdom sayings see Bauckham, 83-93; for the shaping of James by Jesus see Bauckham, 97-108. See also J. S. Kloppenborg, "The Reception of the Jesus Tradition in James," in *The Catholic Epistles and the Tradition* (ed. J. Schlosser; BETL 176; Leuven: Peeters, 2004), 91-139; and "The Emulation of the Jesus Tradition," in Webb and Kloppenborg, *Reading James,* 133-42.

James's use of the "Old Testament" is similar in the style of emulation and intertexture; see R. Bauckham, "James, 1 and 2 Peter, Jude," in *It Is Written: Scripture Citing Scripture. Essays in Honour of Barnabas Lindars, SSF* (ed. D. A. Carson and H. G. M. Williamson; Cambridge: Cambridge University Press, 1988), 306-9; W. Popkes, "James and Scripture: An Exercise in Intertextuality," *NTS* 45 (1999) 213-29; W. H. Wachob, "The Epistle of James and the Book of Psalms: A Socio-Rhetorical Perspective of Intertexture, Culture, and Ideology in Religious Discourse," in *Fabrics of Discourse: Essays in Honor of Vernon K. Robbins* (ed. D. B. Gowler, L. G. Bloomquist, and D. F. Watson; Harrisburg: Trinity, 2003), 264-80; D. A. Carson, "James," in *CNTOT,* 997-1013. A commentary that makes more of this than any other is Brosend.

104. An excellent discussion of this can be found in Johnson, 48-80; Bauckham, *Wisdom of James,* 29-60; see previous note and the two studies listed there by J. S. Kloppenborg.

105. Many words are used by scholars, including "intertexture," "intertextuality," and the German *Vergegenwärtigung.*

106. On this in general, see R. D. Hays, *The Conversion of the Imagination: Paul*

So the evidence about James in the New Testament and in the earliest Christian traditions comports with what we find in the letter, though it cannot be said to prove that the brother of Jesus wrote this letter. Furthermore, the connection of James to the letter from the Jerusalem Council in Acts 15 and a parallel connection to the Jesus traditions make the authorship by James the brother of Jesus credible and even make him the James most likely in mind in the letter's salutation.

JAMES, BROTHER OF JESUS, AND
THE GREEK STYLE OF JAMES

But is the letter pseudonymous? The arguments against the traditional authorship might be the clues needed to finalize that issue. They begin, and for some end as well, with this: the Greek of James is too sophisticated for the brother of Jesus.[107] Since this discussion ultimately rests on whether a carpenter's (or artisan's) son from Galilee could have written sophisticated Greek, we will also mention the other arguments before we examine the language question more carefully.

The "James" of 1:1 does not claim to be the brother of Jesus. While this argument is not infrequently heard, the problem is that nearly everyone argues that the "James" of the pseudonym is the brother of the Lord — so that this argument turns against itself. It is no more likely that the real James omitted his family connection to Jesus than that a pseudonymous author did so. In fact, since pseudonymous authors not infrequently elaborate such connections, perhaps this argument actually favors James being the real author.

The letter also does not mention anything about the life of Jesus. But that also does not favor pseudonymity. Paul gave his life for Jesus, wrote long letters rooted in the so-called Christ-event, and carried on missionary work for decades, but hardly ever mentions events in the life of Jesus or quotes Jesus. If Paul could operate this way, there is no argument for the unlikelihood that the brother of Jesus wrote this letter in its non-mention of events involving Jesus. What it might show is that what we would like to see James do is an indicator that we have not quite grasped what James did.

Some argue that the Torah-observant James of Galatians 2 or Acts 15; 21:18-25 does not fit with the perspective on Torah found in the letter.[108] My

---

as *Interpreter of Israel's Scripture* (Grand Rapids: Eerdmans, 2005); the observation is made by D. A. Carson in *CNTOT*, 997-1013, but outside the main purpose of his sketch.

107. For this discussion, see N. Turner, in MHT, 4.114-20; Johnson, 7-11, 116-18; Frankemölle, 1.52-53, 73-79; Popkes, 13-15; Penner, *The Epistle of James and Eschatology*, 35-47.

108. See Laws, 40-41; Martin, lxx-lxxi.

own analysis of these data is different: the James of the letter is Torah-observant, like Jesus, even if he approaches Torah through a combination of the *Shema* and Leviticus 19:18. For James to have captured (from Jesus, no doubt) Torah through the lens of loving others and loving God does not mean that he is not Torah-observant. It means only that he, like Philo and Paul,[109] is observant from a distinct ethical vantage point. There is no reason to assume that everyone who obeyed Torah did so as the later rabbis did. Furthermore, because this letter is brief and does not address pressing topics in other parts of the earliest churches, it is hard to know what the author of this letter thought about a number of topics, including circumcision. Put differently, since we do not know what James thought, it is possible that he frowned on loose table fellowship as in Galatians 2:11-14 and advocated circumcision for converts. Assuming that James tells us everything in this five-chapter letter is not sound methodologically.

The external evidence that survives — and the surviving bits of information should not be assumed to represent even the most important or general realities that were going on — suggests that James was slowly recognized in the canonical process.[110] The question, the details behind which we are about to sketch, runs like this: if the letter was written by the brother of Jesus, why was it not immediately endorsed?

A brief on the evidence is as follows: Irenaeus quotes James 2:23 in *Against Heresies* (4.16.2) about 180 AD. Origen called James "Scripture," but this is sometime after 200 AD.[111] The letter is not found in the Muratorian

---

109. See Martin, lxxi-lxxii; and Johnson, 58-65, who works hard to show the compatibility of James and Paul. The relationship of James and Paul impinges on this discussion. See our notes at 2:14-26: because it cannot be proven that James is responding to written letters, I conclude that dating cannot be determined by the relationship to Paul's letters. See also Penner, *The Epistle of James and Eschatology,* 47-74, who sifts through the scholarship, including the studies by G. Luedemann, *Opposition to Paul in Jewish Christianity* (trans. M. E. Boring; Minneapolis: Fortress, 1989), 40-63, 140-49, and by Hengel, "Der Jakobusbrief als antipaulinische Polemik," and finds it falling short of the claims made. One of Penner's concluding observations deserves quotation here: "Consequently, the language of James 2 is consonant with the rest of the New Testament, and it is Paul's deviation from that tradition in certain instances which is striking and in need of further elaboration, not the similarities between Paul and James" (p. 68). Penner thinks James and Paul are independent of each other.

110. On canon, see F. F. Bruce, *The Canon of Scripture* (Downers Grove: InterVarsity, 1988); B. M. Metzger, *The Canon of the New Testament* (Oxford: Clarendon, 1987); L. M. McDonald, *The Biblical Canon* (Peabody: Hendrickson, 2007); C. D. Allert, *A High View of Scripture?* (Grand Rapids: Baker, 2007); B. Witherington III, *The Living Word of God* (Waco: Baylor University Press, 2007), 113-35.

111. *Commentary on John* 19.6; *Commentary on Romans* 4.1; *Homilies on Leviticus* 2.4; *Homilies on Joshua* 7.1.

Canon, the African Canon, or the Syriac Canon. But Athanasius lists it in his famous Easter letter of 367 AD. Pelagius used the letter, demonstrating that it was authoritative in Rome prior to 405.[112] Jerome seems to have paved the way for the letter's acceptance in the West, where Augustine found it palatable and where its acceptance at the Council of Hippo (393) led to its inclusion at the third and fourth Councils of Carthage (397, 419). Eusebius, one century later than Origen, assigns James to the *antilegomena* — books against which there is some charge and which are therefore disputed as to status. But he accepts it as Scripture and cites it, appealing to its authority on the basis of its catholicity.[113] Jerome is uncertain and at one point speaks of the letter's possible pseudonymity:[114] "James wrote a single epistle and some claim that it was published by another under his name." And yet there are traces of James in early Christian literature.

It is important to remember that canon consciousness arose over time and that later criteria for inclusion in the canon or for canon-like function and status should not be imposed — as also even with the demand for explicit citation as indication of canonical status — on the earliest period.[115] The doubts about James revolved around four issues: the lack of clarity regarding its provenance, its possible non-apostolic authorship, its addressees, and the nature of its theology.[116] But the doubts appear to be more related to the surging emphasis of Protestant theological concerns and the framing of church teachings according to Paul's theology than to anything else.[117] In other words, this very Jewish letter and its practical, if not also commonplace, teachings were of little use to the concerns with christology and trinity that began to develop in the second century. Nor was the letter of much use for battling Gnosticism. Finally, its Jewishness did not appeal to either Eastern or Western theologians. Tardiness in acknowledgement and doubts about its

---

112. J. Yates, "The Canonical Significance of Citations of James in Pelagius," *Ephemerides theologicae lovanienses* 78 (2002) 482-89.

113. *Eccl Hist* 2.23.24-25; 3.25.3.

114. *De Viris Illustribus* 2; see also *2 Apoc Jas* 44:13-17.

115. Again, see Johnson, 66-80, 126-40.

116. See Mayor, li. This issue was made infamous by Luther, who, in the first edition of his New Testament translation (the *Septemberbibel*), put James, Hebrews, Jude, and Revelation at the back and described James as "an epistle of straw . . . for it has nothing of the nature of the gospel about it." See Mussner, 42-47, who provides the original German text and commentary. Luther's distancing from James was over its apostolicity, meaning its (lack of) preaching of Christ — his death and resurrection. The same *Sachkritik* led Luther to similar remarks about Matthew, Mark, and Luke (see Mussner, 45-46). Modern printings of the *Lutherübersetzung* continue to have Hebrews, James, Jude, and Revelation as the last four books.

117. See Tasker, 19; Robinson, *Redating the New Testament* (Philadelphia: Westminster, 1976), 132.

authorship can be explained adequately by the lack of the letter's usefulness on a number of fronts. At any rate, the rather clear evidence of tardy acknowledgment insufficiently sustains an argument against the brother of Jesus as its author.

If the external evidence yields nothing conclusive, the language may well be the decisive factor. Nigel Turner, one of this generation's finest Greek experts, expresses a common conclusion: "it is widely felt that the style of Greek [in James] is too schooled for the Jerusalem James, the brother of Jesus."[118] Apply to James, *mutatis mutandis,* what was said of the early leaders in Acts 4:13, namely that they were "uneducated and ordinary men,"[119] and some conclude *simpliciter* that James the brother of Jesus could not have been the letter's author. Here we have the logical fallacy of applying what may have been the general situation statistically to a particular person. There are always exceptions to the average. Recent research in the Greek of those who lived in Galilee, not the least of whom would be Jesus and his potential use of Greek, opens up this question in new ways. Furthermore, one must factor into this the likelihood that the brother of Jesus had been living in Jerusalem, and such a setting may well have increased not only his use of Greek but also his capacity to write good Greek.

Perhaps some reminders are in order: Hengel concluded that "Judaea, Samaria, and Galilee were bilingual (or better, trilingual). While Aramaic was the vernacular of ordinary people, and Hebrew the sacred language of religious worship and of scribal discussion, Greek had largely become established as the linguistic medium for trade, commerce and administration."[120] It is simply mistaken to think of the Galileans as rustic hillbillies or as proto-rabbinic separatists who turned away from everything Roman, Greek and "cultural." And it is mistaken to see Galilee as a land of rebellion and anti-Roman or anti-Judean sentiments. It had a thriving economy.[121] Furthermore,

---

118. N. Turner, in MHT, 4.114 (see 114-20); Strecker, *Theology of the New Testament,* 655.

119. ὅτι ἄνθρωποι ἀγράμματοί εἰσιν καὶ ἰδιῶται. On which, see C. K. Barrett, *The Acts of the Apostles* (ICC; Edinburgh: Clark, 1994), 1.233-34, where unprofessional, amateur, or unskilled layperson appears to be the sense. See also T. J. Kraus, "'Uneducated,' 'Ignorant,' or even 'Illiterate'? Aspects and Background for an Understanding of ΑΓΡΑΜΜΑΤΟΙ (and ΙΔΙΩΤΑΙ) in Acts 4.13," *NTS* 45 (1999) 434-49.

120. Hengel, *"Hellenization,"* 8. Hengel allows for a difference between Greek-speaking Diaspora Jews who reside in Jerusalem and bilingual Jews in the Land.

121. I find this stereotype at work in G. Vermes, *Jesus the Jew: An Historian's Reading of the Gospels* (New York: Macmillan, 1974), 42-57. Vast improvements are found in S. Freyne, *Galilee from Alexander the Great to Hadrian, 323 B.C.E. to 135 C.E.* (Notre Dame: University of Notre Dame Press, 1980); Lee I. Levine, ed., *The Galilee in Late Antiquity* (New York: Jewish Theological Seminary of America, 1992); R. A. Hors-

there were Hellenists in Jerusalem, and their numbers were probably considerable (e.g., Acts 6:1). Translators were available both in Jerusalem and abroad (e.g., Josephus, *Against Apion* 1.50).[122] There is a reason that the famous Temple inscription that prohibited Gentiles from advancing deeper into the sacred dimensions was in Greek: many foreigners were present and many who came to the Temple read Greek. In addition, more than a third of the Judean inscriptions surviving from the First Century are in Greek.[123] The Septuagint was not intended exclusively for Diaspora Jews, and we can be confident that the Greek-speaking Jews of the early chapters of Acts were familiar with it. We cannot possibly list all the arguments, but one element that sometimes goes unnoticed is that the apostle Paul was both trained under the rabbinic system and more than competent to write engaging good Greek.[124] To be sure, in the New Testament only Luke and Hebrews show connections to a traditional Greek education,[125] but the commonalities of early Christian writers reveal a widespread facility among early Christians in reading the Septuagint and other more popular literature. To draw these various elements together leads not to the old-fashioned stereotype of Jewish monastic-like conventicles in Galilee and Judea, which in some important ways animates the argument against James as the author of this letter, but to a picture of the Jewish people as more or less fully integrated into a world run by Rome, shaped by Greece, and influenced by any and all who walked its roads. In other words, it is a mistake to infer that residence in Galilee or Judea implies lack of engagement with the reigning trends in culture or an incapacity to speak, read, or write Greek. The early Christian leaders, not the least of whom were James and Paul, were evidently middle-class Jews who had the capacity to read, speak, and write Greek.

---

ley, *Galilee: History, Politics, People* (Valley Forge: Trinity, 1995); Eric M. Meyers, *Sepphoris in Galilee: Crosscurrents of Culture* (Raleigh: North Carolina Museum of Art, 1996). See the excellent sketch of scholarship by M. Rapinchuk, "The Galilee and Jesus in Recent Research," *CBR* 2 (2004): 197-222.

122. See Bauckham, *Wisdom of James,* 24.

123. Hengel, *"Hellenization,"* 9-11.

124. Again, see the exhaustive studies by M. Hengel, *The Pre-Christian Paul* (with R. Deines; Philadelphia: Trinity, 1991); *Paul Between Damascus and Antioch* (with Anna Maria Schwemer; Louisville: Westminster John Knox, 1997).

125. The educational opportunities for someone like Jesus and James are not entirely clear, and it does little good to assert without good evidence that the educational system was as organized and compulsory as it was for the later rabbis. We know very little about education at that time, but it appears to have been private (not public) and often involved adoption into the family of the teacher so that one could live with the teacher. See, e.g., S. J. D. Cohen, *From the Maccabees to the Mishnah* (LEC; Philadelphia: Westminster, 1987), 120-23; J. L. Crenshaw, *Education in Ancient Israel: Across the Deadening Silence* (ABRL; New York: Doubleday, 1998).

In fact, Stanley Porter has recently built upon the path-breaking work of J. N. Sevenster[126] to argue that Jesus himself spoke Greek, and he points to Matthew 8:5-13 par. John 4:46-54; John 4:4-26; Mark 2:13-14 pars.; Mark 7:25-30 par.; Mark 12:13-17 pars.; Mark 8:27-30 pars.; Mark 15:2-5 pars.[127] It is not unreasonable to think that if Jesus was trilingual then his brother James was also. In fact, Porter's conclusion is that "a sizeable number of Jews in Palestine used Greek."[128] Even if Porter's criteria are disputed, the general drift of his argument and the evidence he sketches should make anyone ponder the likelihood that Jesus and his closest associates had some facility in Greek. This makes it reasonable that James, too, had some capacity in Greek.[129] Add to this the long-term presence of James in Jerusalem, where many Jews spoke and wrote Greek and where some Christians would have done the same, and one has a reasonable argument that James could have spoken and written Greek, even Greek as good as is found in the letter of James.

And we cannot neglect the possibility that an amanuensis or compiler had an effect on such matters as style and vocabulary. Add yet more: there is evidence that James's Greek has Semitic elements, such as "doer of the Law" in 1:22.[130] These are not details brought in to salvage traditional authorship but elements of how letters were written in the ancient world. Once again we run up against a stereotype: not only do many of the arguments against the traditional authorship pretend a total bifurcation between Judaism and Hellenism, suggesting in fact that the Greek of James is more sophisticated than it really is, but they pretend to a simplistic theory of authorship. Joseph Fitzmyer long ago outlined the most common methods: (1) write the letter oneself, (2) dictate it word by word, (3) dictate the sense and authorize the secretary to formulate the letter, and (4) authorize a friend or secretary to write in one's name. Recent research has deepened his observations to find three general approaches: the secretary could (1) transcribe as dictated by the author, (2) contribute to the letter to one degree or another, or (3) compose it for the author.[131] Once one factors into consideration matters like these, one is left

---

126. *Do You Know Greek? How Much Greek Could the First Jewish Christians Have Known?* (NovTSup 19; Leiden: Brill, 1968). See further at S. E. Porter, ed., *The Language of the New Testament: Classical Essays* (JSNTSup 60; Sheffield: Sheffield Academic, 1991), especially 126-62, 174-90, 191-204, 205-26.

127. Stanley E. Porter, *The Criteria for Authenticity in Historical-Jesus Research: Previous Discussion and New Proposals* (JSNTSup 191; Sheffield: Sheffield Academic, 2000).

128. Porter, *Criteria,* 141.

129. E.g., P. H. Davids, "Palestinian Traditions in the Epistle of James," in Chilton and Evans, *James the Just and Christian Origins,* 42-45.

130. See the sketch in Davids, "Palestinian Traditions," 44.

131. J. Fitzmyer, "New Testament Epistles," in *The Jerome Biblical Commentary*

on shifting foundations for so much of what one argues about authorship for New Testament books. It is as likely as not that someone like James would commission his letter, read it, proofread it, and then sign it. And this means that its style, content, and vocabulary could be the result of a process.[132]

My conclusion on the language issue is this: dogmatism is unwarranted. More directly, those who argue from language to non-traditional authorship are standing on weak foundations. There is sufficient evidence that James *could* have known and written in Greek, at least with the help of an amanuensis, to dislodge the simple argument that this Greek is too sophisticated for a brother of Jesus.[133] This argument against the brother of Jesus should be laid to rest.

JAMES, BROTHER OF JESUS, AND THEOLOGY

If the style of James offers ambiguity instead of clarity as well as no compelling evidence against the traditional authorship, there is one more question that might tip the balance: does the *theology* of James provide any insight into who wrote this letter? We begin with a sweeping warning: to plot the location of James's theology on a developmental scheme from Jesus to Nicea is impossible because the evidence simply is not available for enough of that plot to enable confidence. Furthermore, mapping James on a Jewish versus Hellenistic axis is no longer useful.[134] The details of the theological question will be found in the Commentary, but we can offer a sketch here. But we need to emphasize that the arguments there for primitivity or lateness will convey only an impression; the evidence is insufficient to map and plot all the developments of early Christian theology. Furthermore, if one factors in a vibrant conservative (and today largely unrecoverable) Jewish Christian tradition that led to such groups as the Nazareans and Ebionites, one could find "early" ideas late in the game and perhaps also "late" ideas appearing

---

(ed. R. E. Brown et al.; Englewood Cliffs: Prentice-Hall, 1968), 2.226. See E. Randolph Richards, *The Secretary in the Letters of Paul* (WUNT 2.42; Tübingen: Mohr, 1991), popularized in *Paul and First-Century Letter Writing* (Downers Grove: InterVarsity, 2004); H.-J. Klauck, *Ancient Letters and the New Testament: A Guide to Content and Exegesis* (with D. P. Bailey; Waco: Baylor University Press, 2006), 55-60.

132. See W. V. Harris, *Ancient Literacy* (Cambridge: Harvard University Press, 1989); A. Millard, *Reading and Writing in the Time of Jesus* (Sheffield: Sheffield Academic, 2000). On letter writing, see W. G. Doty, *Letters in Primitive Christianity* (Philadelphia: Fortress, 1973), 21-47.

133. See the judicious conclusions of Penner, *The Epistle of James and Eschatology,* 44-47.

134. See Penner, *The Epistle of James and Eschatology,* 75-87.

early.[135] Finally, in many cases the accusation that James is not "doctrinal" or "theological" becomes a circular argument: since theology looks like Paul's theology and since James's theology is not like Paul's, James is not really theology.[136] The criticism of this argument is not only simple but also telling: we need to ask ourselves again and again why we must force all theology to look like Pauline soteriology. The simple observation that later Jewish Christians never did look like Paul should wash this argument clean.

Our fundamental contention here is that what we find in James is *less early versus late* and more *Jewish Christian versus the Western re-expression of the gospel that we find in Paul, Hebrews, John, and perhaps Peter.*[137] There is a tendency in scholarship to equate "Jewish" with "early" and "Western developments" with "late." This picture assumes that the march from Jerusalem to Rome and then back to Nicea was the only movement happening. In fact, there were also, at least, those who stayed home and marched in the backyard, that is, the development from Jerusalem that stayed with a more Judean and Middle Eastern perspective and that had its own variations, not all of them to be equated with what was taking place in the West. What we find in James could have been written, so we would argue, anytime from the middle 40s of the first century into the middle of the second century, proper nuances aside.[138]

A few examples should suffice. First, the matter of Torah observance, which clearly characterized the earliest followers of Jesus (Acts 5:33-39; 15:1-5; 21:20). Thus, James's clear commitment to Torah observance (James 2:8-11) connects him to that early Jewish Christian movement. But it also

---

135. There is a rich bibliography to be harvested here, and it includes Dunn, *Unity and Diversity,* 253-87; Pritz, *Nazarene Jewish Christianity;* Stegemann and Stegemann, *The Jesus Movement;* O. Skarsaune, *In the Shadow of the Temple: Jewish Influences on Early Christianity* (Downers Grove: InterVarsity, 2002); Skarsaune and Hvalvik, *Jewish Believers in Jesus,* especially 419-741; R. Bauckham, "The Origin of the Ebionites," in *The Image of the Judaeo-Christians in Ancient Jewish and Christian Literature* (ed. P. J. Tomson and D. Lambers-Petry; WUNT 158; Tübingen: Mohr, 2003), 162-81; M. Jackson-McCabe, ed., *Jewish Christianity Reconsidered* (Minneapolis: Fortress, 2007). See also Klijn and Reinink, *Patristic Evidence for Jewish-Christian Sects,* 19-52; S. Häkkinen, "Ebionites," in *A Companion to Second-Century Christian "Heretics"* (ed. A. Marjanen and P. Luomanen; Supplements to Vigiliae Christianae 76; Leiden: Brill, 2005), 247-78; and in the same volume, P. Luomanen, "Nazarenes," pp. 279-314.

136. See Baker, "Christology," 47-51.

137. See J. E. Botha, "Soteriology under Construction: The Case of James," *Acta Patristica et Byzantia* 17 (2006) 100-118.

138. In general, see two recent important studies: Jackson-McCabe, *Jewish Christianity Reconsidered;* Skarsaune and Hvalvik, *Jewish Believers in Jesus.* Robbins, who eschews the trajectory model (filled as it is with so many unknowns and so much diversity), opts for a culture-making set of categories and concludes that James can be dated anywhere in the first century; see "Making Christian Culture."

connects him to later Jewish Christians. Justin Martyr, in his *Dialogue with Trypho* (47), speaks of Christians who still practice circumcision and Sabbath and other ceremonies.[139] One could quite easily infer that James continued these practices. Thus, Torah observance is not about early versus late but about Jewish Christianity (Christian Judaism) versus the developments of the Christian faith as it moved away from its Jewish roots.

Second, christology. We should not assume that James reveals his full christology in this letter. He mentions Jesus only twice, in 1:1 and 2:1. Jesus is the "Lord," the "Christ," and "the Glorious One" — hardly minimalistic terms. Even if we recognize that the absence does not mean the beliefs were not there, James does not mention the atoning death or the resurrection or our union with Christ — in short, none of the emerging soteriology we find in Paul, Peter, and Hebrews is found in James. Some are prone to infer from these absences to an "early" dating. Perhaps so. But, the christology of later Jewish Christianity does not reveal the same developments we see on the Western side. Of the Ebionites, who had their own christological struggles,[140] Eusebius says this: "The first Christians gave these the suitable name of Ebionites because they had poor and mean opinions concerning Christ. They held him to be a plain and ordinary man who had achieved righteousness merely by the progress of his character and had been born naturally from Mary and her husband."[141] There were others who believed in the virginal conception but not in Christ's pre-existence.[142] Which is merely to point out that the absence of Western soteriological and christological developments in James is no necessary indicator of an "early" date; rather, it could indicate a connection to one or more strands of Jewish Christianity instead of a connection with more Western forms.

Third, the Jesus traditions. One factor that suggests an "early" rather than just a "Jewish" provenance for James is his connection to the Jesus traditions. We sketched some of the evidence above. Two observations: First, this connects James to the sorts of Christians who drew deeply from the Synoptic tradition, perhaps even from the Q traditions or the Matthean form of the Q traditions, more than from the Johannine traditions. This might indicate a Land of Israel provenance, but could hardly prove it. Second, because James does not "quote" the Jesus traditions as we find them in the Synoptics, it could be argued that James is some distance removed from that form of connection to Jesus and he might be more connected to those early Christian

139. See also Epiphanius, *Panarion* 29.7.5; Irenaeus, *Against Heresies* 1.26.2.
140. And their beliefs were not completely clear to their critics: see Irenaeus, *Against Heresies* 1.26.2; Epiphanius, *Panarion* 30.3.3-6; 30.14.4; 30.18.5-6.
141. πτωχῶς καὶ ταπεινῶς τὰ περὶ τοῦ Χριστοῦ δοξάζοντας . . . λιτὸν μὲν γὰρ αὐτὸν καὶ κοινὸν ἡγοῦντο (*Eccl Hist* 3.27.1). See P. Luomanen, "Ebionites and Nazarenes," in Jackson-McCabe, *Jewish Christianity Reconsidered*, 81-118.
142. *Eccl Hist* 3.27.3.

documents, mentioned above, whose practice it is to allude to and incorporate Jesus' statements instead of directly citing them. Our swords get crossed here: a connection to the Synoptics might favor an early date while the form of citation might not eliminate a somewhat later dating.

Fourth, we need to factor in the relationship of James and Paul, which is discussed at the end of the comments on 2:14-26. That evidence, we will argue, is insufficient to compel firm conclusions about the date of James.

We have come to the end of what can be mustered as the best evidence and arguments. We have turned over the rocks, we have smelled the earth afresh, but we have discovered no gold. In my estimation, the arguments against the traditional authorship are inconclusive; the arguments for traditional authorship are better but hardly compelling.[143] I draw two conclusions: First, when the name "James" appears in James 1:1, it is a reference, whether real or pseudonymous,[144] to the brother of Jesus. Second, the traditional view has very few substantial arguments against it, and I will assume the traditional authorship in what follows, knowing that we have failed to prove conclusively that James wrote the letter. In my estimation, the traditional authorship is probably the best conclusion based on the evidence we have and the arguments that can be brought to the table. Following in the wake of a fine German commentator, Franz Mussner,[145] and the prolific German historian Martin Hengel,[146] Luke Timothy Johnson found other arguments in favor of traditional authorship:[147] the absence of signs of late, pseudonymous authorship; a reflection of the early stages of a sect, but here he draws on an emphasis on "morals rather than the manners of the dominant culture," and one could easily imagine a Jewish dominant culture where James's morals would be just as easily described as its manners; proximity to Jesus' teachings and (also!) to Paul's teachings, as well as to local Palestinian color in the letter; and the use of James in *1 Clement*. Johnson postulates that all this means James was written "at a substantially earlier date." I doubt we know enough about how long a text has to be in circulation to be quoted. Our firmest conclusion, then, is that James is Jewish; at a lesser level we can conclude that the traditional view that James the brother of Jesus wrote this letter has many factors in its favor and that the arguments against it are not as conclusive or decisive as is often made out.

143. See Adamson, *James: The Man and His Message,* 3-52; Wall, 5-11. *Pace* P. Davids and R. Wall, I am less inclined to think we can prove that James is the result of sermons and talks edited into letter form.

144. Edgar, *Has God Not Chosen the Poor?* 219-24, prefers a pseudepigraph because of the language problem. See also Hahn and Miller, "Der Jakobusbrief," 59-64.

145. Mussner, 1-8, 237-40.

146. See Hengel, "Der Jakobusbrief als antipaulinische Polemik."

147. Johnson, 118-21, and *Brother of Jesus, Friend of God,* 105-17, provides a critique of the pseudonymous theory. See also Hartin's incisive sketch (pp. 16-25).

It follows from this conclusion that, if James, the brother of Jesus, wrote this letter, we have an early date.[148] James most likely died at the hands of the Sadducean high priest Ananus (or Annas II), which means he died in 62 AD.[149] We can assume that he had been leader of the Jerusalem church for more than a decade, perhaps up to two decades. He wrote the letter probably after Paul's message was either known or beginning to be heard, even if Paul's message was distorted and James was responding to parts of it or to the distortions. It is reasonable then to think James was written in the 50s.[150] It is also reasonable to think the letter was sent from Jerusalem to a number of churches/synagogues of messianic Jews in the Diaspora and that any more specific setting outstrips the evidence.[151] His eschatology or reading of the biblical Story led him to call those dispersed messianists the "twelve tribes." We do not know whether they were in Syrian Antioch, Asia Minor, Greece, Italy, Egypt, Babylon, or even Petra.

148. This conclusion assumes that we cannot prove with confidence that the letter is a later anthology of James's sermons.

149. For a brief sketch see P. W. Barnett, *Jesus and the Rise of Early Christianity* (Downers Grove: InterVarsity, 1999), 322-23.

150. We will not go into all the proposals and theories for the origin of James. Sigal once said that dating James was "an exercise in futility" and that it "defies dating," but he does conclude that it "dates to a very early time, perhaps being the earliest work of the New Testament" (see "Halakhah," 337). Rolland, "La date," dates James in 56 AD, between 1 Corinthians and Galatians/Romans. See also D. C. Allison, Jr., "The Fiction of James and Its *Sitz im Leben*," *RB* 108 (2001) 529-70, who argues that James is a fiction, both in authorship and addressees. As such, it addresses both non-Christian and Christian Jews. His study details the extensive number of scholars who believe that "the twelve tribes in the Dispersion" were ethnic Jews of the Diaspora. I think the proposal is damaged by the use of "Lord Jesus Christ" in 1:1 (and I disagree with the view that 2:1 is an interpolation), since to begin on that note is to stake a claim that none other than Jesus of Nazareth is the Messiah of Israel. Furthermore, the tension of "Lord Jesus Christ" with "twelve tribes" deserves closer scrutiny. I agree with Allison that there is a mixed audience in this letter, and I wonder if that conclusion undoes some of his confidence that "twelve tribes" must refer to Jews and to Jews only. Finally, I am unconvinced that James wears his Christianity too lightly; the letter breathes the teachings of Jesus, and the language is at times far too harsh to be seen as a touchstone approach to Jews.

151. The most ingenious setting proposal is that of Martin, lxi-lxxvii: From 59 AD on, the aristocratic high priests oppressed the lower priests and the latter tended therefore to support those who were inclined toward violence, like the Zealots and sicarii. James's support of the poor involved the lower priests, and his critique of the rich involved the aristocrats. All of this is intelligible and possible, but I am unconvinced that the evidence is clear enough to read James within this social setting. The same applies to K. Syreeni's connection of James to Corinth; see his "James and the Pauline Legacy: Power Play in Corinth?" in *Fair Play: Diversity and Conflicts in Early Christianity: Essays in Honour of Heikki Räisänen* (ed. I. Dunderberg, C. Tuckett, and K. Syreeni; NovTSup 103; Leiden: Brill, 2002), 397-437.

WHAT ARE THE CENTRAL THEMES OF JAMES?

The most significant theological posture of James is that he thinks his audience should not only listen to him but do what he says,[152] however one wants to classify his rhetorical strategy in terms of ancient (or modern) rhetoric or communication theory.[153] Furthermore, he is fond of making his arguments with binary oppositions.[154]

James's audience should listen to him because he is "a servant of God" and a servant "of the Lord Jesus Christ" (1:1). This posture is one of authority derived from Jesus, not of sentimental equality or servanthood. By calling himself a "servant" James aligns himself with Israel's noble heritage of the servants of God, most notably Moses, David, and the prophets. The entailments are many, not the least of which is that James has authority as a distinguished leader in the community that believes Jesus is the Messiah.[155]

Everything that James says flows from this (Christian) source.[156] The theological themes of James are formed in this messianic, Jewish context of a man who has been called by God to be a leader of the messianic community. Scholars today sometimes observe that James's ethics are grounded in theology proper rather than christology or soteriology, but apart from a terse dismissal of both 1:1 and 2:1 as well as the significance of the teachings of Jesus, which have reshaped the entirety of James's ethics, there is a soteriology

---

152. See J. Painter, "James and Peter: Models of Leadership and Mission," in Chilton and Evans, *Missions,* 143-209, where James is the model leader and Peter the model of mission. In the same volume, see W. Popkes, "Leadership: James, Paul, and Their Contemporary Background," 323-54, where an exceptional analysis of leadership is sketched.

153. The discussion is intense. A good example is W. H. Wachob, "The Languages of 'Household' and 'Kingdom' in the Letter of James: A Socio-Rhetorical Study," in Webb and Kloppenborg, *Reading James,* 151-68. He writes: "In the terminology of Graeco-Roman rhetoric, the Epistle of James generally exhibits the characteristics of symbouleutic or deliberative discourse. Such a discourse seeks to make an effective difference in a given social history by using exhortation (προτροπή) and dissuasion (ἀποτροπή) to persuade its addressees to take a particular course of action in the future (Aristotle, *Rhet.* 1.3.39)" (pp. 154-55). From a different angle, Cargal, *Restoring the Diaspora,* speaks of the system of convictions and the micro-semantic universe in which the author lives and wants the readers to live (see pp. 40-44). A nice sketch of James's rhetoric, drawing from it implications for how the text of James was used by Frederick Douglass, is Aymer, *First Pure, Then Peaceable,* 53-73.

154. K. D. Tollefson, "The Epistle of James as Dialectical Discourse," *BTB* 21 (1997) 62-69.

155. See the extensive study by Edgar, *Has God Not Chosen the Poor?* 44-73.

156. Strecker finds allusions to baptism in James at 1:18; 2:5, 7; see *Theology of the New Testament,* 664-65.

in 1:18 and 1:21. In addition, there is an assumption once again in much of this discussion that Paul's way of doing christology and soteriology is the Christian way of doing them; there are, in fact, various ways for a Jesus-shaped theology to emerge.[157] Furthermore, as our comments will show, the ethics of James are not simply contextless listings of advice but theologically and christologically-shaped exhortations.[158]

James raises many themes central to the Jewish world and its interface with the early messianic communities.[159] Such themes include God, messianism, church/community,[160] Torah and halakah,[161] salvation, faith and works, socio-economic justice,[162] speech,[163] prayer, wisdom,[164] and eschatology — and each of these serves his rhetorical intent to shape a community as an alternative to the "world" around him.[165] Short of offering an exhaustive (and perhaps exhausting) sketch of each topic emerging in this letter, I have chosen to sketch the themes of James around two themes: God and ethics. One can organize the teachings of James around other themes. One of the more fruitful such themes in recent discussion is "perfection." Studies of James's use of "perfect" (1:4, 17, 25; 2:8, 22; 3:2; 5:11) perhaps reveal the core of, or at least a window into, his thinking. The most suggestive text for the importance of perfection in James is found at 2:22: "and faith was brought to completion [*eteleiōthē*] by the works."[166] J. H. Elliott masterfully turns this theme over from the angle of a social scientific perspective and examines James's theology through the lens of "holiness-

---

157. See, e.g., M. Hogan, "The Law in the Epistle of James," *Studien zum Neuen Testament und seiner Umwelt* 22 (1997) 79-91.

158. So especially M. Konradt, *Christliche Existenz;* see also the concluding essay in Mussner, 236.

159. A very useful sketch of themes is in Nystrom, 21-26.

160. See, e.g., Burchard, "Gemeinde in der strohernen Epistel."

161. Especially Sigal, "Halakhah," who exposes inadequate Christian framings of the issues; Mussner, 240-50.

162. See B. Noack, "Jakobus wider die Reichen," *ST* 18 (1964) 10-25.

163. Especially Baker, *Personal Speech-Ethics.* One of Baker's more penetrating observations is this: There are thirty-two imperatives in James that deal directly with ethics, and twenty-nine of these are about speech (pp. 6-7).

164. E.g., Hoppe, *Der theologische Hintergrund.*

165. That James seeks to shape an autonomous community is the thesis of G. Theissen, "Éthique et Communauté dans L'Épitre de Jacques. Réflexions sur son *Sitz im Leben*," *ÉTR* 77 (2002) 157-76, especially 163-65.

166. See C. E. B. Cranfield, "The Message of James," *Scottish Journal of Theology* 18 (1965) 182-93, 338-45; Klein, *"Ein vollkommenes Werk";* Hartin, *A Spirituality of Perfection,* who helpfully sketches the various senses of "perfection" in a pastoral vein (pp. 11-15). See also Konradt, *Christliche Existenz,* 267-85; Welzen, "Way of Perfection"; Cheung, *Genre, Composition,* 162-239.

wholeness."[167] Douglas Moo, if from much less of a social-scientific perspective, agrees on the importance of this category for understanding James.[168] Whatever one chooses as the central category, and one should question if there is such a thing and ask why some think there needs to be a "central" category, it is more a logical and explanatory device in the mind of the interpreter than something explicitly stated by James. This category should be held with an honest detachment as one moves through the letter itself.

One might also, as does Rob Wall, sketch the themes of James within a narrative or, put differently, sketch the narrative that precipitates the themes. Wall finds four such themes: (1) the sovereign God, who is able to save and to destroy, (2) who sends forth the word of truth, (3) which saves those who receive it in anticipation of (4) the coming triumph of God's reign. This sketch may appear too Pauline, too soteriological, and too individualistic, but Wall fills out the picture in Jacobite ways.[169]

A reminder: the themes of James are not simply advice. The substance of these themes are life and death (1:12-15), and James's intent in using them is to draw his readers into the world that leads to life and away from the world that leads to death. Historians, commentators, and teachers, then, are lured at times by the demands of a discipline (to explain a text) from the flesh, blood, life, and death realities that animated James in crafting this letter. Todd Penner, and he is a singular voice in this regard, connects James to the Jewish covenant-shaped "two ways" tradition (e.g., Deut 28; 30:15-20; Ps 1; Prov 4:10-27; *Pss Sol* 10:1-4; 1QS 3:13-26; *Did* 1:1-2), revealing the gravity and magnitude of the theology of James as it sits neatly in a robust eschatology.[170] We should not forget here that James's intent is to form a community (or a set of communities) who embody his ecclesial ethic and that the work of God is at stake in this formation.[171] In what follows, then, we have chosen to provide a sketch of two themes.[172]

---

167. J. H. Elliott, "Holiness-Wholeness."

168. See Moo, 43-46.

169. See Wall, 27-34.

170. *The Epistle of James and Eschatology,* 224-33; see also Konradt, *Christliche Existenz,* 287-302.

171. This is where the work of Brian Capper deserves careful consideration. He argues that the earliest communities shared goods. See "The Palestinian Cultural Context of Earliest Christian Community of Goods," in *The Book of Acts in Its Palestinian Setting* (The Book of Acts in Its First Century Setting 4; ed. R. Bauckham; Grand Rapids: Eerdmans, 1995), 323-56; see also the comparison of James to the private feasts of the cultural elite by D. J. Verseput, "Plutarch of Chaeronea and the Epistle of James on Communal Behaviour," *NTS* 47 (2001) 502-18.

172. For studies of the theology of James, see Hoppe, *Der theologische Hinter-*

GOD[173]

James' *theology* appears to be ordinary, Jewish, and Christian. Thus, the quintessential Jewish belief is found in this letter: there is one God (2:19) and that God is the Lawgiver (4:11). Also typically Jewish is that James is a servant of God (1:1) and prays to God (1:5) and that this God is incapable of evil and tempting (1:13). This God gives commands, and the observant who conform to the commands are righteous (1:20, 27) and friends of God (2:23; 4:4). This God elects (2:5) and creates humans as his *eikon*s, or those who are created in God's image (*homoiōsis,* 3:9), and this same God also judges (4:6) and summons his people to do what is right through James's words (4:7-8). The God of James is the Lawgiver (4:11; 5:4) who judges on the basis of that Law, but this God is also merciful, gracious, and forgiving (2:13; 4:6, 7-11).[174] The God of James is single and simple; this God is therefore trustworthy and unchanging (1:5, 17). This God is the Father (1:17, 27; 3:9), an early Christian and Jewish framing of deity in terms of creation, redemption, and provision to all.[175]

All this is typically Jewish or Christian, but James does something that ought to startle any who have concluded that James is early: *there is confusion in this letter at times whether he is speaking of the Father or Jesus when he uses the word "Lord."*[176] Some texts are quite clear. James already calls God "Father" (1:17, 27; 3:9) and sometimes he refers to the Father when he uses the word "Lord" (1:17; 3:9; 4:10, 15; 5:4). But other times he uses "Lord" for Jesus Christ (2:1). Most noteworthy are ambiguous uses of this term (5:7-8, 10-11, 14, 15). One can make a case for these either way, but that is not the point. Rather, we need to observe that use of "Lord" is no lon-

---

grund; Adamson, *James: The Man and His Message,* 259-420; Tamez, *Scandalous Message;* Strecker, *Theology of the New Testament,* 654-82; Moo, 27-43; Johnson, *Brother of Jesus, Friend of God,* 235-59; Martin, lxxvii-lxxxvi; Cargal, *Restoring the Diaspora,* 202-7; Konradt, *Christliche Existenz;* Nystrom, 21-28; Bindemann, "Weisheit versus Weisheit"; Hartin, "Religious Context," 220-24; Welzen, "Way of Perfection"; P. Davids, "James's Message," in Chilton and Neusner, *The Brother of Jesus,* 66-87.

173. See Mussner, 97-98; A. Batten, "God in the Letter of James: Patron or Benefactor?" *NTS* 50 (2004) 257-72, who suggests that James depicts God in terms of the ideal benefactor, a term to be distinguished (as was pointed out in the work of Stephan Joubert, upon whom Batten relies) from patronage. In essence, patronage involved a system of submission and even exploitation, while benefaction was driven more by non-self-interest, goodness, and friendship.

174. Baker, *Personal Speech-Ethics,* 187-248, usefully explores "speech" to God in the context of speech ethics in James.

175. See especially Ng, "Father-God Language," who works against the common pitting of God as creator and as redeemer against one another.

176. See Hahn and Miller, "Der Jakobusbrief," 33-36.

ger a single, traditional referent to YHWH. James's christology is not what it will be with Paul, Hebrews, John, or Peter, but it is in the chrysalis awaiting re-formation.[177] As Bill Baker has outlined, James's christology involves Jesus as teacher (see the comments below at 2:8), but more significantly there is a broaching of the deity of Christ in this use of "Lord" for Jesus and in the use of "the name" (2:7; 5:10), and perhaps also in Jesus as lawgiver and judge (cf. 4:11-12).[178] James sees himself as a "servant" of both God *and* the Lord Jesus Christ; this connection has drawn the interest of those scouting for early christology.[179] This heightened christology is reshaping early Christian theology and makes a cameo appearance when James refers to Jesus Messiah as "the Glorious One" in 2:1.[180]

ETHICS[181]

The ethics of James owe their origins to his soteriological reflection in 1:18, where it is said that God's intent is to give birth to the new creation (life from death; cf. 5:19-20). This conversion occurs through the word of truth[182] and leads to the ethical concerns of the entire letter, whether one wants to see it through the lens of "perfection" or of "friendship with God." It surprises how infrequently one reads of James's central ethical category being "Torah observance," and one wonders if an aversion to Torah observance is reflected in Christian scholarship on James. We should observe that the messianic com-

177. See Frankemölle, 379-84.
178. See Baker, "Christology," 51-57. See also C. Burchard, "Zu einigen christologischen Stellen des Jakobusbriefes," in *Anfänge der Christologie. Festschrift für Ferdinand Hahn zum 65. Geburtstag* (ed. C. Breytenbach and H. Paulsen; Göttingen: Vandenhoeck und Ruprecht, 1991), 353-68; Frankemölle, 376-87; Reumann, "Christology," 133-34; L. W. Hurtado, "Christology," *DLNTD*, 173.
179. See discussions in Vouga, 31, 36; Burchard, 48; Frankemölle, 378-79.
180. See Hurtado, *Lord Jesus Christ;* R. Bauckham, "James and Jesus," in Chilton and Neusner, *The Brother of Jesus*, 134; Reumann, "Christology," 132-33. A recent view proposes that a much more "Jewish" (and less Pauline or Johannine) perception of Jesus can be found in James. So Jackson-McCabe, "Messiah Jesus." In particular, Jackson-McCabe finds an apocalyptic (if not zealotic) worldview, one shaped by the election themes of Genesis–Kings, a Stoic notion of the implanted logos, a lack of soteriology as found in Paul and John, a hope in the restoration of the twelve tribes, and a (sometimes militant) Davidic "christology" connected to that imminent restoration. As we will argue in the commentary, the peace-shaped orientation of James conflicts with the central themes of this view of Jackson-McCabe.
181. The finest sketch of James's ethics I have seen is Hartin, *Spiritualty of Perfection,* 93-127.
182. An emphasis in Konradt, *Christliche Existenz,* 41-100.

munity has the power and obligation to becomes "doers of the word" (1:22-25), and I cannot think of a better ethical category for this expression than Torah observance. Once again, we need to emphasize that Torah observance during the Second Temple period was not always proto-rabbinic. There is a diversity to Torah observance that could easily include James's ethic.

The precise topics James brings to the fore in his Torah-observant ethics are on the surface: trials and testing and perseverance, socio-economic justice, speech ethics, good works, compassion and care for the marginalized, loving God and loving others, resisting the temptation to violence, and pastoral care for the wandering. But he is not offering another proto-rabbinic list of *mitzvot* or commands. Instead, we are drawn back to the opening words of the letter to remember that this is a thoroughly messianic document and that the ethics are also messianic and are shaped to form a new community, a community that embodies a different way of life.

The following points deserve careful consideration in following the origins and contours of the Jacobite Torah-observance ethic.[183] First, there is a *messianic source for the Jacobite ethic* in two respects: first, James is the servant of Jesus Christ and Jesus Christ his Lord and that means that he has self-consciously placed himself under discipleship to Jesus as the Messiah and paradigm for existence (1:1; 2:1). Second, frequently James expresses an ethical concern in interaction with the words of Jesus. Noteworthy examples are the question of oaths (5:12) and his appeal to the *Shema* in the form that Jesus himself articulated (2:8-11). James frames the Law/Torah in ways reminiscent of Jesus' own teachings, and this accounts (as the commentary will show) for the "the perfect law, the law of liberty" (1:25), "the royal law" (2:8), and "the law of liberty" (2:12). But this messianic source need not be understood as replacement ethics. The ethic of James is an expression of Old Testament ethics; hence, his use of the *Shema* (1:12; 2:5, 19) and resonances with the Torah (e.g., 4:6-10). His ethic is Torah observance through the lens of Jesus for a messianic community.

Second, there is a *theological source in the Jacobite ethic.* God is there and the community can go to God because God wants to grace them with divine gifts (1:5). The God who calls them to live out the divine plan, sketched as it is in the Torah and then read through the lens of the Jesus Creed, is altogether good and gracious (1:13-15, 17).[184] This God is the Lawgiver (4:11-12) who has given them the Torah so humans know how to live (2:8-11). Ultimately, Torah observance is relational; James sees the funda-

183. Johnson's focus is the connections of James to the moral traditions of his world; see Johnson, 26-88.

184. On Torah in James, see Hartin, "Religious Context," 210-20; Bauckham, *Wisdom of James,* 142-51; Hoppe, 46-49.

mental relation to be one of loving God (1:12; 2:5). Alongside this theological source is the Torah-Word that God uses for new birth (1:18) and that, once implemented/received, can be drawn upon to live out the life God intends (1:21). Because of this theological origin of ethics, God alone is the Judge for those summoned to observe this messianically-interpreted Torah (2:4; 4:11-12).

Third, there is a *reduction to love in the Jacobite ethic.* There is no theoretical discussion of the greatest commandment or any evidence of the later rabbinic idea of summarizing the Torah while standing on one foot, but James clearly is aware that love is the center of the human responsibility to God, to others, and to self (1:12; 2:8-11). But this reduction of the Torah to love stems from the Torah (2:9), making one wonder if James received it from Jesus or straight from the Torah. (Elsewhere I have called the combination of Deut 6:4-5 and Lev 19:18 as the essence of the Torah "The Jesus Creed," and will do so hereafter.) It suggests also that James has set his understanding of the Torah's essence as love over against those who conceived of it as miscellaneous divine *mitzvot*. To "break one command," which might mean to opt for the *mitzvot* approach to the Torah, means breaking all the commands (2:10). This sounds dramatically like the apostle Paul in Galatians 5. But we need to emphasize that the love ethic of James is a Torah-observant love ethic, a love that leads to the proper observance of the Torah.

Fourth, there is a *communal — new community — shape to the Jacobite ethic.* James does not reveal that he knows of Gentile converts or Gentile participants in the messianic community, but boundaries do appear to be porous for him — hence, his appeal to Rahab as a virtuous woman because of her faith (2:25-26). But throughout the letter we find a community-shaped ethic. Not only does James use the second person plural constantly, but what matters are relational ethics — such as how one treats others and who matters the most (1:9-11, 19-21, 26-27, etc.). One of the fiercest sections in the letter is 3:1–4:12, a section we will explain as devoted to the teachers of the community. James's obvious concern is the impact of their speech on the community. Furthermore, sin is to be confessed within the community (5:13-18), and the wandering are to be restored (5:19-20). The community to which James writes this letter is to be a Jesus-oriented Torah-observant community.

Fifth, like all Jewish and early Christian teaching, there is an *eschatological warrant in the Jacobite ethic.*[185] God is the Lawgiver; God is the Judge; someday God will judge all humans, and that judgment determines salvation or death. This is found throughout the letter (1:2-4, 9-11, 12, 25; 2:12-13, 14-17; 5:1-6, 7-11). What reveals a Christian reworking of the theme of God as Judge is the parousia (5:7-11), and this gives the judgment a

185. See Wachob, "Apocalyptic Intertexture."

45

christological focus found only among the followers of Jesus. Revealingly, once again, the one who judges is the Lawgiver who will judge on the basis of Torah observance.

Sixth, we need to call attention to the *terms used for what matters most in the Jacobite ethic.* If one does not perform or live out the faith, one will not find eschatological salvation (cf. 2:14, 17, 18-19). It is unwise to reify these terms and say one must have one or another, or even to say one must have all. Instead, each of these terms brings to expression a life that is lived properly before God if one is following the Messiah, the Messiah's Torah, and doing so in the messianic community. To further this point, it is also unwise to read any of these terms apart from the wider context of ethics we are sketching here: for James, ethics flow out of what God has now revealed in the Messiah as the community both challenges the systemic injustices of society and awaits the final consummation. I mention some of James's terms now. James calls them to perfection (1:4; 3:2), away from double-mindedness (1:8), toward a focused sanctification of speech (1:19-21, 26; 3:1–4:12). He also clearly opposes the use of violence (1:19-20; 4:1-2) and calls the community to peace (3:17-18). He calls them to be patient and passive but firm in their commitment (1:21; 5:7-11). A singular feature of James is his emphasis on good works (1:22-27; 2:14-26). The flipside of good works is holiness (1:27). If one follows the Jesus Creed of loving God and loving others (1:12; 2:5, 8-11), then one will be impartial and show mercy to all (2:1, 9, 13). Luke Timothy Johnson thinks at the center of James's ethic is friendship with God, and though I think this is overstated, the theme is important to James (2:23; 4:4). One of the hallmarks of James is its connection to wisdom, and one can say that the good life for James is wisdom (3:13-18). Every one of these linguistic signals for ethics emerges from and interacts with the Torah.

Seventh, there is a *consciously important socio-economic shape to the Jacobite ethic.* Liberation theology makes much of this and has much to go on in the letter of James.[186] From beginning to end James has his eye on abuse of the poor, the injustices of the rich, the pride of the merchants, and the need to show mercy to those who are in need (1:9-11, 26-27; 2:1-4, 5-7, 14-17; 4:13–5:6). James is not giving an Aristotelian theory of how society works: the socio-economic shape of his ethics emerges from response to a system of injustice and exploitation (2:6-7; 5:1-6), and the critique he offers emerges from the Torah and the Prophets.[187]

---

186. See Tamez, *Scandalous Message;* Maynard-Reid, *Poverty and Wealth.*

187. See Tiller, "Rich and Poor"; P. Davids, "The Test of Wealth," in Chilton and Evans, *Missions,* 355-84, where it is clearly shown that James and Paul come at the issue of the rich and poor from different angles with significantly different convictions.

Finally, there is an *anthropological element to the Jacobite ethic.* When James informs us that our temptations cannot be blamed on God, he not only anchors his ethic in the nature of the altogether good God but also informs us that human desires are at work in sinfulness because it is their broken system that generates the cycle toward death (1:13-15; 4:1). Humans have the capacity for self-deception (1:23-24, 26) and to be amazingly harsh, hard-hearted, cruel, and brutal (2:1-4, 14-17; 4:1-10; 4:13–5:6). James does not speculate much about human nature, but he describes humans such that one would have to posit that he believes in something not unlike original sin or a corrupt human condition (cf. 3:9-12; 3:13–4:10). He singles out the haughtiness of the merchants (4:13-17) and the abuse of the powerful rich (5:1-6). The good news for James is that God does something to and for humans that makes it possible to live aright (1:18, 21; possibly 4:5). Humans know right from wrong (4:17). Alongside this anthropological element is a *cosmic* dimension to the Jacobite ethic. Genuine wisdom comes from above; bad wisdom comes from below (3:15-17; 4:7). Such wisdom then unfolds into friendship either with the world or with God (4:4). Hence, James has a dualism of humans: either one is on God's side or one is not (1:9-11; 2:8-11; 3:13-18; 4:4, 6; 5:19-20).

The fondness one finds today for the term "perfection" or "friendship of God" makes sense of the book of James, but it is our conviction that it is simpler, more historical, and more in line with the fundamental structures of James's thought to speak of his ethic as a Torah observance in a messianic key. One has to wonder if Luther's ghost haunts even how modern historians choose to conceptualize the ethics of James.

WHAT IS THE STRUCTURE OF JAMES?

Inherent to the interpretation of this letter is an implicit or explicit understanding of its *genre.*[188] However one classifies this letter — allegory on the twelve

---

188. See especially E. Baasland, "Literarische Form, Thematik und geschichtliche Einordnung des Jakobusbriefes," *ANRW* 2.25.5 (1988) 3646-84; Cheung, *Genre, Composition;* also Penner, "Epistle of James," 267-75; Verseput, "Genre and Story." Proposals that move from genre to interpretation of the letter continue to emerge. One of the most interesting is J. S. Kloppenborg, "Diaspora Discourse: The Construction of *Ethos* in James," *NTS* 53 (2007) 242-70, according to which a fictive writer sends a missive to fictive (Diaspora Jewish) readers. Thus it is explained why the letter has so little of the distinctive beliefs and behaviors of the Jesus movement. I am not convinced that James does have a lack of Jesus movement beliefs or behaviors. Instead, this proposal requires more normativity for the Western side of Christianity than is necessary. Kloppenborg argues

tribes, diatribe, Hellenistic Jewish homily, protreptic discourse, paraenesis,[189] or Christian wisdom — a more inductive model of analysis brings to fruition the elements that guide us in comprehending its genre. More importantly, the structural analysis of James puts to the test the widespread tendency to reify genres from the ancient world so that once one has made a conclusion regarding genre one has the key to unlocking the mysterious doors throughout James's winding household. So our focus will be on structure rather than genre, a genre that the insightful study of L. L. Cheung clearly demonstrates to be within the ambit of Jewish wisdom and Hellenistic paraenesis.[190]

There are two extremes to how experts have understood how James put this letter together, that is, how its framing and guiding structure are assembled.[191] First, though not alone in this regard, Martin Dibelius famously argued that the letter is a paraenetic[192] miscellany, a collection of ideas and exhortations with no discernible relations or connections addressed to no discernible context; in fact, Dibelius did not believe it was really a letter. It is, rather, a treasury of a special kind of wisdom characterized by an eclectic use of ethical traditions, sayings loosely strung together, catchwords that sometimes make connections, and motifs repeated in different parts of the letter addressed to an audience that seems to vary from one unit to another.[193] But this view has been largely abandoned today.

A second view finds subtle, overarching rhetorical themes and logical

---

against typical indicators of a Christian audience for James but for the (fictive) author being part of the Jesus movement. He finds a parallel kind of letter in 4QMMT, though it appears to me that that Qumran text much more carefully distinguishes the author's stance from the reader's stance. Kloppenborg's theory that the fictive author appeals to Solomon is both suggestive and in need of further explicit evidence in James.

189. On Dibelius's use of this term and how Peter Davids's 1982 commentary on James began the shift toward overturning the meaning and value of "paraenesis" for understanding James, see Penner, "Epistle of James," 263-67, 270-72, who points to the important study of Perdue, "Paraenesis and the Epistle of James."

190. See Cheung, *Genre, Composition,* 15-52.

191. See especially M. E. Taylor, "Recent Scholarship on the Structure of James," *CBR* 3 (2004) 86-115; Taylor, *Text-Linguistic Investigation,* 8-34, who provides a comprehensive listing of "who's who?" in the debate about structure. Cf. also Cargal, *Restoring the Diaspora,* 9-56, who drives the historical approach to James to what he thinks is its bitter end. Also Ó Fearghail, "Literary Structure"; Penner, *The Epistle of James and Eschatology,* 133-213; Konradt, *Christliche Existenz,* 311-15.

192. On paraenesis, see A. J. Malherbe, *Moral Exhortation: A Greco-Roman Sourcebook* (LEC; Philadelphia: Westminster, 1986), 124-29; "Hellenistic Moralists and the New Testament," in *ANRW* 2.26.1 (1992), 267-333, especially 278-93, who shows that paraenesis is traditional, applicable to a variety of situations, used with an audience that needs reminding, and filled with examples.

193. Dibelius, 1-11.

movements and even a carefully-structured composition.[194] A few attempts to lay out that structure will be sampled below, but one observation needs to be made at this point: a number of units in James are clearly discernible and self-contained, including 2:1-13; 2:14-26; 3:1-12 or 3:1–4:12; and 4:13–5:6. If these units are discernible, the older observation of Dibelius, regardless of how unpopular his larger thesis is today, that the precise connection between units remains disputed if not at times indiscernible finds some support in the text.[195] The result of this simple observation is that most agree on discerning the various units and therefore the various outlines proposed by those studying the structure of James frequently agree. Still, the shift from Dibelius to some of the more recent proposals is notable. Why? As Mark Taylor has chronicled the scholarship on this topic, the shift emerges from at least two factors: more attention has been given to the literary and rhetorical aspects of the text, and the assumptions at work in Dibelius's proposal have been reevaluated.[196] It appears to me that Duane Watson's conclusion speaks for many today: "[James] is a Jewish-Christian work influenced by Hellenistic rhetoric, but is arranged overall in the topic-to-topic fashion of Jewish wisdom texts."[197] We would be wise not to rest too much interpretive weight on any structural proposal.

The outlines that follow are abbreviated; the proponents of each have worked out the details to explain the entire letter in light of their particular structural proposal.[198]

---

194. A good example is H. Cladder, "Die Anfang des Jakobusbriefes," *ZKT* 28 (1904) 37-57, whose interest in chiasm anticipated some more recent proposals but also led to ingenuity beyond the demonstrable. See also J. M. Reese, "The Exegete as Sage: Hearing the Message of James," *BTB* 12 (1982) 82-85; R. B. Crotty, "The Literary Structure of the Letter of James," *ABR* 40 (1992) 45-57; Penner, *The Epistle of James and Eschatology,* especially 133-58, where he gives to 1:2-12 and 4:6–5:12 opening and closing significance; Elliott, "Holiness-Wholeness," 71-73. See also communication theory at work in Cargal, *Restoring the Diaspora;* K. D. Tollefson, "The Epistle of James as Dialectical Discourse," *BTB* 21 (1997) 66-69. Communication theory is at work also in Frankemölle and Popkes, two prominent German commentaries on James (see below). For a much-needed survey of rhetorical features of James, see D. F. Watson, "An Assessment of the Rhetoric and Rhetorical Analysis of the Letter of James," in Webb and Kloppenborg, *Reading James,* 99-120. Rhetorical insights are the salt and pepper of the commentary by Witherington.

195. This cannot be laid exclusively at the door of Dibelius; see Mayor, cxxi; Ropes, 2-4.

196. Taylor, *Text-Linguistic Investigation,* 10-11.

197. D. H. Watson, "An Assessment of the Rhetoric," in Webb and Kloppenborg, *Reading James,* 119.

198. A word of appreciation to Blomberg and Kamell for providing readers with a structural display of each passage. This kind of detailed work works its way into all macro-structural proposals.

F. O. Francis[199]

1. Thematic statements of joy and blessing (1:2-27)
    1.1. Joy (1:2-4), prayer (1:5-8), reversal of roles (1:9-11)
    1.2. Joy (1:12-18), prayer (1:19-21), reversal of roles (1:22-25)
    Hinge: 1:26-27
2. Faith and partiality (2:1-26)
3. Strife from words, wisdom, and position (3:1–5:6)
    3.1. Words bad and good (3:1-12)
    3.2. Two kinds of wisdom (3:13-18)
    3.3. Conflict (4:1-12)
    3.4. Arrogance and injustice (4:13–5:6)
4. Final exhortations (5:7-20), recalling various earlier parts

P. Davids[200]

1. Introduction (1:1)
2. Opening Statement (1:2-27)
    2.1. First segment (1:2-11)
    2.2. Second segment (1:12-27)
3. Excellence of poverty and generosity (2:1-26)
    3.1. No partiality is allowable (2:1-13)
    3.2. Generosity is necessary (2:14-26)
4. Demand for pure speech (3:1–4:12)
    4.1. Pure speech has no anger (3:1-12)
    4.2. Pure speech comes from wisdom (3:13-18)
    4.3. Pure prayer is without anger and in trust (4:1-10/12)
5. Testing through wealth (4:13–5:6)
6. Closing statement (5:7-20)

These first two outlines are formative for the undoing of Dibelius's proposal and include a substantive chiastic/inclusio-like connection between the opening statement and the closing statement. One of the most persistent observations made about this letter is that the first chapter anticipates later developments.[201] For example, what James says about speech and the tongue in 1:26-

---

199. "The Form and Function of the Opening and Closing Paragraphs of James and 1 John," *ZNW* 61 (1970) 110-26, especially 118-24.
200. Davids, 22-28.
201. Another example is Klein, *"Ein vollkommenes Werk,"* 33-41. A problem in this now common approach is ingenuity. That is, what some see in chs. 2–5 strikes me as fancifully connected to ch. 1. In the commentary I will point out some of this, especially in the opening remarks on 5:12-20.

27 (consciously and intentionally) anticipates what he will later say in 3:1–4:12. The observation is valid if one is careful with the word "anticipates." Indeed, themes in the first chapter emerge elsewhere, but "anticipates" suggests that he had a literary, rhetorical, or logical plot in view when he wrote that chapter and that he intentionally sketched his themes and then later filled them in. In my exegetical comments I will push against such theories of conscious, literary, and logical anticipation and will argue that while these themes are natural to James and thus emerge in various locations, the evidence falls short of establishing that ch. 1 is a consciously literary anticipation or whetting of the appetite for what is to come.[202]

Martin borrows from Francis and Davids, backs away from some of their conclusions, and adds an emphasis on the opening chapter providing the major themes of the entire letter. In some ways, this is followed by Luke Timothy Johnson, who has added fresh proposals about the influence of Greek, Roman, and Jewish moral traditions on the letter. Doug Moo's recent revision of an earlier commentary, based as it is on two decades of working in James, picks up what has gone before and avoids the extravagances of some more recent proposals as it works the entire letter through the theme of spiritual wholeness.

R. P. Martin[203]

1. Address and greeting (1:1)
2. Enduring trials (1:2-19a)
3. Applying the word (1:19b–3:18)
    3.1 Obedience of faith (1:19b-27)
    3.2 Problems in the assembly (2:1-13)
    3.3 Faith and deeds (2:14-26)
    3.4 Warning about teachers and tongues (3:1-12)
    3.5 Two types of wisdom (3:13-18)
4. Witnessing to divine providence (4:1–5:20)
    4.1 Community malaise (4:1-10)
    4.2 Community problems (4:11-17)
    4.3 Judgment on rich farmers (5:1-6)
    4.4 Call to patience (5:7-11)
    4.5 Community issues (5:12-18)
    4.6 Final words and fraternal admonitions (5:19-20)

---

202. See Ó Fearghail, "Literary Structure," 68-71, who puts this theory to the test and finds it lacking corroborating evidence.

203. Martin, xcviii-civ, whose proposal is rooted in Francis, Davids, and Vouga, 19-23.

L. T. Johnson[204]

1. Greeting (1:1)
2. Epitome of exhortation (1:2-27)
3. The deeds of faith (2:1-26)
4. The power and peril of speech (3:1-12)
5. Call to conversion (3:13–4:10)
6. Examples of arrogance (4:11–5:6)
7. Patience in time of testing (5:7-11)
8. Speech in the assembly of faith (5:12-20)

D. J. Moo[205]

1. Address and greeting (1:1)
2. Pursuit of spiritual wholeness through trials (1:2-18)
3. Evidence of spiritual wholeness in obedience (1:19–2:26)
4. The community dimension of spiritual wholeness 1: speech and peace (3:1–4:3)
5. Summons to spiritual wholeness (4:4-10)
6. The community dimension of spiritual wholeness 2: speech and peace (4:11-12)
7. Worldview of spiritual wholeness: time and eternity (4:13–5:11)
8. Concluding exhortations (5:12-20)

Communication theory has been at work in the structural analysis of James, and two recent proposals — both in German — can illustrate this method.[206] One comes from Hubert Frankemölle and the other from Wiard Popkes, authors of two of the best commentaries on James.[207]

---

204. Johnson, 11-16.

205. Moo, 43-46. David Nystrom's pastorally rich commentary has a similar approach, though he focuses on building Christian maturity and healthy community; see Nystrom, 29.

206. See also W. Wuellner, "Der Jakobusbrief im Licht der Rhetorik und Textpragmatik," *LB* 43 (1978) 5-66, who finds a prescript (1:1), *exordium* (1:2-4), *narratio* (1:5-11), *propositio* (1:12), *argumentatio* (1:13–5:6), *peroratio* with a *recapitulatio* (5:7-8), and *peroratio* (5:9-20).

207. Another German work, that of Klein, has a more rhetorical shape. Thus there is a double *propositio* (1:2-27) followed by six exhortations in the *argumentatio* (2:1-13, 14-26; 3:1-12, 13-18; 4:1-12; 4:13–5:6) and then by a reprise on the first theme (the "goal" of perfection found at 1:2-18) in 5:7-11. See his *"Ein vollkommenes Werk,"* 39-40.

H. Frankemölle[208]

1. Prescript (1:1)
2. Prologue (1:2-18)
   - 2.1 Christian existence in testing (1:2-4)
   - 2.2 Testing (1:5-11)
   - 2.3 Blessing (1:12)
   - 2.4 God and testing (1:13-18)
3. Body (1:19–5:6)
   - 3.1 Hearing, speaking, anger (1:19-27)
   - 3.2 Partiality and Christian faith (2:1-13)
   - 3.3 Faith without works, faith with works (2:14-26)
   - 3.4 Power of the tongue (3:1-12)
   - 3.5 True wisdom (3:13-18)
   - 3.6 Enmity and its origins (4:1-12)
   - 3.7 Deceitful autonomy of the rich (4:13–5:6)
4. Epilogue (5:7-20)

W. Popkes[209]

1. Prescript (1:1)
2. The correct inner orientation (1:2-15)
3. Association with the Word of God (1:16-27)
4. Faith, love, deeds (2:1-26)
5. Responsible leadership in association with the Word (3:1-12)
6. Relationship to the world (3:13–5:6)
   - 6.1 Wisdom, strife, and their origin (3:13–4:3)
   - 6.2 Friendship with God, world (4:4-12)
   - 6.3 Particular dangers (4:13–5:6)
7. Patience, prayer, and issues in association in the fellowship (5:7-20)

Two proposals applying discourse analysis in such a way that they enable us to take advantage of recent developments in rhetorical and socio-rhetorical criticism, those of L. L. Cheung and M. E. Taylor, round out this survey.[210]

---

208. Frankemölle, 1.62-88, and the structural divisions of his commentary; and see his earlier "Das semantische Netz des Jakobusbriefes. Zur Einheit eines umstrittenen Briefes," *BZ* 34 (1990) 161-97.

209. Popkes, viii-x, and the commentary itself. For a proposal that combines rhetoric with cultural anthropology, see J. H. Elliott, "Holiness-Wholeness."

210. See also Penner's sketch of the rise of rhetorical criticism in James studies: "Epistle of James," 293-96; see also Thurén, "Risky Rhetoric in James."

L. L. Cheung[211]

1. Prescript (1:1)
2. Prologue (1:2-27)
   2.1 Themes associated with the *shema* (1:2-18)
   2.2 Obedience to the law of liberty for true piety (1:19-27)
3. The main body (2:1–5:6)
   3.1 Testing of genuine faith (2:1-26)
   3.2 Manifestation of wisdom from above (3:1–4:10)
   3.3 Eschatological judgment of God (4:11–5:11)
4. Epilogue (5:12-20)

M. E. Taylor[212]

1. Letter opening (1:1)
2. Double introduction: living by righteous wisdom (1:2-27)
   2.1 Trials (1:2-11)
      Transition (1:12)
   2.2 Perils of self-deception (1:13-27)
3. Letter body: living the "law of liberty" (2:1–5:6)
   A Body opening (2:1-11)
      B So speak and so act (2:12-13)
         C Wrong acting, speaking (2:14–3:12)
            D Righteous vs. worldly wisdom (3:13-18)
         C Prophetic rebuke (4:1-10)
      B Do the law, do not judge it (4:11-12)
   A Body closing (4:13–5:6)
4. Conclusion (5:7-20)

I agree with the insight of Richard Bauckham, who observed that Dibelius and his followers too easily connected the lack of a careful, or at least obvious, structure to incoherence. Bauckham simply turned the rock over and discovered that under the rock of a lack of clear structure was coherence.[213]

---

211. Cheung, *Genre, Composition*, 53-85.

212. Taylor, *Text-Linguistic Investigation*; see also M. E. Taylor and G. H. Guthrie, "The Structure of James," *CBQ* 68 (2000) 681-705. Their point is summed up on p. 701: "A key to unlocking the structure of James seems, in part, to lie in the proverbial transitions, significant uses of *inclusio* (most important, the *inclusio* at 2:12-13/4:11-12), and the relationship of chap. 1 to the rest of the letter." I am more inclined to agree with the last paragraph's claim: "The great complexity of the structure of the Letter of James will ensure that discussions on the matter will continue long into the future" (p. 705).

213. Bauckham, *Wisdom of James*, 61-69.

While Dibelius will haunt my own approach to James in not seeing James 1 as an outline of the themes of the book, Bauckham's observation probes more deeply than most.

R. Bauckham[214]

1. Prescript (1:1)
2. Introduction (1:2-27)
3. Exposition (2:1–5:20)

In the commentary I will expound James according to the following outline, and my comments will themselves be my defense:

1. Salutation (introduction) (1:1)
2. The Christian and trials (1:2-18)
3. General exhortations (1:19-27)
4. The Christian and partiality (2:1-13)
5. The Christian and works (2:14-26)
6. General exhortations for teachers (3:1–4:12)
    6.1 Teachers and the tongue (3:1-12)
    6.2 Teachers and wisdom (3:13-18)
    6.3 Teachers and dissensions (4:1-10)
    6.4 Teachers, the community, and the tongue (4:11-12)
7. The messianic community and the wealthy (4:13–5:11)
    7.1 The sin of presumption (4:13-17)
    7.2 The sin of oppression (5:1-6)
    7.3 The messianic community's response to the wealthy (5:7-11)
8. Concluding exhortations (5:12-20)

---

214. Bauckham, *Wisdom of James*, 63-64.

The Letter of James

Commentary

1. SALUTATION (1:1)

The language of the first verse indicates that James is a letter,[1] though there is little in the remainder of the text to lead one to think of James as a letter. Letters in the first-century Jewish and Christian worlds varied in substance (Romans, 2 Corinthians, 1-2 Timothy) and style (Romans, 1 Thessalonians, Hebrews), so one should not infer from James's substance, which is largely hortatory, homiletical, and even sapiential, to its form (letter). There was no prescribed format, especially in the cauldron of a new movement like messianism, that one had to follow for one's writing to be classified as a "letter" or "epistle." Unlike the Pauline and Petrine epistolary form, which have both typical salutations and some kind of introductory thanksgivings, James has only the salutation and from that point on launches into his letter. We should perhaps be careful not to compare this letter to the form of the Pauline and Petrine letter, since those apostolic let-

---

1. The inscriptional evidence shows the normal variations. Nestle-Aland[27] has ΙΑΚΩΒΟΥ ΕΠΙΣΤΟΛΗ, but many manuscripts altered the inscription by adding words or by changing the word order. Some added αποστολου after "James"; some add καθολικη (P33, 1739) after επιστολη. Some clarified the situation by stating that James wrote to Hebrews or Jews or Jewish believers (94, 945), that he wrote from Jerusalem (330), or that he was "holy" (e.g., 2423).

There are of course detractors who think Jas 1:1 was added later, though there is no textual evidence for such a view. What puzzles me is that if someone can later think this book is the sort of thing that can be called a letter (so adding 1:1), then it follows that someone earlier (like James himself) could have thought it a letter. See here S. R. Llewelyn, "The Prescript of James," *NovT* 39 (1997) 385-93. The author's strategy is to contest the defense of the originality of 1:1, but the surer argument is that there is no evidence the letter ever circulated without 1:1.

For textual evidence on James, I have used the *Editio Critica Maior.*

ters and their substantive form were probably only in the infancy of their own developments.[2]

> *James, a servant of God[3] and of the Lord Jesus Christ,*
> *To the twelve tribes in the Dispersion:*[a]
> *Greetings.*

a. TNIV: scattered among the nations.

1 Standard Hellenistic letters included the writer and the addressee (A to B) as well as a greeting ("greetings"), while the evidence that survives suggests that Jewish letters modified the greeting by wishing "peace" *(shalom, eirēnē)* and other blessings *(berakot).*[4] A typical Greek letter, dated to 29 August 58 CE, begins as follows:

> Chairas to his dearest Dionysios many greetings and continual good health.[5]

2. The same applies to how one reads Galatians, for if Galatians is the first of Paul's letters, the "absence" of a thanksgiving section may not be the absence of a form since that form may not yet have been established.

3. Some manuscripts indicate the early Christian trinitarian tendency by adding πατρος (429, 614, 630, *pc*).

4. See Dan 4:1; 6:25; *2 Baruch* 78:2; *b Sanhedrin* 11b.

5. From John White, *Light,* 145. See also S. K. Stowers, *Letter Writing.* Stowers classifies letters into types: (1) friendship, (2) family, (3) praise/blame, (4) exhortation/advice. The fourth type then is subdivided into paraenetic (exhortation and dissuasion), advice, protreptic (exhortation to a way of life), admonition, rebuke, reproach, consolation, mediation, and accusing, apologetic, and accounting. See also Adamson, 19-21; Johnson, 16-26. As long as one does not reify the categories or not allow a letter to use other genres, James would be a letter of exhortation/advice, specifically paraenetic or protreptic. Ropes famously focused on James as a literary letter and diatribe; Ropes, 6-18. Davids, 22-28, finds a set of sermons redacted later into a letter. See also Grünzweig, 22 ("ein schöner Strauss von guten, hilfreichen Worten": "a pretty bouquet of good, helpful sayings"). James resists rigid genre classification.

See also A. J. Malherbe, *Ancient Epistolary Theorists* (SBLSBS 19; Atlanta: Scholars, 1988), on how epistolary theory was understood in the ancient world, with a brief anthology. Malherbe's texts lead one to be more cautious about first-century supposed (and now sometimes reified) categories that must be applied to New Testament letters, not the least James. Behind the rhetoric of letters are logic and the art of persuasion, letters being one example of how logic and persuasion were articulated. Put differently, theoretical reflections on letters and the similarities between letters and rhetorical style are sometimes better explained by the needs of logic and the art of persuasion more than conformity to the ideals of letter writing or rhetorical models. Malherbe's inclusion of Pseudo-Demetrius (pp. 30-41) illustrates our point: there are twenty-one kinds of letters listed by Pseudo-Demetrius, many of which have elements discoverable in James and are

From a Jewish letter, we read:

> Thus speaks Baruch, the son of Neriah, to the brothers who were carried away in captivity: Grace and peace be with you *(2 Baruch* 78:2, *OTP).*

James's salutation is Hellenistic:[6]

> James, a servant of God and of the Lord Jesus Christ, to the twelve tribes in the Dispersion: Greetings.

James's letter conforms in part to reflections on the nature of letter writing as seen now in Seneca's *Moral Epistles* (75.1-2): "You have been complaining," he writes, "that my letters to you are rather carelessly written." And it is here that he ventures a reflection that articulates how James functions: it is the personal presence of James. Seneca begins with the question of why his letters are as they are:

> Now who talks carefully unless he also desires to talk affectedly? I prefer that *my letters should be just what my conversation would be if you and I were sitting in one another's company or taking walks together, — spontaneous and easy;* for my letters have nothing strained or artificial about them. If it were possible, I should prefer to show, rather than speak, my feelings.[7]

This is the sort of letter James has composed: he is speaking, sometimes forthrightly and prophetically and other times more didactically, as if he were in the recipients' presence speaking to them. The letter is not an abstract "epistle" designed for posterity or intellectual reputation. It is a gritty in-your-face pastoral letter zippered up at times with some heated rhetoric.

    The letter says it is from James. But who is "James"? There are no

---

therefore illuminative of the rhetorical intent of James, even if his letter does not conform to any of the models listed. See also Pseudo-Libanius, who gives forty-one types (pp. 66-81). I might sum this up with the observation that one wonders if James consciously sat down with rhetorical models in mind and then worked out his argument within the strictures of such forms. I doubt very much that James, in the heat of his arguments and prophetic rhetoric, did such a thing.

    6. See J. M. Lieu, "'Grace to You and Peace': The Apostolic Greeting," *Bulletin of the John Rylands University Library of Manchester* 68 (1985) 161-78, who points to the need to emphasize the difference between early Christian letters and the standard Greek letters (though James and Acts 15:23-29 are exceptions to this difference).

    7. From Malherbe, *Ancient Epistolary Theorists,* 29, italics added. One is reminded here of what is now known as the familiar, personal essay disseminated for years in *The American Scholar.*

fewer than, to reduce our discussion from the Introduction, three serious candidates for this "James" (Hebrew *Yakov* or Jacob; cf. Gen 25; 27:36).[8] James,
son of Zebedee and one of the twelve original apostles (Mark 3:17; Acts
12:2), was put to death by Herod Agrippa I (c. 44 AD). James, *son of
Alphaeus* and otherwise unknown (Mark 3:18), was also an original apostle.
As we concluded in the Introduction, James, *the brother of Jesus* (Mark 6:3)
and leader of Jerusalem-based messianic Judaism,[9] is most likely the figure
intended here, whether or not "James" is a pseudonym.

That James emerges from the same family as Jesus is not without significance for him, for his socio-religious background, and for the message of
this letter.[10] In particular, as will become clear, the *Magnificat* of Mary has
manifold parallels with both the teachings of Jesus and the letter of James.
Mary, Jesus, and James speak from the world of the *Anawim* (the "pious
poor") and we will mention this socio-economic community and faith tradition at times in this commentary.[11]

That James, brother of Jesus, was an established leader in Jerusalem
— Paul calls him a "pillar" (Gal 2:9) — gave this letter the authority that was
needed to keep it afloat through the canonical process in spite of the tragic
neglect and sometimes biased dismissal of Christian Judaism.[12] Forgotten in
the rise of both Peter and Paul is the fact that James cast a shadow over them
in Jerusalem's earliest messianic community (see Gal 2:12; Acts 15:13-21;
21:18; 1 Cor 15:7).[13] In the Lukan portrayal of James at the Jerusalem Conference, James is depicted as a wise man, a theologically-astute leader, open
to Gentile inclusion in the messianic community with conditions, and desirous of reconciling split parties. It was James who delivered the most effective
speech at that conference (Acts 15:13-21), and in the literary tradition final
speeches are reserved for the most influential leader.

8. For more direct discussion of authorship and a moderate defense of James, the
brother of Jesus, as the author of James, see pp. 13-38 above.

9. Terms are difficult here: some prefer Christian Judaism, others Jewish Christianity, and others opt for a more neutral "messianic Judaism" and "messianic community" (as I have throughout this commentary). Discussion here is intense: Bruce, *New Testament History;* Hengel, *"Hellenization";* Lieu, *Image and Reality; Christian Identity;*
Dunn, *The Partings of the Ways; Jews and Christians;* Pritz, *Nazarene Jewish Christianity;* Chilton and Neusner, *Judaism in the New Testament;* Becker, *Christian Beginnings;*
Crossan, *Birth of Christianity;* Stegemann and Stegemann, *Jesus Movement;* Skarsaune,
In the Shadow; Harland, *Associations;* Boyarin, *Border Lines;* Skarsaune and Hvalvik,
Jewish Believers in Jesus.

10. See now Bauckham, *Jude and the Relatives of Jesus.*

11. For now, see Dibelius, 39-45; E. Bammel, "πτωχός," *TDNT* 6.888-915;
L. Coenen, H.-H. Esser, and C. Brown, "Poor," *NIDNTT* 2.820-29; Brown, *Birth,* 350-65.

12. See the Introduction; also Johnson, 126-40.

13. E.g., Bauckham, "James and the Jerusalem Church"; Painter, *Just James.*

James calls himself a "servant of God," and thereby both evokes his own personal vocation and places himself in a deep and potent Jewish tradition. Elsewhere in the New Testament, letter writers call themselves "servant," "apostle," or "prisoner" and, with others, "servants."[14] Only James and Jude call themselves "servant" with no other designation, thereby possibly indicating their self-awareness that they are not part of the original twelve apostles. What "servant" also indicates is that neither James nor Jude, both traditionally "brothers" of Jesus, used their family status to leverage power. "Servant," however, is not to be understood as some term of extreme humility, as in "not an apostle, but just a servant," or as "simply a believer," but instead points toward two features of James, first, that he sees himself as one who serves the Lord Jesus Christ (confirmed a few words later with the word "Lord")[15] and, second, that he stands in line with some illustrious forbears.[16] Others called "servant" are Moses, David, Amos, Jeremiah, and Daniel.[17] Therefore, using this term of oneself is paradoxical: it is both a claim to subordination to Christ and a claim to privilege and honor in the Jewish messianic community that carries forward the work of Moses, David, and the great prophets of Israel's history.[18] By placing "God and the Lord Jesus Christ" between "James" and "servant," James intentionally sets "servant" in a messianic/Christian context. James is a servant of *both* (the one) God *and* the Lord Jesus Christ.[19]

James, brother of Jesus, sees himself as a servant "of God and of the Lord Jesus Christ."[20] Herein is an early Jacobean glimmer of what was des-

---

14. "Servant" in Romans and Titus. "Apostle" in Romans, 1 Corinthians, Colossians, Ephesians, 1 Timothy, and 1 Peter. "Prisoner" in Philemon. "Servants" in Philippians. 2 and 3 John have just "elder." Jude begins with "servant" and "brother of James." See especially Edgar, *Has God Not Chosen the Poor?* 44-73; also *EDNT* 1.349-53; Mounce, *Dictionary,* 632-33; Spicq, 1.380-86.

15. In Greek, "God and Lord" appear before "servant": θεοῦ καὶ κυρίου . . . δοῦλος.

16. So Martin, 4. Interestingly, at Jas 2:23, a variant found in a few manuscripts connects "servant" with φίλος, thereby distinguishing Abraham with the term "servant." Dibelius, 65-66, thinking the letter pseudonymous, sees the use of "servant" as an exaltation of James, brother of Jesus.

17. Moses in 1 Kgs 8:53; Mal 4:4; Dan 9:11; *1 Clement* 4:12; 43:1; 51:3; *Barnabas* 14.4. David in 2 Sam 3:18. Amos in Amos 3:7. Jeremiah in Jer 7:25; *Did* 9:2. Daniel in Dan 9:10. It is used throughout the apostolic fathers for Christians and Christian leaders (e.g., Hermas, *Mandates* 44.2). For the use of "servant" in the Greco-Roman world, see Dibelius, 65.

18. Ropes, 117-18, contends that the term, as in 1 Pet 2:16, refers to any and all who worship and serve the Lord, though the evidence he cites points instead toward the rather exceptional.

19. See Laws, 45-46.

20. Anarthrous θεοῦ . . . κυρίου Ἰησοῦ Χριστοῦ, were it not standard form to refer

tined to become trinitarian thought. Jesus Christ is defined by "Lord," or better yet, "Lord" is defined by Jesus Christ. As mentioned in the Introduction, that we cannot always be sure whether "Lord" refers to Father/God or to Jesus Christ puts us on the threshold of a profound shift at work in the messianic community's theology. Larry Hurtado's *magnum opus* has demonstrated with full documentation that "Lord" belongs to and emerges from the earliest stratum of Christian worship and theological reflection.[21] We can surmise that ascribing lordship to Jesus Christ is shaped by liturgical practice in the messianic community[22] to which James writes.[23]

But James's line is not to be understood simply as theological reflection. Indeed, James makes a personal confession here that he is one who serves God and the Lord Jesus Christ, thereby making it clear that his allegiance within Judaism has been reshaped by the messianic community and its hermeneutic of reading a messianically-shaped *Tanakh*.[24] It cannot be for-

---

to both Father and Son in non-Jacobite early Christian letters (e.g., Rom 1:7; 2 Cor 1:2; Gal 1:1, 3; 1 Pet 1:2; 2 John 3; Jude 1), might be exploited more for christological purposes. That is, it is possible to render this "servant of the God-Lord, Jesus Christ." Such a rendering could be supported by 2:1, where "the Lord Jesus Christ" is connected to "glory" (see comments at 2:1). In addition, κύριος is used for "God" in 1:7; 3:9; 4:10; 5:10. Further appeal could be made to Tit 2:13 and 2 Pet 1:1. Mayor suggests that oblique cases sometimes omit the article, which would lead to *the* God and *the* Lord Jesus Christ (pp. ccx-ccxxii).

21. *Lord Jesus Christ.* See also his *One God, One Lord* and *At the Origins.*

22. This expression, which has been used mostly until this point for the Jerusalem messianic community, refers not to one community but to a variety of Jewish communities in the Diaspora among whom one finds believers in Jesus as Messiah. Therefore we need to be wary of referring to the community addressed by James as if it were one geographically contained messianic community. The logical corollary to this is that the situations in James are either specific to various communities (and almost certainly unrecoverable) or, which is more likely, typical of a variety of messianic communities. On this, cf. Bauckham, *Wisdom of James,* 25-28.

23. The single most interesting text in earliest Christianity in the growth of high christology, a text often only at the margins of the discussion, is 1 Cor 8:4-6, where the *Shema* is exegeted in such a manner that "God" refers to "Father" and "Lord" refers to "Jesus Christ." The oneness of God permitted (at least) binitarian thinking. See also Boyarin, *Border Lines,* 89-147; P. Rainbow, "Monotheism and Christology in 1 Corinthians 8:4-6" (D.Phil. thesis, Oxford 1987); C. J. Davis, *The Name and Way of the Lord* (JSNTSup 129; Sheffield: Sheffield Academic, 1996).

24. The literature here is enormous, but one cannot fail to mention the following: Dodd, *According to the Scriptures;* Goppelt, *Typos;* Lindars, *New Testament Apologetic;* Longenecker, *Biblical Exegesis in the Apostolic Period;* Carson and Williamson, *It Is Written;* Juel, *Messianic Exegesis;* Ellis, *The Old Testament in Early Christianity.* For the larger discussion, see especially Fishbane, *Biblical Interpretation.* For James's own use of the Old Testament, see now R. A. Bauckham, "James, 1 and 2 Peter, Jude," in Carson and Williamson, *It Is Written,* 306-9; D. A. Carson, in *CNTOT,* 997-1013.

gotten that earliest Christianity was driven to the Scriptures for a variety of reasons, not the least of which were (1) Jesus' own use of Scripture, (2) the necessity of following and worshiping and comprehending a crucified and risen Lord, (3) the inevitable discussions around their new understanding of Israel's history and the work of God through Jesus Christ, and (4) the need for explanations of their own experiences and persecution. The formative shape of the messianic community was derived from its hermeneutic of Scripture. For James (see 2:1-12), for instance, the entire Torah is to be read through the lens of Leviticus 19:18, the second half of what I have elsewhere called the Jesus Creed,[25] and the figures of the Old Testament are exemplary for the messianic community (see 2:21-23, 25; 5:10, 11, 17). The hermeneutic of James is that of Jesus.[26]

James, then, is a servant of God and the Lord Jesus Christ as he has come to know both through experience and Scripture interpretation. This confession may well put James in jeopardy on two separate fronts: because he "serves" the Lord Jesus Christ, he sets himself apart from other Jews who do not serve Jesus and from all those Gentiles who serve neither the God of Israel nor Jesus as Messiah. In light of exegesis of the meaning of "poor" in James, this confession by James places him among the "poor" who find themselves dominated by the "rich." To confess Jesus as Lord could be a confession of solidarity with the economic condition of the messianic community of James.

James addresses his letter "to the twelve tribes in the Dispersion,"[27] an address that has led to great consternation and little consensus among exegetes. Does this pregnant expression describe

an ethnic body *(Jews* or messianic *Jews)* or
a metaphorical body (*anyone* Jewish or messianic or Christian)?

And does "Dispersion" refer to

25. See *The Jesus Creed.* The first half of the Jesus Creed (the traditional *Shema*) can be found in Jas 1:12 (τοῖς ἀγαπῶσιν αὐτόν) and 2:19 (σὺ πιστεύεις ὅτι εἷς ἐστιν ὁ θεός).

26. See Bauckham, "James, 1 and 2 Peter, Jude," 309.

27. ταῖς δώδεκα φυλαῖς ταῖς ἐν τῇ διασπορᾷ. On the last term, see BDAG, 236. Scholars have waged battles over this expression. In addition to the commentaries (e.g., Hartin, 50-51, 53-55), see Bauckham, *Wisdom of James,* 14-16; Cargal, *Restoring the Diaspora,* 45-51, who connects 1:1 to 5:19-20 on the basis of his rhetorical, structural theory and sees the "Diaspora" of 1:1 to be hinted at in the wandering from the truth in 5:19-20; McKnight, "A Parting within the Way," 111-13; Edgar, *Has God Not Chosen the Poor?* 96-101 (figurative, and pointing to the sheer impossibility of the letter going to the whole Diaspora Jewish community as well as to the particularities of contextual information in James).

physical distance from the Land (in the *physical* Dispersion) or
the metaphorical sojourn life on this earth the Christian is called to
endure (in the *spiritual* Dispersion)?

The principles for detection of a metaphor are critical here. For a term to be
metaphorical, there need to be some clues:[28] the presence of a metaphor or of
a simile signifier, "as" or "like"; the impossibility of rendering something literally, as in the rich man "withering away" in 1:11; low correspondence between metaphor and analogue, as would be the case if we knew that James
was addressing the messianic community in Jerusalem as the "Dispersion";
and an expression so clearly developed that one must conclude it is metaphorical, as when James describes temptation in 1:13-15.

Do any of these apply to either "twelve tribes" or to "Dispersion"?
First, this language is typical for Jews when referring to themselves as an ethnic body in the Dispersion — in other words, this is ethnically- and
geographically-oriented language, and there is nothing that indicates it is a
highly developed metaphor.[29] It is customary for Jews to see themselves as
the twelve-tribe-people,[30] and Dispersion nearly always refers to the land
outside the Land of Israel. The verbal form of this word can be used for those
who were scattered from Jerusalem into other parts of Judea and Samaria
(Acts 8:1).[31] Second, this language is dropped from this point on, foreclosing
any chance of peering into the mind of the author through other evidence.

Third, the expression "twelve tribes" could be seen as almost *per
definitionem* metaphorical: ten of those tribes have been lost since the Assyr-
ian captivity. But it is not that easy: Jews with plausible connections back to
the eighth-century deportation were present in the Diaspora in the first century, and the hope of their return was a routine feature of Jewish eschatology.
So, since that return is expected but has not yet occurred in the ethnic sense,
"twelve tribes" must be a reference to all of Israel, and this expression probably also included the eschatological hope of reunion.[32] This is how Jesus

28. See Caird, *Language and Imagery,* 183-97, for a discussion of how to detect a
metaphor.

29. See Matt 19:28; Acts 26:7; Rev 7:4-8; *1 Clement* 55:6; Hermas, *Similitudes*
9.17.1-2. Also John 7:35; 1 Pet 1:1 with Deut 28:25; Ps 147:2; Isa 49:6; Jdth 5:19; 2 Macc
1:27. E.g., Verseput, "Genre and Story," 99-101.

30. See McKnight, "Jesus and the Twelve," 211-20.

31. Acts 8:1: πάντες δὲ διεσπάρησαν κατὰ τὰς χώρας τῆς Ἰουδαίας καὶ
Σαμαρείας πλὴν τῶν ἀποστόλων: "That day a severe persecution began against the church
in Jerusalem, and all except the apostles were scattered throughout the countryside of
Judea and Samaria."

32. See Isa 11:11-16; Jer 3:18; 31:8; 2 Chron 29:24; 30:1; 34:9; *Pss Sol* 17:28;
1 Esdras 7:8; *2 Esdras* 13:34-47; *Sibylline Oracles* 2.170; *Testament of Abraham* 13.6;

used "twelve" (Mark 3:13-19; Matt 19:28), and for Jesus there is a reconstitution of that twelve-tribe group for those who follow him and his apostles. Which means, in light of our comments about James stemming from a messianic community shaped by a messianic hermeneutic, it is highly likely that he is writing to the "twelve tribes" in the sense of those ethnic Jews who are part of the apostolically-led messianic community.[33] The single text that should clinch this for understanding James is found in Acts 15:13-21, where James addresses the Apostolic Conference in these words from Amos 9:11-12:

> After this I will return,
> and *I will rebuild the dwelling of David,* which has fallen;
>   from its ruins I will rebuild it, and I will set it up,
> so that all other peoples may seek the Lord —
> even all the Gentiles over whom my name has been called.
> Thus says the Lord, who has been making these things known from
> long ago. (Acts 15:16-18a)

Clearly, James sees the work of Jesus to be one of restoring Israel, and the specific shape of that restoring work is the messianic community of Jerusalem.

Fourth, a slight clarification of the Christian emphasis given in the previous point: the border between this messianic community and the rest of the Jewish community is amorphous. James 2:1-13 unveils a community that still meets in a "synagogue" (2:2), and the rest of James uses "church" only once (5:14). This means that "twelve tribes" is both messianic and still ethno-religiously inseparable from the Jewish community. Finally, there is very little evidence, outside Hebrews,[34] that early Christians, especially the early messianic community, had begun to use the language of pilgrimage for life on this earth.[35]

We conclude then that on balance it is more likely that James writes his letter to the messianic Jewish community or communities, which remain attached to the non-messianic Jewish community, which are residing in the Dis-

---

1QS 8:1; 1Q28a 11-12; 4Q159 frgs. 2-4:3-4; 1QM 2:1-3; 4Q164 2:1-3. See Brant Pitre, *Jesus, the Tribulation, and the End of Exile* (Grand Rapids: Baker, 2005); Penner, *The Epistle of James and Eschatology,* 181-83.

33. See Ropes, 118-20, 123-27; Dibelius, 66-67; Davids, 63-64; Laws, 48-49; especially Martin, 8-9; Popkes, 71-73; Frankemölle, 1.125-28.

34. 11:13; 13:14.

35. On Peter's use of "aliens and strangers," I follow the conclusions of J. H. Elliott, *Home for the Homeless,* for whom these terms describe the social status of the Christians.

persion, and which James understands to be the foretaste of the kingdom of God.[36] James sees such a community as part of Israel in the ethnic and covenant senses of that term. Thus, Patrick J. Hartin: "the recipients of James's letter are those from the house of Israel who have embraced Jesus' message."[37]

A final point, hardly demonstrable, deserves consideration: Why were the messianists scattered into the Dispersion? It is not impossible that James refers here to the dispersed Jerusalem-based messianists who fled persecution in the Holy City.[38] One thinks here of Acts 8:1 (see 9:31; 11:19, 29). In fact, if one presumes James is in Jerusalem writing to dispersed messianists, a text like Acts 8:1 is remarkably like the situation found in James.[39]

"Greetings to you!" James says after all this. The use of the cognate for "grace" reflects customary rather than early Christian, especially Pauline, theology. This is the same greeting we find in Acts 15:23, which may mean nothing for authorship, but which is (at least) attributed to James as well.[40]

2. THE CHRISTIAN AND TRIALS (1:2-18)

James quickly launches[1] into the substance of his letter, and trials are one of his central themes (cf. 2:1-7; 4:13-17; 5:1-6). The issue for understanding 1:2-18, and even 1:2-27, is the relationship among the various paragraphs — is this a loosely connected series of exhortations on a variety of topics or a largely coherent unit dealing with the same situation (poverty) and offering a variety of exhortations (patience, wisdom, etc.)? This commentary will propose that 1:2-27 is a single unit addressed to a specific audience: the poor messianic community that is being oppressed by persons in positions of power.

36. Martin, 9-11, contends that there is an emphasis on preservation under persecution when the term "Dispersion" is used; Frankemölle, 1.127.

37. P. J. Hartin, "The Religious Context," in Matt A. Jackson-McCabe, *Jewish Christianity Reconsidered* (Minneapolis: Fortress, 2007), 210.

38. Hengel, *Acts and the History of Earliest Christianity,* 74-75, famously argued that Acts 8:1 refers to the Hellenists fleeing Jerusalem. Craig Hill, *Hellenists and Hebrews: Reappraising Division within the Earliest Church* (Minneapolis: Fortress, 1992), 32-39, subjects Hengel's thesis to critique.

39. For a theology rooted in the African "dispersion," see the comment by Byron, 463.

40. On the ellipsis and syntax of the imperative χαίρειν, see BDF §§389, 480.5; MHT, 3.78. I consider the reality of an ellipsis to mean that the infinitive can be complementary.

1. Paul's letters and 1 Peter characteristically turn here to God in thanksgiving or praise for the church to which the apostles write (e.g., Rom 1:8-15; 1 Thess 1:2-10; 2 Tim 1:3-7; 1 Pet 1:3-9). James does not, much like 1 Tim, Titus, 2 Pet, and Jude.

Structurally, James states that the *purpose* of trials is to produce mature Christian character (1:2-4), but, knowing that discerning the purpose of trials is no easy matter even for the spiritually mature, James then exhorts the messianic Jewish community to ask God for *wisdom* when they encounter trials (1:3-8). Revealing just what he has in mind, James now turns to the specific form of trial the messianic Jewish community is encountering: it is facing poverty in the context of others having wealth (1:9-11). And James clearly sides with the poor who can learn to glory in their (paradoxical) exaltation. In his "plausibility structure,"[2] to be poor means to be on the right side of God's work.[3] Finally, because James knows that his community will ask the penetrating question and that some are already questioning the goodness of God, he turns to *how God relates to trials* (1:12-18). God is good, James teaches, and trials are an opportunity for the community to be tested. Sin emerges from the human condition and can be overcome by the "new birth" (1:18) as it creates a new community as a foretaste of what is to come.

2.1. THE PURPOSE OF TESTING (1:2-4)

2 *My brothers and sisters*[a], *whenever you face trials of any kind*[b], *consider*[4] *it nothing but*[c] *joy,* 3 *because you know that the testing*[5] *of your*[6] *faith*[d] *produces endurance*[e]; 4 *and let endurance have its full effect*[f], *so that you may be mature and complete,*[7] *lacking in nothing.*

2. On this, see P. Berger and T. Luckmann, *The Social Construction of Reality: A Treatise in the Sociology of Knowledge* (New York: Anchor, 1967).

3. Paul uses the argument from persecution to legitimacy in Gal 4:21-31.

4. A significant number of ninth- to eleventh-century manuscripts, including 33, 607, 621, and 1735, have ηγεισθε instead of ἡγήσασθε.

5. δοκίμιον, a substantival adjective (BDAG: "the process or means of determining the genuineness of someth." or "genuineness as a result of a test"), appears in some manuscripts as δόκιμον (BDAG: "pert. to being genuine on the basis of testing . . . worthy of high regard . . . valuable"); see 110, 1241 *pc;* Did[pt]. The meaning is distinct: in the former the focus is *process* (the testing of the genuineness) while the latter is the *result* (the genuineness). The manuscript evidence is overwhelmingly in favor of the former. The former term appears in the New Testament at 1 Pet 1:7 and the latter term appears at Jas 1:12; also at Rom 14:18; 16:10; 1 Cor 11:19; 2 Cor 10:18; 13:7; 2 Tim 2:15. There is an important discussion in A. Deissmann, *Bible Studies,* 259-62, where clarity is also brought to LXX Ps 11[12]:7[6]; Prov 27:21.

6. The word order varies: ὑμῶν τῆς πίστεως is altered to τῆς πίστεως ὑμῶν (629), the possessive is omitted (429, 614, etc.), only the possessive appears (B[2]), and one tradition omits all three words (sy[h] Aug[pt] Arn). The vast majority of the manuscripts prefer ὑμῶν τῆς πίστεως (01, 02 with MajT and MaxConf, PsMaxConf, PsOec).

7. καὶ ὁλόκληροι is omitted altogether as a redundancy in several manuscripts

69

a. The inclusive translation of TNIV and NRSV[8]

b. TNIV: many kinds

c. TNIV: pure joy

d. You know that "whatever is genuine in your faith" produces (Deissmann).

e. TNIV: perseverance

f. TNIV: finish its work

The structure of James 1:2-4 is simple: after a rhetorical connection (1:2a), James describes a condition (1:2b), gives an exhortation (1:2c: "consider it nothing but joy"), and then gives a reason that is made of a chain of connecting virtues (1:3-4).

1:2   Since James, like most authors of letters in the early Christian world, assumed a connection with his audience and also assumed shared information, the informed reader recognizes such assumptions and does what he or she can do to fill in the gaps. James makes a connection to his audience now with "my brothers and sisters."[9] Rhetorically, this phrase is suspended in Greek until after "consider it nothing but joy" and, though neither unusual nor special, envelops the audience with a sense of community fellowship as it comes to terms with the injunction James gives to them. "Brothers and sisters" could refer *inclusively* to an *ethnic* body (the Jewish community), whether limited only to messianic Jews or not. Thus, Leviticus 25:46 and Deuteronomy 15:3 are typical examples of Jews seeing their fellow nationals as family "brothers." The early Christian community continued this same language when the audience was both messianic and non-messianic "brothers" (Acts 2:29; Rom 9:3). Others have suggested that "brothers and sisters" is to be rendered in a more *exclusive* sense as referring to the messianic Jewish community, which has been referred to as the "twelve tribes" in 1:1.[10] There is plenty of evidence from earliest Christianity and from James himself

---

(400, 1270, and some Coptic manuscripts), but found in P74V, 629C, 631f, 1595Z, with Cyr, Did, MaxConf, PsMaxConf, PsOec, most Latin manuscripts, and some Coptic, Syriac, and Ethiopic manuscripts).

8. In general, see Johnson, *Brother of Jesus, Friend of God,* 221-34. James's depiction of leadership is not, according to Johnson, along typical male qualities but instead deals with meekness and service; James uses "giving birth" of God — the Father! — in 1:18; and note the lack of "generational kinship language" (father/son etc.) in James. These are traces of what is sometimes called a "redemptive trend/hermeneutic" with respect to sexuality and equality. This would justify the NRSV's and TNIV's inclusive translations. See, more broadly, Ng, "Father-God Language."

9. ἀδελφοί μου. The term ἀδελφός is used 19x in James. When the personal pronoun is added, as here, the term indicates the community of Jesus to which James is writing. See BDAG, 18-19.

10. This, too, is early Christian: cf. Mayor, 33; Ropes, 131-32; Mussner, 63; Burchard, 54.

for understanding the community as a "brotherhood community" (Matt 23:8; 25:40; Jas 1:9, 16, etc.).[11]

The Greek text differs from the English translation in that James suddenly commands[12] the messianic Jewish community to "consider"[13] their condition, one marked by trials, as an occasion for joy. To "consider" trials as an occasion of joy involves an act of faith, for instead of looking *at* the trial, the messianic Jewish community is instead encouraged to look *through* the trial to its potential outcome. As Paul considered his trial before King Agrippa an opportunity for defense, preaching, and potential release (Acts 26:2), as he urged believers to "consider" others better than oneself (Phil 2:3; cf. 1 Thess 5:13), as Christ did not "consider" equality something to be grasped but to be surrendered for the redemption of others (Phil 2:6), as Paul "considered" his former glory an actual loss (3:7), as

---

11. Also 1:19; 2:1, 5, 14; 3:1, 10, 12; 4:11; 5:7, 9-12, 19. It is therefore unlikely that the term is simply rhetorical or homiletical vocabulary (see Vouga, 38), though it is undoubtedly rhetorically shaped (Ropes, 132).

12. ἡγήσασθε, BDAG, 434, is an aorist imperative. Throughout this commentary an aspectual theory of Greek syntax will be assumed; our approach is closest to the work of Stan Porter (see below). For the aorist in our passage, one should not understand the "command" as punctiliar or ingressive but instead as "global" or an "action viewed completely" or an "action viewed from outside." In this case, it is the "thatness" of considering it all joy rather than the "howness" of the considering that leads James to the aorist. Along with this, then, the focus is on the vocabularic meaning of the aorist rather than when or how something happens or happened. On aspectual theory and imperatives, see Porter, *Verbal Aspect,* 335-63; Fanning, *Verbal Aspect;* for a readable introduction to aspect theory, see A. D. Naselli, "A Brief Introduction to Verbal Aspect in New Testament Greek," *DBSJ* 12 (2007) 17-28; see also S. E. Porter, "Greek Grammar and Syntax," in *The Face of New Testament Studies* (ed. S. McKnight and G. R. Osborne; Grand Rapids: Baker, 2004), 76-103.

A new, courageous introduction to aspectual theory, taking "aspect" as "viewpoint" and seeing aspect as either "outside" (perfective — aorist and future) or "inside" (imperfective — present [proximate], imperfect [remote], perfect [heightened proximity], and pluperfect), can be seen in the altogether useful brief textbook of C. R. Campbell, *Basics of Verbal Aspect in Biblical Greek* (Grand Rapids: Zondervan, 2008). One of the best features of this book is its brief discussion of the history of aspectual theory (pp. 26-33). Campbell slides the "stative" aspect (roughly the perfect tense) into the "imperfective" aspect and sees the perfect as "heightened proximity" so that it functions as a "superpresent" tense (p. 51).

The implications of aspect theory for New Testament scholarship are enormous. For instance, aspect theory leads us to think in terms of the author's subjective depiction or viewpoint and runs against the sorts of observations like that of Ropes, 131, who thinks the aorist is used to indicate each specific example of trial.

13. See also at Acts 26:2; 2 Cor 9:5; Phil 2:3, 6, 25; 3:7-8; 1 Thess 5:13; 2 Thess 3:15; 1 Tim 1:12; 6:1; Heb 10:29; 11:11, 26; 2 Pet 1:13; 2:13; 3:15.

Abraham "considered" God faithful and powerful enough to enable Sarah to conceive (Heb 11:11), as Moses "considered" suffering for Christ more valuable than the treasures of Egypt (11:26), and as the author of 2 Peter wanted his readers to "consider" the patience of the Lord as salvation (3:15), so James urges the messianic Jewish community to "consider" their trials an occasion for joy as they look *through* their trials to their purgative and sanctifying impact.

The Christian attitude toward trials and suffering is legendary, and while it found story-shaping examples like those of Perpetua, Felicitas,[14] and Macrina[15] in the pre- and post-Constantinian period, the foundations were laid in Israel's history — whether one thinks of Job or of the suffering of the prophets. In addition, the lives of John the Baptist, Jesus, and first martyrs of the faith filled the Christian imagination with hope.[16] Some explained such trials as something that would only be overcome in the eschaton (Matt 5:10-12; 1 Pet 4:12-14), as destiny (1 Thess 3:3), or as an opportunity to imitate Christ (Acts 5:41), but James finds the silver lining in what trials accomplish in moral formation and character.

James is fond of using catchwords to make connections. He joins his salutation in 1:1 to the beginning of the body of the letter in 1:2 with "greetings"/"joy," which are cognates.[17] He speaks of the "ground" for this "joy" in the messianic community in spite of impoverishment and oppression, which far transcends any optimism or "positive thinking."[18] What James has in mind is an inner confidence that permits fidelity to follow Jesus because of one's confidence in the goodness of God, in God's sovereign control of history and eternity, and in one's inner transformation, which wells up into a sense of joyfulness (4:5). Translations have done their best to make "all joy"[19] meaningful in English, and interpreters need to set it in the context of

14. *The Martyrdom of Perpetua and Felicitas,* ANF 3.697-706.

15. Gregory of Nyssa, *The Life of Saint Macrina.*

16. Frend, *Martyrdom.*

17. χαίρειν — χαράν. For other instances, cf. 1:4 and 1:5; 1:12 and 13; 1:15-18; 1:26 and 27; 2:12 and 13; 3:11 and 13; 3:17 and 18; 5:9 and 12; 5:13-16; 5:19 and 20. On χαρά, see BDAG, 1077; *EDNT* 3.454-55; W. G. Morrice, *Joy in the New Testament* (Grand Rapids: Eerdmans, 1984).

18. See here Mayor, 33; Ropes, 131; Johnson, 176-77; Popkes, 80-81; Blomberg and Kamell, 48-49.

19. πᾶσαν χαράν in Greek. The adjective πᾶς with an anarthrous noun indicates "every in the sense of any (or each)"; see BDF §275.3. As such, it intensifies χαράν and it is this "intensification" that requires English translation. It means "full" or "sheer" or "utter" or "pure" or "complete"; cf. Ropes, 129-31; Dibelius, 72 n. 11; Davids, 67. Mayor sees it as equivalent to μεγάλην or πολλήν and suggests abundance (p. 32). See also Phil 2:29; 1 Pet 2:18; 1 Tim 2:2, 11; Tit 2:10, 15; 3:2; Acts 17:11; 23:1. For joy in trials, see 2 Macc 6:12-17; *4 Maccabees* 7:22; 11:12; Matt 5:11-12; Acts 5:41; 1 Pet 1:6-7.

an early Christian sense of hope (1:2, 9-11, 12, 25; 2:5; 4:6; 5:10-11), as does Elsa Tamez.[20]

A significant question becomes *why* James urges the messianic Jewish community to face trials with joy, and there are two fundamentally different approaches. The first is to see the Christian life as a pilgrimage and the ground for joy in an eschatological reward. Such a motivation is threaded through the entire fabric of earliest Christianity, and eschatology is a foundational element of earliest Christianity. Thus, the Apostle Paul can say in Romans 5:2-5 that sufferings produce hope, and Peter can say in 1 Peter 1:6-7 that sufferings prove faith for the day Jesus is revealed. James himself holds hands with such an eschatological basis for facing trials for in 1:12, and in 2:5 he states that the one who endures testing is promised a crown of life.[21] While this eschatological focus of final redemption and release from trial ought not to be minimized, this is perhaps not all that James has in mind. He seems to have more earthly things in mind as well: suffering should promote endurance (1:2-4), justice (1:20), a life full of love and compassion (1:26-27; 2:1-13, 14-17), and peacemaking (3:18). When James focuses on the eschaton he speaks of it as judgment (2:12-13; 4:12; 5:1-6, 7-9) and as death that brings to an end the messianic community's opportunity to realize the will of God (1:15; 3:13-18; 4:7-11, 13-17; 5:7-9, 10-11, 20). Thus, to focus "joy" in this text on one's heavenly reward seems out of step with what James has in mind.[22]

On the other hand, a second view of why the messianic community ought to be joyous should not be quickly discounted: Acts 5:41 relates that the apostles left the Sanhedrin, after being flogged for their faith, *"rejoicing"* because "they were considered worthy to suffer dishonor for the sake of the name." 2 Corinthians 8:1-9 connects suffering to generosity and to the example of Jesus Christ, and does so in language similar to James 1:2-4, 9-11.[23] The connections in James 1:2 to such an early Christian tradition are as sub-

---

20. She is mostly alone in this emphasis: see Tamez, 27-41.

21. See especially Penner, *The Epistle of James and Eschatology,* who focuses on the testing and eschatology (especially 183-210). He points to a number of texts, including Zech 13:9; Dan 11:35; 12:10; Mal 3:1-5; 1QS 4:5; 8:3; 1QM 16:17–17:9; Rev 2:26-27; 3:10.

22. Once again, though, this is not to deny a future eschatological reward for James; see 1:12 and commentary there. For a recent suggestive study of the importance of life on earth against a preoccupation with an otherworldly heaven, see N. T. Wright, *Surprised by Hope* (New York: HarperOne, 2008).

23. The following connections, both verbal and thematic, need to be observed: (1) χάριν in 2 Cor 8:1, 2; (2) δοκιμῇ in 8:2, 8; (3) the theme of suffering/trial in 8:2; (4) πτωχεία in 8:2, 9 [see exegesis at Jas 1:9-11]; (5) πλούσιος in 8:9 and Jas 1:9-11; and (6) the interchange of wealth and poverty in 2 Cor 8:8-10.

stantial as those in Romans 5:2-5 and 1 Peter 1:6-7, and it needs to be observed that in 1:2-4 James does not delve into eschatology: the focus is on discipleship as character and moral formation. Thus, a *discipleship* or *imitatio Christi* ground for this joy has every reason to be considered part of the thought-world of James.[24]

The *condition* for this exhortation to joy is "whenever[25] you face trials of any kind" (1:2). James's perception, at this point in his text, of the sort of trial the messianic Jewish community is facing is not directly clear, in part because he describes it with such open-endedness: "whenever" and "trials of any kind."[26] But, what for James is open-ended need not be taken by moderns to include everything they want to include in "trials of any kind," as our exegesis will show. NRSV "face" masks a more evocative term. *peripiptō*[27] indicates an *unexpected encounter,* as when the "man" going from Jerusalem to Jericho "fell" into the hands of robbers (Luke 10:30; cf. Acts 27:41). As well, it is an encounter with something that puts a person to the test by taking one to the end of and beyond one's means.[28] Such unexpected encounters, according to 2 Maccabees 6:13, are used by God to "discipline" his people.[29] In

24. Col 1:24 has an entirely different perspective, but participation in the sufferings of Christ in a salvific sense has no parallel in James.

25. The temporal conditional particle ὅταν with the subjunctive περιπέσητε indicates randomness and indeterminacy and the need to respond to any such circumstance with a readiness to see through the circumstance to what God may accomplish.

26. James does not say that all will be tested in this life, though it would be a rare person indeed who did not find life's rolling waves to be an occasion for the testing of faith. There is a tendency among some Christians to operate with what is often called an "attribution theory" of life that emerges out of some form of theological determinism, that is, they sense a need to "attribute" a divine purpose in everything that occurs to them (and others) and they seem to know just what that purpose is. The perspective of James is more humble: the test itself leads one to discover that the test provoked endurance and the development of character. See McKnight, *Turning to Jesus,* 92-95; see more at B. Spilka, P. Shaver, and L. A. Kirkpatrick, "A General Attribution Theory for the Psychology of Religion," *JSSR* 24 (1985) 1-20; W. Proudfoot and P. Shaver, "Attribution Theory and the Psychology of Religion," *JSSR* 14 (1975) 317-30. For a pastorally sensitive discussion, see A. Hamilton, *Seeing Gray in a Black and White World* (Nashville: Abingdon, 2008), 121-32.

27. περιπίπτω; cf. BDAG, 804; Spicq, 3.97-99; W. Michaelis, in *TDNT* 6.173; Mussner, 64.

28. 2 Macc 9:7: ". . . and the fall (περιπεσόντα) was so hard as to torture every limb of his body." 1 Clem 51:2 is strikingly bold: "For those who conduct themselves with reverential awe and love prefer to *undergo* (περιπίπτειν) torture themselves than to have their neighbors do so."

29. NRSV: "In fact, it is a sign of great kindness not to let the impious alone for long, but to *punish them* (περιπίπτειν ἐπιτίμοις) immediately" (6:13). The Gentiles, so the writer contends, do not experience such "mercy" (6:16). "Although he disciplines us with calamities, he does not forsake his own people" (6:16). See also 10:4.

addition, for James this "encounter," if not seen *through,* can lead to the inner compulsion to sin and moral collapse (1:13-15).[30]

What might James have meant by "trials of any kind"?[31] Various options have been offered by the church's many commentators, including *daily* trials such as food shortage, being laid off, or a fire in the home,[32] *internal* trials in the sense of moral temptations,[33] which in James revolve often enough around verbal sins and violent reactions (1:19-21; 3:1-12) and political mongering (3:13–4:12), or *external* trials in the sense of persecution.[34] Attached to the view that the "trials of any kind" are external trials are two other ideas: that such trials are the lot of the pious, as in 1 Peter 1:6,[35] or that they are the inevitable lot of those thrust into the eschatological distress of the last times, as is probably the case in the Lord's Prayer (Matt 6:13) and clearly the case in Revelation 3:10.[36] In other words, one may encounter unexpectedly some kind of external trial because that is what happens to the Lord's people as he disciplines them or because we are in the last days.

Can we know more?[37] I think we can. To begin with, "trials" translates *peirasmoi,* which refers both to external tests that are found within the providence of God — as in Jesus' tests (Matt 4:1-11; cf. Luke 22:28) and to internal or external temptations to sin — as in the *locus classicus,* 1 Corinthians 10:13, and in 1 Thessalonians 3:5 or 2 Peter 2:9.[38] Second, since James sees *benefit* in these "trials," we can only conclude that he is speaking about unexpected encounters that put both individuals and the whole of the messianic Jewish community to the test. This leads many to suggest that with "trials of any kind" James is thinking of *persecution* because of faith in Jesus Christ.[39] Furthermore, if one scans James one finds that the *kind* of persecution he has in mind in this letter has to do with *economic injustice and oppression.* It is unwise to narrow words when such narrowing is not shaped by

30. Cf. Prov 11:5; Josephus, *Ant* 4.293. See also Gal 6:1; 1 Tim 6:9.

31. See P. Davids, "Why Do We Suffer? Suffering in James and Paul," in Chilton and Evans, *Missions,* 435-66; also Popkes, 81-83; Burchard, 54-55 (who prefers "Anfechtung" in the sense of testing).

32. So Laws, 52, 67, 69.

33. Cf. 1:13-14.

34. This is the standard view of Jas 1:2-4; cf. Mayor, 33; Ropes, 133; Dibelius, 71. See also Josephus, *B.J.* 1.653; *Pss Sol* 10:1-3.

35. See Gen 22; Num 14:20-24; Job 36:8-12; Prov 3:11-12; Sir 2:1, 5; Jdth 8:25; *4 Maccabees* 16:19; 1QS 10; 17; 1QH 5:15-17; 1QM 16:15–17:3; Matt 5:11-12.

36. See especially Allison, *The End of the Ages,* 5-25. On the Lord's Prayer, see R. E. Brown, *New Testament Essays,* 275-320.

37. See P. Davids, "James's Message," in Chilton and Neusner, *The Brother of Jesus,* 69-71; Guthrie, 212.

38. See Spicq, 3.80-90; *TDNT* 6.23-36.

39. So Davids, 67; Martin, 15.

textual evidence, but it is also unwise to broaden terms when the texts do not permit that. In "trials of any kind" one might think James has everything and anything in mind, but the text is not this general.[40]

James mentions these manifestations of persecution: stresses connected to economic poverty (1:9, 27; 2:15-16), favoritism for the wealthy and against the poor (2:1-4, 9), economic abuse and injustice (2:5-7), blasphemy of Jesus Christ by those with sufficient political power (2:7), and economic exploitation of the poor by the rich (5:1-6). And it is precisely at 5:7, after James has excoriated the rich for economic injustices, that he returns to the theme he opened with, namely, enduring suffering. In 5:7 he says, "Be patient," and in 5:10-11 he says, "As an example of suffering and patience, beloved, take the prophets who spoke in the name of the Lord . . . [and] Job. . . ." And in 5:13, as in 1:2-4 and 5-8, he connects suffering and prayer. Put together, it appears that James has socio-economic suffering in mind when he thinks of the social situation of the messianic Jewish community. In other words, the "trials of any kind" of 1:2 seem crystallized in 2:6-7:

> But you have dishonored the poor. Is it not the rich who oppress you? Is it not they who drag you into court? Is it not they who blaspheme the excellent name that was invoked over you?

But it is not enough to stop here: for James the "trial" is not just what the messianic community is being forced to endure, but also *how they respond.* And here we have to read James in context. In this letter, the concern is that the messianic community not turn to verbal abuse of others or to volatile anger at the physical level. Now, this surprises the gentle and largely cultured (Western) church of the twenty-first century, but a closer look at James shows that the messianic community was, in fact, tempted to use violence to bring about the will of God. This is seen in 1:19-21 and 4:1-2, it is hinted at in the "desire" of 1:13-15, and it is the inevitable implication of the abuse the Christians are experiencing according to 2:5-7 and 5:1-6. The trial then is twofold: the socio-economic privation of the messianic community and their need to resist the desire to resort to violence (4:1-2) to establish justice (1:20) and peace (3:18).

This robust conclusion to the meaning of "trials" in 1:2 means we have faced a fork in the interpretive road and have taken one path: James has in mind a more specific than general notion in this term. This conclusion will have an impact on what follows, but in carrying through with this interpretive decision, this commentary will regularly provide an alternative viewpoint

---

40. ποικίλοις could refer to "any kind one might think of" or to "a variety of a given type" (say, economic).

when the evidence can be so interpreted. In light of this conclusion, we need to pause momentarily to consider how close the theme of James 1:2 is to the Magnificat (Luke 1:46-55) and the Beatitudes (Luke 6:20-26). The *Anawim* theology found in such texts is also found in James, and it is this context that makes most sense of the text of James.

1:3   After his pastoral injunction and the clarification of the condition, James now provides the *reason* that the messianic Jewish community ought to find in their tests an opportunity to see *through* them in joy. This reason unfolds into a chain of virtues that have a goal: "maturity." The capacity to see through a test to character formation at the hand of God's grace is based on *knowledge*.[41] One can surmise that the messianic Jewish community learned to see through tests to what they could do for them from their Jewish or messianic Jewish catechetical traditions,[42] that it was "stock" knowledge for the community,[43] or that James is rhetorically assuming what he is about to teach.

What the messianic Jewish community "knows" is that "the testing of your faith produces endurance." James is more interested in the *result* of tests/trials than he is in getting hung up on words, but "testing" carries with it an inherent ambiguity because *dokimion* is an adjective without a noun to modify. C. F. D. Moule translates it as "the tested (i.e. genuine) part."[44] The general sense appears to be "the process of testing will determine the *genuineness* of your faith, and *what is genuine* emerging from that test" will produce "endurance,"[45] although others think *to dokimion* refers only to "the means of testing" or to "the test itself" which itself produces "endurance."[46] The economic (or moral) trials of the messianic Jewish community will test its faith and what survives that test will lead toward endurance. After James the apostle had been killed, and earlier John the Baptist and Jesus, while Saul was breathing fire on those who adhered to Jesus, and while endurance was

41. The present active adverbial participle, γινώσκοντες, can be interpreted generically ("knowing that"), causally ("because you know"; so NRSV, NIV), or imperativally ("Know that . . ."; so Martin, 14, though his translation there and on p. 15 shows little connection to the imperative mood). The present tense of the participle favors a generic interpretation, suggesting that "knowing" is a "concurrent" or "progressive" or "characteristic" feature of "considering." In grammatical terms, its aspect is "imperfective" or unfolding. On this, see especially Porter, *Verbal Aspect*, 75-109.
42. So Davids, 68.
43. So evidently Dibelius, 72.
44. Moule, *Idiom Book*, 96. See also BDF §263.2.
45. See Mayor, 34; Ropes, 134; Davids, 68; Martin, 15; Burchard, 55-56 (sees an emphasis on purification); M. E. Isaacs, "Suffering in the Lives of Christians: James 1:2-19a," *RevExp* 97 (2000) 183-93. Important evidence includes Prov 27:21; Rom 5:4; 2 Cor 8:2; 13:3; 1 Pet 1:7.
46. Dibelius, 72-73; Davids, 68.

not something read about but experienced daily, *to dokimion* and the moral exhortation to become a person marked by "endurance" were of obvious relevance.

What is tested by these trials is "faith."[47] In the Christian tradition, "faith" has been connected to "what one believes" (*creedal* faith) as well as to the personal *act* of believing and trusting God to get one through a test, and surely James has the latter in mind.[48]

James envisions, as do 1 Pet 1:6-7 and Rom 5:3-5 but also 2 Pet 1:5-8 and Rom 8:28-30, a linkage from one virtue or condition to another[49] because he describes it as a theologically-driven and progressive operation of conversion *(katergazetai),* as if it were going on before his eyes.[50]

James 1:2-4	*1 Peter 1:6-7*	*Romans 5:3-5*
Test	**Test**	Stress
faith	**faith**	**(faith)**
endurance		**endurance**
		character
		hope
mature/complete	**love**	**love** of God
	eschatological glory	
	salvation	

47. ὑμῶν τῆς πίστεως. On "faith" in James, the discussion is enormous; see the succinct summary of Burchard, 56; the lengthier discussion in Frankemölle, 1.222-31, and notes at 2:14-26.

48. This is the sense at 1:6; 2:5; and 5:15.

49. On the links and differences, some leading scholars today think there is no connection between these texts; see Davids, 65-66. Most discussions neglect 2 Pet and Rom 8, and inasmuch as they link one virtue or condition to another, they deserve consideration.

50. On this term, BDAG, 531: "to cause a state or condition, bring about, produce, create." See Rom 5:3-5; 7:8, 13, 15, 20; 15:18; 2 Cor 4:17; 5:5; 7:10-11; 9:11; Eph 6:13; Phil 2:12. At the bottom of a Christian "theology of effects" is the grace of God working through the Holy Spirit to "effect" the community in which humans are restored for the good of the world. See McKnight, *Embracing Grace.* James touches on this very theme in 1:18, there attributing the enablement to the implanted word, and 4:5-6, where the enablement is the grace of the Holy Spirit residing in the community. On conversion, see McKnight, *Turning to Jesus,* 27-114. On the centrality of community (ecclesiology), see Stegemann and Stegemann, *Jesus Movement,* 249-407; Patzia, *Emergence;* Banks, *Paul's Idea;* from a more theological angle, Grenz, *The Social God,* 304-36; Volf, *Exclusion and Embrace.*

James 1:2-4	2 Peter 1:5-8	Romans 8:28-30
Test		
faith	**faith**	**love**
endurance	goodness	foreknowledge
	knowledge	predestination
	self-control	called
	perseverance	justified
	godliness	glorified
	brotherly kindness	
mature/complete	**love**	

In vocabulary, James is close here to 1 Peter 1 and Romans 5, though only James and Romans tie together "faith," "endurance," and "produces." Formally, 1 Peter 1 is less of a chain text than either James 1:2-4; Romans 5:3-5; 2 Peter 1:5-8; or Romans 8:28-30. Substantially, James 1:2-4 is closest to 2 Peter 1:5-8, then Romans 8:28-30, and then Romans 5:3-5 in providing a list where one virtue or condition leads to or triggers another. Teleologically, James finds its *telos* in being "mature and complete, lacking in nothing," while both Romans 5:3-5 and 2 Peter 1:5-8 finish with "love";[51] 1 Peter 1:6-7 and Romans 8:5-8 finish in a more theological vision: eschatological glory. Theologically, God's work is in view in each of these lists, though 2 Peter 1:5-8 appears at first blush to see the virtues as something a human works at (but cf. 2 Pet 1:3-4). The implication of the list in James, along with these other chain passages in early Christian writing, is that God has a design for his people and he provides both the enablement and the assurance that that design will be accomplished.

Because James understands "endurance" to be needed in the context of persecution, his concern is less with the development of a list of moral virtues — as in 2 Peter 1:5-8; Romans 5:3-5; 2 Corinthians 1:6; 1 Timothy 6:11; or even Galatians 5:22-23 — than with the acquisition of the virtue of "endurance" so that the messianic Jewish community can become "mature." Even here, because of the *telos* of these virtues, "endurance" for James differs markedly from the Stoic sense of quiet, passive absorption because it derives from confidence in final justice (5:11)[52] and the importance of moral development.[53] Thus, for James "endurance" is not a goal, as with the Stoics, but a means to a goal.

---

51. But see Jas 1:25; 2:8-11.

52. See Turner, *Christian Words,* 318-19; Nystrom, 48-50. See also the sense of enduring hope at Qumran: 1QHa 14:6; 17:12, 14; 18:22; 19:31; 4Q88 8:1; 4Q171 f1 2:2, 9; 4Q437 f2 1:14; 4Q521 f2 2; 4:4; 11Q5 19:16.

53. See also at Matt 24:13; Luke 8:15; 21:19; Rom 2:7; 5:3; 8:25; 2 Cor 1:6; 6:4; Col 1:11; 2 Thess 1:4; 1 Tim 6:11; 2 Tim 3:10; Tit 2:2; Heb 10:36; 12:1; Rev 1:9; 2:2; 13:10; 14:12; *Did* 16:5. One needs also to think of 1-2 Macc.

The genuineness of the faith that emerges out of the sea of testing produces "endurance," and this term describes the capacity to respond to that test with virtues intact — the virtue is active and is more than "submission."[54] Instead of fading away (cf. 1:5-8), such genuineness produces fidelity, stability, and the ability to retain one's faith in spite of the stress persecution might cause. Commentators are prone to speak here of the development of character,[55] but "endurance" is like love and faith: they are not something acquired so much as *ongoing acts* that conform to God's design.[56] In particular, in James "endurance" needs to be understood concretely instead of as just a general virtue. "Endurance" and "patience" are nearly synonymous (see 5:7). Which means that James is not so concerned with the moral trait of fidelity as he is with its concrete manifestation in sustaining one's messianic discipleship. Once again, we need to turn to the evidence of James: the community is enduring socio-economic oppression, and the singular temptation it faces is to strike back verbally and physically. This much is clear from 1:19-21 and 4:1-12. "Endurance," then, may well describe the decision on the part of the messianic community to refuse the option of violence to establish justice and to learn to wait for God's work to be accomplished in God's timing (1:9-11). We should not envision passivity so much as a confident moral rectitude and concrete behaviors of love in the face of opposition.

1:4 If the messianic Jewish community meets its tests with a genuine faith, it will be stable and faithful to its vocation. Endurance itself will lead the messianic believer to "maturity": "and[57] let[58] endurance have its full[59] effect so that you may be mature and complete, lacking in nothing." There is an emphasis here on personal or communal responsibility: James urges the community to permit "endurance" to do what it is designed by God to do by consciously being aware of what the test of faith entails and letting that entailment come into fruition. James does not explain how this occurs, but only *that* it is to occur. He assumes responsibility on the part of humans, as he will make clear in 1:13-15 as well.

Endurance has the splendid capacity ("full effect") to produce matu-

---

54. See *Martyrdom of Polycarp* 19:2; Ignatius, *Romans* 10:3.

55. So Mayor, 36; Ropes, 135-36; Davids, 68; Martin, 15-16. See Tamez, 43-46, who speaks of "militant patience."

56. Laws, 53.

57. δέ is either continuative ("and"; Ropes, 137) or a slight adversative ("but it does not stop with endurance; it must be permitted to have its way so maturity can develop"; Martin, 16).

58. On ἐχέτω in the sense of "surrendering to its powers," "entailment," see Jas 2:17; Heb 10:35; 1 John 4:18; see also the similar ideas at Rom 6 and Gal 5:6.

59. The translation of τέλειον with "full" is colorless; the word speaks of excellence, maturation, and splendid virtue. ἔργον refers to "effect" or "impact."

ration, or moral perfection.[60] A more literal translation, which would reveal the special catchword style James is using, would be "let endurance do its *maturing/perfect* work so that you may be *mature/perfect.*" The Greek term *teleios* ("mature" or "perfect") has played mind games with Christians for two millennia,[61] and the following need to be kept in mind:[62] First, James does not adhere to a sense of universal Christian sinlessness since 3:2 says, in the context of verbal sins, "all of us make many mistakes." Second, the sins dealt with in James are sufficient to indicate that he sees evidence of them in the community (e.g., 1:19-21, 22-25, 26; 2:1-13, 14-17; 3:1-12, 14-16; 4:1-6, 11-17; 5:1-6, 15). But, third, James believes the messianic Jewish community should strive for a *maturity* level where verbal sins do not occur (3:2: "Anyone who makes no mistakes in speaking is perfect [*teleios*]") and where violence is not manifested (1:19-21). Perfection for James is not just eschatological or an inner orientation toward God but concretely behavioral. Fourth, *teleios* can be used of both God (Jas 1:17; Matt 5:48) and humans (Jas 1:4; 3:2; Matt 19:21; Ignatius, *Smyrnaeans* 11:3).[63] Fifth, Paul refers to a group of people to whom *teleios* applies (1 Cor 2:6), and this spiritual group have God's Spirit (vv. 6-16; cf. also Phil 3:15; Col 4:12). The same is seen in Hebrews 5:14. In addition, there is a sense in which *teleios* describes the eschaton (1 Cor 13:10; cf. Eph 4:13; Col 1:28). All of this derives in some measure from the Hebrew word *tamim* or "completeness" (see Gen 6:9; 17:1; Deut 18:13) of devotion to God or relationship with God.[64]

---

60. The grammar suggests three *telic* orientations for endurance: (1) τέλειος, (2) ὁλόκληρος, and (3) λειπόμενοι ἐν μηδενί. It is likely that the first two are a hendiadys and that the third is a sweeping clarification.

61. A most influential work of John Wesley stands out: *Plain Account of Christian Perfection.* See also Tamez, 66-72, who sees a different emphasis in James than is found in Wesley, namely in James's "trans-individual relationships in the practice and demonstration of the faith" (p. 71). One ought also to consider S. Kierkegaard, *Purity of Heart Is to Will One Thing* (trans. D. V. Steere; New York: Harper, 1956).

62. On τέλειος, see R. Schippers, in *NIDNTT* 2.59-65; G. Delling, in *TDNT* 8.49-87; H. Hübner, in *EDNT* 3.342-44; Turner, *Christian Words,* 324-29: "one who obeys the will of God and responds to Him, totally submitted, absolutely dependent, devoted to His service" (p. 327). Turner shows that such a category is a part of inaugurated eschatology (p. 328). See also Tamez, 46-56; an excellent sketch of evidence can be found in Hartin, *Spirituality of Perfection,* 17-39; Klein, *"Ein vollkommenes Werk";* Cheung, *Genre, Composition,* 163-77 (background) and 177-94; Konradt, *Christliche Existenz,* 267-85; Popkes, 84-85; Hoppe, 21-24.

63. In James it also describes *gifts* from God (1:17) and the *Torah* (1:25). For Paul it can describe the will of God (Rom 12:2) and orthodox thinking (1 Cor 14:20). For John it applies to love (1 John 4:18).

64. See also LXX 3 Kgdms 8:61; 11:4; 15:3, 14; 1 Chron 28:9; 1QS 1:1-8; 3:3, 9; 5:24; 8:1, 18, 21; 9:19.

For James, as we try to put this together, we may safely conclude that he believes the messianic Jewish community is to strive for a level of morality (character and behavior)[65] where particular forms of sin are not manifested and that this morality derives from a perfect God, who gives perfect gifts, not least of which is new birth (1:18), and from a royal, perfect Torah, so that the messianic community can be noted for its Torah observance.[66] Such an understanding of perfection is Jewish[67] and at the same time consistent with Jesus (Matt 5:48; 19:21), with the Pauline notion of "living in the Spirit" (Gal 5:13-26; cf. also Phil 3:15; Col 1:28; 4:12; 1 Cor 14:20), with the Johannine notion of "walking in the light" (1 John 1:5-7; 2:9-11; 3:9), and with the notion of "perfection" in Hebrews (5:14). What James says, therefore, is neither unusual for the messianic community nor something to be explained away as left over from his Torah observance past, but neither should we radicalize it to the point of seeing sinlessness spoken of here.

When "endurance" works itself out properly in the messianic Jewish community, it will be "mature" (or "perfect"), and such maturity is defined as "complete, lacking in nothing."[68] To be "complete" (holoklēros)[69] means to be intact, undefiled, undamaged — like a stone that has not been chiseled (Deut 27:6), "complete justice" (Wis 15:3), or a healthy body (Acts 3:16).[70] Thus, a teleios is someone who is also completely sound. Such a person therefore lacks nothing — and this in a comprehensive rather than exhaustive sense.

James will now proceed, with "lacking" as a catchword, to make sure that one virtue not lacking is "wisdom" (1:5; the catchword will return in 2:15).

65. So many commentators, who focus a little more on the static concept of "character" or "personality trait," as if "perfection" is a state; it is more a consistent form of behavior. See Mayor, 36; Davids, 69-70; Laws, 53-54; Martin, 16-17.

66. It goes without saying that James, if typical, would have thought such a state of perfection would be established in the Eschaton, but that is precisely not how James uses the term: for him, when it describes believers, it refers to the present existence of Torah observance. Pace Martin, 16; Mussner, 67.

67. Important references in the Old Testament include Gen 6:9 (Noah); Deut 18:13; 2 Sam 22:26; 1 Kgs 15:14; 1 Chron 28:9. So Davids, 69, who points to Gen 6:9; Sir 44:17; Jubilees 23:10; and many places in the Dead Sea Scrolls: see תָּנִיע at CD 7:5; 1QS 4:22; 1QM 14:7; 4Q266 f3iii.6.

68. καὶ ὁλόκληροι ἐν μηδενὶ λειπόμενοι. See n. 60 above.

69. On which, cf. BDAG, 703-4; Spicq, 2.578-79; New Docs 4.161-62.

70. See Spicq, 2.579.

2.2. THE NEED FOR WISDOM DURING TESTING (1:5-8)

5 *If any of you is lacking in wisdom,*[71] *ask God, who gives to all generously*[72] *and*[73] *ungrudgingly*[a]*, and it will be given you.*[74] 6 *But ask in faith, never doubting,*[75] *for the one who doubts is like a wave of the sea, driven and tossed by the wind;* 7 [8][b] *for the doubter,*[76] *being double-minded*[77] *and unstable in every way, must not expect to receive anything*[78] *from the Lord.*[79]

a. TNIV: without finding fault.

b. TNIV is closer in word order to the Greek.

Knowing that one can look *through* testing to the impact it will have on one's moral formation enables the messianic Jewish community to press forward. But *theoria* does not necessarily produce *praxis* just as *scientia* does not inevitably generate *sapientia*. James, knowing that many will struggle with discernment to see *through* the event to its more enduring impact, exhorts his readers to seek wisdom from God, but to do so in faith (*pistis*, v. 6, as before in v. 3).

Structurally, 1:5-8 is clear: a *condition* is given (1:5a) that can be resolved by following the *advice* of James (1:5b). In this advice, James *com-*

---

71. The Georgian tradition has πνευματικῆς σοφίας.

72. The meaning of ἁπλῶς has been rendered as πλουσίως in a few Latin, Armenian, Georgian, and Slavic manuscripts.

73. The Maj and other manuscripts negate the participle ὀνειδίζοντος with the unusual οὐκ.

74. A few manuscripts omit καὶ δοθήσεται αὐτῷ.

75. The manuscript evidence varies: (1) the printed text has an early and wide-ranging support; but (2) some manuscripts have διακρινομενος οτι ληψεται (206, 522, 1490*, 1799, and 2080) while (3) a few others have απιστων οτι ληψεται (429T, 630, and 2200).

76. In Greek, ὁ ἄνθρωπος ἐκεῖνος is clearly anaphoric to the ὁ διακρινόμενος of 1:6.

77. Some manuscripts (61, 326, 378, 621, Chrysostom, Cyril, Syriac Harclean, Armenian) add γαρ between ἀνήρ and δίψυχος. The use of ἀνήρ in James (1:8, 12, 20, 23; 2:2; 3:2) can be used of "males" or "generically" (1:20?). The NRSV consistently removes any suggestion that James has in mind a male. James knows the generic usage of ἄνθρωπος (cf. 1:7!), and it has been suggested that for James ἀνήρ is also generic. I am inclined to think James has "males" in mind when he uses ἀνήρ, but he does so from a first-century cultural context, and translating it generically is to me an acceptable updating.

78. Sinaiticus (א) and the fifth-century C*vid omit τι.

79. Some manuscripts have του θεου or θεου, making the vocabulary between 1:7 and 1:5 identical and clarifying that for the messianic community κύριος often directs one's mind to the Lord Jesus Christ (2:1).

ments on God's character. Next, he *elaborates* on the meaning of "ask" in 1:5b by clarifying the nature of genuine asking. This elaboration is unfolded first in a positive direction (1:6a) and then more completely in a negative direction (1:6b-8), with each line of these verses taking up and extending the previous line.

The connection between 1:2-4 and 1:5-8 is not clear to all. Some, for instance, think the connection is simply literary and that the only substantial element in its favor is the catchword "lacking" (1:4-5).[80] Others think the connection is substantial in one of two ways. First, 1:5-8 is taken as expressing a mode of *enduring tests and trials:*[81] that is, gaining wisdom will empower the messianic community to understand and endure its trials. Or second, 1:5-8 is taken as a mode of *attaining perfection:*[82] that is, seeking wisdom is how a person becomes "perfect" or "mature." That elsewhere in the early Christian tradition trials and wisdom are brought together suggests that the first is to be favored,[83] though I see no great distinction between these two views. What James has in mind is the wisdom needed so that the trials of life can lead to a moral *telos.*[84] He does not make the connection obvious by drawing his readers back into the topic of attaining *perfection* (1:4; but see immediately below), and neither 1:9-11 nor 1:12-18 draws us back into that *telos.*

In 1:9-11 James draws his readers back into the theme of poverty, which our exegesis of 1:2-4 showed to be uppermost in his mind when he speaks of testing and trials. This suggests that 1:5-8 may not have left that theme. The need for wisdom it speaks of could be connected to the theme of economic destitution and exploitation as the *means* by which the messianic community learns to see *through* the tests to discover the long-term value in moral formation, namely, wisdom from God.

1:5   The most prized attribute, we are suggesting, of the messianic community as it faces tests is "wisdom," and that is why James brings it up in 1:5-8.[85] To anticipate what James will say, "wisdom" is supernatural in origin

---

80. So Dibelius, 70, 77, who calls the connection "superficial" (77). For other instances, cf. 1:12 and 13; 1:15-18; 1:26 and 27; 2:12 and 13; 3:11 and 13; 3:17 and 18; 5:9 and 12; 5:13-16; 5:19 and 20.

81. So Mayor, 38.

82. So Ropes, 138; Davids, 71-72.

83. See also at 1 Cor 2:6-13; Col 1:21-28; see also Wisd 9:6.

84. Hermas, *Mandates* 9, draws the language of Jas 1:5-8 into an extensive discussion of the believer wondering if the Lord's mercy extends to those who have sinned. The mercy of God is the foundation for the Shepherd's instruction.

85. On which see especially the wisdom articles in *DOTWPW,* especially 842-912; J. Goetzmann, C. Brown, and H. Weigelt, in *NIDNTT* 3.1023-38; Blenkinsopp, *Sage, Prophet, Priest,* 9-65; W. P. Brown, *Character in Crisis; Character and Scripture.* If the

(3:15), is manifested through deeds of mercy and holiness (3:17), and leads toward a community noted by "peace" (3:18), perhaps the most important virtue/gift James could want for a community tempted by oppression to violence.[86] The supernatural origin is thought of now as James urges the messianic community to ask God for wisdom. This invokes the timeless theme of wisdom from Proverbs (1:1-7 and 2:6-8):

> The proverbs of Solomon son of David, king of Israel:
> For learning about wisdom and instruction,
>   for understanding words of insight,
> for gaining instruction in wise dealing,
>   righteousness, justice, and equity;
> to teach shrewdness to the simple,
>   knowledge and prudence to the young —
> Let the wise also hear and gain in learning,
>   and the discerning acquire skill,
> to understand a proverb and a figure,
>   the words of the wise and their riddles.
> *The fear of the LORD is the beginning of knowledge;*
>   fools despise wisdom and instruction.
>
> *For the LORD gives wisdom;*
>   from his mouth come knowledge and understanding;
> he stores up sound wisdom for the upright;
>   he is a shield to those who walk blamelessly,
> guarding the paths of justice
>   and preserving the way of his faithful ones.

---

practical and ethical subordinated the purely intellectual quest in ancient Israel, such a conclusion does not suggest that "wisdom" has been democratized or assigned to the uneducated or simple folk. Wisdom was a mark of honor throughout Israel's history; in addition, wisdom was increasingly personified in Jewish literature. J. A. Kirk connects James's use of "wisdom" with the use of the "Holy Spirit" in other New Testament writers; see "The Meaning of Wisdom in James: Examination of a Hypothesis," *New Testament Studies* 16 (1970) 24-38. His connection of Jas 1:5-8 with Matt 7:7 (par. Luke 11:13) and Jas 3:13-18 with Gal 5:19-21 is indeed suggestive. See also Frankemölle, 1.80-88, 1.211-15; and especially Blomberg and Kamell, 178-79, where we find a sketch of Kamell's master's thesis conclusions with this statement: "If James does not fully equate Wisdom with the Spirit, he nevertheless appears to understand them in similar ways and probably would have agreed that the Spirit is the preeminent (and perhaps exclusive) dispenser of the Father's wisdom for Christian living" (p. 179).

86. This suggests, as our exegesis in 1:2-27 will show, that "wisdom" here is not just the wisdom of the grey-haired sage who spins riddles and attracts intellectual guests, but the wisdom that manifests itself in a certain kind of community life (see especially 1:19-21; 3:13-18; 4:1-12).

And Wisdom 8:21:

> But I perceived that I would not possess wisdom *unless God gave her to me.*

To thus set wisdom in James in context means that we see him more along the lines of Proverbs (e.g., 9:1-6), Sirach (e.g., 4:17), Wisdom (e.g., 6:12-14; 7:15, 23-26; 8–9), and Job and less along the lines drawn at Qumran, where wisdom is esoteric and eschatological revelation.[87] Wisdom is for James, at least in part, what faith is for Paul, what love or life is for John, and what hope is for Peter.[88] It is, as Ropes states, "the supreme and divine quality of the soul whereby man knows and practices righteousness."[89] While I cannot agree completely with the eschatological emphasis of Davids on 1:2-4 or 1:5-8, that the Holy Spirit is involved in the reception of wisdom nonetheless deserves consideration: 1:18 speaks of a "new birth" of sorts that gives rise to a community that practices the will of God, and this thought is not far from a Pauline doctrine of the indwelling Holy Spirit.[90] When this wisdom dawns on the messianic community, it will see through the tests to the formative influence of the tests.

There is yet more to this sense of "wisdom" in James. It will become clear in this letter that a pressing issue was the hotheaded reactions of some in the messianic community. This occurs first most clearly in 1:19-21, though it is also present in 1:13-15 and perhaps in 1:2-4; it then occurs in full force in 3:13–4:12. In both 1:5-8 and 3:13-18 James is an advocate for "wisdom." And in both contexts it can be discerned that "wisdom" is more than an intellectual sagaciousness that has the capacity to spin out potent proverbs for specific situations: it is a kind of life that pursues "justice" (1:20), "love" (2:8-11), and "peace" (3:18) along properly moral lines — that is, without resorting to violence or volatile language. To ask for "wisdom" is almost to ask for an ability to "endure" with the ethic of Jesus (justice, love, and peace) when pressure is put on people to live otherwise.

The narrative flow suggests that for James "endurance," being "mature" (1:4), and having "wisdom" are nearly synonymous: the mature community member is the one that both endures and has wisdom. That both wisdom and maturity manifest themselves in community virtue (cf. 3:13-18 with 1:25 and 3:2) suggests the same conclusion. To come around the circle, then, one might say that the supposed *dis*connection of themes between 1:2-4 and

---

87. For a brief survey, Martin, lxxxii-lxxxiv, lxxxvii-xciii; Johnson, 33-34.
88. So Mayor, 38.
89. Ropes, 139.
90. Davids, 71-72. For evidence about the eschatological wisdom, cf. *2 Baruch* 44:14; 59:7; *4 Ezra* 8:52; *1 Enoch* 5:8; 100:6; 1QS 11; CD 6:3.

1:5-8 may in fact be a connection.[91] An identical synonymity is found in 1 Corinthians 2:6 and Colossians 1:28:

> Yet among the mature *(teleios)* we do speak wisdom *(sophia).*

> . . . teaching everyone in all wisdom *(sophia),* so that we may present everyone mature *(teleios)* in Christ.

And in Wisdom 9:6 we see "mature" (or "perfect") transcended by "wisdom":

> for even one who is perfect *(teleios)* among human beings will be regarded as nothing without the wisdom *(sophia)* that comes from you.

The evidence then is solid enough to permit an interpretation that finds the "wisdom" of 1:5-8 to be the same goal that James has in mind with "mature" in 1:2-4.

Those who want to pursue the path of perfection discover their need[92] and are told to "ask God."[93] Request is an inherent attribute of prayer in the Bible, and includes noteworthy examples in Abraham interceding for Sodom (Genesis 19), David praying for his child with Bathsheba (2 Sam 12:16-23) and for forgiveness (Psalm 51), and Solomon's global prayer for wisdom (1 Kgs 3:1-14; 2 Chron 1:7-13).[94] And the reason the messianic Jewish community is to "ask" is that God is the one "who gives." James continues that, if you ask, "it will be given you."

For James, prayer is rooted in theology proper: God is "generous" or, as we will now argue, gives "singlemindedly." God is ready to give[95] because he "gives to all generously and ungrudgingly." As Ralph Martin has put it: prayer is "universal (God gives to all who petition him), it is beneficent, it is without regard to merit, and it is a response with no equivocations."[96] Prayer that is confident (cf. 5:15-16) receives what it asks because of who God is.

Behind "generously" is a debate: does the adverb *haplōs* mean "generously" (NRSV) or "simply" (BDAG)?[97] The word occurs only here in the

---

91. So Davids, 71.

92. The Greek term is λείπεται and is present, like the verb αἰτείτω, and both indicate action that is incomplete or ongoing or characteristic of a condition: "If a person lacks wisdom, that person should be asking God for wisdom." See Ropes, 140; BDAG, 590.

93. αἰτείτω παρὰ τοῦ . . . θεοῦ. The present tense is chosen to make the request vivid and visible to the readers' minds.

94. See Miller, *They Cried to the Lord,* 55-134.

95. See Ps 145:15-19; *Pss Sol* 5:13-15.

96. Martin, 19.

97. Scholarship favors "simply." For "generously," see Ropes, 139-40; Laws, 55; Johnson, 179; for "simply," see Mayor, 30; Davids, 72-73 ("without mental reservation");

New Testament, but two cognates, the adjective *haplous* and the noun *haplotēs,* occur ten times and can mean either "generous/generosity" or "simply/simplicity, (with) singleness of intention or integrity."[98] The noun clearly means "generosity" in Rom 12:8 and 2 Cor 8:2; 9:11, 13, but elsewhere "simplicity" or "with integrity" seems more likely (2 Cor 1:12; 11:3; Eph 6:5; Col 3:22). Because James is connected to the teachings of Jesus, one needs to bring the use of the adjective in Matt 6:22 par. Luke 11:34 into account, and there the sense of "single-minded" is clear. When one factors in the wisdom literature of the LXX (e.g., Prov 10:9; Wis 1:1-2), the balance shifts toward James 1:5 saying that God gives with "simplicity" or "integrity" or "single-mindedness." And, since James will quickly speak of the "double-minded" doubter, it is quite possible that the single-mindedly generous God drawing from the community a single-minded trust is in view (cf. 1:6-8).

So if someone asks of God in faith, God responds simply, with integrity, and with the single-minded intent of answering that request. Or, as James goes on to say negatively, "ungrudgingly,"[99] taking *haplōs* partly as the positive equivalent of *mē oneidizontos.* Once again, one thinks of the teachings of Jesus in Matthew 7:7-11:

> Ask, and it will be given you; search, and you will find; knock, and the door will be opened for you. For everyone who asks receives, and everyone who searches finds, and for everyone who knocks, the door will be opened. Is there anyone among you who, if your child asks for bread, will give a stone? Or if the child asks for a fish, will give a snake? If you then, who are evil, know how to give good gifts to your children, how much more will your Father in heaven give good things to those who ask him!

Or of Jeremiah 29:12-14:

> When you call upon me and come and pray to me, I will hear you. When you search for me, you will find me; if you seek me with all your heart, I will let you find me, says the LORD, and I will restore your fortunes and gather you from all the nations and all the places where I have driven you, says the LORD, and I will bring you back to the place from which I sent you into exile.

And of Sirach 20:14-15:

Martin, 18; Johnson, 179; Moo, 58-59; Popkes, 88-89; Blomberg and Kamell, 51. See also Mussner, 68-69.

98. See Matt 6:22; Luke 11:34; Rom 12:8; 2 Cor 1:12; 8:2; 9:11, 13; 11:3; Eph 6:5; Col 3:22.

99. καὶ μὴ ὀνειδίζοντος. See BDAG, 710-11.

A fool's gift will profit you nothing,
  for he looks for recompense sevenfold.
He gives little and *upbraids* much;
  he opens his mouth like a town crier.
Today he lends and tomorrow he asks it back;
  such a one is hateful to God and humans.

Humans may give grudgingly, either wishing they had not or only because they feel obliged, but God's grace flows in one direction.[100] There is no back-tracking or second-guessing in God, nor is there any criticism or backstabbing after giving.

1:6   The flow of God's grace toward the messianic Jewish community is dependent, so James says, on one condition, and we find this in James's elaboration of the meaning of "ask": "But ask in faith, never doubting."[101] In James, "faith," found in both 1:2-4 and 1:5-8, when positive, refers to "the act of trusting God," while when it refers to "faith as content" it appears to be used negatively.[102] What James has in mind is that the messianic Jewish community, when it finds itself afloat and buffeted by trials, is to be like God in mono-focal single-mindedness,[103] trusting God single-mindedly, simply, and with integrity *for wisdom*[104] and letting trust shape the entirety of their relationship to God. If God is one who simply gives and does not upbraid, then the community is to be one that simply trusts, "never doubting."[105] As God would regard humans as an object of scorn if he gave to them and then criticized them, so humans would heap scorn on God by trusting in God and doubting at the same time. To doubt here would mean either to

---

100. See Sir 18:15-18; 41:22; *Did* 4:7; Hermas, *Mandates* 9.

101. αἰτείτω δὲ ἐν πίστει μηδὲν διακρινόμενος. Aspectually, the present tenses focus on vividness of description, in appeal to the imagination, rather than ongoingness of petitions, in appeal to steadfastness in prayer.

102. More discussion about πιστεύω and πίστις will be found in the *locus classicus,* Jas 2:14-26. "Faith as content" is found at 2:1, 14, 17, 18, 20, 22, 24, 26. "Faith as the act of trusting God" can be found at 1:3, 6; 2:19, 23; 5:15.

103. So Mayor, 40.

104. Some suggest James has moved from the specific need of σοφία to global interests in prayer; the τι of 1:7 can support this view (Moo, 59-60). But this view depends on one's view of the connections of the paragraphs in 1:2-18, and this commentary contends they are integrally and thematically related.

105. Διακρινόμενος, the nominative masculine singular active substantival participle of διακρίνω, has two primary senses: "to discriminate" in the sense of judge or make a distinction (Matt 16:3; Acts 11:2, 12; 15:9; 1 Cor 11:29, 31; 14:29; Jas 2:4; Jude 9), and "to discriminate" in the sense of a lack of decisiveness or uncertainty or to be at odds within oneself (Matt 21:21; Acts 10:20; Rom 4:20; 14:23; 1 Cor 6:5; Jude 22). See BDAG, 231. Again, the present aspect indicates a vividness of description, rather than constant doubt, and leads to the gnomic statement in 1:6b.

question one's allegiance to the Lord and the messianic community (global doubt leading to apostasy) or to find oneself unable to trust God simply and with integrity as one endures the testing of faith (internal doubt). James will take up the theme of apostasy in the last two verses of the letter,[106] but the proximate context of the "double-minded man" of 1:7-8 suggests that here he is thinking in terms of "internal doubt."

James now provides an explanation of his elaboration: the reason the messianic community should not doubt is that the doubting person is unstable and in a precarious position: "for the one who doubts[107] is like[108] a wave of the sea, driven and tossed[109] by the wind" (1:6b). James, who grew up near the Sea[110] of Galilee, would know the sudden surges of waves from experience, though anyone familiar with Scripture and the various Jewish traditions would also know other frames of reference.[111] The messianic believer who comes to God both trusting *and* doubting is in a precarious position with respect to getting the *sophia* ("wisdom") he or she needs to see *through* the testing to the moral formation it is designed to effect.

1:7 "Therefore,[112] the doubter, being double-minded and unstable in

106. See notes at 5:19-20.

107. Substantival present (characteristic) participle: ὁ διακρινόμενος. The present participle here is more open-ended and less categorical than a perfect or even aorist participle, and therefore used because James is exhorting the community to see the fullness of doubt.

108. ἔοικα, a perfect form of εἴκω, means "to resemble" (BDAG, 355). The term is a cognate of εἰκών, an *Eikon* or image. One might say that as humans are *Eikons* of God, so waves are *Eikons* (visible manifestations) of the Doubter, and so also is the man who observes his face in a mirror and pays no attention a visible manifestation of the one who is not a Doer (1:23 where we also see ἔοικεν).

109. ἀνεμιζομένῳ καὶ ῥιπιζομένῳ is a hendiadys and dramatically impressionistic of instability.

110. θαλάσσης here could refer to any body of water. The term is often anarthrous when used with another noun; see MHT, 3.175.

111. E.g., Isa 57:20; Sir 33:2; Wis 14:5; 19:7; 1 Macc 6:8-13. Pride of place, of course, is given to Jon 1:4. Early Christians also used the same image: cf. Matt 11:7; Luke 8:24; Eph 4:14; Jude 12-13.

112. The structure is not entirely clear. In 1:6 James says that the believer is to ask in faith, not doubting; the explanation or reason for asking in faith is that a doubting person is unstable; and now 1:7-8 adds a second γάρ. Is the second one epexegetical for 1:6b (explaining the instability even further) or is it a second explanation of why a person should ask in faith? Some manuscripts add yet a third γάρ after ἀνήρ in 1:8. Neither grammar nor syntax permits a simple answer: the logical flow seems to me to be along the line of an ever-deepening explanation; thus, it appears to be epexegetical. Thus:

Ask for wisdom in faith, not doubting (1:6a);
for a doubting person is unstable (1:6b);

every way, must not expect[113] to receive anything[114] from the Lord."[115] The focal term of vv. 7-8 is "double-minded" *(dipsychos),*[116] or as J. H. Ropes borrows from John Bunyan's *Pilgrim's Progress,* "Mr. Facing-both-ways."[117] The word, literally "two-souled," grows out of Jewish soil, especially Old Testament language of the "double-hearted" person.[118] Daily recital of the

---

for an unstable doubting person will not receive wisdom from God (1:7);
[for] the unstable doubting person is double-minded (1:8).

Jas 1:7 resumes the "doubter" of 1:6b and extends the thought; 1:8 extends 1:7. See discussions in Mayor, 43; Ropes, 142; Laws, 58; Davids, 74. This sort of restatement with subtle difference and development is the essence of Hebrew parallelism. See especially Kugel, *The Idea of Biblical Poetry.*

113. οἴεσθω (from οἴομαι) with ὅτι means "to consider something to be true but with a component of tentativeness" (BDAG, 701; BDF §336.3; MHT, 3.76). But the present does not indicate that one should desist from what one is already doing but that one should not be characterized by such thinking.

114. τι could suggest the prayer request is general — any kind of request at all. But, in light of contextual flow, τι could refer to the general of which σοφία is a particular instance.

115. Κύριος has an unclear referent. It can refer to "God" (1:5, 17; 4:15; 5:10, 11) and to "Jesus Christ" (1:1; 2:1; 5:14, 15). Since 1:5 has "God" in view, "Lord" in 1:7 probably refers to "God." For discussions, see Mayor, 42; Ropes, 142; Davids, 74; Popkes, 91.

116. Grammatically, there are several points to make: (1) δίψυχος is the implied subject of λήψεται by repetition, or (2) in apposition to ὁ ἄνθρωπος of 1:7a, a repetition of the subject of μὴ οἰέσθω, or (3) the predicate of ἀνήρ with an implied εἰμί, or (4) the subject predicate of the implied εἰμί to which ἀκατάστατος is the predicate. Some manuscripts add γάρ, suggesting that a new sentence begins with 1:8, leaving us with either (3) or (4). The balance is for (3) because there would be a less abrupt change in "Such a man is double-minded, unstable . . ." than in "A double-minded man is unstable," for the latter implies a previous use of "double-minded." On the expression, see Cheung, *Genre, Composition,* 196-222, who explores the ramifications of an approach to James through doubleness.

117. Ropes, 143, which comes from Christian's encounter with By-ends. There are many editions of Bunyan's classic.

118. See בְּלֵב וָלֵב in Ps 12:1-2 (Hebrew, 12:3), the *lev va-lev.* Also at Deut 6:5; 13:3; 18:13; Ps 101:2, 4, 6; 1 Chron 12:38 [12:39]; 2 Chron 31:21; Hos 10:2; *Testament of Asher* 1:3–6:2; *Testament of Benjamin* 6:5-7; Sir 1:28; 15:11-14; 2:12; Wis 1:1; 1QS 3:17-18; 4:23. The language was picked up in the early churches: see BDAG, 253; *Did* 4:1-4; 5:1 (διπλοκαρδία); Hermas, *Mandates* 9:4-5; *Barnabas* 19:5; 20:1 (διπλοκαρδία); *1 Clement* 11:2; 23:1-2; *2 Clement* 11:1-7; 19:1-4 (where persecutions are the context). See S. Porter, "Is *dipsuchos* (James 1, 8; 4, 8) a 'Christian' Word?" *Biblica* 71 (1996) 469-98, who critiques Turner's study in his *Christian Words,* 116-18, though he does see the term as a Christian word coined by James. Porter helpfully distinguishes the senses of 1:8 and 4:8 and explores fully the use of this term in the patristic period. For an earlier study, see W. I. Wolverton, "The Double-Minded Man in the Light of Essene Psychology," *ATR* 38 (1956) 166-75. The issues here are not simply linguistic and vocabularic; they include the interac-

Shema[119] makes a "whole heart" devoted to love of God a moral preoccupation, thus setting a divided heart into the context of covenantal fidelity with respect to *Torah* observance. Also, Jewish anthropology, as found in Romans 7, frequently understands the human heart as twofold, containing a good impulse *(yetzer hatov)* and a bad impulse *(yetzer hara').*[120] But James is less concerned here with the "evil" out-boxing the "good" than he is with a person's heart being split in its allegiance and in the integrity of simply trusting God to provide wisdom. The double-minded person does not love God wholeheartedly, does not love the neighbor properly, and does not live out the Torah as God intends. The opposite of the "double-minded" person is the "single-mindedness" of God, which the messianic community is to follow in single-minded trust of God's provisions.

1:8 The "double-minded man" is "unstable in every way."[121] "Unstable" *(akatastatos)* refers to the condition of the person who, because he (or she) does not simply trust God for wisdom, finds himself (or herself) wavering and incapable of handling the stress created by opposition to the messianic community. While it might refer to the sort of instability that could lead to apostasy, it more likely refers to the instability created by lack of simply trusting God for wisdom to endure trials. However, like the "anything" of 1:7, the "in every way"[122] could suggest a general disruption of all of life, even of the social order, when a person fails to center down into simply trusting God.[123] In this sense, one needs to connect "unstable" to the lack of wisdom and the pursuit of such things as desires and violence (see 1:13-15, 19-21; 4:1-12).

Once again, however, this must be read in context. This is less of a Sunday School lesson for children than an urgent warning for the messianic Jewish community being severely stressed by, for instance, economic sanctions against them, and the need for them to see *through* the persecution to its moral effects and to find harmony with God by simply trusting in him for

tion of various anthropologies. See also Burchard, 61-63: the person who is simultaneously focused on God and the world.

119. See Deut 6:4-9; Montefiore, "Thou Shalt Love"; Edgar, "Love-Command."

120. See especially Davies, *Paul and Rabbinic Judaism,* 17-35; Str-B 4.1:466-83.

121. Again, the ἀκατάστατος is an epexegetical explanation of δίψυχος. On ἀκατάστατος, cf. BDAG, 35. Cognates are found in important parallels: 1 Cor 14:33; 2 Cor 6:5; 12:20. Jas 3:8 sees the tongue as a restless evil, and 3:16 includes "disorder" as the result of envy and selfish ambition. A wonderful collection of theological and pastoral insights can be found in *ACC: James,* 8-9.

122. The language is stereotypical of the Bible ("in every way" translates ἐν πάσαις ταῖς ὁδοῖς αὐτοῦ), borrowing from the language of the "walking" and the "path." The later rabbinic "halakhah" emerges from this and other expressions; see *EJ* 1.340-66. See Pss 91:11; 145:17; Prov 3:6; Wis 2:16; Sir 11:26; 17:15, 19; Jer 16:17; Ezek 7:8, 9; Acts 14:16; 1 Cor 4:17.

123. See Ropes, 144; Martin, 21.

wisdom. This sort of wisdom pursues "justice" (1:20), "love" (2:8-11), and "peace" (3:18) in ways consistent with the path walked by Jesus. The unstable person abandons these very things in the heat of opposition, perhaps becoming the oppressor (cf. 5:1-6).

2.3. POVERTY AND WEALTH AS A TEST (1:9-11)

9 *Let the*[124] *believer*[a] *who is lowly*[b] *boast in being raised up,* 10 *and*[125] *the rich*[c] *in being brought low, because the rich will*[126] *disappear like a flower in the field.* 11 *For the sun rises with its scorching heat and withers the field*[d]; *its*[127] *flower falls, and its*[128] *beauty perishes. It is the same way with the rich; in the midst of a busy life, they will wither away.*

a. TNIV: believers (NIV: brother)

b. TNIV: in humble circumstances

c. NRSV does not clarify if "the rich" is a "believer" or not; neither does the TNIV.

d. TNIV: plant; NRSV "field" is incomplete and seems to mean "the field of flowers" (?) since the next expression, "its flower falls," does not grammatically follow from "field."

James shifts from seeking wisdom from God about testing to the morally formative powers of that testing, and he shifts from warning about the necessary single-mindedness in the quest for wisdom to a warning about wealth. For some the apparent change of topics indicates that James proceeds rather loosely from one topic to another with little thought of connection,[129] while for others there is in fact no change in topic but a return (after a digression on prayer) to the theme of testing from 1:2-4.[130] The issue of the connection of

---

124. Various "editors" of the manuscripts spent a great deal of energy with the word order. Thus, ὁ ἀδελφὸς ὁ ταπεινὸς was rearranged, or ταπεινὸς (631, 808) was inserted before ἀδελφός (P74). P74 also omitted δέ.

125. While standard texts today have δέ as the particle at Jas 1:10, some early versions (Coptic, Armenian, Georgian) have καί and thereby correlate 1:9 and 1:10, which is what the NRSV does. The TNIV translates 1:10 adversatively.

126. Some versions reflect οὕτως here (Latin, Syriac, Peshitta, and Georgian).

127. Some manuscripts (614, 630, 1505, Syrian, Harclean, Armenian, and Georgian) omit αὐτοῦ.

128. B omits αὐτοῦ.

129. So Dibelius, 70-71, 83-84; Laws, 62.

130. Ropes, 144. Moo, 63-64, leaves the matter open.

1:9-11 to what precedes hangs on one's specific understandings of crucial phrases and terms.

To begin with,[131] it is unlikely that James would begin a letter with random thoughts. It is a commonplace that the early parts of letters establish the lines of thinking for the entire letters. Furthermore, the theme of poverty and wealth or socio-economic oppression was, as our exegesis showed, implicit in the "trials" (tests) in 1:2-4, was most likely carried through in the reason for praying for wisdom in 1:5-8, and is now brought into the open in 1:9-11. What carries the day for the thematic cohesion of 1:2-11 is that James elsewhere is preoccupied with the issue of economic privation and how the messianic community should respond to the temptations that emerge from oppression.[132]

If we ask what issue was most pressing for the messianic Jewish community, we must admit that economic stress and how best to respond to it were foremost on the list. A common thread running through *Anawim* piety is economic justice. One can observe this by reading the Magnificat (Luke 1:46-55), Jesus' inaugural sermon (4:16-30), the (Lukan) Beatitudes (6:20-26), Jesus' comment to the disciples of John the Baptist (7:18-23), and the parable of the rich man and Lazarus (16:19-31) and by finding the same in the concerns of the early *Anawim* community in Jerusalem (Acts 2:43-47; 4:32-35). If, then, we ask the nature of the trials (1:2-4) or for what issue that sort of community most needed God's wisdom, it would again be economic oppression and how best to respond to it (1:5-8). So it should not surprise that 1:9-11 brings the issue up: the tension of the poor and wealthy is uppermost in the mind of James, the *Anaw*.[133]

Therefore, the connection of 1:2-11 is tight: in contrast to being a "double-minded doubter," the reader/hearer should be "lowly," able to "boast" of "being raised up," and able, through the acquisition of wisdom (1:5-8), to find the strength to endure trials (1:2-4) and resist the desire to use violence or abusive language (1:13-21). The "boast" of 1:9 is synonymous with the "joy" of 1:2 and the gentleness of 1:21 and 3:18. Within our paragraph, we find a correlative exhortation: the "lowly" and the "rich" are to boast, but, vv. 10-11 go on to explain, perhaps in scorn, the "rich" is to boast over the perishing of his (or her) riches.

Structurally, James 1:9-10a contains a twofold *injunction:* the poor

131. James does not introduce new topics with δέ; so also Davids, 75.
132. See commentary at 1:26-27; 2:1-7, 14-17; 3:13-18; 4:6; 4:13–5:6. See especially Maynard-Reid, *Poverty and Wealth in James,* 24-37. On 1:9-11, see pp. 38-47. For the context, see also M. Hengel, *Property and Riches in the Early Church* (trans. J. Bowden; Philadelphia: Fortress, 1974), especially 15-19.
133. Martin, 22-23, finds here a warning to the wealthy that wealth is a test of faith (cf. 4:13-17).

are to boast in their exaltation and the rich in their humiliation. This is then followed by an *elaboration* (1:10b-11d) and a summary *conclusion* (1:11e) of why wealth will dissipate.

1:9 The NRSV forces a discussion when it translates *ho adelphos ho tapeinos* (literally "the humble/lowly brother") in 1:9 with "the *believer* who is lowly." But some contend that "brother" could refer either to the *Jewish* brotherhood or to *universal* brotherhood, and that therefore "believer" is reductive. However, since every other reference to "brother" in James refers to the "brotherhood of community,"[134] "believer" is probably accurate even if it subtly masks the family imagery in the word "brother." James is speaking to the messianic Jewish brotherhood (and sisterhood).

A knottier issue comes with the injunction's first concern: the "lowly."[135] Does this describe one's *social* or *spiritual* condition? While *tapeinos* can at times indicate the "humble" in contrast to the "haughty" and therefore a moral quality,[136] three considerations decisively point to a socio-economic condition behind the word.[137] First, the antonym in context is not the "haughty" or "powerful" but the "rich" (1:10). Second, *tapeinos* and *ptōchos* ("poor") are nearly synonyms in James, and the latter is clearly a socio-economic term.[138] Third, the socio-economic status of the messianic Jewish community shows so many connections to the (prophetic) *Anawim*

134. Cf. 1:2, 16, 19; 2:1, 5, 14; 3:1, 10, 12; 4:11; 5:7, 9, 12, 19. See Frankemölle, 1.242-43.

135. ὁ ταπεινός, on which see BDAG, 989; Spicq, 3.369-71; *TDNT* 8.1-26; Mussner, 76-84; Tamez, 14-21; Maynard-Reid, *Poverty and Wealth in James,* 24-37; R. L. Williams, "Piety and Poverty in James," *Wesleyan Theological Journal* 22 (1987) 37-55, who follows Martin's setting proposal to see three groups in James's audience: the poor, the synagogue member, and the rich; Cheung, *Genre, Composition,* 254-60. See also D. Flusser, "Blessed Are the Poor in Spirit . . . ," in his *Judaism and the Origins of Christianity* (Jerusalem: Magnes, 1988), 102-14; L. E. Keck, "The Poor among the Saints in the New Testament," *ZNW* 56 (1965) 100-129; "The Poor among the Saints in Jewish Christianity and Qumran," *ZNW* 57 (1966) 54-78, who famously argued that the Jerusalem church did not call itself "the poor." R. Crotty, "Identifying the Poor in the Letter of James," *Colloquium* 27 (1995) 11-21, ties the meaning of "poor/humble one" to the socially, economically marginalized one who humbly receives wisdom. Also O. E. Alana, "A Word with the Rich (James 5:1-6)," *Verbum et ecclesia* 24 (2003) 1-14. Edgar's suggestion, that the poor in James are the socially marginal prophetic itinerants, intrigues but fails to persuade on the basis of a lack of compelling evidence; cf. his *Has God Not Chosen the Poor?* 106-33.

136. So Jas 4:6; see also Luke 1:52; Matt 11:29; Rom 12:16; 2 Cor 7:6; 1 Pet 5:5.

137. So the majority of commentators: Mayor, 45; Ropes, 145; Laws, 62; Davids, 76; Martin, 25; Maynard-Reid, *Poverty and Wealth in James,* 38-47; Mussner, 73-74; Hoppe, 30-35; Blomberg and Kamell, 54-55. This makes for a substantial connection to the addressees of 1 Peter.

138. Jas 2:2-6. But see Burchard, 64, who focuses more on social location.

(not Wisdom) tradition[139] in Israel that one is led to think that James has them specifically in mind with this term. In fact, the term *tapeinos* is found in the Magnificat of Mary, where it again has elements of both social location and economic deprivation (Luke 1:48, 52-53):

> for he has looked with favor on the *lowliness* of his servant.
>   Surely, from now on all generations will call me blessed.

> He has brought down the powerful from their thrones,
>   and lifted up the *lowly;*
> he has filled the hungry with good things,
>   and sent the *rich* away empty.

The theme of reversal[140] inherent in the correlative exhortation of James 1:9-10 belongs to the same *Anawim* tradition in which Mary's Magnificat gets its magic from one reversal after another.[141] One must consider once again the impact of Mary, mother of Jesus, on the messianic Jewish community through the influence of James.[142]

The lowly believer, James continues in 1:9, is to "boast in being raised up."[143] Again, the boasting[144] of 1:9 correlates with the "joy" of 1:2[145] and, therefore, the intended result of the exhortation here puts us immediately in touch with the goal of 1:2-4. That is, James intends for the *tapeinos* to "boast" in the sense of learning to see through the economic tests to the morally for-

---

139. See R. E. Brown, *Birth,* 350-65. The Wisdom tradition focuses more on correlation of righteousness and wisdom with wealth and foolishness with poverty. R. Gordis, "The Social Background of Wisdom Literature," *Hebrew Union College Annual* 18 (1943-44) 77-118.

140. See Prov 3:34; Pss 18:27; 138:6; Isa 54:11-17; Sir 11:1; 29:8-9; 1 Macc 14:14.

141. On the Magnificat, see J. Nolland, *Luke 1–9:20* (WBC 35A; Dallas: Word, 1989), 59-77, with extensive bibliography; J. B. Green, *The Gospel of Luke* (NICNT; Grand Rapids: Eerdmans, 1997), 92-105; *IVPWBC* 565-66, with 453-54.

142. See R. E. Brown et al., *Mary in the New Testament* (Philadelphia: Fortress, 1978); J. McHugh, *The Mother of Jesus in the New Testament* (Garden City: Doubleday, 1975); D. F. Wright, ed., *Chosen by God: Mary in Evangelical Perspective* (London: Marshall Pickering, 1989); E. A. Johnson, *Truly Our Sister* (New York: Continuum, 2004); A.-J. Levine, ed., *A Feminist Companion to Mariology* (London: Clark, 2005); S. McKnight, *The Real Mary* (Brewster: Paraclete, 2007); T. Perry, *Mary for Evangelicals* (Downers Grove: InterVarsity, 2006).

143. Καυχάσθω δὲ ὁ ἀδελφὸς ὁ ταπεινὸς ἐν τῷ ὕψει αὐτοῦ.

144. On this term, cf. Rom 5:2-3; also 1 Cor 1:31; 2 Cor 12:5, 9; BDAG, 536-37. If Jer 9:23-24 is behind this passage, that connection would be most likely in 1:10 and not in the use of "boast" in 1:9.

145. So Ropes, 145. See also Martin, 25.

mative influence such tests will bring as well as the potential benefits that in-fluence will bring to the messianic community.[146] It is normally stated that James's intended goal of 1:9 is for the "lowly believer" to see the exalted sta-tus of being destined for eternity or being in the ecclesial family[147] or being reconciled with God,[148] but James shows no signs of such a meaning. The lan-guage of 1:9 (with 1:2-4) is so similar to Romans 5:2-3 that one must think they are borrowing from a similar tradition about inaugurated eschatology:[149]

> . . . through whom we have obtained access to this grace in which we stand; and we boast in our hope of sharing the glory of God. And not only that, but we also boast in our sufferings, knowing that suffering produces endurance.

Again, as the goal of the "joy" in 1:2-4 was "perfection" in moral for-mation, so the "in being raised up" here probably means the same thing: moral formation and wisdom, and by extension also a life dedicated to pursu-ing "justice" (1:20), "love" (2:8-11), and "peace" (3:18). To be sure, as 1:12 will connect the goal to the eschaton, so also here: to be "raised up" is a proleptic realization (through moral and community formation) of the eschaton. And also again, the implication of 1:9's "boast" is not triumphalism in the sense that the believer is to recognize his or her exalted status or future vindication, but to "boast" or have "joy" in the transformative experience of the socio-economic tests through which the messianic Jewish community is presently going. Thus, as 2:5 indicates that God's elective grace of the "poor" is so that they will "be rich in faith and . . . heirs of the kingdom," so the "being raised up" also indicates the same sense of being in-augurated into the kingdom with the morally formative powers connected to that reception of grace.

1:10 If the *tapeinos* is to "boast in being raised up," the "rich"[150] has a completely different ground for his (or her) "boast": "in being brought low."[151] It seems likely that Jeremiah 9:23-24 is behind the words of James 1:9-11:

146. So Ropes, 145.
147. Mayor, 44.
148. Moo, 65.
149. See Davids, 76; Martin, 25.
150. ὁ πλούσιος. See BDAG, 831; P. H. Furfey, "ΠΛΟΥΣΙΟΣ and Cognates in the New Testament," *CBQ* 5 (1943) 243-63, who sees the term describing those who were freed from manual labor by their capital and income; *EDNT* 3.114-17; M. Hengel, *Property and Riches in the Early Church* (trans. J. Bowden; Philadelphia: Fortress, 1974); C. L. Blomberg, *Neither Poverty Nor Riches* (Grand Rapids: Eerdmans, 1999).
151. ἐν τῇ ταπεινώσει. BDAG, 990; *EDNT* 3.333-35.

Thus says the LORD: Do not let the wise boast in their wisdom, do not let the mighty boast in their might, do not let the wealthy boast in their wealth; but let those who boast boast in this, that they understand and know me, that I am the LORD; I act with steadfast love, justice, and righteousness in the earth, for in these things I delight, says the LORD.

The meaning of this verse hangs on the answer to one significant question: is the "rich" a "believer/brother" or not? If so, then his being "brought low" will be connected to the being "raised up" of the *tapeinos,* and will be a paradoxical statement of humiliation and dependence on God.[152] If not, "brought low" could be connected once again to the sort of result we find in the Magnificat: brought down from high and haughty places in the dramatic reversal of God's restoring justice. The ideological intent of the rhetoric of James in this context is obvious: he wants to bolster the poor and critique the rich.[153]

In favor of the view that the "rich" is a "brother,"[154] in 2:2 it appears that a brother is well off enough to dress luxuriously and extravagantly, and in 4:13-17 a brother is wealthy enough to make business arrangements. "Brother" with "poor" in 1:9 might carry over to the "rich [brother]" in 1:10 just as "boast" carries over in parallel fashion. Zacchaeus, who was rich but gave it all away, would form a noteworthy illustration (Luke 19:1-10). In other words, James subtly urges the rich brother to take the heroic option and give up the possessions. David Nystrom offers a compelling analogy: if the "rich" are Christians, then "rich" functions as "cows of Bashan" do in Amos 4:1-3.[155]

---

152. See S. E. Wheeler, *Wealth as Peril and Obligation* (Grand Rapids: Eerdmans, 1995), 102-3.

153. A. Batten, "Ideological Strategies in the Letter of James," in Webb and Kloppenborg, *Reading James,* 6-26, shows that "rich" and "poor" are not just economic terms but social honor terms, and she argues for James thinking of the "honourable poor" (p. 26). Most importantly, she tunes her ear to hear the rhetorical impact — sociologically studied — of James's language in 1:9-11, 2:1-13, and 5:1-6 to hear these themes: he unifies the audience in opposition to the rich; he legitimates his own teaching; he exhorts to action in not wanting to live as the rich do; and he rationalizes his point of view.

154. See Mayor, 44; Ropes, 145-46; Moo, 66-67; Burchard, 64; Popkes, 95; Hartin, 69; Blomberg and Kamell, 57-58. A recent study by H. H. Drake Williams III, "Of Rags and Riches: The Benefits of Hearing Jeremiah 9:23-24 within James 1:9-11," *TynBul* 43 (2002) 273-82, argues that reading Jer 9:23-24 intertextually suggests that the "rich" are believers. The impact of this text on Judaism can be found in his discussion on pp. 278-81. I am not convinced that the use of this text for Israelites tips the balance away from the evidence of the remaining texts in James where the rich are clearly unbelievers, and Williams's suggestion does not square as well with the significance of the rich man's perishing in 1:11.

155. Nystrom, 55.

More have sided with the view that, in his use of deep and strong irony in the verse, the "rich" person is not a brother.[156] There is considerable doubt that the fancy dresser of 2:2 is actually part of the messianic community since messianic and non-messianic Jews might have assembled in the same synagogue. Also, while it is possible that the grammar implies that the rich man is a brother, it is hardly necessary, and one is tempted to ask why James would omit the word "brother" in referring to the "rich." In James, the "rich" are those who treat the "poor" unjustly (2:6-7) and who, because they are guilty of serious economic injustices, are warned of judgment (5:1-6).[157] Perhaps more significantly, 1:11 explicitly states that the rich man "will wither away." If we explore the teachings of Jesus on the matter, we are drawn once again to the stereotypical contrast between the righteous poor and the unrighteous rich (Luke 6:24).[158]

We need to press further and ask, if the rich is not a brother, who the rich might be. In light of our suggestion below on "flower" in 1:11, it is possible that James has in mind the Jewish priestly establishment. This suggestion carries with it other suggestions: the priestly establishment had a foothold in the courts (cf. 2:1-13), they had the funds to dress well (2:2-4), they were those who made trips abroad (4:13-17), they were the ones who could withhold wages (5:1-6), and they, as caretakers of the Temple, would be those most in danger when the predictions of Jesus about the Temple's downfall came to pass (5:7). There were few options in James's society for who might be called "rich": the Roman rulers, the priestly establishment, or the retainers for the economic system — that is, those who did not have to do manual labor. If we were to ask which group most likely would be present in the situations James finds troubling about the rich, the priestly establishment are the most likely.[159] However, there is probably no need to isolate this term onto one group: anyone who did not need to do manual labor to put bread on the table and anyone who had sufficient economic power to oppress would be in mind. In light of this evidence, it is hard to avoid two conclusions: James sees the "rich" as enemies to the kingdom inaugurated by Jesus, and his

156. See Dibelius, 85; Laws, 63-64; Davids, 76-77; Martin, 25-26; Maynard-Reid, *Poverty and Wealth in James,* 44; Tamez, 21-26; Wall, 56.

157. It is noteworthy that 5:1-6 is followed up by an exhortation to "patience," not unlike that of 1:2-4 and 1:12, connecting patience, endurance, and economic injustices.

158. See also Matt 19:23-24; Mark 12:41; Luke 12:13-21; 16:19-31.

159. And there is a further possible familial connection: John the Baptist is the son of a priest according to early traditions (Luke 1–2); John evidently broke with the prevailing priestly vision of purity and saw purity transmitted through water at the Jordan; Jesus joined this movement of John's, and it is not unlikely that James did as well — and all this gives a possible, but no more than that, setting for an anti-priestly movement centered in the *Anawim* around Mary, the brothers of Jesus, and the messianic community.

words must be taken as tongue-lashing (prophet-like) irony: the "boasting" and "exaltation" of the rich will shortly turn to humiliation!

The implications of one's exegetical conclusion on whether the "rich" is a "brother" determine the meaning of "brought low." If the "rich" is a "brother," then "brought low" is a Christian paradox, not unlike what Jesus means by seeing service as ruling (Mark 10:35-45).[160] If the "rich" is not a "brother," as our exegesis has concluded, then "brought low" is a warning to the wealthy in the Jewish community who use their economic power to create systemic injustice that their day is coming. Not unlike the ruling wealthy of the Magnificat, they will be brought down from their unjust ruling and sent away empty. Their fancy clothing (2:2), unjust rulings (2:6-7), blasphemies against the name of Jesus (2:7), and economic exploitation (5:1-6) will be brought to ruin before the bar of God's justice. If our suggestion above has any strength, James may well have in mind (prophetically) the destruction of Jerusalem in 70 AD and its stripping of power from the priestly establishment. If our exegesis of 1:19-21 below is correct, then the being brought low here is an act of God, not of the messianic community, for James sees the necessity for the messianic community to pursue community formation (1:18) and a quiet life of deeds of mercy as the means to accomplishing the justice, love, and peace of God.[161]

James's next few lines clarify the debate for most: "the rich man will disappear like a flower in the field." Here James creates a chiasm: he begins with direct ironical (if not sarcastic) language about the rich man (1:10a), moves to a general statement in the imagery of a fading flower (1:10b) to a more complete explanation of the imagery of the fading flower (1:11a), and then turns back to direct language about the rich man withering away (1:11b).

The subject of 1:10b, "because *the rich* will disappear," is implied. Again, there is some matter of disagreement. If the "rich" is a "brother," then the implied subject could be the "riches" themselves rather than the "rich" himself.[162] Our exegesis up to this point favors the "rich" as the implied subject.[163] The word "because"[164] supports such an interpretation since it gives the reason that James can (ironically) claim that the rich person can "boast"

---

160. Cf. Mayor, 44-45; Moo, 66-67. Support could be found in Sir 3:18; 1 Tim 6:17; Luke 22:26; Phil 3:3-8.

161. In other words, it is not inappropriate to see James as a social tract on how best to live as a messianic community that seeks justice for the land.

162. So Ropes, 148.

163. Again, the implied subject would carry over from 1:10a; had a shift from πλούσιος to πλοῦτος been intended the author would most likely have indicated it by changing to that term in the second half of v. 10.

164. ὅτι modifies the implied verb καυχάσθω and therefore introduces an adverbial, causal clause.

(implied and ironical) in his humiliation (ironical). Why? Because he, the person, will perish.

Such a person, we are contending that James is saying, "will disappear like a flower in the field." Here James draws on a stock image from both experience in the Land of Israel and in the Scriptures. Three texts come to mind immediately: Psalms 90:3-6 and 103:15-16 and Isaiah 40:6-8:

> You turn us back to dust,
>> and say, "Turn back, you mortals."
> For a thousand years in your sight
>> are like yesterday when it is past,
>> or like a watch in the night.
> You sweep them away; they are like a dream,
>> like grass that is renewed in the morning;
> in the morning it flourishes and is renewed;
>> in the evening it fades and withers (Ps 90:3-6).[165]

> As for mortals, their days are like grass;
>> they flourish like a flower of the field;
> for the wind passes over it, and it is gone,
>> and its place knows it no more (Ps 103:15-16).

> All people are grass,
>> their constancy is like the flower of the field.
> The grass withers, the flower fades,
>> when the breath of the LORD blows upon it;
>> surely the people are grass.[166]
> The grass withers, the flower fades;
>> but the word of our God will stand forever (Isa 40:6-8).[167]

---

165. LXX: "to dust" in Greek is εἰς ταπείνωσιν; in 90:6 [LXX 89:6] we find another verbal link: ξηρανθείη. What James explains by heat, the psalmist explains as time (implying weather).

166. LXX: "grass" in Greek is χόρτος, and the second line of the text in the LXX also has another link: ἄνθος. Isaiah attributes the withering to wind, James to the sun's scorching heat. There are other links: Isa 40:2 has ταπείνωσις. See Martin, 23-24, who points to the undeniable differences in emphasis between James and Isa 40.

167. LXX: a verbal link is found in Isaiah with χόρτος and very notably in ὡς ἄνθος χόρτου, while LXX Isa 40:7 is nearly quoted in Jas 1:11. Perhaps more significantly, the LXX rendering of Isa 40:6cd ("all flesh is grass [hatsir], all its goodness like flowers [tsits] of the field [sadeh]") shows an irregularity that James picks up, which confuses the interpretation: LXX renders both hatsir and sadeh with χόρτος ("grass"). If the LXX translation is considered as little more than a poetic reuse of one term, then it becomes possible to see a more obvious analogy: comparison is being made with the wildflowers and meadow flowers, like the anemone. See Laws, 64; Martin, 26.

If James has Psalm 103 in mind, he may also think the verses that follow about the steadfast love of the Lord may apply to the "poor" who remain faithful. As in Psalm 90, so James speaks of flourishing in the morning and perishing in the evening. Even more, James compares the rich to a single "flower in the field," and that language is most like Isaiah 40. Since it seems apparent that he has Isaiah 40 in mind, he may also think that the abiding and effective power of the word of God applies to the poor as well.[168]

Most importantly, James's emphasis is that the rich "will disappear"[169] the way a wild "flower"[170] dissipates and wilts under the heat of the sun. It is the withering away of the "rich" that most concerns James as he unfolds the withering of the flower in 1:11a. The brevity of life is evident from the quick turns of nature (Matt 6:19-34).

1:11 James mentions four phases in the withering of the flower. First, "the sun rises[171] with its scorching[172] heat." Second, the sun's heat "withers the field [or flower]."[173] Third, "its flower falls."[174] James is describing the "rich" in these terms, and it is worth noting that Hebrew *tsir* in Isaiah

---

168. See also Job 14:2; 15:30-33; Pss 37:2; 102:11; 129:6 (describing the temporary grass that grows in the dirt used to seal housetops); Isa 51:12. 1 Peter uses Isa 40:6-8 to speak to the eternality of rebirth (1:22-25).

169. παρελεύσεται, a deponent future; see BDAG, 775-76.

170. Various concrete images could be in view: wildflowers, the flowers of grapes or olives, or the buds on wild grasses. See n. 167 above for the view that James's term may be describing wildflowers.

171. The aorist indicative active of ἀνατέλλω. The aorist tense, focusing as it does on the action itself rather than how or when the action occurs, enables the reader to focus on the inevitability of the flower's fading by the end of the day. Grammarians, however, differ. Mayor, 46, and Ropes, 148, see a gnomic aorist; Moule, *Idiom Book,* understands a "perfective" aorist: "has happened before you can look around." MHT, 3.73, agrees. Porter, *Verbal Aspect,* 223, sees it more accurately as "omnitemporal."

172. It is not clear if σὺν τῷ καύσωνι refers to "heat" or "blowing wind." For the former, see Laws, 65; Davids, 77-78; for the latter, see Mayor, 47; Martin, 27. On σύν as μετά, see BDF §221. Davids presents the case for a "sirocco" and then, because the concern is with the "sun" and not a wind, contends that James has in mind the scorching heat. Martin, 27, disagrees. See "scorching heat" at Gen 31:40; Isa 25:5; Sir 18:16; Jon 4:8; LXX Dan 3:67 (Θ); Matt 20:12; Luke 12:55. On the hot east winds of the land of Israel, cf. Ps 103:16; Jer 18:17; Ezek 17:10; 19:12; Hos 12:1; 13:15; Jon 4:8. A potent commentary on Jas 1:11 is Job 27:13-23. I am inclined to think the winds are involved in the imagery.

173. ἐξήρανεν τὸν χόρτον. If one sticks to the vocabularic meaning "grass," then James has in mind the buds of wild grasses. However, if we consider the LXX to be a loose rendering of Isa 40:6 (see discussion above), where clearly a wildflower is in mind, then we could render this expression as "withers the flower."

174. καὶ τὸ ἄνθος αὐτοῦ ἐξέπεσεν. Isa 40:7 has "fade" or "droop" *(navel);* James picks up the LXX translation here. In light of what James will make of the "rich" at the end of v. 11, "falls" is more devastating than drooping or fading.

40:7 ("flower") was also used of the artificial golden flowered frontlet of the priestly headgear (Exod 28:36; 39:30; Lev 8:9). It is possible, as we intimated earlier, that James has the priestly establishment in mind with the "rich."[175] Fourth, "its beauty[176] perishes."[177]

The chiasm is complete (see above): "It is the same way with the rich; in the midst of a busy life, they will wither away."[178] "In the midst of a busy life" will be explained further in 4:13-17 as the activity of business.[179] But the NRSV is a little more explicit here than the Greek, which merely says "in their ways" (ἐν ταῖς πορείαις). Some have suggested that, instead of a description of the business life of the rich, this is a description of the rich person's overall "way of life."[180] That this refers specifically to a lifestyle of travel is supported by Luke 13:22, where the same term is used for Jesus' travel. Along with James 4:13-17, two parables of Jesus, the Parable of the Rich Fool (Luke 12:13-21) and the Parable of the Great Banquet (14:15-24), are close enough in content to suggest that James has in mind the overall lifestyle of the rich man, who plans and plots how to increase riches instead of living each day before God. The characterization is damning, and so also is the rich person's future. Such a man, James says, "will wither away." While some have suggested that James is referring here to no more than the loss of riches[181] or to death (4:14), it is much more likely that James has in mind the Day of the Lord. Notably, when James turns to this theme again in 4:13–5:6, it is immediately followed up with a warning to be ready for the imminent coming of the Lord, which I take to be a reference to the destruction of Jerusalem in 70 AD.[182] Once again, another parable comes to mind: the Parable of the Days of Noah (Luke 17:26-31).

175. See Baltzer, *Deutero-Isaiah,* 58.

176. ἡ εὐπρέπεια τοῦ προσώπου αὐτοῦ. In the LXX εὐπρέπεια is used for the Temple (Ps 26:8) and Zion (50:2) and YHWH (93:1). See Ropes, 149. Not translated "in its beauty" is the Semitic τοῦ προσώπου αὐτοῦ, which is a rendering of *panim* and refers to the surface appearance of something. See Luke 12:56.

177. ἀπώλετο is a strong term. This same term is used in parables for the destruction of Jerusalem (Matt 21:41; 22:7; Luke 17:27, 29; cf. also John 11:50), and it refers as well to final eschatology (Matt 5:29-30; Luke 13:3, 5; John 6:27; 10:10, 28; Rom 2:12; 1 Cor 1:18-19; 2 Cor 2:15; 2 Thess 2:10; Jas 4:12).

178. οὕτως καὶ ὁ πλούσιος ἐν ταῖς πορείαις αὐτοῦ μαρανθήσεται. A notable feature is the change from aorists to the future in μαρανθήσεται (future passive of μαραίνω). On the "eschatological passive," which indicates a certain sensitivity about pronouncing the active agent in such judgments and at the same time throws weight on the act itself (here, "final withering"), see Reiser, *Jesus and Judgment,* 266-73.

179. See Mayor, 47.

180. So Ropes, 149; Laws, 65; Davids, 78; Popkes, 98.

181. Ropes, 149.

182. See McKnight, *A New Vision for Israel,* 120-55; for those with a similar view of Jas 1:11, see Davids, 78.

The language of James 1:9-11 is sharp and biting, even ironical or sarcastic. It owes its ultimate genesis to the prophetic tradition of the Tanakh. James knows full well the power of the rich, and he finds the rich to be those who blaspheme the name of the Messiah and abuse their power over the poor messianic Jewish community. Within his overall covenant framework of knowing the people of God as continuous from Abraham to the messianic community, James warns the rich that they will find nothing but judgment on the Day of the Lord. The irony is that the venom he uses against the rich turns to soothing balm when he approaches the same economic situation from the angle of what God is doing through such trials: for the messianic community, what the rich are doing in an unjust manner is designed (by God?) to be an opportunity to trust in God for moral formation. In other words, as he is about to divulge, their economic persecution, met by endurance, will paradoxically earn them a "crown of glory."

2.4. GOD, TRIALS AND TESTING (1:12-18)

12 *Blessed is anyone*[183] *who endures*[184] *temptation.*[a] *Such a one has stood the test and will receive the crown of life that the Lord*[b][185] *has promised to those who love him.*[186] 13 *No one, when tempted, should say, "I am being tempted by*[187] *God"; for God cannot be tempted by evil and he himself tempts no one.* 14 *But one is tempted by one's own desire, being lured and enticed by it;*[c] 15 *then, when that desire has conceived, it gives birth to sin, and that sin, when it is fully grown, gives*[188]

183. Instead of ἀνήρ a few manuscripts read the more generic ανθρωπος (A, Y, 1448, and Cyr). The universalizing of this term in modern translations is understandable in light of the interchange of the two terms in 1:7-8; see BDAG, 79, "a person." See also at 1:8, 20, 23; 2:2; 3:2. Of the three major terms, ἄρσην, ἀνήρ, and ἄνθρωπος, the first is the most sexualized and the last the most generic. See Blomberg and Kamell, 69.

184. Many manuscripts read a future (K, L, P, Armenian, and Slavonic) as some also read πειρασμόν as a plural (056, 0142, Slavonic, and Armenian).

185. Various manuscripts insert either κυριος (C, P, 0246, Byz, and Harclean) or Θεος (4, 33[vid], 323, 945, 1241, 1739, *al* vg Peshitta, Ethiopic, Did[pt], and Cyr) to clarify the subject.

186. Some think this is an unrecorded saying of Jesus *(agrapha).* So Adamson, 68. They appeal to 1 Cor 9:25; 1 Pet 5:4; 2 Tim 4:8; and Rev 2:10. Such a promise, in explicit terms, does not appear in the Old Testament (though Exod 20:6 is close). Such a view is a possibility, but the evidence permits only guesswork.

187. To clarify agency instead of source, some manuscripts have υπο (ℵ, 81, 206, 429, 522, 630, 1505, 1611, 1799, 2138, and 2495).

188. As with ὑπομένει in v. 12, so in v. 15 some manuscripts have a future for ἀποκύει (L, Y, 5, 33, 93, *et permulti*).

birth to death. 16 *Do not be deceived, my beloved.*[d] 17 *Every generous act of giving, with every perfect gift,*[e] *is from above, coming down*[189] *from*[190] *the Father of lights,*[f] *with whom there is*[191] *no variation*[192] *or shadow due to change.*[g] 18 *In fulfillment of his own purpose he*[h] *gave us birth*[193] *by the word of truth, so that we would become a kind of first fruits of his creatures.*

a. TNIV: who persevere under trial

b. TNIV: God

c. TNIV: when you are dragged away by your own evil desire and enticed

d. TNIV: my dear brothers and sisters

e. NRSV is grammatically clumsy; TNIV: Every good and perfect gift

f. TNIV: heavenly lights

g. TNIV: who does not change like shifting shadows

h. TNIV: he chose to give us birth

This new section is either a simple resumption of what was started and dropped in 1:2-4 (the effects of testing)[194] or, as we have been arguing, a re-capitulation of a theme that has moved from 1:1-4 through 1:5-8 and 1:9-11 in order to move to the related topic undertaken in 1:13-18.[195] It is more diffi-cult to think the author would bring up a topic on tests, drop it suddenly, only so quickly to resume it again. It is more likely that he is not shifting and thus has never left the topic of being tested by economic stress and learning to re-spond to it properly. That is, interpreting 1:5-11 as wandering into new topics is less justifiable than seeing 1:2-15 as variations on a single theme, with 1:2-4 and 1:12 coupling the entire section. Terms from 1:2-4 (or their cognates) reappear: "test" *(peirasmos),* "testing" *(dokimion),* and "endurance" *(hypo-*

189. Instead of καταβαῖνον (P74, 424, etc.) some manuscripts read κατερχομενον (322, 323, Georgian).

190. Some manuscripts have παρα (K, 056, 0142, Cyr, Dam, etc.) instead of ἀπό.

191. The ἔνι (=ἐνεστιν) is spelled more completely (εστιν) in some manuscripts (ℵ, P, 522, etc.).

192. There is great variation in word order in the tradition, with the translated text reflecting not only the widespread text found in Nestle-Aland[27] but also the general con-sensus of the variations. See commentary notes below.

193. Some manuscripts have εποιησεν ("made"; see 206, 378, 429, and Harclean) instead of the more widespread and early ἀπεκύησεν ("gave birth"). The motive is perhaps discomfort with a feminine image for God. See J. David Miller, "Can the 'Father of Lights' Give Birth?" *Priscilla Papers* 19 (2005) 5-7.

194. So Laws, 66; Davids, 79.

195. However, Penner, *The Epistle of James and Eschatology,* 143-49, sees 1:12 as the second part of a chiasm with 1:2. He thus separates 1:12 from 1:13 and that which follows at the structural level.

monē). Thus, there is an undeniable link between 1:2-4 and 1:12, and we argue that this coupling is an indicator that, at least in his mind, James has never shifted from this concern with economic testing.

Structurally, as the exegesis will show, 1:12 summarizes the direction James has been going in 1:2-11. This recapitulation establishes the theme: God rewards those who endure testing. Because that testing stretches one's perception of God's inherent goodness and providential care of his people, James must clarify its source and the relationship of God to what the messianic community is experiencing (1:13-18). In the process of doing this, James lays full responsibility for sin on the individual and his (or her) choices. There is no need for a theodicy.

2.4.1. Recapitulation (1:12)

The recapitulation of the themes of 1:2-11 involves three elements: a blessing (1:12a), the condition of the blessing (1:12b), and the reason for the blessing (1:12c). We begin with a brief sketch of the background to the term "blessed."

EXCURSUS: MACARISMS IN CONTEXT

This beatitude, or macarism, is similar in form and substance to the Beatitudes of Jesus.[196] The Lukan Beatitudes (Luke 6:20-26) are a clue to the comparative nature of beatitudes: when one group is praised for its behaviors, another group is denounced for failing to exhibit such behaviors.[197] The same is found in Jewish parallels:[198]

> "Cursed be anyone who makes an idol or casts an image, anything abhorrent to the LORD, the work of an artisan, and sets it up in secret." All the people shall respond, saying, "Amen!" . . . (Deut 27:15).

> Blessed shall be the fruit of your womb, the fruit of your ground, and the fruit of your livestock, both the increase of your cattle and the issue of your flock (28:4).

---

196. Matt 5:3-12; Luke 6:20-23 (with woes at 6:24-26). On μακάριος, see n. 204 below.

197. This is explicit in Luke, implicit in Matthew. At a deep level, this is inherent to a macarism: to bless one group/virtue is to set it above other groups/virtues or to compare it favorably to another group/lesser virtue. See Dodd, *More,* 1-10.

198. Deut 27:11–28:68 and Lev 26; Isa 3:10-11; Eccl 10:16-17; Dan 12:12; Tob 13:12, 14; 4Q286 f. 7, 2.5, 7, 11; 4Q403 f 1. col 1.10-25; *1 Enoch* 58:2-3; *b. Berakoth* 61b; *b. Yoma* 87a.

These curses and blessings, which are simply lifted from a long list of both, are rooted in a covenant formula with a clear sense of conditionality. Disobedience incurs curse and obedience incurs blessings. So it begins with this:

> Then Moses and the levitical priests spoke to all Israel, saying: Keep silence and hear, O Israel! This very day you have become the people of the LORD your God. Therefore obey the LORD your God, observing his commandments and his statutes that I am commanding you today (Deut 27:9-10).

The same theme can be seen in Ecclesiastes 10:16-17:

> Alas for you, O land, when your king is a servant,
>   and your princes feast in the morning!
> Happy are you, O land, when your king is a nobleman,
>   and your princes feast at the proper time —
> for strength, and not for drunkenness!

And in Tobit 13:12, 14:

> Cursed are all who speak a harsh word against you;
>   cursed are all who conquer you
>   and pull down your walls,
> all who overthrow your towers
>   and set your homes on fire.
>   But blessed forever will be all who revere you. . . .
> Happy are those who love you,
>   and happy are those who rejoice in your prosperity.
> Happy also are all people who grieve with you
>   because of your afflictions;
> for they will rejoice with you
>   and witness all your glory forever.

R. Akiva, when imprisoned, was joined by Pappus b. Judah, who said,

> Happy are you, R. Akiva, that you have been seized for busying yourself with the Torah! Alas for Pappus who has been seized for busying himself with idle things! (*b. Berakoth* 61b)

Frequently interwoven in macarisms is a reversal theme: those who are promised great things presently do not have those great things. The Jesus tradition, for instance, promises the kingdom to the poor and persecuted and threatens destruction on the rich (Matt 5:3, 11; Luke 6:24-26).[199] This com-

---

199. Notice Jas 2:5: "Has not God chosen the *poor* in the world to be rich in faith

parison and reversal establish a significant link with James 1:9-10, where the poor are promised exaltation and the rich are promised humiliation, providing yet more evidence that we are dealing with a cohesive unit from 1:2 to 1:15. C. H. Dodd observed that the language of James reflects "a well marked attitude or frame of mind, characterized by an acute sense of the miseries of an oppressed class, and by the expectation of a *peripeteia* ['reversal']."[200] This macarism of James also breathes the spirit of the Magnificat and longs for the establishment of justice (cf. 1:20) and peace (3:18).

With this historical sketch in mind and before we return to James 1:12, a word about the *form* of a macarism. It is a brief set of two parts: a blessing is pronounced on a person or group, and then the reason, or blessing, is provided.[201] As illustrated above, this form of a blessing is found throughout Judaism.[202] In the form we find in James, the Hebrew term behind Greek *makarios* would be *ashre* and not the much more liturgically-shaped form we see in the *baruk*-tradition.[203] The distinction between the general blessing and the liturgical blessing is notable: James's macarism is less about a divine liturgical blessing. Instead, James is concerned either with moral wisdom that brings deep joy, justice, and peace or with eschatological confidence in spite of current conditions.

•   •

1:12 What does "blessed" in James 1:12a mean? The term, as rich in suggestion as it is varied in application, describes the special favor of God on his people both physically and spiritually and the resultant state or sphere in which they dwell. Several elements combine to give *makarios* its meaning.[204] First, the *source* of this joy is God or, as a fuller Christian theology would say, the triune God. Second, there is an *eschatological orientation* to the macarism: it is not so much that life on earth is abandoned, for James clearly does not permit such exclusiveness or withdrawal, but that fullness and final justice await the follower of Jesus in the kingdom of God, whether this is an earthly inauguration of that kingdom or the future ultimate manifestation in the new heavens

---

and to be heirs of the *kingdom* that he has promised to those who love him?" And 5:1: "Come now, you *rich* people, weep and *wail* for the miseries that are coming to you."

200. Dodd, *More*, 5.

201. Matthew's macarisms are in the third person, Luke's in the second. James is like Matthew in this regard.

202. Beside the evidence above, see also some other good parallels at Pss 1:1; 2:12; 119:1; Isa 30:18; Sir 25:8-9; *b. Haggith* 14b. See Zimmerli, "Seligpreisungen"; see Davies and Allison, *Matthew* 1.431-34.

203. Again, see Zimmerli, "Seligpreisungen."

204. On μακάριος, see *TDNT* 4.362-70; *EDNT* 2.376-79; *NIDNTT* 1.215-16; Spicq, 2.432-44; in James, see Burchard, 69.

and new earth.[205] Third, the notion of *reversal* shapes the entire context and substance of the macarism.[206] Fourth, the experience of this macarism is *conditional:* the messianic community is exhorted to love God and others and to live faithfully under trial, to use one's words with wisdom, to care for the poor and widows, etc.[207] Those who do such things will find the joy James promises. James 1:12 brings this to the surface in "who endures," "one has stood the test," and "to those who love him." Fifth, the eschatological shape of the macarism has already been *inaugurated:* James does not have in mind simply a hope in heaven but a reality into which the messianic Jewish (and poor) community can now enter.[208] Notice that James speaks of one who "has stood the test." This also draws us back to 1:2-4, where James focused on the moral formation that can occur if one responds to tests properly. Sixth, the *nature* of this blessing in James 1:12, in contrast to the classical formulations of Deuteronomy 28 or the wisdom literature, is that one may see God's blessing not in *material* abundance but in an inner confidence that God will bring to fruition his promises and kingdom and in a morally-formed character and community.

The *condition,* so typical in macarisms, is spelled out: the blessing is for "anyone who endures temptation." Generically, "endures" *(hypomenei)* means to sustain one's strength or courage or moderation or self-mastery through difficulty, and the term takes on heroic, philosophic, and Stoic dimensions.[209] In Judaism, the source for strength to endure is God (Pss 39:7 [LXX 38:8]; 71:5 [70:5]) and waiting on his promises in faith. Thus, because God made himself known in covenant and Torah, the heroic dimension of endurance comes to fruition as fidelity to the Torah (Ezra 9–10) even to the point of martyrdom (so 1 and 2 Maccabees). So Daniel 12:12: "Happy are those who *persevere* and attain the thousand three hundred thirty-five days." Jesus builds on this deep Jewish tradition by summoning his followers to run the gauntlet with him and warns those who fail to run it of dire consequences

205. See Matt 11:6; 13:16; Jas 1:12; 2:5. This is an emphasis of many commentators; see Davids, 79; Martin, 33. For James, see Penner, *The Epistle of James and Eschatology;* for the broader sweep, see R. Bauckham and T. Hart, *Hope against Hope* (Grand Rapids: Eerdmans, 1999); H. Schwarz, *Eschatology* (Grand Rapids: Eerdmans, 2000); B. E. Daley, *The Hope of the Early Church* (Peabody: Hendrickson, 2003); C. F. Hill, *Regnum Caelorum* (2d ed.; Grand Rapids: Eerdmans, 2001).

206. See Luke 6:20-26 and Jas 1:9-10, 12; 2:5.

207. See Pss 1:1, 3-6; 32; 89:15; 94:12; 106:3; 112:1; 119:1, 2; Prov 8:32, 34; Isa 30:18; 56:2.

208. Recent scholarship on James from the angle of James's rhetoric and the rhetorical intent clarifies this point. James writes in order to create a new world for those who will follow his vision. E.g., A. Batten, "Ideological Strategies in the Letter of James," in Webb and Kloppenborg, *Reading James with New Eyes,* 6-26.

209. See Spicq, 3.414-20.

(Mark 8:34–9:1; 13:13; Matt 10:22; Heb 12:2-3). Early Christian theology reflects the same need for fidelity (Rom 2:7; 12:12; 1 Thess 1:3; 2 Tim 2:10, 12; Heb 10:32; 12:7; 1 Pet 2:20). There is no disputing the necessity of endurance in early Christian *praxis* (Mark 13:13; Rom 2:7; 2 Cor 12:12; Col 1:11), and James fits snugly into this stream of conditional thinking.[210]

Once again, James uses the term *peirasmos* in his description of the condition (cf. 1:2). It can mean either "test" or "temptation," and James moves from one to the other in 1:12-18. By 1:13 he clearly means "tempt." Does he in 1:12 as well? Is the blessing for the one who successfully endures through *temptations* or through the *tests* of life? Once again, there are few options and they are mostly shaped by whether one reads 1:2-18 as a unity (so that 1:2 and 1:12 have the same concern) or as a series of topics, in which case 1:12b could refer to "temptation." Put differently, is *peirasmos* in 1:12b a play on *peirasmos* in 1:2, or is it the same word with the same meaning? Many favor the view that the meaning shifts, that *peirasmos* refers to "temptations" here, and that it sets up 1:13-18.[211] Others see it as a general reference to anything that threatens one's fidelity to Christ as a "test."[212] Both options are reasonable explanations in this context, but it is hard to think that either James or his readers would be dabbling in general moral considerations when their survival was at stake. We should perhaps recognize the emotional heat of 1:9-11: there is more than a hint of vindictiveness, triumphalism, and perhaps even sarcasm that will carry over into what the author has to say in 1:12. Contextual flow, then, suggests that James has "test" (particularly the financial tests that press the issue of fidelity to the Messiah) in mind here as in 1:2. Because these tests are so severe (again, 2:5-7; 5:1-6), the promise of eternal reward, the ultimate trump card in economics, is all the more appealing.

The *reason* for James's blessing is spelled out in 1:12c: "has stood the test and will receive the crown of life."[213] The *telos* of the "test" shifts in this section: in 1:2-4 it was moral formation, but in 1:12-14 it is eschatological reward. And a similar shift is seen in "has stood the test":[214] in this term we

---

210. There is an entire history of theology in the issue of perseverance; cf. Marshall, *Kept by the Power of God;* McKnight, "Warning Passages"; on Paul, see especially Gundry Volf, *Paul and Perseverance.* For James, see Calvin, 287, who wrestles expressions like this in James into claims like this: "our fighting only renders us fit to receive" what God has "gratuitiously appointed"; also Davids, 79-80. In context, the one who is finally blessed is the one who is δόκιμος (1:12b).

211. So Martin, 30, 32; Laws, 67, 69.

212. Moo, 70.

213. ὅτι δόκιμος γενόμενος λήμψεται τὸν στέφανον τῆς ζωῆς. The aorist participle is used to provide the assumption (in a global manner) of receiving the crown rather than to specify that the approval occurs before the reception of the crown.

214. δόκιμος γενόμενος, roughly "in, or by, becoming approved." The "has stood"

find a reference back to a cognate in 1:3 *(dokimion),* where the emphasis was process, while in 1:12 *dokimos* is used of the person who has already successfully endured that process.[215] Other New Testament uses of this term reveal a notable gravity, putting the emphasis on divine and final approval. A good parallel can be found in 1 Peter 1:6-7:

> even if now for a little while you have had to suffer various *trials,* so that the *genuineness* of your faith — being more precious than gold that, though perishable, is tested by fire — may be found to result in praise and glory and honor when Jesus Christ is revealed.

The connection between fidelity and reward, or the focus on the conditionality of blessing, is therefore typical of early Christian thinking. Those who meet the conditions, if one begins to compare the literature, "will receive"[216] a variety of rewards or, perhaps better, such rewards are described with a variety of images. The word common in the Gospel tradition, *misthos,*[217] is not found here, but its theology is assumed. Those who are persecuted will receive a great reward (Matt 5:12); deeds done to be noticed will not be rewarded (6:1); rewards are granted for service to servants of Christ (10:41); Jesus radicalizes rewards by turning them into gifts in the Parable of the Workers in the Vineyard (20:1-16); that reward is already inaugurated (John 4:36). Paul sees rewards based on carrying out one's gifts (1 Cor 3:8, 14). 2 John 8, like James, speaks of reward for fidelity, as do Rev 11:18 and 22:12.[218]

James 1:12 is more like Jesus and 2 John and Revelation than like Paul. Here the issue is one of the stress that puts fidelity to the test and the consequent reward for endurance. Those who endure the "test" will receive "the crown of life."[219] In context, the "crown of life" needs to be associated

---

is a strong translation of the aorist middle participle. The aorist here is less concerned with the state or the process, and more with the "thatness" of "being *dokimos.*" We might translate: "Blessed is the person . . . because, as the approved one, that person will receive. . . ." This adjectival participial clause modifies the implied subject of the verb λήμψεται.

215. Seven times in the New Testament: Rom 14:18; 16:10; 1 Cor 11:19; 2 Cor 10:18; 13:7; 2 Tim 2:15; and here. The verb δοκιμάζω, "to make a critical evaluation of someone or something," is common; see BDAG, 255-56.

216. λήμψεται, future indicative of λαμβάνω. See also Matt 19:29; 20:9-11; John 16:24; Acts 2:38; 1 Cor 3:8, 14; 9:24-25; Heb 9:15; 11:8; Jas 3:1; Rev 22:17. Jas 3:1 uses λαμβάνω for "receiving a greater judgment" for teachers.

217. See Spicq, 2.502-15.

218. Again, a theology is involved: Is this "merit" or "disinterestedness" finding its natural correlation? Among the scores of studies, see Mohrlang, *Matthew and Paul,* 48-71.

219. τὸν στέφανον τῆς ζωῆς, an epexegetical genitive ("the crown that consists of life"); see Laws, 68; Davids, 80; Martin, 33. The noun στέφανος is modified by both τῆς ζωῆς and the adjectival ὃν ἐπηγγείλατο κτλ clause.

with "raised up" in 1:9 and "the kingdom" in 2:5. A "crown," known so well through the poetry of Pindar and others, could be a victory wreath or a royal crown or even the garland worn on occasions of joy.[220] Since the crown is given to the one who endures the tests, it is most likely that James has in mind the crown given to winners in competitions (cf. Heb 12:1-3).[221] That crown is "life" itself,[222] the promise that those who endure the tests will inherit the kingdom of God and obtain eternal life (James 2:5).

Such a reward is what "the Lord has promised."[223] Early Christians regularly conceptualized the work of God through Jesus Christ and the Spirit as the fulfillment of the Abrahamic promise,[224] but the focus of the promise in James is "eternal life."[225] By bringing up promise, James touches here on the center of biblical theology.[226] Three terms are interrelated, though with different degrees of emphasis, in the Old Testament — Torah, Covenant, and Promise — and none can be considered separately without doing violence to the others. These terms function as hermeneutical grids through which a person reads the Bible and understands history. Even more: these are the terms through which a person or a community received identity, and identity had more than one crystallization among Jews and early Christians.[227] James evidently read the Bible through the lens of Torah, but he does so as one who sees Torah as fulfilled in Jesus' teaching of the centrality of neighbor-love from Le-

220. See Ps 21:3; Wis 2:8; 5:16; 1 Cor 9:25; Phil 4:1; 1 Thess 2:19; 2 Tim 2:5; Rev 4:4, 10; 6:2; 9:7; 14:14. See Ropes, 150-52; Laws, 68. On Pindar, see *The Odes* (trans. C. M. Bowra; London: Penguin, 1969). Pindar was famous for his victory odes in honor of the victors of the panhellenic games.

221. Davids, 80, suggests it is "useless" to speculate whether this is a victor's crown or a royal crown, even though he then suggests that the former would be more appropriate. What is useless is to speculate whether James thought this would be a "physical" or a "metaphorical" crown; cf. here Prov 1:9; 12:4; 16:31; 17:6; Sir 1:11; 1 Cor 9:25; 1 Thess 2:19; 2 Tim 4:8.

222. Other such "crowns" include "righteousness" (2 Tim 4:8), "glory" (1 Pet 5:4), and "life" (Rev 2:10).

223. See above on whether to read "Lord" or "God." In context, "God" would be preferred as it is the subject of 1:13-18 and the similar expression in 2:5.

224. Abraham: Acts 7:17; 13:23, 32; 26:6; Rom 4:16; 9:4, 8; Jesus Christ: Rom 4:13-14, 16, 20; 15:8; 2 Cor 1:20; Gal 3:14-18, 21-22, 29; Holy Spirit: Luke 24:49; Acts 1:4; 2:33, 39; Eph 1:13.

225. As in texts such as 1 Tim 4:8; 2 Tim 1:1; Heb 6:12; 9:15; 10:36; 2 Pet 3:4, 9; 1 John 2:25.

226. See Ollenburger, Martens, and Hasel, *The Flowering of Old Testament Theology,* especially Part 2 (pp. 43-370). There is a dearth of studies on this theme in the New Testament and early Christianity; see the sketch by E. Hoffmann in *NIDNTT* 3.68-74.

227. On which, see especially Lieu, *Christian Identity;* Gruen, *Heritage and Hellenism;* Cohen, *The Beginnings of Jewishness.* These books show that identity is forged on the anvil of hermeneutics.

viticus 19:18 (see below on 2:8-11). Thus, it is a Torah-through-Jesus–shaped identity that James discovers and passes on to the messianic community.

James's sense of endurance and fidelity is clarified at the end of 1:12: "that the Lord has promised *to those who love him.*" In 1:2-18 James has used two primary terms for how the messianic community is to live: "faith" and "endurance" (1:3). Now he shifts to "love" (the verb *agapaō*),[228] making it clear that faith and endurance are dimensions of love. As will be clear in the commentary at 2:8-11, James practiced the *Shema* as taught by Jesus: every morning and every evening, and perhaps on every entrance into or exit from the home, Jews recited the *Shema.* Though we are not sure of the specifics of first-century Jewish liturgical customs, it is likely that Jews recited the Ten Commandments and other scriptural texts along with the *Shema.*[229] Jesus amended the Jewish practice of reciting Shema by adding Leviticus 19:18 (neighbor-love) to the recital (cf. Mark 12:28-32 pars.).[230] In reciting the *Shema,* one was afforded the opportunity to reflect on one's relationship with God as one of love, and it is likely that this enabled James to see love as the global response to God.[231] In the Ten Commandments is a promise that God's "steadfast love" *(hesed)* will be shown to those who "love me *(le'ohavay)* and keep my commandments" (Exod 20:6; cf. Deut 5:10).[232] Instead of "steadfast love," James promises "the crown of life" to those who have "stood the test."

---

228. See Spicq, 1.8-22, where he makes the case for understanding ἀγάπη as a "demonstration of love" (p. 12). See also *NIDNTT* 2.538-51; Morris, *Testaments of Love,* 169-72.

229. See Hoffman, *The Sh'ma and Its Blessings;* Edgar, "Love-Command." See 1QS 10:1-3, 10; and especially the later *m. Tamid* 5:1:

A. The superintendent said to them, "Say one blessing."
B. They said a blessing, pronounced the Ten Commandments, the Shema [Hear O Israel (Dt. 6:4-9)], And it shall come to pass if you shall hearken (Dt. 11:13-21), and And the Lord spoke to Moses (Num. 15:37-41).
C. They blessed the people with three blessings: True and sure, Abodah, and the blessing of priests.
D. And on the Sabbath they add a blessing for the outgoing priestly watch.

230. See my *The Jesus Creed;* also Konradt, *Christliche Existenz,* 179-84; Cheung, *Genre, Composition,* 119-20 n. 67.

231. The use of the present active participle here intends to describe love as the "characteristic" of the messianic community, as something where the action is incomplete. James's use of the present then makes loving God more vivid to the mind of his listeners/readers.

232. Ps 145:20; Sir 1:10; *Pss Sol* 4:29; 6:9; 10:4; 14:1; *1 Enoch* 108:8; Rom 8:28; 1 Cor 2:9 (echoed in *1 Clement* 34:8; *2 Clement* 11:7; *Gospel of Thomas* 17; *Acts of Peter* 39); *1 Clement* 59:3; see also Eph 6:24.

Evidently, however, some in James' audience saw this *testing* by God as an act whereby God was actually *tempting* humans to sin. James responds to this pastoral problem by appealing to the total goodness of God in what can only be called an extended discussion of God and temptations.

2.4.2. Tests and Temptations (1:13-15)

As a paragraph, James 1:13-18 can be a footnote response to a pastoral problem, attached because James has brought up the word "test" again and because some blame God for their temptations or tests.[233] Or this paragraph may begin another topic altogether, even if it is connected to the previous verse by a play on terms.[234] Regardless, James's logic seems to be this:[235]

1:13a: The problem stated: God (cannot be all good since God) tempts.

1:13b: The problem denied: God is not temptable and God does not tempt.

1:14-15: An explanation of the origins of temptation: internal desires.

1:16: Pastoral warning concerning deception about God's goodness.

1:17: A theological foundation: God is good, perfect, and unchanging.

1:18: God's goodness extended to formation of the community.

While interpretation of specific parts of this passage is notoriously difficult, the general direction seems clear. James shifts from *peirasmos* as "test" to *peirasmos* as "temptation" because someone has called God's goodness into question.[236] James counters the statement: God is altogether good and, what is often not noted in this discussion in 1:13-18, has a beautiful design for the messianic community: to be "a kind of first fruits of his creatures" (1:18). Furthermore, almost as a teaser, James hints at his own theological anthropology.[237]

1:13 For James, every test carries with it the possibility of the be-

233. So Davids, 80-82.
234. So Laws, 69.
235. The presence of present tenses (imperfective aspect) makes the ideas vivid and almost timelessly true in depiction.
236. James responds to others elsewhere, but nowhere as clearly as in 2:18.
237. On this, cf. W. T. Wilson, "Sin as Sex and Sex with Sin: The Anthropology of James 1:12-15," *HTR* 94 (2002) 147-68, who connects James to Philo in this regard. For the broader discussion, see F. LeRon Shults, *Reforming Theological Anthropology* (Grand Rapids: Eerdmans 2003).

liever failing that test and turning it into a temptation. As stated above, at some point in this movement from 1:2-18 James evidently shifts the meaning of *peirasmos* from "testing" to "temptation."[238] There are three possibilities in v. 13a, where cognate verb *peirazō* is used, which can be visualized on the following chart:

> **Option A**: *peirazō* as "test" only:
>> No one, when *tested,* should say, "I am being *tested* by God."
>
> **Option B**: *peirazō* as both "test" and "tempt":
>> No one, when *tested,* should say, "I am being *tempted* by God."
>
> **Option C**: *peirazō* as "tempt" only:
>> No one, when *tempted,* should say, "I am being *tempted* by God."

Option A seems unwarranted. Since James denies that God "tempts" in 1:13b, then something about temptation must be in 1:13a.[239] The meaning "tempt" could be in both uses of the verb in 1:13a or only the second. Option B is possible: 1:2-4 and 1:12 use *peirasmos* in the sense of "test." It is indeed possible that 1:13a first uses *peirazō* to mean "test," as a way of summing up 1:2-12, and then shifts in a play on words to a problem that has arisen pastorally. Some are failing in their test and are blaming God for "tempting" them. Option C is also possible, since it may be that the new topic of "temptation" comes up with the opening line: "No one, when *tempted,* should. . . ." Such a view does not preclude understanding 1:2-12 as presenting a continuous theme (as this commentary has done).[240] Therefore, either the first or the second use of the verb in 1:13a shifts the meaning to "tempt." It makes the most sense to read the first, which sums up 1:2-12, as "when tested" and the second as "tempt." Thus, I prefer Option B.

James's concern with "temptation" needs to be seen in wider context of both Jesus and Paul, though we would be hard-pressed to think the evidence that survives adequately represents the "theology of temptation" of either. James no doubt repeated the Lord's Prayer as framed by Jesus, including "do not bring us to the time of *trial,* but rescue us from the evil one" (Matt 6:13).[241] The Lord's Prayer expresses an *eschatological* sense — the fi-

---

238. So Dibelius, 90.

239. *Contra* Davids, 80-82. It is not possible to deny that God "tests" in scriptural Judaism: Abraham and Isaac in Genesis 22 and the wilderness wanderings of Exodus–Deuteronomy are driven by such a theme, and Job is filled with it. Jewish apocalyptic literature often sees tribulation as a testing ground to prove the fidelity of God's people. On tribulation, see Allison, *The End of the Ages Has Come,* 5-25.

240. See Schrage and Balz, 19; Ropes, 153-54.

241. Luke 11:4 has only "And do not bring us to the time of trial." Matthew's extension of the prayer brings in the Evil One. In contrast, James lays blame on the individ-

nal ordeal — of *peirasmos*,[242] but this request could be related to James inasmuch as the tests already facing the messianic community may anticipate the fuller and more severe tests of the final tribulation (cf. 5:7-11). A different, more *pastoral,* line of thinking is taken by Paul in 1 Corinthians 10:13:

> No testing has overtaken you that is not common to everyone. God is faithful, and he will not let you be tested beyond your strength, but with the testing he will also provide the way out so that you may be able to endure it.

Jesus sees God behind the oncoming tribulation and prays that he and his disciples will be spared from it.[243] Both Jesus and Paul see God as sovereign, Jesus in God's control of history and Paul in a more pastoral sense in that God cares for each of his people and prevents them from being stretched beyond their limits. The teachings of Jesus and Paul could (*could,* I say) lead one to connect God to the evil that comes from testing and temptations. In the history of thought many have made such a connection in discussions of theodicy.[244] But, in classic biblical fashion, James quickly wrests the problem from God: God is altogether good and, therefore, temptation and sin are to be blamed on the human who chooses to sin. James's "theory" of temptation, as we will see in these verses, is more *anthropological:* humans are to blame (not God). With these structural observations and this wider perspective now cleared away, we can now turn to the exegesis of 1:13-18.

A concrete question confronts the attentive reader: What sort of "temptation" does James have in mind?[245] Most commentators simply pass this question by or suggest that it is temptations in general. As will be evident in this commentary, we need to think more contextually and to do so on the basis of what James does say. Several considerations come to mind. First, the messianic community or at least the poor in the messianic community are being oppressed by the rich and are suffering economically. Second, this condition promotes "desires" for revenge and violence (1:13-15, 19-21). Third,

---

ual and his or her desires (1:14-15), excuses God (1:13b, 17-18), and avoids the Evil One (but cf. Jas 3:15).

242. See R. E. Brown, *New Testament Essays,* 314-20.

243. See also Mark 14:36, 38.

244. An excellent text for the discussion is T. Tiessen, *Providence and Prayer: How Does God Work in the World?* (Downers Grove: InterVarsity, 2000); see also C. J. H. Wright, *The God I Don't Understand* (Grand Rapids: Zondervan, 2008); A. Hamilton, *Seeing Gray in a World of Black and White* (Nashville: Abingdon, 2008), 121-32.

245. Whatever the merits of J. L. P. Wolmarans's wide-ranging sketch of misogyny as an expression of "desire," there is no evidence that sexual temptation is specifically in mind in Jas 1:12-18. See his "Misogyny as a Meme: The Legacy of James 1:12-18," *Acta patristica et byzantina* 17 (2006) 349-61.

James mentions just these sorts of "desires" in 4:1-12, where he brings up such things as murder, disputes, and slander. I suggest therefore that we at least consider, whether we land firmly on this view or not, that James has something far more concrete in mind with the idea of temptation. He responds to a messianic community where some are being tempted to use violence against their oppressors in order to establish justice (1:20). He makes it clear that such desires do not come from God. In fact, he analyzes such a process of thinking as diabolical (3:13–4:12).[246]

A general pastoral comment is in order: one tendency in reading 1:13 is to see humans underestimating themselves, and it may well be. But sometimes excessive humility, as Mary Evans points out, leads to an underestimation of the image of God in humans, and Evans is quick to notice the significance of this for women.[247] James's point cannot be reduced to self-deprecation.

James enters here for the first time into an imaginary dialogue with someone,[248] which continues elsewhere (e.g., 2:3, 16, 18; 4:13). He *denies the problem* (1:13b) posed in a quotation from someone: "I am being tempted by God." To return to a previous point, though some think the word *peirazō* here means "test," I find it nearly impossible to think James would deny that God tests — and what he does deny is inherent to his response in 1:13b-18. God regularly tests in Scripture.[249] However, James vehemently denies, *tempting* does not come from God.[250]

Why? Because God is altogether good and holy and loving: "for God cannot be tempted by evil[251] and he himself tempts no one" (1:13b). Tech-

---

246. Which connects James closer with the Lord's Prayer in the Matthean form: "and deliver us from the Evil One."

247. Evans, 776.

248. λεγέτω.

249. See Gen 3:12-13; 22; Job 1:12; 2:6; 1 Chron 21:1; 2 Sam 24:1; Prov 19:3; Sir 15:11-20; *Jubilees* 17:16. See especially Sir 15:11-20:

> Do not say, "It was the Lord's doing that I fell away"; for he does not do what he hates. Do not say, "It was he who led me astray"; for he has no need of the sinful. The Lord hates all abominations; such things are not loved by those who fear him. It was he who created humankind in the beginning, and he left them in the power of their own free choice. If you choose, you can keep the commandments, and to act faithfully is a matter of your own choice. He has placed before you fire and water; stretch out your hand for whichever you choose. Before each person are life and death, and whichever one chooses will be given. For great is the wisdom of the Lord; he is mighty in power and sees everything; his eyes are on those who fear him, and he knows every human action. He has not commanded anyone to be wicked, and he has not given anyone permission to sin.

250. I lay emphasis on ἀπό.

251. κακῶν; see BDAG, 501.

nically, the line reads "for God is without temptation."[252] This term can be either active — "God does not tempt" — or passive — "God is untemptable."[253] In this context, however, the sense is clearly passive because the next clause is in a correlative contrast with this clause: thus, "God is not temptable, nor does he tempt."[254] This double denial of temptation on the part of God serves to make God's goodness all the more clear.[255]

1:14-15   The anthropological focus of James comes to the fore now as James *explains the origins of temptations.*[256] Jesus says in Mark 7:21, "For it is from within, from the human heart, that evil intentions come. . . ." So also James traces "evil" not to God or even to Satan, but to the seductive power of human desires: "But one is tempted by one's own desire." Paul speaks to the same issue in the much-disputed section on inner struggle in Romans 7. Thus, Romans 7:19: "For I do not do the good I want, but the evil I do not want is what I do."[257] James emphatically distributes the responsibility to each person: "But *one*[258] is tempted by *one's own*[259] desires." By appealing to "desires,"[260] James lands firmly in the Jewish *yetzer* thinking (e.g.,

---

252. ὁ γὰρ θεὸς ἀπείραστός ἐστιν κακῶν. The NRSV's "cannot" is permissible. The present tense makes the statement especially vivid and uncompleted (thus, characteristic of God's behavior and being).

253. See BDAG, 100, on this verbal adjective.

254. So Laws, 71. For those who maintain that "test" is still the translation, further complications arise. Davids, 83, harking back to Spitta, 34, contends that the text means that God thinks back to Deut 6:16, where it is clear that God ought not to be tested or provoked by evil people. The ingenuity of this interpretation is overcome by the clarity that comes by understanding *peirasmos* as temptation. See Mussner, 87-88; Martin, 34-35; Moo, 73-74; Popkes, 103-4.

255. See Moo, 73-74.

256. See Klein, *"Ein vollkommenes Werk,"* 82-91.

257. See also Rom 13:10; 1 Cor 10:6; 2 Cor 13:7; Col 3:5; 1 Pet 3:9-12.

258. ἕκαστος.

259. ὑπὸ τῆς ἰδίας.

260. ἐπιθυμίας. See also at Mark 4:19; John 8:44; Rom 1:24; 6:12; 7:7-18; 13:14; Gal 5:16, 24; Eph 2:3; 4:22; Col 3:5; 1 Thess 4:5; 1 Tim 6:9; 2 Tim 2:22; 3:6; 4:3; Tit 2:12; 3:3; 1 Pet 1:14; 4:2-3; 2 Pet 1:4; 2:10, 18; 3:3; 1 John 2:16; Jude 16. Klein, *"Ein vollkommenes Werk,"* p. 116 (my translation): Desire "leads the person into temptation (1:14), awakens the person's longings according to the evil things of this world (above all, according to possession and wealth; 4:1-2) and tempts the person in such a way that, when the person surrenders, it leads to sinful behavior (1:15; 4:8; 5:20) that leads in the End to damnation at the Judgment (1:10-11; 3:6) and to (eternal) death (1:15; 5:20)." He develops this even further, but the citation above clearly illustrates the magnitude of "desire" in Klein's perception of James's anthropology. Klein sees little metaphysics in James's anthropology and sees instead a "two-way" ethic of human response and responsibility. Indeed, James does emphasize responsibility, but it is noteworthy that James does not focus on "will" but on "desire," and the existence within humans of this "de-

Gen 6:5; 8:21; see also 4:7).[261] To make sense of life by avoiding chaos, Jews had three options to explain evil: God is the cause of evil, Satan is the cause of evil, or humans are the cause of evil. Jewish *yetzer* thinking focused on the third while not denying the second as a contributing factor.[262] Anchoring their thoughts to an expression in Genesis 6:5 *(yetzer hara', the evil inclination)*, Jews constructed the belief that in each human heart are two *yetzers*: the evil desire *(yetzer hara')* and the good desire *(yetzer hatov)*.[263] A crystal-clear, even if late, example is found in *b Berakoth* 61b:

> R. Jose the Galiean says, The righteous are swayed by their good inclination, as it says, *My heart is slain within me* (Ps 109:22). The wicked are swayed by their evil inclination, as it says, *Transgression speaketh to the wicked, methinks, there is no fear of God before his eyes* (Ps 36:1). Average people are swayed by both inclinations, as it says, *Because He standeth at the right hand of the needy, to save him from them that judge his soul* (Ps 109:31).

This thinking is clearly evident in Galatians 5 and Romans 7.[264] If the rabbis find the resolution to the *yetzer hara'* in the study of the Torah and Paul finds it in the indwelling presence of the Holy Spirit, James seems to find it in three interlocking ideas: the necessity of Torah observance and obedience (the *yetzer*), rebirth through the Word (1:18), and (only possibly) the indwelling Spirit and work of God (4:5-10).

Each person is tempted, James in carrying on his anthropological focus says, by "being lured and enticed by it [desire]."[265] This is a happy mix-

---

sire" is not very far from the Pauline anthropology of Gal 5 and Rom 6–8. On θέλω in James, cf. 2:20 and 4:15.

261. See early studies in Davies, *Paul and Rabbinic Judaism,* 17-35; Str-B, 3.330-32; but the singular study here is that of J. Marcus, "The Evil Inclination in the Epistle of James," *CBQ* 44 (1982) 606-21. Also Davids, 83; Martin, 30, 36-37; *pace* Popkes, 106. One must also consider Jas 4:2. W. T. Wilson, "Sin as Sex and Sex with Sin: The Anthropology of James 1:12-15," *HTR* 94 (2002) 147-68, focuses on desire in James as the feminine seductive power vs. the manly ideology of resistance. Popkes, 105-6, questions the likelihood of the sexual understanding of "desire" here.

262. See Sir 15:11-20, especially v. 14; *4 Ezra* 3:21; 4:30-31; *Test Ash* 1:3-9; 1QH 10:22-23. Other texts include Deut 31:21; 1 Chron 28:9; 29:18; Isa 26:3; 29:16; Hab 2:18.

263. Cf. *b. B.B.* 16a: "Satan, the *yetzer hara',* and the Angel of Death are one and the same." *Gen Rab* 9 suggests that the *yetzer hara',* when properly sublimated, leads to good: like marriage, building a house, having children, and engaging in business.

264. Rom 7 is intensely debated; see the commentaries and Pauline theologies. The most reasonable view takes the autobiographical view of Rom 7 seriously, while also recognizing that there is a clear salvation-historical orientation to the language.

265. ἐξελκόμενος καὶ δελεαζόμενος; see BDAG, 347 ("taken in tow by his own desires") and 217 ("to arouse someone's interest in someth. by adroit measures, *lure, en-*

ing of images, though the order is not particularly satisfying: to be drawn out as if by a hook ("being lured") and then to be aroused seems backward.[266] Some suggest the two are indeed a single process.[267] Davids is probably accurate in asking readers to let these fishing images be mixed, as can be seen in a similar instance at Qumran (1QH 3:26; 5:8).[268] Instead of seeing a process here, perhaps we see two images: in the first the human is lured onto a hook and dragged to the ground by desire, while in the second the person is enticed by desires. The focus of James is not a technical analysis of the process of sin but a rhetorical laying of blame on the individual for succumbing in various ways to desire.[269]

The larger movement of temptations, however one understands the two metaphors of 1:14, is mapped by James:

A. desire *(epithymia)* → B. sin *(hamartia)* → C. death *(thanatos)*

Desire "gives birth" to sin after it "has conceived."[270] Sin "gives birth" to death after it is "fully grown."[271] We will look at each of the three elements of the creative and poetic image of giving birth to death.[272] In context, this process from desire to death may well be describing the poor among the messianic community who cave in to pressures to deny the faith and the potential disaster they could experience. It could also explain the fate of the rich (1:10-11). There are three phases in James's paradoxical but pregnant expressions of the "birth of death."

First, the desire phase.[273] Desire is seen here, perhaps in light of Prov-

---

tice"). See Davids, "James's Message," in Chilton and Neusner, *The Brother of Jesus,* 71-75; Johnson, 193; Burchard, 73.

266. Adamson, 72.

267. Martin, 36.

268. Davids, 84; Moo, 75; but see also Martin, 36, who finds a process here.

269. The imagery is found elsewhere and may not be fresh imagery from the local fishing world; cf. Philo, *De Agricultura* 103; *Quod omnis Probus Liber sit* 159; Epictetus, *Fragment* 112.

270. "Gives birth" (τίκτει) and "has conceived" (συλλαβοῦσα), casting the first more vividly and the second as the assumption.

271. "Give birth" (ἀποκύει) and "fully grown" (ἀποτελεσθεῖσα), again casting the present as vivid and the aorist participle as the assumption for giving birth. The point is not that the aorist means either singular event in the past or historical priority, as in "first this, then this," but a more global assumption for the present tense verb.

272. For Old Testament illustrations, one thinks of Gen 3:1-7; 4:5-16; 16; 25:19-34; 27; 37; 38:12-30; Exod 2:11-22; 17:1-7; 32; Lev 10:1-3; Num 16; Josh 7; Judg 16; 1 Sam 15; 2 Sam 11; 13:7-14; 2 Kgs 17; Pss 32; 51; 130; Mark 7:17-23; 14:66-72; Luke 15:17-21; Acts 5:1-11. For an insightful study of sin, see Plantinga, *Not the Way.*

273. On the term ἐπιθυμία see on 1:15.

erbs 5 and 7, as a power that seduces the Christian from faithful obedience or as the internal impulse of a human being (Sir 15:11-20), as mentioned above in our comments about the *yetzer.* The desire does its work by conceiving within the person a plan for sin.[274] Desire "gives birth"[275] to sin.

Second, the sin phase. James defines sin relationally — anything contrary to love of neighbor (2:8-9, 12-13) — and judicially — an infraction of the Torah (2:10-11) — but ultimately he defines it theologically — something out of tune with God's will (2:11). Sin, James says, needs to be "fully grown" or "perfected."[276] He dabbles in a vividly evocative irony here: "sin gives birth to death" and "sin is perfected." It is likely that intends a contrast with the "perfection" of faith,[277] which is manifested in fidelity through stress (1:2-4), in the freedom of good deeds (1:25-26), and in control of the tongue (3:2), while the "perfection" of sin is death (1:15). Again, there is a contrasting set of links in 1:2-12 and 1:15:[278]

1:15:   desire →   sin   →   death
1:2-12: test   →   endurance →   life

Third, the death phase. Sin, when it is fully formed and the desired deed has been done, "gives birth"[279] to death. The process is now over: desire conceives sin, and sin, when it is grown up, delivers death. The image is not

---

274. On συλλαμβάνω, see BDAG, 955-56: "conceive." The term can also mean "to take into custody" (Matt 26:55), "to catch" (Luke 5:9), or "to support" (Phil 4:3). There is no reason why "take into custody" couldn't be the meaning here: "desire, when it has taken hold of the person, gives birth to sin." Martin, 36-37, however, observes that the imagery moves along the line of conception and giving birth. The aorist participle does not indicate that the "conception" occurs before the "giving birth," however true that must be, but that the action of "conceiving" is depicted simply and globally. The combination of "conception" and "giving birth" is common in the Old Testament: cf. Judg 13:7; Ruth 4:13; Ps 7:14.

275. τίκτει; see BDAG, 1004, which observes a fondness for this image in Philo; see also Johnson, 194. The present tense is omnitemporal; the concern is not that conception always leads to giving birth but that giving birth is seen without respect to time categories but in a remarkably vivid manner.

276. ἀποτελεσθεῖσα, see BDAG, 123. The idea is one of running its course or coming to a completion. Again, James reverts to the aorist participle to modify or prepare for the present verb (ἀποκύει).

277. See also at 1:25 and 3:2.

278. See Davids, 85.

279. ἀποκύει, see BDAG, 114. κύω means "to be pregnant," and so this term refers to "delivery." This could indicate that for James "giving birth" to sin could refer to the phase of pregnancy, and it is only at the "delivery" phase (ἀποκύω) that the child (death) is born.

entirely clear:[280] when is the (metaphorical) child born in this process? Is the child sin or death? Is there the birth of one child (sin), who then gives birth to another (death)? And why does James change vocabulary from *tiktei* to *apokuei?* He might have in mind desire impregnating the person with sin, which grows until it is ready for birth, and sin then delivers death as a child. In that case the only child born is death. Or, as it is more commonly understood, the child is sin, in which case desire conceives and gives birth to the child, sin, who, when grown up, delivers yet another child, death. The first view has much to say for it but is weakened by the use of "gives birth" *(tiktei)* with respect to sin, while the second suffers from the difficulty of what it means for sin to "give birth" *(apokyei)* to death. These questions are probably unanswerable, but the general drift of the argument is clear: desire conceives/ *gives birth* to sin; sin grows up/*gives birth* to death. Finally, the ideas here are most likely connected to the Fall narrative in Genesis 3 and to what Paul says in Romans 7:7-13.[281]

2.4.3. God and Temptations (1:16-18)

1:16 James now abruptly interjects an exhortation (a prohibition): "Do not be deceived."[282] While this may be rhetorically abrupt, the theme of 1:12-18 remains coherent and flowing: James continues to address the issue of the origins of temptation. Having assigned it to the human will in 1:13-15, he now provides a theodicy: God is not at all involved in sin.

He does this by an abrupt introduction (1:16) and then by asserting that all gifts from God are good (assuming that God is good) in 1:17a and that God never changes in 1:17b. Then he simply *specifies* a singularly good gift: new birth (1:18). This specification carries with it yet another assumption: God's goodness is especially manifested in creating the messianic community.

James's rhetorical stance with his audience, indicated by "my beloved,"[283] is nonetheless at the same time a stance over against them: those (of us) who think tests are actual devious attempts by God to seduce us into

---

280. See Popkes, 107-9; Blomberg and Kamell, 72.

281. The singular, and by no means small, difference is that Paul sees desire provoked by Torah when used by sin, where James seems to lay that blame on the human will. The term βουληθείς does not appear until 1:18a, but it is possible that "God's will" is in contrast to the human will of 1:14-15.

282. μὴ πλανᾶσθε, see BDAG, 821-22. The present imperative indicates a prohibited action conceived of as unfolding or in progress, but without regard to time. See 1 Cor 6:9; Gal 6:7; 1 John 1:8; 4:6; 2 Pet 3:17. Some suggest that μὴ πλανᾶσθε introduces a quotation: see Davids, 86; Laws, 72.

283. ἀδελφοί μου, "my brothers." The NRSV renders this inclusively, as it should for contemporary readers. This is followed by ἀγαπητοί, on which see also 1:19; 2:5.

sin are gravely mistaken. Evidently, God's goodness is under question for some in the messianic community, and there are some traces of what they were thinking: God's simple response of goodness has been questioned (1:5), some have suggested that God is temptable and tempts (1:13), and there is the suggestion that God shifts like shadows (1:17). Thus we are led to think that 1:16-18 is a commentary on a motif found in 1:2-15: the poor messianic community is undergoing (economic) suffering and is tempted to react with violence and verbal abuse. At least some in the community are tempted to think God is not good, that he does not dispense his wisdom to those who trust him, that he does incite his people into sin, and that he is hard to trust because he changes.[284] The tendency of some to idealize the earliest messianic community can, in light of these points from James 1 alone, be laid to rest. James was a pastor to a community filled with typical human questions, problems, and sins.

But James thinks some in the community were deceived. The deception on the part of the community James has in mind is neither simply cognitive nor moral: it is also a deception at the level of faith and love. Those who are succumbing to the idea that God is not altogether good are failing to love and trust God through their trials.[285] The gravity of James's pastoral introduction is now clear: trials are leading some to question God. There is enough evidence in the flow of the argument so far to think that the concern we see in 1:13-15, and now seen as deception in 1:16, is not a random topic, but should be used to understand even what was said in the opening paragraph (1:2-4). The "trials of any kind" involve, but cannot be limited to, the temptation to blame God for the oppression of the messianic community. The "wisdom" needed in 1:5-8 involves the need to understand the goodness of God. To be sure, James began positively at 1:2-4 and only hinted at the lurking problems, but 1:16-18 clarifies a significant issue that has been addressed from the beginning. What the community is going through is not designed by God to break them, but is an opportunity for their moral formation as they learn to draw on God's reliable goodness.

1:17   For moral formation to take place in this situation, James now states, the messianic community must know that God is altogether good. James makes three basic points. In making these points, he *assumes* that God is good and does not even begin to attempt to prove it.[286] First, James con-

284. Philo responds to the same issue: *De Fuga et Inventione* 79-80.
285. See Davids, 86.
286. It is possible that James is quoting a poetic fragment in πᾶσα δόσις ἀγαθὴ καὶ πᾶν δώρημα τέλειον. Hexameters (a six-beat rhythm) were common in Greek, and it is possible that James wanted to begin with this, which led him away from demonstrating God's goodness first. See BDF §487; Dibelius, 99-100. Don Verseput, "James 1:17 and the Jew-

tends that everything good is from God (1:17a); second, that God does not change in his dispensing of good gifts, that is, in his faithfulness (1:17b); and third, that this same good God has formed the readers into a community by the new birth (1:18).[287] This third part reuses *apokyei* ("gives birth") from 1:15, and shows what God is actually doing. The contrast could not be clearer: as desire leads to sin and sin gives birth to death, so God "gives birth" to "us" through his Word (1:18). The metaphorical children are death or the community, depending on whether a person chooses "desire" or the goodness of God. We turn now to the assertion that all gifts from God are good because God is constant.

James 1:17 seems to operate with some form of dualistic thinking: some things are attributable to God (good things like wisdom), and some things are not (bad things). The latter would be either the persecutions the readers are experiencing or (more likely) their turning tests into temptations. James begins with this: "every generous act of giving, with every perfect gift"[288] comes from God. There is a neat parallelism here, perhaps stemming from some poetic fragment, which suggests to many that the interpreter should not make fine distinctions between these terms but instead should synthesize what is intended to be a double statement of one thing:

> every giving good
> every gift perfect

One therefore need not distinguish "giving" *(dosis)* and "gift" *(dōrēma)* as one need not distinguish "good" *(agathē)* from "perfect" *(teleion).*[289] But it is interesting that James begins this line by speaking of "gifts." The notion of

---

ish Morning Prayers," *NovT* 39 (1997) 177-91, connects the words in 1:17 to recited morning prayers, i.e., the *Shema,* which began (in some traditions) with "He who forms light and darkness" and closed with "Creator of luminaries." See 4Q503; *b. Berakoth* 11b-12a; Jerusalem Talmud *Berakoth* 1:8. Verseput's suggestions stand (and fall) with our ability (or inability) to know the precise form of *Shema* at work in the messianic community.

287. There are other ways to approach James's logic. It is possible that 1:16 calls for the community not to be deceived by their experiences and then 1:17 claims that all experiences are good. I doubt James believes this. The emphasis in 1:17 on the "good" and the "perfect" could be stating that what God gives is always good and perfect; the listeners/readers are recipients of God's gifts, and therefore what they are experiencing is somehow connected to God's goodness. 1:16 responds to the issue of 1:13, which was clarified in 1:14-15. Namely, God is not the source of evil; humans are. Do not be deceived about God's goodness, etc. Critical here is that James *assumes* God's goodness.

288. The NRSV is too subtle; the TNIV is better here: "every good and perfect gift." The Greek is πᾶσα δόσις ἀγαθὴ καὶ πᾶν δώρημα τέλειον. πᾶς as an attribute and as anarthrous indicates "every." See Moule, *Idiom Book,* 94-95; Porter, *Idioms,* 119-20.

289. So also Laws, 72.

gifts has not been on the table, and it suddenly enters here. What I am suggesting is that James wants to begin with this snippet of (what may be) poetry[290] so that he can let this language carry the assumption that God is good and then suggest that the messianic community has experienced and continues to experience God's goodness in a variety of gifts. That James begins with gifts is a possible window into both his mind and the messianic community itself.

The word "good" with "gift" is often understood as "beneficial" or "generous"[291] rather than just morally good. This permits a connection from 1:17 back to 1:5, where *haplōs* was understood as God's simple or generous giving of wisdom to those who ask. When *agathos* is connected to *haplōs* in the sense of "beneficial" or "generous," it permits also an important connection to Matthew 6:22-23 and 7:7-11, where "evil/bad" is understood as stingy and "good" as generous. A similar more economic sense can possibly be found in the root *telei-* ("mature" or "perfect") in James 1:4 and 17. If the "perfect" person of 1:4 is one who responds properly to economic stress, then the "perfect" gift of 1:17 might be that which prods the poor to see these (economic non-)gifts as from the hand of a good God who is at work for their redemption and moral formation. At any rate, the connections of 1:17a to 1:2-8 are suggestive.[292]

Most commentators observe that the singular "gift" the readers need is "wisdom" (*sophia*, 1:5), and 3:15, 17 uses nearly identical language as is found here. Thus,

1:17: Every good giving and every perfect gift is *from above, coming down.* . . .

3:15: Such wisdom does not *come down from above.*

3:17: But the wisdom *from above.* . . .

Wisdom may be seen in James as an antidote to persecution — in that it can protect from persecution, grant the readers wisdom through persecution, or help them endure persecution (as in *4 Maccabees*).[293] And, since they are experiencing tests of all sorts (1:2) and need wisdom for each test (1:5), it is ap-

---

290. See further at C. B. Amphoux, "A propos de Jacques 1,17," *RHPR* 50 (1970) 127-36; Popkes, 120.

291. See BDAG, 3 ("beneficial"); also Hagner, *Matthew* 1.158.

292. Full commitment to such an interpretation of 1:17 could lead to this translation: "every generous gift and every perfect (moral-forming) gift. . . ."

293. See J. C. Poirier, "Symbols of Wisdom in James 1:17," *JTS* 57 (2006) 57-75, who buttresses the wisdom understanding of these gifts by appealing to Philo, *Questions on Genesis* 3.43. Furthermore, Poirier finds an allusion to the Qumran use of *Urim and Thummim* in the sense of wisdom for enduring persecution (pp. 62-75).

propriate to speak of "gifts" in the plural (1:17). It is also possible, and rarely observed, that James is thinking of economic gifts, namely, Paul's "gifts" from Diaspora Christians for the poor saints in Jerusalem, for, that is, the messianic community to which James is writing (Phil 4:15; Gal 2:10; Acts 11:27-30).[294] The implications of this view for reading James 1:2-18 are significant, since then, once again, what James has in mind throughout this section is the economic stresses on the messianic community.[295] James, if this view be accepted, may understand these gifts as a token of the eschatological nature of the messianic community (cf. 1:18: "first fruits").[296]

James believes God is always good and that it is God's grace that makes these "gifts" good; in fact, everything from God is good.[297] These gifts, however they might be understood, are "from above, coming down from the Father of lights" (1:17b).[298] James uses "from above" *(anōthen)*[299] three times (1:17; 3:15, 17), and it describes what is "heavenly" or "from God" in contrast to what is "earthly" and "demonic" (3:15).[300]

If the general image is clear — all good things come from God in heaven — the specifics are not. Trouble confronts the interpreter of "the Father of lights." In general, there are three options: that "lights" refers to (1) "stars" and planets,[301] (2) human rulers,[302] or (3) angels.[303] Few consider the second option viable, and closer scrutiny reveals that the first and third are more similar than they might first appear. The ancients considered the

---

294. See McKnight, "Collection for the Saints." Gal 6:6-10 is suggestive of a parallel to Jas 1:17a: ἐν πᾶσιν ἀγαθοῖς (Gal 6:6), μὴ πλανᾶσθε (6:7a), τὸ ἀγαθὸν πρὸς πάντας, μάλιστα δὲ πρὸς τοὺς οἰκείους τῆς πίστεως (6:10), which leads one to wonder if the "household of faith" might not be the Jerusalem community. See Hurtado, "The Jerusalem Collection."

295. This could be implicit in the use of τέλειον in 1:4 and 1:17. If the "perfect" person of 1:4 is the one who handles economic stress properly, then the "perfect" gift of 1:17 might be that which prods the poor to see these gifts as from the hand of a good God who is at work for their redemption.

296. Cf. Rom 11:9-26; 2 Cor 9:10-12.

297. Philo, *De Sacrificiis Abelis et Caini* 63; *De Posteritate Caini* 80; *De Migratione Abrahami* 73 ("all his gifts are full and complete [τέλεια]").

298. καταβαῖνον could either modify ἄνωθεν or be a periphrasis with ἐστίν. The former is more likely (see discussions in Davids, 86-87; Laws, 66, 72). The presents sketch the descent of gifts from God in a vivid manner.

299. BDAG, 92.

300. John is similar: cf. John 3:3, 7, 31; 19:11, 23.

301. Davids, 87; Martin, 38; Burchard, 75; Johnson, 196; Blomberg and Kamell, 74.

302. H. Conzelmann, in *TDNT* 9.319-27.

303. See the informed study of Allison, *Studies in Matthew,* 17-41, on whom I rely here.

stars to be angels (cf. Judg 5:20; Job 38:7). In fact, as Dale Allison observes, "in antiquity stars were widely thought to be alive."[304] As stars fall from the sky out of the heavens, so do angels and demons (Genesis 28; Isa 14:12; *3 Macc* 6:16-29; *Joseph and Aseneth* 14:1-7; Revelation 12:4; 18:1; 20:1).[305] James then affirms that God is good/faithful and that every good thing comes down from the Father[306] of the angelic lights. Of course, there is inherent to this a reflection on God/Father as creator, and one thinks of the series of similar expressions in Psalm 136 (LXX 135).[307]

The issue for James is not that we can now discern his cosmology. Rather, the stars represent a dramatic exhibition either of the routine, consistent, and constant or of the constantly changing and shifting pattern of the angelic bodies in the skies. With the first, God is like the faithfulness of these fixed bodies in the heavenlies, his goodness can therefore be counted on, and the temptations the community faces are not from God. Or God is *unlike* the astral bodies with their constant change and is not both a testing and a tempting God.[308] Either way, "the Father of lights" is one "with whom[309] there is no variation or shadow due to change,"[310] and the temptations do not derive

304. Allison, *Studies in Matthew,* 22. Allison points to the following four texts in Philo: *De Plantatione* 12; *De Gigantibus* 8; *De Somniis* 1.135; *De Opificio Mundi* 73.

305. For further texts, see especially Allison, *Studies in Matthew,* 36-41.

306. On Father, see 1:17, 27; 3:9. In these texts, God as Father evokes mercy for humans as their creator and redeemer. See Ng, "Father-God Language," 43-48. The discussion on God as Father has been recently summarized in Dunn, *Jesus Remembered,* 548-55.

307. Cf. Jas 1:17a with LXX Ps 135:1, 25, 26; 1:18a with LXX Ps 135:10, 25. This is pointed out in Ng, "Father-God Language," 47.

308. Moo, 78-79.

309. παρ᾽ ᾧ means "in whom" or "with whom." See Davids, 87; Martin, 39.

310. The condition of the text is problematic. A good discussion can be found in Metzger, *Textual Commentary, ad loc;* Johnson, 196-97; also Ropes, 162-64. The texts for each can be found in *Novum Testamentum Graecum: Editio Critica Maior* IV, p. 14. The options are:

(1) παραλλαγη η τροπης αποσκιασμα

(2) παραλλαγη ουδε τροπης αποσκιασμα

(3) παραλλαγη η τροπος αποσκιασμα

(4) παραλλαγη η τροπης αποσκιασματος

(5) παραλλαγη η τροπη αποσκιασματος

(6) παραλλαγης η τροπης αποσκιασματος

(7) παραλλαγη η ροπη αποσκιασματος

(8) παραλλαγη η ροπης αποσκιασμα

(9) ουδεν αποσκιασματος η τροπης η παραλλαγης

(10) παραλλαγη η τροπη η τροπης αποσκιασμα ουδε μεχρι υπονοιας τινος υποβολη αποσκιασματος

from God. The logical flow seems to favor the view that James sees God and the stars alike in their constancy, for it would be hard to know why he would bring up the stars if only to say God is not like them. The vocabulary, however, favors the more common view that James has brought up the stars in their changes only to deny their similarity to God. Thus, James sees God as does John in 1 John 1:5: "God is light and in him there is no darkness at all."[311]

So both "variation" and "shadow due to change" probably (though not certainly) come from language used to describe stars and heavenly bodies in their various sorts of changes and shifts across the sky.[312] Thus Sirach 27:11: "The conversation of the godly is always wise, but the fool changes like the moon." And, since wisdom from James 1:5 may still be in view, observe that James could be connected to Wisdom 7:29-30:

> She [wisdom] is more beautiful than the sun,
>   and excels every constellation of the stars.
> Compared with the light she is found to be superior,
>   for it is succeeded by the night,
> but against wisdom evil does not prevail.

James is saying either that humans can be like the planets and stars in their motion and change by doubting God and accusing him of tempting them (cf. 1:5-8, 13), or that God creates and controls the changes of the stars but does not himself change in his faithfulness and so is constantly good and therefore not the one causing these temptations. Or, and there is no reason to choose between the two, James could be saying both: the messianic community can either trust God's goodness, which never changes in its faithfulness, or be like the stars in their constant fluctuations.[313] A verse like Malachi 3:6 is behind all this: "For I the Lord do not change."

1:18 Perhaps the most remarkable statement here is that the "Father

---

(11) παραλλαγη η τροπης αποσκιασμα ουδε μεχρι υπονοιας τινος υποβολη αποσκιασματος

(12) καταλλαγη η τροπης αποσκιασμα.

Nestle-Aland uses (1) with good reasons: the text is the least problematic; the readings are widespread and early (except for being found in the corrector of Sinaiticus and not in B); and it probably explains the origins of the others. In spite of this diversity, the general sense of the text remains the same.

311. See Isa 60:19-20; Wis 7:29-30; Job 15:15; 25:5-6.

312. παραλλαγή, BDAG, 768 ("change, variation"). τροπῆς ἀποσκίασμα, BDAG, 1016 ("turn, turning, change") and 120 ("shadow"). Hence, "no change or shifting of shadow." A good discussion can be found in Davids, 88; Burchard, 76-77.

313. See Martin, 38-39.

of lights," that is, their creator, who does not change in his goodness while the stars go about all their changes, has chosen to give to the messianic community a new birth. This new birth, so the logical flow of 1:2-18 would suggest, enables the messianic community to be like God in constancy and fidelity as it undergoes testing. His goodness is available to the community because he is the Father of the community.

James does not always spell out his logic as clearly as Paul, Peter, and the author of Hebrews do.[314] He has moved from testing to temptations, and through what he says we see that some were questioning God's constant goodness. He began his critique of such questioning in 1:16, and in its place he offers a vision of the constant goodness of God. Everything good, he argues, comes from God (1:17) and this God does not change like the angelic stars above. Now, to show that this constancy needs to take root in the community, James argues that this constantly good God has given the members of the community birth.[315] James looks at this birth in three stages: (1) God's *choice of regeneration* (1:18a), (2) the *means* of that new birth (1:18b), and (3) the *intended goal* of that new birth (1:18c). We will look at the first and third before the second.

First, God's choice of regeneration (1:18a). God's constancy is anchored in the community because God, "in fulfillment of his own purpose," has created this community. "In fulfillment of his own purpose" is a fulsome translation of the Greek word *boulētheis*[316] and is not completely understood until it is tied to the last words of the verse: "so that we would become a kind of first fruits of his creatures." Clearly, God's *boulē* is in contrast to the messianic community's tendency to express itself in *epithymia* ("desire").[317] The emphatic position is given to *boulētheis* as a way of introducing "gave us birth": God's global *intention* is to give birth to the messianic community. *Human* "desire" *(epithymia)* leads to sin and death; *God's* "desire" *(boulētheis)* leads to new birth and a community.[318]

---

314. Further, the sentence opens up with an asyndeton.

315. For other views, see Davids, 88-90, who sees 1:18 as an example of God's goodness; Laws, 75, who sees here a commentary on what "Father" means; Martin, 39, who sees a contrast here between God's desire (βουληθείς) and human desire (1:14-15).

316. On βούλομαι, see BDAG, 182. Philo, *De Opificio Mundi* 16, 44, 77; *De Plantatione* 14. Philo was fond of this term. The aorist is the global assumption more than the cause.

317. Interestingly, the two major translations of βούλομαι are "desire" and "intention." See also at 3:4; 4:4, and the categories in *GEL* 1.357-59.

318. The theology connected to God's *boulē* of a people continues to be fruitful; see D. Novak, *The Election of Israel: The Idea of the Chosen People* (Cambridge: Cambridge University Press, 1995); R. Kendall Soulen, *The God of Israel and Christian Theology* (Minneapolis: Fortress, 1996); C. E. Braaten and R. W. Jenson, eds., *Jews and*

With "he gave us[319] birth" James reuses a term *(apokyeō)* from 1:15 and sets in contrast again human desire and divine intent and creation: the human desire that produces sin gives birth to (or "delivers") death, but the divine intent is to "deliver" the eschatological community ("gave *us* birth") to the world. What John expresses as a "birth from above" (John 1:12-13; 3:3), Paul as a Spirit-created new life (Gal 3:21; Rom 4:17; 8:11; 1 Cor 15:22, 36, 45; 2 Cor 3:6; 5:17; Tit 3:4-7), and Peter as a "new birth" (1 Pet 1:3-5, 23; 2:2-3), James sees as "divine delivery" of the ecclesial community into the world.[320]

Second, the intended goal (1:18c). James says God's delivery of the first fruits pertains to "his creatures."[321] There are three possible ideas connected to this: it could refer to created matter in distinction to humans, to created matter including humans, or more narrowly to the global ecclesial community or the future ecclesial community as distinguished from the messianic community. Since James does not offer us any other evidence, we cannot be confident of any of these options. Since he has just mentioned astral phenomena (1:17), the rest of the created order is not out of question, though I am inclined to think that James is closer here to the Apostle Paul than to any other person of antiquity. In other words, I suspect James is referring here to the messianic community as a harbinger of a universal ecclesial community — perhaps even the kingdom of God. This would include all of creation.[322] James is not alone in giving cosmic significance to this divine birthing of the messianic community: Matt 19:28 speaks of the "renewal of all things," Peter's speech in Acts refers to the restoration of "everything" (Acts 3:19-21), and Paul speaks of "the whole creation groaning" and of creation itself being liberated (Rom 8:19-24), and nothing compares to 2 Peter 3:10-13 or to John's

Christians: People of God (Grand Rapids: Eerdmans, 2003); C. J. H. Wright, *The Mission of God* (Downers Grove: InterVarsity, 2006), 191-264; B. K. Waltke, *An Old Testament Theology* (with C. Yu; Grand Rapids: Zondervan, 2007), 305-75.

319. I doubt this refers to humans as the peak of creation (e.g., Jas 3:9; Luke 3:38; Acts 17:28-29; etc.) or to Israel as "God's son" (Deut 32:18; Hos 11:1; etc.); rather, it refers to the community, indeed the messianic community, as the "first fruits." See here L. E. Elliott-Binns, "James I.18: Creation or Redemption?" *NTS* 3 (1956-57) 148-61; Laws, 75-78. Contrary to Laws, the critical factors here are to be found in ἀπαρχή, where the "newness" of a "new" birth is found, and in this new birth occurring through λόγῳ ἀληθείας, which is not a creation category. See also Hort, 33-35; Popkes, 123-24.

320. See Anglican theologian Peter Toon, *Born Again: A Biblical and Theological Study of Regeneration* (Grand Rapids: Baker, 1987). Davids, 88-89, rightly contests the notion that this must refer to a primordial god. See also M. J. Evans, 777, and J. David Miller, "Can the 'Father of Light' Give Birth?" *Priscilla Papers* 19 (2005) 5-7, both of whom call our attention to a feminine image here for God as mothering.

321. κτισμάτων, BDAG, 573. See also 1 Tim 4:4; Rev 5:13; 8:9.

322. See Davids, 90.

final words (Rev 21:1-4). James says the divine delivery of the messianic community was so that it would be "a kind[323] of first fruits of his creatures."

Understanding the messianic community as a kind of first fruits[324] is a profound indicator of James's inaugurated eschatology and makes for a close connection to a theme in the Apostle Paul.[325] The "new birth" of James is both intensely personal and structurally ecclesial: God's intent is to restore individuals in the context of a community that has a missional focus on the rest of the world.[326] Paul speaks of one of his converts as "the first fruits in Asia for Christ" (Rom 16:5), of "the house of Stephanas" as "the first fruits of Achaia" (1 Cor 16:15), and of the Thessalonian Christians as "the first fruits for salvation" (2 Thess 2:13). Further, "not only the creation, but we ourselves, who have the first fruits of the Spirit, groan inwardly while we wait for adoption, the redemption of our bodies" (Rom 8:23). And "If the part of the dough offered as first fruits is holy, then the whole batch is holy; and if the root is holy, then the branches also are holy" (Rom 11:16). The relationship of James to Paul has been the subject of intense debate, but in this instance James and Paul are quite similar: both see the ecclesial community as the "first fruits" of God's large-scale redemption of the world.[327] However, if our understanding of James's audience is accurate (cf. 1:10), then it is possible that James and Paul differ at a substantive level: it is possible that James thinks the *aparchē* is the Jewish messianic community, while for Paul it is the first-generation, including Gentile, Spirit-indwelt ecclesial community.[328] The language is remarkable: the first fruit offering was always a Jewish obligation to respect God's ownership of the *Land,* but here that language has perhaps become the act of God (not Israel) for the sake of the world (not the Land).

Third, the means (1:18b). God gives birth to the messianic community into the world as a kind of first fruits "by the word of truth."[329] The first

323. See BDF §301.1.
324. On ἀπαρχή, see BDAG, 98. Spicq, 1.145-52. The allusion is in the first instance to the Jewish offering (Deut 18:3-5; 26:1-10; Num 18:8-12; *m. Bikkurim*) but it does not imply a universalistic theory of redemption; see F. H. Palmer, "James i.18 and the Offering of First-Fruits," *TynBul* 3 (1957) 1-2.
325. See Dibelius, 104-5; Davids, 89; Martin, 40.
326. A good discussion can be found in Grenz, *Renewing the Center,* 287-324.
327. James's use of ἀπαρχή is similar to Paul's use of ἀρραβών. See also Heb 12:23.
328. An indicator of this is that Paul sees Christ as the first-fruits: 1 Cor 15:20, 23. It is entirely possible that Rom 11:16 refers to the messianic community as well.
329. λόγῳ ἀληθείας. The genitive is epexegetical. See on this expression Ludwig, *Wort als Gesetz;* Klein, "Der vollkommene Werk," 129-34; Cheung, *Genre, Composition,* 86-92.

thought that comes to mind for a first-century Jewish reader would be Genesis 1, where God stanched the flow of the *tohu wa-bohu* and turned it all into a pleasing order through his word.[330] God's creative word surrounds everything in James 1:18. The addition of "of truth" *(alētheias)*[331] could well indicate that James is thinking of the gospel message, perhaps the gospel of the kingdom,[332] for the early Christians were clearly convinced that Jesus unraveled the meaning of history and life. "Word" as gospel and "truth" is common enough in the New Testament to make one think that it is in James's mind.[333] For the early Christians, "truth" was both substantive (certain statements were more or less true, 2 Cor 6:4-7) and relational (God alone is Truth; knowing God enlightens humans to that Truth, John 14:6). As Ceslaus Spicq said it, "In a word, the Christian religion is a cult of the truth."[334]

James 1:18 ties together what James has been working to deny: some think God's goodness is inconstant. James thinks God's goodness is constant and that this goodness is grounded in the messianic community by God's word-inspired deliverance: God has himself chosen to create a community that testifies to his eschatological redemption now at work. Thus, there is an ontology or an ontic presence of God at work in the community that can evidently unleash the power for the messianic community to trust God's goodness and to live above and through the stresses they are experiencing at the hands of the rich.

330. Gen 1:3; Pss 33:6; 107:20; 147:15; Isa 55:11; Wis 18:15; Sir 43:26. See also Deut 22:20; Ps 119:43; Prov 22:21; and Jer 23:28 for other uses of "word of truth," though none of them provides the context for Jas 1:18.

331. On ἀλήθεια, see BDAG, 42-43; Spicq, 1.66-86.

332. Blomberg and Kamell, 75, outstrip the evidence of James when they render "word of truth" as "the gospel message — the story of Christ's incarnation, death, and resurrection — and its significance" (p. 75), but they raise a fundamental question: In what way, or ways, was the gospel message (here "word of truth") articulated by James? Clearly James sees a redemptive work in Jesus Christ, in a new birth, in a new community, and in a Torah observance shaped by Lev 19:18, but beyond that we do not know. See Johnson, 197-98; Popkes, 124-25.

333. See Davids, 89. One thinks of common expressions like Matt 7:24, 26, or of Jesus' creative powerful word (8:8, 16), or of the "word of the Kingdom" (13:19). In John we have a similar usage: "anyone who hears my word and believes him who sent me has eternal life" (John 5:24). Most notably, we think of John 1:1-14. The "word" is part of early Christian preaching: Acts 2:40-41; 4:4, 29, 31; 6:7; 8:4; etc. Paul's is a ministry of the word: Rom 15:18; 1 Cor 1:17, 18; 15:2; 2 Cor 2:17; Eph 1:18; 6:19; Col 1:5, 25; 3:16; etc. Johnson, 198.

334. Spicq, 1.75.

3. GENERAL EXHORTATIONS (1:19-27)

Once again, the structural flow of James is unclear, so a variety of options have been proposed, none of them compellingly clear and therefore a flexible caution is in order. The thesis that James contains a series of loosely connected wisdom reflections often appeals to ch. 1 and can discover evidence in its favor in the supposed change of subject at 1:19. This commentary has argued that there is a thematic coherence in 1:2-18, namely the economic oppression of the poor and how they might respond best. I will argue below that the three paragraphs in 1:19-27 fit together into a coherent thematic network and are related to 1:2-18. Therefore, 1:2-27 is not a collection of disconnected ideas but a focused address about how to live under economic oppression.

The three topics of 1:19-27 — speech behavior, hearing *and* doing, and deeds of mercy as pure religion — are clearly important to James and appear elsewhere in the letter. How the messianic community is to conduct its speech patterns comes up throughout 3:1–4:12. Hearing and doing is the focus not only of 1:22-25, but also 2:14-26 and probably also 2:1-13, as 2:12 hints. And the issue of pure religion seems to be what 2:1-13 is all about, if not other sections as well. However the separable units of 1:19-27 are connected, they clearly raise important issues for James elsewhere. To return to a point made in the Introduction about structural proposals: that 1:2-27 can be shown to be James's words about how to deal with economic oppression does not entail the more rigorous suggestion of others that 1:2-27 is a conscious, deliberate anticipation of themes to be developed elsewhere in James. It might be wiser to think that James has one major concern on his mind that emerges regardless of the topics he discusses. (That theory, too, is probably beyond proof.)

It might be suggested at this point that, to read James in context, we could "read back" the specifics of 1:19-27 into 1:2-18 — thus, perhaps "tests," "maturity," "perfection," "wisdom," "poor" and "rich," "blessed," "temptation," and God's goodness (or vacillating goodness) could each be related to speech control, hearing *and* doing, and pure religion. The pure religion of looking after the marginalized in 1:26-27 might be the alternative to the violent speech mentioned in 1:19-21. Also requiring attention is what James really means by "maturity" and "wisdom" in 1:2-4 and 5-8. It is as likely, if not more, that James is speaking to his context throughout than that he is offering for his readers a new set of timeless and context-less proverbial wisdom sayings.

The three parts of 1:19-27, the exhortation on speech (1:19-21), the exhortation on hearing *and* doing (1:22-25), and the exhortation on pure religion (1:26-27), are most likely intertwined by the context of the messianic community, but we will let the exegesis demonstrate the probability of such a conclusion.

3.1. AN EXHORTATION ON SPEECH (1:19-21)

19 *You[1] must understand this, my beloved:[a] let[2] everyone be quick to listen, slow to speak, slow to anger;* 20 *for your anger does not produce[3] God's righteousness.[b]* 21 *Therefore rid yourselves of all sordidness[c] and rank growth[4] of wickedness,[d] and welcome with meekness[e] the implanted word that has the power to[f] save your[5] souls.[g]*

a. TNIV: my dear brothers and sisters

b. TNIV: the righteousness that God desires

c. TNIV: moral filth

d. TNIV: the evil that is so prevalent

e. TNIV: humbly accept

f. TNIV: which can

g. TNIV: save you

The logical flow from 1:12-18 to 1:19-21 is neither smooth nor clear. Some suggest that 1:19a actually finishes off 1:12-18,[6] while the vast majority keep 1:19a in the unit with 1:19b-21. We can think backward to a satisfactory understanding. 1:19b-21 is concerned with communal harmony, and this is ex-

---

1. Some manuscripts have δε (cf. P74, A, 629, 2464, and some Coptic manuscripts). Other manuscripts omit Ἴστε (1838, and many Latin manuscripts). Others have ὥστε instead (P, Y, Maj, 93, 312, and 1842). Nestle-Aland[27] prints the most likely reading, found in ℵ*, B, C, 81, and elsewhere. An interesting reading, supporting those scholars who think James has a double introduction, is found in 631 and two Georgian manuscripts: λοιπον αδελφοι μου αγαπητοι.

2. Again, some omit the δε (cf. majority tradition). See here C. B. Amphoux, "Une relecture de chapitre I de l'Épître de Jacques," *RHPR* 50 (1970) 554-61, here pp. 554-56.

3. Some manuscripts have made a compound of the verb: οὐκ ἐργάζεται becomes οὐ κατεργάζεται (C, P, 0246, 1739, and Maj).

4. Some manuscripts read περισσευμα instead of περισσείαν. One of these is very early; the others are from the tenth century or later: A 33, 436, 442, 1409, 2344, 2541, and L596.

5. The evidence is neatly divided, as it often is, between ὑμῶν and ἡμῶν. The early and major manuscripts read ὑμῶν.

6. Martin, 41, 44. The singular problem is that normally ἀδελφοί μου ἀγαπητοί begins a section.

actly what 1:18 was leading to: as God has given birth to the messianic community as the "first fruits," so that community is to live together in justice.[7] If this approximates the mind of James, then it is quite likely that "you must understand this" should be rendered "you already understand this" — that is, they already understand themselves as the "first fruits" of God's redemptive plan.[8]

This paragraph begins with a rhetorical introduction (1:19a), gives three commands about speech (1:19b-d), and then James gives the reason for the three commands (1:20). An inference is then drawn in 1:21 that sums up the three commands from a different angle (1:21a) and leads to yet a different command that itself re-expresses the three commands with yet another image (1:21b). The structure could be chiastic:[9]

introduction (1:19a)
1. three commands about speech (1:19b-d)
   2. the reason for the commands (1:20)
   2'. inference that sums up the three commands (1:21a)
1'. command that re-expresses the three commands (1:21b)

1:19 In the introduction James assumes what the messianic community knows and connects himself to them with "my beloved."[10] Because they know the divine origins of their community and that their destiny is to be the first fruits, they are to live a life of justice. Their eschatological destiny is to shape their present existence. If the life setting of the messianic community was oppression by the rich, then a singular temptation for each of them would have been revenge and even violence.[11] James makes the point clear:

7. On "justice," see below at 1:20.

8. Ἴστε derives from οἶδα/εἴδω. See BDAG, 693-94; ἴστε can be either imperative ("you must understand") or indicative ("you already understand"). See also 1:3; 3:1; Heb 12:17; Eph 5:5. Most see it as imperative; cf. Dibelius, 109; BDF §99.2; Davids, 91; Martin, 44. But I think it is indicative: see Mayor, 64-65; Johnson, 198-99; Popkes, 128. Understanding ἴστε as an indicative makes for the smoothest logical movement from 1:18 to 1:19a and then on to 1:19b. The issue is abruptness: if ἴστε is an imperative, it becomes prospective (looking forward to 1:19b) and makes for a more sudden and abrupt change of subject. The indicative permits a smoother transition, though smooth transitions should not be the only factor considered.

9. Many are generally skeptical of chiastic structural proposals by New Testament scholars, since more often than not they seem to suggest the ingenuity of the interpreter more than the explicit intention of the author. In this case, I am proposing a general, structural chiasm. On chiasms in general, see N. Lund, *Chiasmus in the New Testament: A Study in the Form and Function of Chiastic Structures* (Peabody: Hendrickson, 1992).

10. See on 1:16.

11. See 3:13–4:12, and commentary on 1:13.

they are the offspring of God and are to live out of that new birth into a new life in the context of a community that forms an alternative society.

James breaks this down into three quick commands: "let everyone be[12] quick to listen, slow to speak, slow to anger." The commands are for "everyone."[13] There is nothing tricky about any of these commands inasmuch as they deal with the basics of a community life in which relationships are characterized by mutual love (2:8-11) as it would be expressed in speech in a Jewish messianic community.[14] It is also clear that James has not simply lapsed into general wisdom comments for anyone who might care to listen. This letter addresses real humans in concrete situations, and we are required to think in terms of its evidence.[15] For James, the justice, not to mention integrity and security, of the messianic community is threatened by some hotheads who are tempted to use violence against the rich. Words and "desires" need to come under the control of the "implanted word."

"Quick to listen."[16] It is true that the language of 1:19b sounds like the wisdom literature of ancient Judaism. Thus, Sirach 5:11: "Be quick to hear, but deliberate in answering."[17] But what is said in the context of a list of sayings of wisdom appears differently when such sayings are baptized into the

12. ἔστω δέ. The present tense indicates the imperfective aspect, that is, the author chooses the present in order to depict action in a way that is uncompleted. The point is not that this is something they are to be doing "now" but more that it is characteristic and timeless. The particle could be a mild adversative or, as I prefer, a mild inference: "So, let everyone be. . . ." It is difficult to make 1:19b an adversative to either an imperatival or indicative ἴστε. It is too speculative (e.g., Davids, 91) to infer that δέ came to James from a pre-James tradition and that he clumsily kept it. No one is that slavish to traditions, especially in Judaism. On all this, see now the thoroughgoing analysis of Dunn, *Jesus Remembered,* 139-336.

13. πᾶς ἄνθρωπος. See Gal 5:3; Col 1:28; John 1:9; 2:10. πᾶς with anarthrous noun in the sense of "each" or "every"; see BDAG, 782 (1[a]).

14. For the background to James's speech ethics, see Baker, *Pesonal Speech-Ethics,* 23-83; for this verse, cf. pp. 84-87.

15. See Introduction; also, again, 1:19-21; 2:5-7; 3:13–4:12. See also Prov 16:32; Eccl 7:9; Sir 5:11; and the discussions in Baker, *Personal Speech-Ethics,* 23-83, who canvasses the ancient literature on controlled speech, listening-words-deeds, and the power of words.

16. ταχὺς εἰς τὸ ἀκοῦσαι. On ταχύς, cf. BDAG, 993; see Matt 5:25; 28:7-8; Luke 15:22; John 11:29; Rev 2:16; 11:14; 22:7, 12, 20. One is tempted to hear the *Shema* behind ἀκοῦσαι, for that is the word so often used to introduce grave utterances in the Old Testament. But the wisdom context is too notable to permit such speculations. The aorist is chosen to depict the hearing as a summative act.

17. Γίνου ταχὺς ἐν ἀκροάσει σου καὶ ἐν μακροθυμίᾳ φθέγγου ἀπόκρισιν. See also Sir 1:22; 6:33, 35; 11:8. It is common also to Proverbs: 12:15; 19:20; 28:9. A full listing can be found in Davids, 92. Bauckham, *Wisdom of James,* 83-84, uses this as a text to build his case for how James has used Jewish wisdom through the lens of Jesus.

waters of James's situation. If the context is the sort of condition we find in James 2:1-7 and 3:13–4:12, as well as 5:1-6, then to be "quick to listen" pertains to the control of the desires (1:13-15) that are leading to conflicts, disputes, and even murders (4:1-2). Just what the members of the community are to listen *to* is not clear, though one thinks here that it might be to one another and to the "other" in the community,[18] to James's own counsel, to the gospel, to the Torah, to wisdom,[19] or, what is contextually immediate, to the "implanted word" of v. 21.[20]

"Slow to speak."[21] This is a counsel less about casual conversation than about reactive verbal confrontations with one another and with the "other" in the community. Again, the language is both common in Proverbs (cf. 17:27) but anchored contextually in a specific situation for James. For James, the wise and perfect person — which is what the messianic community was advised about in 1:4-5 — is one who controls his tongue by not cursing others (3:1-12), who lives with gentleness (3:13), and who avoids strife (3:14). Such a person brings justice (1:20) and peace (3:18). Pointed verbal jabs produce a community at war against itself (4:1-3, 11-12). It is wise, then, to expand "slow to speak" to include at least the counsel to avoid verbal disputes with those with power, that is, the rich.

"Slow to anger."[22] Since James has dealt with interpersonal relations, seemingly at the level of the verbal, in his first two commands, it is likely that he now moves on from the verbal to a more comprehensive view. Some limit this to "verbal" anger and others suggest that it is general,[23] but there are contextual reasons once again to think more concretely. Again, we think of the context of the oppressed poor and the abusive rich (5:1-6), and we need to consider the concrete concerns of James in 3:13–4:12. Some in the messianic community had already or were tempted to rise up in physical violence. James 4:1-2 speaks of "conflicts and disputes among you" and "murder." The same connection is made in *Didache* 3:2: "Do not become angry, for anger

18. Schrage and Balz, 21-22.
19. So Dibelius, 109-10.
20. See Ropes, 168.
21. βραδὺς εἰς τὸ λαλῆσαι. On βραδύς, see BDAG, 183. Only elsewhere in the New Testament at Luke 24:25. The infinitive limits the adjective's compass; see MHT, 3.143. For more references in the Old Testament, cf. Baker, *Personal Speech-Ethics,* 27-42.
22. βραδὺς εἰς ὀργήν. On ὀργή, see BDAG, 720-21; also Mark 3:5 (Jesus); Eph 4:31; Col 3:8; 1 Tim 2:8. Normally, this term in the New Testament refers to the wrath of God (e.g., Rom 1:18; Rev 19:15). See also references in *1 Clem* 13:1; 39:7; 63:2; Ignatius, *Ephesians* 10:2; *Philadelphians* 6:1 (significant parallels to James); 8:1; *Did* 3:2; 15:3; Hermas, *Mandates* 34.4.
23. So Ropes, 169; Dibelius, 110; Laws, 80; Popkes, 129.

leads to murder." It is doubtful that this kind of extension is simply an exaggerated *ad infinitum.* In James 4, as in the context at 1:21, James appeals to an inner spiritual work: "God yearns jealously for the spirit that he has made to dwell in us" (4:5). And in that context, as here, James counsels humility (4:6) and that it is God who will "exalt" the hearer (1:12). The connection between 1:19-21 and 3:13–4:12 is too clear; it is most likely therefore that these verses clarify the social conditions of 1:19b. James worries the messianic community is being tempted to use physical violence and verbal abuse against the rich to establish justice.

1:20 Having gone through three commands,[24] James now comments on *orgē* ("wrath") and states that *orgē* does not effect (produce) *dikaiosynē* ("justice").[25] Here he crosses the line into a pacifistic strain of thought: "for your anger does not produce God's righteousness [or 'justice']." Logically, 1:20 provides the *reason* for the three commands of 1:19b: the readers are to be quick to listen and slow in speech and anger *because* anger does not bring justice.

It is simplest to begin with *orgē* ("anger"). "Your anger"[26] is in bold contrast with "God's righteousness." The NRSV's use of "your" damages the gnomic quality of James's language since a more accurate rendering would be "human anger does not effect God's justice."[27] Again, the language is paralleled in proverbial wisdom,[28] but need not be limited to that context. The "anger" James has in mind is not the routine displays of frustration that attend human life but the violent anger that disrupts communities and leads to physical violence (see 3:13–4:12, especially 4:1-2).[29]

James states that human anger "does not produce"[30] justice. The concern is with "effects," that which one produces (cf. 2:9). Jesus judged people by their effects (Matt 7:23; Mark 14:6), and John roots such effects in the

24. Dibelius speculates on the traditional origins of these three; cf. 111-12.

25. See Baker, *Personal Speech-Ethics,* 88-89.

26. ὀργὴ γὰρ ἀνδρός, "the wrath of man." On ἀνήρ, see comments on 1:12. Also at 1:23; 2:2; 3:2. Mayor, 65, thinks males are in view. Emphasis on males leads one to think of *Lysistrata* by Aristophanes, who wrote the play in response to the crumbling power of Athens in 411 BC. But see also the wry comment of Brosend, 49; Johnson, 200.

27. See also Johnson, 200, who translates "a man's anger."

28. See Sir 1:22: "Unjust anger cannot be justified" (οὐ δυνήσεται θυμὸς ἄδικος δικαιωθῆναι). The debilitating anger of Moses is famous: Ps 106:32-33.

29. Reicke long ago connected this "anger" to the rage of the Zealots (pp. 20-21). There is no evidence in James that the messianic community was worried about Rome. The power group of most concern to James is the "rich," and perhaps the priestly establishment.

30. οὐκ ἐργάζεται; see BDAG, 389 ("bring about, give rise to"). So Dibelius, 110; Martin, 48. The present tense (imperfective aspect) is used to render the verb/action timeless and vivid.

work of God (John 3:21; 5:17; 6:28-29; 9:4). Paul, too, focused on effects (Rom 2:10; 13:10).[31] A direct parallel is Hebrews 11:33, where the Jewish saints are those who "administered [*ergazomai*] justice [*dikaiosynē*]." Anger, James says, does not effect the justice God wants.

With the expression "justice of God" (NRSV, TNIV: "righteousness") we enter a New Testament quagmire.[32] The term *dikaiosynē theou* ("righteousness/justice of God") has two possible meanings: (1) God's *own* righteousness in the sense of (a) God's being morally righteous/just or (b) God's salvation-creating power and saving action, or (2) God's righteousness *given to humans* (c) as a standing[33] or (d) as a behavioral moral attribute that emerges from redemption.[34] In (2) one need not choose between (c) and (d) since God's saving activity both grants a status and prompts righteous/just behaviors. James 1:20 uses the term in the first sense, as an attribute of God ("the justice *of God*"), but this attribute of God is what God is accomplishing in this world, so (b) seems the most likely meaning. In addition, because one cannot demand that only one sense is operating, (d) becomes a likelihood as the human response mirroring God's work of establishing righteousness. Thus, "righteousness/justice of God" refers to the inability on the part of humans to use "anger" to bring about God's saving action as these same humans seek to establish God's will in society.

The use of *dikaiosynē* (b) in this context is, then, nearly synonymous with Jesus' use of *kingdom (baseileia/malkut)* since it is "God's" justice that is being established. Thus, it is at the same time nearly synonymous with "salvation" or "God's saving action." Thus, James 1:20 is much like LXX Isaiah 46:13: "I bring near my deliverance [*dikaiosynē*], and my salvation will not tarry; I will give my salvation in Zion, to Israel for glory." But, there is much to be said for (d) as well. James is countering some messianists who think they can bring about God's saving action/justice by means of "anger," so clearly James has in mind something humans are involved in. I have translated this term "justice" since "righteousness" shifts the term into Reformation debates, tends to narrow it to individual sanctity or forensic status, and blunts the community force of what James is saying. Once again, we need to think in context. In James 3:18 we have a nearly identical idea: "And a harvest [effect] of justice [*dikaiosynē*] is sown in peace for those who make peace." In the Bible and Judaism, *tsedeq/dikaiosynē* has always been a description or category of humans whose behavior conforms to the covenant re-

---

31. Paul's theology was shaped by divine provision as well: Rom 4:4-5.

32. See Reumann, *Righteousness,* 148-58.

33. Mayor, 66, emphasizes the gift element in James (see 1:5, 18; 3:17).

34. A good chart can be seen in N. T. Wright, *What Saint Paul Really Said,* 101; see also Dunn, *Theology,* 334-89; Moo, *Romans,* 79-90.

lationship with God and to the Torah as an expression of that covenant (see Phil 3:6). That is, the "righteous person" is Torah-observant. It is only with Paul that the notion of a legal standing, that is, an imputed or forensic righteousness, comes to the fore. Without clear evidence to the contrary, the term means what it always meant (Judaism's usage) — and thus we are led to think that James is describing here, in addition to (b) above, either an individual conformity to the will of God or to a community/society living within that will of God. The contexts in James are concerned preeminently with social discord and peace at the community level. We conclude that James is thinking about social harmony, where things are done right, that is, about *dikaiosynē* as "justice," and he opposes that to thoughts that God's kind of society can be produced through violent actions and force.[35] In the context of James's emphases, one would have to think that "justice" is the saving action of God that brings about behavior and conditions that conform to "the perfect law, the law of liberty" (1:25; 2:12), which could be the same as the "royal law" of love for neighbor (2:8-9).[36] James's standard, then, is loving relations with others, and "justice" is behavior and conditions[37] that conform to that standard.

1:21   Now James clarifies the conditions he is most concerned about by urging the messianic community, in substantive parallel with 1:19b, to do two things: to put away sin and to receive the implanted word.[38] "Therefore" grounds these exhortations on 1:19-20:[39] they know better, they are to communicate in love, and justice cannot be established through anger, so *therefore* they are to get rid of the sins that prevent justice. As this verse builds on what has been said before, it also restates in different language the commands of 1:19b. There, James was concerned with communication and anger; here he is concerned with "all sordidness and rank growth of wickedness." The language trades in the world of purity and James sees purity in fig-

35. The Hebrew *tsedeq* is behind all of this discussion; the discussion here is immense, but the two best studies remain Sanders, *PPJ*, 183-205; Przybylski, *Righteousness in Matthew*. The term means "behavior that conforms to the will/Torah of God." This is the meaning of the term in Matthew (e.g., 3:15; 5:6, 10, 20; 6:1, 33; 21:32) and here in James. Paul develops the idea that "righteousness" is a declared standing with God on the basis of the righteousness of another (Christ). *Tsedeq/justice/righteousness* always is a relational term in that it speaks of a standard and whether a person lives according to that standard or relationship. The standard in James is "God," which probably is explained by the Torah as interpreted/understood by Jesus and James, and a "righteous/just" person is one who lives according to that understanding.

36. For discussions, cf. Mayor, 66; Ropes, 169; Dibelius, 111; Laws, 81; Davids, 93; Martin, 47-48.

37. Seen more accurately by Martin, 47-48.

38. One thinks here of a similar set of injunctions in 1 Pet 2:11-12.

39. *Contra* Dibelius, 112, who connects 1:21 with 1:22-25. See Davids, 93.

urative categories.[40] The import of the social setting is largely the same, as we have already seen.

James's use of "rid yourselves"[41] draws on the catechetical moral tradition of earliest Christianity, and it may derive from a baptismal ceremony or perhaps circumcision.[42] The new life of the follower of Jesus includes both renunciation of vices and assumption of virtues[43] and ought not include "sordidness" *(ryparian)*[44] or "rank growth of wickedness" *(perisseian kakias)*.[45] The NRSV translation is archaic: TNIV's "moral filth" and "prevalent evil" is clearer. But it is not clear whether James has two specific sins in mind or is using synonyms for one.[46] General terms like this do not make for tidy distinctions.[47]

Structurally, if 1:21a parallels 1:19b, then by *pasan ryparian kai perisseian kakias* James would be speaking of verbal sins and anger, and this

40. See Lockett, *Purity and Worldview,* 108-12. Lockett's focus in his study is on the figurative use of the category of purity and how James rhetorically uses the category to frame two opposing worldviews, one focused on Christ and the other on the world. See also J. Klawaans, *Impurity and Sin in Ancient Judaism* (New York: Oxford University Press, 2000).

41. ἀποθέμενοι, from ἀποτίθημι. See BDAG, 123-24 ("lay aside"). See Rom 13:12; Eph 4:22; Col 3:8; Heb 12:1; 1 Pet 2:1. The aorist middle participle is sometimes taken to be "imperatival." See Porter, *Idioms,* 181-93; *Verbal Aspect,* 370-77. It is best to see it as ranking behind δέξασθε in importance in this verse but taking on some of its imperatival force. It is more than simple adverbial modification ("receive by/in/while ridding oneself"). Both participle and verb are aorist, indicating global perception of the action. "Ridding" and "receiving" are contemporary actions; neither precedes or follows the other if one approaches the issue through aspectual theory (*pace* Baker, *Personal Speech-Ethics,* 89).

42. The definitive study here remains E. G. Selwyn, *The First Epistle of St. Peter* (New York: Macmillan, 1961), 363-466; his view is endorsed in J. H. Elliott, *1 Peter* (AB 37B; New York: Doubleday, 2000), 395-96. Allison, "Exegetical Amnesia," 165-66, calls our attention to the older view that this line in 1:21 could refer to circumcision.

43. Renunciations: cf. 1 Pet 2:1-2; 4:1; Rom 13:12, 14; Col 3:5-10, 12; Eph 4:17-19, 22, 24-26, 29, 31; 1 John 2:15; Heb 12:1; also 1 Thess 5:8; Gal 3:27. On assumptions: cf. e.g., Rom 12–13; 1 Pet 2:3-4; 3:8-9; 4:8-11.

44. πᾶσαν ῥυπαρίαν, BDAG, 908. The πᾶσαν indicates "all" as in "any kind at all" or "every."

45. περισσείαν κακίας, BDAG, 804-5. κακίας is epexegetic with περισσείαν, for James cannot think they need to get rid only of the "surplus" of evil while holding on to the rest. See Paul's use of περισσεία for the gifts of redemption and fellowship: Rom 5:17; 2 Cor 8:2; 10:15. Luke 6:45 uses a cognate for what comes from the heart and out of the mouth and in this regard is probably most like Jas 1:21.

46. So Mayor, 67. On parallelism, see Kugel, *Idea of Biblical Poetry.*

47. This undercuts the attempt by many to see a specific image here: "rank growth" of vice (surviving from pre-Jesus days?) that needs to be lopped off. See discussions in Dibelius, 113; Laws, 82; Davids, 94.

is confirmed from other contexts. The only other passage where James uses general moral language is 3:1-18, where there are clear similarities, and 4:1-2 and 11-12, where again there are similarities. In these contexts, the issue is communal division, verbal fisticuffs, interpersonal strife, and potential physical violence. In particular, "meekness" *(praütēs)* and "justice" *(dikaiosynē)* are what James commends in both 1:21 and 3:13, 18. The language of 4:10 ("humble yourselves") is along the same line. Thus, there is reason to think James is using general language in 1:21a for what he has already spoken against in 1:19b-d. To be sure, it has frequently been argued that James is speaking simply of general moral filth.[48] The context, however, suggests that he has something more specific in mind: his worry is anger and retaliation; his exhortation is toward justice, peace, and love in both emotion and speech.[49]

There is some debate over where "with meekness" belongs. Does it belong with "rid yourselves . . . with meekness" (Nestle-Aland) or with "welcome with meekness" (NRSV, TNIV).[50] Both make sense, for in the first case "meekness" would virtually define what getting rid of vices means, while in the second it would refer to the vulnerability needed in reception of the Word. The evidence from how "meekness" *(praütēs)* is used with such verbs and participles elsewhere in the New Testament[51] suggests that "with meekness" goes with what precedes: "rid yourselves . . . with meekness,"[52] but the case is not closed. "Meek" people, those who avoid the social strife James is so concerned about (3:13), correspond to the *Anawim* mentioned, for instance, in Luke 1–2 and in Jesus' Beatitudes. We are dealing here then, most probably, with more than a simple moral virtue, with a social class, the poor of 1:9 and elsewhere in James, who need to be reminded that they can wait on God for his redemptive justice and peace to be established (cf. 5:1-6, 7-11). As such, these "meek" *Anawim* are to be distinguished from those characterized by "anger" *(orgē,* 1:19-20), who may well have aligned themselves with the Zealot movement. It is important to understand that both the *Anawim* and the Zealots had the same vision for Israel and the kingdom of God: they differed widely on how to achieve that kingdom.[53]

James moves on to a positive exhortation with "welcome."[54] The

---

48. Ropes, 170; Dibelius, 113. See Job 14:4; Isa 64:6; Zech 3:4; Rev 22:11.

49. Laws, 81.

50. Davids, 94; Martin, 44; Popkes, 133.

51. See Gal 6:1; 1 Cor 4:21; 2 Cor 10:1; Eph 4:1-2; 1 Pet 3:15-16. The only exception is 2 Tim 2:25; but see also Sir 3:17.

52. A substantial parallel is found in Gal 6:1-5.

53. On the historical context, see Hengel, *The Zealots;* W. Heard and C. A. Evans, "Revolutionary Movements, Jewish," in *DNTB* 936-47.

54. δέξασθε, from δέχομαι. See BDAG, 221-22. The imperative is used four times in the New Testament: 2 Cor 11:16; Eph 6:17; Col 4:10; Jas 1:21. The verb is found with

translation could be stronger: "receive" or "absorb" or "surrender to." It describes letting the Word have its way with one's heart and life so that a person learns to live in accordance with that Word as a Torah-observant person.[55] One who "welcomes" is, then, is like the "doer of the word" of 1:22.

The Word is identified as "the implanted word," to which there is no clear parallel.[56] But "implanted" *(emphytos)* is used figuratively in *Barnabas* 1:2 and 9:9: "you have received such a measure of his grace *planted within you*"; "the one who has placed the *implanted* gift of his covenant in us knew these things." The word can also mean "innate,"[57] which might suggest that James has in mind the Judaic notion of God's image struck in the heart of every human, to which each person is summoned to respond (3:9), or to a more Stoic notion of inborn reason.[58] What discounts the latter most is that James uses *logos* elsewhere as a near equivalent to Torah (see especially 1:18, 22-25), and one would probably not be told to receive something that is innate. James could also have in mind a counter-power to "inborn wickedness" in Wisdom 12:10: "though you were not unaware that their origin was evil and their wickedness inborn."[59] Or even the wisdom they received from their teachers.[60] It is more likely, given James's concern for Torah, Logos, and Torah observance, that he has in mind the idea of having the Torah in one's soul (cf. Deut 30:1, 11-14; Jer 31:33). But, this understanding probably has shifted focus for James.

"*Im*planted word" is the most likely meaning and implies that God has done a work in the believers. But this gives us only a general idea. More particularly, does James use this expression for (1) the "new birth," (2) the "new covenant" of Jeremiah 31, (3) the "Holy Spirit" as a received gift or (4) the "Word of God" when appropriated or incorporated or acted upon in faith? The evidence could support options 1, 2, and 3 in light of passages like Joel 2:28-32; Isaiah 32:15; 34:16-17; 59:21; Deuteronomy 30:11-14; Jeremiah 31:31-34; Ezekiel 36:22-38;[61] 4Q504 (fragments 1-2, column 2); and James

---

λόγος: cf. Matt 10:14; Luke 8:13; Acts 8:14; 11:1; 17:11; 1 Thess 1:6; 2:13. In these other instances it refers to a response to the "gospel" in an initiatory way. See Laws, 83. The aorist does not indicate "once and for all" but is used in order to depict the action in a global manner. The emphasis is *that* they are to receive, not *when* or *how*.

55. See Dibelius, 114; Ropes, 171; Davids, 95.

56. τὸν ἔμφυτον λόγον. On ἔμφυτος, see BDAG, 326-27; also Klein, *"Ein vollkommenes Werk,"* 135-37; Cheung, *Genre, Composition,* 86-92.

57. See the discussions in Adamson, 98-100; Laws, 82-85; Popkes, 134-35.

58. See Jackson-McCabe, *Logos and Law.*

59. οὐκ ἀγνοῶν ὅτι πονηρὰ ἡ γένεσις αὐτῶν καὶ ἔμφυτος ἡ κακία αὐτῶν. See Cheung, *Genre, Composition,* 90.

60. Wall, 73.

61. See McKnight, "Covenant and Spirit," 49-53. One thinks also of John 14:26; 1 John 2:20; 1 Cor 2:13.

1:18, 22-25; and perhaps 2:8-11. For James the "implanted word" is the "word of truth" (1:18), the "saving word" (1:21), "the perfect law, the law of liberty" (1:25), and the "royal law" (2:8). As well, we need to consider the parallel at 4:5: "God," according to some Scripture,[62] "yearns jealously for the spirit that he has made to dwell in us." If James is using this notion, then the "implanted" word of 1:21 refers to the indwelling of the Holy Spirit. We cannot be sure that James is thinking of any of these four options in particular. What we have is a glimpse here into some of the earliest messianic thinking about Torah, Word of God, gospel, and Spirit.

The "implanted word" has the effective "power to save your souls."[63] James seems to consider the "implanted word" one of the gifts of the eschatological age for the messianic community. "Power" is one of the features of that age because of the presence of God, who is Power.[64] With "save" James lands on a term that will become fundamental to Pauline theology, but if we read James in context, then we are led to see this term as an eschatological reward, since that is what it most likely means in 2:14; 4:12; and 5:20.[65] We need to be careful to use the evidence we find in James: if 1:21b is largely synonymous with 1:20, then this salvation and "God's justice" could be the same thing — in which case James would be describing the establishment of the kingdom of God.

Similar considerations are to be kept in mind when we look at "soul" in 1:21b. James could refer to the "self" or to "life" or to "soul."[66] Which means that he could be thinking in altogether earthly terms: if you do this you will stay alive, or in eschatological terms: the word will grant you the kingdom of God. We cannot be sure, but the emphasis so far would at least open the possibility that James is counseling the messianic community to avoid violence and volatility in order to stay alive as it seeks to establish and waits for God's kingdom.

---

62. See commentary on 4:5.

63. τὸν δυνάμενον σῶσαι τὰς ψυχὰς ὑμῶν. The present participle is used to indicate a characteristic property of the ἔμφυτον λόγον: it saves.

64. The two major terms are δύναμις and ἐξουσία. While the majority of such references are to miracles (e.g., Mark 6:2, 14; Acts 1:8; 2:22; 3:12; 4:7, 33; 8:10; 10:38; see also Jas 5:15), in James the notion is the eternal effective saving power of God (2:14; 4:12; 5:20). See also Rom 1:16; 1 Pet 1:9; Heb 10:39. On God, see Mark 14:62.

65. At 5:15 it refers, as it often does in the Gospels, to physical healing.

66. On this, see especially H. W. Wolff, *Anthropology of the Old Testament* (trans. M. Kohl; London: SCM, 1974), 7-79. Ψυχή, which normally translates נֶפֶשׁ *(nephesh),* can be rendered "soul" or "life" or "person." See H. Seebass, in *TDOT* 9.497-519.

3.2. AN EXHORTATION ON HEARING AND DOING (1:22-25)

22 But be doers of the word,[67] and not merely[68] hearers who deceive themselves.[a] 23 For[69] if any are hearers of the word[70] and not doers, they are like those who look at themselves[b] in a mirror; 24 for they look at themselves and, on going away, immediately forget what they were like. 25 But those who look[c] into the perfect law, the law of liberty, and persevere,[d] being not hearers who forget[71] but doers who act — they will be blessed in their doing.

    a. TNIV alters the word order: Do not merely listen to the word, and so deceive yourselves. Do what it says.

    b. TNIV: their faces

    c. TNIV: intently

    d. TNIV: continue in it

The move from 1:19-21 to 1:22-25 is a natural one, if also artistic. As the focus there moved to the "implanted word" (1:21b), so here James picks up on the term "word" (1:22) and develops it. And, as the exhortation in 1:21b was to "welcome" the implanted word, which re-expressed ridding oneself of sin (1:21a), so here James maintains that the messianic community are to be "doers of the word, and not merely hearers." Those who hear only, like the "angry" and volatile of 1:19b, are deceiving themselves and will never see jus-

---

    67. Manuscripts show two options: λόγου and νόμου. The former is supported by a widely and early-attested set of manuscripts (P74, ℵ, A, B, C, P, Ψ, 5.81, and Maj), while the second conforms to Jas 4:11 and has some good support (C [sixth-century variant], 88, 398, 1845, and 1874). Internally, 1:18, 1:21, and 1:23 support λόγου, while 1:25 supports νόμου.

    68. Word order is an issue: μόνον is an adverb, and its suspension until after ἀκροαταί lessens its force. This harder reading, though not chosen in Nestle-Aland[27], is found in *Editio Critica Maior,* one of only two differences between these two editions of James. The suspension, besides being the *lectio difficilior,* is supported by B, 206, 398, 1611, and 2138 and found in Latin, Syriac, and Georgian manuscripts. The earliest manuscripts support the Nestle-Aland[27] reading. Understanding the text as "be . . . not merely hearers" or "be . . . not hearers only" carries a subtle difference between an adverbial and adjectival emphasis.

    69. Translates ὅτι, which is omitted in some good manuscripts (P74, A, 33, 81, etc.). Its presence in most of the early manuscripts as well as in Maj favors its inclusion.

    70. Again, as in 1:22, some manuscripts, though fewer, have νόμου.

    71. Some manuscripts add οὗτος before οὐκ, thereby clarifying the sentence by resuming the subject (and creating a suspended subject clause). The manuscripts adding it include P, Ψ, 398, 623, and a Byzantine manuscript (467), Harclean, and some Georgian and Slavonic manuscripts.

tice. Those who hear and do are the ones who pursue God's justice peacefully and will see it. Logically, "be doers of the word" of 1:22 re-expresses 1:21b, but is at the same time nearly synonymous with "welcome . . . the implanted word" in 1:21.

James moves through this small section in a chiastic structure: first, there is a substantive claim about the need for hearing *and* doing (1:22), then an illustration by way of a parable (1:23-24), and then a return to his substantive claim, only this time he steps up the clarity by specifying the "word" as the "perfect law, the law of liberty" (1:25). The first substantive point ended negatively with a warning about self-deception, while the second ends with a positive blessing for the one who both hears *and* does what the "perfect law" teaches.

1. the need to hear *and* do (1:22), with warning about deception
   2. illustration (1:23-24)
1'. the need to hear *and* do (1:25), with promise of blessing

This passage is a favorite for many readers of James and is in fact a singular emphasis of James: genuine faith is a faith that works.[72] If the famous passage in 2:14-26 garners all the attention, 1:22-25 sets the stage.[73]

1:22 James begins this section with an exhortation to be a hearer *and* doer. "Be[74] doers of the word" is the positive, with the negative expressed as "not merely hearers."[75] The emphasis on being a "doer"[76] of the word[77] conforms to the teachings of Jesus in Matthew 7:12-27 and 25:31-46 (cf. John 13:17) but is also nearly identical to Romans 2:13: "It is not the hearers of the law who are righteous in God's sight, but the doers of the law

72. I take this from Jim Wallis, *Faith Works: Lessons from the Life of an Activist Preacher* (New York: Random, 2000); see also R. J. Sider, *Good News and Good Works: A Theology for the Whole Gospel* (Grand Rapids: Baker, 1993).

73. See Baker, *Personal Speech-Ethics,* 92-96; Johnson, *Brother of Jesus, Friend of God,* 168-81.

74. Γίνεσθε, present middle imperative of γίνομαι, expresses "imperfective" action: thus, the action is conceived by the author as uncompleted. The focus is on the practice of doing. Older perspectives can be seen in Mayor, 69; Ropes, 174; Dibelius, 114. For James, see also at 3:1. But see also at Matt 6:16; 10:16; 24:44; Luke 6:36; Rom 12:16; 1 Cor 4:16; 7:23; 11:1; 15:58; Gal 4:12; Eph 4:32; 5:1; Phil 3:17; Col 3:15.

75. I prefer the translation "not hearers only" (in accordance with the text-critical decision made above).

76. ποιηταί, see BDAG, 842. This substantive comes from the Hebrew verb עשׂה. See Jas 1:22, 23, 25; 4:11.

77. On "word," see commentary at 1:21. "Word" here means the same as it did in 1:21, where it is the implanted word that evokes at least the eschatological Torah implanted in the heart (Jer 31:31-34).

who will be justified."[78] It is a historical mistake to assign James 1:22 to messianic or Jewish Christianity only; the teaching here is entirely Jewish, and it was only with the rise of a non-Jewish focus, and frankly at times anti-Semitic framing of issues, that his sort of Torah observance became nearly impossible for Christian communities, pastors, and theologians.[79] *Torah* and "do" *('asah)* are brought together so often in the Hebrew Bible that instinct ought to lead us to see here a form of Torah observance.[80] As E. P. Sanders summarized it, "As such it [Judaism] embraced what people *did* more than what they thought. . . . This emphasis on correct action in every sphere of life, technically called 'orthopraxy,' is a hallmark of Judaism."[81] Thus Josephus: "Piety governs all our actions and occupations and speech; none of these things did our lawgiver leave unexamined or indeterminate" (*Against Apion* 2.171). If this is the case in Judaism, it finds its climax among the Essenes at Qumran. A fragment of 4Q470 says it well: "to live by the whole Law, and to cause others to do so."[82] What makes James's view of doing the

78. Rom 2:14-16 spells out the presence of the inner law in the hearts for Gentiles.

79. See especially Johnson, 140-43.

80. See Exod 18:20; Deut 17:19; 27:26; 28:58; 29:29 (29:28); 31:12; 32:46; Josh 1:7-8; 22:5; 23:6; 2 Kgs 17:34, 37; Jer 32:23; Ps 40:8; Ezra 7:10; Neh 10:29; 2 Chr 14:4. See especially Sanders, *JPB,* 190-240.

81. Sanders, *JPB,* 191.

82. 4Q470 f 1:4. See also CD 4:8; 6:14; 16:8; 1QS 5:3; 8:2, 15; 1QpHab 8:1; 11Q Temple 56:3, 7, 14. An emphasis on עשה is found in *m. Horayoth* 1:1:

A. [If] the court gave a decision to transgress any or all of the commandments which are stated in the Torah,

B. and an individual went and acted in accord with their instructions, [so transgressing] inadvertently,

C. (1) whether they carried out what they said and he carried out what they said right along with them,

D. (2) or whether they carried out what they said and he carried out what they said after they did,

E. (3) whether they did not carry out what they said, but he carried out what they said —

F. he is exempt,

G. since he relied on the court,

H. [If] the court gave a decision, and one of them knew that they had erred,

I. or a disciple who is worthy to give instruction,

J. and he [who knew of the error] went and carried out what they said,

K. (1) whether they carried out what they said and he carried out what they said right along with them,

L. (2) whether they carried out what they said and he carried out what they said after they did,

M. (3) whether they did not carry out what they said, but he carried out what they said —

Law/word *distinct within Judaism* is that in the next chapter he will invoke the Jesus Creed (Deut 6:4-5 + Lev 19:18) as the summary of the Law (cf. Jas 2:8-11 with 1:12). Understanding the Law through the hermeneutic of the double commandment is distinctly Jesus' teaching, even if it is also clearly within the ambit of Judaism.[83]

With "merely hearers" Mayor suggested long ago that James had in mind a person in a synagogue who only listened, and Laws suggested that the Jewish debate about the value of hearing the Torah read was in mind.[84] But James's point is rather simple: there is a glaring contrast between "hearing only"[85] and "hearing *and* doing," and James claims that only the second is acceptable to God. It is no different from the word of Simeon, son of Rabban Gamaliel, who said, "not the learning is the main thing but the doing" (*m Abot* 1:17). But pride of place goes to the later but illustrative *m Abot* 5:14:

A. There are four sorts among those who go to the study house:
B. he who goes but does not carry out [what he learns] — he has at least the reward for the going.
C. He who practices but does not go [to study] — he has at least the reward for the doing.
D. He who both goes and practices — he is truly pious.
E. He who neither goes nor practices — he is truly wicked.

Jesus (Matt 7:12-27), James, and this anonymous rabbinic voice agree that the aim is "D": hearing *and* doing. For James there are only two alternatives: "hearing *and* doing" or "hearing only."[86]

N. lo, this one is liable,
O. since he [who knew the law] did not in point of fact rely upon the court.
P. This is the governing principle:
Q. He who relies on himself is liable, and he who relies on the court is exempt.

83. On which, see Sanders, "Jesus and the First Table"; *Judaism: Practice and Belief,* 230-35. What Sanders does not account for is the sudden presence and centrality of this hermeneutic of love with Jesus and his followers. See further at 2:8-11; cf. Mark 12:28-32; John 13; Gal 5:14; Rom 13:9; 1 John.

84. Mayor, 70; Laws, 85.

85. ἀκροαταί is found here, 1:23, 1:25, and at Rom 2:13. The term is also found at Isa 3:3; Sir 3:29: "The mind of the intelligent appreciates proverbs/and an attentive (ἀκροατοῦ) ear is the desire of the wise." Similarly, the words of 1 Kgs 18:26: those who called on Baal: "'O Baal, answer us!' But there was no voice, and no answer (ἀκρόασις)." See also 2 Kgs 4:31; Isa 21:7: "let him listen diligently, very diligently (ἀκρόασαι ἀκρόασιν πολλήν)"; Sir 5:11.

86. Rom 2 clearly addresses the issue of the *ger tsedeq,* "the righteous gentile" of rabbinic legislations. Here we find yet a third option: the one who "does what is right

To be a hearer and doer, in context, is to be the person who perseveres into moral formation (1:2-4), who seeks God's wisdom in trials (1:5), who knows that the poor will be exalted and the rich rendered powerless (1:9-11), who avoids impulses toward violence to establish God's will (1:13-15, 19-21), who pursues God's justice in meekness and receptivity (1:21), and who is shaped in the context of God's "first fruit" messianic community (1:18).

Those who can be classed as "hearers only," James makes clear, are making a colossal mistake: they "deceive themselves."[87] Jesus, too, was intensely concerned about self-deception, but the word he normally chose to hang this concern on was "hypocrisy."[88] What is closest to James is perhaps Matthew 7:21-23. Just what might they be deceived about? Most understand this to be deception about final redemption,[89] and that is perhaps the best way to understand the verse, but there are reasons to think James may once again be thinking about the messianic age that is dawning now and its opportunity to establish justice and peace. In James, the *promise* the messianic community is given is both a here *and* then sort. In 1:4, James is concerned with being "perfect/mature"; in 1:5 he is concerned with "wisdom"; the alternative to wisdom is double-mindedness and instability (1:7-8); in 1:9-11 James sees something good now for the poor and something bad now for the rich; the "crown" of 1:12 is no doubt mostly an eternal perspective, but "life" is something experienced now for the messianic community. The community is *now* the "first fruits" (1:18), and the "justice of God" that the community is to strive for is something that can come now (1:20). And we suggested that "saving the soul" in 1:21 may be the eschatological redemption, but it may also be earthly survival and flourishing. If we skip ahead to 1:25, the "blessings" come in the doer's deeds and, like most macarisms, pertain as much to life now as they do to life in eternity. In other words, while we would be hasty to dismiss an eschatological future (as judgment) from the deception in 1:22, it is just as likely that James has in mind the person who "hears but does not do" and that such a person is deceived if he or she thinks God's will can be established in such a manner. Their deception, in other words, could be about how to bring about God's kingdom.

---

only" but does not have a proper hearing (of the gospel, of the Torah). See also Acts 10:35. Thus, one thinks also of Amos 9:7; Isa 19:25; Mic 6:8. See F. F. Bruce, *The Book of the Acts* (NICNT; Grand Rapids: Eerdmans, 1988), 211-12; Witherington, *The Acts of the Apostles,* 356.

87. παραλογιζόμενοι ἑαυτούς. See BDAG, 768. The present middle expresses in a vivid manner a characteristic of those who think they can hear and not do. Col 2:4 pertains to being deceived by others.

88. See especially Matt 6:1-18; 23:1-33; Mark 7:1-23. The terms are distinct; for "hypocrisy" see D. E. Garland, *The Intention of Matthew 23* (NovTSup 52; Leiden: E. J. Brill, 1979), 91-123.

89. Davids, 97.

1:23-24 Having made his substantive point through an exhortation (1:22) — that hearing *and* doing must remain together — James now moves on to *illustrate* the point with a parable about a mirror (1:23-24): "For if any are hearers of the word and not doers"[90] restates 1:22, which itself incorporates 1:21, while the parable of vv. 23b and 24 fleshes out "who deceive themselves." James does this by sketching the general point (a person sees himself in a mirror) in 23b, and then elucidating the specifics: the person sees himself, walks away, and forgets what he saw (v. 24).

The parable: "they[91] are like[92] those who look at themselves in a mirror; for they look at themselves and, on going away, immediately forget what they were like." Many have made much of the present tense of "look at themselves"[93] and have suggested that it means "stare for a long time," but the present tense, as the "imperfective aspect," indicates the characteristic of the person and is used to create a more vivid, ongoing scene: this person observes and moves on. The point is not how long or when but the kind of action the author chooses to depict: it is depicted as uncompleted or "imperfective." The looking is depicted as uncompleted, perhaps because it does not accomplish the divine intent of doing. There could be a contrast in verbs between 1:23 ("look at," *katanoeō* in the present tense) and 1:24 ("look at," *katanoeō* in aorist tense), but the change in tense would seem to be related to the author's concern for the general overall image in 1:23b (present) in comparison to the more specific features of that image in 1:24.[94]

What does the one who looks into the mirror see? James says that they look at "themselves," though this simple translation hides a more profound issue for interpreters. The Greek behind "themselves" is *to prosopon tēs geneseōs,* and the addition of *tēs geneseōs* is significant even though both NRSV and TNIV avoid translating it. A base definition for *genesis* is "one's coming into being at a specific moment, birth" or "existence."[95] It is used in

90. ὅτι εἴ τις ἀκροατὴς λόγου ἐστιν καὶ οὐ ποιητής, a first class conditional sentence (with indicative in protasis), makes an assertion for the sake of an argument. The ὅτι is synonymous here with γάρ (Mayor, 70; Davids, 97). It is normal for the negative of a protasis to be μή, but in this instance οὐ is used because it is a negation of ποιητής (thus a "non-doer"; see Moule, *Idiom Book,* 149).

91. Resumptive οὗτος. See 1:25; 3:2.

92. The verb here is ἔοικεν (ἔοικα; see 1:6), BDAG, 355. The author uses the perfect to depict the action as completed.

93. κατανοοῦντι; "at themselves" translates τὸ πρόσωπον, a common translation of the Hebrew פָּנֶה ("face").

94. The attentive stare is seen in 1:23 (κατανοοῦντι) by Martin, 50; Davids, 97. But the contrast in tenses between 1:23 and 1:24 (κατενόησεν) has to do with how the action is conceived: in the first it is "imperfective" or in process, while in the second it is captured globally.

95. BDAG, 192.

in Matthew 1:18 of Jesus' "birth," and the verb *gennaō* is found throughout Matthew 1:1-17. If *genesis* can refer to "birth," it can also refer to "existence," as can be seen in Judith 12:18 ("the greatest day in my whole life [*tēs geneseōs mou*]") and Wisdom 7:5-6 ("For no king has had a different beginning of existence; there is for all one entrance into life, and one way out"). Neither possibility in James 1:23 is captured in the simple translation "themselves." The *ontological* view understands here a reference back to the "image of God" in Gen 1:26-27:[96] the person who hears the Word but does not listen is like one who sees *what God has made him or her to be*, the *imago Dei*, but does not let the *imago Dei* shape his or her life. The *moral* view finds in "themselves" a reference to the human sinful nature,[97] an alternative expression for Paul's "natural man" theology:[98] the person who hears the Word but does not do is like the person who sees *his or her own sinfulness* but does nothing about it.

The ontological view finds a parallel in Wisdom 7:26:

> For she [wisdom] is a reflection of eternal light,
> a spotless mirror of the working of God,
> and an image of his goodness.

And in *Odes of Solomon* 13:1:

> Behold, the Lord is our mirror.
> Open (your) eyes and see them in him.[99]

James 3:9's reflection on the tongue must also come into play here: "With it [the tongue] we bless the Lord and Father, and with it we curse those *who are made in the likeness of God.*" In other words, it is contextually sound to suggest that in *to prosōpon tēs geneseōs* James has in mind humans made in the *imago Dei*.[100] It should also be observed that each view implies the other: one who sees humans as made in the *imago Dei* also sees their moral confusion,

---

96. So Laws, 86; Martin, 50.

97. So Davids, 98.

98. See especially Gal 5:13-26; Rom 6–8; 1 Cor 1–3; and Paul's use of σάρξ. See Dunn, *Theology of Paul the Apostle,* 62-70; H. R. Ridderbos, *Paul: An Outline of His Theology* (trans. J. R. De Witt; Grand Rapids: Eerdmans, 1975), 91-158.

99. Some point to *1 Clement* 36:2, but this reflection on Christ as the perfect one does not use "image" or "mirror."

100. This theme has been explored by theologians, and I recommend especially P. E. Hughes, *The True Image: The Origin and Destiny of Man in Christ* (Grand Rapids: Eerdmans, 1989); L. Stevenson and D. L. Haberman, *Ten Theories of Human Nature* (4th ed.; New York: Oxford, 2004); J. R. Middleton, *The Liberating Image* (Grand Rapids: Brazos, 2005); McKnight, *Embracing Grace,* and *A Community Called Atonement,* 17-22.

and one who sees human moral failures understands them against the backdrop of the *imago Dei.*

What perhaps clinches our ability to understand this expression in context is the *location* where the person sees himself or herself, namely, the "Word" (1:21, 22-23) or "Law" (1:25), which James parabolizes into "mirror."[101] Mirrors, made of silver or a mixture of copper and tin, were used in the ancient world primarily (as they are now) to inspect or to find personal beauty.[102] In Paul, the imperfect image in the mirror reflects our fallen condition, while in the eschaton we will see face to face (1 Cor 13:12), but here James is speaking of "knowledge" as such and not self-evaluation. Plutarch makes the same point with regard to students listening to lectures, and he, too, appeals to the image of a mirror as something where students can see their faults and learn from them:

> There is no point in his getting up out of a barber's chair, standing by a mirror and touching his head to check on the haircut and the difference it has made, but failing, as soon as he leaves a lecture or lesson, to observe himself and inspect his mind, to see whether it has lost any of its troublesome and unnecessary features, and has become less burdensome and distressing.[103]

The evidence, while it is far from overwhelming, can be rendered in either of the two interpretations sketched above, but the mirror image tips the interpretation in favor of a moral rather than ontological interpretation. One who sees but does nothing about it is like one who sees his or her moral condition in a mirror and walks away without changing. But again, each view implies the other.

The parable now explains the general image created in 1:23b with *specifics.* Some of those who observe themselves[104] in the mirror abort the process: "for they look[105] at themselves and, on going away, immediately for-

---

101. ἔσοπτρον, BDAG, 397. See especially Johnson, 207-8; also his *Brother of Jesus, Friend of God,* 171-78. N. Denyer, "Mirrors in James 1:22-25 and Plato, *Alcibiades* 132C-133C," *TynBul* 50 (1999) 237-40, suggests that Plato provides the closest parallel with the famous "know thyself" discussion between Socrates and Alcibiades. Denyer sees the knowledge of the self perceived in a mirror, as a vivid but evanescent perception, to be an inferior grasp of self-knowledge.

102. See Josephus, *Ant* 12.81.

103. Plutarch, *Essays* (trans. R. Waterfield; New York: Penguin, 1992), 37. See also Plutarch, *Moralia* 1 (42 B).

104. The Greek is singular and has been pluralized to facilitate inclusion.

105. Some see the aorist as gnomic (Mayor, 72; Ropes, 176-77; Davids, 98; Martin, 50; and BDF §344). This interpretation is focused on trying to figure out how an aorist tense (understood as simple past) can be used for what appears to be a timeless act or a

get what they were like."[106] This image resembles the logical flow of 2:10: "For whoever keeps the whole law but fails in one point has become accountable for all of it." In 1:24, the person immediately forgets "what they were like."[107] Here again we are back to the question of what the person saw in the mirror — the ontological vision of Adam as the *imago Dei* or the moral vision of human sinfulness, and "what they were like" permits either view. In light of our conclusion above that the moral view is to be preferred, we would paraphrase 1:24 as: "they forget the moral corruption they saw in the word." This forgetting is a form of "self-deception" (1:22c).

1:25 As stated above, James now comes full circle. He is back to the point made in 1:22 but now provides greater specificity to "word," and the warning turns into a promise. So, to welcome the implanted word (1:21) is to become hearers and doers of the word (1:22); those who hear but do not do deceive themselves (1:22b, 23-24). In contrast[108] to this self-deceiver, those who hear *and* do will be "blessed in their doing" (1:25). There are three parts to 1:25:

> *Subject:* "But those who look into the perfect law, the law of liberty, and persevere" (25a),
> *Comment:* "being not hearers who forget but doers who act" (25b),
> *Promise:* "will be blessed in their doing" (25c).

---

proverbially timeless process. The issue is not time, however; the issue is how the action is conceived by the author. In the aorist James is capturing the whole action at once and moving through three stages: seeing, walking away, and forgetting. Translating it as a timeless present, of course, is fine, but not because it is timeless but because the action is globally depicted and therefore omnitemporal. The perfect ἀπελήλυθεν could reflect the Hebrew perfect tense, and thus could speak to the "completeness" of the action, as stated by Moule, *Idiom Book,* 12, though his "suddenness" is not indicated by tense. Any notion of suddenness is in the third verb where the deictic indicator εὐθέως is present. Moule's comments pertain to 1:11, but he sees the same Hebrew perfect influencing 1:24. On this, see Porter, *Idioms,* 38-39; *Verbal Aspect,* 221-25.

106. Grammatically, the three verbs in the NRSV ("look," "going away," "forget") are structural equivalents connected by καί: aorist, perfect, and aorist. If the first and third depict actions as "perfective" (complete, holistically), the second depicts action that has given rise to a state of affairs. Thus, the person looks, now in a state of being away from the mirror, and forgets. BDF §344, operating as it does with a time-based theory of tense, sees the tenses as "incorrectly mixed." Mayor, 72, and Ropes, 177, see a proleptic perfect.

107. εὐθέως ἐπελάθετο, BDAG, 374 ("forget"); second aorist middle of ἐπιλανθάνομαι. On "what they were like," ὁποῖος ἦν, see BDAG, 716-17 ("of what sort"); cf. MHT, 3.49, for the correlative pronoun used as an interrogative. See Gal 2:6 ("what they actually were makes no difference to me"); 1 Thess 1:9 ("what kind of welcome"); 1 Cor 3:13 ("what sort of work").

108. δέ.

Subject (v. 25a). This "look" into the perfect law involves a change of vocabulary. "Look" in 1:23b-24a is *katanoeō,* while "look" in 1:25a is *parakyptō.*[109] The verb itself means "take a look" or "look into" and can have the sense of bending over something to look into or down onto something.[110] Inasmuch as James is talking about Torah at some level, it could refer to bending over in order to read,[111] but reading was neither the norm for ancient Jews nor does the context suggest the specifics of Torah study — the images of 1:25 strike one as hearing *and* doing the "law" (Torah observance) rather than reading it or studying it. Thus, *parakyptō* could be an unconscious synonym of *katanoeō.*[112] Regardless, it is best to read the verb contextually: it needs to be brought into the ambit of "welcome" in 1:21b, of "hearing" in 1:22-23a, and of "looking" in 1:23b-24a and to be connected to "persevere" in 1:25a. "The one who looks" is clearly in contrast to the one who "hears" but does not do in 1:22-24 and the one who looks, walks away, and forgets in 1:24. As such, the sense of *parakyptō* here is "look into something in a receptive mode,"[113] the way an art lover meanders through the paintings of an exhibition, a music lover attends to the music of an orchestral performance, an actress participates in a theatrical performance, a parent listens to the words of a child, or a lover absorbs the words of the one she loves. This person stands in contrast to the one who does not find maturity and wisdom (1:2-4), who does not see the temporality of wealth (1:9-11), who is led by desires (1:13-15), who questions God's goodness (1:16-18), or who resorts to verbal abuse and emotional outbreaks of anger (1:19-21).

The secret to this person is that he or she not only looks in a receptive mode but also "perseveres."[114] While the theological issue of perseverance has commanded attention (e.g, John 8:31), the notion here is simpler: it refers

---

109. παρακύπτω, BDAG, 767.

110. Peter ran to the tomb, "stooping and looking in" (Luke 24:12; see John 20:5); Mary does the same in John 20:11. The angels want to look into gospel matters (1 Pet 1:12). See also Gen 26:8; 1 Chron 15:29; Prov 7:6; Sir 14:23, for peering through windows at something. So Mayor, 72; Laws, 86.

111. On this, see W. V. Harris, *Ancient Literacy* (Cambridge: Harvard University Press, 1989); A. R. Millard, *Reading and Writing in the Time of Jesus* (Biblical Seminar 69; Sheffield: Sheffield Academic, 2000). It is common to conclude that 10 percent of the Jewish population could read, so it is unwise to assume that this is exclusively about reading a text.

112. See Ropes, 177.

113. Martin may overdo it with his agreement to a "penetrating absorption" (p. 50).

114. παραμείνας, the aorist of παραμένω; see BDAG, 769. The person is described with two participles: "the one who looks and perseveres." Both participles are aorist, denoting the action holistically. The "persevering" is thus described not as an inceptive action but in its totality.

to the person who sees what the "law" says and practices it over time, as in Deuteronomy 27:26: "Cursed be anyone who does not uphold the words of this law by observing them."[115] This sense of "perseveres" is established by the comment in v. 25b ("doers who act"). What they look at and persevere in is "the perfect law, the law of liberty."[116] It is surprising to see "law" here: James has been using "word" *(logos)* up to this point (1:18, 21, 22, 23). There would seem to be only one real possibility here for James: he is referring to the Torah of Moses,[117] but just how he understands that Torah is the subject of intense discussion.

Three options are available for understanding "the perfect law, the law of liberty." First, there is a (supposedly) Hellenistic Judaism view: it refers to a free life in accordance with reason, with "reason" being a way of describing the Law of Moses.[118] Second is a nomistic Judaism view: it refers to the Law of Moses as that which brings freedom to the obedient.[119] Third is a Christian Judaism view: it refers to the Law of Moses as understood by and interpreted by Jesus in accordance with the double commandment to love God and others.[120] Before making a case for one view, we will lay out some of the evidence and argumentation for each view, but we must keep in mind that James is a Torah-observant messianist.[121]

That "the perfect law, the law of liberty" could derive from what has traditionally been called Hellenistic Judaism, not unlike that found in Philo, finds support in the ancient world. A good example would be Philo, *Every Good Man Is Free* 45-46:[122]

> Further again, just as with cities, those which lie under an oligarchy or tyranny suffer enslavement, because they have cruel or severe masters, who keep them in subjection under their sway, while those which have laws to care for and protect them are free, so, too, with men. Those in whom anger or desire or any other passion, or again any insidious vice

---

115. See 1 Cor 16:6; Phil 1:25; Heb 7:23. Some point to the treasuring in the heart of Luke 2:19, 51.

116. εἰς νόμον τέλειον τὸν τῆς ἐλευθερίας. E. Stauffer, "Das 'Gesetz der Freiheit' in der Ordensregel von Jericho," *TLZ* 77 (1952) 527-32; Hartin, "The Religious Context," 215-17; McKnight, "A Parting within the Way," 117-23; Cheung, *Genre, Composition,* 92-129. Sigal, "Halakhah," 344-46, sees an allusion to Ps 19:8 (LXX 19:7), along with similar ideas in Philo and the Mishnah.

117. M. Hogan, "The Law in the Epistle of James," *Studien zum Neuen Testament und seiner Umwelt* 22 (1997) 79-91, especially 86-87.

118. See here Dibelius, 116-20.

119. Johnson, 209; see the extensive discussion in Hartin, 111-15.

120. See with variations, Davids, 99-100; Moo, 93-94.

121. See the extensive study in Wall, 83-98.

122. See also Philo, *De Opificio Mundi* 3; *De vita Mosis* 2.48.

holds sway, are entirely enslaved, while all those whose life is regulated
by law are free. And right reason is an infallible law engraved not by
this mortal or that and, therefore, perishable as he, nor on parchment or
slabs, and, therefore, soulless as they, but by immortal nature on the immortal mind, never to perish.

Or the ejaculatory praise in *4 Maccabees* 14:2: "O reason, more kingly than
kings, more free than freemen!" This view is also found in Epictetus, *Discourses* 4.1:[123]

He is free who lives as he wishes to live; who is neither subject to compulsion nor to hindrance, nor to force; whose movements to action are
not impeded, whose desires attain their purpose, and who does not fall
into that which he would avoid.

And in Seneca, *The Good Life* 15:7: "to obey God is freedom."

Favoring the view that the "law of liberty" is the Torah of Moses, beside the obvious evidence of James's use of "law" *(nomos)* here and in 2:8-
11, is that the Torah was so highly valued as God's definitive revelation for
his elect people. From at least Ezra onward the Law was a focal point of
praise. We can begin with Psalm 1:2: "but their delight is in the law of
YHWH." Nothing is quite like Psalm 19:7-11:[124]

The law of the LORD is perfect,
    reviving the soul;
the decrees of the LORD are sure,
    making wise the simple;
the precepts of the LORD are right,
    rejoicing the heart;
the commandment of the LORD is clear,
    enlightening the eyes;
the fear of the LORD is pure,
    enduring forever;
the ordinances of the LORD are true
    and righteous altogether.
More to be desired are they than gold,
    even much fine gold;
sweeter also than honey,
    and drippings of the honeycomb.
    Moreover by them is your servant warned;
    in keeping them there is great reward.

123. Trans. G. Long; GBWW 12.213.
124. See also Pss 40:8; 119; Sir 6:23-31; or the reflection on wisdom in 51:13-22.

Psalm 119:45 is close:

> I shall walk at liberty,
> for I have sought your precepts.

That the Essenes of Qumran (e.g., 1QS 10) or the rabbis had a profound joy in the Torah and praised its virtues goes without saying.[125] Thus, *m Avot* 1:1: "Simeon the Righteous . . . would say: 'On three things does the world stand: (1) 'On the Torah, (2) and on the Temple service, (3) and on deeds of loving kindness.'"[126] Rob Wall has proposed that with "liberty" James evokes the richly-textured Jubilee theme of Leviticus 25.[127]

Third, and here we move toward a view that sees here a Christian Judaism well-known for its commitment to the Torah, the Temple, and Israel. James is himself, according to Hegesippus as quoted by Eusebius, an example:[128]

> He was called "Just" by all men. . . . He drank no wine or strong drink, nor did he eat flesh; no razor . . . ; he did not anoint himself . . . did not go to the baths. He alone was allowed to enter into the sanctuary, for he did not wear wool but linen, and he used to enter alone into the temple and be found kneeling and praying for forgiveness for the people, so that his knees grew hard like a camel's because of his constant worship of God, kneeling and asking forgiveness for the people.

Some dispute the veracity of this report about James; none disputes that these are the sort of characteristics one finds in some of the pious of Christian Judaism in the first messianic community. This community, however, was not just committed to Torah. It was also committed to the interpretation of that Torah by Jesus. Thus, we must think of Mark 12:28-32, as well as Matthew 5:17-20; 15:1-20. Paul, too, in Galatians 5:13-14:

> For you were called to freedom, brothers and sisters; only do not use your freedom as an opportunity for self-indulgence, but through love become slaves to one another. For the whole law is summed up in a single commandment, "You shall love your neighbor as yourself."

125. Mussner, 108-9; Frankemölle, 1.344-57; Blomberg and Kamell, 91-92.
126. Some editions of *m. Avot* 6:2: "Read not *haruth* (graven) but *heruth* (freedom), for you find no free man except him who occupies himself with the study of Torah."
127. Wall, 92-97. The concept of "Jubilee" stretches what is said explicitly in James.
128. Eusebius, *Eccl Hist* 2.23.4-6. See B. T. Viviano, "La loi parfaite de liberté: Jacques 1,25 et la loi," in *The Catholic Epistles and the Tradition* (ed. J. Schlosser; Leuven: Leuven University Press, 2004), 213-24.

Or Romans 8:2: "For the law of the Spirit of life in Christ Jesus has set you free from the law of sin and of death." John, too, saw the fulfillment of the Law in Jesus' love commandment, and he calls it the "new commandment" (John 13:34-35).[129]

Of the three interpretations of "the perfect law, the law of liberty" the third is favored. A variety of observations lead to the conclusion that James has a Christian hermeneutic of the Torah in mind here. (1) James speaks of a law defined by "liberty" and "perfection."[130] In earliest Christianity both terms are connected to the Torah as taught by Jesus (cf. Matt 5:17-20, 48; Gal 5:13-14). (2) The notion of "liberty" is not prominent in this letter, but in 2:8-11 James appeals to the Jesus Creed of Mark 12:28-32 (law and love) as how the Torah is to be understood, and at that point he finishes off by saying that the Torah is the "law of liberty."[131] Thus, in 2:8-12 we see that James understands the "law of liberty" as the Christian reinterpretation of the Torah through the Jesus Creed. The "liberty" of 2:12 must be connected to the "liberty" of 1:25a. (3) Even more, the "law of liberty" in 1:25 must be connected to the "implanted word" of 1:21 and to the conversion sense of "word" in 1:18, and all this makes for a connection to Jeremiah 31:31-34 and therefore to the Spirit of Pentecost (Acts 2).[132] Again, the connections here are to a Christian reinterpretation of the Torah in the New Age. James is Torah-observant in a Jesus kind of way.[133]

James's point is this: those who look into the Law as understood by Jesus, which can be called the "word," is "perfect," and brings "liberty," and persevere in their following of that understanding of the Law, are those who will be blessed (1:25c). After making this statement, James comments in order to clarify what it means to "*look* into the perfect law, the law of liberty, *and persevere.*"

Comment (v. 25b). "Those who persevere" is clarified in light of 1:22 and 1:23-24: "being not hearers who forget but doers who act."[134]

129. *Barnabas* 2.6: "the *new law of our Lord Jesus Christ,* which is without the yoke of compulsion. . . ."

130. On τέλειον, see notes at 1:4 and 1:17. See also Matt 5:48; 19:21; Rom 12:2.

131. For James, either the law was characterized by "freedom" or (what is more likely) the law promoted freedom or liberated. See Martin, 51. The genitive is objective. A similar sense of ἐλευθερία is found at 2:12: "the law of liberty." See Cheung, *Genre, Composition,* 93-96. For further texts in history on "freedom," see GBWW 2.991-1012.

132. From a different angle, see Calvin, 297-98.

133. Calvin, 298, captures the Reformation's distinct angle and debate about the law in the Christian life: "The teaching of the law, let it no longer lead you to bondage, but, on the contrary, bring you to liberty; let it no longer be only a schoolmaster, but bring you to perfection: it ought to be received by you with sincere affection, so that you may lead a godly and holy life."

134. οὐκ ἀκροατὴς ἐπιλησμονῆς γενόμενος ἀλλὰ ποιητὴς ἔργου. On ἐπιλησμονή, see BDAG, 375; BDF §109 (on -μονη form). The genitive is adjectival. It is found in Sir

The connection of "forget" with "law" is typical of the Old Testament. For example:

> Deuteronomy 4:23: "So be careful not to forget the covenant that
> YHWH your God made with you."
> Deuteronomy 6:12: "take care that you do not forget YHWH."[135]
> Deuteronomy 26:13: "I have neither transgressed nor forgotten any of
> your commandments."[136]
> Psalm 119:16: "I will not forget your word."

Each of these uses of "forget" translates the same Hebrew term,[137] and that term is also found frequently in the Dead Sea Scrolls. A noteworthy parallel, because it also comes from a situation of persecution, is 4Q525 fragment 2, column 2, lines 3-7:

> Blessed is the man who attains wisdom, and walks in the law of the
> Most High: establishes his heart in its ways, restrains himself by its cor-
> rections, is continually satisfied with its punishments, does not forsake
> it in the face of [his] trials, at the time of distress he does not abandon it,
> *does not forget it* [in the day of] terror, and in the humility of his soul he
> does not abhor it. But he meditates on it continually, and in his trial he
> reflects [on the law, and with al]l his being [he gains understanding] in
> it, [and he establishes it] before his eyes so as not to walk in the ways
> [of injustice, and . . .].

Forgetting becomes extreme (in language, of course) for the rabbis:

> A. R. Dosetai b. R. Yannai in the name of R. Meir says, "Whoever *for-
>   gets* a single thing from what he has learned — Scripture reckons it to
>   him as if he has become liable for his life,
> B. as it is said, Only take heed to yourself and keep your soul diligently,
>   lest You *forget* the words which your eyes saw (Dt. 4:9)."
> C. Is it possible that this is so even if his learning became too much for
>   him?
> D. Scripture says, Lest they depart from your heart all the days of your
>   life.

11:27: "An hour's misery makes one *forget* past delights. . . ." The term comes from ἐπιλανθάνομαι, which is found in Matt 16:5; Luke 12:6; Phil 3:13; Heb 6:10; 13:2, 16; and Jas 1:24. The aorist participle γενόμενος fits with the aorist substantival participles of 1:25a, and the aorist is used to conceive the action holistically.

135. See also Hos 2:13; 8:14; 13:6; Jer 2:32; 3:21; 18:15; Pss 44:17, 20; 50:22.
136. See also Hos 4:6.
137. שׁכח, see *TDOT* 14.671-76; *TLOT* 3.1322-26.

E. Thus he becomes liable for his life only when he will sit down and actually remove [his learning] from his own heart.

And, to complement the quotation of *m Avot* 3:8 above, here is 5:12:

A. There are four types of disciples:
B. (1) quick to grasp, quick to forget — he loses what he gains;
C. (2) slow to grasp, slow to forget — what he loses he gains;
D. (3) quick to grasp, slow to forget — a sage;
E. (4) slow to grasp, quick to forget — a bad lot indeed.

Those who persevere not only do not forget but are "doers who act."[138] James uses two of his favorite terms here: "doers" and "act" (from *ergon,* "work").[139] The rather colorless use of "act" in the NRSV as well as in the TNIV ("doing it") surprises: one would have thought with the frequency of the use of *erg-* in James that the translation would be "a doer of work." Thus, 2:14: "if you say you have faith but do not have *works*"; and 2:17: "faith by itself, if it has no *works,* is dead." And not to be forgotten here is how important this is to James in 2:24: "You see that a person is justified by *works* and not by faith alone." Finally, in a passage not dissimilar to our context, in 3:13 it reads: "Who is wise and understanding among you? Show by your good life that your *works* are done with gentleness born of wisdom." In light of the context in James, it is best to translate *ergon* in 1:25 ("doers who act") as "doers of work [works]."[140]

What might such a "work" be? 1:26-27 both answers that question and provides further evidence that *ergon* in 1:25b is not a colorless word: "to care for orphans and widows in their distress, and to keep oneself unstained by the world." The "work" of 1:25b is most likely, then, compassion (deeds of mercy)[141] and holiness, and it needs to be seen in the context of a letter written to the poor and for the poor. James is here expressing the need for solidarity among the poor and care for one another.[142] The substance of his letter emerges as we read this in context: those who follow Jesus' interpretation of the Torah (1:25a) care for the poor, as he did, and know that God's plan is to establish justice, as is seen in the Magnificat (Luke 1:46-55).[143] Such people

138. ποιητὴς ἔργου. On ποιητής, see also at 1:22-23 and 4:11.
139. On ἔργον, see BDAG, 390-91 ("deed, action").
140. In 2:14-26 and at 3:13 ἔργον is plural; here it is singular. The genitive ἔργου in 1:25b is objective.
141. On which see especially Str-B, 4.1.559-610; Sanders, *JPB,* 230-35.
142. A good example would be Acts 6:1-7.
143. These connections need to be made to put James's teaching in proper context: Luke 1:46-55; 4:16-30; 6:20-26; Matt 11:2-6; and then Acts 2–4. There is a solid line

do not lash out in violence (1:13-15, 19-20) but pursue God's justice in humility (1:21) and peacefulness (3:18). To speak of "persevering in the Law" is not a proto-rabbinic wisdom saying but a summons for the messianic community to stick together as the first fruits (1:18), to remain faithful to Jesus and the Jesus Creed, to avoid succumbing to the pressures of the rich (1:12), and to pursue God's justice in peace and humility (1:21; 3:18). J. H. Elliott sums up the perspective of James well: "fidelity to the complete and royal law of freedom, inspired by the wisdom from above, entails an integrity of *hearing*-completed-in-doing, of *seeing*-completed-in-doing, of *speaking*-completed-in-doing, and of *faith*-activated-in-love."[144]

Promise (v. 25c). Those who persevere do not forget what they have learned, they do works, and for this reason "they will be blessed in their doing."[145] As in 1:12, so here: "blessing" pertains to God's favor on a person.[146] A blessing is from God, is often promised to those whose conditions will be socially reversed, is conditioned upon loving fidelity to God, and is either eschatologically future or both inaugurated and future. The first three of these characteristics of a *macarism* are easy to see in 1:22-25, but there is some discussion as to whether the blessing will be both here and now or just in the future. The future tense "will be" is one indicator that it is for the eschaton, as in 1:12. But as the reward theme of James involves the present life, so it is possible here that the "blessing" is inaugurated in the here and now and experienced as God's protection and preservation (1:3-4, 12), community fellowship (1:18), moral formation (1:2-4, 5-8), reversal (1:9-11), and the establishment of justice (1:20) and peace (3:18). That the doers will be blessed "in their doing" makes this "blessing" concrete in the present world.[147] Whatever that means "in the process of the doing" or "as a product of the doing,"[148] it pertains to life on earth: they will be blessed not *because of* the "doing" but *in* the "doing." Therefore God's favor on those who do God's works of mercy is as much something experienced in the here and now as in the kingdom.

---

from Mary to Jesus to James on the theme of the Kingdom of God as a society in which the will of God is established.

144. J. H. Elliott, "Holiness-Wholeness," 78; I have omitted his many references to the book of James to focus on his excellent sweep of categories.

145. οὗτος μακάριος ἐν τῇ ποιήσει αὐτοῦ ἔσται. The future tense presents problems for aspect theory. C. R. Campbell, *Basics of Verbal Aspect in Biblical Greek* (Grand Rapids: Zondervan, 2008), sees it as perfective (action depicted as completed) and also temporally referring to the future.

146. See notes at 1:12.

147. ἐν τῇ ποιήσει αὐτοῦ ἔσται. On ποίησις, see Sir 19:20; 51:19.

148. The term ποίησις can mean either "process" or "the product" of one's doing; see BDAG, 842. See also Sir 19:20; 51:19. Ropes is not alone in stating that this term describes the whole of a person's conduct (p. 180).

3.3. AN EXHORTATION ON PURE RELIGION (1:26-27)

*If[149] any think they are religious,[150] and do not bridle[a] their[151] tongues
but deceive their hearts,[b] their religion is worthless. 27 Religion[152] that
is pure and undefiled before God, the Father, is this: to care[153] for orphans and widows in their distress, and to keep oneself unstained[c] by
the world.*

a. TNIV: keep a tight rein
b. TNIV: themselves
c. TNIV: from being polluted

Once again, while some like to divide the various sections of James into at
most loose connections, this section, if read in context, carries on the themes
that have been present with us since 1:2-4: the poor, the need to live properly,
speech practices, the need to resist the desires of this world, and the potency
of a kingdom community. In fact, 1:26-27 is the summary statement of the
whole of ch. 1 and in some ways a way of conceptualizing the entire letter's
ethical position. It is a commentary on and clarification of what it means to
be a doer of the work and to persevere in the Law, and the themes of speech
ethics are never far from view.[154] If the temptation of the messianic community was toward impulsive or unsavory language and violent establishment of
justice, James offers an alternative to the "religious" person. If the deceived
person of 1:22[155] thought he or she could hear the word and walk away unchanged, James contends that the person who stares into the perfect Law of
liberty should be a "doer of works." Here James clarifies what those works
are: bridling the tongue, deeds of compassion for the marginalized, and a
community noted by holiness.[156]

149. Some good manuscripts add δε, including the fourth-century C (04) and the
fifth-century 0173. See also P, 2464, and Peshitta. The addition reveals that at least these
manuscripts saw a slight adversative of 1:26a with what precedes, and that is the interpretation that best makes sense of the text.

150. The Maj tradition adds εν υμιν.

151. The NRSV pluralizes for inclusion. The original text is αὐτοῦ, with some
manuscripts having εαυτου (B, P, and 0173).

152. Some manuscripts add γαρ to clarify the logical flow as explanatory.

153. Nestle-Aland[27] has ἐπισκέπτεσθαι, while some manuscripts have the second
person plural επισκεπτεσθε (P74, א, L, 33, and some Ethiopic). P74 also converts ἄσπιλον
to υπερασπιζειν αὐτους.

154. Baker, *Personal Speech-Ethics,* 96-99.

155. Self-deception is also found at 1:16, and there it has to do with an improper
view of God.

156. See Mayor, 75; Martin, 52. See also Ropes, 181; Johnson, *Brother of Jesus,
Friend of God,* 155-67.

1:26 is a general statement, and 1:27 makes it more specific by giving it concrete implications for the community. V. 26 has two parts, the protasis (or "if" clause) in which James spells out a condition of a person who "thinks" he or she can be "religious" and practice a lack of control in speech, and the apodosis (or "then" clause) which simply pronounces in a negative fashion that such a condition is "worthless." 1:27 gives the positive side of what genuine "religion" looks like.

1:26 The *general statement* begins with "if any think[157] they are religious, [then . . .]." Paul made use of the same rhetorical device:

> Galatians 6:3: For if those who are nothing think they are something, they deceive themselves.
> 1 Corinthians 3:18: If you think that you are wise in this age, you should become fools so that you may become wise.
> 1 Corinthians 10:12: So if you think you are standing, watch out that you do not fall.

James pulls together everything in ch. 1 in one term: "religious."[158] We find this term *(thrēskos)* in three places in the New Testament. In Acts 26:5, Paul uses the cognate noun *thrēskeia* for Judaism and declares that he was in a "sect" (Pharisaism) within Judaism. In Colossians 2:18, we have a notorious *crux interpretum* where the NRSV translates "worship [thrēskeia] of angels." The cognate *thrēskeia* also occurs twice in James 1:26b and 27a. These terms seem to be used most often for specific acts of worship.[159] Thus, Wisdom 14:27: "For the worship of idols not to be named is the beginning and cause and end of every evil." Sometimes it sums up one's "piety." Also Josephus, *Ant* 12.271: "Whoever," Mattathias cries out in the heat of his rebellion against Antiochus Epiphanes, "is zealous for our country's laws and worship of God *(tēs tou theou thrēskeias),* let him come with me!" Early Christians also appropriated this term for their own faith and its practices. We find this use in *1 Clement* 62:1: "We have written enough to you, brothers, about the things which pertain to our religion *(peri . . . tē thrēskeia hēmōn)* and are particularly helpful for a virtuous life, at least for those who wish to guide their steps in holiness and righteousness."[160]

---

157. The personal use of the protasis with δοκεῖ with infinitive is not the norm in the New Testament (see BHT 3.147). See also John 5:39; 1 Cor 8:2; 14:37.

158. On which, see *TDNT* 3.155-59; Spicq, 1.200-204; *GEL,* 532; Burchard, 91-92; Popkes, 147-48.

159. See LSJ, 806.

160. See *Diognetus* 3:2.

Thrēskos can be used pejoratively for formalism, but James is concerned with "pure and undefiled" *thrēskeia,* and he sees that in deeds of compassion and holiness (1:27). These qualities stand in contrast to volatility in speech, heartlessness in response, and being stained by the world. In light of this evidence, it is best to see *thrēsk-* as James's term for what is *visible* about one's faith.[161]

As he has done in 1:19-20 and will do in 3:1-12, James is willing to reduce (for pointed rhetorical reasons) "religion" to whether or not people "bridle their tongues."[162] As in 3:2-3, control of the tongue can be compared to the bridle that controls the entire horse. Some take the image of bridling the tongue to be simply a general moral comment about persons who offer pious platitudes without good works,[163] while others think something more specific is mind. Peter Davids made the case for this verse anticipating what will be said to a factional group of teachers in 3:1-12.[164] Contextually, I suggest that we look back to 1:19-20 and infer from those verses that James is concerned in 1:26a with the control of the *volatile* tongue for those who want to establish justice. If a case can be made, though hardly with a high degree of probability, for 3:1-12 being about divisive teachers, a stronger case can be made for James worrying about verbal speech patterns that are connected to anger and violent outbursts by leaders.[165] His willingness to reduce moral exhortations to bridling the tongue is best understood in a specific rather than general context: this control is needed by hotheads who are tempted to indulge their desires with angry verbal abuse. In other contexts, James might reduce it to something else for rhetorical reasons.

James's next comment appears to be logically disruptive: "but deceive their hearts."[166] One would expect this clause, as something like it did in

---

161. So Dibelius, 121; Davids, 101; Johnson, 210, 211.

162. μὴ χαλιναγωγῶν γλῶσσαν, see BDAG, 1076. This term is found in Jas 1:26a and 3:2-3. The present participle is used to provide characteristic behavior. Even the accumulation of presents in 1:26 should not be used to conclude that this behavior is currently going on; it is the "action" that concerns James, not the time. The absence of any particle renders the two present participles circumstantial. Thus, one might translate "the one who thinks this and, while thinking this, does not bridle the tongue but deceives the heart, this person's religion. . . ." On the historical context, see Johnson, *Brother of Jesus, Friend of God,* 155-56 nn. 3-7, and 157-64; see also Baker, *Personal Speech-Ethics.*

163. See Martin, 52; also Ropes, 182.

164. Davids, 101.

165. See commentary on 1:13-15, 19-20, and especially at 3:1–4:12.

166. ἀλλὰ ἀπατῶν καρδίαν αὐτοῦ. On ἀπατάω, see BDAG, 98-99 ("deceive, mislead"). There is little distinction between ἀπατάω here and παραλογίζομαι in 1:22 or πλανάω in 1:16. See also at Eph 5:6; 1 Tim 2:14. The note on p. 367 of *GEL* is the opposite of how James is using terms; they suggest the πατ- words would have to do with mis-

1:22, to be the closure to the point: "If any thinks . . . he deceives his own heart." But James lets this clause finish the protasis (with a preliminary climax) and then he goes on to a fuller closure with "their religion is worthless." So on this interpretation of the syntax, James has a double-pointed protasis: "*If* any think they are religious and (1) do not bridle their tongues but (2) deceive their hearts, *then.* . . ." James is perhaps a little more subtle than that. Since he supplies no particle prior to "do not bridle," it may be better to render this conditional sentence as follows:

> If persons think they are religious, and while thinking this do not bridle their tongues but instead choose to deceive their hearts, their religion is worthless.

In other words, James does here as he did in 1:13-15: he lays full blame on the person and accuses the person of *intentionally* deceiving himself.[167]

And yet there is another possibility that may eliminate the logical disruption: sometimes the word *apataō* (translated here "deceive") means "enjoy oneself, live pleasurably," and this leads Johnson to suggest that James means "indulging their hearts."[168] Once again, this points to the intentionality of the action as well as to what James was saying in 1:13-15 on "desire."[169] Furthermore, this concern with desire anticipates 4:1-3, and the self-satiety of the protasis stands in strong (and thoroughly credible) contrast to the self-sacrifice of 1:27. This leads to an improved translation of 1:26:

> If persons think they are religious, and while thinking this do not bridle their tongues but instead indulge their hearts, their religion is worthless.

This interpretation should be given a favorable hearing even if it is based on less than compelling evidence.

Such a person's "religion is worthless." The meaning of "worthless"

---

conceptions while the πλαν- words would have to do with general deceptive behavior. Jas 1:16 is clearly misconception (of who God is) while 1:26 is more general (with καρδία). On καρδία, see comments on uses at 1:26; 3:14; 4:8; 5:5, 8.

167. Thus, the manuscript tradition has a variety of evidence, including early evidence, in favor of εαυτου (see B, C, with a dozen or more later manuscripts).

168. Johnson, 210-11. BDAG, 98, lists such a meaning only in the middle, but Johnson finds support in the active at LXX Sir 14:16 and 30:23. The noun ἀπάτη can also mean "pleasure" (cf. Mark 4:19; 2 Pet 2:13; Hermas, *Similitudes* 6.4.4; 6.5.1; *Mandate* 11.12). Johnson has sufficient evidence to establish the case that the term in Jas 1:26a can mean "indulging their hearts."

169. Against this view is (1) that James uses καρδία instead of ἐπιθυμία, and (2) that καρδία is normally used for more positive yearnings. However, in 3:14; 4:8; and 5:5 there is a negative sense to καρδία.

(mataios)[170] once again brings in the nuance of contextual reading. It usually bears the sense of "idle, fruitless, powerless." Thus, in Acts 14:15 Paul sees the Lystrans worshiping "useless" gods; in 1 Corinthians 3:20 the wisdom of the so-called "wise" is called "useless"; in 1 Corinthians 15:17, Christian faith is said to be rendered "useless" if Jesus is not raised; and in 1 Peter 1:18 Peter sees the pre-conversion religio-cultural heritage of his converts to be "useless."[171] On this, nearly everyone is agreed: *mataios* refers to "effects," a concern of James in 1:20. The *thrēskeia* he has described "effects" nothing good, or it does not bring about the desired conditions, or it is "worthless" for bringing about good. This theme will be developed in another way in 2:14, 17, 20, 22, 26, and this evidence taken together raises a concrete question that is not asked often enough: what conditions are not brought about if a person chooses to deceive/indulge his or her heart by not controlling the tongue? The standard answer is that James sees the messianic community, or more often individuals, in danger of jeopardizing eternity with God or, more generally, displeasing God,[172] as it is put in 1:12, the "crown of life." This could all be true, but contextually we are led to reconsider this traditional view by asking what James says elsewhere about the tongue. Again we need to look back to 1:19-20 and forward to 3:1-12. What does not come about because of the volatile tongue and violent action is "justice" (1:20) or "peace" (3:18). In other words, while *mataios* might be used of jeopardizing one's relationship to God either here or in the eschaton, it more particularly pertains to jeopardizing the social conditions created (or not created) by those who choose (or choose not) to control the tongue and refrain from violence and anger. Not controlling the tongue is "worthless" for establishing the kingdom of God because violent anger, whether expressed physically or verbally, does not "effect" the justice of God (1:20).

170. μάταιος, see BDAG, 621; *GEL,* 625, where it is associated with both ἀργάς and νεκρός; *EWNT* 2.396; Johnson, 211; Popkes, 149.

171. On which see especially W. C. van Unnik, "The Critique of Paganism in 1 Peter 1:18," in *Neotestamentica et Semitica: Studies in Honour of Matthew Black* (ed. E. E. Ellis and M. Wilcox; Edinburgh: Clark, 1969), 129-42. Here is his noteworthy conclusion about Peter's apologetic against ancestral faiths and their being μάταιος: "The ancient tradition of home and nation is broken, not for the sake of opposition but because of the work of Jesus Christ who had set them free. In this case the Christians did not take over, as far as we can see, the criticism of Jewish apologetics; but they struck a blow of their own. Transition from paganism to Judaism meant a transition from one system of ancestral traditions to another. *Here it proclaimed a completely new life in Christ*" (p. 141, italics added).

172. So Davids, 102. It would not be inappropriate to connect μάταιος with νεκρά in 2:17 and with the implied negative of μὴ δύναται ἡ πίστις σῶσαι αὐτόν (v. 14). Thus, there is evidence in James for reading this in the traditional manner. But it can at least be asked here (and partly answered in the exegesis of 2:14-26) whether "dead" and "save" have to refer to the eschaton or heaven.

1:27 James now moves from a general observation about useless religion to *the specifics* of "pure and undefiled religion" (1:27).[173] Purity was for many Jews, especially those whose faith was centered in the Temple, the core concern of Judaism and life.[174] Furthermore, purity was defined by Torah, and James was well-known for his Torah piety.[175] And there is every reason to believe that, even if James sees purity figuratively (as did Jesus, Mark 7:1-23) and as an internal condition that transcends or is "more important than" the external manifestation, James was both Torah-observant and concerned to live within the laws of purity. It has often been inferred, at times without careful consideration, that because James (like Jesus) saw purity as deeds of mercy he must have rejected the typical sense of purity in Judaism. This is a *non sequitur.* To see purity as an internal condition does not necessarily eliminate the desire to follow the Torah's purity guidelines. For James, to be pure means to be marked off in worldview from those who are unjust, oppressive, and worldly, and the marking off was more internal-moral versus external-moral. But being marked off is not just separation: it is the devotion to compassion and Torah observance that determines the separation.

A text like Hermas, *Parables* 60.1 (5.7.1) is apposite for James 1:27:

173. καθαρὰ καὶ ἀμίαντος. BDAG, 489, 54. This is hendiadys. On purity in James, see McKnight, "A Parting within the Way"; J. H. Elliott, "Holiness-Wholeness," 74-77; but see further the more extensive research of Lockett, *Purity and Worldview,* and "'Unstained by the World': Purity and Pollution as an Indicator of Cultural Interaction in the Letter of James," in Webb and Kloppenborg, *Reading James,* 49-74. Apart from Jas 1:26-27, Lockett helpfully works with 3:6, 3:13-17, and 4:8 to contend that purity is worldview demarcation. His analysis bears resemblance to what Johnson calls "friendship" in "Friendship with the World and Friendship with God: A Study of Discipleship in James," in Johnson, *Brother of Jesus, Friend of God,* 202-20. See the older exchange: D. J. Roberts, "The Definition of 'Pure Religion' in James 1:27," *Expository Times* 83 (1972) 215-16; and B. C. Johanson, "The Definition of 'Pure Religion' in James 1:27 Reconsidered," *Expository Times* 84 (1973) 118-19. Roberts made much of P74's use of ὑπερασπίζειν in the sense of "shielding them [widows and orphans] from the world during their affliction." Roberts's theory is that such stand-offishness is inconsistent with James's practical religion, but one would think Jas 4:4 would be sufficient to rebut his aversion to the standard reading of the text. M. Black found this "corruption" a "particularly happy one" in "Critical and Exegetical Notes on Three New Testament Texts: Hebrews xi.11, Jude 5, James i.27," in *Apophoreta: Festschrift für E. Haenchen* (ed. W. Eltester and F. H. Kettler; BZNW 30; Berlin: A. Töpelmann, 1964), 39-45, here p. 45.

174. See the summary of B. D. Chilton, "Purity," in *DNTB,* 874-82; J. E. Hartley, "Holy and Holiness, Clean and Unclean," in *DOTP,* 420-31; McKnight, "A Parting within the Way," 84-89.

175. Besides Acts 15:16-18 (cf. Lev 17–18), see Gal 2:11-14; Jas 1:25; 2:8, 12; Eusebius, *Eccl Hist* 2.23.3-8. See Evans, "Jesus and James: Martyrs of the Temple."

"Keep this flesh of yours clean and undefiled,[176] in order that the Spirit that lives in it may bear witness to it, and your flesh may be justified." James after all is rooted more in Torah than in anything else. So, when he says "pure" one thinks of Genesis 8:20 ("clean animal"); Leviticus 4:12 ("clean place"); 7:19 ("clean" flesh), and for "undefiled" one thinks of Leviticus 18:24 ("defile yourselves") or Deuteronomy 21:23 ("defile the land"). Thus, "pure and undefiled" are purity terms to describe the condition of a person and his or her aptness to live in the Land or enter the Temple for worship in utter fidelity to God and Torah. Not only are these terms derived from the Torah, what James contends constitutes that purity is also from the same source. Thus, to anticipate the next section, James says "pure and undefiled religion . . . is this: to care for orphans and widows," which itself comes from Torah legislation:

Exodus 22:22: "You shall not abuse any widow or orphan."
Deuteronomy 10:18: "who executes justice for the orphan and the widow, and who loves the strangers, providing them food and clothing" (cf. James 2:14-17).

James's appeal to "unstained" in 1:27b is of the same cloth.

The specifics of the positive side to what James is getting at are now deepened by contending that the purity James is concerned with is one that has to do with God. It is not impossible to understand "before God, the Father"[177] polemically and interpret it as a contrast with "before the Temple" or "before the Torah." But there is very little evidence that James fashions the messianic community as anything other than a fully functioning Jewish community, including Temple worship, that believes Jesus is the Messiah. A life before God the Father, who is the creator (cf. Sir 4:10), can be a life of Torah-keeping purity, even if that purity is understood to transcend the outwardly observant and to include deeds of mercy. In other words, there is nothing non-Jewish about what James is saying here.

James defines "pure and undefiled religion" as follows: "to care[178] for

176. καθαρὰν καὶ ἀμίαντον.
177. παρὰ τῷ θεῷ καὶ πατρί, on which see Ropes, 183-84; Martin, 53. On "father" as language for God, see McKnight, New Vision, 49-65. The use of "father" for God was not "distinct" to Jesus, but it was "characteristic" of Jesus; nor does it carry the freight that Jesus was the first to see God in relational terms. Nonetheless, this is characteristic and emphatic language for Jesus and the early Christians. See further at Ng, "Father-God Language," 48-50.
178. ἐπισκέπτεσθαι, see BDAG, 378. The term is cognate with ἐπίσκοπος. The present tense indicates vivid or characteristic action and behavior. The infinitive defines αὕτη and thus functions as a complement of the predicate. It is structurally equivalent with τηρεῖν at the end of 1:27.

orphans and widows in their distress, and to keep oneself unstained by the world." Early Christian visitation was anchored in the goodness of God, who is the Father and creator, and in Jesus' practice of ministering to the marginalized and hurting. Thus, in Luke 1:68 and 78, Zechariah extols God's "visitation" of the last days.[179] Jesus cared for the marginalized (see Matt 8–9) and urged his followers to participate in visitations and care for the naked, sick, and imprisoned (Matt 25:36, 43), and many have made of this the very presence of Christ among the marginalized.[180] The example of Jesus, buttressed as it is by such teachings from James, has led many to a life dedicated to the poor and wounded, and one thinks here both of St. Francis and the founders of hospitals and hospice ministries.[181]

The first manifestation of a "pure and undefiled religion" for James is care for "orphans and widows."[182] The connection of "orphans and widows" is typical for the Old Testament (e.g., Ezek 22:7) and Judaism.[183] This injunction flows from Old Testament legislation into the glowing prescriptions of Isaiah 1:17:

> learn to do good;
> seek justice,
> rescue the oppressed,
> defend the orphan,
> plead for the widow.

Turning from idolatry meant turning to mercy for the orphan:

> Assyria shall not save us; we will not ride upon horses; we will say no more, 'Our God,' to the work of our hands. In you the orphan finds mercy (Hosea 14:3).

Tobit, too, described his own piety by his treatment of the orphan and widows:

> A third tenth I would give to the orphans and widows and to the converts who had attached themselves to Israel (1:8; cf. 1:3-9).

179. See also Luke 7:16; Acts 15:14; Heb 2:6.

180. See also Josephus, *Ant* 9.178 (Joash, king of Jerusalem, visiting Elisha).

181. It is a sad irony that scholarship on the cognates of ἐπισκέπτεσθαι is obsessed with the question of authority inherent to the office rather than the pastoral ministry of visitation. Popkes, 150, gets this right.

182. On orphans, see Exod 22:22; Deut 10:18; 24:17, 19-21; 27:19; Job 6:27; 24:9; 31:18, 21; Pss 10:14, 18; 82:3; 94:6; 146:9; Isa 1:23; Jer 5:28; 7:6; 22:3; Ezek 22:7; Zech 7:10; Mal 3:5; Sir 35:14; 2 Esdr 2:20.

183. See 1QHa 13:20 (where orphan is attached to the poor); 4Q255 f3 2.22; 4Q434 f 51.2; *m. Maaseroth S* 5:10 ("to the stranger, the orphan, and the widow").

Josephus tells us that the Essenes nurtured orphans in their community.[184]

The annexation of "widows" to "orphans" sheds light on the meaning of the latter. Recent study of papyri has shown that to be called an "orphan" requires only that one has lost one parent and not both.[185] In other words, "orphan" often meant "fatherless" (or "motherless") rather than "parent-less,"[186] bringing into sharper focus why for the "fatherless" James may be pointing to God as "Father" in this text. Here is an example from a funerary inscription for a man where the term does not mean "parentless":

> (Envious fortune has done you wrong and)
> given tears to your mother in her old age,
> widowhood to your wife,
> as well as making an orphan of your poor child.[187]

Clearly, the deceased leaves behind a wife and child, and the child is called an "orphan."

"Widows,"[188] too, were a special concern of Jesus and of the early messianic community, and this concern extended into the first few centuries.[189] There is no reason to assign a source for James's concern: it is biblical, it is found in Jesus' ministry, and it is socio-economically present for the first messianic community. Anyone who practices the Jesus Creed of James 2:8-11 will see the needs of the orphans and widows and will respond with compassion.

James says the messianic community is to be characterized by com-

184. *J.W.* 2.120; see also *m. Qidd* 4.1-3 (for the *asufi,* or "foundling"). See S. McKnight, *A Light among the Gentiles: Jewish Missionary Activity in the Second Temple Period* (Minneapolis: Fortress, 1991), 66-67.

185. *m. Bek* 9:4 specifies that an "orphaned" (יתום) beast is not tithed, and the term is defined as "the dam of which has died or been slaughtered," and then R. Joshua says, "Even if its dam is slaughtered, but the hide is whole, this is not deemed an orphan." Here clearly the issue pertains to motherlessness.

186. See *New Docs* 4.162-64.

187. *New Docs* 4.163.

188. On widows, see *EDNT* 3.465-66; D. C. Verner, *The Household of God: The Social World of the Pastoral Epistles* (SBLDS 71; Chico: Scholars, 1983), 161-66. F. Scott Spencer, "Neglected Widows in Acts 6:1-7," *CBQ* 56 (1994) 715-33, finds four alienations for widows: economic, practical, social, and emotional. He sees an appropriate tension between the apostles in Acts 6:1-7 and 9:41.

189. For Jesus: see Mark 12:38-43; Luke 7:12; 18:3, 5. For the messianic community: see Luke 2:37 *(Anawim);* Acts 6:1; 9:39, 41. Also see 1 Tim 5:3-5, 9, 11, 16; Justin, *1 Apologia* 67.7; Ignatius, *Smyrnaeans* 6.2. See also Exod 22:22; Deut 10:18; 24:19-21; 27:19; 1 Kgs 17:9-10; Job 24:21; 31:18; Pss 94:6; 146:9; Isa 1:17; Jer 7:6; 22:3; Ezek 22:7; Zech 7:10; Mal 3:5. See also Jdth 8:4; 9:4, 9; Sir 35:14-15; Bar 6:38; 2 Esdr 2:20.

passion for orphans and widows, and he adds "in their distress."[190] What sort of distress is James talking about? Some recent commentators have observed that the word *thlipsis* ("distress") is often connected to the eschatological tribulation or final ordeal[191] and have suggested that James has this in mind here.[192] Others opt for the more normal sense of *thlipsis* when connected to both widows and orphans: either bereavement[193] or poverty.[194] James does not directly describe any of the distress of the messianic community as part of the eschatological woes; instead, he blames persecution on the persecutors[195] as part of his broader emphasis on human responsibility.[196] The eschaton is the time of establishing justice and reward, while the present time is one of testing and trials in order to form the moral character (1:2-4) as the messianic community pursues justice and peace. If the eschatological view of "in their distress" with "orphans and widows" does not have much in its favor within the text of James, it can also be considered a customary expression referring to poverty and possibly to bereavement.[197] It seems most likely, then, that with "in their distress" James is describing the socio-economic and emotional condition of the widows and orphans rather than the eschatological location of those sufferings.

The second indicator of pure and undefiled religion is "to keep[198]

---

190. ἐν τῇ θλίψει, on which see BDAG, 457; *EDNT* 2.151-53; Allison, *The End of the Ages Has Come,* 5-25. As eschatological "distress," see Matt 24:9, 21, 29; Col 1:24; Rev 1:9; 2:9-10, 22; 7:14. As persecution or another form of distress, see Matt 13:21; John 16:33; Acts 7:10-11; 11:19; 14:22; 20:23; Rom 2:9; 5:3; 8:35; 12:12; 2 Cor 1:4, 8; 2:4; 4:17; 6:4; 7:4; 8:2, 13; Eph 3:13; Phil 1:17; 4:14; 1 Thess 1:6; 3:3, 7; 2 Thess 1:6; Heb 10:33. I have chosen to leave many in the second grouping because it would take considerable work to demonstrate the eschatological nature of many of these.

191. There is a tendency to see the term θλῖψις and think only and immediately of eschatological tribulation. A balanced discussion can be found in *EDNT* 2.152-53.

192. See Laws, 89-90; Martin, 53.

193. Ropes, 184.

194. Johnson, 212.

195. Observe 2:5-7; 4:1-12, and the emphasis on blame of those who do not act properly. In 5:1-6, James sees the eschaton as a time when justice will be established against those who persecute and oppress. 5:7-11 emphasizes patience until the eschaton but does not explain their distress as part of the final ordeal.

196. See notes at 1:13-15.

197. See Matt 5:4. Widows and orphans and distress are part and parcel of the *Anawim* conditions. On linguistic paradigms, see A. C. Thiselton, "Semantics and New Testament Interpretation," in *New Testament Interpretation: Essays on Principles and Methods* (ed. I. H. Marshall; Grand Rapids: Eerdmans, 1977), 75-104.

198. On τηρεῖν, see BDAG, 1002. Also at Matt 19:17; 23:3; 28:20; John 8:51-52, 55; 14:15, 21, 23-24; 15:10, 20; 17:6, 15; Acts 15:5; 1 Cor 7:37; Eph 4:3; 1 Tim 5:22; 6:14; 2 Tim 4:7; 1 John 2:3-5; 3:22, 24; 5:3, 18; Rev 1:3; 2:26; 3:3, 8, 10; 14:12; 22:7, 9. The present tense emphasizes characteristic behavior; it is "imperfective" in as-

oneself unstained by the world."[199] The concern to be "unstained" *(aspilon)* expresses the reverence of earliest Christianity and its commitment to holiness.[200] In 1 Timothy 6:14, "without spot *(aspilon)* or blame" is used of confessional purity, and in 2 Peter 3:14 "without spot *(aspiloi)* or blemish" is used of moral purity. What James says is like the latter since his concern is with being unstained "by the world."[201] "The world" stands in contrast to "the kingdom" in 2:5 and to "God" in 4:4.[202] And, though in 3:15 James does not use "world," the sense is similar: "Such wisdom does not come down from above [God? kingdom? heaven?], but is earthly *(epigeios),* unspiritual *(psychikē),* devilish *(daimoniōdēs).*" And this "wisdom" refers back to 3:14 where James is most concerned with "bitter envy and selfish ambition in your hearts" and being "boastful." Which stands in contrast to 3:13: "Show by your good life that your works are done with gentleness born of wisdom." Once again, we are in touch with themes that resonate throughout James 1: wisdom, good works, and a gentle life of good works — and this in contrast to social disruption, violence, and arrogance. Worldliness for James pertains to human forceful efforts to establish justice, peace, or God's will.

Throughout 1:26-27 James has utilized cultic imagery, or at least language that seems suited especially for the Temple. This language is intended to compel the messianic community to strive for holiness in the sense of moral fidelity and compassionate behavior.

---

pect. BDF §337.2 calls it categorical with an ingressive element mixed in. The infinitive is a complement of the predicate and is the second such complement (along with ἐπισκέπτεσθαι).

199. ἄσπιλον ἑαυτὸν τηρεῖν ἀπὸ τοῦ κόσμου. On ἄσπιλον, see BDAG, 144. The alpha-privative of σπίλος means "spotless" or "untainted" or "pure." The term is not found in the LXX or Josephus or Philo, but is found in *2 Clement* 8:6 ("keep the flesh pure and the seal unstained [ἄσπιλον]"); Hermas, *Visions* 24.5 ("those who have been chosen by God for eternal life will be spotless [ἄσπιλοι] and pure"); *Similitudes* 59.7 ("For all flesh in which the Holy Spirit has dwelled — and which has been found undefiled and spotless [ἄσπιλος] — will receive a reward").

200. A theology of holiness is in need of renewal today. See J. Webster, *Holiness* (Grand Rapids: Eerdmans, 2003); D. G. Peterson, "Holiness," in *NDBT,* 544-50. A. W. Tozer, one devoted to the holiness of God, provides an example: see L. Dorsett, *A Passion for God: The Spiritual Journey of A. W. Tozer* (Chicago: Moody, 2008).

201. κόσμος is found often in the New Testament, especially in John's writings. In James, cf. 1:27; 2:5; 3:6; 4:4. On the moral sense, see also Ropes, 184-85; Laws, 90-91; Davids, 103; Martin, 53. The genitive is one of separation: cf. MHT, 3.215.

202. Jas 3:6 is metaphorical; see notes there.

4. THE CHRISTIAN AND PARTIALITY (2:1-13)

This section is divided into three subsections.[1] James begins by describing the *inconsistency* of faith in the glorious Jesus Christ, who was himself poor, with treatment of the poor with contempt and the rich with partiality. Impartiality blocks the avalanche of grace that is designed to treat the poor with compassion (2:1-4). This is followed by a rhetorical *interrogation* of readers who have become partial in their treatment of others (2:5-7). James's strategy is to examine this treatment, now in light of the pattern of God's electing grace. Has not God persistently chosen the pattern of grace for the poor? The messianic community, however, has broken the pattern. Furthermore, they have not used their commonsense: Who is it that oppresses the messianic community? Is it the poor or the rich? Follow suit, he argues. Third, James provides *instruction* (2:8-13). First, he appeals to the ever-present Jesus version of the *Shema*. As Jesus amended the sacred creed of Judaism, the *Shema*, by adding Leviticus 19:18 to Deuteronomy 6:4-9, so now the brother of Jesus revitalizes the significance of that amendment. The essence of the Torah is to love your neighbor as yourself. That *mitzvah*, that commandment, is broken whenever the messianic community shows partiality.[2] James's reflection on breaking that commandment, now one of the two central *mitzvoth* for the messianic community, leads to a digression on breaking the Torah wherein he establishes that each breaking of the Torah incurs judgment. Breaking the Torah ought to lead the messianic community back to their knees and generate a repentance that leads to a life lived in obedience to "the law of liberty." Such a life will triumph in the end (2:8-13).[3]

---

1. The rhetorical and logical moves are traced in Wachob, *Voice of Jesus*, 59-113; Hartin, 124-28. Wisdom themes in 2:1-13 are traced in Hoppe, *Der theologische Hintergrund*, 72-99. It is entirely possible that James criticizes the Roman patronage system; see Batten, "God in the Letter of James," 264-65. No studies of rhetoric in James are as defined as Duane Watson's learned case for James 2's relationship to the Greco-Roman models of rhetoric in "James 2 in Light of Greco-Roman Schemes of Argumentation," *NTS* 39 (1993) 94-121. I have made a case above that conscious use of rhetorical models, which is often implicit in studies like this, and the general art of persuasion need to be more carefully analyzed. Watson, in my opinion, if he does not show that James knew models of rhetoric and that specific verses can now be labeled more accurately, clarifies at least the art of persuasion of James 2.

2. See Maynard-Reid, *Poverty and Wealth in James*, 48-67.

3. For the entire passage, see Wachob, *Voice of Jesus*.

4.1. INCONSISTENCY (2:1-4)

1 *My[4] brothers and sisters, do[5] you with your acts of favoritism[6] really believe in our glorious[7] Lord Jesus Christ?*[a] 2 *For if* [b] *a person with gold rings[c] and in fine clothes comes into your[8] assembly,[d] and if a poor person in dirty clothes also comes in,* 3 *and[9] if you take notice[e] of the one wearing the fine clothes and say,[10] "Have a seat here, please,[f] " while to the one who is poor you say, "Stand there," or, "Sit[g] at[11] my feet,"[12]* 4 *have you not made distinctions[h] among yourselves, and become judges with evil thoughts?*

a. TNIV: believers in our glorious Lord Jesus Christ must not show favoritism
b. TNIV: Suppose . . .

4. Some lectionary-influenced manuscripts omit μου (e.g., 1251).

5. The Greek grammar of 2:1 creates opportunity for dynamic equivalent translations. The NRSV finds a question while the TNIV finds an imperative. The verb ἔχετε, besides finding its way in some manuscripts into a subjunctive (61, 94, 459), could be rendered either as an imperative or an indicative interrogative with an implied negative answer. The interrogative (NRSV) does not make logical sense, for why would James deny that they are showing partiality only to explain specific instances of partiality? So Mussner, 115 n. 1; Popkes, 158. Somehow Johnson, 220, cites Ropes (p. 46) as maintaining the interrogative view, and that same reference is found in Popkes, but Ropes, p. 46, does not discuss Jas 2:1, and on p. 186 Ropes clearly affirms the imperative mood for the verb in 2:1.

6. Frequently spelled προσωποληψιαις (copyist 2 of B; also 025, 044, etc.). The plural προσωπολημψίαις is probably poetic and may suggest "instantiations of partiality" (see MHT, 3.27-28).

7. Some manuscripts (206, 429, along with some Coptic and Syriac manuscripts) place τῆς δόξης before τοῦ κυρίου ἡμῶν Ἰησοῦ Χριστοῦ. Nestle-Aland[27] prints the order of words most likely original. A few manuscripts (33, 631, and Antiochus Monarchus) omit τῆς δόξης altogether.

8. Some manuscripts, including one variation in ℵ as well as B, C, Y, and others, omit την before σψναγωγην. Other early and important manuscripts include it (ℵ, A, P, 33, and many Maj manuscripts). Nestle-Aland[27] omits the article.

9. Some good manuscripts have και επιβλεψητε (P74V, ℵ, A, 33, and Maj manuscripts). The δὲ is most likely not an adversative but continuative (Martin, 62).

10. A number of manuscripts insert αυτω to make clear the obvious (P, 5, 88, 323, 1739, etc.).

11. Many manuscripts have επι instead of υπο; thus B², P, Y, 33, and Latin, Syriac, and Sahidic texts.

12. There are a variety of readings for "Stand there" or "Sit at my feet." (1) The translated text reflects σὺ στῆθι ἐκεῖ ἢ κάθου ὑπὸ τὸ ὑποπόδιόν μου (A, C*, Y, 33, etc.); (2) some prefer συ στηθι η καθου εκει υπο το υποποδιον μου (B, 945, 1241, 1243, 1739, etc.); (3) συ στῆθι ἐκεῖ ἢ κάθου ὧδε (P74, ℵ, P, and Maj texts).

c. TNIV: a gold ring

d. TNIV: meeting

e. TNIV: show special attention

f. TNIV: Here's a good seat for you

g. TNIV: on the floor

h. TNIV: discriminated

How James 2:1-4 fits with 1:19-27 remains unclear and any strong claims to structural clarity outrun the evidence. In general, James's concern with the marginalized, such as widows and orphans (1:27), and his overriding focus on critique of the oppressive wealthy, on God's favor toward the oppressed poor (1:9-11),[13] and on potential violence and injustice in the community (1:19-20; 2:14-17; 3:13-18; 4:1-10; 5:1-6) lead James to focus on a specific instantiation of systemic injustice: the messianic community is treating the poor unjustly and showing favoritism toward the wealthy in public settings. They are caving in to a way of the world that James knows is wrong and that he learned about from Jesus (e.g., Mark 10:35-45).

James begins with a prohibition (not a question) in 2:1[14] and then expounds that prohibition with a graphic and almost ridiculous example of injustice in the community (2:2-3) that ends with a question implicating the messianic community (2:4).[15] 2:1 is filled with exegetical questions, some of which could be partly or completely resolved if we knew more of the precise context.[16]

2:1   A pastoral theology rooted in fellowship and family routinely prompts instruction and exhortation: "My brothers [and sisters by implication]."[17] The verb of the main clause in 2:1 is "have" *(echete),*[18] and this imperative needs to be connected to 2:18, where the same verb occurs twice: "You *have* faith and I *have* works." One need not think of possession here so much as simultaneous disposition: this messianic community "had" faith, that is, they were laying claim to redemption in Jesus Christ. Simultaneously they also "had," or better yet "were exercising," partiality. More importantly, the grammar shows that the object of *echete* is "faith." Their dominant disposition was one of faith in Jesus Christ, but, contradictorily, while believing in

13. So Davids, 105.

14. See above at the notes on translation and text.

15. On the use of δέ for coordination, see C. B. Amphoux, "L'emploi du coordonnant dans l'Épître de Jacques," *Biblica* 63 (1982) 90-101, especially p. 94.

16. The precise social setting is under debate. Kloppenborg Verbin, "Patronage Avoidance," for instance, interprets this text as responding to patronage. Ward famously focused on a judicial setting; see his "Partiality in the Assembly."

17. See also 1:2, 9, 16; 2:5, 14; 3:1, 10, 12; 4:11; 5:7, 9, 10, 12, 19.

18. See also 1:4; 2:17; 3:14; 4:2 *bis;* see also BDAG, 421 (7.a.β).

Jesus Christ they were showing favoritism toward the wealthy. This social exigency, namely partiality, is the situation into which the words of 2:1-13 are sent on a mission to change behavior.

"Favoritism."[19] God, it has been laid down, "shows no partiality and accepts no bribes" (Deut 10:17; cf. James 1:17) so God's people ought not to be partial. Though James has no need to offer a proof-text since the ethical code of impartiality had been worked so deeply into the Jewish conscience (Prov 18:5), he might have had this text in mind: "You shall not render an unjust judgment; you shall not be *partial to the poor or defer to the great:* with justice you shall judge your neighbor" (Lev. 19:15).[20] James refers to Leviticus 19 several times in the letter; the following are the major instances: James 5:4 (Lev 19:13); 5:9 (Lev 19:18a); 5:12 (Lev 19:12); 5:20 (Lev 19:17b). Because of this clear use of Leviticus 19, it can be inferred with reasonable probability that the messianic community's instantiations of "favoritism" are wrong because they are not in accordance with the Jesus Creed's reformulation of the *Shema* in adding Leviticus 19:18 to the standard morning recitation of Deuteronomy 6:4-9. Thus, favoritism is unloving in that it does not treat the neighbor as oneself (cf. James 2:8 and 1:25).

The NRSV has chosen to translate our sentence as a question: "Do you . . . really believe . . . ?"[21] This interrogative, along with the inserted word "really," just might let readers off the hook. In fact, James wants them on the hook and, as his rhetoric will reveal, he wants them to be seen for all they are doing in order to shame them into reform. The logic of 2:1-4 requires that the messianic community has in reality resorted to deferring to the rich and prejudice against the poor. Hence, the TNIV's translation "believers . . . must not show" is preferable.

Another translation decision concerns "believe" and "our Lord Jesus Christ." The Greek syntax is a connection of genitives: *echete tēn pistin tou kuriou hēmōn Iēsou Christou.* Some today conclude that "faith *of* our Lord Jesus Christ" is a subjective genitive and translate "the faith that Jesus Christ

---

19. On προσωπολημψία, see BDAG, 881; EDNT 3.179-80; Kloppenborg Verbin, "Patronage Avoidance," 764-65. The word translates the Hebrew נשׂא פנים ("to lift the face"; see BDB, s.v. נשׂא), which is a graphic expression for lifting up the face of the prostrated one. The expression in the Christian literature always connotes inappropriate favoritism, bias, or prejudice; since God is impartial, so too ought his people to be (Acts 10:34; Rom 2:11; Gal 2:6; Eph 6:9; Col 3:25; see also Matt 22:16; 1 Tim 5:21; *1 Clement* 1:3). See also Job 34:17-20; Ps 82:2; Mal 2:9; Sir 35:14.

20. Lev 19, this time citing v. 18, will appear later in this section at Jas 2:8-9, where προσωπολεμπτεῖτε will also be used. See L. T. Johnson, "The Use of Leviticus 19 in the Letter of James," *JBL* 101 (1982) 391-401.

21. See above under notes on translation and text.

himself had."[22] There are three insurmountable problems for this view, in spite of its rising popularity. First, while we cannot dismiss the observation often made that in James faith is directed to God (cf. 2:19, 23), when one calls Jesus Christ "Lord" and "Glorious" (2:1), faith in Jesus Christ is entailed at some level. A translation that sees here a reference to a person's faith in Jesus Christ is therefore not at all impossible. Second, the actor in the "partiality" is a messianist who is doing two things simultaneously: holding faith and partiality in the same hand. This form of double-mindedness expects both faith and partiality to be performed by the same person. Third, we can develop this second point a little more completely. The overall picture must be observed: according to the simple Greek structure, we are to see that the "you" in the "you have faith"[23] is the same "you" who has faith "in partiality." It is much more difficult to suggest that this person holds "Jesus Christ's own faith in partiality" than to think that he or she is holding two things at the same time: his or her own faith and own partiality.

The contradiction and hypocrisy James sees in the messianic community is an act of favoring the rich. The problem for James arises because the community claims it has *faith* "in our glorious Lord Jesus Christ." James, it is true, can envision a kind of "faith" that is not genuinely productive but, as he goes on to say, he believes good works will inevitably become manifest for the one with genuine faith (cf. 2:20-26).[24] One could conclude that, since James knows of deficient faith, their faith still saves. But that logic would give them permission to ignore his words, and he does not surrender to them at all. Instead, James assumes both that their faith is genuine and that their praxis of favoritism contradicts genuine faith, and so he calls them to repent and be transformed.[25]

Even though the expression "believers in our glorious Lord Jesus Christ" is unusual, leading some to suggest an interpolation, all the evidence

22. A good example is Hartin, 117. A recent attempt to connect the new perspective of Paul, *pistis Christou,* and Jas 2:1 can be found in Bruce A. Lowe, "James 2:1 in the Πίστις Χριστοῦ Debate: Indecipherable or Indispensable?" in *The Faith of Jesus Christ: Exegetical, Biblical and Theological Studies* (ed. Michael F. Bird and Preston M. Sprinkle; Carlisle: Paternoster/Peabody: Hendrickson, 2010).

23. Thus, "you have faith" is a ground level translation that is denied: "You should not have faith along with partiality."

24. The wording of 2:18 is similar: σὺ πίστιν ἔχεις.

25. There is some dispute over what James means by "faith" and how that meaning relates to Paul's understanding of "faith." It is common to say that by "faith" James means no more than creedal faith and then to define that by monotheism. While this might explain all of 2:14-26, Jas 2:1 shows that those monotheists about whom James is so concerned in 2:14-26 are the ones who also affirm some kind of "orthodox" faith in Jesus Christ, the Glorious One (2:1).

of the surviving manuscripts suggests that this text is original.[26] Faith in the Lord Jesus Christ is a thoroughly Christian expression, but the addition of "glorious" is unusual and could derive from early hymnic or creedal lines (e.g., 1 Tim 3:16) and it could be a combination of "our Lord Jesus Christ" with the "Lord of glory" (1 Cor 2:8).[27] Several issues arise: Which word or words does "glorious" modify, or does it stand on its own? What does "glorious" mean in this context? Here are some options:

> "faith in our Lord Jesus (glorious) Christ"
> "faith in our glorious Lord, Jesus Christ"[28]
> "faith in our glorious Lord Jesus Christ"[29]
> "faith in our Lord Jesus Christ, the glorious one"[30]
> "faith in the glorious one, the Lord Jesus Christ"[31]

The most decisive element of the evidence is word order: "glorious" is the last word and could be emphatic and so favor the last translation in our list, or "glorious" might stand on its own epexegetically since its fit with "Jesus Christ" would be so unusual. We cannot find confident ground, but I would favor "faith in our Lord Jesus Christ, the glorious one" if pressed to decide. We quote Mayor: "We may suppose that the reason why the word *doxa* stands here alone . . . is in order that it may be understood in its fullest and widest sense of Him who alone comprises all glory in Himself."[32]

Of even more interest is what "glorious" in this context might mean.[33]

---

26. Davids, 106, mentions both Spitta and Windisch as concluding that ἡμῶν Ἰησοῦ Χριστοῦ is interpolation, and Davids offers arguments against the speculative textual emendation.

27. So R. Bauckham, "James and Jesus," in Chilton and Neusner, *The Brother of Jesus*, 133-34, where Jewish parallels are listed. Burchard's discussion of the genitives here is called "Zur Genitivkette in Jakobus 2,1" (Burchard, 97-98), that is, "on the chain of genitives in James 2:1." See Wall, 109-10, who sees a subjective genitive: the faith Jesus Christ exhibits.

28. One could find support in 1 Cor 2:8: οὐκ ἂν τὸν κύριον τῆς δόξης.

29. Ropes, 187; Dibelius, 128; Davids, 106-7; Martin, 60.

30. Laws, 95-96. Mayor, 81, appeals to 1 Tim 1:1; some appeal to Jas 1:12, where τῆς ζωῆς could also be epexegetical. On "glory" used this way, see also Luke 2:32; John 1:14; 17:22; Eph 1:17; Col 1:27; Heb 1:3; 1 Pet 4:14; 2 Pet 1:17. See also the formative text Psalm 24. Popkes, 152, is similar in German.

31. One might appeal here to Acts 4:33; 2 Cor 4:4; Rom 5:2.

32. Mayor, 81; he then appeals to the Greek's rhythm, which makes a natural pause before τῆς δόξης.

33. On "glory," see Spicq, 1.362-79; Turner, *Christian Words*, 185-89; Mounce, *Dictionary*, 289-90; *NIDNTT* 2.44-52; J. Freeborn, "Lord of Glory: A Study of James 2 and 1 Corinthians 2," *Expository Times* 111 (2000) 185-89; also Popkes, 158-59.

Glory *(doxa)* could be a translation of Hebrew *kabod* or perhaps *hod, shekina,* or *tip'eret.* The term could be (1) incarnational or theophanic (e.g., 1 Cor 2:8) and suggest the very splendor and presence of God, which would render favoritism especially hypocritical.[34] Or it could be (2) eschatological and suggest the resurrection and exaltation of Jesus Christ after his humiliation and poverty (e.g., 2 Cor 8:9; cf. John 3:14; 8:28; 12:32), which would in turn put the behavior of the messianic community under the threat of judgment.[35] In which case, the text of James echoes texts like Deuteronomy 10:17-18 and Sirach 35:10-15:

> For the LORD your God is God of gods and Lord of lords, the great God, mighty and awesome, who is not partial and takes no bribe, who executes justice for the orphan and the widow, and who loves the strangers, providing them food and clothing (Deut 10:17-18).

> Give to the Most High as he has given to you,
>   and as generously as you can afford.
> For the Lord is the one who repays,
>   and he will repay you sevenfold.
> Do not offer him a bribe, for he will not accept it;
>   and do not rely on a dishonest sacrifice;
>   for the Lord is the judge,
>   and with him there is no partiality.
> He will not show partiality to the poor;
>   but he will listen to the prayer of one who is wronged.
> He will not ignore the supplication of the orphan,
>   or the widow when she pours out her complaint
>   (Sir 35:10-15; cf. also 10:30-31; 11:1, 4, 12-13).

If one favors the suggestion of the previous paragraph and translates "the glorious one," there is a slight tip of the hat toward the first interpretation since the weight of the expression is on an attribute of the Lord Jesus Christ — he is the glorious one and therefore the one deserving of honor. Nonetheless, that con-

---

34. Thus, Exod 16:10; 2 Chron 7:1-3; Isa 6:1; Ezek 8:4. In the New Testament, one thinks of Luke 2:9; Mark 9:1-8; 2 Cor 3–4, especially 3:18; 4:6; John 1:14; 17:5; Heb 1:3; 2 Pet 1:17.

35. Thus, Mark 8:38; 13:24-27; Matt 19:28; 25:31; Luke 24:26; John 17:5; Acts 7:55; 1 Cor 15:40-43; Phil 2:11; 3:21; Col 3:4; 1 Tim 3:16; Heb 2:9; 1 Pet 1:11, 21; 4:13; Rev 4:11; 5:12-13. With appropriate nuances by each, the theophanic sense is favored by Hort, 47; Popkes, 158; Blomberg and Kamell, 106-7; and the eschatological sense is favored by Davids, 107. A more neutral sense can be seen in Brosend, 57-58. The emphasis on wisdom in James might lead some to see a connection here to Jesus as Wisdom, which is sometimes connected to glory (e.g., Prov 21:21; 22:4).

sideration does not compel either interpretation and can be made to fit with either the theophanic or eschatological view. Sophie Laws is right: "James is not here concerned with the definition of christology [which the theophanic view emphasizes] but with the relation between faith and behaviour."[36]

Inasmuch as James has no other references to glory and no christology outside this passage, we are left with the option of leaving the two views in balance. If we take the theophanic view, contextually James could be emphasizing that the Lord Jesus Christ left the glorious presence of God, entered exemplarily into the impoverished state of the human condition, and has now returned to that glorious state of splendor: he is the poor and now exalted one. Therefore, the messianic community should be shamed in not identifying with the doubly glorious one who humbly identified with the poor. If we take the eschatological view, James could be exhorting the messianic community to recognize that they will have to render an account for their deference to the rich and their systemic mistreatment of the poor to the all-glorious Lord of the judgment, who, after his earthly ministry, was exalted to the right hand of God (cf. 5:7).

The *grammar* of 2:1 reveals the emphasis of James. A paraphrastic rendering would be "do not . . . in partiality . . . confess faith in the Lord Jesus Christ, the glorious one." By putting "in partiality" between "do not" and "confess" James shoves the community's glaring problem to the fore: the utter incompatibility of faith in Jesus Christ and favoritism toward the rich at the expense of the poor. And the *vocabulary* of 2:1, with its suspension of *doxa* until the end of the sentence, scores a dramatic victory: the Old Testament/Hebrew backdrop in *kabod* evokes wealth and fame (e.g., Gen 31:1; 45:13; 1 Chron 29:25) bound together into the weighty presence of a person, but now all that resides in the Lord Jesus Christ. His weight, his wealthy glory, come after his impoverishment. One can easily understand why our minds are drawn back to the paradoxes of 1:9-11: wealth leads to humiliation and poverty to exaltation.

2:2-4 Having prohibited the stunning behavior of the messianic community and set forth the theme of this section, now James elucidates or illustrates[37] the prohibition with a graphic instance of favoritism. Martin Dibelius famously suggested that this example of favoritism cannot be used to discern actual behaviors within the community, and he has been followed to some degree by both Sophie Laws and Peter Davids.[38] But more believe it ei-

---

36. Laws, 97, though she tends toward a more theophanic emphasis. Yet, one must ask if she has not framed this into a false dichotomy.

37. ἐὰν γάρ. Martin, 60: "To illustrate. . . ." Use of examples is characteristic of deliberative rhetoric; see Wachob, *Voice of Jesus,* 71-90.

38. Most take the condition as real (Reicke, 27; Martin, 60), with the indicative in

ther is real or borders on the real.[39] Both Laws and Davids suggest that the hypothetical example bears some relationship to actual events in the messianic community and could be an example with some caricature involved. Wall turns that view around and finds concrete realities at work in the community itself.[40] What then, we are led to ask, might that actual situation be but something just like what is described in 2:2-4? That James uses indicatives in 2:4 suggests that he not only thinks the discrimination in 2:2-4 is a great rhetorical, hypothetical example but he also wants to depict it as an actuality so that the readers can see, hear, and sense the event. Touching up his example with some Flannery O'Connor–like caricature[41] serves only to show the inconsistency in a Christian praxis that affirms the lordship of the poverty-stricken Jesus Christ and that includes their own poverty over against the glaring mistreatment of others who are poor. These verses contain a lengthy protasis (vv. 2-3) with five separable actions (*eiselthē, eiselthē, epiblepsēte, eipēte, eipēte:* "comes," "comes," "take notice," "say," "say") spanning the sketch of the scene.[42] This protasis is then followed hard by a question designed to denounce the behaviors previously sketched as inconsistent with faith in Jesus Christ, the glorious one who, like the readers, was poor.

2:2 Martin translates the opening of 2:2 with "To illustrate."[43] The inconsistency occurs in the readers' "assembly." The oddity of this expression is that here, and here alone, the word normally translated "synagogue" is used *(synagōgē),*[44] pressing upon us all sorts of questions: Was the messianic

---

2:4 (and the implied reality of vv. 4-7), while Dibelius (128-30) and Laws (97-98) suggest a hypothetical method for James. See also Mussner, 116-17. But see Popkes, 160-61, for a view similar to what we argue here.

39. So Reicke, 27; Martin, 60-61. The subjunctive mood, depicting as it does potentiality, does not necessarily mean that what is depicted is merely hypothetical; it is "rhetorically" hypothetical in this instance because the action of the verb must be suspended until the indicatives and interrogatives of 2:4.

40. Wall, 103-5.

41. See the short stories of Flannery O'Connor, a master of Southern grotesque, in her *Collected Works* (New York: Library of America, 1988).

42. James sketches the scene with typical aorists that are shaped to describe the action without regard to completion or incompletion. These aorists stand in descriptive contrast with the bolder, more vivid present tense of 2:1, which describes the moral problem of gripping faith and partiality in the same set of hands.

43. Martin, 60. Nigel Turner, in MHT, 3.115, says ἐάν with the aorist subjunctive "represents a definite event as occurring only once in the future, and conceived as taking place before the time of the action of the main verb. It is expectation, but not fulfillment as yet. It is very near the meaning of ὅταν, and is often more than mere probability (see LXX Isa 24:13 *when;* Am 7:2)." Turner thus straddles the views of Dibelius (hypothetical) and those who see the example as real.

44. There is now a rich fund of study on synagogues, which frequently were not

community still in a synagogue? Was the "synagogue" mixed with both non-messianic and messianic Jews? Did the messianic Jews adopt the word "synagogue" for either their building or their gatherings? Was it a dedicated building or, which is far more likely, a home? We cannot answer each of these questions with any kind of conviction, but we can sort through what we do know.

The word *synagōgē* could refer to three things:

1. *A place:* a physical building like a house, in which case it could refer to a non-messianic Jewish building, to a building housing both messianic and non-messianic Jews, or to a building now used only by the messianic community. There is support for a building being called a "synagogue" by Josephus (*B.J.* 2.285, 289; 7:44) and Philo (*Every Good Man Is Free* 81) and apparently in the New Testament (Mark 12:39; Matt 23:6). We should not think of a synagogue always as a building constructed exclusively for public worship, instruction, and prayer.
2. *A gathering of people:* "assembling" or "gathering."[45] Again, this could refer to any of our three groups. Laws, for instance, sees this usage in Acts 6:9; 9:2; Revelation 2:9; 3:9.[46] The evidence is not as clear as one might think. Inasmuch as the vast majority of New Testament

much more than a house or a convenient meeting place. I mention only these in chronological order: M. Hengel, "Proseuche and Synagoge: Jüdische Gemeinde, Gotteshaus und Gottesdienst in der Diaspora und in Palästina," in *Tradition und Glaube. Das Frühe Christentum in seiner Umwelt. Festgabe für Karl Georg Kuhn zum 65. Geburtstag* (ed. J. Jeremias; Göttingen: Vandenhoeck und Ruprecht, 1971), 157-84; Lee I. Levine, "The Sages and the Synagogue in Late Antiquity: The Evidence of the Galilee," in *The Galilee in Late Antiquity* (ed. Lee I. Levine; Cambridge: Harvard University Press, 1992), 201-22; P. Richardson, "Early Synagogues as Collegia in the Diaspora and Palestine," in *Voluntary Associations in the Graeco-Roman World* (ed. J. S. Kloppenborg and S. G. Wilson; New York: Routledge, 1996), 90-109; H. C. Kee and L. H. Cohick, eds., *Evolution of the Synagogue: Problems and Progress* (Harrisburg: Trinity Press International, 1999); Lee I. Levine, "The Development of the Synagogue Liturgy in Late Antiquity," in *Galilee through the Centuries: Confluence of Cultures* (ed. E. M. Meyers; Winona Lake: Eisenbrauns, 1999), 123-44; various articles in *CHJ* 3.267-401; Harland, *Associations;* R. W. Gehring, *House Church and Mission* (Peabody: Hendrickson, 2004); Ritva H. Williams, *Stewards, Prophets, Keepers of the Word: Leadership in the Early Church* (Peabody: Hendrickson, 2006), 8-54; S. K. Catto, *Reconstructing the First-Century Synagogue* (LNTS 363; Edinburgh: Clark, 2007).

45. So Davids, 108.

46. Laws, 100; Davids, 108, holds a similar view. Johnson, 221-22, and Popkes, 161-62, admit that the evidence is not entirely clear. See also the sketch in Blomberg and Kamell, 110-11.

uses of the word refer to a place of Jewish worship, and inasmuch as the second meaning is inherent to the first, it is most likely that it means "synagogue" in its expected sense of a place of worship and teaching.

3. Three other factors, however, lead me to think *synagōgē* here refers more narrowly to *the messianic place of worship.*[47] First, James clearly borrows Jewish language in 1:1 to refer to the messianic community and this lends (potential) credibility to the view that he sees their meeting place in similar terms, as a (messianic) "synagogue." Second, James knows the word "church" *(ekklēsia)* as is seen in 5:14; it is reasonable to think he can use either term for the messianic community. Third, in James 2:2 James calls the *synagōgē* "your" *synagōgē.* That "your" must refer to the messianic community.

So while the evidence is hardly compelling, it is reasonable to see "assembly" or "congregating place" *(synagōgē)* in 2:2 as a term referring to the messianic community's worship and learning center, which for whatever reasons visitors sometimes attended.[48] The stance taken here, however, does not mean that James belongs to an earlier stage of the growth of Christianity; it only means that he and the messianic community "borrowed" typical language to refer to their gathering place.

James sketches two persons entering into the assembly, a rich man and a poor man, and the impact of his teaching is to subvert an element of the honor-shame culture of that day. "Clothing," Jerome Neyrey reminds us, "was not mere body covering, but indicated one's role and status."[49] It could indicate gender (Deut 22:5; 1 Cor 11:14-15), nationality (2 Macc 4:12), and occupation (Eph 6:14-17). The rich man[50] is stereotyped by his jewelry and

---

47. So BDAG, 963. See R. Riesner, "Synagogues in Jerusalem," in *The Book of Acts in Its Palestinian Setting* (The Book of Acts in Its First Century Setting 4; ed. R. Bauckham; Grand Rapids: Eerdmans, 1995), 179-211, here especially 207-8. Riesner provides later Christian evidence for calling congregating rooms "synagogues" and for an architectural connection with preferential seating arrangements from Sanhedrin to synagogue to basilica — as one can see today, for instance, in Ostia antica in Italy. See the comments of Witherington, 454-55.

48. Some think the language of 2:3 suggests that the gold-fingered man and the poor man are visitors since they need directions. I doubt that the language of 2:3 needs to be pressed into directions. Instead, the language speaks of labels and judgments of worth and status, in which case the gold-fingered man and the poor man may well be Christians.

49. J. Neyrey, in *Biblical Social Values and Their Meaning*, ed. John J. Pilch and Bruce J. Malina (Peabody: Hendrickson, 1993), 20; see pp. 20-25; also Burchard, 98; Popkes, 162.

50. I agree with Davids, 108, and Popkes, 163, that one need not suppose a Ro-

clothing, both symbolizing his social rank and wealth. He is wearing "gold rings" or, better yet, is a "gold-fingered man."[51] When Jesus defended John and his clothing he described the clothing of the wealthy: "What then did you go out to see? Someone dressed in soft robes? Look, those who put on fine clothing and live in luxury are in royal palaces" (Luke 7:25). One also thinks here of the opening of a parable of Jesus: "There was a rich man who was dressed in purple and fine linen and who feasted sumptuously every day. And at his gate lay a poor man named Lazarus, covered with sores, who longed to satisfy his hunger with what fell from the rich man's table; even the dogs would come and lick his sores" (Luke 16:19-21). And the Apocalypse excoriates Babylon's sins by revealing what becomes, among other things, of her clothing when the day of doom comes on her: "And the merchants of the earth weep and mourn for her, since no one buys their cargo anymore, cargo of gold, silver, jewels and pearls, fine linen, purple, silk and scarlet, all kinds of scented wood, all articles of ivory, all articles of costly wood, bronze, iron, and marble, cinnamon, spice, incense, myrrh, frankincense, wine, olive oil, choice flour and wheat, cattle and sheep, horses and chariots, slaves — and human lives" (Rev 18:11-13). Perhaps the rich man is wearing brilliant white clothing since *en esthēti lampra* ("fine clothes") could refer to that, or perhaps it refers to the kind of cloth, like the flashiness of silk or satin. It could indicate the superiority a patron might feel toward those in need of his patronage. Specifics may remain unclear, but the rhetorical thrust is not: the man is wealthy and socially empowered through that wealth.

More importantly, is the gold-fingered man a Christian? Peter Davids, knowing well the evidence of 1:9-11 and 2:5-7, where "the rich" *(plousios)* are depicted as non-Christians, contends that both 2:2 and 4:13 use circumlocutions because in these two instances the well-to-do persons are Christian and James prefers not to call them "rich."[52] One might suggest that *en heautois* ("among yourselves") in 2:4 favors his view since the gold-fingered man could be one "among yourselves." However, since 1 Corinthians 14:23 reveals that visitors attended Christian assemblies, and assuming for the moment that our passage is describing a Christian assembly, one cannot assume that his presence means the gold-fingered man is part of the messianic movement. Later evidence from Sardis, where the "synagogue" was nearly an

---

man equestrian or a political motivation on the part of such a person for entering into the assembly. The point seems to be the exhibition of superiority; cf. Kloppenborg Verbin, "Patronage Avoidance," 765.

51. χρυσοδακτύλιος, BDAG, 1092; M-M, 694.

52. Davids, 108; Moo, 103, suggests that the gold-fingered man is a recent convert. Mussner thinks James's emphasis is on the reaction of the community (p. 117).

open-air meeting in the heart of the political and economic arena, also suggests that presence does not indicate commitment or membership; it could indicate curiosity and seeking.[53] If "gold-fingered" is simply a rhetorical contrast with "poor" and thus equivalent to "rich" in 1:10-11, then the gold-fingered man could be a non-messianic Jew. Still, the evidence is not clear enough to render a confident verdict. I suspect James is casting into bold relief the behavior of Christians toward one another, but his emphasis is on the *behavior* of those who claim to have faith, not on the religious status of those to whom they are showing partiality.

While "gold-fingered" is a circumlocution for "rich," the "poor man" is called just that. He is absent of any jewelry and has only "dirty" *(rypara)* clothing.[54] The messianic community to which James writes is filled with the poor (1:9; 2:1-7, 14-16; 4:6; 5:1-6), giving to that term a certain dignity. Ironically, however, the poor messianic community treats one of their own with contempt while treating those who oppress them with respect — which is why James erupts as he does in 2:1, 5-7.

By the time we complete 2:1-4 it will be obvious that James has subverted the labels "poor" and "gold fingered," as he did in 1:9-11. He turns them upside-down: the poor are God's people and the rich are withering away, not simply because of their economic standing but because of what each of these labels represents. It is how the messianic community responds to each of these two men that reveals a preposterous inconsistency, and James will have none of it.

With the messianic community now gathered and with a rich man and a poor man assigned a status, we have to ask what the messianic community was assembled for, (1) worship, education, and formation or (2) to render a legal verdict about something?[55] Typically, first-century local synagogues were used for public reading, study, and instruction in Scripture (Acts 15:21) and for prayer (16:13), but were also where judicial decisions (e.g.,

---

53. On Sardis, see especially A. T. Kraabel, "The Diaspora Synagogue: Archaeological and Epigraphic Evidence since Sukenik," *ANRW* 2.19.1:477-510; "The Impact of the Discovery of the Sardis Synagogue," in *Sardis from Prehistoric to Roman Times: Results of the Archaeological Exploration of Sardis, 1958-1975* (ed. G. M. Hanfmann and W. E. Mierse; Cambridge: Harvard University Press, 1983), 178-90.

54. On ῥυπαρᾷ, see BDAG, 908.

55. The majority of scholars have favored the judicial setting; Ward, "Partiality in the Assembly," usually gets the credit for the ecclesial-judicial setting; his argument is rooted in later rabbinic evidence. He has been followed by Davids, 109-10; Martin, 57-58; Johnson, 223-24; Maynard-Reid, *Poverty and Wealth in James,* 54-61; Blomberg and Kamell, 110-11. Allison points out that this view was held already in the seventeenth century; see his "Exegetical Amnesia," 162-65. Popkes, 161, suggests that much of this discussion extends beyond what the evidence permits.

b Shebuot 30a, 31a)[56] were rendered[57] and funds and goods were distributed. A good description of synagogue life comes from Philo:[58]

> Even now this practice is retained, and the Jews every seventh day oc-cupy themselves with the philosophy of their fathers, dedicating that time to the acquiring of knowledge and the study of the truths of nature. For what are our places of prayer [*proseuchtēria*] throughout the cities but schools of prudence and courage and temperance and justice and also of piety, holiness and every virtue by which duties to God and men are discerned and rightly performed?

While traces of ancient evidence tease one into considering the event in James 2:2-4 as a judicial assembly, I wonder if we are not pressing James's words well beyond their intent. If he has at all caricatured the situation, we are pressed to look more to rhetorical intent than to historical description. In other words, James is describing partiality in glowing colors and bold im-ages. As Jesus used a rich man over against poor Lazarus in a parable without indicating a specific context (Luke 16:19-31), so perhaps James paints with similar bold, caricatured patterns. Suggestive parallels to judicial courts in other literature may have nothing to do with what James is describing. Fur-thermore, there is nothing in the synagogue assembly in James 2:2-4 that suggests the presence of a judge. The emphasis here is on the community's prejudicial response to the gold-fingered man and the poor man. There is no sketch of a judge, defendants, and litigants. Had James been concerned with judicial "favoritism," his words would focus on a judge rather than "distinc-tions among yourselves" (2:4).

Finally, the language of 2:6 suggests a setting other than the synagogue assembly in 2:2-4. In 2:6 the rich are using their power to drag poor members

---

56. Readers of commentaries that list rabbinic and non-canonical evidence with-out recourse to the texts themselves might be impressed by the references, but closer in-spection of even these texts creates problems. To begin with, the emphasis of *b Shebuot* 30a-31a is on the importance of the witnesses and litigants standing (see also *Tosephta Sanhedrin* 6:2), which is clearly not the case in Jas 2:3. However, there is a case in *b Shevuot* 30a-31a of a rabbi being permitted to sit while a poor person, because it does not matter, can either sit or stand. This text also brings up the issue of the wealthy outdressing the one with whom they are in legal dispute. This text in the Talmud counsels dressing similarly or discarding advantageous dress. Furthermore, this evidence is several centuries later, by which time the synagogue's customs may have developed well beyond anything we find in the first century.

57. This also occurred in the *ekklēsia:* cf. Matt 18:15-20; 1 Cor 5:3-5; 6:5-6 (which suggests the inappropriateness of Christians disputing with one another in a public court).

58. *Life of Moses* 2.216.

of the messianic community to what appears to be a new setting, a *court* (not to "synagogue") where slander (2:7) occurs. Moreover, the rich are described in two different ways: in 2:2-4 the rich are treated with deferential respect and favoritism while in 2:6-7 they are seizing control. The greater the difference between 2:2-4 and 2:6-7, the less likely the former portrays a judicial setting.

2:3 James now continues to sketch the scene of how the messianic community responds to the gold-fingered man and the dirty-garbed man.[59] The verb "take notice of" *(epiblepsēte)*[60] is used only for how the messianic community views the man with fine clothing. The other two uses in the New Testament (Luke 1:48; 9:38) refer to a gaze upon a person in need that leads to an act of mercy and healing. The messianic community gazes upon the rich man but, whether star-struck, envious, manipulative, or hoping to gain something, it chooses to break down its essential commitment to showing mercy to the poor. Instead of treating a person according to his or her God-given eikonic status, the community chooses to honor the wealthy man for what his ostentatious attire represents. The elevation is found in these words: "Have a seat here, please."[61] One could translate this with "You, honorable one, belong in a prominent seat like this one!" Jesus' words about the Pharisees and scribes are similar and just as comical and caricatured as those in James: "They love to have the place of honor at banquets and the best seats in the synagogues, and to be greeted with respect in the marketplaces, and to have people call them rabbi" (Matt 23:6-7). Jesus subverted the social rank evident in some meals as unjust rigmarole in the Parable of the Banquet (Luke 14:7-14).[62] The messianic community confessed this Jesus to be the Messiah, the glorious one, but they were not listening to his teachings or following his customs.

In addition,[63] to the poor man they say:[64] "Stand there" or "Sit at my feet." The focus here is on the traditionally honorable location: a seat. The

59. The protasis of 2:2 continues through 2:3. The apodosis comes in 2:4.

60. ἐπιβλέψητε. BDAG translates: "to pay close attention to, with implication of obsequiousness, *show special respect for, gaze upon*" (p. 368).

61. σὺ κάθου ὧδε καλῶς. The σὺ is emphatic; καλῶς is adverbial, meaning "well" (as in "this seat suits you well") or "please" (as in "sit here, won't you please"). See Ropes, 190.

62. See J. H. Neyrey, "Ceremonies in Luke-Acts: The Case of Meals and Table-Fellowship," in *The Social World of Luke-Acts: Models for Interpretation* (ed. J. H. Neyrey; Peabody: Hendrickson, 1991), 361-87. A good example of this can be found at 1QSa 2:11-17.

63. καί here could be adversative, but it is just as likely that James intends for his readers to add the response to the finely dressed man and the response to the poor man together to form a scenario in which they both show favoritism toward the wealthy and against the poor. That scenario creates the apodosis in 2:4.

64. Again, the verb ἐπιβλέπω is not repeated for the messianic community's response to the poor man since it involves looking admirably at someone.

THE LETTER OF JAMES

gold-fingered and finely-attired man gets a seat, the poor man gets to stand or sit at someone's feet. Instead of honor and proximity, the poor man is assigned to a place of dishonor and distance.[65]

2:4 The scenario — all contained in the protasis from 2:2 through 2:3 — is now sketched. In v. 4 (the apodosis) James pulls the rug hard and subverts everything the messianic community has been doing. Not only has the messianic community denied Jesus Messiah, the glorious one who was poor, but its actions have become divisive and sinful. In fact, as James will say in 4:11-12, they have usurped the prerogative of God.

James's question in 2:4 is not simply a question: it comes loaded with an answer and that answer is "Yes, indeed."[66] The two-edged question is simultaneously a two-edged accusation:

(1) Have you not made distinctions among yourselves?
(2) [Have you not] become judges with evil thoughts?

Thus, the two accusations are: you have made distinctions among yourselves and you have become judges with evil thoughts.

These two accusations must be tied back to 2:1: What James has in mind with "acts of favoritism," spelled out in 2:2-3, is an act of judgment that cuts the messianic community in two and is also an act of sin. We must not lose contact with the inconsistency of three things then: the inconsistency of their actions with faith in Jesus Christ; the act itself being favoritism toward the rich and prejudice against the poor; and it being captured by James as an act of judgment. Furthermore, it is wise to keep in mind the rest of James as we read 2:4.

First, the messianic community is divided by this public act of judgment against the poor and in favor of the rich (2:4a). The operative word is "made distinctions" *(diekrithēte)*,[67] a word with either the sense of doubt (cf. 1:6-7) or the sense of rendering a decision about something or someone.[68] In

---

65. One need not think James is thinking of a specific Old Testament passage, like Ps 110:1, when he says κάθου ὑπὸ τὸ ὑποπόδιόν μου. Sitting at one's feet (on the footstool) is a common enough image for submission and subordination, either in a good sense (as a learner; Luke 10:39; Acts 22:3) or in a sense of disgrace.

66. Thus, the οὐ of 2:4 implies an affirmative answer.

67. The form is aorist passive, but ἐν ἑαυτοῖς leads Laws, 102, to see a middle force to the act of judging.

68. The word has two primary senses: "to discriminate" in the sense of judging or making a distinction (Matt 16:3; Acts 11:2, 12; 15:9; 1 Cor 11:29, 31; 14:29; Jas 2:4; Jude 9), and "to discriminate" in the sense of showing a lack of decisiveness or uncertainty or being at odds within oneself (Matt 21:21; Acts 10:20; Rom 4:20; 14:23; 1 Cor 6:5; Jude 22). See BDAG, 231.

the passive, as here, it would mean "become divided."[69] What James has in mind is at least the sundering of the community into the haves and have-nots by this one symbolic act. And surely we can extend this also to include using a standard for judgment that is at odds not only with the great prophetic tradition (e.g., Isaiah 58), but also with Jesus' own teachings and practice (e.g., Luke 6:20-26; see also Luke 1:46-55). And, if we keep 2:1 in mind, James intends for his readers to know that Jesus himself was poor and was raised to glory and that faith in that Jesus as Messiah involves commitment to those like him — the poor.

James addresses other issues surrounding unity and division, including the need to watch how one speaks (1:19-21; 3:1-12; 4:11-12), how one treats the marginalized (1:26-27), how one treats the poor (2:14-17), and how one thinks about and relates to others in the messianic community (3:14-16, 18; 4:1-3; 5:8-9). 3:9 opens up another possible explanation for the seriousness of his words: "With it we bless the Lord and Father, and with it we curse those who are made in the likeness of God." Here James is appealing to Genesis 1:26-27 and the creation of all humans in God's image. Recognizing the poor (and the rich) as made in God's image ought to prohibit slanderous communications between brothers and sisters in the messianic community. To anticipate what comes at 2:8-9, the partiality James denounces in 2:1-4 contradicts the second half of the Jesus Creed (Mark 12:28-32), the command to love neighbor as self, which comes from Leviticus 19:18, which also prohibits prejudice against the poor: "You shall not render an unjust judgment; you shall not be partial to the poor or defer to the great: with justice you shall judge your neighbor" (Lev 19:15). In this emphasis, then, on unity in the community James is continuing the teachings of Jesus (John 15:12; 17:11, 21-23) and is in harmony with Paul's great vision of a church formed into a unity by the Spirit's indwelling (1 Cor 12–14; Eph 4:1-5).

Second, they have "become judges with evil thoughts" (2:4b).[70] Again, the operative word is "judges" *(kritai)*. The expression "evil thoughts" *(dialogismōn ponēron)* is abstract but is found in one or more forms in the New Testament:

> Matt 15:19: "out of the heart come *evil intentions*" (cf. Mark 7:21)
> Luke 2:35: "the *inner thoughts* of many will be revealed"
> Luke 5:22: "when Jesus perceived their *questionings*"
> Luke 9:47: "Jesus, aware of their *inner thoughts*"
> Luke 24:38: "why do *doubts* arise in your hearts?"

---

69. Martin, 63.

70. κριταὶ διαλογισμῶν πονηρῶν. Moule, *Idiom Book,* 175, sees here an adjectival genitive and translates "judges with wicked thoughts."

Romans 1:21: "they became futile in their *thinking*"
Romans 14:1: "not for the purpose of quarreling over *opinions*"
1 Corinthians 3:20: "the Lord knows the *thoughts* of the wise, that they are futile"
Philippians 2:14: "do all things without murmuring and *arguing*"
1 Timothy 2:8: "lifting up holy hands without anger or *argument*"

What James has in mind with "evil thoughts," then, is corrupt mental processes. Besides severing the unity of the messianic community, such processes include at least (1) usurping the place of God (4:11-12), (2) using a worldly standard that roots honor in wealth and status (2:2-3), and (3) corrupting the mind of Christians to render judgment on God's will for the community.

The judge in James is God (4:11-12), and Jesus is the judge's agent (5:7-9). James's strong denunciation of favoritism is rooted in faith in Jesus Christ, the glorious one, who was poor and was glorified after his death and resurrection. Faith in this kind of Messiah implicates the messianic community in a life of advocacy for the poor, commits its members to live with one another in love, and summons the rich to generosity and justice. Sadly, the messianic community has become infected with favoritism. James will now appeal to a simple, pragmatic argument: experience.

4.2. INTERROGATION (2:5-7)

5 *Listen, my beloved[a] brothers and sisters. Has not God chosen the poor in[71] the[b] world to be rich in faith and to be heirs of the kingdom that he[72] has promised to those who love him? 6 But you have dishonored the poor. Is it not[73] the rich who oppress[c] you? Is it not they who drag you into court? 7 Is it not[74] they who blaspheme the excellent[d] name that was invoked[75] over you?[e]*

71. A few manuscripts (322, 323, 808, and perhaps the Vulgate) add εν. Many manuscripts (A corrector, C corrector, P, Y, 5, etc.) have του κοσμου instead of the dative, and a few manuscripts have τουτου after κοσμου (61, 180 addition, 326*, 398, etc.).

72. Many manuscripts add ο Θεος (614, 629, 1292, 1505, with some Latin, Coptic, Syriac, Georgian, and Slavonic manuscripts), while others inserted κυριος (1243 and 2492).

73. A number of manuscripts strengthen ουχ into ουχι (A, probably C, 88; also P74, etc.).

74. Many manuscripts change ουκ to και (P74, A, Y, 33, 81, etc.) to form a coordination with "drag you into court" (2:6).

75. επικληθέν suggests "invoke" (NRSV) instead of the simpler "called" (but see BDAG, 372; also TNIV); since many think the latter is the meaning here, it is not surpris-

a. TNIV: dear
b. TNIV: eyes of the
c. TNIV: are exploiting
d. TNIV: noble
e. TNIV: of him to whom you belong

The inconsistency of the messianic community's living out of its faith in Jesus Christ, the glorious one, seen in its overt favoritism toward the wealthy and casual dismissal of the eikonic status of the poor, now leads James to nothing less than a public interrogation. "Listen, my beloved brothers and sisters!" he exclaims. With little comment and with heavy assumptions, he asks four questions, each of which assumes an affirmative answer:

1. Has not God chosen the poor in the world to be rich in faith and to be heirs of the kingdom that he has promised to those who love him?[76]
2. Is it not the rich who oppress you?
3. Is it not they who drag you into court?
4. Is it not they who blaspheme the excellent name that was invoked over you?

Between the first and second questions, James utters a description that is simultaneously a denunciation clothed with kindness: "But you have dishonored the poor." There is no time for answers; there is simply a barrage of questions. The "Yes" to each points out the readers' inconsistency and instructs them to reconsider behaviors. The first question stands as the head and contrasts with the rest of the questions. God's choice of the poor flies in the face of the rich, who despise the poor. Furthermore, God's choice of the poor contrasts with the messianic community's choice to favor the rich and disparage the poor. The second, third, and fourth questions form a crescendo: oppression leads to court injustice and to overt blasphemy of Jesus Christ, the glorious one.

2:5 The opening introduction contains the audience ("my beloved brothers and sisters")[77] and the imperative "Listen!" James customarily opens new sections or creates special rhetorical space for an urgent message by appealing to "brothers" as the community's unique familial connection.

---

ing that many early manuscripts saw it the same way and have κληθεν (206, 254, 429, 522, etc.). See commentary on 2:7.

76. On this verse and the unpacking of its rhetoric and context, see the penetrating study of Wachob, *Voice of Jesus*.

77. Ἀκούσατε, ἀδελφοί μου ἀγαπητοί, with "my sisters" added to clarify the generic "brothers."

Thus, "brothers [and sisters]" is found at 1:2, 16, 19; 2:1, 5, 14; 3:1, 10, 12; 4:11; 5:7, 9, 12, 19.

The community is addressed with the imperative "Listen!," a word that emerges from Israel's rich heritage of God speaking and God's people needing to listen. The word also emerges from Israel's literary and rhetorical traditions that intend to grab the listener's attention to what is about to be said (Deut. 6:3-5; 9:1; Mic 1:2; Joel 1:2; Isa 7:13; Matt 13:18; 15:10; 21:33; Luke 8:18; 18:6).[78] The apostles carried on the tradition (Acts 15:13; 22:1) even though James's use of the imperative here in 2:5 is rare in the New Testament. The closest parallel is Acts 15:13, where Luke interestingly attributes the same word to James. At a fundamental level Israel believed that God, YHWH, actually spoke to Israel either directly or through God's prophets like Moses. The most common disposition of God's people to God's speaking finds expression in the Hebrew word *shema* and the Greek word *akouō*. This conviction that God speaks makes the Bible — or Tanakh — not only sacred writings but the very words of God, creating the need for all reading to be listening in relationship to the God who speaks.[79]

The word "hear" or "listen" in the Bible operates at at least three levels: attention, absorption, and action. *Attention* refers to the ears being open and attentive to words, especially God's words. Thus, 1 Corinthians 14:2: "For those who speak in a [spiritual] tongue do not speak to humans but to God. Humans do not *attend to* what they are saying [because they cannot understand it]; they are speaking mysteries by the Spirit." A second, deeper level of meaning is *absorption,* when God's people's ears let God's voice in so that it fills their being. This can be found in Solomon's great prayer on becoming king: "So give your servant a *hearing* heart" (1 Kgs 3:9). And God did give Solomon a "wise and discerning heart" (3:12), a heart that fully absorbed what God was saying. The third level is *action.* As Jesus says: "Therefore everyone who *hears* these words of mine and *does* them" (Matt 7:24). Or when the Father says to the disciples of Jesus when he was transfigured: "*Listen* to him!" (17:5). Both Hebrew *shema* and Greek *akouō* move from attentiveness to concrete actions: to "listen" often means to "do."

---

78. Johnson, 224.

79. See especially Klyne Snodgrass, "Reading to Hear: A Hermeneutics of Hearing," *Horizons in Biblical Theology* 24 (2002) 1-32. See also J. Goldingay, *Old Testament Theology,* vol. 1: *Israel's Gospel* (Downers Grove: InterVarsity, 2003), 49-61, 732-40; A. Jacobs, *A Theology of Reading: The Hermeneutics of Love* (Boulder: Westview, 2001); K. Vanhoozer, *Is There a Meaning in This Text? The Bible, the Reader, and the Morality of Literary Knowledge* (Grand Rapids: Zondervan, 1998); T. Work, *Living and Active: Scripture in the Economy of Salvation* (Grand Rapids: Eerdmans, 2002); J. K. Brown, *Scripture as Communication: Introducing Biblical Hermeneutics* (Grand Rapids: Baker, 2007).

In 2:5 James may be focusing on attentiveness, but absorption and action are close at hand.

The first question, "Has not God chosen the poor," puts the rest of the questions in proper context: God's perspective deconstructs the perspective of the rich in vv. 6b-7. God's choice to elect the poor[80] emerges from a deep, identity-forming tradition in the Hebrew Scriptures: God's election of Israel.[81] Fundamental statements include:

> Deuteronomy 4:37-38: And because he loved your ancestors, he chose their descendants after them. He brought you out of Egypt with his own presence, by his great power, driving out before you nations greater and mightier than yourselves, to bring you in, giving you their land for a possession, as it is still today.
>
> Deuteronomy 7:7-8: It was not because you were more numerous than any other people that the LORD set his heart on you and chose you — for you were the fewest of all peoples. It was because the LORD loved you and kept the oath that he swore to your ancestors, that the LORD has brought you out with a mighty hand, and redeemed you from the house of slavery, from the hand of Pharaoh king of Egypt.
>
> Deuteronomy 14:2: For you are a people holy to the LORD your God; it is you the LORD has chosen out of all the peoples on earth to be his people, his treasured possession.[82]

God's election, clearly concerned mostly with choosing Israel as a nation and not individual Israelites, as emerges later in systematic theology, nonetheless can be spoken of both of individuals and of the designation of an individual — such as Peter — to carry out a specific mission. Peter was chosen to preach the gospel to Gentiles (Acts 15:7). Inasmuch as the earliest Christians

---

80. ὁ θεὸς ἐξελέξατο τοὺς πτωχοὺς τῷ κόσμῳ. ἐξελέξατο is a third person aorist middle from ἐκλέγω/ἐκλέγομαι (BDAG, 305-6). Its common Hebrew form is בחר ("to choose"; see BDB, 103-4). That James uses the middle voice may indicate that God chose the poor "for himself" or that God's special involvement is in mind (see Martin, 64). τῷ κόσμῳ is an adverbial dative of reference: "poor *in* this world" or "poor *of* this world." The aorist depicts the action globally instead of as either completed or uncompleted. On the poor, see commentary on 1:9.

81. See above on 1:18; in addition, cf. Goldingay, *Israel's Faith*, 192-209; Seock-Tae Sohn, *The Divine Election of Israel* (Grand Rapids: Eerdmans, 1991); for the modern ambiguity of election, created in part by Spinoza's inversion of election to something Israel did of God, see David Novak, *The Election of Israel: The Idea of the Chosen People* (New York: Cambridge University Press, 1995).

82. See also Acts 13:16-25.

were convinced that they were the fulfillment of God's promises to Israel, they too become the chosen people (1 Pet 2:9; Eph 1:4).

But the circle narrows for James: God chose "the poor in this world." God's choice of the poor is prevalent in the Tanakh. It was anchored in God's liberation of Israel from Egypt and became the touchstone for Israel's treatment of the poor, resident aliens, and the marginalized. Furthermore, the messianic era becomes the day when justice for the poor is established. Thus,

> Deuteronomy 26:7: we [Israel in Egypt] cried to the LORD, the God of
> our ancestors; the LORD heard our voice and saw our affliction, our
> toil, and our oppression.
> Psalm 9:18: For the needy shall not always be forgotten,
>   nor the hope of the poor perish forever.
> Psalm 10:14: But you do see! Indeed you note trouble and grief,
>   that you may take it into your hands;
>   the helpless commit themselves to you;
>   you have been the helper of the orphan.
> Psalm 18:27: For you deliver a humble people,
>   but the haughty eyes you bring down.
> Isaiah 11:3-4: He shall not judge by what his eyes see,
>   or decide by what his ears hear;
>   but with righteousness he shall judge the poor,
>   and decide with equity for the meek of the earth;
>   he shall strike the earth with the rod of his mouth,
>   and with the breath of his lips he shall kill the
>   wicked.

This theme is also central to the Magnificat of Mary (Luke 1:48, 52-53), the songs of Simeon and Anna (2:25-38), and Mary's son's famous Beatitudes (6:20-26) and praxis (7:22). Paul, in a passage not unlike this passage in James 2, knows the reality of the poor responding to the gospel (1 Cor 1:27-29):

> But God chose what is foolish in the world to shame the wise; God chose what is weak in the world to shame the strong; God chose what is low and despised in the world, things that are not, to reduce to nothing things that are, so that no one might boast in the presence of God.

The earliest messianic community in Jerusalem lived out this vision for a just economy (Acts 2:42-47; 4:32-35). All these passages tend to locate the messianic community to which James writes in the *Anawim* tradition (see James 1:9-11) where "poor" and "pious" become nearly synonymous.[83] Thus, it is

83. Popkes, 165.

not simply that God loves the poor, though that is true, but that "poor" *and* "pious" (*Anawim* is the Hebrew term) combine to refer to one group of persons[84] — and the *Anawim* either became messianic or the messianic community chose this term as one way of self-identification.

Indeed, God has chosen the poor "to be rich in faith." As in James 1:9-11; Luke 1:52-53; 6:20-26, reversal occurs in the messianic community. The poor *(ptōchoi)* become the rich *(plousioi)*. But, reversal here is incongruent: they remain materially poor but they become rich "in faith."[85] And, since the messianic community lives by faith in the Messiah, the glorious one (2:1), they can rest in their richness-by-faith while their oppressors take comfort in their richness-in-the-world, which simultaneously becomes poverty-in-faith. Faith here contrasts with world.[86] Why are they "rich" in faith? Because the poor messianic community will be "heirs of the kingdom."[87]

This kingdom has been promised to those who love God, and it is they who will "inherit" it.[88] That God has promised the kingdom leads many to think of Matthew 5:3 or Luke 6:20, which surely is in the background to James's statement.[89] Kingdom here refers to the society, the Davidic society, long promised and anticipated and now beginning to be present in the messianic community.[90] What is perhaps least noted is that for James the poor

84. So Martin, 64-65; Davids, 112; Laws, 103; Blomberg and Kamell, 112.

85. Parallels need to be noted: "in faith" contrasts with "in the world." See Andria, "James," 1512.

86. Dibelius, 138. Note also Rev 2:9; 3:17. *Testament of Gad* 7:6: "The man who is poor but free from envy, who is grateful to the Lord for everything, is richer than all, because he does not love the foolish things that are a temptation common to mankind." See also Hermas, *Similitudes* 51:4-7.

87. κληρονόμους τῆς βασιλείας. κληρονόμους is the second (predicative) of the double accusatives with τοὺς πτωχούς. The genitive τῆς βασιλείας is objective: "they inherit the kingdom."

88. ἧς ἐπηγγείλατο τοῖς ἀγαπῶσιν αὐτόν. The aorist ἐπηγγείλατο does not indicate that God made this promise once and hence does not drive modern interpreters to search and find that one text. The aorist indicates that James conceives of God's loving, promissory word in its totality without reference to time or to the number of times God made such a promise. The middle could indicate God's personal involvement in the promise, which seems obvious — middle or not. On "inheritance," see especially Gal 3:29; 4:7; Rom 8:17; Eph 1:14, 18; Tit 3:7.

89. See also *Gospel of Thomas* 54; Polycarp, *Philippians* 2:3. Cf. Davids, 111; Laws, 103-4; Wachob, *Voice of Jesus,* 138-51; Tiller, "Rich and Poor," 911-14.

90. A favorite hermeneutical term for Jesus, who saw the entire sweep of God's plan through this term, "kingdom" is not as significant to James, Paul, Peter, or John. Of the 154 references, it is found 8x in Acts, 14x in Paul, 3x in Hebrews, 9x in Revelation and only here in James. On kingdom, see G. R. Beasley-Murray, *Jesus and the Kingdom of God* (Grand Rapids: Eerdmans, 1986); *DJG,* 417-30 (C. Caragounis); McKnight, *New Vision,* 70-155.

are now defined as those who love God.[91] To love God, which clearly echoes James 1:12 — in fact, the words are identical in Greek — emerges from the daily recital of the *Shema*.[92] Twice now James sums up the response of the messianic community to God — in Christ, in Torah, in morality — as love toward God, as Torah observance is best understood. To repeat what was said at 1:12, James practiced the *Shema* as taught by Jesus: every morning and every evening, and perhaps upon every entrance or exit from the home, Jews recited the *Shema*. Though we are not sure of the specifics of first-century Jewish liturgical customs, it is likely that Jews recited the Ten Commandments and other scriptural texts along with the *Shema*.[93] Jesus amended the Jewish practice by adding Leviticus 19:18 (neighbor-love) to the customary recital (cf. Mark 12:28-32 par.).[94] In practicing the *Shema* one was afforded the opportunity to reflect on one's relationship with God as one of love, and it is likely that this enabled James to see love as the global response to God. In the Ten Commandments is a promise that God's "steadfast love" *(hesed)* will be shown to those who "love me *(le'ohavay)* and keep my commandments" (Exod 20:6; cf. Deut 5:10).[95] Instead of "steadfast love" (Exod 20:6) or "crown of life" (James 1:12), James now promises a substantial (Jesus-shaped) equivalent, the "kingdom," to those who love God.

2:6 For reasons left unexplored, the Bible verse markers put the pointed observation of James — "But you have dishonored the poor" (2:6a) — in a new verse with the next question. Technically speaking, 2:6a belongs with 2:5 more than with 2:6b-7 because the observation is designed to contrast with God's election of the poor — God chooses the poor but the messianic community, by favoring the rich and disparaging the poor, "dishonor" the poor.[96] The messianic community thus steals the honor God has granted to the poor. The "you" is emphatic and in definite contrast to what God has chosen to do. James's language draws again on the Bible (LXX):[97]

---

91. τοῖς ἀγαπῶσιν αὐτόν. The present tense indicates characteristic behavior since it depicts uncompleted action (imperfective aspect).

92. See notes at 1:12.

93. See Hoffman, *The Sh'ma and Its Blessings;* Edgar, "Love-Command."

94. See my *The Jesus Creed.* But see Montefiore, "Thou Shalt Love."

95. See also Ps 145:20; Sir 1:10; *Pss Sol* 4:29; 6:9; 10:4; 14:1; *1 Enoch* 108:8; Rom 8:28; 1 Cor 2:9 (echoed in *1 Clement* 34:8; *2 Clement* 11:7; *Gospel of Thomas* 17; *Acts of Peter* 39); *1 Clement* 59:3; also Eph 6:24.

96. ὑμεῖς δὲ ἠτιμάσατε τὸν πτωχόν. The aorist, again, does not refer to a one-time act of dishonor in the past; rather, from James's perspective, it sums up into one word what they have done, and surely he has 2:2-3 in mind.

97. For other references to ἀτιμάζω, cf. Gen 16:4-5; Deut 27:16; 1 Sam 17:42; Isa 53:3; Ezek 28:26; Mark 12:4; Acts 5:41.

Proverbs 14:21: Those who despise [*atimazōn*] their neighbors are
                  sinners,
                but happy are those who are kind to the poor.

In fact, one could put this verse at the door to the messianic community,
which needed to hear its words:

Proverbs 22:22: Do not rob the poor because they are poor,
                or crush [*atimasēs*] the afflicted at the gate.

James has now made his point: God elects the poor but the messianic community has dishonored the poor — in public — by its contemptible mistreatment of the poor and inexplicable favoring of the rich. He now asks questions
designed to bring them to clarity about the rich. His three questions assume
three affirmations, and these three affirmations are that the rich oppress the
messianic community, drag its members into court, and blaspheme the name
of the glorious one (2:1).

With the second question, "Is it not the rich who oppress you?"
James's argument shifts now to the pragmatic.[98] Not only was the glorious
one poor, not only is God the final and only judge, not only does favoritism
break down the command to love, and not only has God chosen the poor, but
the messianic community's own experiences with the powerful rich reveal
that the rich *(plousioi)* have severely mistreated them. Again, we ask if the
plousioi are believers and in the messianic community.[99] The behaviors of
the rich in 2:6-7 are both more intense than what we find in 2:2-3 and wholly
inconsistent with following Jesus Christ. If James has a crescendo in mind in
the actions of 2:6b-7, then injustice is bad enough but blaspheming the very
name of Christ falls headlong over the edge. The *plousioi* of 2:6b-7 are not in
the messianic community. In addition, there is no reason to identify the
plousioi of 2:6b-7 with the gold-fingered man of 2:2-3.[100] The word James

98. Laws, 104, accurately points then to four reasons for the messianic community not to judge or act judgmentally: (1) it is inconsistent with the faith, and here Laws
could have drawn more on christology; (2) Lev 19:18's command to love; (3) God's
choice of the poor; and (4) experience at the hands of the rich. I would add, in light of
4:11-12 as it begins to come to expression in 2:4, that judgment is wrong because it usurps
the prerogative of God.

99. See also the discussions at 1:9-11 and 2:2.

100. Laws, 104, sees no hostility toward the rich in James. Her view in part
founders on equating the *plousioi* of 2:6b-7 with the man of 2:2-3. If one factors in 1:9-11
as well as 5:1-6, one is hard-pressed not to find hostility, even if prophetic, toward the
rich. Davids, 112, carefully observes that James holds back from calling the gold-fingered
man (2:2-3) and the wealthy businessmen of 4:13-17 *plousioi*. Including those two pas-

197

uses for the actions of the *plousioi* against the poor messianic community, "oppress" *(katadynasteuousin),*[101] implies overpowering physically, economically, socially, and legally. A good example comes from Habakkuk 1:4:

> So the law becomes slack
>   and justice never prevails.
> The wicked *surround* the righteous —
>   therefore judgment comes forth perverted.

Another passage (Mal 3:5) evokes not only James 2:6b but also 5:1-6:

> Then I will draw near to you for judgment; I will be swift to bear witness against the sorcerers, against the adulterers, against those who swear falsely, against those who *oppress* the hired workers in their wages, the widow and the orphan, against those who thrust aside the alien, and do not fear me, says the LORD of hosts.

It might be asked *why* the *plousioi* were oppressing the poor. Was it because they were poor or was it because they were messianic? Probably a combination of both. In 2:7 the *plousioi* blaspheme the name, a clear indicator of religious intolerance and persecution for messianic faith, while the accent of James falls on economic exploitation (see especially 5:1-6). What might also be asked is what James has in mind with the word "oppress." The next question answers that question, at least in part.

Two particular instances of oppression now appear as questions — one about court injustice (2:6c) and the other about abuse of the messianic community's most sacred name, that of Jesus the Messiah (2:7). Perhaps the best commentary on James 2:6c is the description of Paul's actions in Acts 9:1-2:

> Meanwhile Saul, still breathing threats and murder against the disciples of the Lord, went to the high priest and asked him for letters to the synagogues at Damascus, so that if he found any who belonged to the Way, men or women, he might bring them bound to Jerusalem (see also 9:14).[102]

---

sages in the sketch of the *plousioi* might suggest that there are rich in the messianic community, but it does not explain how forthright James's language is in 1:9-11 and 2:6-7.

101. καταδυναστεύουσιν. See BDAG, 516. The term is found only one other time in the New Testament: Acts 10:38, where it refers to Jesus liberating those "oppressed by the devil." The term is used often enough in the LXX for the exploits of the powerful rich against the marginalized, including orphans, widows, proselytes (resident aliens), and the poor: Lev 19:15; Jer 7:6; 22:3; Ezek 18:7, 12, 16; 22:7, 29; Amos 4:1; 8:4; Hab 1:4; Zech 7:10; Mal 3:5; Wis 2:10; 17:2. Wis 1:16–2:20 is filled with the mirror opposite of James's own theology.

102. Communication from Jerusalem and Judea to outlying districts and synagogues is common enough (see for similar ideas 2 Cor 3:1 and 1 Macc 15:15-24).

Opposition to the messianic community begins in its embryonic form already with Jesus (Matt 10:16-25; Mark 13:9-13; Luke 12:11-12). In addition, Jesus himself gave explanations for why persecution would arise, not the least of which was that prophets were persecuted (Matt 5:10-12), that following Jesus meant sharing his fate (Mark 8:34–9:1), and that public trials would benefit the spread of the gospel (Matt 10:19-20). Persecution and martyrdom characterized the church and still does.[103]

Oppression found expression in being "dragged" *(helkousin)* into court.[104] As Peter and John were arrested and taken into custody (Acts 4:1-4), Paul and Barnabas driven out of Pisdian Antioch (13:50), Paul and Silas "dragged" into the marketplace (16:19), and Paul dragged out of the Temple (21:30), so the poor in the messianic community are being dragged into court (James 2:6c). Those using force against the poor messianists to prosecute are the *plousioi,* and this alone should give them pause about showing deference or preference to the rich. But it gets worse in James's stunning depiction.

2:7   Oppression moves from the general (2:6a) to a specific legal action (2:6b) and now to a religious, covenantal action: "Is it not they who blaspheme the excellent name that was invoked over you?" Once again, it is "they" — the *plousioi* — who are emphasized (with emphatic αὐτοί). Three expressions deserve attention: the act of blasphemy, the use of "the excellent name," and the idea of invocation of a name over someone.[105]

To "blaspheme" means to speak contemptuously, irreligiously, or scurrilously of someone, some faith, or some sacred object. The rhetorical in-

---

103. Frend, *Martyrdom and Persecution;* Rodney Stark, *The Rise of Christianity;* J. L. Gonzalez, *The Story of Christianity,* vol. 1: *The Early Church to the Dawn of the Reformation* (San Francisco: HarperSanFrancisco, 1984), 31-48, 82-109; T. M. Johnson, "Martyrdom," in *DMT* 220-22, which includes a link address to the World Christian Database where numbers of martyrdoms are assessed.

104. καὶ αὐτοὶ ἕλκουσιν ὑμᾶς εἰς κριτήρια. The use of αὐτοί serves to emphasize the *plousioi.* On ἕλκω see BDAG, 318; also Ps 10:9. The present tense is used to depict the action with vividness — as if it is passing by the listener/reader on the way into the court. It is impossible to know if this persecution is "official" or not. On εἰς κριτήρια, see BDAG, 570. An instance of a Christian tribunal is perhaps found at 1 Cor 6:2, 4. For the Jewish context, see Schürer, 2.199-226 (on the Sanhedrin and judicial procedures); Safrai, *JPFC,* 1.1.377-419; L. A. Jervis, "Law/Nomos in the Greco-Roman World," in *DNTB,* 631-36. One needs also to read the heavy dose of historical commonsense and reality in Sanders, *JPB,* 458-90.

105. οὐκ αὐτοὶ βλασφημοῦσιν τὸ καλὸν ὄνομα τὸ ἐπικληθὲν ἐφ' ὑμᾶς; the present tense (βλασφημοῦσιν) indicates characteristic action in a timeless sense: "Is it not they who are blaspheming the name?" or "Is it not they who blaspheme the name?" In the former, one watches the action unfold before one's eyes; in the latter one frames that action as timeless. See McKay, *New Syntax,* 40-41.

tent of such language is to slander, malign, discredit, and even destroy or de-construct.[106] The term is often narrowed to mean blasphemy of God, as in Mark 2:7 or Revelation 13:6 or blasphemy of Jesus as in Matthew 9:32-34 and 12:22-24. But the act of verbal violence can also be directed at humans, as in Matthew 27:39 or Acts 13:45 and 18:6. If successfully attached to a per-son, in this case Jesus, the person blasphemed will be labeled as a deviant and considered taboo. Blasphemy, then, is a social weapon designed for so-cial control. The decision to haul the poor messianists into court fulfills what Jesus said would occur (Matt 10:16-25). Not only were the *plousioi* blas-pheming Christ, but they involved the messianists in the same label, render-ing them deviant and powerless.[107]

What the *plousioi* were blaspheming was "the excellent name." Be-cause the second commandment (Exod 20:7) was extended to include using the sacred name of God, *ha-shem* (Hebrew for "the Name") was a customary way of referring to God in the first century (see also Exod 23:20-21).[108] Without mentioning God's name or the sacred name, the tetragrammaton (YHWH), the pious Israelite could speak of God by saying "the Name." This is reflected in passages like Matthew 5:34-35 and in the Lord's Prayer: "May your name be hallowed." Jewish reverence before God prompted the proliferation of circum-locutions like "the Highest One" (Luke 6:35), "the Blessed One" (*m Berakot* 7:3; Mark 14:61), and "the Powerful One" (14:62), but the driving force for such linguistic moves was the sacredness of God's very name. That name, not held in the same honor among contemporary Christians as among ancient Jews and current messianic Jews, was YHWH. Thus, Deuteronomy 28:10: "you are called by the name of the LORD [YHWH]." Those who follow the covenant YHWH made with Abraham are "called by my name," says God (Isa 43:7). Gentiles are "not called by your name" (63:19). 2 Maccabees 8:15 manifests confidence in God's protection "because he had called them by his holy and glorious name." The earliest Christians picked up this same practice. When

---

106. See BDAG, 178. The verb is found 34x in the New Testament, including Matt 9:3; 26:65; Luke 12:10; 23:39; John 10:36; Acts 13:45; 18:6; 19:37; 26:11; 1 Cor 10:30; 1 Pet 4:4; 2 Pet 2:2, 10, 12; Jude 8; Rev 13:6; 16:9. See D. Bock, *Blasphemy and Exaltation in Judaism: The Charge against Jesus in Mark 14:53-65* (Grand Rapids: Baker, 2000); B. J. Malina and J. H. Neyrey, *Calling Jesus Names: The Social Value of Labels in Matthew* (Sonoma: Polebridge, 1988); S. McKnight and J. B. Modica, *Who Do My Opponents Say That I Am?* (LNTS 358; Edinburgh: Clark, 2008).

107. The debate over whether they are blaspheming Christ by blaspheming his followers (Laws, 104-5) misses the accusative direct object of the verb: they are blas-pheming the "excellent name." Thus, they are not blaspheming so much the messianic community as Christ; indirectly, they are blaspheming all those connected to him.

108. The "name" is found throughout the Dead Sea Scrolls: see CD 2:11; 4:4; 15:2-3; 20:34; 1QS 6:27; 1QM 14:8; 4Q175 1:7.

Ananias was summoned to incorporate Saul (Paul) into the church, God told him, "Go, for he [Paul] is an instrument whom I have chosen to bring my name before Gentiles" (Acts 9:15). But, there is a subtle shift among the earliest Christians, expressing no doubt their growing perception of christology,[109] by which Jesus Christ gets connected to the sacred name. The one who holds the lampstands, none other than Christ, is the one who also says "yet you are holding fast to *my name*" (Rev 2:1, 13; see also Rom 10:13). "Just as 'the name' was a pious Jewish surrogate for God, so for the early Jewish Christians it became a designation for Jesus, the Lord's Christ. And as in its earlier usage, so with the Christians it connoted the divine presence and power."[110]

So, when James refers the "excellent name" to Jesus Christ (2:1),[111] the glorious one, we gain a glimpse into the emerging high christology of the earliest messianic, Land-of-Israel, community. Jesus Christ is the name whereby they are named, giving the community its identity, and he is — to use the worship hymn Paul uses — given the name above all names (Phil 2:9-11):

> Therefore God also highly exalted him
>> and gave him the *name*
>> that is above every *name,*
> so that at the *name* of Jesus
>> every knee should bend,
>> in heaven and on earth and under the earth,
> and every tongue should confess
>> that Jesus Christ is Lord,
>> to the glory of God the Father.

The "name" Jesus is "invoked" upon early Christians at their baptism.[112] If Matt 28:16-20 may indicate a trinitarian formula at baptism, other

---

109. See Hurtado, *Lord Jesus Christ,* who has for decades expounded the view that high christology emerged from worship.

110. R. N. Longenecker, *The Christology of Early Jewish Christianity* (London: SCM, 1970), 45-46.

111. Some think "God" or "YHWH" is still in view; e.g., Frankemölle, 396-98. The use of 5:10, 14 to support a "theocentric" instead of a "christocentric" understanding of name fails on two accounts: first, there it is clearly "the Lord" that is in view while in 2:7 that is not clear; second, the name most likely at work in 2:7 is the name of 2:1. Furthermore, there is clear early Christian evidence for "name" being transferred to Jesus (Phil 2:9-11). There is a nearly unanimous agreement that "Jesus" is the "excellent name" here; see, e.g., Popkes, 170.

112. τὸ ἐπικληθὲν ἐφ' ὑμᾶς. The subject of the aorist passive is unclear; it could be simply undefined, a divine passive, or, which is more likely, a reference to the one administering the baptism who invokes upon them "the name of Jesus." On ἐπικαλέω, see BDAG, 373; see also Hurtado, *Lord Jesus Christ,* 202.

texts indicate a baptism "in the name of Jesus." Thus, Acts 2:38: "Repent, and be baptized every one of you in the name of Jesus Christ so that your sins may be forgiven; and you will receive the gift of the Holy Spirit."[113] It is the only name by which one is saved (4:12). The word "invoked" either indicates that the baptisand calls upon Jesus for mercy or, which is more likely, the baptizer himself (or herself) invokes that name "upon" the person so that the newly baptized is now known by that name — as followers of Jesus, as "Christians."[114] James does not make this clear, but other early Christian evidence may, and we should not fail to stand before this development with clear eyes: never before had baptism led to the invocation of the divine name like this. Two texts come to mind: 1 Peter 4:14-16 and Hermas, *Similitudes*. Both deserve citation as connecting baptism and invocation of the name of Jesus Christ, the Son of God:

> If you are reviled for the *name of Christ,* you are blessed, because the spirit of glory, which is the Spirit of God, is resting on you. But let none of you suffer as a murderer, a thief, a criminal, or even as a mischief maker. Yet if any of you suffers as a *Christian,* do not consider it a disgrace, but glorify God because *you bear this name* (1 Pet 4:14-16).

> It will be of no use for you to receive the name alone without receiving the clothing [by the virgins] from them. For these virgins are the powers of the Son of God. If you bear the name but not his power, it will be in vain (*Similitudes* 9.13.2-3).

> The one who bears these names and the name of the Son of God will be able to enter the kingdom of God (*Similitudes* 15.2).

> And so these who had died received the seal of the Son of God. . . . For before a person bears the name of God . . . but when he receives the seal. . . . And so the seal is the water. They go down into the water dead, therefore, and rise up living (*Similitudes* 16.3-4).

To sum up: The *plousioi* oppressed the messianic community, dragged its poor into court, and in front of everyone blasphemed the name of Jesus

---

113. See also Acts 10:48; but also 3:6; 4:7, 10, 12, 18; 5:40; 9:27; 16:18. The oddity of 19:13-15 probably reveals early Christian liturgical language. Rev 3:12 indicates that they will receive the "name of my God" as well as the "name of the city of my God" and, in addition, "my own new name." Identity-forming names are invoked over the baptisand and by the one being baptized. See J. D. G. Dunn, *Baptism in the Holy Spirit* (Philadelphia: Westminster, 1970), 90-102; R. N. Longenecker, *Christology,* 41-46; Hurtado, *Lord Jesus Christ,* 143-44, 200-203; L. Hartman, *"Into the Name of the Lord Jesus": Baptism in the Early Church* (Edinburgh: Clark, 1997).

114. James uses the plural ὑμᾶς; his intent is to speak to the whole community because of its inconsistent behavior.

Christ. The messianic community confessed this same Jesus as the Messiah, the glorious one, and had evidently transferred the sacredness of the name YHWH to the very name of Jesus. But, for inexplicable reasons, these same poor confessors of Jesus were favoring the rich and showing prejudice against the poor. James now calls them to what he learned from Jesus: the significance of Leviticus 19:18 for understanding the entirety of the Torah as either love of God or love of others. Love, James now will reveal to the messianic community, charts a path much different than the path of favoritism and prejudice.

4.3. INSTRUCTION (2:8-13)

8 *You do well if you really fulfill the royal law according to the scripture,*[115] *"You shall love your neighbor as yourself."*[a] 9 *But if you show partiality,*[b] *you commit sin and are convicted by the law as transgressors.*[c] 10 *For*[116] *whoever keeps*[117] *the whole law but fails*[d][118] *in one point has become accountable*[e] *for all of it.* 11 *For the one who said,*[119] *"You shall not commit adultery," also said, "You shall not murder." Now if you do not commit adultery but if you murder, you have become*[120] *a transgressor*[c] *of the law.* 12 *So speak and so act as those who are to be judged by the law of liberty.*[f] 13 *For judgment will be without mercy*[121] *to anyone who has shown no mercy;*[122] *mercy triumphs over judgment.*

115. Some manuscripts, now seeing collected Scriptures as authoritative text, have the plural κατα τας γραφας: 322, 323, the Latin Vulgate, some Coptic manuscripts, and the Syriac Peshitta and Harklensis.

116. Some manuscripts, sensing the need for an adversative, have δε.

117. The subjunctive τηρήσῃ, because it sounds identical, becomes future in many manuscripts (τηρησει). There are other variants where τηρήσῃ morphs into various forms of τελεω (τελεσει and τελεση) as this verb conforms to 2:8a.

118. Again, the subjunctive becomes future in many manuscripts (025, 044, 5, etc.).

119. The manuscript tradition behind "You shall not commit adultery," also "You shall not murder," varies enormously because of the repetition of words and the variations from subjunctive to future. The translated text reflects accurately the vast majority and the best of the manuscripts. For a full display, see *ECM* 4.1.33.

120. The Alexandrian witnesses, P74 and Alexandrinus, are interesting here. Instead of γέγονας the reading is εγενου, and instead of παραβάτης we find αποστατης, the latter reading favored by G. D. Kilpatrick, "Übertreter des Gesetzes, Jak. 2,11," *TZ* 23 (1967) 433.

121. In many manuscripts ἀνέλεος is spelled ανιλεως (including the important Byzantine manuscripts L, Y, and 056).

122. In the "shown no mercy" clause, some manuscripts have ελεον instead of ἔλεος (K), but in the last clause this change is frequent (C, Y, 5, 33, 322, 323, etc.). See MHT, 2.126; LSJ, 532.

a. TNIV differs considerably: If you really keep the royal law found in Scripture, "Love your neighbor as yourself," you are doing right.

b. TNIV: favoritism

c. TNIV: lawbreakers

d. TNIV: stumbles

e. TNIV: guilty

f. TNIV: the law that gives freedom

James 2:8-13 extends the teachings of 2:1-7 by exploring the significance of love as the central virtue through which all behaviors, including those involving the oppressing rich and the needy poor, are judged. The first two verses of this paragraph (2:8-9) form a double set of conditions, with the second in contrast to the first. The first condition sets out what James wants — a community shaped by the Jesus Creed (Lev 19:18) and already made visible in 1:25-27 — and the second spells out the contrasting consequences of the messianic community's recent glaring behaviors.

> If you *love,* you are doing what is right.
> But if you are *partial,* you become "transgressor."

With this *condition* set up, James then *explains* why he can label such a person "transgressor" in 2:10-11. His explanation is twofold: first, the one who commits to the Torah becomes accountable to the whole Torah; second, the one who gave one law also gave the others. Which means, if you keep one law but break another, you are a "transgressor" in the eyes of the divine lawgiver. 2:11 then leads us back to the conclusion of 2:9.

James follows this strong language about becoming a "transgressor" by *exhorting* the messianic community to love (2:12), and thus he returns back to 2:8 (and to 1:25-27). But, instead of using the word "love," in 2:12 James speaks of "the law of liberty," drawing us back to 1:25. His final lines in this section (2:13), though, turn the exhortation of 2:12 into a threat of judgment if one does not live by mercy. Thus, we are prepared to see a variety of ways of looking at the proper way for the messianic community to shape its behaviors: love, the law of liberty, and mercy. These are distinguishable terms but inseparable in substance.

2:8-9 These two verses work in tandem to express the *condition* upon which James now builds toward an exhortation in order to get the messianic community beyond the sinful behaviors of 2:2-4: *mentoi* (translated as "really" in NRSV and TNIV) in 2:8 works with *de* ("but") in v. 9. The first sketches proper behavior; the second improper. Furthermore, the quotation of Leviticus 19:18 in James 2:8b assumes the prohibition of partiality in Leviticus 19:15, which is what James brings up in 2:9 (repeating

2:1).[123] James 2:9 essentially recapitulates 2:2-7, while 2:8 serves to provide the positive counterpart both to the behaviors of 2:2-4 and the strong critique of 2:5-7 while it also repeats the good behaviors seen in 1:25-27. Thus, 2:8-9 *together* pull together everything from 1:25 to 2:7 to form the condition that leads to the exhortation in 2:12-13. Between 2:8-9 and 2:12-13 comes an explanatory parenthesis (2:10-11). Skipping the explanatory parenthesis, we have this logic: if you love, you will do well; but if you are partial, you are "transgressor." So, James exhorts in 2:12-13, live by the law of love (2:8, 12) and not by the law of partiality (2:9) because God's judgment scrutinizes a person's mercifulness (2:13) and sees the lack of mercy (= partiality) as cause for judgment.

2:8 A good translation of 2:8 can open with "If you *really* do fulfill the royal law. . . ."[124] James both assumes that the messianic community really is following the royal law and also knows that it does not follow it consistently and that he is about to speak once again to their failures (in 2:9). Once we recognize that "really" in 2:8 belongs with the messianic community's salutary practices in 1:25-27,[125] where a very similar expression occurs ("the perfect law, the law of liberty"), we can see more clearly what James is saying. He wants to remind them of 1:25-27 in order to get them to move beyond what he has just described in 2:2-4. Thus, if they *really* do live as described in 1:25-27, they will be fine. But James knows better. This verse then sets up the messianic community for one more strong critique about their favoritism. 2:9 will begin that critique.

The use of present tenses in "you do well" and "if you really fulfill" paints a picture of an event occurring before our eyes, and that picture is found in the community's benevolence toward orphans and widows (1:26-

---

123. Lev 19:18: love your neighbor as yourself (Jas 2:8b); Jas 2:9: against partiality (assuming Lev 19:15's use of partiality).

124. Εἰ μέντοι νόμον τελεῖτε βασιλικὸν. The particle μέντοι must be taken together with 2:9; the two verses in 2:8-9 as a whole form a contrast with what James has advocated in 2:1-7 because 2:9 (manifesting partiality) is the true condition of the community. But the assumption of the truth of 2:8 needs to be connected to the obviously similar idea at 1:25 and its practices in 1:26-27. Thus, 2:8 itself contrasts with 2:2-7 and therefore needs a positive counterpart similar to what is seen in 1:25-27. See BDAG, 630; Moo, 110-11. Burchard, 103, connects 2:8 back to 1:27 (and therefore also to 1:25). To see the contrast of μέντοι with 2:6's ὑμεῖς δὲ ἠτιμάσατε τὸν πτωχόν is too obscure (Mussner, 123). Popkes, 171, knowing the significance of μέντοι, finds its emphasis to be in contrast with 2:9, but this requires that 2:8 follow 2:9. It is the beginning of 2:8 with this particle that deserves special attention.

125. Not enough commentators go back to 1:25-27, in spite of the grammatical likelihood that 2:8 describes a reality about the messianic community that contrasts legitimately with 2:2-7. When Davids, 114, finds 2:8 to be "semi-ironic," I sense he has felt the inconsistency of 2:8 with 2:2-4 but not the consistency of 2:8 with 1:25-27.

27).[126] To "fulfill" means (1) to bring to completion (Matt 7:28; 11:1; Luke 2:39; 12:50; John 19:28, 30; 2 Cor 12:9), (2) to "pay" (Matt 17:24), or (3) to "observe" or "do" or "keep" (Rom 2:27; James 2:8).[127] Here, "fulfill" is synonymous with "keeps" in 2:10.[128] Even more it has the sense of doing the Torah completely, which helps set up the emphasis in 2:10-11 on doing all of the Torah. In fact, one might detect a tone of arrogance, not uncommon in this letter (cf. 1:19-21; 2:14-17; 3:1-12, 13-18; 4:1-4, 11-12, 13-17), in the descriptions of the community's actions or claims to do the Torah.

What they were "fulfilling" was the "royal law."[129] We might be tempted to forget that James is referring here to the Torah, the law or laws of Moses. But even that is not without its own history and development, and the fulfillment of the Torah in Jesus Christ (Matt 5:17-20) feeds into what James is saying here. In what sense then is the law "royal"? Three components come into play and need not exclude one another. First, it could refer to the "capital" or "preeminent" of all the laws, which would suggest that the connection of "royal law" to Leviticus 19:18 in this verse (James 2:8) and that the law of loving others is that preeminent law.[130] James would then be agreeing with Jesus (Mark 12:28-32), Paul (Rom 12:19; 13:9; Gal 5:14), John (1 John 3:11, 23; 4:17), and Peter (1 Pet 4:8). But there may be residual traces of christology here. Inasmuch as Jesus is the Messiah and the Messiah is the royal king and the Messiah's rule is the kingdom, then, secondly, the Messiah's law is royal and designed for his kingdom (2:1). We can extend this slightly to a third consideration: if the law is the Messiah's (royal) law, then the law itself is the royal law for the king's subjects as they live in the kingdom. It is unwise to dwell heavily on the second and third aspects of "royal law" for one primary reason: in James the focus of the evidence is not on the "royal" = kingly law but on the "preeminent" nature of this singular law found in Lev 19:18 and raised to prominence by Jesus Messiah (Mark 12:28-32). The only other passage of significance in James is 1:25, where we have "perfect" *(teleion)* as in 2:8 ("fulfill" comes from *teleō*) and where the Torah is connected to "freedom."[131] And, in that location "word" needed to be connected to "implanted word" in 1:18, 21 and perhaps to the Spirit of the new covenant. Furthermore,

126. ποιεῖτε, τελεῖτε; in Greek, the second verb occurs first. Many seem to interpret the verbs as futures or even as subjunctives — as if they depicted action that the messianic community wants to do in the future or that they hope to do.

127. BDAG, 997-98.

128. As noted above in the translation and textual notes, τηρέω is sometimes changed to τελεω in some of the manuscripts.

129. νόμον . . . βασιλικὸν. See Burchard, 103-4; Hartin, "The Religious Context," 217-20; Cheung, *Genre, Composition,* 97-99.

130. Emphasized by Martin, 67; see also Dibelius, 142-43.

131. See notes at 1:25 where "freedom" is explained.

in 2:12 we find that 1:25's sense of freedom has been brought into our passage: "So speak and so act as those who are to be judged by the law of liberty."

I suggest then that "royal law" refers (1) to Jesus' highlighting of Lev 19:18 as the preeminent command of all commands, alongside loving God, (2) to this interpretation of the Torah bringing the Torah to its destined completion (1:25), (3) to this law of love actually creating freedom for the messianic community,[132] and (4) to the empowering implanted presence of word and Spirit in the messianic community. James is Torah-observant. What we find in James does not lead us to think that he believes the messianic community has been set free from the works of the Torah as we see in Pauline theology in Galatians and Romans. What James implies might not be clear, but the significance of the Torah coming to a new expression in Jesus surely sets the groundwork for buildings to be constructed later by (Gentile) Christians.[133]

We need now to fill in some of the lines mapped in this discussion so far. The "royal law" of James 2:8, where James spells out what the messianic community is doing right, is "according to scripture." Are we to see this as an introductory formula that sets up the quotation, or is this an adverbial expression[134] that clarifies James's major point? That is, should we translate as: "If you really fulfill the royal law, as found in Leviticus 19:18, *as the Scripture intends you to live it,* you will do well."[135] Since Leviticus 19:15 prohibits partiality and prejudice against the poor, this view has much in its favor because it would then be saying that the fully scriptural way of living out Leviticus 19:18 includes Leviticus 19:15. Which leads to 2:9 nicely.

Leviticus 19:18, a text not quoted in Jewish literature from the time of Leviticus until the time of Jesus, was raised a notch in importance when Jesus attached it to the daily recital of the *Shema.* Thus, Mark 12:28-34:[136]

132. More on "freedom/liberty" at 2:12.

133. I resonate with the observations of Martin, 67-68.

134. Thus "according to scripture" modifies "fulfill" and could be rendered: "if you fulfill this law in the way Scripture intends you to fulfill it. . . ."

135. So, roughly, Johnson, 231.

136. See parallels at Matt 22:34-40 and Luke 10:25-28, whose differences need not trouble us in this context. One can find numerous parallels in Jewish literature to the importance of loving God or loving others (*Testament of Simeon* 4:7; *Testament of Issachar* 5:2; *Testament of Dan* 5:4; Philo, *Specialibus legibus* 1.299-300, 324), or to the importance of love (*Odes of Solomon* 41:1-6), but something about Jesus and his followers remains distinct: the connection of Lev 19:18 to Deut 6:4-5. The daily recitation of *Shema* as followed by Lev 19:18 forms that distinction. See Montefiore, "Thou Shalt Love"; Sanders, "Jesus and the First Table of the Jewish Law," 55-73; Johnson (with Wachob) speaks of the "abundance of Jewish and Christian sources that corroborate the use of Lev 19:18 as a summary of the whole law," but cites much later rabbinic texts and New Testament and early Christian texts (Johnson, *Brother of Jesus, Friend of God,* 151). The appeal to later rabbinic texts does not count for an "abundance" of texts for determin-

One of the scribes came near and heard them disputing with one another, and seeing that he answered them well, he asked him, "Which commandment is the first of all?" Jesus answered, "The first is, 'Hear, O Israel: the Lord our God, the Lord is one; you shall love the Lord your God with all your heart, and with all your soul, and with all your mind, and with all your strength.' The second is this, 'You shall love your neighbor as yourself.' There is no other commandment greater than these." Then the scribe said to him, "You are right, Teacher; you have truly said that 'he is one, and besides him there is no other'; and 'to love him with all the heart, and with all the understanding, and with all the strength,' and 'to love one's neighbor as oneself,' — this is much more important than all whole burnt offerings and sacrifices." When Jesus saw that he answered wisely, he said to him, "You are not far from the kingdom of God." After that no one dared to ask him any question.

Several New Testament writings, surprisingly, quote Leviticus 19:18 in such a manner that demonstrates their awareness of the elevation of Lev 19:18 by Jesus. Thus, Paul explicitly makes it the fundamental rule of life (Rom 12:19; 13:9; Gal 5:14), while Peter hedges in that direction (1 Pet 4:8) and John explodes into full focus on love (John 13:34-35; 1 John 3:11, 23; 4:17). It is not without significance that James is the only person in the New Testament after Jesus who quotes both sides of the Jesus Creed: loving God in 1:12 and 2:5 and loving others as oneself here in 2:8.

Several observations about James's use of Leviticus 19:18 are in order. First, it is exactly what is now printed in standard editions of the Septuagint. And this translation is a simple, clear, direct translation of the Hebrew.[137] Second, the use of the future — "you shall love" — is a common way of translating the Hebrew imperfect. It can also be translated as an imperative: "Love your neighbor as yourself." Third, in context, it is more than likely that James has the poor (*ptōchoi*) in mind when he says "neighbor" (*plēsion*).[138] Fourth, as we have already mentioned, Leviticus 19:18 implies conformity also to Leviticus 19:15: "You shall not render an unjust judgment; you shall not be partial to the poor or defer to the great: with justice you shall judge your neighbor." Thus, James's reading of Leviticus 19:18 in this context could be rendered: "If you really live out the royal law of Jesus in its full intent, the law

---

ing whether Jesus' use of Lev 19:18 was simply part of his Jewish context. Methodologically, concluding that Jesus was evidently the one who raised Lev 19:18 to a central location does not make him non-Jewish, nor does it make the other groups of Judaism less Jewish or less loving. We return to the main point: it is connecting Lev 19:18 to the Shema that marks Jesus' distinctive use of Lev 19:18.

137. וְאָהַבְתָּ לְרֵעֲךָ כָּמוֹךָ → ἀγαπήσεις τὸν πλησίον σου ὡς σεαυτόν.

138. Davids, 115; Martin, 68.

to love your neighbor as yourselves as the companion to loving God with everything you have, you will love the poor whom you have recently despised."

James closes the positive side of this condition with this statement: "You do well."[139] The NRSV puts this clause first in its sentence, though in the Greek it finishes up the sentence. This statement, like that in 2:19, means that James sees living out the second half of the Jesus Creed is a noble, excellent, and proper rule of life for the messianic community. Such a way of life meets the high standards expected of the messianic community by James. The expression "do well" is similar to the word "blessing" (Deut 28; Lev 26–27; James 1:12, 25). James assumes the community lives like this — and some evidence suggests just that (1:25-27).

2:9 James turns now to the second half of the condition, which describes the messianic community's negative behaviors. If 2:8 hearkens back to 1:25-27, 2:9 returns to the inappropriate behaviors described in 2:2-4.[140] The focus of James in 2:8-13 is on the second half of this condition (2:9), on the messianic community's acts of partiality. The consequences for the community's behaviors are detailed: if living out Leviticus 19:18 means a life of blessing (2:8), living out partiality means becoming a "transgressor" (2:9).

Again, James's use of the present tense is notable: "if you show partiality" and "you commit sin" and "are convicted."[141] It is not that James is describing something currently going on in the church but, as aspectual theory is now teaching us, the actions are *depicted as* incomplete and *depicted as* going on before our eyes.[142] When this event occurs is not important to James; he wants us to see it going on. If the messianic community shows partiality, then consequences follow. The act of partiality effects sin.[143] James uses the word "sin" *(hamartia)* six times. Sin is the perverse desire and choice not to do what one knows is good (1:14-15; 2:9; 4:17) and is an act

---

139. καλῶς ποιεῖτε. On καλῶς, see BDAG, 505-6. See also Mark 7:37; 12:28 and 32 (where Jesus first attaches Lev 19:18 to Deut 6:4-5); Gal 4:17; 5:7; 1 Tim 3:4. A slightly different expression is found at Jas 4:17. It is important to note that this term is an adverb modifying the verb ποιεῖτε, describing something about *how* they are doing, not *what* (good acts) they are doing. Jas 4:17 does that. The clause could be rendered "living the right way" or "conducting yourself properly."

140. The relationship of 2:9 to 2:8 is adversative (δέ).

141. προσωπολημπτεῖτε, ἐργάζεσθε, and ἐλεγχόμενοι. On προσωπολημπτεῖτε, see notes at 2:1.

142. Again, see Porter, *Verbal Aspect,* 83-97, especially 91; McKay, *New Syntax,* 27-34, here pp. 29-30 (where the present along with the imperfect are "imperfective" aspect).

143. The Greek verb ἐργάζεσθε means to "do, accomplish, carry out" (BDAG, 389). The NRSV translation "commit" is not as clear or as strong as "effects sin" or "produces sin" or simply "works sin." The middle may well capture the person's personal involvement in what is produced: sin. It is not unlike Jas 1:20, where human wrath does not produce God's will or righteousness. See Popkes, 175.

against God's will (2:11) and against relational love and mercy (2:8-13); upon confession and prayer, sin can be forgiven by God (5:15); sins are to be confessed to one another (5:16); sin leads to death (1:15), but the messianic community's restoration of sinners leads to their sins being covered over (5:20).[144] By using *ergazomai* (NRSV: "commit"), James draws us back to 1:14-15 and the mysterious, desirous forces of sin to lead humans from their eikonic design to the inevitability of destruction and death. The singular act of partiality unleashes the powers of sin in the messianic community.

Not only are sin's powers turned loose, but the act of partiality leads to a status: "transgressors." The term is plural. James's concern is the community and not just an individual: the messianic community becomes complicit in the act of partiality and renders the entire community "transgressors." Some translations mask the Greek construction as in the NRSV: "you commit sin *and* are convicted," which translates a verb and a participle. The participle *elenchomenoi* could indicate, as in NRSV and TNIV, simply an attendant circumstance, translated virtually as an equivalent to the main verb "commit" by using "and convicted," or it could extend the thought by defining what James means by "commit sin." In such a case, a more accurate translation could be "commit sin, leading to your conviction as 'transgressor'" or "commit sin, that is, be convicted as a transgressor."[145]

Critical to James's point is the word "convict" *(elenchō),*[146] which suggests confrontation of a person or the community with the facts of the case in such a way that they are proven in the wrong.[147] Partiality, when examined "by the law,"[148] convicts the messianic community and renders the community "transgressors." It might be tempting to see "by the law" as little more than a Torah-sweeping statement — "in general, the law would say such behavior is wrong." But because the context so clearly focuses on Leviticus 19:18 and its companion law about partiality in 19:15, it is far more likely that with "by the law" James means "by this specific prohibition in the Torah of Moses," that is, Leviticus 19:15 and 18. What this specific text in the Law says is that James's readers are to live by the law of loving others as themselves, and that entails

144. See also notes at 1:14-15. On sin, see Plantinga, *Not the Way;* T. Peters, *Sin: Radical Evil in Soul and Society* (Grand Rapids: Eerdmans, 1994); M. Biddle, *Missing the Mark* (Nashville: Abingdon, 2005); McKnight, *A Community Called Atonement,* 22-24, 46-48.

145. The decisive factor is that James chose to use not a second verb but a participle. The participle is most probably a redefinition (epexegetical or appositional participle) of the main verb. See Davids, 115.

146. BDAG, 315.

147. For other New Testament references, see Matt 18:15; Luke 3:19; John 3:20; 16:8; Eph 5:11; 1 Tim 5:20; Tit 1:9; Jude 15; Rev 3:19.

148. ὑπὸ τοῦ νόμου.

not treating the poor with contempt. Because they are not living up to Torah in this way, the Torah proves that they have behaved inadequately. Thus, the Torah labels them as "transgressors,"[149] those who break or violate specific commands of God or cross over God's established boundaries.

James has now set forth the condition of the messianic community: claiming to live up to the teachings of Jesus but demonstrating by action that they are transgressors. We expect an exhortation, and we will get it, but first James must explain what he means by "transgressor." Vv. 10 and 11 are an explanatory gloss by James on that term. Once done with this explanation, James will proceed to the exhortation (2:12-13).

2:10-11 James's point is perhaps more difficult to comprehend than a Protestant reader might suppose, and so his context needs to be sketched. Following the Reformation, which filtered Augustine's anthropology into a bold set of categories, Protestants tend to read James 2:10-11 like this: God gave the Law to reveal his will and to reveal sin; humans listen to the Law but, instead of confessing their sins, use it to establish their own righteousness. James steps into this anthropological blindness and contends that, since God gave not only individual laws but the whole Law, anyone who transgresses any specific commandment is guilty of it all. Why? Because, whether one transgresses all of it or only one aspect of it, one is proven to be a transgressor. Since God demands either utter perfection or the alien righteousness that comes from Christ's own obedience to the Law, any transgression puts one outside the bounds of redemption until one accepts alien righteousness. Something close to this is the common assumption by which many Protestants tend to read James 2:10-11. It is considered the way Paul dealt with the legalism of Judaism. So, a brief digression into these themes in Judaism will set up our comments on 2:10-11.

Many appeal to texts like Galatians 5:3[150] to support the demand of perfection and the need for an alien righteousness as the very heart of the gospel. The distinct problem with this view is that, while the Jewish world clearly expected all Jews to follow all the Law, the Torah itself wrote into its very fabric a mechanism that released Israelites from the demand of total perfection: that mechanism was *Yom Kippur,* the Day of Atonement. In other words, while the Torah demands obedience it also provides forgiveness through confession and sacrifice. The scholar who argued this doggedly for

---

149. ὡς παραβάται. This word is rare in the LXX and in the New Testament (Rom 2:25, 27; Gal 2:18, and twice in James [2:9, 11]). The noun παράβασις is found at Rom 2:23; 4:15; 5:14; Gal 3:19; 1 Tim 2:14; Heb 2:2; 9:15. See *NIDNTT* 3:583-85; *EDNT* 3:14-15.

150. "Once again I testify to every man who lets himself be circumcised that he is obliged to obey the entire law."

more than a decade was E. P. Sanders.[151] Sanders lays bare what many have taken to be the view of "normative" Judaism, and it is my view that this is at work in how many try to read James 2:10-11: "one must keep it [the Law] all; one cannot do so; there is no forgiveness of transgression; therefore accepting the law necessarily leads to being cursed." But Sanders observes that "the middle terms of this thought-sequence are never stated by Paul, and this sequence of views cannot be found in contemporary Jewish literature." "All the rabbis . . . took the position that all the law must be accepted," but "No rabbi took the position that obedience must be perfect." "It is equally un-Jewish to think that the law is too difficult to be fulfilled." Thus, "It would, in short, be extraordinarily un-Pharisaic and even un-Jewish of Paul to insist that obedience of the law, once undertaken, must be perfect." "[T]he law is not too difficult to be satisfactorily fulfilled; nevertheless more or less everybody sins at some time or other . . . ; but God has appointed means of atonement which are available to all." "Paul may very well simply have been reminding his converts [Gentiles] that, if they accepted circumcision, the consequence would be that they would have to begin living their lives according to a new set of rules for daily living." Such a conclusion for Gal 5:3 is similar to what needs to be seen in James 2:10-11.

Judaism did not tolerate a "pick and choose" mentality when it came to Torah observance.[152] A commitment to observance meant (for some anyway) commitment to observe the whole Torah. A line from the later Babylonian Talmud, *Horayot* 8b, illustrates this conviction: "Ulla said: What is the reason of R. Jose the Galilean? Scripture said: *And it shall be when he shall be guilty in one of these things* [Lev 5:5]; whoever is subject to liability for every one of these is liable for any of them, and whosoever is not subject to liability for every one of these is not liable for any of them." And in a discussion of Sabbath regulations, R. Johanan put it this way: "[It is to teach] that if one performs all of them in one state of unawareness he is liable for each separately" (*Shabbath* 70b). A text from a time closer to the New Testament, *4 Maccabees* 5:16-34, records the conviction of Eleazar, a pious Jew, when it came to Torah observance, as he faced Antiochus, and this text embodies the ideals of the kind of Judaism that shaped the world of James:

> We, O Antiochus, who have been persuaded to govern our lives by the divine law, think that there is no compulsion more powerful than our obedience to the law. Therefore we consider that we should not transgress it in any respect. Even if, as you suppose, our law were not truly divine and we

151. See *Paul, the Law, and the Jewish People* (Philadelphia: Fortress, 1983), 27-29. The quotations that follow come from these pages.
152. See Laws, 111-12.

had wrongly held it to be divine, not even so would it be right for us to invalidate our reputation for piety. Therefore do not suppose that it would be a petty sin if we were to eat defiling food; to transgress the law in matters either small or great is of equal seriousness, for in either case the law is equally despised. You scoff at our philosophy as though living by it were irrational, but it teaches us self-control, so that we master all pleasures and desires, and it also trains us in courage, so that we endure any suffering willingly; it instructs us in justice, so that in all our dealings we act impartially, and it teaches us piety, so that with proper reverence we worship the only living God.

Therefore we do not eat defiling food; for since we believe that the law was established by God, we know that in the nature of things the Creator of the world in giving us the law has shown sympathy toward us. He has permitted us to eat what will be most suitable for our lives, but he has forbidden us to eat meats that would be contrary to this. It would be tyrannical for you to compel us not only to transgress the law, but also to eat in such a way that you may deride us for eating defiling foods, which are most hateful to us. But you shall have no such occasion to laugh at me, nor will I transgress the sacred oaths of my ancestors concerning the keeping of the law, not even if you gouge out my eyes and burn my entrails. I am not so old and cowardly as not to be young in reason on behalf of piety. Therefore get your torture wheels ready and fan the fire more vehemently! I do not so pity my old age as to break the ancestral law by my own act. I will not play false to you, O law that trained me, nor will I renounce you, beloved self-control.

And prior to the writing of James the Qumran community famously expected each member to live completely according to its interpretation of the Torah. This text illustrates their rigor:

This means the expounding of the Law, decreed by God through Moses for obedience, that being defined by what has been revealed for each age, and by what the prophets have revealed by His holy spirit. No man belonging to the Covenant of the Community who flagrantly deviates from any commandment is to touch the pure food belonging to the holy men. Further, he is not to participate in any of their deliberations until all his works have been cleansed from evil, so that he is again able to walk blamelessly. They shall admit him into deliberations by the decision of the general membership; afterwards, he shall be enrolled at an appropriate rank. This is also the procedure for every initiate added to the Yahad (1QS 8).

If this sketch is anywhere near the world in which James wrote, namely a situation where obedience was expected and forgiveness granted

213

but also where a firm commitment to doing *all* of the Torah was the expectation, it leads to some modifications of what some think is said in James 2:10-11. Once again, we need to remind ourselves that these verses are a digression that define the meaning of "transgressor" in 2:9. James has accused his community of being transgressors because it, a community convinced it is committed to the (whole) Torah, has broken the law of Leviticus 19:15, 18 — the command to love others as oneself. The person who does not love others, as the community has failed to love the poor (2:2-4), has broken the law of love from Leviticus. This infraction of the Law makes them not observant but *transgressors.* If one keeps the whole Law (2:10a) but breaks just one commandment (2:10b), one is assigned to the category of a transgressor who has, in effect, broken the whole (2:10c). Why? Because there are only two options: one is either observant or a transgressor.[153]

James comes to this conclusion in 2:10-11 by converting his argument into concrete details: the God who gave the commandment not to commit adultery also prohibited murder. If one does not commit adultery, but one murders, one is judged as a "transgressor" by the commanding God. As we will seek to show, James has not just pulled two random commands from the Torah: he has chosen "murder" because he thinks the behavior of the messianic community with respect to the poor is murderous, or he knows of actual murders in the community. In 5:6 murder is again connected to the poor. The turbulence of the context of this letter cannot be left aside. What is more subtle is that James here assumes that the messianic community is committed to the Torah, is Torah-observant, and is proud of its observance. Either they are unaware that their behavior breaks the Torah of Leviticus 19:18 or, what is only remotely possible, they are persuaded that such a commandment is insignificant in the larger picture. Into that bubble of their pride of observance James now pokes a hole so that he can get them to realize how serious their mistreatment of the poor actually is. Calling them "transgressor" is potent rhetoric in a Torah-drenched and Torah-observant community. James is not simply labeling and classifying. His intent is to gain the attention of his community so that he can motivate them to end such unloving behaviors and move into a life of love. Therefore, following these two verses James will begin to make an appeal to live in light of God's final judgment, when God will judge by a new law, the "law of liberty" (2:12).

---

153. It is worth pondering why James does not move here to themes connected to atonement and forgiveness, which he does do in 5:13-20. It is true that Judaism is bathed in the mechanism of sin and atonement, but James's interest is otherwise here. His interest is with the implication that commitment to Torah entails observance of the whole Torah. Hence, his focus here is not on Torah/transgression/forgiveness, but on Torah/commitment to all of Torah/exhortation.

2:10 At the level of specifics one is led to ask how v. 10 fits with what precedes. Does *gar* ("for") indicate that v. 10 explains vv. 8-9, in that the "whole law" of 2:10 is the same as the "royal law" of 2:8-9? Or does *gar* indicate that v. 10 provides proof for what has been said in v. 9 by clarifying the meaning of "transgressors"? Since vv. 10 and 11 are concerned with the word "transgressor," the second of these options makes most sense.[154]

James now contends something typical, though not unique,[155] in the Jewish world: observance is an all or nothing approach to life. Thus, "For whoever keeps the whole law but fails in one point has become accountable for all of it." The one who commits herself or himself to the Torah, as his messianic community has, is obligated to all of it. But James's point of view is stronger, if not extreme, in his world: he extends obligation to culpability. Anyone who is committed to Torah observance and "keeps"[156] the whole Law *but* "fails[157] in one point,"[158] has become guilty[159] as if he or she had broken every commandment and must appear before God. In other words, and this will be his conclusion at the end of the next verse, the person who trips up even over one commandment is a "transgressor" of God's (whole) Law. James's intent is to classify the messianic community as transgressors, and his rhetoric is focused to get them to see the gravity of what they are doing.

This verse is about more than "a forceful way of stating that every command is important."[160] To be sure, the importance of every command factors into James's point, but he has extended importance into final culpability. Indeed, the messianic community may well be contending that they,

154. Dibelius, 144.

155. Marjorie O'Rourke Boyle, for instance, sees Jas 2:10 in Stoic context: see "The Stoic Paradox of James 2.10," *NTS* 31 (1985) 611-17. She observes that, from Augustine to Luther to Dibelius, a connection to Stoic thought was often observed, and then it disappeared. Lucius Annaeus Seneca said, "He who has one vice has all" (see O'Rourke Boyle, p. 612) in the context of benefactions without regard to status; O'Rourke Boyle sees Jas 2:10 as a Judaic context expressing a Stoic paradox. What perhaps counts against this interpretation is that James surrounds it with citations of Jewish Torah (2:8-11).

156. τηρήσῃ, perhaps a gnomic aorist subjunctive. The focus, however, is on how James depicts the action: it is conceived without regard to either time or progress and is conceived in its totality. James's grammar reflects shifts in the development of indefinite constructions: the expected indefinite ἄν is not present. On this, cf. MHT, 3:106-8.

157. See BDAG, 894; the word is more pictorial than "fails" and evokes "trip, stumble, or lose one's footing." See also 3:2; Rom 11:11; 2 Pet 1:10.

158. ἐν ἑνί. In this context, the one specific commandment would be Lev 19:18.

159. The term ἔνοχος means more than "accountable" (NRSV); the TNIV's "guilty" is more accurate. The expression conveys culpability before God for nonobservance of Torah. See Mark 3:29; 14:64; Matt 5:21-22; 26:66; 1 Cor 11:27; Heb 2:15.

160. Davids, 117.

after all, are thoroughly committed to the Torah and are observing it, and James's words will be reinforcement of their commitment. But, to repeat our point, his language carries the point beyond the need to follow every commandment. He contends that transgression against even one command makes a person guilty for breaking every commandment. What we have in this passage, then, is something not unlike the radical conception of sin and sinfulness found in Paul's theology — a kind of proto-Pauline anthropology or at least a parallel Pauline anthropology. James has argued here not for original sin, but instead for the final culpability for everyone and anyone who breaks even one commandment — and we are on sure grounds to think that James believed each person in the community he addresses had done that.

2:11 Here the logical connection provided by "for" *(gar)* is causal:[161] that person who violates one command becomes guilty/accountable before God[162] *because* the God who gives one command gives the others as well. So James now draws this argument into a personal theology: the Law is not just an impersonal document; it is God's word and God's will, and those who listen to it both enter into relationship with God and become accountable to God.

James now plays with two prohibitions — against adultery and against murder.[163] A very important question is: Why these two?[164] They could be

161. Martin, 69.

162. There is a possible circumlocution here: "the one [One] who said" is God. See Davids, 117. The use of the aorist participle (ὁ εἰπών) sums up the God of Sinai as the God who speaks or who spoke.

163. μὴ μοιχεύσῃς, μὴ φονεύσῃς. The LXX in both Exod 20:13 and Deut 5:17 uses the future as an imperative. James here uses the negated aorist subjunctive. It is only remotely possible that James takes two purely hypothetical examples that bear no resemblance to anything going on in the community. That is, it is unlikely that James means something like this: "The One who said, for instance, 'Don't commit adultery' is the same One who said, for instance, 'Don't murder.' If you (hypothetical you) do not, for instance, commit adultery but you (hypothetical you) do, for instance, commit murder (which you really are not doing), then you — the one who hypothetically is murdering (but which you really are not doing) — are a transgressor of the law." While a purely hypothetical example is possible, it is highly unlikely. James actually narrows the kind of transgressor his community is by turning toward "murder," and he thereby clarifies what he has in mind in 2:9.

164. Because the order of the commands in James differs from the Hebrew Bible's order in Exod 20:1-17 and Deut 5:6-21 and is the same as the order of the commands in the LXX, Philo, Luke 18:20, and Rom 13:9, Laws, 115-16, contends that James derives from a Greek-speaking *Sitz im Leben*. Laws presses the evidence beyond its intent. There is no reason to assume that James's order derives from a text or from memory; it is more likely that James puts murder second because of rhetoric. James leads the community into agreement with the prohibition against adultery and then, once he has them in agreement, reveals their shortcomings in murder.

randomly chosen, as one finds evidently in Romans 13:9. Or, what is more likely, James's intent is more subtle and rhetorically potent: he gains agreement with his community over adultery — they are clean here. Then he turns agreement into critique by bringing up a sin they are guilty of: "murder." Which leads to a second question: Are these commands figurative or literal? In light of 4:2-4 some have argued that James is concerned here with relational problems: the community is adulterous in the sense of unfaithful to God and the Torah, and the community is murderous in the sense that they are at war with one another.[165] Before we can answer this question, though, we face this issue: James has chosen two odd commands if he is randomly choosing prohibitions. It is far more likely that either both or at least one of these commands is chosen because it (or they) emerges (or emerge) from his specific context in this chapter. In other words, there is something breathtakingly real about murder in this messianic community.

James sets up his readers with something they do not do (adultery) in order to accuse them of what they are doing (murder).[166] Whatever one thinks "murder" means in James 2:11, the logic of vv. 10-11 only makes sense if murder is something the community is committing.[167] Adultery means sexual congress with someone other than one's spouse, of which (in the logic of James) the community is not guilty. But, when it comes to murder, they are guilty. Does "murder" here mean relational murder, as we see in Jesus' redefinition (Matt 5:21-22),[168] or does it refer to actual bloodshed? The former view fits the context well: the community's treatment of the poor amounts to what Jesus calls murder in the Sermon on the Mount, which is like what has shaped the need for James to drive home the point that his community are transgressors. Another view is, in my judgment, reasonable even if it stretches the imagination of modern Christian sensitivities. If one factors into the word "murder" James 1:19-21; 4:1-2; and especially 5:6, one could infer that James has in mind actual murders and violence occurring in the community on the part of some hot-headed people who are seeking to establish justice through violence. I consider this interpretation just as likely as the figu-

---

165. A nuanced example is Davids, 117.

166. The conditional sentence (*ei* with the present indicative) indicates that James depicts the behaviors — not committing adultery but committing murder — as incomplete (imperfective) actions. They are depicted as going on before the eyes of his readers, whether they were going on in reality at the present moment or not.

167. εἰ δὲ οὐ μοιχεύεις φονεύεις δέ, where the present indicatives are timeless but used to depict action vividly. One should not press these present tenses to suggest that James has in mind persistent practices of adultery and murder and that it is only the persistence of such practices that makes a person either observant or transgressor. The view I here advocate is tied to recent discussions of aspectual theory.

168. A standard view; e.g., Johnson, 233; Wall, 127; Blomberg and Kamell, 119.

rative interpretation of "murder."[169] What must be noted is that 5:1-6 connects mistreatment of the poor with murder. Perhaps, and we are pressed to leave this as a suggestion, oppression was leading to the death of poor members of the messianic community, and complicity with the rich on the part of some was contributing to those deaths.

The logic now comes to its intended goal: as 2:9 accused the community of being "transgressors," now James concludes that, if an individual is not an adulterer but is a murderer, that person has "become a transgressor of the law." It is worth observing that, if taken simply at face value, James's point is curiously weak: Does anyone doubt that a murderer is a transgressor of the Law? But he is saying more than what we find at face value. His rhetorical intent is to label the community with a genuine legal status; his goal is to show that they are transgressors of the Law so that he can move them from their current behaviors to another level. Labeling them as "transgressors" has been his intent since he digressed at 2:10. His intent clear and his point now made, James can move on to exhort the community to more circumspect Christian behavior in their treatment of the poor.

2:12-13 The logical flow of 2:1-13 now comes to its telos in an exhortation to change (2:12) and an eschatological warrant (2:13). The moral point of these two verses was made in negative form in 2:1, where James prohibited favoritism. What he meant by favoritism was then fleshed out in 2:2-4 in the graphic behaviors of the community: they were favoring the rich and abusing the poor. James then asked a series of questions that were designed to get the messianic community to see that mistreatment of the poor is inconsistent with faith in Jesus Christ. Following this James offered wisdom on how the messianic community was to live: by the "royal law" of loving one's neighbor as oneself (2:8), which was blatantly at odds with prejudicial behaviors. Indeed, James says that violators of this law are "transgressors" (2:9). But he must now back up to explain how he can call a supposedly observant group of messianists "transgressors," because they do see themselves as observant. So, James pulls out a standard definition of observance in Judaism: to observe Torah is to observe all of Torah. Anyone who avoids adultery but murders is a transgressor (2:10-11). Now James is ready to state again, this time a little more directly, what he has already indicated in this passage: the messianic community should live by the law of love (2:12-13). As such, 2:12-13 both makes a summary exhortation for the whole passage and draws a conclusion to the passage.

2:12 "So" in "*So* speak and *so* act"[170] is more than a logical conclu-

---

169. See Martin, 70.

170. Οὕτως λαλεῖτε καὶ οὕτως ποιεῖτε. Do these present imperatives indicate ongoing behaviors or are they, as aspectual theory teaches us, commanded actions that are

sion to 2:1-11; "so" *(houtōs)* also adverbially intensifies "speak" and "act" as it connects speaking-doing to the *hōs* ("as") introducing the rest of the verse. Speaking and doing are shorthand for everything a human does (Acts 1:1; 7:22; 1 John 3:18). It might be tempting to ask which of the two is emphasized,[171] but James is one book in the New Testament that emphasizes both speaking (3:1-12) and doing (1:19, 22-25).[172] James's concern here is with how one's speech and behaviors impact the poor.

Not only does the Bible frequently bring up the theme of judgment, but the biblical sense of judgment is far more severe than what is commonly said in pulpits and in devotional books that focus on God's unconditional grace and love. The final judgment for James, as for Jesus (e.g., Matt 12:36; 16:27; 25:31-46) and Paul (1 Cor 3:10-15; 2 Cor 5:1-10), will be established on the basis of both what the messianic community says (James 1:19, 26; 3:1-12; 4:11-16; 5:12) and what it does (1:27; 2:1-26; 4:1-10; 5:1-6).[173] Another feature of the early Christian understanding of judgment was its seeming imminence (5:7-8; cf. also Matt 10:23; Mark 9:1; 13:30; 1 Thess 4:15, 17).[174] That sense of imminence was more rooted in the uncertainty of the time and hence the need for readiness than in some kind of clear knowledge of the precise time and date of the parousia or, worse yet, in wishful thinking or grandiloquent disillusionment.[175] So, when James uses the expression "to be judged," which could be translated "about to be judged,"[176] we are led to think in terms of confidence in a certain judgment rather than immediacy that has turned out to be temporary.

What perhaps surprises a Christian reader is James's next expression:

---

depicted as imperfected or incomplete? Because we have tied tense so closely to time in our accustomed grammar theories, we fail to observe that time is not the point for Greek tenses. Instead, James's point is not so much "keep on speaking" and "keep on acting" but the open-endedness of the actions; thus, "speak" and "act" translate accurately without over-translating. It is morphologically possible but contextually (nearly) impossible for the two verbs to be indicatives.

171. Popkes, 179.

172. Davids, 118.

173. Among recent studies these can be mentioned: Reiser, *Jesus and Judgment;* Dunn, *Theology of Paul,* 487-93; A. A. Hoekema, *The Bible and the Future* (Grand Rapids: Eerdmans, 1979), 253-64; J. A. Motyer, "Judgment," in *NDBT,* 612-15.

174. See McKnight, *A New Vision,* 128-39; cf. B. Witherington III, *Jesus, Paul and the End of the World* (Downers Grove: InterVarsity, 1992).

175. An important point of G. B. Caird's brilliant study of eschatological language is that our interpretation of apocalyptic language may not be at all what the original authors meant; see his *The Language and Imagery of the Bible* (Philadelphia: Westminster, 1980), 243-71; see also N. T. Wright, *Jesus and the Victory of God,* 320-68.

176. μέλλοντες κρίνεσθαι. On μέλλω, see BDAG, 627-28 (2a); Martin, 70; Davids, 118; Popkes, 180.

"by the law of liberty." Judgment is based on the "law," which of course refers to the Mosaic Torah, but James adds a modifier: "of liberty."[177] And, instead of using the more common "on the basis of" *(kata),* James uses
"through/by" *(dia),* leading some to suggest that he is not saying that the
community will be judged on the basis of the law of liberty but that the law
of liberty is "the state or condition in which [the community's action] is performed."[178] In other words, James means the community will be judged by
whether or not it lives out the "law of liberty." This is a difference with little
distinction and that is why most commentators see "by" *(dia)* as equivalent
to "on the basis of" (either *kata* or *hypo* — as in 2:9).[179] By attaching "of liberty" to "law," though, James changes the game of the yardstick by which
one is judged. Yes, Torah observance is the yardstick, but James's Torah has
been clarified by Jesus. Several factors come into play in James' expression:
first, we are led to think of Jesus' own interpretation of the Torah in terms of
the Jesus Creed (Mark 12:28-32; Matt 5:17-48; 7:15-23); second, we are
drawn back to James 1:25, where James similarly connects "law" to "liberty" and where the connotation is deeds of mercy to the poor and marginalized; third, the sense of "liberty" here may well have to do with the
courage to break down boundaries between rich and poor or powerful and
powerless as an act of Christian solidarity with all; and finally it is worthy of
our attention to think of the "law of liberty" as the "implanted word" (1:21)
and see this as James's early sketch of the Spirit of God at work. Above all,
though, we must let each of these considerations flow into the central theme
for James: the law of liberty is the law of loving your neighbor as yourself
(2:8). Now we can take note of what James teaches: the messianic community will someday face God, perhaps soon; soon or not, it will certainly face
the God of judgment. God's judgment will be based on the Torah. But that
Torah is to be seen as the revelation from God that the messianic community
is to live according to the teaching of Jesus to love others as themselves.
There are no substantive differences, then, between James 2:12 and Matthew 25:31-46.

   2:13   The warrant for James's assertion that the messianic community needs to live in light of a judgment based on mercy and loving others is
found in v. 13.[180] Two statements are made, but how they are connected is not
as clear as one might like:

   177. It is impossible to know with certainty what kind of genitive James uses
here, but somehow the word "liberty" defines or characterizes the "law." It could be the
law (1) that brings freedom or (2) that is characterized by or defined by freedom.
   178. Laws, 116.
   179. So Davids, 118; Popkes, 180. See also Rom 2:12-13.
   180. γὰρ connects v. 13 as the reason for v. 12. See *ACC: James,* 25-26, for theological and pastoral observations on mercy.

> Live in light of a judgment based on the "law of liberty" . . . *because*
> Judgment will be without mercy to anyone who has shown no mercy.
> Mercy triumphs over judgment.

Peter Davids contends that the shift from the second person to the third person (from "so speak" to "will be"), the proverbial pithiness of 2:13, and the change from "the law of liberty" (as love) to "mercy" in 2:13 indicate that 2:13 was a free-floating statement that James quotes at this point because it fits his argument.[181] Several considerations slow down this conclusion for me. First, James thought the connection was tight enough that he used the word "For" *(gar)*. Second, I am not so sure that the appearance of "mercy" expresses a change. While "love" is found in 2:8, it is not used elsewhere in James for how the messianic community is to relate to others or to the poor in particular. No particular words — other than perhaps "do" — rise to the surface as James's favorite in 1:19-27, and that text addresses the same concerns as 2:1-13. Third, "mercy" appears not only twice in 2:13, but also in 3:17, where James provides words expressing specific Christian behaviors. To be sure, Davids and others recognize the pithiness of these two statements, but perhaps we should recognize the diversity of James's vocabulary and enter the word "mercy" into the entire discussion of 2:1-13 and not wait for it until this verse. Perhaps what James has in mind in 2:2-4 is not just "love" but also "mercy." Perhaps, too, he had the capacity to be pithy all on his own.

Which leads us now to the connection of 2:13 to 2:12. Even if we admit that 2:13's statements could be "free-floating" proverbs, both the use of "for" and the appropriateness of "mercy" lead to the conclusion that 2:13 is the ground of the exhortation in 2:12. The messianic community is to speak and act toward the poor and marginalized in light of the judgment because the judgment will not show mercy to those who do not show mercy. This negative warrant is followed without a conjunction by the alternative, a glimmer of hope and optimism: "mercy triumphs over judgment." That is, if they become merciful toward the poor, they will escape the judgment.

God's judgment[182] will be "without mercy" to those in the messianic community who persist in prejudice against the poor and marginalized.[183] The Torah gave rise to a strong Jewish tradition of showing mercy, and when that mercy was not shown the prophets spoke on behalf of the poor and im-

---

181. Davids, 118; Laws sees even less connection (p. 117); see also Johnson, *Brother of Jesus, Friend of God,* 152-54; also Wachob.

182. The personification of judgment here speaks of its majesty, not to say reverence before God. See here Martin, 71-72.

183. See Dibelius, 119.

plored Israel to show mercy.[184] Hence, even if Jesus is the one who brought into fresh light Leviticus 19:18, the essential behavior of mercy toward the marginalized is written into the fabric of the Hebrew Bible and the Jewish tradition. A good example is found in Sirach 28:1-9,[185] a book that here and elsewhere reflects the themes and language of James:

> The vengeful will face the Lord's vengeance,
>   for he keeps a strict account of their sins.
> Forgive your neighbor the wrong he has done,
>   and then your sins will be pardoned when you pray.
> Does anyone harbor anger against another,
>   and expect healing from the Lord?
> If one has no mercy toward another like himself,
>   can he then seek pardon for his own sins?
> If a mere mortal harbors wrath,
>   who will make an atoning sacrifice for his sins?
> Remember the end of your life, and set enmity aside;
>   remember corruption and death, and be true to the commandments.
>
> Remember the commandments, and do not be angry with your
>   neighbor;
>   remember the covenant of the Most High, and overlook faults.
> Refrain from strife, and your sins will be fewer;
>   for the hot-tempered kindle strife,
> and the sinner disrupts friendships
>   and sows discord among those who are at peace.

Jesus' contribution to this discussion was the centralization of love of God and love of others as well as his prophetic critique of those who were not fulfilling the double commandment.[186] These are not pious platitudes on James's part: he has in mind the sort of incident mentioned in 2:2-4 and 2:9, and he expects both speaking and doing to be merciful (2:12).

Thus, James gives the messianic community two options: to experience the merciless judgment of God (2:13a) or to experience victory in the judgment through acting mercifully toward those in need (2:13b). Repentance from their prejudices will lead to God's gracious forgiveness and atonement. The turnabout effected leads to a life of mercy toward the poor and, in the end, a life of mercy will hear the salutary blessing of God at the Last Judgment.

---

184. See J. K. Bruckner, "Ethics," in *DOTP*, 224-40; E. E. Urbach, *The Sages: Their Concepts and Beliefs* (Jerusalem: Magnes, 1979), 448-61.

185. See also Tob 4:9-11; *Testament of Zebulon* 5:1, 3; 8:1-6.

186. See Matt 5:7; 6:14-15; 18:23-35; Luke 10:25-37; 15:1-2.

"Mercy" here refers to the behaviors of the messianic community with respect to the poor. One thinks of 1:26-27; 2:2-4; and 2:14-17. That is, one thinks of care for widows and orphans and of not asking the poor to sit subordinately but, like everyone else, to sit alongside the others. Mercy is both verbal, which concerns James at 3:1-12, 13 and 4:1-12, and behavioral, which concerns James especially at 1:19-27 and 2:14-17. Others think both "mercy" and "justice" are attributes of God, and that this saying refers to God's own mercy triumphing over God's own justice.[187] Two factors weigh against this: first, the reason for God becoming (suddenly) merciful to those who are transgressors is omitted; if "mercy" refers to the messianic community's repentance from prejudice and consequent change of behaviors, then that change of verdict is clarified. Second, "without mercy" in 2:13a referred to the behaviors of the messianic community and not to God, so an easier flow is established if both "without mercy" and "mercy" refer to behaviors by the same group (the messianic community). Furthermore, the entire focus in 2:1-13 has been on the need for the messianic community to show mercy toward those in need.

A strong word that needs comment is "triumphs."[188] It is translated in Romans 11:18 as "boast," and the same word is used again in James 3:14, leading one to think that there is an assurance and confidence along with some figurative chest-pounding and fist-raising on the part of the personified mercy in the face of the personified justice. This word describes the posture of the victor, even the gladiator, as he or she stands over the defeated on the battlefield. Paradoxically, it is mercy that stands as the conquering victor in this battle. The image is breathtaking — and dropped suddenly. A new topic is in order.

James does not know it, but he is about to record a set of thoughts that would torment Luther and many in the Protestant movement that flowed from him. However difficult they might be to square with some ways Protestants frame faith and works, James's words flow naturally from 2:1-13 and fit snugly in both a Jewish and a messianic Jewish world. If 2:1 asserted that faith in Jesus Christ was inconsistent with prejudice against the poor, 2:14-17 (and 18-26) will expound the meaning of "faith" as something that involves "works" of mercy.[189] Professor Thorwald Lorenzen says what needs to be said: "It is very seldom that this text is taken seriously." In fact, he observes,

187. See the discussion at Martin, 72-73, who seems to get God's mercy and our mercy all bundled together. I agree with Moo, 118. See also Dyrness, "Mercy Triumphs over Justice."

188. κατακαυχᾶται. See BDAG, 517. The present tense depicts the action in a timeless or vivid manner.

189. See the clear exposition of D. V. Palmer, "James 2:14-26: Justification as Orthopraxy," *Caribbean Journal of Evangelical Theology* 9 (2005) 54-78.

"Luther for example took this text seriously." That is, Luther "let his [James's] message stand, although he criticized it from his 'Pauline' perspective."[190] Augustine said it well: "I do not understand why the Lord said, 'If you want to enter into eternal life, keep the commandments,' and then mentioned the commandments relating to good behavior, if one is able to enter into eternal life without them."[191] And as everyone quotes his famous line, we will too: "Paul said that man is justified through faith without works of the law, but not without those works of which James speaks."[192]

5. THE CHRISTIAN AND WORKS (2:14-26)

The word "mercy" in 2:13, expressing as it does the "law of liberty" in 2:12 (cf. 1:25) and the law of loving one's neighbor as oneself in 2:8, both contrasts with the partiality of the messianic community's behaviors (2:2-4, 9) and leads James to a robust defense of works. In brief, "mercy" is expounded in 2:14-26 in the term "works" and, because James connects faith and works, one can also say that "mercy" is expounded in what James means by a proper faith. 2:1 established that "faith" in the Lord Jesus Christ, the glorious one, is inconsistent with prejudicial behaviors against the poor. What James meant by "faith" there was not entirely clear, but he now clarifies it: faith involves works of mercy.[1] All of this to say that the prejudicial, partial behavior of the messianic community (2:1-4) is inconsistent both with Judaism and the gospel of Jesus.

James drives his conclusion home repeatedly in 2:14-26, beginning with an interrogation (2:14-17) in which the questions imply sharp rebuttal and then proceeding to a set of challenges (2:18-26). He begins with two questions about the saving inadequacy of a faith that is not simultaneously at work in deeds of mercy (2:14): "What good is it, my brothers and sisters, if you say you have faith but do not have works? Can faith save you?" The implied answers to these questions — "no good" and "no" — are then elaborated with a graphic, almost comic, example (2:15-16): "Go in peace. . . ." The example is couched in a conditional sentence, the concluding apodosis being a question that repeats what was asked in v. 14: "What good is it?"

---

190. See T. Lorenzen, "Faith without Works Does Not Count before God! James 2:14-26," *Expository Times* 89 (1978) 231-35, quoting here from p. 231.

191. From *ACC: James*, 29.

192. From *ACC: James*, 31.

1. An excellent summary of the Jewish evidence can be seen in Str-B, 4/1.536-58, 559-610. For a study that anchors faith and works in wisdom, see Hoppe, *Der theologische Hintergrund*, 100-118.

James then draws his conclusion (2:17), which becomes the focus of yet more questions and repeated conclusions in 2:18-26.[2]

An issue of form and style arises in 2:18-19. The letters of the New Testament, especially those of Paul, occasionally reflect a response to a question, leading readers today to think we are hearing one end of a conversation. James 2:18-19 evidently is a response of James to a question. Even if James gives us his version of the query in 2:18 (18a or 18ab?), scholars remain unsure just what James understands the question to be, despite many efforts to resolve the issues. If we are unclear about the questions his opponents are asking, we are nonetheless on firmer ground in discerning his response, even if there is some debate where it begins (2:18b or 2:19?). The impact of 2:18-19, though, is clear: faith and works are an inseparable couple. What James implied in 2:14 remains the single conclusion throughout 2:20-26.

Once again, James furthers his argument with questions in 2:20: "Do you want evidence that faith without works is useless?" James answers this question by appealing to two figures — a most likely candidate, Abraham, and a most unlikely candidate, Rahab. Following his sketch of how each of these two illustrates the necessity of works, James concludes yet again: "As the body without the spirit is dead, so faith without deeds is dead" (2:26). He is making one point in this passage, and we will do well to stick to his point, which he makes with four words. Faith without works:

> is *useless* (*ophelos,* 2:14, 16),
> cannot *save* (2:14),
> is *ineffective* (*argē,* 2:20), and
> is *dead* (*nekra,* 2:17, 26).

It fascinates theologians, pastors, and lay persons to tease out the relationship of faith and works: Is the former the foundation of the latter? If so, why does James not say it quite that way? Are works a dimension of faith? Is faith nearly the same or identical with works? Is faith a work? Are works faith itself or a demonstration of the presence of faith? Why, then, do non-followers of Jesus have as many works as faith-focused Christians? These are important questions, but they do not drive what James is arguing here.[3] He is argu-

2. For an alternative, more poetic approach to these verses, see G. M. Burge, "'And Threw Them Thus on Paper': Recovering the Poetic Form of James 2:14-26," *Studia Biblica et Theologica* 7 (1977) 31-45; see also J. D. N. Van der Westhuizen, "Stylistic Techniques and Their Functions in James 2:14-26," *Neotestamentica* 25 (1991) 89-107, who pursues a rhetorical strategy; J. G. Lodge, "James and Paul at Cross-Purposes? James 2,22," *Biblica* 62 (1981) 195-213, finds a chiasm with 2:22 at the center.

3. See D. Bonhoeffer, *Discipleship* (Dietrich Bonhoeffer Works 4, trans. B. Green

ing that faith without works is useless, unable to save, ineffective, and dead. Whatever relationship there is between faith and works or works and faith, there is a relationship — but what concerns James is not analysis of the relationship but the *ineradicable necessity of works in faith*.

5.1. INTERROGATION (2:14-17)

> 14*What good is it, my brothers and sisters, if you*[a] *say you have faith but do not have works? Can faith*[b] *save you?* 15*If*[4] *a brother or sister is naked*[c] *and lacks*[5] *daily food,* 16*and one of you says to them, "Go in peace; keep warm and eat your fill*[d]*," and yet you do not supply their bodily needs, what is the good of that?* 17*So*[e] *faith by itself, if it has no works*[f]*, is dead.*

a. TNIV: people
b. TNIV: such faith
c. TNIV: without clothes
d. TNIV: well fed
e. TNIV: In the same way
f. TNIV: if it is not accompanied by action

James 2:14-17 begins with two questions, each of which assumes its answer: (1) What good is it . . . if people claim to have faith but have no deeds? (2) Can such faith save them? The first assumes the answer that such faith is no (saving) good and the second that such (workless) faith cannot save. Then James elaborates the answer he has assumed — the uselessness of faith without works — by offering a graphic, comic example (2:15-16). I say "comic" because we hope (and trust) that no follower of Jesus would behave this way in an overt, conscious manner. Then James, in 2:17, draws his conclusion — the conclusion he assumed in the answers to his questions in 2:14.

2:14 The "good" in "What *good* is it?" is *ophelos,*[6] which could also mean "benefit," but the more important observation is that it draws its mean-

---

and R. Krauss; ed. G. B. Kelly and J. D. Godsey; Minneapolis: Fortress, 2001); A. C. Thiselton, *The Hermeneutics of Doctrine* (Grand Rapids: Eerdmans, 2007), 19-42, on the disposition of belief; see also pp. 352-54.

4. Numerous manuscripts, including A and C, insert δε.

5. A number of manuscripts insert the subjunctive of ειμι, ωσιν, at this point (A, P, Y, etc.), but the verb ὑπάρχωσιν is the more original verb with λειπόμενοι.

6. Many observe the popularity of this term in diatribes; see Johnson, 237. Jas 2:14 is a conditional sentence with the protasis second ("if you say you have faith . . .") and the apodosis first ("what is the good of it?").

ing from its context. That is, it draws on the word "save" in the last part of v. 14 to clarify what kind of "good" is involved. Thus, the "good" or "benefit" in James's question is salvation or saving benefits for the messianic community.[7] "What good is it?" assumes the content of the conditional construction "if you say. . . ." James challenges throughout this letter the *assumption,* or the *claim,*[8] of faith that is not accompanied by works (1:22-27), and many other places in the New Testament show that faith must become manifest in love and obedience (Luke 3:7-14; Matt 7:15-27; Rom 1:5; 2:6-8; 6:17-18; 1 Cor 13:2; 2 Cor 10:5-6; Gal 6:4-6; Heb 5:11–6:8; 1 John 1:6).

This universal person claims "faith,"[9] but does not have "works."[10] James 2:14-26, not to mention the whole of James, is concerned with the disparity of this claim and this absence. The disparity was demonstrated by the prejudicial behaviors of the messianic community (2:1-4), but the issue runs deeper and may also have been seen in the sorts of insensitivities mentioned in 2:14-17. The disparity is expressed by the contrast of two verbs, "claim to have" *(legō echein)* and "have" *(echō).* There is perhaps a subtle distinction between claiming to have and just claiming, but the emphasis in the text emerges in the word *echō/echein:* it is about what one *has* or does not *have.* James knows that his universal person *does not have* works, even if he or she

---

7. See BDAG, 743; Davids, 120; otherwise with Popkes, 192. See also Job 15:3 (LXX); 1 Cor 15:32; Sir 20:30; 41:14; Philo, *De Posteritate Caini* 86; Josephus, *Ant* 1.263; 2.107; 4.90; 6.81, 209, 341; 10.112; 17.154; 18.210; *War* 3.111. The expression ἀδελφοί μου refers to the messianic community (see 1:2, 9, 16; 2:1, 5, 14; 3:1, 10, 12; 4:11; 5:7, 9, 10, 12, 19).

8. The verb here is λέγω, frequently translated "claim" (BDAG, 590 [2e]), and James universalizes with τις. The casting of the verbs in the present tense is for the sake of vividness; that James uses the present tense does not mean there are folks saying these very things in the community as James writes. Nor does the subjunctive mean this is a purely hypothetical case (Moo, 122).

9. πίστιν. In Jas 1:3, 6; 2:1, 5, 14, 17, 18, 20, 22, 24, 26; 5:15. See the note on Jas 2:1; cf. Frankemölle, 1.222-31.

10. ἔργα. In Jas 1:4, 25; 2:14, 17, 18, 20, 24; 3:13. This term and the Pauline expression "works of the law" have been at the forefront of the New Perspective debates. A recent insightful study of this debate in James can be found in F. Avemarie, "Die Werke des Gesetzes im Spiegel des Jakobusbriefes: A Very Old Perspective on Paul," *ZTK* 98 (2001) 282-309. Avemarie argues that James debates Paul and that James's understanding of what Paul meant by "works of the law" was the active fulfillment of the law rather than boundary markers as defended in the New Perspective, most notably in the many writings of James D. G. Dunn. There is no disputing that James understands "works" as "works of the Torah," even if that Torah is read through Lev 19:18; furthermore, there is no indication in James that "works" means boundary markers. The issue, of course, is the precise sense in which James is interacting with Paul's mature reflections on "works," the importance of "faith" to James, and whether Avemarie appreciates the nuanced differences in terms between James and Paul. See the excursus below after 2:26.

claims to have faith.[11] James knows this, in this context, because of what happened in the encounter with the poor person (2:2-4). And, no matter how hard we Protestants might try to work this out, the bottom line for James is *having* works. Works may well indicate the presence of faith, but the absence of works proves the absence of a faith that can bring about what James calls the "good."

There are basically two options for what James means by "works": either he means "works of the Torah," as in Paul, which would bring James into material conflict with Paul, or he means generally good "works," which means James and Paul could be harmonized. There can be no dispute that James does not speak of "works" as does Paul, for whom "works" often refers to boundary markers between Jews and Gentiles and represents covenant fidelity.[12] Nor can there be dispute that James's essential angle is good works in general or that these general good works are mapped out in the Torah and expressed in Torah observance. This is what we find in texts like 1:25 and will find in 2:14-26. For some this seems to let James off the hook, but I am unconvinced it is as simple as an either-or. James is Jewish, and he writes to a messianic Jewish community. It would be impossible for such a person or such a readership to hear the word "works" and not connect it to the Mosaic Torah. In fact, I propose that James means "works of the Torah" when he says "works," but he understands works through the lens of the Jesus Creed, and that means he generalizes "works" into a life shaped by following Jesus' teaching about doing Torah through love of God and others. That is, for James "works" means a life of loving God and loving others, and loving others means deeds of compassion toward those in need. This rendering of "works" is established by 2:8-13.[13]

The second question functions to clarify the first one. If "good" could be general enough to mean little more than "what good is it?" the second question narrows the meaning of "good" to the most crucial question the

11. Some suggest the absence of the article with πίστιν in 2:14a indicates an anaphoric reference back to 2:1, but there are three problems with this view: (1) James approves of the word "faith" in 2:1, but in 2:14 he does not; (2) both "faith" and "works" are anarthrous and for a good reason: to emphasize the qualitativeness of these nouns; (3) the universalizing of τις fits into the universalizing of everything in 2:14. On the other hand, I do not think "faith" can be reduced to the affirmation of monotheism here; even if 2:14 is disapproved and 2:1 approved, the "faith" that concerns James is the faith of the messianic community, and they believed in the one true God of Israel, indeed, but they also believed in Jesus as Messiah, the Glorious One.

12. On which, see the excellent monograph by Tom Holmén, *Jesus and Jewish Covenant Thinking* (BIS 55; Leiden: Brill, 2001), especially 37-87.

13. A good discussion, one that sides with "works" meaning general good works and to be distinguished from Paul, is Davids, "James and Paul," *DPL*, 458.

messianic community can ask: "Can [that kind of workless] faith[14] *save* you?"[15] The answer is an assumed "No, that kind of faith cannot save that person." So we are left to define what James means by "faith." In this context, and we need to keep our eye on both 2:1 and 2:19, "faith" evidently means — for the one with this kind of faith — "confessional" faith in God as one and Jesus as the Messiah as sufficient for redemption but not necessarily accompanied by deeds of mercy toward the marginalized. In 2:19 James will make it clear that this person confesses monotheism, and here James refers to the *Shema* (Deut 6:4-5: "God is *one*," Hebrew *echad*). If the emphasis in 2:14 is not on *what* one believes but on the claim to believe, that emphasis entails the absence of mercy, love, and compassion for the poor. In James's view, that kind of faith is not able[16] to save that kind of person.

What does James mean by "save"?[17] God is the Savior because God is also the Judge (4:12), and God saves, at least in part, through the "implanted word" (1:21), James's early version of the theology of regeneration. In light of 1:21, we can say that "save" involves moral transformation, but clearly for James salvation is eschatological since it is connected to the final judgment (4:12). This is spelled out more concretely in 5:20, where it is the "sinner's soul" saved "from death" because salvation will "cover a multitude of sins." Salvation, then, is regenerative, morally transforming, and eternal[18] — and the tragedy for James is that those who claim to have faith but do not have works will not be saved. Most Protestants do not believe this today.

2:15-16 James now offers a comic example, and it would be humorous if it were not so tragic. These two verses are one long conditional sentence, and can be diagrammed like this:

> *If* a brother or sister is naked and lacks daily food, and one of you says to them, "Go in peace; keep warm and eat your fill," and yet you do not supply their bodily needs,
>
> *then* what is the good of that?

---

14. The articular ἡ πίστις in 2:14b is anaphoric to the πίστιν of 2:14a. Thus, "Can *that kind of faith* . . . ," namely the kind of faith mentioned in 2:14a that did not involve works.

15. The NRSV converts the third person singulars in 2:14 to second person: from "someone" to "you." That translation mimics the vividness of the present tenses by making it even more vivid. James's actual wording (third person) is a little more clinical and distant, making it easier to be critical — "Can that kind of faith save that kind of person?"

16. δύναται . . . σῶσαι αὐτόν. See Popkes, 212-13. The action of the first verb is depicted imperfectively (or not yet completed), while the second is depicted in its totality.

17. See 1:21; 2:14; 4:12; 5:15, 20. See G. B. Caird, *New Testament Theology* (completed by L. D. Hurst; Oxford: Clarendon, 1994), especially 118-35.

18. Popkes, 212.

The protasis ("if") clause contains three elements: the condition of neediness (2:15), the condition of response to the needy (2:16a), and the summary evaluation of the response by James (2:16b).

The neediness of the "brother and sister," family terms for the messianic community,[19] is clothing and food. The need for *clothing* comes to expression with a graphic image: "If a brother or sister is *naked.*"[20] Inasmuch as blatant nudity was shameful in the Jewish world (e.g., Rev 16:15; 17:16),[21] this expression is merely a graphic image of the inadequacy of clothing, or it refers to being poorly dressed (Matt 25:36, 38, 43-44) or incompletely dressed (John 21:7).[22] Nakedness is an image of shame and defenselessness. The need for *food* ("lacks daily food")[23] focuses on the basics — "daily."[24] This brother or sister does not have even a daily allotment (see Acts 6:1; 1 Tim 5:3-20).

James contrasts[25] his description of the neediness of someone in the messianic community with the incomprehensible response on the part of others in the community as he turns to the second of three elements in the protasis: the person both wishes the poor well and does nothing to help them. James spares finger-pointing by saying "one of you." If the specific persons are not clear, such a person's "faith" is: this is the person who has faith but no

19. This is the only time James uses the word ἀδελφή. In light of 2:5's contrast of brothers with the rich in 2:6, it is likely that "brothers and sisters" in 2:15 refers to the messianic community as a family fellowship (Popkes, 192). If this is accurate, whether James thought the messianic community should respond to the needs of those outside the community is not at issue. One can assume he thought they should. This text reminds one of Matt 25:31-46, where those to whom the followers of Jesus are to show compassion are also in the family of Jesus' followers, leaving unstated how they were to respond to those outside the community. Gal 6:10 speaks for the whole first century's response to those in need. On images for the church, see P. S. Minear, *Images of the Church in the New Testament* (Philadelphia: Westminster, 1975), 165-67; P. D. Hanson, *The People Called: The Growth of Community in the Bible* (San Francisco: Harper and Row, 1986); J. H. Hellerman, *The Ancient Church as Family* (Minneapolis: Fortress, 2001).

20. γυμνοὶ ὑπάρχωσιν. The verb ὑπάρχω is stronger than εἰμι and speaks about the condition of one's existence (BDAG, 1029-30), and the present tense makes the condition vivid and graphic.

21. See BDAG, 208; *EDNT* 1.265-66; *ISBE* 3.480.

22. Laws, 120-21; Popkes, 193.

23. λειπόμενοι τῆς ἐφημέρου τροφῆς. The change from a verb (ὑπάρχωσιν) to a participle λειπόμενοι is connected with καὶ; the grammar probably indicates coordination instead of subordination, and this view is reflected in manuscripts that insert ωσιν. Again, the present tense makes the situation especially vivid instead of attempting to describe this as an ongoing condition.

24. ἐφημέρου, from which we get the word "ephemeral." A similar word is used in Luke 1:5, 8 for the daily assignments of priests.

25. He uses δέ, and it coordinates with μὴ δῶτε δὲ in the second section of 2:16.

works (2:14). As the person with this kind of faith "claims to have faith" (2:14), so now this kind of person "says" to the naked and hungry brother or sister three things: "Go in peace; keep warm and eat your fill."[26] Following the person's speech will be the person's behaviors (2:16b).

"Go in peace." This common Jewish form of greeting, farewell and blessing also emphasizes confidence that a person's wishes will be granted (Judg 18:6; 1 Sam 1:17; 20:42; 29:7; 2 Sam 15:9; Mark 5:34; Luke 7:50; 10:5; Acts 16:36). Though we should be wary of overtheologizing the word "peace" (Hebrew *shalom*), the common usage of this expression suggests the peace and blessing of God upon a person.[27] Because "keep warm" (Greek *thermainō*) is either passive or middle, and because the "go in peace" connotes God's peace, many read this as a divine passive in the form of a prayer: "May God warm you." This may be overinterpretation but, if so, not by much: the false piety, the false claims, and the false religion of those who have faith but do not have works are palpable in this letter (e.g., 1:26-27) and so a more religious reading of "keep warm" is not far from the mark.[28] The brother or sister is in need of clothing and food; the pious-sounding but cold-hearted messianists respond to the first with "keep warm" and to the second with "eat your fill." The word suggests eating to the point of being sated (Matt 5:6; 14:20; 15:37; John 6:26; Phil 4:12; Rev 19:21). Again, there is an air of piety surrounding the community's response: "May God's peace be upon you; may God warm you; may God fill you up."

The neediness of the brother or sister shocks us when we see the contrasting behaviors of the messianists: they say things that sound pious (2:16a) but *do nothing* (2:16b): "and yet you do not supply their bodily needs."[29] Their lack of "daily" food (2:16a) is met by a fierce refusal to respond to the needs requisite to the body. The description here is tragic: the messianic community is connected to the Messiah who became poor in order to make others rich and who taught in word and deed to show mercy to those in need; the community is connected to the Scriptures of Israel, which from beginning to end advocate mercy and compassion for those in need; and the community is filled with poor who know the underside of oppression. Yet — and this is what perplexes James into strong words — this group of those who say they have faith in Jesus the Messiah, the glorious one who became poor, does nothing for those who make their needs obvious.

26. ὑπάγετε ἐν εἰρήνῃ, θερμαίνεσθε καὶ χορτάζεσθε. Again, all three are present tense to carry on the vividness of image.
27. On this, see now W. M. Swartley, *Covenant of Peace: The Missing Peace in New Testament Theology and Ethics* (Grand Rapids: Eerdmans, 2006), 27-52, 259-62.
28. See Laws, 121; Popkes, 193-94. Davids disagrees (122).
29. μὴ δῶτε δὲ αὐτοῖς τὰ ἐπιτήδεια τοῦ σώματος. The aorist is a summary statement of their action. On ἐπιτήδεια, see BDAG, 383-84.

"What is the good of that?" James asks. This question rounds off 2:14-16 by framing the whole with the same question. The "good," again, is the "saving good." The implied answer is "No good, none whatsoever."

2:17 James now draws his conclusion in 2:17, and it is the conclusion that has quietly lurked behind everything James has said from the beginning of this paragraph: "So faith by itself, if it has no works, is dead." This conclusion is clearer than the implicit answer of 2:14 and is spoken of in four ways: faith without works is useless (2:14), cannot save (2:14), is dead (2:17), and is ineffective (2:20).[30] It is wiser to synthesize the four than to drive wedges between them. Perhaps the most weighty is the second: faith without works cannot save.

"So faith."[31] As claims and wishes and prayers that are not met by actions do no good for those in need (2:15-16), so faith that does not have works is dead. What is the meaning of "faith" *(pistis)* here? As in 2:1, the word here is neutral. In 2:5 and 2:22 (and 1:3, 6; 5:15) "faith" does what faith is designed to do: it trusts God and obeys God. But, in 2:1, 14, 17, 18, 20, 24, faith is the right word but is stalled in its design from moving into full-blown works. It is best to understand this kind of stalled faith as a claim of faith that, because it does not manifest good works, cannot save. That faith was in God as one and Jesus as the Messiah.

The NRSV moves forward the last two words of the Greek sentence: "by itself."[32] This raises an interesting, if minor, question: Does "by itself" modify "faith" in "So faith [by itself]"? Or does its suspension until the end lead to a different kind of modification, namely, "Faith is dead *by itself* [or *on its own* or *in itself*]"? There is a subtle difference between the two and the grammar of the Greek sentence favors the second option. The major point, though, is that faith here stands alone with no works. There would be (and are) precious few who would (do) claim to have faith and have absolutely no works, so it is wise for us to understand James describing an absolute condition in order to make his appeal more persuasive. Had he moved into how many works are requisite, the point would die the death of nuances.

Faith, "if it has no works,"[33] is *dead.* For James, the options are two: ei-

---

30. In 1:26, "religion" without works is "vain" (μάταιος).

31. οὕτως καὶ ἡ πίστις. The TNIV has "In the same way," which is slightly better than NRSV's "So faith." The analogy of the comic behaviors of 2:15-16 emerges from both οὕτως καὶ, so I prefer a translation that brings this out: something like "so also faith" (BDAG, 495-96). See also 1:11; 2:26; 3:5.

32. καθ' ἑαυτήν.

33. Again, the Greek is slightly different with no difference in meaning: ἐὰν μὴ ἔχῃ ἔργα. "If it does not have works" is not quite the same as "If it has *no* works." By using the subjunctive, James pulls back slightly from a direct accusation of those who have mistreated the poor; the present tense makes the hypothetical situation more vivid.

ther one has the kind of (claimed) faith that does not live out in works or one has the kind of (saving) faith that lives out in works. The former (claimed) faith is dead. As sin is "dead" without the Law to give it life (Rom 7:8), so faith is dead without works. Again, the focus here is not so much that such faith is simply ineffective in this life alone, which it is. It is "vain" (1:26), "useless" (2:14), and "ineffective" (2:20). But there is more: James stretches the now into the eternal — "dead" means "cannot save" (2:14). As Rob Wall puts it, "those whose confidence rests on routine professions of faith in God but whose lives do not embody the mercy of God are destined for 'death' instead of 'life' at day's end (cf. 5:19-20)."[34] We must also respect what James is saying: there are those who claim faith, who are connected to the community of faith, who confess an orthodox faith, and who may well be supports of the faith, but who do not have works — and their faith cannot save.[35]

James now turns to a rhetorical, imaginative debate with an unidentified (and perhaps unidentifiable!) interlocutor. His main point is already clear from 2:17, but he must deepen his argument, sharpen the polemic, and lay bare his objections to the kind of faith that does not produce works. Martin Dibelius, it should be observed as we enter into this next little room in James, once said that James 2:18 "was one of the most difficult New Testament passages."[36] Even if it is easy to get lost in the thicket of problems, we cannot lose sight of James's major point: that faith without works cannot save.

5.2. CHALLENGE AND RESPONSES (2:18-26)

18*But someone will say, "You have faith and I have works." Show me your faith apart[37] from your works, and I by my works will show you my faith.* 19*You believe that[38] God is one;*[a] *you do well.*[b] *Even the de-*

---

34. Wall, 134-35. Calvin reasons: "We hence conclude that it is indeed no faith, for when dead, it does not properly retain the name" (p. 311).

35. See S. S. Taylor, "Faith, faithfulness," in *NDBT*, 487-93; D. J. Treier, "Faith," in *DTIB*, 226-28. A Christian understanding of faith is far more complex than discerning both the difference and relationship of faith and works. An exceptionally fine study of the scope of faith and faithfulness, and their fundamental expression in both Christ's own faithfulness and our faith in him, is that of S. S. Taylor just mentioned.

36. Dibelius, 154.

37. Numerous manuscripts have "by" (ἐκ) instead of "apart from" (χωρίς); thus James is stalemated with his interlocutor. See 5, 218, 322, etc.

38. The variants here are numerous. Here is a partial listing, the presence of the article being the major issue:

1. εις εστιν ο θεος: P74, ℵ, A, 442, etc.
2. εις εστιν Θεος: 945, 1241, 1739, 2298

mons believe^c — *and shudder.* 20*Do you want to be shown, you senseless*^d *person, that faith apart from works is barren*^e? 21*Was not our ancestor*^f *Abraham justified*^g *by works when he offered his son Isaac on the altar?* 22*You see that faith was active along with his works, and faith was brought to completion by the works.* 23*Thus the scripture was fulfilled that says, "Abraham believed God, and it was reckoned*^h *to him as righteousness,"*[39] *and he was called the friend of God.* 24*You see that a person is justified by works*ⁱ *and not by faith alone.* 25*Likewise, was not Rahab the prostitute also justified*^g *by works when she welcomed*^j *the messengers and sent them out by another road*^k? 26*For just as the body without the spirit is dead, so faith without works*^l *is also dead.*

a. TNIV: that there is one God

b. TNIV: Good!

c. TNIV: believe that

d. TNIV: foolish

e. TNIV: useless

f. TNIV: father

g. TNIV: considered righteous

h. TNIV: credited

i. TNIV: by what they do

---

3. εστιν Θεος: Y, Athanasius

4. εις ο Θεος: Cyr., Latin text types F, T

5. εις ο Θεος εστιν: C, 33 (evidently), 81, 1175, 1243

6. εις Θεος εστιν: B, 206, 254, 429, 522

7. ο Θεος εις εστιν: 5, 88, 218, 322, 323

8. θεος εις εστιν: 88 (additional reading), 43, 69, 93, 319, 321

9. ο Θεος εστιν: K*, 2197*

10. θεος εστιν: 365, Photius

The variants all witness to the standard Jewish creed, the *Shema* (Deut 6:4-5). Metzger observes that 5 and 6 are Christian assimilations to 1 Cor 8:6; Eph 4:6; and 1 Tim 2:5 and that 1 stands with Jewish orthodoxy. He also observes that 7 is a later Christian framing of the words. See *Textual Commentary*, 681; Omanson, 472.

39. There are differences between James's quotation of Gen 15:6 and both the MT and the LXX. With respect to the MT: (1) "Abraham" is added both in the LXX and in James, though their spellings of Abraham's name differ; LXX has Ἀβράμ while James has Ἀβραάμ. (2) The LXX and James have an aorist passive while the Hebrew for "reckon" is a Qal imperfect. (3) Perhaps most notable is that both the LXX and James have θεός for the tetragrammaton. With respect to the LXX and James: (1) James spells "Abraham" differently because he knows the name was changed (cf. Gen 17:5). (2) James uses a different conjunction: the LXX has καί but James δέ. James has basically used a text like that of the LXX; there is no sign he has used the MT.

j. TNIV: when she gave lodging to the spies
k. TNIV: in a different direction
l. TNIV: deeds

This brief sketch of differences between the NRSV and the TNIV in 2:20-26 manifests an evangelical unease with the language of James with respect to both the terms "justified" and "works."

James 2:18-19 interrupts the flow by providing the response of an imagined interlocutor to whom James then responds, and this style is a form of ancient rhetoric.[40] I begin with an outline of our section which will guide the comments.

1. The Interlocutor's Challenge (2:18a).
2. The Responses of James (2:18b-26)
   2.1. Regarding faith and works (2:18b)
   2.2. Regarding creedal faith (2:19)
   2.3. Regarding biblical proof (2:20-26)

The debates on vv. 18 and 19 are legion, and it would gobble up space to list the options and their proponents. Since it is unlikely that any theory will dispel all the problems, I will do my best to make my view clear.[41] These questions have been raised: (1) Is the speaker in 2:18a (Greek *tis,* NRSV: "someone") an interlocutor, James himself, or an ally of James? (2) Where does this speaker's statement end? With 2:18b or 2:19? Or from the other angle, where does James begin to respond? At 2:18b, 2:19, or 2:20? (3) Are the personal pronouns of 2:18a to be given full weight? Does "you" mean James or someone he is facing and the "I" refer to himself? Or, are they generic personal pronouns? (4) What is the logical relationship of 2:18b to 2:18a and 2:19 to what precedes? (5) The most significant question, and one not asked often enough, is this: Why does the interlocutor, who supposedly is speaking in 2:18a, use

40. On rhetorical criticism, see C. Clifton Black, "Rhetorical Criticism," in *Hearing the New Testament* (Grand Rapids: Eerdmans, 1995), 256-77. In spite of his expertise in the field and the framing of his commentary in terms of rhetoric, Witherington, 475-76, sheds little light on the rhetoric of these verses. The fact is that the "you" of 2:18 does not refer to a known position of James because the opening sentence, beginning with "You have faith . . . ," asserts a view of the relationship of faith and works that is not the view of James.

41. See McKnight, "Unidentifiable Interlocutor." One of the advantages of working on and teaching a book like James throughout one's career is looking back at previous conclusions. When I reread the above piece for the commentary, I was pleased (if not surprised) to conclude that I still agree with myself! See the detailed discussion of the issues and options in C. E. Donker, "Der Verfasser des Jak und sein Gegner. Zum Problem des Einwandes in Jak 2:18-19," *ZNW* 72 (1981) 227-40 (who sees all of vv. 18-19 as the opponents' view); Popkes, 196-98; Konradt, *Christliche Existenz,* 217-21; Blomberg and Kamell, 132-34.

the term "works" *(erga)* for himself when one would expect the interlocutor, because he or she must disagree with James, to use "faith" and assign the word "works" to James or his allies? I suggest that the answer to this question provides the clue to answering, at some level of probability, the other questions.

5.2.1. The Interlocutor's Statement (2:18a)

This verse stands in strong contrast to the preceding ("but")[42] and, as is commonly recognized for a diatribe format,[43] introduces an interrupting interlocutor. Who is this "someone"? The options include: (1) James or an ally of James,[44] (2) a Jew who affirms a former generation's understanding of Jewish theology and who sees Christian works as different from works of the Torah and therefore unacceptable,[45] (3) an imaginary opponent,[46] (4) an objector who actually speaks James's mind,[47] or (5) someone who either affirms the validity of two approaches to redemption[48] — "one has pre-eminently

42. Ἀλλ' ἐρεῖ τις. See Hort, 60; Dibelius, 149-50; Ropes, 208; H. Windisch, *Die katholischen Briefe* (Handbuch zum Neuen Testament, 15; Tübingen: Mohr, 1930), 17; J. Schneider, *Die Briefe des Jakobus, Petrus, Judas und Johannes* (Neue Testament Deutsch; Göttingen: Vandenhoeck und Ruprecht, 1961), 19; Laws, 123. Importantly, Mayor, 99, thinks ἀλλά is emphatic — something like "Indeed, let me make my point now even more clear." The strength of this position is that it makes the pronouns natural. But the problem that arises is fatal: the next two words indicate another person (not James) speaking, and that favors the adversative interpretation. That James has become adversarial is proven by 2:20a: "you senseless person." See also 1 Cor 15:35-36; Rom 9:19; 11:19; Luke 4:23; Josephus, *War* 8.363; *4 Maccabees* 2:24; *Barnabas* 9:6; Xenophon, *Cyropaedia* 4.3.10.

43. See D. F. Watson, "James 2 in Light of Greco-Roman Schemes of Argumentation," *NTS* 39 (1993) 94-121, especially 118-20, for observations about diatribe.

44. Mayor, 99, but his "Further Notes," 31-32, concede that this use of ἀλλά is without textual support; Mussner, 136-37; Cantinat, 145; Adamson, 124-25, 135-37; Konradt, *Christliche Existenz,* 219 ("Bundesgenosse" who needs correction and who says to James mistakenly, "You, too then, understand salvation to be by faith!").

45. See, with differences, the views of T. Zahn, *Introduction to the New Testament* (3 vols.; Edinburgh: Clark, 1909), 1.97-98, n. 4; Hort, 60-61. This view strains the meaning of ἔργα in this text and asks the interlocutor's words to extend to the end of 2:18.

46. Dibelius, 156; Laws, 124. A problem here is the reality of this view in 2:2-4 and 2:15-16 and the bold accusation in 2:20a.

47. J. E. Huther, *Critical and Exegetical Handbook to the General Epistles of James, Peter, John, and Jude* (New York: Funk and Wagnalls, 1887), 123-24; M. Meinertz, *Der Jakobusbrief und sein Verfasser in Schrift und Überlieferung* (Biblische Studien; Freiburg: Herder, 1905), 32-33; B. S. Easton, "The Epistle of James," in *The Interpreter's Bible,* vol. 12 (New York: Abingdon, 1957), 42-43.

48. Ropes, 208. The problem here is not in how Ropes understands 2:18a; it is in how James responds because his response is not to the problem Ropes articulates. James responds to the relationship of faith and works and the necessity of the former being con-

faith, another has pre-eminently works," and both are equally valid in the way that different gifts are valid in 1 Cor 12:9-10, or affirms that faith and works are completely distinguishable — "one has faith, and then again, another person has works, but the two are separable and different."[49] Furthermore, what is the extent of the interlocutor's statement? One would think there would be more debate on this, since clarity evades us at every turn in these two verses, but nearly everyone agrees that the interlocutor's statement is no more than the opening line: "You have faith and I have works."[50]

To resolve the issues in 2:18-19, I propose the following vantage points and a brief translation to clarify each point. The *first* is that the "someone," since the grammar clearly favors a diatribe style,[51] is an opponent of James and the words that immediately follow are from that opponent and reflect that opponent's view.[52]

Now my opponent will respond . . .

Second, if we consider the words of 2:18a and 2:18b, it is clear that 2:18b expresses the view of James. Thus, it is safe to conclude that the opponent's view is found in 2:18a.[53]

2:18a "You [James] have faith, and I [your opponent] have works."
2:18b James: "Show me your faith apart from works and I will show you my faith by my works." (2:18b)

But seeing 2:18a as the view of the opponent presents a problem. One expects the opponent of James to take the view that he or she has "faith" and James has "works," since that is what James has argued from 2:1 on. Thus,

---

nected to the latter. James criticizes, not toleration, but separation of faith from works. See also Martin, 86-89.

49. McKnight, "Unidentifiable Interlocutor."

50. So Ropes, 208-11; Dibelius, 154; A. Schlatter, *Der Jakobusbrief und die Johannesbriefe ausgelegt für Bibelleser* (Stuttgart: Vereinsbuchhandlung, 1895), 194-95; Schneider, 18-19; Mitton, 108-9. An alternative view is conjectural emendation; O. Pfleiderer, *Primitive Christianity: Its Writings and Teachings in Their Historical Connections* (New York: Putnam, 1911), 4.304, n. 1. He suggested that we read "you have works, I have faith." It solves most of the problems except the lack of manuscript evidence.

51. S. K. Stowers, "The Diatribe," in *Greco-Roman Literature and the New Testament* (ed. D. E. Aune; SBLSBS 21; Atlanta: Scholars, 1988), 71-83; see the judicious summary in D. E. Aune, *The New Testament in Its Literary Environment* (LEC; Philadelphia: Westminster, 1987), 200-202; D. F. Watson, "An Assessment of the Rhetoric," in Webb and Kloppenborg, *Reading James,* 110-11.

52. Dibelius, 150; Davids, 123; Johnson, 239; *contra* Adamson, 124-25, on whom one should also read BDF, 448.1, 448.3.

53. So Hort, 60; Ropes, 208-9, 211; Dibelius, 154; Mitton, 108-9.

we would expect "You have works and I have faith." And it is not clear how James's response in 2:18b contests what is said in 2:18a.

This leads to a *third* vantage point: the personal pronouns need not be taken as referring to specific persons or to different persons. J. B. Mayor argued that the two pronouns, "You" and "I," "may be a more vivid expression for *ho men* and *ho de*," that is, "on the one hand one person says . . . and on the other hand another person says. . . ."[54] And J. H. Ropes fully supported Mayor by observing that "With any other mode of interpretation [than Mayor's softening of the pronouns] it seems impossible to gain a satisfactory sense from the passage."[55] Martin Dibelius, too, and he translates "the one has faith, the other has works."[56] What this position deals with is the incomprehensible nature of the opponent's words if those words are a quotation of James's view and his/her view. In the simplest of terms, one cannot reasonably say James has faith and the opponent has works if his opponent opposes his belief in the ineradicable connection of faith and works — that makes no sense of the context. Since it is a near certainty that 2:18a introduces an opponent and since the opponent's words are found in 2:18a, then we are driven to ask if the *prima facie* reading needs adjustment, which is what Mayor, Ropes, and Dibelius do. If we let the pronouns be more general, we are let off the hook and sense flows in all directions. So, instead of *"You [James] have faith, and I [your opponent] have works,"* I propose, building on the work of these three scholars, something like this: *"One has faith and one has works."* Now we have what looks like an abstract but analytical claim of some kind of pluralistic views on faith and works:

2:18a Interlocutor: "One has faith and one has works."
2:18b James: "Show me your faith apart from works and I will show you my faith by my works."

For 2:18b to make sense, James must have understood 2:18a as separating faith and works.[57] Thus, something like this: "One has faith and one has works and both are equally acceptable ways of living out the covenant God has with Israel." James responds with a "No!" because he will not accept a workless faith as an acceptable way of life before God.[58] Thus, when James

54. Mayor, 100. That is, "on the one hand one says . . . and on the other hand another says."
55. Ropes, 31.
56. Dibelius, 156.
57. Again, see Hort, 61; Ropes, 209; Dibelius, 155; Cantinat, 145.
58. It is altogether tempting here to wonder if the faith person is the Pauline Gentile Christian and the works person the messianic Jew. If this is the case, James cuts deeply into the claim of his opponent by saying that such a representation of Paul or such a view is entirely unacceptable.

says "Show me your faith apart from works," he believes he has the opponent on the hook because it is impossible to have saving faith and not have works. The interlocutor, who stands in for the messianists of 2:2-4 and 2:15-16, believes one can have faith and no works. The interlocutor, therefore, believes faith saves and works are an option or, put differently, that faith and works are two different things. Perhaps the interlocutor believes something like this: "Some Christians have only faith; others have (both faith and) works." It is likely that the interlocutor believed that a Jesus-shaped confession of the one God of Israel (2:19) was enough for salvation. However one wants to work out the particulars, the opponent separates faith and works, and James will now show that faith and works are not only inseparable but the former without the latter cannot save (2:21, 24).[59] James, it should be observed, does not personally prove his faith by appealing to his own works. The absence of that kind of proof indicates that the "I" of this verse is more representative than personal.

5.2.2. The Responses of James (2:18b-26)

James now responds to the claims that faith and works are separable items and that some persons have only faith while others have (faith and) works. James offers two stiff challenges. First, he challenges the interlocutor to show his faith without works; James, for his part, will back up his words by showing his faith by his works. The second challenge concerns creedal faith. Having creedal faith alone, James states, is not enough; even demons have that. The third response concerns biblical proof for his point, which he finds in both Abraham and his unlikely ally, Rahab.

5.2.2.1. Regarding Faith and Works (2:18b)

This is a face-to-face, rhetorically speaking, challenge. James says "Show me your faith apart from your works, and I by my works will show you my faith."[60] He challenges his opponent, who represents the workless believers who have no deeds of mercy, to show (prove by revealing)[61] his faith without

---

59. As for details, the present tenses (ἐρεῖ, ἔχεις, ἔχω) are used to make the scene vivid and do not seek to depict repeated or ongoing action. The absence of articles with both πίστιν and ἔργα throws emphasis on the qualities of the nouns instead of serving to focus on some particular form of faith (orthodox, creedal faith) or works (Torah-shaped).

60. The Greek is neatly balanced, though not poetically so:

δεῖξόν μοι τὴν πίστιν σου χωρὶς τῶν ἔργων,
κἀγώ σοι δείξω ἐκ τῶν ἔργων μου τὴν πίστιν.

61. The aorist of δείκνυμι is constative or global. See BDAG, 214-15; Moo, 219. Other instances in the New Testament: Matt 4:8; 8:4; Mark 14:15; Luke 20:24; 24:40;

works. James knows that the opponent, should he try, would be attempting the impossible. He knows this because he believes that genuine, saving faith is inseparable from works. James could be asking his opponent for either of two things: that he show James his faith-without-works or that he show his faith without pointing to any works.[62] The second is more likely. The first option would be a stalemate. James would be saying, "Show me your workless faith and I will show you my working faith."[63]

In contrast to his opponent, who without works simply cannot prove his faith, James will show his faith by, on the basis of, or out of his works.[64] We should listen to what James says here: James proves faith by works. Faith for James cannot be reduced to trust or to creedal orthodoxy; faith for James flowers into full-blown acts of mercy toward the poor and marginalized, or it is not saving faith.[65]

5.2.2.2. Regarding Creedal Faith (2:19)

Once again James gets in the rhetorical face of his interlocutor: "You believe that God is one." This challenge, too, responds to the interlocutor's claim that faith and works are separable and that faith alone is saving. What that faith is now seems clear: it is faith that there is one God, the God of Israel.[66] This text, even with all its variants (see above), witnesses to the daily presence of the *Shema* in the lives of Jews and of ordinary messianists. The *Shema*, a later liturgical rendition of not only Deuteronomy 6:4-5, but also including 6:6-8: 11:13-21; and Numbers 15:37-41, supplemented evidently in the first century with the Ten Words (Exod 20:1-17; Deut 5:6-21), was a daily confession.[67] Observant Jews recited the *Shema* at daybreak, at the time of the after-

---

John 5:20; 10:32; 14:8-9; 20:20; Acts 7:3; 10:28; 1 Cor 12:31; 1 Tim 6:15; Heb 8:5; Rev 1:1; 4:1; 17:1; 21:9; 22:1, 6. The only other use in James is at 3:13. See Popkes, 199.

62. In the first option, χωρίς modifies τὴν πίστιν; in the second, it modifies the verb δεῖξον.

63. This second option creates another possibility, namely, the interlocutor's depersonalized pronouns running through 2:18b. Thus, "One has faith, and another has works. Someone can show me their work-less faith and someone else can show me their working faith. It doesn't matter."

64. The general sense of ἐκ can be rendered accurately with any of these translations. The works, in other words, are the source of the information that leads the observer to infer that faith is present.

65. Calvin rightly observes that James is not suggesting that everyone who has works has faith; cf. p. 312.

66. See further at Philo, *On the Creation* 171; Gal 3:20; 1 Cor 8:4-6; Eph 4:6; 1 Tim 2:5. We should not forget Jas 2:1 in this context: yes, the interlocutor believed in monotheism, but the interlocutor is a messianist as well. See Edgar, "Love-Command."

67. See also *Testament of Issachar* 5:2; *Did* 1:1; *Barnabas* 19:2.

noon sacrifice, and in the evening — and probably whenever they entered or left their homes. More importantly for the messianic community, Jesus affirmed the *Shema* and attached to it an important, and horizontalizing, reminder from Leviticus 19:18, the command to love one's neighbor as oneself (Mark 12:28-32), in what I call the Jesus Creed.

The *Shema,* in its Jesus Creed form, figures more prominently in James than in any other book in the New Testament, witnessing again to the Jewish location of this book. Only James has all of the Jesus Creed. There are traces of it in:

1:12: "to those who love him."
2:5: "to those who love him."
2:8: "You shall love your neighbor as yourself."
2:18: "You believe that God is one."

More schematically, it looks like this:

God is one	Deuteronomy 6:4-5	James 2:18
Love God	Deuteronomy 6:4-5	James 1:12; 2:5
Love others	Leviticus 19:18	James 2:8

With this context, then, James's challenge to his interlocutor, "You believe that God is one," is probably more than the simple creed of Judaism but is instead a lead-in for someone who not only recites the *Shema* but recites it in the Jesus Creed form. His concern is with someone in the messianic community, someone who recites the Jesus Creed daily, who thinks that a person can affirm the one God and follow Jesus and yet remain oblivious to the needy around him or her.[68]

The claim to believe[69] that the God of Israel is the one and only God is insufficient. James turns to biting sarcasm or at least irony: "you do well."[70] Some suggest James means to agree with the interlocutor as in, "So, you are right."[71] James, however, is not kind to his opponent — 2:14-16 uses words like "useless," and 2:20 calls the opponent a "senseless person." It is more than likely that

---

68. Too much scholarship is fascinated with the absence of christology here, in spite of 1:1 and 2:1. See Popkes, 200.

69. πιστεύεις ὅτι. This is creedal: to believe "that" is a way of affirming *what* one believes and the content of what one believes. This is not the same as believe "in" (εἰς, ἐν), in the sense of trusting in saving faith.

70. καλῶς ποιεῖς. Again, as with so much of this, the present tenses serve to make the action vivid in the eyes of the readers and listeners. See Ropes, 216; Davids, 125; Popkes, 200.

71. E.g., Laws, 126.

"you do well" is a biting comment.[72] The next two lines pull the legs out from under the opponent. First, he says, "Even[73] the demons believe," and then he adds, as if adding a kicking blow to a wounded body, "and shudder." Demons, too, believe that there is but one God — and they know that the one God is YHWH, the God of Israel (see Mark 1:24; 3:11; Acts 16:17; 19:15). But — and here one must fill in the lines to express James's tone — at least they shudder and shake[74] in God's presence! James's example is *ad absurdum.* While it is possible that James uses the shuddering of the demons as evidence that faith produces some kind of action (works),[75] it is more likely that he is casting the interlocutor — and therefore the workless followers of Jesus — in negative light.[76] They are worse than demons! Demons shudder in the presence of God, but the workless messianists are seemingly oblivious to the superficiality of their faith and the doom they face if they do not turn from their callousness.[77] James has tied together genuine faith in God, loving God, and loving others.

5.2.2.3. Regarding Biblical Proof (2:20-26)

James continues his diatribe in 2:20-26 with a third response to the interlocutor's challenge. He now turns to proving the ineradicable connection and inseparability of faith and works in Scripture, and he finds two unlikely allies: Abraham (2:21-24)[78] and Rahab (2:25).[79] Before these two examples, James asks the question he wants to answer (2:20), and afterward he concludes the entire chapter, section, and subsection with the conclusion that has been shaping everything (2:26).

5.2.2.3.1. Question about Proof (2:20)

James's opening words, "Do you want to be shown?"[80] come from the world of rhetoric, persuasion, and argumentation. One finds similar expressions in

72. Blomberg and Kamell, 135.
73. καί in the sense of "even."
74. φρίσσουσιν. See BDAG, 1065. The word is used also for the shuddering of the body and demons upon exorcism; see the discussion in Laws, 126-28.
75. See Laws, 126.
76. See Johnson, 241; Popkes, 201.
77. Popkes, 201.
78. See Siker, *Disinheriting the Jews.* Siker's thesis is straightforward: the Jewish Christian Paul and the Gentile Christian Luke used Abraham for *inclusionary* purposes; later the Jewish Christian John and the Gentile Christian Justin used Abraham for *exclusionary* purposes.
79. I doubt Abraham and Rahab, male and female, are designed to draw out the "brother or sister" of 2:15, as some have suggested.
80. Θέλεις δὲ γνῶναι. The present tense θέλεις continues the vividness created by

Paul (Rom 6:16; 11:2; 1 Cor 3:16; 5:6; 6:2-3, 9, 15, 16, 19; 9:13, 24). This style is not prone to wait for the interlocutor's answer. James's question, in other words, is not genuine. I have for more than a decade wondered how the author of James 3:1-12, where we find strong warnings about strong words, can say things like "You senseless person" (2:20) or, even more accusatory, "Adulterers!" (4:4), which is followed shortly by "Do not speak evil against one another" (4:11). The only satisfactory solution is that the rhetoric of that world saw no disrespect or problem in moral denunciation of those in the wrong. However one explains the language, James calls the interlocutor "You senseless person."[81] He thinks the interlocutor's attempted combination of faith in Christ (2:1) and monotheism (2:19) with indifference toward the poor and needy is "senseless," which of course it is. The kind of senselessness he has in mind is both intellectual and moral (see e.g., Judg 9:4).

The question James asks the interlocutor concerns, once again, the supposed separability of faith and works: Is it not true that "faith apart from works is barren"? The question betrays James's answer: he thinks such a faith is useless (2:14), unsaving (2:14), dead (2:17), and futile (2:20).[82] Furthermore, his pitting of faith against works is structurally parallel to his pitting of hearing against doing in 1:22. As with hearing without doing, so faith without works: they are "useless." The word behind "useless," *argē*, combines "non" and "working"[83] to be both a play on words ("works" that are "workless" are worthless) and a deconstruction of the interlocutor's theological position. It means "workless" in the sense of "ineffective" or "barren" in production.[84] What James has in mind, then, is that faith without works cannot save (2:14) and does not effect God's will in this world either. Not only does he have it in mind, he has proof: Abraham and Rahab prove his point.

Before we proceed to those examples, though, a comment about how

---

the other present tenses in 2:14-19; the aorist γνῶναι does not emphasize "come to know" or suggest a singular act of knowing through a powerful proof. Instead, the aorist indicates the act of knowing viewed in its totality. The aorist active is better translated "to know" (Adamson, 127) than "to be shown" (Davids, 126). There are other, and better, Greek words for "show" (e.g., δείκνυμι in 2:18). On θέλω with γινώσκω, see Mark 7:24; 9:30; Acts 17:20. There are no strict parallels to this expression in the New Testament.

81. ὦ ἄνθρωπε κενέ, where James unusually combines ὦ with the vocative. Jesus and Paul trade in the same rhetoric: see Matt 23:17 (with 5:22); Luke 24:25; Gal 3:1; Rom 2:1; 1 Cor 15:36. See also Hermas, *Visions* 3.8.9; Epictetus, *Discourses* 1.21.2; 2.16-17. On κενός, see BDAG, 539; the word means "empty." Some think the expression in James is unemotive (MHT, 3.33), while others (and I agree) see some emotion (BDF, 146.1b).

82. The manuscript tradition uses other words that James has already used: νεκρά and κενή.

83. α privative with ἔργα.

84. Moulton and Milligan provide evidence for a derivative of this term meaning "holiday" or "vacation" (M-M, 74). See also Wis 13:13; 14:5.

to express the relationship of faith and works in James. I see a tendency, which seems to me to be a subtle attempt to let the Reformation have too much influence on exegesis, to prefer this formula: faith is *demonstrated* by works.[85] What this does is salvage faith as the *sine qua non* of salvation, which may well be sound theology, but it lacks the nuance of James. (Some have argued that it is James who lacks the nuance and is in need of help.) Instead of locking into the term "demonstration," I suggest we use each of the four terms James himself uses, and I suggest we use these terms liberally:

Works *show* faith (2:18).
Faith *works with* works (2:22a).
Faith *is perfected by* works (2:22b).
Works *fulfill* faith (2:23).

While we may be most comfortable with the first and least comfortable with the second, both the third and fourth are instances as much, if not more, of the second as of the first. Yes, works demonstrate faith, but they also perfect and fulfill faith and, as James goes to great pains to emphasize, the two work together to produce a working faith that saves. His emphasis is on their inseparability, not on distinguishing them or on their sequential relationship.[86]

What needs reiteration is that James *interprets* both Abraham and Rahab through his own theological grid of how faith and works work together to produce salvation.[87] Neither the *Aqedah,* the binding of Isaac, nor the story of Rahab, uses the word "justify," and that happens to be the term James uses to summarize how he understands their stories. In other words, James cannot and does not prove from those texts that the word "justify" is present to support his argument. Instead, assuming he has the relationship right, he illustrates how both Abraham and Rahab evince a faith — and Rahab's faith is not even mentioned by James — that works with works to produce justification and salvation. James finds the words "faith" and "justification" in Genesis 15:6 and ties that text to Genesis 22; the glue that holds them together is how he understands the saving faith that justifies. That Abraham and Rahab were *justified* by their works is James's *interpretation.* No one doubts that both had faith, or that both had works. James interprets that relationship between faith and works as the kind of relationship that jus-

---

85. Calvin, 314: James "is speaking of the proof he [Abraham] gave of his justification."

86. Hence, the following statement by Blomberg and Kamell separates what James does not: "Thus both Abraham and Rahab . . . were shown, in history, to be righteous by their actions, giving proof of their prior spiritual state" (p. 136).

87. See discussion in Popkes, 187-89.

tifies. That Paul could interpret Genesis 15:6, or the *Aqedah* for that matter, for other purposes would neither surprise James nor upset his argument.

5.2.2.3.2. First Proof: Abraham (2:21-24)

2:21   Since Abraham is the "father"[88] of Israel, appeal to Abraham is not only first but also perhaps the weightiest argument James might find. Most New Testament writers found a way to appeal to Abraham in either theology or polemic, and they did so within fundamentally covenantal and Judaistic categories, but by the time of Justin Martyr Abraham became a figure of intense separation and supersessionism.[89] The NRSV's "ancestor" is not enough; Abraham is more than an "ancestor." He is *the* ancestor — in other words, the "father" of Israel[90] and the father of the messianic community.[91] Not only is he the primordial ancestor, for James goes one more step to ask: Was not Abraham "justified by works when he offered his son Isaac on the altar?" (2:21).

Our understanding of justification has either gone a revolution since the

---

88. Ἀβραὰμ ὁ πατὴρ ἡμῶν. Torah-centric Judaism, however, emphasizes not Abraham but Moses. A good example of this is M. Fishbane, *Sacred Attunement* (Chicago: University of Chicago Press, 2008), 156: "Jewish theology begins at Sinai." In appealing here to Abraham instead of Moses, James may be showing another connection to the apostle Paul; cf. Gal 3:15–4:7; Rom 4.

89. See Siker, *Disinheriting the Jews,* 28-143, 163-84; also R. B. Ward, "The Works of Abraham," *HTR* 61 (1968) 283-90; I. Jacobs, "The Midrashic Background for James II. 21-23," *NTS* 22 (1976) 457-64, who sketches the Jewish evidence linking Abraham's love of God, fear of God, and obedience; R. N. Longenecker, "The 'Faith of Abraham' Theme in Paul, James and Hebrews: A Study in the Circumstantial Nature of New Testament Teaching," *Journal of the Evangelical Theological Society* 20 (1977) 203-12; M. L. Soards, "The Early Christian Interpretation of Abraham and the Place of James within that Context," *IBS* 9 (1987) 18-26; on the fecundity of Abraham, both past and present, see W. Baird, "Abraham in the New Testament: Tradition and the New Identity," *Int* 42 (1988) 367-79.

90. To say "our father" solidifies the connection of James to his Jewish ancestors as well as to, if James 2 reflects Pauline theology, the push of early Christians like Paul to trace their heritage in faith to Abraham (cf. Gal 3:7-8, 29; Rom 4:11-12, 16). So "our" is not simply Jewish but also Jewish-Christian. I suspect, furthermore, in light of 1:1 and expressions like "my brothers," that James has the messianic community in mind, exclusively, in the expression "our" father Abraham. Laws believes Abraham and Rahab are brought to the attention of the interlocutor because they were both proselytes (p. 138). She appeals to Philo, *Virtues* 211-16, 218; *1 Clement* 10:7; 12:1. No doubt Abraham was perceived by many as the primordial proselyte. The problem with this view is that neither the interlocutor nor the larger context betrays any interest in either of them being proselytes. Nor is there any suggestion that James's audience is composed of proselytes. The issue at hand is faith and works.

91. See Isa 51:2; *4 Maccabees* 16:20; Matt 3:9; John 8:33, 39; *m Avot* 5:2.

publication of E. P. Sanders's *Paul and Palestinian Judaism* in 1977 or has been under attack since that time. How one sees this shift in understanding will impact what one sees in James 2:21-24.[92] Every commentator on James is tempted to write a minor dissertation on the relationship of James 2:20-26 to Paul's theology of justification. Few resist. I shall try, because my focus here is on what James says in his context and not on battles best fought elsewhere.[93] I begin with this: To be called "righteous"[94] is to be described, in general, as one who conforms to a standard. But life is not lived simply in the general; we live in particular worlds. So, to be called "righteous" *in the Bible* means that one's behavior and life conform to the Torah, the standard of God (Gen 38:26). To be called "righteous" *in Judaism* means that one's behavior and life conform to the Torah as interpreted by one's authorities — e.g., the Teacher of Righteousness at Qumran or Hillel or Shammai. To be called "righteous" *in the messianic community of James* means that one's behavior and life conform to the Torah as interpreted by Jesus (Luke 18:14) and the leaders of that messianic community, most especially James (1:26-27; 2:8-13, etc.). To be called "righteous" *in the world of Paul* means to be conformed to the standard of God by union with Christ (Gal 3:11-12; Rom 2:13; 3:23-26; 4:5). Even if Paul uses this term in an innovative way, the sense of judgment by God and moral conformity to God's will are in one way or another always present.

92. The bibliography continues to grow as the opinions increasingly polarize. I recommend the following: Sanders, *PPJ;* B. Przybylski, *Righteousness in Matthew and His World of Thought* (SNTSMS 41; Cambridge: Cambridge University Press, 1980), 13-76; T. Laato, "Justification according to James: A Comparison with Paul," *Trinity Journal* 18 (1997) 43-84 (the irony of this piece is that it concludes that James's understanding of justification is actually Lutheran); Dunn, *Theology of Paul the Apostle,* 334-89; Wright, *What Saint Paul Really Said,* 95-133; P. Stuhlmacher, *Revisiting Paul's Doctrine of Justification* (with D. A. Hagner; Downers Grove: InterVarsity, 2001); S. Kim, *Paul and the New Perspective* (Grand Rapids: Eerdmans, 2002); F. Watson, *Paul and the Hermeneutics of Faith* (London: Clark, 2004); S. Westerholm, *Perspectives Old and New on Paul* (Grand Rapids: Eerdmans, 2004); D. A. Campbell, *The Quest for Paul's Gospel* (London: Clark, 2005); C. Van Landingham, *Judgment and Justification in Early Judaism and the Apostle Paul* (Peabody: Hendrickson, 2006); B. L. McCormack, ed., *Justification in Perspective* (Grand Rapids: Baker, 2006); M. F. Bird, *The Saving Righteousness of God* (London: Paternoster, 2007); J. Piper, *The Future of Justification* (Wheaton: Crossway, 2007); N. T. Wright, *Justification* (Downers Grove: InterVarsity, 2009).

For James, a recent exceptional discussion is W. Popkes, "Two Interpretations of 'Justification' in the New Testament: Reflections on Galatians 2:15-21 and James 2:21-25," *ST* 59 (2005) 129-46, who by tweaking Paul's theology of justification in a personal/relational direction sets a different stage for understanding James as depicting justification as friendship with God.

93. See the observations of Johnson, 246, on the disproportionate attention given to this text and, therefore, the distortion that results.

94. Greek δίκαιος, δικαιοσύνη; Hebrew צדק in various forms.

Some question here whether "Was not our ancestor Abraham *justified . . . ?*" means that he had eschatological, judicial salvation[95] or, in a more limited sense, was "declared righteous" or "approved" as one who is in the right in how he lives.[96] The difference is probably minimal since most will admit that, even if one can distinguish God declaring that a person is righteous — like the one who does deeds of mercy — from the one who is forensically declared righteous in the final courtroom (or even in an inaugurated manner at conversion) — that final court's decision is undoubtedly connected to the more earthly recognition by God. If we keep in mind the thrust of James's argument, namely that faith and works are inseparable and that faith without works is non-saving faith, then we can answer the focus of the word "justified" by returning to James's own words. "Justified" is the opposite of "useless" (as in "what *good* is it?" in 2:14), unsaving (2:14), dead (2:17), shaken in God's presence (2:19), and barren or ineffective (2:20). To be justified, then, is to have useful, saving, life, delight in God's presence, and fruitfulness — all with an eye to the final courtroom in which the work-full believer is declared in the right by God (on the basis of what one has done?).[97] To be justified is to be brought into a saving relationship with God through the new birth (1:18), in which one lives out God's will as taught by Jesus, particularly in showing mercy to those in need.[98]

What shocks the post-Reformation reader of James 2:21 is "by works."[99] James says Abraham was justified — brought into a saving relationship with God or declared righteous by God — *on the basis of* his

---

95. See Ropes, 217-18.

96. Davids, 127-28: "a declaration by God that a person is righteous" (p. 127). Davids stretches too far when he goes on to say that the "point of James's argument, then, has nothing to do with a forensic declaration of justification" (p. 127). See also Davids, "James and Paul," *DPL*, 459-60, where this point seems to be softened. Further at Konradt, *Christliche Existenz,* 234-40; Verseput, "Reworking the Puzzle."

Those who find in the aorist (ἐδικαιώθη) an indication of a one-time event are missing the point of the timeless aorist aspect: the aorist is chosen precisely because time is not relevant. What is relevant is the *thatness* of being declared right by God. It is a summary description of what God decided about Abraham.

97. The connection of final judgment to works reverberates throughout the Jewish and early Christian world. E.g., Matt 16:27; 2 Cor 5:10. A relentless book on this topic is Van Landingham, *Judgment and Justification in Early Judaism and the Apostle Paul* (see note 92 above).

98. One of the most careful thinkers of this language, Moo, sees in James the meaning of "vindicate in the judgment" (pp. 133-35); I agree so long as one does not make this entirely in the future, for surely James thought Abraham was justified during his life (he quotes Gen 15:6 at Jas 2:23), and the *Aqedah* itself is the perfection of his faith and the moment when his justification, too, was brought to completion.

99. ἐξ ἔργων, in the sense of "on the basis of."

works.[100] And James tells us exactly which work (singular) of Abraham's it was that justified him: "when he offered his son Isaac on the altar."[101] We need to understand the "binding" (Hebrew *aqedah,* from Gen 22:9) of Isaac in order to understand why James says Abraham was justified "by works." "The extraordinary prominence of the story of the binding of Isaac in Gen 22:1-19 in rabbinic Judaism," Jon Levenson observes, "stands in stark contrast to the utter absence of direct references to it anywhere else in the Hebrew Bible."[102] James fits somewhere along the line from the rather clear unimportance of the *Aqedah* to the obvious major significance of the *Aqedah* in later Judaism. To see where James fits, we need to sketch some of this evidence.

It begins with Genesis 22:1-19, known for the haunting question of Isaac, "Where is the lamb for a burnt offering?" and father Abraham's believing response, "God himself will provide the lamb for a burnt offering, my son." Attached to this scene is the angelic commentary on Abraham's faithfulness: "Because you have done this, and have not withheld your son, your only son, I will indeed bless you . . . because you have obeyed my voice" (22:16-18). The theme of the faithfulness of Abraham is found in Nehemiah 9:8 ("you found his heart faithful before you") but even more completely in Sirach 44:19-20:

100. It is not necessary here to expand this expression into deeds of mercy; James defines what he means by this in Abraham's sacrifice of Isaac.

101. ἀνενέγκας Ἰσαὰκ τὸν υἱὸν αὐτοῦ ἐπὶ τὸ θυσιαστήριον. The participle expresses time or means; the aorist summarizes the action of Abraham. The θυσιαστήριον was one Abraham constructed (Gen 22:9); see BDAG, 463.

102. Jon D. Levenson, *The Death and Resurrection of the Beloved Son* (New Haven: Yale University Press, 1993), 173. I am dependent on Levenson's two fine chapters on this theme (pp. 173-219). For other studies, see A. C. Swindell, "Abraham and Isaac: An Essay in Biblical Appropriation," *Expository Times* 87 (1975) 50-53; P. R. Davies and B. D. Chilton, "The Aqedah: A Revised Tradition History," *CBQ* 40 (1978) 514-46; R. Hayward, "The Present State of Research into the Targumic Account of the Sacrifice of Isaac," *JSS* 32 (1981) 127-50; A. F. Segal, " 'He Who Did Not Spare His Own Son . . .': Jesus, Paul and the Akedah," in *From Jesus to Paul* (ed. P. Richardson and J. C. Hurd; Waterloo: Wilfrid Laurier University, 1984), 169-84; G. Vermes, "New Light on the Aqedah from 4Q225," *JJS* 47 (1996) 140-56; A. Segal, "The Akedah: Some Reconsiderations," in *Judentum* (ed. P. Schäter; vol. 1 ot *Geschichte — Tradition — Reflexion,* ed. by H. Cancik, H. Lichtenberger, P. Schäfer; Tübingen: Mohr, 1996), 99-116; B. N. Fisk, "Offering Isaac Again and Again," *CBQ* 62 (2000) 481-507; E. Noort and E. Tigchelaar, *The Sacrifice of Isaac* (vol. 4 of *Themes in Biblical Narrative;* Leiden: Brill, 2002). For a brief sketch of the atonement discussion, see J. A. Fitzmyer, *Romans* (AB 33; New York: Doubleday, 1993), 531-32. We are not concerned here with the significance of the *Aqedah* in atonement theology, a theme that has been occasionally exaggerated, but with the *Aqedah's* significance for Jas 2:21, where its emphasis is on the justifiable faithfulness of Abraham.

> Abraham was the great father of a multitude of nations,
>> and no one has been found like him in glory.
> He kept the law of the Most High,
>> and entered into a covenant with him;
> he certified the covenant in his flesh,
>> and *when he was tested* he proved faithful.

And in Wisdom 10:5:

> Wisdom also, when the nations in wicked agreement had been put to confusion, recognized the righteous man and preserved him blameless before God, and kept him strong in the face of his compassion for his child.

And in 1 Maccabees 2:51-52:

> Remember the deeds of the ancestors, which they did in their generations; and you will receive great honor and an everlasting name. Was not Abraham found faithful *when tested,* and it was reckoned to him as righteousness?[103]

And *Jubilees* 17–18: "And it came to pass . . . that words came in heaven concerning Abraham that he was faithful in everything which was told him and he loved the LORD and was faithful in all affliction. And Prince Mastema came" and asked God to test Abraham by requiring the sacrifice of his son. God knows that Abraham is faithful because he has already "tested" him in regard to land, famine, wealth, the taking of Sarah, circumcision, and the departure of Hagar and Ishmael. "And in everything in which he tested him, he was found faithful" (17:15-18). *Jubilees* goes on to give a slightly expanded version of Genesis 22 with the notable addition that the incident takes place on "Mount Zion" (18:13).[104] And in Hebrews 11:17-19:

> By faith Abraham, when put to the *test,* offered up Isaac. He who had received the promises was ready to offer up his only son, of whom he had been told, "It is through Isaac that descendants shall be named for

---

103. The text goes on to list others who were tested: "Joseph in the time of his distress kept the commandment, and became lord of Egypt. Phinehas our ancestor, because he was deeply zealous, received the covenant of everlasting priesthood. Joshua, because he fulfilled the command, became a judge in Israel. Caleb, because he testified in the assembly, received an inheritance in the land. David, because he was merciful, inherited the throne of the kingdom forever. Elijah, because of great zeal for the law, was taken up into heaven. Hananiah, Azariah, and Mishael believed and were saved from the flame. Daniel, because of his innocence, was delivered from the mouth of the lions" (vv. 53-60).

104. A messianic community in Jerusalem might take courage from Abraham's obedience.

you." He considered the fact that God is able even to raise someone from the dead — and figuratively speaking, he did receive him back.

These texts repeat over and over the theme of God's testing of Abraham in the *Aqedah* and the emphasis is squarely on Abraham's faithfulness. This incident, then, became the summary act of obedience in Abraham's life of faith.[105] Abraham's *pistis,* his faith, was faithfulness.[106] The *Aqedah,* then, is not just an important act of faith in a series of acts of faith, but the primordial or preeminent or capstone act of faith: that is, it is *this* act of faith and obedience that the angel says led to the blessing of Abraham. All of this now leads to this point: when James says Abraham was justified by works when he acted as he did in the *Aqedah,* James is drawing on a deep Jewish tradition that this act of obedient faithfulness by Abraham was *the singular event* in Abraham's life that led to God's blessing him (a variant on "justified") and to the formation and blessing of the people of Israel.[107]

But why then does James use the plural "works"? Perhaps because the one act of the *Aqedah* sums up all the other works in the testing of Abraham's faith — and Jewish tradition (*Jubilees* 19) finds ten such tests of Abraham.[108] In particular, and this is why I think James also brings up Rahab (see below),[109] we need to recall that just prior to the *Aqedah* was an incident in which *Abraham showed hospitality to strangers* (Genesis 18) and it was this incident that led to the birth of Isaac.[110] It is not fanciful to think of Genesis 22, then, as another instance of God *providing* (22:8) for the one who was merciful to others by providing life's necessities. Once we connect Abraham's "works" back to the hospitality theme in Genesis, we realize that James has touched on a moment of brilliance: Abraham, the one who was hospitable to those who had needs, was tested by God the (hospitable) Provider. The Jewish

105. See how details are sometimes filled in both in Philo, *Abraham,* especially 191-99, and Josephus, *Ant* 1.220-36. See also the variant in the account of Jephthah's daughter in Ps.-Philo 40.2, 5. The connection of the *Aqedah* and atonement is spelled out much later: see *Mekhilta de R. Ishmael,* pisha 7; *Exodus Rabbah* 15:11; *Targum Neofiti* on Lev 22:27. Levenson traces as well the transformation of what looks like a passive Isaac into a noble man of courage (J. D. Levenson, *The Death and Resurrection of the Beloved Son: The Transformation of Child Sacrifice in Judaism and Christianity* [New Haven: Yale University Press, 1993],187-99).

106. Adapted from Dunn, *Theology of Paul the Apostle,* 375.

107. See also P. Davids, "Tradition and Citation in the Epistle of James," in *Scripture, Tradition, and Interpretation* (ed. W. S. LaSor; Grand Rapids: Eerdmans, 1978), 113-26.

108. On this, see Wall, 145-48; Siker, *Disinheriting the Jews,* 99.

109. See Johnson, 249.

110. It is worth observing that the promise of Gen 22:18 is connected to the same promise in Gen 18:18.

tradition famously saw Abraham as an example of hospitality.[111] Abraham survived the test by remaining faithful and God provided for him. God the Provider justified Abraham on the basis of that kind of faithfulness (works). And what lies latent in all of this is that James has urged since 1:19-27, but especially in ch. 2, that the messianic community — like Abraham — should be acting with compassion and mercy toward those in need.

Justification by works, then, is not by "works of the law" so much as it is by "works of mercy" as the way to interpret genuine Torah observance. As James calls the messianic community to such (1:19-27; 2:1-4, 14-17), so he appeals to Abraham as one whose entire life came to expression in acts of hospitality that led to his own act of sacrificing his son to God the Provider. For James, Abraham's faith, his lifelong faithfulness, is found in that word "works." What James will not tolerate is a kind of "faith" that is not like Abraham's faithfulness.

2:22 James wrote before the intense debates about works and faith developed in the Reformation. But in some ways James 2:22 anticipates the important distinction the Reformers drew between faith and works. Even if James wants to affirm strongly that saving faith couples faith and works, his words show that faith and works are distinguishable. Since James can assume agreement with his point that Abraham was not justified until he laid Isaac on the altar, he can assume that his readers will draw the conclusion he has drawn. That is the point of "You see that."[112] And what should they see? Abraham's faith[113] "co-worked with his works"[114] in the sense that they inter-

---

111. See Philo, *Abraham* 167; *Avot de R. Natan* 7; *Testament of Abraham* 1:3; 4:1-11. Also see R. B. Ward, "The Works of Abraham: James 2:14-26," *HTR* 61 (1968) 283-90.

112. βλέπεις ὅτι. On βλέπω with the meaning of perceiving mentally, see BDAG, 179 (7b). BDAG point also to Rom 7:23; 2 Cor 7:8; Heb 3:19. The tenses are interesting in Jas 2:22-24: βλέπεις (present), συνήργει (imperfect), ἐτελειώθη (aorist), ἐπληρώθη (aorist), ἐκλήθη (aorist), ὁρᾶτε (present), δικαιοῦται (present). If anything shows that time is not the central point of tense usage but that instead aspect is, these three verses do. James's logical inferences ("you see" and "you see") can be made with two present tenses (2:22, 24). He can draw out the action with an imperfect (the "imperfective" aspect wherein the action is not conceived as complete but as in progress) because he wants to show two things working together; the imperfect συνήργει is used here because the action is conceived as background to the point of the aorist ἐτελειώθη, while a timeless present does the same in v. 24 (δικαιοῦται). The aorists, which emphasize not past time but action conceived in its totality, are where James focuses: ἐτελειώθη, ἐπληρώθη, ἐκλήθη. I am grateful to my colleague Joel Willitts for a conversation we had about the tense variations in these verses.

113. The articular πίστις is probably possessive: "his faith."

114. My attempt to bring out the play on words in the verb and noun. That James again uses the plural for "works" points back to the works of Abraham that came to perfection in the *Aqedah*.

mingled with one another (Rom 8:28; 1 Cor 16:16; 2 Cor 6:1). It is not so simple that we could say first he had faith and then he had works, and once he had both he had what it takes to get salvation. The faith of Abraham, the faith itself, worked itself out in works and it is the faith itself that is completed by works. It was a working faith, not a faith plus works.[115] As a side point, Peter Davids is probably right: James fastens onto Abraham's faith because, like that of his interlocutor and those he represents, Abraham's faith was monotheistic (*Jubilees* 11–12; Philo, *Legum Allegoriae* 3.228; *de Virtute* 216; Josephus, *Ant.* 1:154-57): "You believe that God is one" (2:19). But, unlike the interlocutor and those who think works are unimportant, Abraham's faith was a working faith.

It was *on the basis of his works* that Abraham's faith was "brought to completion." Again, as in v. 21, why does James use the plural "works"? Possibly he is responding to the sorts of things said by Paul or by those around Paul, and Paul often used "works" to express commitment to the Torah (Gal 2:15-21). But more likely he is simply reusing the term he used in 2:20. Or we should back up some and wonder if we can explain this simpler: perhaps the instinctual term is plural. Still, James belongs to the Jewish tradition that sees the *Aqedah* as the summation of all of Abraham's works, including his hospitality to strangers. We should observe again how ingenious this example becomes in James's context: the combination of the father of Israel, overt confession of monotheism, and works of mercy to those in need is exactly what James needs. It is worth observing that great rhetoric and preaching trades in this sort of insightful example.

Everything in James's logic hinges on "brought to completion."[116] To begin with, a more accurate term would be "brought to *perfection.*" Faith finds its intended shape when it is working; the idea is something being brought to its full realization, its divinely-intended design and form. We see this idea at work in 1:4 and 1:15. This sense is also found in Philo's description of Jacob as "him who was made perfect through practice."[117] James's point is not unlike what Paul says in Gal 5:6: "For in Christ Jesus neither circumcision nor uncircumcision counts for anything; the only thing that counts is faith working through love." And it is like that of John in 1 John 4:12: "If we love one another, God lives in us, and his love is perfected in us." As the sacrificial system finds its intent in the cross and as the Torah finds its intent

115. Moo, 136.
116. ἐτελειώθη. See BDAG, 997-98. The passive here is impersonal; faith itself is acted upon by works to reach its intended goal. See also Phil 3:10; Heb 2:10. For further study, see D. Peterson, *Hebrews and Perfection* (SNTSMS 47; Cambridge: Cambridge University Press, 1982).
117. *Confusion* 181; see also *Husbandry* 42.

in the teachings of Jesus (Matt 5:17-20) and life in the Spirit (Gal 5:18), so faith finds its intent when it becomes active in deeds of mercy (Jas 2:14-17).

2:23   What perhaps surprises Protestants the most is that James does not think the job was complete when Abraham trusted God in Genesis 15:6; it was the *Aqedah* that brought the trust of Abraham to its intended goal. Genesis 15 finds its perfection in the narrative of Genesis 18–22. Simple trust and believing the right things is not saving faith in the mind of James.

Paul used Genesis 15:6 as potent evidence that justification occurs solely by faith, by trusting in the word of God, apart from works. Because Abraham was justified (Gen 15:6) prior to circumcision, Paul says, the promises to his seed were received by faith alone (Gal 3:6, 16; Rom 4:9-11, 18, 22). Therefore, since justification occurred prior to circumcision and prior to any works, works do not figure into the act of God in making a person righteous (Gal 3:10-11; Rom 3:20, 28; 9:31-32). Furthermore, because the proper response is trust in the word of God, Paul knows that justification can occur for Gentiles without them having to enter into Judaism through circumcision (Gal 3:7-9; Rom 4:11-12). Having had his say in this way, however, Paul still knew the importance of works (Gal 5:22; Rom 12:1-2; 1 Cor 3:13; 2 Cor 5:10).

James comes at this topic from a different angle.[118] Paul faces some who think of Jewish status as sufficient or even as an exclusive privilege, but James faces those who think confessional/creedal faith is sufficient. These different issues lead to different uses of both the faith versus works language and the example of Abraham, even if both can appeal in their own way to Genesis 15:6. For James, Abraham is not the model of faith-*before*-works but of faith-*with*-works. Paul wants to show justification prior to circumcision, and James wants to show that Abraham's justification was not perfected until the *Aqedah*. It was there, and here James banks on the potency of the Jewish traditions about Abraham's testing, that Abraham's faith reached the divine intent. It seems to me that James knew of Paul's teaching.[119] This is not a matter of who got Abraham right; this is a matter of hermeneutics in a Jewish world.

Hence, James says, it was at the *Aqedah* that Genesis 15:6 was "fulfilled."[120] The verb means to fill up (Matt 13:48; John 12:3) but it could also

---

118. This is one of the most important issues in understanding biblical theology: it is always *occasional* or *contingent*. I appeal here to M. Fishbane's *Sacred Attunement* (Chicago: University of Chicago Press, 2008), who draws this out on several occasions (e.g., pp. 160-62); here he extracts a hermeneutical spirituality from the theoretical foundation laid in *Biblical Interpretation*.

119. See the discussions in Davids, 130-31; Laws, 131-32; J. T. Sanders, *Ethics in the New Testament* (London: SCM, 1986), 115-28.

120. ἐπληρώθη. BDAG, 828, defines this usage as "to bring to a designed end, fulfill" and "of the fulfillment of divine predictions or promises." Martin, 93, disagrees and defines it as confirming James's point.

mean to "fulfill prophetically" or "confirm" in the sense that this text confirms the point James is making. It seems that another view is more likely: since James is showing that Abraham's Genesis 15:6 faith was "perfected" (Jas 2:22) in the *Aqedah,* it stands to reason that "fulfilled" means nearly the same. That is, the *Aqedah* consummated or brought to full realization ("fulfilled") the faith of Genesis 15:6. This view approximates "fulfill prophetically" (see Matt 2:17; 5:17).[121] Thus, the *Aqedah* brings to full completion the faith Abraham exercised in Genesis 15 when he complained that the promise of a child was unfulfilled. YHWH showed him the stars in the sky and declared that Abram's progeny would be as numerous, and Abram simply trusted that YHWH would indeed do what was said. The faith that trusted YHWH's word came to completion when Abraham lifted Isaac to the altar.

When Abram so trusted God, YHWH "reckoned" his faith as righteousness.[122] It could be that Abraham's faith was considered a kind of work and that it was that kind of work that was reckoned in the divine tribunal as righteousness (a life of Torah observance). But this is not how James is using these terms: for James, faith is distinguishable from works. Faith is not a work. Rather saving faith works or moves into acts of mercy. So, it is more likely that Abraham's trusting of YHWH's word was an act that YHWH considered good and so therefore assigned Abraham to the class of those who were "righteous," that is, those who did God's will.[123] What James is emphasizing, though, is that this act of trust by Abram did not come to its perfection or completion until the *Aqedah.*[124]

Not only is Scripture fulfilled, but Abraham was "called the friend of God."[125] James sums up God's view of Abraham with the summary word

---

121. Ropes, 221, though I am not sure that James sees Gen 15:6 as a prophecy. See also Mayor, 104; Moo, 138.

122. The image is one of a ledger and a mental act of assigning a *quid pro quo,* a "this for that."

123. It is possible that James shares the Reformers' emphasis on an alien righteousness, namely Christ's, being imputed to Abraham. But it is impossible to demonstrate from the book of James that this is how he understands "reckoned to him as righteousness." Somehow God considers Abraham righteous on the basis of his faith.

124. It is difficult to know what to make of 1 Macc 2:52: "Was not Abraham found faithful when tested, and it was reckoned to him as righteousness?" Does this text, as some think, show that Gen 15:6a (Abraham's believing YHWH) and 15:6b (reckoned as righteousness) are separable? It appears that the author applies Gen 15:6 to the *Aqedah* testing of Gen 22, as does James, more than that he separates faith from deeds, which the latter considered righteousness (see Dibelius, 164-65).

125. καὶ φίλος θεοῦ ἐκλήθη. By whom? By Scripture (2 Chron 20:7; Isa 41:8) and tradition (e.g., Philo, *Abraham* 273). The aorist passive is not a divine passive so much as impersonal: Scripture (or tradition) calls Abraham the friend of God. The aorist is not used to speak to the moment at which he became God's friend but to sum up the action

"called."[126] "Friend" *(philos)* brings together three words James has already used that express divine approval: "justified" (2:21), "brought to completion" (2:22), and "fulfilled" (2:23a). When James calls Abraham the "friend of God" he could be quoting verses like 2 Chronicles 20:7; Isaiah 41:8; or Wisdom 7:27, or, more likely, he simply sums up the Jewish view of Abraham.[127] To be God's friend is to be in the people of God (cf. Luke 12:4; John 3:29; 11:11; 15:13-15; 3 John 15), to be in the right, to be saved, and to be a person who in fellowship with God lives out the life God designs for those on earth. Inasmuch as friendship with God (cf. Jas 4:4) involves love, one can find echoes of the Jesus Creed as the friend of God acts in friendship toward others (2:8-13).

2:24 James now sums up his point one more time and repeats what he said in 2:20. Here we are justified in hearing James responding either to Paul or to someone around Paul. From the perfection and fulfillment of Abraham's Genesis 15:6 faith in the *Aqedah,* James concludes[128] that "a person is justified by works and not by faith alone." James now universalizes with "a person,"[129] which is used in the same way in Galatians 2:16, along with the equivalent "flesh."[130]

James's conclusion has a positive and a negative element:

A person is justified:
        positive: by works
        negative: not by faith alone

Justification is forensic: it is to be declared in the right by God in the courtroom of God. Those who are in the right are so by virtue of works (like Abra-

---

globally. The anarthrous φίλος Θεοῦ could be translated "the friend of God," but the quality of the relationship is evoked by "and he was called 'friend of God.'"

126. ἐκλήθη. The aorist captures summary action.

127. James is not quoting (explicitly) the words of 2 Chron 20:7; Isa 41:8; or Wis 7:27. Thus, we can also include Philo, *Abraham* 273; *Moses* 1.28; *Allegorical Interpretation* 3.27; *Sobriety* 56; *Jubilees* 19:9; CD 3:2; 30:20; 2 Esdr 3:14. Abraham as friend of God continued into the early churches: see *1 Clement* 10:1; 17:2; Tertullian, *Adversus Judaeos* 2:7; Irenaeus, *Adversus Haereses* 4.14.4; 16.2. See Martin, 94; Johnson, 243-44. Classical sources on friendship, most notably Aristotle's *Nicomachean Ethics* 8, Cicero's *De Amicitia,* or Plutarch's *How to Tell a Flatterer from a Friend,* while they fill out what might be involved in *koinonia* or *ecclesia,* are of only tangential use to what James means by "friend of God."

128. James uses ὁρᾶτε ὅτι, "you see that." In this James uses the plural, moving beyond the singulars in 2:20-23.

129. The use of the word ἄνθρωπος and the present tense δικαιοῦται effect a universalizing point, with the present drawing the action before our eyes.

130. See also Matt 4:4; Acts 4:12; Rom 3:28.

ham in Genesis 18–22). And, like Abraham, no one can be justified by "faith alone." "Faith alone" is confession of monotheism (2:19) and thinking one is in the right before God even if one does not respond to those in need (2:1-17). It is confessional, creedal, and workless faith. This point should not surprise the reader of the New Testament: Matthew 7:15-21; Galatians 5:6; 6:4; 1 Corinthians 13:2; 2 Corinthians 9:8, Hebrews 11; 1 John 2:3-6. Saving faith, then, is a trusting faith that flows into deeds of mercy; non-saving faith is creedal faith without deeds of mercy. In this setting, James may distinguish faith from works, but he leaves no room for a saving faith that does not involve works. Faith finds its perfection and fulfillment in acts of mercy.

5.2.2.3.3. Second Proof: Rahab (2:25)

It is not clear that James returns to direct confrontation with the interlocutor. Still, we can infer that moving from his first example, Abraham, to a second, Rahab, indicates the interlocutor is at least in the corner of his eye. His intent is to demonstrate the inseparability of faith and works and to deconstruct the arguments of those who think one can have faith and not have works (deeds of mercy). The perfection of Abraham's faith in the *Aqedah* now gives way to the active faith of Rahab. This shorter example then is followed by a summary conclusion (2:26).

"Likewise"[131] ties what James has to say about Rahab to what he has said about Abraham as a second proof that faith and works are inseparable. The Canaanite prostitute Rahab, whose story of hospitality is told in Joshua 2 and whose reward is described in Joshua 6:16-25, creates problems for modern interpreters and historians while she resolves a faith-works relationship for James.[132] The writer of Hebrews also saw Rahab as an example of faith

---

131. ὁμοίως δὲ καί. This could be translated "Likewise also" or "Likewise even," but καί is probably pleonastic. I cannot think James would see Rahab as at the bottom end of a scale ("*even* Rahab got this one right") from Abraham. The manuscript tradition shows enough variation to think that others struggled with the inclusion of both δὲ and καί, and in that order. Many manuscripts omit δὲ, while a few instead omit καί. At least two sources (C and Peshitta) change it all to οὕτως.

132. Among the problems include why the two spies took up space at a prostitute's home (Josh 2:1, 4), her prostitution being mentioned without repentance, her lying (2:5-6), how she knew of the God of Israel (2:9-11), and the complicity of the spies in deceit (2:14). On the other hand, there are some dramatic resemblances of Rahab to the midwives of Egypt, not the least of which are the word "hid" (Josh 2:4; cf. Exod 2:2) and the marking of a home with red to protect the home and its inhabitants from destruction. On Rahab, see the brief sketch by Tikva Frymer-Kensky, Amy-Jill Levine, and Mary Rose D'Angelo, *WiS*, 140-42; Philippa Carter, *IVPWBC*, 116-20. Carter lists these as other examples of deception: Gen 27:1-40; 38:1-26; Judg 4:1-24; 5:24-31. See also D. J. Wiseman, "Rahab of Jericho," *TynBul* 14 (1964) 8-11, on the linguistic elements of defining *zonah* ("harlot" or one

and hospitality (11:31), while Matthew seems to depict her as a sinful Gentile woman who played a role in the Messiah's genealogy (1:5). Josephus makes her an innkeeper instead of a prostitute, and therefore the spies are only there for dinner (*Ant.* 5.7-15). In *1 Clement* 12 we discover a prophetic type of atonement in the red cord, and in later Judaism Rahab was classified as a proselyte, but none of this is James's point.[133] For James, Rahab was (1) a prostitute,[134] (2) justified by works, who (3) welcomed the spies[135] and sent them off surreptitiously.

What does James mean here by "justified"?[136] It means to be judged in the right by God or to made righteous or to be vindicated before God. And, as with Abraham, James boldly claims — in the face of his interlocutor — that God judges Rahab to be in the right *on the basis of works.* Once again, James uses the plural "works." He could be referring to the double act of reception and sending away in safety, but it is more likely that he is using typical language, whether he has one thing in mind (hospitality) or more. It is not without significance that James sees Rahab's works in her hospitality,[137] that is, in her treatment of Israelites in need, and sets her behavior before the messianic community as a standard (cf. 2:1-4).

5.2.2.3.4. Conclusion (2:26)

There is nothing new in James's conclusion because he has made his point implicitly and explicitly since he opened this section at 2:1.[138] Furthermore,

---

who traded with foreigners in a variety of ways; cf. Josephus, *Ant* 5.74); A. T. Hanson, "Rahab the Harlot in Early Christian Tradition," *JSNT* 1 (1978) 33-41.

133. Str-B, 1.20-23.

134. ἡ πόρνη. See also Matt 21:31-32; Luke 15:30; 1 Cor 6:15-16; Heb 11:31. On prostitution, see T. Ilan, *Jewish Women in Greco-Roman Palestine* (Peabody: Hendrickson, 1996), 214-21; C. S. Keener, "Adultery, Divorce," *DNTB,* 11-12.

135. Heb 11:31 uses τοὺς κατασκόπους ("the spies"), but James calls them τοὺς ἀγγέλους. They were not supernatural beings so the term means "messengers."

136. ἐδικαιώθη. The aorist is chosen, not because the act of God declaring her just is over and done, but because James chooses to depict the act in summary form. The passive is divine ("God declared her just").

137. James uses the word ὑποδέχομαι (BDAG, 1037). An exceptional study of hospitality can be found in A. Arterbury, *Entertaining Angels: Early Christian Hospitality in Its Mediterranean Setting* (Sheffield: Phoenix, 2005); see also C. D. Pohl, *Making Room: Recovering Hospitality as a Christian Tradition* (Grand Rapids: Eerdmans, 1999); A. G. Oden, ed., *And You Welcomed Me: A Sourcebook on Hospitality in Early Christianity* (Nashville: Abingdon, 2001). At a more popular level and focusing on house churches, see R. and J. Banks, *The Church Comes Home* (Peabody: Hendrickson, 2006).

138. Davids suggests that some might wonder if James has indulged in "rhetorical overkill" (p. 133).

the same point was made in 1:19-27, especially vv. 22-27. Implicitly, James has argued that, since faith and works are inseparable, (1) the messianic community's prejudice against the poor and favoritism toward the rich are contrary to faith (2:1-4), (2) experience itself should inform the community's members that God is with the poor, while the rich are oppressing the community (2:5-7), and (3) the royal law to love one's neighbor as oneself demands care for the poor, while the community's disrespect for the poor proves that its members are transgressors (2:8-13). Following this implicit argument, which is hardly subtle, James turned more aggressive at 2:14. Faith without works is useless (2:14a) and it cannot finally save (2:14b). With the help of an exaggerated example, James asserts that such a workless faith is dead (2:15-17). The interlocutor now interrupts with a question that assumes that faith and works are totally different responses to God and that the former without the latter saves (2:18a). James responds with three points: faith can only be shown to be saving by works (2:18b), creedal faith is not enough because even the demons have that (2:19), and the examples of the unquestioned faith of Abraham (2:21-24) and Rahab (2:25) prove that they had the kind of faith that worked. Explicit statements that faith and works are inseparable and that only a working faith saves can be found, then, in 2:14, 17, 20, and now 26.

James concludes this last time with an analogy:[139] "For just as the body without the spirit is dead, so faith without works is also dead." The anthropology at work in this analogy assumes that the spirit animates and gives life to the body (Gen 2:7; 6:17; Ps 31:5 [LXX 30:6]; Ezek 37:8-10; Luke 8:55; 23:46; 1 Cor 7:34).[140] It would stretch the evidence to suggest that we must strictly compare faith (alone?) to the body and works (as the perfection of faith?) to the spirit, with in this instance works being what gives life to faith or what brings faith to its completion, since James is com-

---

139. He uses ὥσπερ γὰρ. This is the only time James uses this term; see also Matt 12:40; 13:40; 24:27; John 5:21, 26; Rom 5:12, 19, 21; 6:4, 19; 1 Cor 11:12; 15:22; 2 Cor 8:7; Gal 4:29.

140. Anthropology is a major preoccupation with theologians and philosophers today. See F. LeRon Shults, *Reforming Theological Anthropology* (Grand Rapids: Eerdmans, 2003); Ellen Charry, "Human Being, Doctrine of," in *DTIB*, 310-13; K. Corcoran, *Rethinking Human Nature* (Grand Rapids: Baker, 2006); A. C. Thiselton, *The Hermeneutics of Doctrine* (Grand Rapids: Eerdmans, 2007), 177-308. A sweep of history can be found in L. Stevenson and D. L. Haberman, *Ten Theories of Human Nature* (4th ed.; New York: Oxford University Press, 2004). The biblical material has been discussed by P. E. Hughes, *The True Image* (Grand Rapids: Eerdmans, 1989); H. W. Wolff, *Old Testament Anthropology* (London: SCM, 1974), especially 11-79; U. Schnelle, *The Human Condition* (trans. O. C. Dean, Jr.; Minneapolis: Fortress, 1996); J. B. Green, *Body, Soul, and Human Life* (Grand Rapids: Baker, 2008). For the anthropology of rabbinic texts, see Neusner, *EJ* 3.1419-28.

paring one whole situation with another and not dissecting. From beginning to end this chapter has had one central theme: the inseparability of faith and works if the faith is to be saving and the works justifying. One can clearly discern a difference: faith is confessional and works behavioral, but for James a saving faith is one in which the confession is manifest in works of mercy toward those in need. Faith alone, by which he means a minimal creedal faith, cannot save. It is useless, ineffective, and dead. Christian theologians might synthesize James and Paul with this line: "as faith without works is dead, so are works without faith dead."[141] True enough, but neither James nor Paul was in situations where the niceties of such theological syntheses were needed.

BRIEF EXCURSUS: JAMES AND PAUL[142]

We perhaps need to remind ourselves that neither James nor Paul defined their terms; they used words that came from various settings with meanings

---

141. I take this from Johnson, 245, who is quoting John Chrysostom.

142. The bibliography here is endless. I have chosen a few representative discussions: Margaret Mitchell's taxonomy and article is a good place to begin; see "The Letter of James as a Document of Paulinism?" in Webb and Kloppenborg, *Reading James,* 75-98. See also J. Jeremias, "Paul and James," *Expository Times* 66 (1954-55) 368-71, whose view represents pre–New Perspective categories; R. Y. K. Fung, "'Justification' in the Epistle of James," in *Right with God* (ed. D. A. Carson; Grand Rapids: Baker, 1992), 146-62, who emphasizes that James teaches a "probative justification of works"; M. Hengel, "Der Jakobusbrief als antipaulinische Polemik," in *Tradition and Interpretation in the New Testament* (ed. G. F. Hawthorne and O. Betz; Grand Rapids: Eerdmans, 1987), 248-78; for a more radical view, cf. K. Syreeni, "James and the Pauline Legacy: Power Play in Corinth?" in *Fair Play: Diversity and Conflicts in Early Christianity: Essays in Honour of Heikki Räisänen* (ed. I. Dunderberg, C. Tuckett, and K. Syreeni; NovTSup 103; Leiden: Brill, 2002), 397-437. See also Martin, xxxiii-xli, lxxvi-lxxvii, 82-84; Konradt, *Christliche Existenz,* 241-46; Popkes, 182-90, 211-14; Penner, *The Epistle of James and Eschatology,* 47-74; P. Davids, "James and Paul," *DPL,* 457-61; Strecker, *Theology of the New Testament,* 669-76; Bauckham, *Wisdom of James,* 113-40; Verseput, "Reworking the Puzzle"; R. Wall, "Law and Gospel, Church and Canon," *Wesleyan Theological Journal* 22 (1987) 38-70, especially 53-55; Frankemölle, 2.461-74; Hartin, 163-72; Chilton and Evans, *Missions,* 235-486 (various authors, various topics); W. Popkes, "The Mission of James," in Chilton and Neusner, *The Brother of Jesus,* 90-92; K. Berger, *Theologiegeschichte des Urchristentums. Theologie des Neuen Testaments* (Tübingen: Francke, 1994), 188-90; Cheung, *Genre, Composition,* 194-96; T. Schreiner, *New Testament Theology: Magnifying God in Christ* (Grand Rapids: Baker, 2008), 597-605; Witherington, 466-70.

A recent proposal by K. Jason Coker, "Nativism in James 2.14-26: A Post-colonial Reading," in Webb and Kloppenborg, *Reading James,* 27-48, revives the ghost of the Tübingen school in the garb of post-colonial criticism and makes the argument that James is nativist and argues against the hybridity of Paul, who is a "threat from imperial

that were assumed, and sometimes they tweaked the assumptions. We are in constant need of reminding ourselves that we do our best with our mental lexicons to approximate the lexicons of the earliest Christians, but our definitions are not the same as theirs.

There is nothing distinctly Pauline about calling that first generation of beliefs "faith in Jesus Christ" (cf. Jas 2:1), nor is there anything distinctly Pauline about speaking of "works." Once we accept that "faith" and "works" are not exclusively Pauline words, that all Christians expressed themselves with these terms, and that the terms grew rather naturally out of Jewish soil, we can no longer leap to the conclusion that, since both James and Paul are talking about faith and works, they must be talking at one another, with one another, or past one another.

Furthermore, at issue in this passage is not "faith" *or* "works" but "faith without works" over against "faith with works." James fashions a theology in which the Torah remains in force and therefore works remain in force, but he does so in a way that sets faith and works into a tension. And as Don Verseput has recently reminded us, we cannot explain James by simply appealing to a causal relationship of faith and works.[143] For James they are distinguishable realities, connected to be sure, but not simply as cause (faith) and effect (works).

The need to exhort Jews or messianic Jews to a working faith was not a Pauline problem. John the Baptist does it in Matthew 3:7-10, and Jesus did it frequently (7:21-27; 25:31-46). John does the same much later in 1 John. In fact, the entire theme is Jewish to the core.

It is likely that Paul and James knew one another (Gal 1:19; 2:9; Acts 15; 21:17-26). Galatians suggests that their first encounter came very early in Paul's career (Gal 1:18-19, ca. 37 AD). Paul later encountered some "men from James" who were concerned about his teaching (Gal 2:12), and Paul also visited Jerusalem in approximately 48 AD. The opportunities for encounter were many and varied, and we can surmise that the two men had serious discussions, probable compromises, and firm convictions. This point is often ignored in the discussion of the relationship of James 2:14-26 and Paul's distinctive theology and makes it much more difficult to argue

---

assimilation" (p. 44). As well, Margaret Mitchell contends that it is James who is the hybrid response to Paul though he should not be seen as "early catholicism" but instead as a dimension of Paulinism. See her essay "The Letter of James as a Document of Paulinism?" in Webb and Kloppenborg, *Reading James,* 79, though "hybrid" is not her term.

143. See "Reworking the Puzzle." Also M. Proctor, "Faith, Works and the Christian Religion in James 2:14-26," *Evangelical Quarterly* 69 (1997) 307-22. For an alternative, see W. Nicol, "Faith and Works in the Letter of James," *Neotestamentica* 9 (1975) 7-24.

for the independent interpretation of Abraham faith traditions by both James and Paul.[144]

The concentration on "faith" and "works" and on their relationship is a peculiarly Pauline problem, and James has the same problem. No one else in the New Testament enters into this verbal and theological struggle as do James and Paul. Both also appeal to Abraham and Genesis 15:6, even if they use texts and terms differently (a fact not always given its deserved space). This commonality is there even if we embrace an early date for James (prior to Paul's second visit to Jerusalem): the Pauline problem (e.g., something like Galatians 2 or Acts 15) surely raised its head in Jerusalem before Paul wrote his letters. Therefore, what we see in James would be another manifestation of the reception of and response to Paul's message, whether in its earliest oral forms or its later more mature written forms. James could well represent one reaction among others to Paul's teachings or to an exaggeration of his teachings, not unlike the themes and circumstances we see in Galatians 2:4-5, 7, 10 and Acts 15:1-5. If we assume an early date, we must also assume an oral form of Paul's teaching, and we cannot be certain what that looked like. We can assume that it would have been easier at that date to misrepresent and use strong rhetoric. It is more than probable that Paul's teaching was often misunderstood and misrepresented (e.g., Rom 6:1-12).

It is therefore unwise, in our estimation, to see James 2:14-26 as responding to the more mature and fuller and written presentations of these issues in Galatians or Romans. It might be more accurate to see a four-step development at work in the relationship of James and Paul:[145]

1. Paul's conversion and early articulations of theology (33-48 AD),
2. James's response to what he was hearing (ca. 45+ AD; cf. Gal. 2:12!),
3. a public discussion at which James endorses Paul (Gal 2:9),
4. Paul's later more mature articulation, taking into consideration his discussions with James.[146]

---

144. See also Avemarie, "Werke," 289-94 (see note 10 above), who interacts with the work of Konradt.

145. Another proposal that intertwines James and Paul is P. Rolland, "La date."

146. See H. P. Hamann, "Faith and Works: Paul and James," *Lutheran Theological Journal* 9 (1975) 33-41. See also Popkes, "Two Interpretations," 137-38 (see note 92 above), who sees more in common than many today because he has reshaped Paul's theory of justification in more relational terms. K. Haacker finds James more in dialogue with the Gospels' sense of salvation and in dispute with Peter, but stands alone in this view: see "Justification, Salut et Foi. Étude sur les rapports entre Paul, Jacques et Pierre," *ÉTR* 73 (1998) 177-88.

Once one admits this connection, that James 2:14-26 articulates a fundamentally important theme in James — namely faith and works, and that this theme appears in various locations in the letter, we are driven to conclude that the "response" to Paul that emerges with forcefulness in 2:14-26 actually appears throughout and shapes the entire letter.[147]

The following two-line comparison serves to illustrate an important point: James and Paul are using language so close to each other and in such different ways that one must posit some kind of connection:[148]

James 2:24
A person is justified by *works*   and not by *faith* alone.

Romans 3:28
a person is justified by *faith*   and not by *works* of the law.

Regardless of how one works to harmonize or compare these two early Christian leaders, the fact remains that James does not cede to the word "faith" the same importance as is found in Paul. Or, from the other angle, Paul does not cede to "works" the same importance as is found in James. These two authors come at things from two different settings with different theological

---

147. The emphasis of those who agree with this conclusion is on James as anti-Pauline polemic; see Hengel, "Der Jakobusbrief as antipaulinische Polemik"; Popkes, 36-39; V. Limberis, "The Provenance of the Caliphate Church: James 2.17-26 and Galatians 3 Reconsidered," in *Early Christian Interpretation of the Scriptures of Israel: Investigations and Proposals* (ed. C. A. Evans and J. A. Sanders; JSNTSup 148; Sheffield: Sheffield Academic, 1997), 397-420; M. Tsuji, *Glaube zwischen Vollkommengeit und Verweltlichung. Eine Untersuchung zur literarischen Gestalt und zur inhaltlichen Kohärenz des Jakobusbriefes* (WUNT 2.93; Tübingen: Mohr, 1997). But see the nuanced view of comparing James and Paul to the options around them in G. Boccaccini, *Middle Judaism: Jewish Thought, 300 B.C.E. to 200 C.E.* (Minneapolis: Fortress, 1991), 213-28; also Adamson, *James: The Man and His Message,* 195-227; Johnson, 58-63.

148. Moo, 140; see his excellent discussion (pp. 140-42), though I think he presses a distinction between James and Paul on the meaning of "justify" a little too neatly. Here is Moo's final summary: "If a sinner can get into relationship with God only by faith (Paul), the ultimate validation of that relationship takes into account the works that true faith must inevitably produce (James)" (p. 141). A similar view can be found in Guthrie, 241-42. For James, faith is not simply something that produces works in a kind of one-step, two-step format, but faith and works co-work in a way that leads to salvation. M. Mitchell contends that James knows of a collection of Paul's letters, dating James much later than do I, but her point reveals the awareness of Paul on the part of James ("Document of Paulinism?" 88-95 [see note 142 above]). Bauckham's point that James and Paul are independently interpreting Genesis 15 and Abraham (see *Wisdom of James,* 127-31), is possible but not as likely. A similar view is found in Penner, *The Epistle of James and Eschatology,* 47-74.

orientations and intents, making their teachings more complementary than identical or contradictory.[149] In the words of Sharyn Dowd, "James is using Paul's vocabulary, but not his dictionary."[150] And one should not ignore Romans 2:6-16 in this discussion, a text that connects Paul more closely to James and that many have done their best to reinterpret or ignore.[151] More reflection needs to take place over the significance of a proto-Augustinian or overtly Augustinian anthropology for framing and defining the debates that occur among Christians and theologians when it comes to comparing James and Paul. I suspect that James did not operate with that sort of anthropology.

Something that deserves more elaboration than can be given here but must be mentioned is that James shows more connection in these issues to the rest of the New Testament, say Jesus (or Matthew), Hebrews, and 1 John in their own ways than does Paul. Paul is the outlier here.[152] If post-Reformation Christians struggle with James, the earliest Christians would have had the same struggle at times with Paul.

My conclusion is that James is responding either to Paul in the flesh or, which is slightly more likely, to the early Paul or to early followers of Paul who had embraced his message and driven it to some distortions,[153] or, which is safer but less likely, to a common Jewish Christian environment where the emphasis on faith provoked conversations and poor theology concerning how faith and works are related. It is not impossible, but less likely, that both James and Paul independently developed the Jewish traditions about Abraham and faith.

•   •

149. This is the older view of the relationship and is sustained after generations of examination; see Jeremias, "Paul and James," 370-71 (see note 142 above); Longenecker, "The 'Faith of Abraham,'" 207 (see note 89 above); T. Lorenzen, "Faith without Works Does Not Count before God! James 2:14-26," *Expository Times* 89 (1978), 234-35; Fung, "Justification" (see note 142 above); D. Ryan Jenkins, "Faith and Works in Paul and James," *BibSac* 159 (2002) 62-78; Bauckham, *Wisdom of James,* 120-27, who offers a strong defense of the different senses but compatible teachings of the terms used by both James and Paul. See also Popkes, 213-14; Strecker, *Theology of the New Testament,* 675-76; Dyrness, "Mercy Triumphs over Justice," 15-16; Mussner, 152-57; Nystrom, 156-61; Guthrie, 241-42.

150. S. Dowd, "Faith That Works: James 2:14-26," *RevExp* 97 (2000) 195-205, here p. 202.

151. See especially the exceptional piece by my colleague K. R. Snodgrass, "Justification by Grace — To the Doers: An Analysis of the Place of Romans 2 in the Theology of Paul," *NTS* 32 (1986) 72-93. Snodgrass's wry comment hints at deeper issues for interpreters: "I would like to suggest that Romans 2 means exactly what it says."

152. See Penner, *The Epistle of James and Eschatology,* 67-70.

153. See Moo, 121; Davids, "James and Paul," *DPL,* 458; Siker, *Disinheriting the Jews,* 100-101.

6. GENERAL EXHORTATIONS
FOR TEACHERS (3:1–4:12)

6.1. TEACHERS AND THE TONGUE (3:1-12)

1*Not many of you should become[a] teachers, my brothers and sisters, for[1] you know that we[2] who teach will be judged with greater strictness. 2For all of us make many mistakes.[b] Anyone who makes[3] no mistakes[c] in speaking is perfect, able[4] to keep the whole body in check with a bridle.[d] 3If[5] we put bits into the mouths of horses to make them obey us, we guide their whole bodies.[e] 4Or look at ships: though they are so large that it takes strong winds to drive them, yet they are guided by a very small rudder wherever the will of the pilot directs. 5So also[6] the tongue is a small member,[f] yet it boasts[7] of great exploits.[g]*

How great[8] a forest is set ablaze by a small fire![h] 6And the tongue is a fire. The tongue is placed among our members as a world of iniquity;[i] it stains the whole body, sets on fire the cycle of nature, and is itself set on fire by hell.[j] 7For every species of beast[k] and bird, of reptile and sea creature, can be tamed and has been tamed by the human species, 8but no one can tame the tongue — a restless[9] evil, full

---

1. Two Latin text types (S and Augustine) omit εἰδότες, and so convert οτι as object of the participle to causal ὅτι; instead of "knowing that we shall receive," it becomes "because we shall receive."

2. A number of later manuscripts use the second person plural λημψεσθε (436, 1067, and some Latin and Coptic manuscripts).

3. A number of manuscripts use the future πταισει (614, 1292, 1505, Antioch, Cyr, Dam, Did, HessS, PsOec, and some Latin and Coptic manuscripts).

4. Many manuscripts change the adjective δυνατός to the participle δυναμενος (ℵ, 18, 35, 206, 254, 429, some lectionaries, Cyril of Alexandia, and John of Damascus).

5. Many manuscripts have the imperative ιδε instead of the conditional εἰ δὲ. A good discussion can be found in Omanson, 473. The conditional sentence, being more difficult (since there is no apodosis), is more likely the original reading. The imperative arose in conformity to vv. 4 and 5 or because of similar pronunciation.

6. Good manuscripts have ωσαυτως, including probably P74, A, Y, 5, 81, etc.

7. Some manuscripts have, instead of μεγάλα αὐχεῖ, the verb μεγαλαυχει (P20, ℵ, a copyist of C, Y, and many others). The difference is "boasts great things" versus "boasts" (BDAG, 154, 622).

8. James's play on words with ἡλίκον . . . ἡλίκην (BDAG, 436) was not detected and so altered in some manuscripts to ολιγον . . . ηλικην (evidently uncial A and the first hand of C, Y, and many others).

9. Many manuscripts have "uncontrollable" (ακατασχετον) instead of "restless" (ἀκατάστατον). The more unusual ἀκατάστατον is probably original; it also has the weightier manuscripts in its favor (see Omanson, 473).

of deadly poison. 9With it we bless[l] the Lord[10] and Father, and with it we curse those[m] who are made[11] in the likeness of God. 10From the same mouth come blessing[n] and cursing. My brothers and sisters, this ought not to be so. 11Does a spring pour forth from the same opening both fresh and brackish water? 12Can a fig tree, my brothers and sisters, yield olives, or a grapevine figs? No more can salt water yield fresh.[o12]

a. TNIV: presume to be

b. TNIV: stumble

c. TNIV: never at fault

d. TNIV: omits *with a bridle*

e. TNIV: we can turn the whole animal

f. TNIV: small part of the body

g. TNIV: great boasts

h. TNIV: small spark

i. TNIV: The tongue also is a fire, a world of evil among the parts of the body.

j. TNIV: It corrupts the whole person, sets the whole course of one's life on fire, and is itself set on fire by hell.

k. TNIV: All kinds of animals

l. TNIV: praise

m. TNIV: humans beings

n. TNIV: praise

o. TNIV: a salt spring produce fresh water

The letter of James is not organized like a Pauline or Petrine epistle, which follow a more linear, logical line of thinking. Nor is it like 1 John with its rondo-like features. Instead, James is organized by topics that, while they are related to what precedes and unfold with a variety of rhetorical features, are not logical inferences or ordered progressions. 3:1–4:12 illustrates this most. Its relationship to what precedes is a source of contention. Some, rather fancifully I think, connect them through an English term that sounds better than it is logical: the "works" of 2:14-26 become the "words" of 3:1-12. That is, "words" are "works." This proposal serves to illustrate the problem of the relationship rather than clarify it. In fact, it is probably this sec-

10. Most extant manuscripts have θεον instead of κύριον, which is found in the earliest and better manuscripts. See Omanson, 474.

11. Some manuscripts have γεννάω (A, 5, 33, 218, 365, 623, etc.) instead of γίνομαι.

12. The readings on this last line vary enormously, with the major difference between the later addition of ουτως and the later Majority Text tradition adding material. On this, see *ECM,* 59; Omanson, 474.

tion that most shapes how exegetes and historians have come to terms with James's structure and rhetorical strategy.[13] It is not without value to observe that the wildly differing proposals for the letter's structure could be an indication that James did not have a thought-out order when he sat down to write. Innovative insights into the structure and movement of James, each of which seems to teach us something about the letter, have their place, but in a commentary designed for pastors, preachers, and students seeking to elucidate the text for the church, it is not necessary to push a structural proposal that, on a windy day, might be knocked over. So we will examine the various units of 3:1–4:12 by topic and make structural considerations footnotes to the exposition.

3:1-12 sets out the first of four themes that may or may not be connected to speech in the messianic community. I say "may not be" because it is not clear that either 3:13-18 or 4:1-10 is centrally focused on speech patterns, though each can be interpreted in that way. (And we would do well to remind ourselves that how we put a few paragraphs together might make sense to us and to our friends but not to others or, and this matters most, to the original author.) The four themes, taken at face value for what they say in and of themselves, can be ordered like this:

1. Teachers and the tongue (3:1-12)
2. Wisdom (3:13-18)
3. Dissensions (4:1-10)
4. Community and the tongue (4:11-12)

As we proceed we will make comments about connections, but a few are in order now. If 3:1-12 is about teaching and the tongue and if 3:13 suggests that we are still talking to teachers, then it makes sense that the whole of ch. 3 is shaped toward addressing teachers. Furthermore, 4:1-10 carries forward an implicit theme of 3:13-18, namely, dissension, just as it carries forward a theme about the tongue. But it should be observed that the word "teacher" occurs only in 3:1 and never again. So, when James turns in 4:11 to "brothers," we can either assume that the brother is the teacher (as in 3:1) or we can conclude that James has expanded his audience from teachers to all males or, more generically, to anyone in the community, which is how both the NRSV and the TNIV render 3:13. In which case, then, 3:1–4:12 would not be entirely directed toward the teachers of the messianic community. Had James intended to speak exclusively to the teachers for the entire section, he could

13. See Introduction. Perhaps the most informed analysis of the structure of James is summarized in Guthrie, 203-7. For full discussion of the options, see Taylor, "Recent Scholarship."

have made that more clear. Still, the balance of the evidence, especially the apparent continuing focus on teachers in 3:13, suggests that the entirety of 3:1–4:12 is addressed to the teachers of the messianic community.[14] But, these are the sorts of questions we will have to sort out as we move from line to line.

Turning now to 3:1-12, which clearly connects back to 1:19, 26 and 2:12, we observe the following structural flow.[15] James begins with a negative warning in 3:1a and immediately gives a reason for the warning (3:1b). He then gives the same warning, this time with a subtle concession about the inevitability of everyone stumbling (3:2a) but a special status for those who manage not to stumble in speech patterns (3:2b).[16]

At this point James simply begins to expound on the magnitude of the impact of the tongue (3:3-12), and he does not properly bring what he has said in 3:1-2 to a close, or if he does, not explicitly. He begins addressing the problem of the tongue's magnitude by giving three clever, concrete examples: a bit and a horse (3:3), a rudder and a ship (3:4), and a spark and a fire (3:5b-6). In the middle of this, he makes his analogy clear by saying that the tongue is a small member of a big body (3:5a). Then he turns from observation of the magnitude of the tongue's impact to say that it is hard to tame the tongue (3:7-8), and he makes his point once again with analogy, now from domestication of animals. Fatigued either by the teachers or the flow of his examples, James gasps about the tragedy of how the tongue is used. Thus, he challenges his readers/teachers simply to stop using the tongue for destruction (3:9-12).

The use of indirect and direct forms of communication are noticeable in 3:1-12. Vv. 1-2 are direct. Vv. 3-4 are indirect, inviting the reader/listener to explore speech patterns through the images of the bit and the rudder. V. 5a is direct, though James does not speak directly of the kind of speech pattern he has in mind. V. 5b resumes the use of metaphor, once again inviting the reader to explore negative speech patterns in the image of a spark that sets a fire ablaze. V. 6a makes the analogies direct: "And the tongue is a fire." This leads to three metaphors about the negative power of the tongue in what remains of v. 6. V. 7 uses images to set up a direct comment in v. 8a about no one being able to tame the tongue, but then v. 8b gives metaphors of the

14. See the alternative in Moo, 147-48, and the pastoral observations in Byron, 467.

15. Duane Watson has a study of the rhetoric of 3:1-12 in "The Rhetoric of James 3:1-12 and a Classical Pattern of Argumentation," *NovT* 35 (1993) 48-64. Whether one accepts his specific labels for verses and verse fragments, he has at least unveiled the persuasive art of James's rhetoric.

16. See especially Baker, *Personal Speech-Ethics,* 105-38, for a careful study of the evil tongue.

267

tongue's negative impact. Only vv. 1-2 rivals the directness of vv. 9-10a, where the forms of speech pattern James has in mind are referred to as "blessing" and "cursing." Vv. 10b-12 once again explores these two terms through the use of metaphor. The randomness of the length of clauses and variety of images echo the chaotic use of the tongue in the community by the teachers.

6.1.1. The Warning (3:1-2)

3:1 James begins with a simple prohibition: "Not many of you should become teachers, my brothers and sisters."[17] NRSV and TNIV's "my brothers and sisters" makes the text inclusive, but may cloak the simple "my brothers" with a viewpoint that is not in James's mind. Perhaps he means by "brothers" simply "male teachers." 3:13, which might refer to the same group, might support a more exclusive translation. We cannot be sure, but we should at least be aware of what happens when we translate such texts in an inclusive manner.[18]

When James urges individuals in the messianic community not to become teachers,[19] he may be concerned not so much with the number of teachers in the community or even with candidates for the teaching office[20] as he is

---

17. See *ACC: James,* 36-37, for good reminders of the significance of this text.

18. See the note to this effect by Ross S. Kraemer, in *WiS,* 497; also Evans, 778; Blomberg and Kamell, 154-55. I should perhaps clarify my own view, which is strongly supportive of women in ministry (see my *The Blue Parakeet* [Grand Rapids: Zondervan, 2008]). In the avalanche of studies on this topic, see also four recent books with which I resonate: R. T. France, *Women in the Church's Ministry* (Grand Rapids: Eerdmans, 1997); W. Webb, *Slaves, Women, and Homosexuals* (Downers Grove: InterVarsity, 2001); J. Stackhouse, *Finally Feminist* (Grand Rapids: Baker, 2005); R. W. Pierce and R. M. Groothuis, eds., *Discovering Biblical Equality* (Downers Grove: InterVarsity, 2005). Another recent book about women's participation in religion is C. E. Schultz, *Women's Religious Activity in the Roman Republic* (Chapel Hill: University of North Carolina Press, 2006). The issue here is not one's overall view but how best to interpret Jas 3:1 in context.

19. Μὴ πολλοὶ διδάσκαλοι γίνεσθε. The present (imperfective aspect) negated imperative here almost certainly does not say "do not keep on being teachers," in the sense of turning in their cap or not adding to their number if some are standing in line for the office, but instead is a simple prohibition: "do not become teachers." It is not the present tense that shows there is a problem in the church (Martin, 107), but the attention James gives to these concerns in the letter. See McKay, *A New Syntax,* 77-81. The present tense is used, perhaps, because it can vividly and adequately sketch before the eyes of the messianic community that teaching involves public speech that itself is a significant problem in the community. Some read πολλοί as an adverb, hence as if it were πολύ, and render it as the prohibition of teaching every opportunity they get; see Mussner, 159 n. 3; BDF, §243. But it is more likely a subject and predicate; so Martin, 107.

20. See R. Riesner, *Jesus als Lehrer. Eine Untersuchung zum Ursprung der Evangelien-Überlieferung* (WUNT 2/7; Tübingen: Mohr, 1981); A. F. Zimmermann, *Die*

with the impact of too many talking and teaching in irresponsible, unloving ways.[21] We say this because of how 3:1-12 develops and, if there is a strong connection to the next section, how 3:1–4:12 develops. Not once does James bring up again how many teachers there are; instead, he is concerned with the impact of speech patterns in the community, and here particularly with the crucial role teachers play in such a community. His concern shifts from the number of teachers to the impact of teachers. This verse fits with Matthew 23:6-8: "They love to have the place of honor at banquets and the best seats in the synagogues, and to be greeted with respect in the marketplaces, and to have people call them rabbi. But you are not to be called rabbi, for you have one teacher, and you are all students." If Jesus perceived the desire for power and prestige to be a vice for teachers, James augments those two desires with the desire to dominate verbally.

Teaching has always been necessary and, to one degree or another, prestigious because knowledge and power go hand in hand, especially in that world, where only about 10% could read.[22] From the glories of Cicero and Quintilian[23] and on to Moses and the sages and prophets[24] and the early churches[25] and the rabbis,[26] teaching carries with it the capacity to know, guide, and offer wisdom, not to mention criticism and rebuke.[27] At the time

---

urchristlichen Lehrer (WUNT 2/12; 2d ed.; Tübingen: Mohr, 1988), 198-201; Edgar, *Has God Not Chosen the Poor?* 50-57.

21. See the various comments in *ACC: James,* 36-37.

22. See W. V. Harris, *Ancient Literacy* (Cambridge: Harvard University Press, 1989); A. Millard, *Reading and Writing in the Time of Jesus* (Sheffield: Sheffield Academic, 2000).

23. It is worth the extra effort for a pastor to spend some time reading the essays of these classical teachers, so I mention an item or two for each: Cicero, *Brutus, Orator* (LCL; Cambridge: Harvard University Press, 1997), 297-509; Quintilian, *The Orator's Education* (LCL; 5 vols.; Cambridge: Harvard University Press, 2001) or his *Lesser Declamations* (LCL; 2 vols.; Cambridge: Harvard University Press, 2006). These would be a good place to start for the classical prototypes.

24. See Jeremias, *Jerusalem in the Time of Jesus,* 233-45; W. Barclay, *Educational Ideals in the Ancient World* (Grand Rapids: Baker, 1974); Blenkinsopp, *Sage, Priest, Prophet;* J. L. Crenshaw, *Education in Ancient Israel* (ABRL; New York: Doubleday, 1998).

25. See Dunn, *Jesus and the Spirit,* 186, 236-38, 282-84; A. F. Zimmermann, *Die urchristlichen Lehrer* (see note 20 above); M. Hengel, *The Pre-Christian Paul* (with R. Deines; Philadelphia: Trinity, 1991), 18-62; R. A. Campbell, *The Elders: Seniority within Earliest Christianity* (SNTW; Edinburgh: Clark, 1994); an older study that sets some of this discussion in context is E. Schweizer, *Church Order in the New Testament* (London: SCM, 1961).

26. On rabbis, see the valuable sketch of B. D. Chilton, "Rabbis," *DNTB,* 914-17.

27. For an elegant statement on the teaching profession, see D. P. Verene, *The Art of Humane Education* (Ithaca: Cornell University Press, 2002).

of James, and the evidence is not entirely clear, education took place in the home and in schools and in synagogues.[28]

In the New Testament we see the gradual development of a class of teachers in the church, though we need to be careful to avoid thinking of them in terms of official qualifications and credentials as we would today with seminary and university degrees. It is possible that "teachers" were more local and prophets more itinerant.[29] For instance, we see teachers in Acts 13:1, and they are mentioned with "prophets." This fits with Paul's listing of the gifts of the Spirit: "God has appointed in the church first apostles, second prophets, third teachers" (1 Cor 12:28). Paul also lists "teachers" with "pastors" and "elders": "The gifts he gave were that some would be apostles, some prophets, some evangelists, some pastors and teachers" (Eph 4:11; see 1 Tim 6:3; 2 Tim 4:3). Peter depicts the elders as teachers (1 Pet 5:1).

The church carried on what we find already in the New Testament. Thus, *Didache* 13:1-2 and 15:1-2:

> But every genuine prophet who wishes to settle among you is worthy of his food. Likewise, every genuine teacher is, like the worker, worthy of his food.

> Therefore appoint for yourselves bishops and deacons worthy of the Lord, men who are humble and not avaricious and true and approved, for they too carry out for you the ministry of the prophets and teachers. You must not, therefore, despise them, for they are your honored men, along with the prophets and teachers.

And the dying Polycarp is called "an apostolic and prophetic teacher" (*didaskalos apostolikos kai prophetikos*):

> When the lawless men eventually realized that his body could not be consumed by the fire, they ordered an executioner to go up to him and stab him with a dagger. And when he did this, there came out a large quantity of blood, so that it extinguished the fire; and the whole crowd was amazed that there should be so great a difference between the unbelievers and the elect. Among them most certainly was this man, the most remarkable Polycarp, who proved to be an apostolic and prophetic teacher in our own time, bishop of the holy church in Smyrna. For every

---

28. An excellent sketch can be found in D. F. Watson, "Education: Jewish and Greco-Roman," in *DNTB*, 308-13; see also S. Safrai, "Education and the Study of the Torah," *JPFC* 1.2, 945-70. Hovering over most of this discussion, however, is the singular problem of finding evidence for the first century. It is unwise simply to import evidence from the third- and fourth-century rabbis into the first-century contexts.

29. See Laws, 142.

word which came from his mouth was accomplished and will be accomplished (*Martyrdom of Polycarp* 16:1-2).

James's problem, however, transcends the issues of power and prestige. It is the status of a teacher that leads James to turn toward them. He prohibits the rise in numbers of teachers because of the abuse of the teaching position with irresponsible speech. We take it as entirely likely that some of the "elders" of 5:14 were also the teachers at whom James here must point his finger (1 Tim 5:17; Tit 1:9). The fundamental problem is that these teachers, who explained God's Word and God's ways for the messianic community and who brought "a new insight into an old word from God"[30] could also abuse that vulnerable charismatic authority by saying the wrong thing at the wrong time to the wrong persons or about another person and so lead to the destruction of the delicate relationships that characterize the Christian community.

James now begins to clarify why they should not become teachers: "for you know that we who teach will be judged with greater strictness" (3:1b).[31] His concern is an abuse of power, but the abuse — so unlike many warnings in the rest of the New Testament — is not false teaching but bad manners leading to a fractured and fractious community.[32] The long-term impact of these teachers is not heresy but a community at odds with itself (3:13-18). One might wonder how James's community had learned about the strictness of judgment for teachers, and since Paul also uses "you know" of tradition that was passed on orally (Rom 5:3; 6:9; 13:11; 1 Cor 15:58; 2 Cor 4:14), it is reasonable to think there were traditional codes of behavior for the teaching office that came with special warnings. Perhaps something like Matthew 23 was part of that code.[33]

Teachers will be judged more strictly[34] because of those to whom much is given much will also be required (Luke 12:48).[35] Not only are teach-

---

30. Dunn, *Jesus and the Spirit,* 237.

31. The aorist participle sums up the "knowing" into one act. It is an adverbial participle of cause: "because you know."

32. See 1 Tim 1:7; 2 Pet 2:1.

33. See Martin, 108; Zimmermann, *Die urchristlichen Lehrer,* 194-208 (see note 20 above).

34. It is highly unlikely that James means "judgment as condemnation" with the word κρίμα; his concern at this point is to warn of future accountability before God. Hence, the future of λημψόμεθα is less conditional than some suggest; see Martin, 107. The teachers will be scrutinized more carefully because they know more. Moo proposes that James means that teachers expose themselves to "greater *danger* of judgment" (p. 150).

35. Other New Testament texts include Matt 12:36-37; Rom 2:17-23; 1 Cor 3:10-15; 9:27.

ers "in the know," but their knowledge leads to responsibility for both what they teach and how they live. This, after all, is precisely the point Jesus makes in Matthew 23 when he excoriates the scribes and Pharisees for both knowing and not doing. In the words of Daniel Doriani, teachers

> are especially vulnerable to failures of speech because their role demands that they speak so much. More words mean more errors. As we grow accustomed to public speaking, we can become careless. When asked to offer opinion, we tend to comply, even if we have scant qualifications and little factual basis. Humor is a dangerous gift. It pleases the crowd, but can easily wound or mislead. Too many laughs come at someone else's expense.[36]

3:2 James concedes now, but only slightly. Once his concession is made, he returns to his exhortation to challenge the "brothers [and sisters]," or teachers, to a life of verbal purity. The concession is simple, a timeless bit of wisdom: "For all of us make many mistakes."[37] Even if one can never render confident judgment, "all of us" might suggest that James has now gone beyond an exhortation to teachers alone, unless he means "all of us teachers." If the emphasis of the language of 3:1 is not how many teachers are present in the community but on the danger of the tongue, then "all of us" is best rendered as referring to teachers and anyone else speaking publicly.

To observe that we all sin is a commonplace. Thus:

> Can mortals be righteous before God?
> Can human beings be pure before their Maker? (Job 4:17)

> But who can detect their errors? (Ps 19:12)

> Who can say, "I have made my heart clean;
> I am pure from my sin"? (Prov 20:9)

> The heart is devious above all else;
> it is perverse —
> who can understand it? (Jer 17:9)

Both Proverbs and Sirach apply the same understanding of human nature to the tongue:

---

36. Doriani, 105-6.

37. πολλὰ γὰρ πταίομεν ἅπαντες. The present tense is especially suited to gnomic wisdom statements. The statement has three plosives that reflect its proverbial origins. The γὰρ provides the reason for the statement in 3:1a: teachers are more prone to speech sins.

> Rash words are like sword thrusts,
>> but the tongue of the wise brings healing (Prov 12:18).
>
> Those who guard their mouths preserve their lives;
>> those who open wide their lips come to ruin (13:3; see 18:7).
>
> Death and life are in the power of the tongue,
>> and those who love it will eat its fruits (18:21).
>
> A person may make a slip without intending it.
>> Who has not sinned with his tongue? (Sir 19:16)

Some of the more interesting comments are found in the Dead Sea Scrolls:

> You [God] have taught me Your covenant and my tongue is as one of Your disciples (1Q Hodayot[a] 15:10).
>
> with a clean heart and does not slander with his tongue (4Q525 f2ii + 3:1)
>
> with your lips, and be very careful against a slip of the tongue . . . lest you be caught by your own lips and trapped together by the tongue (4Q525 f14 ii:26)

Jesus' own teaching moves in the same circle. If he recognizes that humans are evil (Matt 7:11), he is particularly concerned about sins of the tongue:

> It is what comes out of a person that defiles. For it is from within, from the human heart, that evil intentions come: fornication, theft, murder, adultery, avarice, wickedness, deceit, licentiousness, envy, slander, pride, folly. All these evil things come from within, and they defile a person (Mark 7:20-23).

and how one uses the tongue to label others:

> You have heard that it was said to those of ancient times, "You shall not murder"; and "whoever murders shall be liable to judgment." But I say to you that if you are angry with a brother or sister, you will be liable to judgment; and if you insult a brother or sister, you will be liable to the council; and if you say, "You fool," you will be liable to the hell of fire (Matt 5:21-22).

Commonplace statements like these form the context for James's words in 3:2-12 because he, too, ties inevitability of sin to the need to control the tongue as he focuses his attention on the teacher and the tongue. NRSV's "make many mistakes" renders a more literal "stumble in many ways" less metaphorically. "Stumble" (Greek *ptaiō*)[38] is found three times in James (2:10; twice in 3:2) and elsewhere in the New Testament only in Romans 11:11, where it refers to Israel's overall relationship with the God of the covenant, and in 2 Peter 1:10, where it refers to the need for moral perseverance. The word is used in the Septuagint for moral lapse (Deut 7:25) and military defeat (1 Sam 4:2-3, 10; 7:10; 2 Sam 10:19; 1 Kgs 8:33). A striking parallel is found in Sirach 37:12:

> But associate with a godly person whom you know to be a keeper of the commandments, who is like-minded with yourself, and who will grieve with you if you fail *(ptaiō)*.

While one might be tempted to see gravity in this term, it seems James is using it more for peccadilloes since he says "all of us" trip up in "many" ways (adverbial *polla*). James here scans the teachers and says that all of us trip up in many ways and often.[39] Rhetorically he gains their attention without pushing too hard.

But he is not done. His concern is not to let his community, or much less the teachers, off the hook by giving them a platitude they can bank on when they sin. Instead, he concedes a point — that we all sin — in order to sharpen his focus on his favorite subject: verbal sins. He is scouting for the messianic teacher who can avoid those sins: "Anyone who makes no mistakes in speaking is perfect, able to keep the whole body in check with a bridle." The NRSV masks the grammar: the entire sentence is a conditional construction.[40] James does not believe in sinlessness, nor does any writer in the New Testament (cf. 1 John 1:8), but he does believe that those who have the implanted word (James 1:21) can obey the royal law of love (1:25-27; 2:8-13). The royal law of love manifests itself in verbal purity. James puts it this way: "Anyone who makes no mistakes in speaking." Speech purity is a central concern of James: 1:19-21 brings the matter up and 3:1–4:12 is shaped by this concern. But does James perhaps mean "in teaching"[41] instead of just "in speaking" (in general)? Again, since it is not clear that James ever leaves the teachers from 3:1 to 4:12 and since 3:13 returns to the teachers, the more accurate translation would be "in teaching." However, inasmuch as 3:3-12

---

38. BDAG, 894.

39. So Dibelius, 184 n. 16.

40. εἴ τις with the apodosis beginning with οὗτος. In that James uses a real condition, the NRSV's choice of turning it into a simple statement is accurate. See also 1:5 and 2:26.

41. So Mussner, 160. Martin, 109, thinks it applies both to teachers and to speech sins in general.

will illustrate 3:1-2 and "in speaking" *(en logō)* is considered by some a near equivalent for "tongue" *(glossa)* in 3:5, some think "in speaking" is preferred. We are back to the same issue: Does James retain his focus on the teacher? Since he started with a direct interest in them (3:1), since teachers are prone to verbal sins and specifically verbal sins that fracture communities (4:1-10), and since 3:13 is about teachers, it remains a stubborn exegetical accuracy to think James has in mind the teachers when he says "Anyone who makes no mistakes in speaking." Teachers and preachers know full well how difficult it is to avoid verbal sins.

The teacher (or person) who avoids stumbling in speaking is "perfect."[42] By now the careful reader of James is familiar with this term. James has spoken of believers being "mature and complete" in 1:4, of God's gifts as "perfect" in 1:17, and more importantly of the "law of liberty" being the "perfect law" in 1:25. The law of liberty in 1:25 is a synonym for the "royal law," the second half of the Jesus Creed (e.g., Lev 19:18) in 2:8. Thus, when James speaks of a "perfect" teacher in 3:2, his concern is more focused than on just Torah observance. This person is a fully developed follower of Jesus' own teachings of the Torah as the Torah of loving God and loving others. The perfect teacher is one whose love shapes how he or she teaches and speaks of others. Indeed, the term speaks of maturity and completeness or, even better, of having arrived at the destined goal designed by God.[43] This was the point about Abraham (2:22), and it makes one wonder if James has not almost incorporated behavior and deeds into what he means by avoiding speech sins (cf. 3:13).[44]

Such a teacher, because he or she is shaped by God's own design, is "able to keep the whole body in check with a bridle" (3:2b).[45] This inelegant NRSV phrasing seeks to keep James's metaphor of the bit that guides the horse in view while rendering it into English. The point is that the teacher who controls the tongue controls everything. This seeming overstatement is expounded in 3:3-12, where it is shown that James is not in fact overstating his point. James really does believe that control of the tongue is a sign that

---

42. τέλειος ἀνήρ, "a perfect man." The use of ἀνήρ (BDAG, 79-80) is considered by most to be pleonastic (as at 1:12; see Davids, 137), but it is not impossible that James is speaking to males because only males were teachers in this messianic community. Even if there were women who taught (e.g., Priscilla in Acts 18:26), few dispute that the vast majority of teachers in the early churches were males. For James to have thought of males would have been a rule with exceptions. On τέλειος see the notes at 1:4 and pp. 80-82 above.

43. See Laws, 145; Davids, 137; Martin, 109.

44. See Johnson, 256; Popkes, 222.

45. δυνατὸς χαλιναγωγῆσαι καὶ ὅλον τὸ σῶμα: "able to bridle even the whole body." This language forms a bridge to similar words in 3:3.

one can control one's moral life. We have spoken here of the "whole body," the physical body, and of "everything" and "one's moral life," making "body" a metaphor for one's moral life. Is this the case? Clearly James uses "body" *(sōma)* for the physical body and speaks of the tongue as a part of that body (cf. 3:2-3, 6). But the exegetical conclusion that James is speaking to teachers could guide us to a fresher and more accurate perspective on what he means in 3:2b. If James is speaking to teachers and if "speaking" refers to "teaching," it is not impossible that James refers to the messianic community or "messianic body" with "body." The teacher who controls the tongue is one who can guide the whole messianic body.[46] While there is no evidence that James uses the word "body" as Paul does (e.g., 1 Corinthians 12–14), the emphasis of James 3:1–4:12 is not on individual piety but on ecclesial peace and harmony (3:13-18; 4:1-10, 11-12). The same ecclesial shape was seen the first time James brought up speech sins (1:19-21). We consider "body" in 3:2 to be an image for the messianic community.

6.1.2. The Magnitude of the Tongue's Impact (3:3-12)

6.1.2.1. The Problem: Three Analogies (3:3-6)

James launches now into an exposition of the magnitude of the tongue's impact: though small, it has an influence grossly out of proportion to its size. James does not explain his point so much as give analogies — three of them. He begins with the bit and the horse (3:3), moves to the rudder and the ship (3:4), and then turns to the spark and the fire (3:5b-6). Just prior to the spark and fire analogy, though, James explains the point of his analogies: "So also the tongue is a small member, yet it boasts great exploits" (3:5a).

James's three analogies were commonplaces in the ancient world, showing James to be at home in the Hellenistic world. Plutarch, a first-century Greek moralist and priest at Delphi, in his essay *Concerning Talkativeness* (10), urges his readers to guard their words because trusting them to others turns those words loose. "Thus, then, the story goes on increasing and multiplying by link after link of incontinent betrayal." Only a "story confined to its first possessor is truly secret; but if it passes to another, it has acquired the status of rumour." Words, he learned from Homer, have wings. At this point, then, Plutarch compares words let loose to boats caught by winds that shipwreck and sparks caught by winds that set off fires. It is Plutarch's combination of boats and fire that catches our attention. Philo connects horses and bits, but what strikes the reader of his *On the Creation* is that these are set in a context of humans being made in God's image and having the capacity to tame

46. Martin, 103-7.

animals (83-86). In his *Allegorical Interpretation of Genesis,* Philo connects the rudder and boat to a mind set ablaze by irrational sense like a fire (3.224). One could easily conclude that these were stock examples of small things with huge impacts instead of thinking that James had recently read or consulted either Plutarch or Philo. In the words of a classicist, David Nystrom, "Therefore, no specific parallel is in view. James simply appropriated what he knew to be stock phrases and crafted them to his own ends."[47]

If James's rhetoric connects to the style of others in the ancient world, it also illustrates something every good speaker, preacher, or teacher knows: the power of a graphic image to convey a message. One is reminded here of Jesus' graphic images (yokes, kings, crucifixion) as well as the power of images in the prophets, like Hosea's use of a harlot.

3:3 Teachers, James tells them, need to be aware that their tongues are like a bit that can direct and misdirect the entire messianic community. We concluded in the translation above that the original text of 3:3 was a conditional sentence. Thus: "If we put[48] bits[49] into the mouths of horses to make them obey us, we guide their whole bodies." It is the smallness of the bit that captures James's attention: in comparison to a horse a bit is tiny, but that tiny bit can be used to guide the large animal. Plutarch again trades in the same themes we find in James: "And again," he says quoting, "'Tis character persuades, and not the speech.' No, rather it is both character and speech, or character by means of speech, just as a horseman uses a bridle, or a helmsman uses a rudder, since virtue has no instrument so humane or so akin to itself as speech" (*How to Study Poetry* 12).

James's point is that the bit enables the rider to "make them [the horses] obey us."[50] The bit is placed into the mouth so we can "guide their whole bodies."[51] That he uses "guide" both here and in v. 4 suggests that he is thinking of the teacher's tongue as the guide of the church. But, we need to

---

47. Nystrom, 176.

48. βάλλομεν is present and is used to sketch the image more vividly. See BDAG, 163-64 (3b). James uses three presents in 3:3, and each enables a more vivid illustration: the actions of his sketch are happening before our eyes.

49. James here connects back to 3:2 with the word χαλινούς. Perhaps this illustration led to his choice of words in 3:2, or perhaps the analogy of 3:2 led to his choice of illustrations in 3:3.

50. εἰς τὸ πείθεσθαι αὐτοὺς ἡμῖν. This could be taken to be a passive in this sense: "so they (accusative subject) are persuaded by us (dative of means)" or a deponent in this sense: "so we might persuade them to our advantage."

51. This is the apodosis. The use of σῶμα connects back to 3:2, but it should not (and cannot) be used to determine if "body" in 3:2 was a metaphor for the church. That would permit the horse to guide the bit. (It is not the bit itself that controls the horse, of course; it is the use of the bit by a skilled rider that can guide the horse.)

remind ourselves that James makes his point in 3:5a: "So also the tongue is a small member, yet it boasts of great exploits." His concern is the smallness of something having a large destructive impact. The bit and the horse and the guidance illustrate his point: as a little bit can guide a large horse, so the little tongue can destructively impact the entire messianic community.

3:4 The tongue of a teacher, James adds, can be compared to the rudder of a ship: as the small rudder guides a big ship, so the tongue can direct and misdirect the messianic community.[52] James describes ships as "so large that it takes strong winds to drive them." A question arises as to whether James is speaking of the size of wind that large ships require in order to sail effectively or how a violent[53] wind that buffets a boat can be mastered by even a small rudder.[54] Since James defines "boats" with two clauses ("so large" and the strong winds that drive them) in order to sketch the image, leaving us with a big boat driven by wicked winds, the second view seems more likely. His emphasis remains the contrast of small with large. The use of "strong winds," even if not neatly parallel, evokes the violence done by the tongue. The oddity here is that the rudder is used to control a violently blown ship, but James's own logic is the rudderlessness of the teachers' tongues. This shows that his emphasis is on the contrast of a small object influencing a much larger object.

James indirectly throws the responsibility back on the will of the teachers in his extension of this analogy to include the sovereign control of the helmsman: "wherever the will of the pilot directs."[55] The pilot, even if the

---

52. James begins this analogy with ἰδοὺ καί, which could be rendered "Notice also" or, as the NRSV has it, "Or look." The grammar of 3:4 involves a neuter plural noun (τὰ πλοῖα) that is modified by both τηλικαῦτα ὄντα and ἐλαυνόμενα, and this participle has an adverbial prepositional phrase (ὑπὸ ἀνέμων σκληρῶν) modifying it. The neuter plural noun's verb is the present passive μετάγεται: "the boat is guided." The verb then has its own adverbial prepositional phrase (ὑπὸ ἐλαχίστου πηδαλίου) and an indefinite verbal clause (ὅπου ἡ ὁρμὴ τοῦ εὐθύνοντος βούλεται). The present tenses of v. 4 work, as did the presents of v. 3, to make the action vivid. The demonstrative correlative τηλικοῦτος means "so great, so large" and, in this construction, can be translated in relationship to the strong, violent winds and such a small rudder, which is described with an elative superlative adjective (ἐλάχιστος). Hence, "Though they are so large. . . ." See other uses of this correlative at 2 Cor 1:10; Heb 2:3; Rev 16:18.

53. The word σκληρός could mean "strong," but other New Testament references suggest "violent" winds (see LXX Prov 27:16; Matt 25:24; John 6:60; Acts 26:14; Jude 15).

54. See Moo, 153-54; Johnson, 257.

55. The substantival participle of εὐθύνω throws weight on the action: "the steerer" or "the one piloting." See BDAG, 406. Again, James's use of the present tenses is vivid: "wherever the will of the one piloting is choosing." There are good resources for the images here: the classic study of James Smith, *The Voyage and Shipwreck of St. Paul* (4th

winds are more than he can control, controls the impact of the winds on the sails by operating the rudder with expertise. By moving into the will of the pilot, James now prepares the messianic community to hear more explicitly the point he is making. As Luke Timothy Johnson states, James has his audience now prepared: "James makes all three components [of his rhetorical point] explicit: the guiding desire (the steersman), the means of control (the rudder), and that which is controlled (the ship), corresponding in turn to human desire, the tongue, and the body."[56]

3:5 Before James trots out his third analogy (3:5b), he breaks in to make the analogies clear:[57] "So also the tongue is a small member, yet it boasts of great exploits."[58] The focus, once again, is small versus large, and his intent is to press home to the teachers that their tongue is a small instrument with potentially devastating effects. James's wording is alliterative and mnemonic: *hē glōssa mikron melos estin kai megala auchei*. Perhaps surprising is James's choice of the word "boasts" *(auchei)*.[59] Johnson says "James does not denounce such boasting" because, in fact, what the tongue boasts about is in fact correct — that is, it says true things.[60] Another way of putting this is to say that James means nothing more than that this small tongue does great things. True enough, but I doubt that James would give so much away at his crucial point in his argument. Instead of thinking that James here says the tongue actually says right things, the context suggests that he is more concerned with the vaunting pride and vituperative rhetoric characteristic of teachers who are destructive in the community. His use of "tongue" here is negative.[61] Not only do the analogies suggest that James sees a dramatically negative impact on the community, but the rest of this section (3:13–4:12) trades in similar ideas, even if it does not use the word "boast." Thus, we should look to 3:14-16 and 4:1-6, 11-12, and 16-17. The boasting of which James speaks in 3:5, then, is most likely the arrogant and

---

ed.; Grand Rapids: Baker, 1978, a reprint of the 1880 edition); B. M. Rapske, "Acts, Travel and Shipwreck," in *The Book of Acts in Its Graeco-Roman Setting* (The Book of Acts in Its First Century Setting 2; ed. D. W. J. Gill and C. Gempf; Grand Rapids: Eerdmans, 1994), 1-47; see also L. Casson, *Travel in the Ancient World* (Baltimore: Johns Hopkins University Press, 1994), 149-62.

56. Johnson, 258; but see Popkes, 225, who disagrees with this anthropological comparison.

57. The inference is made with οὕτως καί; see 1:11; 2:17, 26.

58. James chooses not to state clearly what these teachers were boasting about. The word "exploits" in the NRSV is fair enough, but James is less explicit; he has only μεγάλα.

59. See BDAG, 154.

60. Johnson, 258, who appeals also to Hort, 70, and Mayor, 112.

61. So Davids, 140; Martin, 112; Popkes, 225.

divisive warmongering on the part of some of the teachers and leaders in the messianic community.

James then resumes by moving briefly to a third analogy, to fire, and this analogy will lead to a more complete exposition in vv. 6-12. James wants the teachers to realize that their tongues are like a spark setting on fire a forest: "How great a forest is set ablaze[62] by a small fire!"[63] Anyone familiar with the American West these days knows that even a spark at the wrong time can threaten the lives and homes of thousands. It might also be observed that forests are uncommon in the Land of Israel, and this leads some to suggest that *hylē,* "forest," might have its more common meaning "wood," suggesting brush fires instead of the conflagration of a forest (cf. Isa 10:17).[64] The best commentary is perhaps Philo, with whom James shares so many similarities in this passage. In speaking of desire *(epithymia),* Philo says that from desire "flow the most iniquitous actions, public and private, small and great, dealing with things sacred or things profane, affecting bodies and souls and what are called external things. For nothing escapes desire, and as I have said before, like a flame in the forest, it spreads abroad and consumes and destroys everything."[65]

The emphases of James's three analogies varies: the bit and horse emphasized small size and great impact, the rudder and ship emphasized not only small and great but also guidance, while the spark and forest now emphasizes small and great along with destructiveness.

3:6 James 3:6 is a commentary on 3:5. As 3:5 connected the tongue to fire indirectly, 3:6 clarifies that connection. Thus, James moves from the tongue being a "small member" with "great exploits" to a great forest being set ablaze by a "small fire" (v. 5) to "the tongue is a fire" (v. 6) and in the process he moves from simile to metaphor. But, as is sometimes the case in the New Testament, what is intended to be a clarification can become a source of contention.[66]

To begin with, there are *textual* problems. Is the standard text used for translations, as in the NRSV above, accurate, or is it in need of emendation? Even if textual emendation is rarely compelling, Ropes was unafraid to sug-

---

62. Again, the verb is present and vivid: ἀνάπτω. BDAG, 71; Luke 12:49.

63. James uses a single Greek term with opposite meanings: ἡλίκος here means both "how great" and "small."

64. So Moo, 155; Hort, 104-6; L. E. Elliott-Binns, "The Meaning of ὕλη in James iii.5," *NTS* 2 (1955) 48-50.

65. *Decalogue* 173.

66. Moo, 157-58, discusses the options. See also R. Bauckham, "The Tongue Set on Fire by Hell (James 3:6)," in his book *The Fate of the Dead: Studies on the Jewish and Christian Apocalypses* (NovTSup 93; Leiden: Brill, 1998), 119-31; J. Duncan M. Derrett, "The Epistle of James and the Dhammadpada Commentary," *STK* 82 (2006) 36-39, especially 37 n. 17.

gest that "as a world of iniquity" was a later scribal gloss and not the words of the original text.[67] Franz Spitta went further yet and suggested that "And the tongue is a fire, a world of iniquity" was all a gloss.[68] Dibelius went even further: "as a world of iniquity, the tongue is established among our members" is added to the original.[69] Ropes knew full well the attraction of this sort of speculative game: "Exegesis by leaving out hard phrases is an intoxicating experience."[70] It is indeed the case that oddities in a text *could* indicate corruption; but it is far more likely that the more difficult reading indicates authenticity. Apart from textual evidence, the interpreter of the text of the New Testament is wiser to interpret the text we have than to speculate, without evidence, what may have been the text and then interpret that.[71]

If we take the text as printed as reliable, there remain *exegetical* problems because the syntax is unusual.[72] To begin with, what does "as a world of iniquity" mean? Does it mean an "ornament" that is evil, or does it mean an "iniquitous world"? And, is "a world of iniquity" an appositive ("the tongue is a fire, a world of evil; the tongue . . .") or the predicate of "is placed" (as in NRSV)? And, what is the meaning of "is placed" *(kathistatai)* — "is made, becomes" or "appoints itself"? And, entering into an even deeper thicket, what is the meaning of "sets on fire the cycle of nature"? Is this a use of the technical and pessimistic Hellenistic expression for the endless transmigrations of the soul from body to body with no hope for deliverance, or does it denote the more general ups and downs of the cycle of nature? Monographs have

67. Ropes, 234.
68. See the discussion in Ropes, 234.
69. Dibelius, 193-94 n. 64.
70. Ropes, 234. See also Martin, 113-14.
71. Westcott and Hort noted about sixty texts in the New Testament where emendation was possible, but did not include Jas 3:6. Bruce Metzger's words are wise: "the amount of evidence for the text of the New Testament . . . is so much greater than that available for any ancient classical author [where emendations are occasionally compelling] that the necessity of resorting to emendation is reduced to the smallest dimensions." See B. M. Metzger, *The Text of the New Testament: Its Transmission, Corruption, and Restoration* (3d ed.; New York: Oxford University Press, 1992), 182-85, quoting here p. 185. Kurt Aland says, "Textual difficulties should not be solved by conjecture," in K. Aland and B. Aland, *The Text of the New Testament* (2d ed.; trans. E. F. Rhodes; Grand Rapids: Eerdmans, 1989), 280. See also the cautions of L. Vagany and C.-B. Amphoux, *An Introduction to New Testament Textual Criticism* (2d ed.; trans. J. Heimerdinger; New York: Cambridge University Press, 1991), 84-86.
72. The sentence begins with a simple predicate (καὶ ἡ γλῶσσα πῦρ), interjects a masculine noun with a qualifying genitive (ὁ κόσμος τῆς ἀδικίας) and then resumes with the original predicate's subject (ἡ γλῶσσα) in what is apparently another predicate construction (ἡ γλῶσσα καθίσταται ἐν τοῖς μέλεσιν ἡμῶν), which is itself followed by three adjectival participles that help to define ἡ γλῶσσα (ἡ σπιλοῦσα, φλογίζουσα, φλογιζομένη).

been written and will be written on the ideas and expressions in this short verse, but it is our task to set out an interpretation that seems most compelling.

"And the tongue is a fire." From verse 3 James has been analogizing about the tongue and its impact on a community when teachers use it unwisely. Now he sees the teacher's impact as analogous to a spark loose in a forest, and this means that his focus is on the destructive impact of loose words.[73] Several passages can serve to illustrate James's point, namely the disastrous impact of abusive speech.

> Scoundrels concoct evil,
>> and their speech is like a scorching fire (Prov 16:27).

> As charcoal is to hot embers and wood to fire,
>> so is a quarrelsome person for kindling strife (26:21).

> See, the name of the LORD comes from far away,
>> burning with his anger, and in thick rising smoke;
> his lips are full of indignation,
>> and his tongue is like a devouring fire (Isa 30:27).

> Curse the gossips and the double-tongued,
>> for they destroy the peace of many.
> Slander has shaken many,
>> and scattered them from nation to nation;
> it has destroyed strong cities,
>> and overturned the houses of the great.
> The blow of a whip raises a welt,
>> but a blow of the tongue crushes the bones. . . .
> Many have fallen by the edge of the sword,
>> but not as many as have fallen because of the tongue.
> Happy is the one who is protected from it,
>> who has not been exposed to its anger,
> who has not borne its yoke,
>> and has not been bound with its fetters.
> For its yoke is a yoke of iron,
>> and its fetters are fetters of bronze;
> its death is an evil death,
>> and Hades is preferable to it.
> It has no power over the godly;
>> they will not be burned in its flame (Sir 28:13-14, 18-22).

---

73. See the excellent collection of ancient comments on this text in Bray, *ACC: James,* 39-40.

The NRSV suspends the words "a world of iniquity" until the end of the next clause: "The tongue is placed among our members as a world of iniquity." But in Greek these words follow "And the tongue is a fire": *ho kosmos tēs adikias hē glossa kathistatai en tois melesin hēmōn.* Should this be taken as "The tongue is a fire, a world of iniquity; the tongue is placed among our members"? Or as "The tongue is a fire. The tongue is placed among our members as a world of iniquity"? The first option is possible but unlikely.[74] "A world of iniquity" is not simply an appositional phrase with "the tongue is a fire," but is instead the "object" of the near predicative verb "is placed."[75] The grammar suggests that the tongue is divinely appointed among the members of the body[76] and that its placement as the speaking instrument gives it potency for abuse when humans choose to use it for what it was not intended to accomplish. When it is used improperly it "becomes" a "world of iniquity."[77]

But to speak of "abuse" implies an interpretation of "a world of iniquity." James uses the word "world" *(kosmos)* five times (1:27; 2:5; 3:6; twice in 4:4). If we leave our verse to the side, we find a uniform meaning of "world" in James: as in Paul, it refers to this world's system, which is opposed to God and to God's kingdom work in this world. It is likely then that in 3:6 it has the same meaning and clarifies what James means when he says the tongue is a "fire." That is, the tongue is a world of injustice[78] that (can) stand opposed to God's designs. The TNIV uses "evil" and the NRSV "iniquity," and both lack the spe-

---

74. See Mussner, 163, who offers a variant of this appositional take on "a world of iniquity"; cf. Popkes, 226.

75. καθίσταται. See BDAG, 492. The verb is stronger than most translations let on. As can be seen in other similar uses in the New Testament (e.g., Matt 24:45, 47; 25:21, 23; Luke 12:14, 42, 44; Acts 6:3; 7:10, 27, 35; Rom 5:19; Titus 1:5; Heb 5:1; 7:28; 8:3; Jas 4:4), the word suggests divine appointment and assignment. In the passive, it softens into "become," but a translation of the term should not be divorced from its divinely appointed intentions. The use of the term in Jas 4:4 shows a near parallel with ἔστιν. Moo sees the verb as a middle, both here and in 4:4 (Moo, 158), and translates "appoints itself." So also Popkes, 228. The present tense (καθίσταται) makes vivid the picture James chooses to sketch.

76. James has in mind the various parts, or members, of the body, and by "body" he means the physical body, not the messianic community. But see Martin, 115.

77. James's language, if the passive voice is pressed hard into a divine passive, could be construed to suggest that God designs the tongue for abusiveness; this is contrary to everything James says elsewhere in this letter. We are to fill in such things as divine appointment, human freedom, and choice to use the divinely appointed tongue appropriately or inappropriately; furthermore, the tongue is personified here and can be seen as a middle voice.

78. James uses τῆς ἀδικίας, "injustice" or that which is contrary to God's will, only here. See Luke 16:9.

cial connection this passage has with ch. 2's reference to unjust treatment of the poor in the messianic community. It is the tongue, James could be interpreted to mean, that gives rise to the *injustices* in the community.

James now sketches the image of the teacher's tongue set loose as a fire in the community with three adjectival participles, the second of which ("sets," *phlogizō*) appears both as an active and a passive, and each of these participles modifies the word "tongue":

> The tongue (thus) becomes a world of injustice among our members:
> ↓
>   staining,
>   setting on fire, and
>   being set on fire.

First, the tongue is a world of injustice in that it "stains the whole body,"[79] or can stain the whole body if it is used to destroy. We are probably to see here an allusion back to 2:10, "whoever keeps the whole law but fails in one point has become accountable for all of it," and perhaps also to 1:19-21 and 27, where James connects moral stains to the world and rhetorically urges his readers to mark themselves off from the world. In context, James has been concerned with the big influence of a small item — a bit, a rudder, and a spark. A singularly small word, spoken harshly or with ruthless abandon, can stain or spot the entire body and person. It is reasonable, though difficult to establish with force, that "body" here could refer metaphorically here to the messianic community.[80]

Second, the tongue is a world of injustice in that it "sets on fire the cycle of nature."[81] There is nothing like this elsewhere in James or the New Testament; furthermore, the language is far from common in the ancient Greek world. Thus, an overly confident interpretation needs to be checked at the gate. To begin with, James does use the word "nature" *(genesis)* in 1:23, "they are like those who look at themselves in a mirror," which could be rendered "they look at their *natural* face in a mirror." There "face of nature" represents perhaps the sinful human condition or, more likely, the face that one has or was born with. Structurally, we need to keep in mind that the singular article (with "stain"; *hē spilousa*) could be used to unite all three adjectival

---

79. ἡ σπιλοῦσα ὅλον τὸ σῶμα. See BDAG, 938. On the verb, see especially Lockett, *Purity and Worldview,* 120-24, who argues that the figurative sense of purity here marks off the community from the world, that is, it concerns ideological location.

80. Martin, 115.

81. Again, the present tense makes James's image vivid and memorable, as if it is happening before one's eyes. On τροχός, "cycle," see BDAG, 1017-18; the primary sense is "wheel" as in ongoing revolutions.

participles. Whether that is the case or not, "sets on fire" here is parallel to "stains the whole body" and expands that sense from one's body to nature itself. The exaggerated rhetoric, for of course a teacher's misuse of the tongue does not undo all of nature, makes clear to the messianic community and its teachers that misuse of the tongue has dramatic and disastrous effects.

Does James intend to evoke the Orphic literature[82] where "cycle of nature" (kyklos tēs geneseōs) meant the circle of becoming in the ongoing transmigrations of souls on their way toward full actualization? A few texts suggest that this view is not as un-Jewish as it might sound. Philo, in his On Dreams, speaks of Pharaoh's treatment of Joseph:

> In the next place he puts round his neck "a golden collar," a manifest halter, a circlet and a hoop of unending necessity,[83] not a life of orderly sequence, not the chain which marks Nature's doings.

The Sentences of Pseudo-Phocylides, from the approximate time of James, seeks to demonstrate that the best of the Greek world is consistent with Judaism and the Jewish law (line 27):

> Suffering is common to all; life is a wheel; prosperity is unstable.

And in the Jewish Sibylline Oracles:

> All have a common lot, the wheel of life, unstable prosperity (2.87).

The pessimism inherent to these lines, along with the rather pessimistic view of James in ch. 3, lends credibility to James's use of a trope from the Jewish world. Since he is using a metaphor and is concerned with the tongue and not the soul, it is better to leave this expression as a metaphor for disaster in life[84] than to think of him trading in soul migration. What should be observed here is the almost apocalyptic nature of his rhetoric: the teachers are about to undo the very course of God's design for nature, namely redemption.[85]

Third, James explains the tongue's disastrous impacts by converting his active voice participle into a passive voice: "and is itself set on fire by hell." The tongue is a world of injustice in that it is stoked by hell. The word "hell" translates the Greek word gehenna (from "valley of Hinnom," 2 Kgs 23:10; Jer 7:31), the fire pit where rubbish was burned outside Jerusalem. The term became an idiom, not for the dwelling place of Satan or demons,[86]

---

82. See Dibelius, 196-98.
83. κύκλον καὶ τροχὸν ἀνάγκης ἀτελευτήτου.
84. Bauckham, "Tongue," 130-31 (see note 66 above).
85. Johnson, 260.
86. A point made sharply by Bauckham, "Tongue," 120-23.

but for the place of condemnation because it was an everlasting fire (Matt 5:22; 18:9).[87] Hell inspires the abusive tongue, and James personifies hell as something "on the march" because he wants to drive home to the teachers that they will be held accountable to God for what they say. The punishment, then, fits the crime: if it sets things on fire, it, too, will be set on fire (e.g., Jas 2:13; 1 Cor 3:17; cf. Prov 16:27; Sir 28:22-23; *PssSol* 12:1-4).[88] "Far easier," Doug Moo wisely reminds us, "to heal are the wounds caused by sticks and stones than the damage caused by words."[89]

6.1.2.2. The Difficulty: Taming the Tongue (3:7-8)

Having sketched in vivid detail and with clever analogies the problem the tongue presents to the teachers — its propensity to evil — James now proceeds to the difficulty[90] of taming the tongue. James 3:7-8 form a dual sentence, mentioning first the positive capacity of humans to control all the animals of the world (perhaps James did not know about Cairn Terriers) and second the negative incapacity of humans to control the tongue.

Perhaps backing up puts this in better perspective. James's fundamental point was established in 3:1-2: teachers carry the load of speaking the truth in love, and one who controls the tongue is "perfect." From that point on James amplifies his points by sketching the problem of controlling the tongue (3:3-6), by exploring the difficulty of controlling the tongue (3:7-8), and by laying out his point again and buttressing that with a series of questions (3:9-11). Once again we need to keep in mind how James proceeds: he is not offering an inductive argument. He states his point first and then elaborates and clarifies it from a variety of angles, but always with a view to exhorting the teachers to guard the tongue.[91] James's rhetoric, it needs to be emphasized, is decidedly negative and pessimistic, but that rhetoric does not reflect a pessimistic attitude about what he expects from the teachers. The negative rhetoric is designed to gain the hearing of the teachers.

---

87. See BDAG, 190-91. See also D. C. Allison, *Resurrecting Jesus* (New York: Clark, 2005), 56-100; A. E. Bernstein, *The Formation of Hell* (Ithaca: Cornell University Press, 1993).

88. Again, see Bauckham, "Tongue," 123-24.

89. Moo, 160.

90. Both pastoral and personal theologies are racked by the incapacity of humans to disable addictions and sins and fleshly patterns. If James's language here strikes the optimist Christian as pessimistic, it may well strike the pastor as radically refreshing and profoundly realistic.

91. See comments by Laws, 152-53; Davids, 144. The γὰρ of Jas 3:7 is explanatory, but in a more general sense instead of a precisely rational reason for 3:6. Jas 3:7-8 is connected both to "the tongue is a fire" in 3:6a and to the general thrust of 3:3-6. See Popkes, 230.

3:7   Humans, and we see this today in zoos, can muster their energies to tame the animal world.[92] This is James's rhetorical claim, and it will form the foundation for a contrary claim about the human capacity to tame the tongue in v. 8. A few lines from Philo express the ancient first-century pride in what humans had accomplished in taming animals:

> Properly, I should say to them, "beasts ought to become tame through association with men." Indeed I have often known lions and bears and panthers become tame, not only with those who feed them, in gratitude for receiving what they require, but also with everybody else, presumably because of the likeness to those who give them food. That is what should happen, for it is always good for the inferior to follow the superior in hope of improvement.[93]

The NRSV's "every species" ably translates *pasa physis* ("all nature").[94] It could be rendered "take your pick, humans have tamed them all," and James seems to be indiscriminately referring to any particular species of animal.[95] He mentions four categories: "beast and bird, reptile and sea creature." We are led to think here that he is drawing on the creation mandate to form the foundation for his argument about the tongue: "and let them have dominion over the fish of the sea, and over the birds of the air, and over the cattle, and over all the wild animals of the earth, and over every creeping thing that creeps upon the earth . . . and have dominion over the fish of the sea and over the birds of the air and over every living thing that moves upon the earth" (Gen 1:26, 28). Neither "beasts" nor "sea creatures" are mentioned in Genesis.[96] And though "tamed"[97] is also not in Genesis,[98] that James brings up a listing like that in Genesis 1:28 and uses "likeness of God" in 3:9 suggests that the

---

92. Job 38:39–39:12, 26-30, though, reminds humans of their limitations and checks vaunting pride.

93. Philo, *Decalogue* 113.

94. When πᾶς is used before an anarthrous noun, as here, it means "*every* in the sense of *any* . . . [that is,] any you please." So Turner, *MHT* 3.199.

95. See Davids, 144; BDAG, 1070. Philo, *Special Laws* 4.116; *4 Maccabees* 1:20; Aristotle, *On the History of Animals*.

96. See also Gen 9:2, where "beasts" (θηρίοις) is used. See further at Deut 4:17-18; Ps 8:6-8; Sir 17:4; *Jubilees* 3:1-2, 15-16; Acts 10:12; 11:6.

97. James uses δαμάζω, where the LXX has ἀρχέτωσαν (from ἄρχω). The Hebrew term in Gen 1:26 is רְדָה, and in 1:28 the word כְּבָשֻׁ is used. Neither of these terms is ever translated with δαμάζω in the LXX. One word is a near equivalent, though, and that is the LXX expression in Gen 1:28: κατακυριεύσατε αὐτῆς. James may have this term in mind.

98. See J. Stackhouse, *Making the Best of It* (New York: Oxford University Press, 2008); S. Steer, "Ecology/environment," in *DMT*, 104-6.

creation text and God's mandate to humans to govern the world lurks behind 3:7-8. It is the *success* of humans with animals that both impresses James and his readers (and us), and that success will form the foil for the human inability to control the tongue. In fact, James flourishes in his praise of success: he says any animal species "can be tamed and has been tamed"[99] by the human species.[100] Some have suggested that "can be tamed" refers to the human appropriation of the Genesis mandate to govern the world for God, while the perfect tense "has been tamed" refers to God's governance of animals at creation.[101] But James's choice to see the agent of the taming in "by[102] the human species" contradicts that suggestion and, in context, James is not concerned with divine control of the world but with the human capacity and success in controlling animals and their incapacity to control the tongue.

3:8 In hyperbole, James now makes his case for the problem the teachers are facing: "but no one can tame the tongue."[103] 3:2 claimed that the one who does, in fact, control the tongue is "perfect" and now James forces the urgency of the situation in the hyperbolic claim that no one can do so. Thus, James once again sounds like the Jewish wisdom tradition, even if his rhetoric is stronger:[104]

Rash words are like sword thrusts,
but the tongue of the wise brings healing (Prov 12:18).

Those who guard their mouths preserve their lives;
those who open wide their lips come to ruin (13:3).

A gentle tongue is a tree of life,
but perverseness in it breaks the spirit (15:4).

She opens her mouth with wisdom,
and the teaching of kindness is on her tongue (31:26).

99. δαμάζεται καὶ δεδάμασται. James uses the "imperfective" aspect (present tense) and the "perfective" aspect (perfect tense) to indicate both ongoing and accomplished action.

100. τῇ φύσει τῇ ἀνθρωπίνῃ: "by the human species." On φύσις, see BDAG, 1069-70; on the adjective ἀνθρώπινος, see BDAG, 80. Here James contrasts the human with the animal species.

101. E.g., Moo, 161; Martin, 117.

102. Laws, 153, suggests "for" instead of "by," but Martin is right in seeing there the agent (p. 117).

103. The use of the present δύναται, "is able," makes James's claim even more vivid. The infinitive complement is aorist, and it globally depicts the action of taming and throws weight on the vocabularic meaning.

104. Hermas, *Mandates* 12.1.1-2; 12.4.2-3, borrows James's language here and applies it to taming desires and living out the commandments.

The translation above, "no one can tame," perhaps obscures a subtle nuance that compares taming the animal and inability to tame the human world. This nuance can be seen in a more literal rendering that focuses on James's comparison of species: "but no one can tame the tongue *of humans*."[105] If humans can tame wild animals of all sorts, they still cannot tame the little tongue inside the human. As George Guthrie says it, "Yet, irony of ironies, that small beast, the tongue, defies subjugation."[106]

Furthermore, James says the tongue is also "a restless evil" and "full of deadly poison,"[107] and both expressions are primarily concerned with the impact of the tongue on the community. James uses "restless" *(akatastatos)*[108] and its noun cognate in 1:8 ("the doubter, being double-minded and *unstable* in every way") and 3:16 ("where there is envy and selfish ambition, there will also be *disorder* and wickedness of every kind"). Here he combines it with "evil" *(kakon)*. In light of 1 Corinthians 14:33, where the noun cognate *(akatastasia)* is contrasted to "peace" and where God is dissociated from this restlessness and chaos, the restless evil James has in mind is communal: the teacher who uses his or her tongue to tear apart destroys the stability of the messianic community. Again, we can look to the letter of James itself, that is, to 1:19-21; 2:2-4; 3:13-18; and 4:1-12 for concrete examples of this restless evil.

The tongue is also "full of deadly poison." Davids is surely right here: the image is so appropriate and so common one should avoid seeking a specific origin of the expression.[109] Perhaps disclosed in James's use of death-

---

105. Most think the genitive "of humans" modifies "no one [of humans]" (Moo, 161; Popkes, 231). In light of James's interest in species, I prefer "the tongue of humans." Martin, 117, has this statement: "The use of ἀνθρώπων, after ἀνθρώπινος v 7, appears somewhat redundant, but this repetition may be for added emphasis." I agree, but it seems to favor the "tongue of humans" interpretation rather than "no human being." It is unlikely that Augustine's interpretation was in the mind of James: Augustine thought that James's emphasis was on no one *of men,* but in the power of God, the tongue can be tamed. *On Nature and Grace,* 16 [xv]. Jas 3:2 contrasts with this, and Jas 3:8's rhetoric is hyperbolic (see Popkes, 231).

106. Guthrie, 247.

107. Martin, 117, sees these as ejaculatory nominatives: "Disorderly evil! Replete with lethal poison!" Others prefer to see ellipsis of something like "because it, the tongue, is . . . ," but the meaning is not affected by the suggestion. The nouns do not agree with the accusative τὴν γλῶσσαν at the beginning of the verse. The word ἰός could mean "rust" (Jas 5:3) or "arrow," but here it means "poison." See BDAG, 477; W. Weiser, "Durch Grünspan verdorbenes Edelmetall? Zur Deutung des Wortes 'IOS' im Brief des Jakobus," *BZ* 43 (1999) 220-23. The adjective θανατηφόρος means "death-bringing" or "death-dealing"; see BDAG, 442; LXX Num 18:22, where the sons of Israel are warned about approaching the tent of meeting lest their sin become death-dealing.

108. See BDAG, 35.

109. Davids, 145. See also Laws, 154.

dealing "poison" is a snake bite. Thus, Psalm 140:3: "They make their tongue sharp as a snake's, and under their lips is the venom of vipers" (see also Ps 58:3-4; Rom 3:13). And from Qumran, "a lying tongue; as the poison of serpents it bursts forth continuously" (1QH^a 13:27).[110] The sources for the abusive tongue are both hell (James 3:6) and the serpent (3:8), and in 3:15 James traces sinful behaviors back to their "earthly, unspiritual, devilish" origin.

James knows control of the tongue marks holiness and love. He also knows that humans have more capacity to tame animals than their tongues, and this is especially important for the teachers of the messianic community. When the tongue is unleashed from its hinges, it destabilizes and deals death to the community. For this reason, James piles on rhetorical exaggeration to gain the attention of the teachers and to press them to perfection.[111]

6.1.2.3. The Challenge: Tragedy and the Tongue (3:9-12)

Now James deepens the problem of the misuse of the tongue by unmasking the tragedy and incomprehensibility of unkind words. First, in 3:9-10a James restates the problem as a contradiction in its use for both blessing and cursing. In the core of this restatement, he brings in a profound anthropological argument: humans are made in God's image. In 3:10b James becomes direct in his exhortation: "My brothers and sisters, this ought not to be so." Then he illustrates the problem of the misuse of the tongue with, once again, metaphors, now of a spring (3:11), a fig tree (3:12a), a grapevine (3:12b), and salt water (3:12c). Each of these explores the inappropriateness of teachers using words to destroy those who are made in God's image.

6.1.2.3.1. The Problem Restated (3:9-10)

As observed at the outset of ch. 3, vv. 9-10a rival vv. 1-2 in direct communication while most of vv. 1-12 explores James's warnings and teachings about the use of the tongue through metaphor. Furthermore, James turns to first person speech in 3:9 — his pastoral identification with the teachers is affective and persuasive — and this shift in style ties his words back to the directness of 3:1-2.

3:9 James begins with "with *it*" and assumes "with *the tongue*."[112]

---

110. A handful of commentaries cite 1QH 5:26-27, but that text is now found at 1QHa 13:26-27. See also *Testament of Gad* 5:1. Fragment 3 of *Sibylline Oracles* (3:32-33): "There are gods which by deceit are leaders of mindless men, from whose mouths pour deadly poison."

111. A point made well by Byron, 467.

112. The antecedent of ἐν αὐτῇ could be γλῶσσα in 3:5 or 3:6 or 3:8.

The same tongue brings forth two kinds of words: those that bless the Lord and Father[113] and those that curse humans made in God's image. James will return to these two kinds of words at the beginning of 3:10a to round off his rhetoric.

The incongruity of this behavior might remind the reader of the double-mindedness of 1:8, but that connection is neither necessary nor compelling. The incongruity at 1:8 had to do with trusting and not trusting God instead of blessing God and cursing humans. Blessing and cursing have to do with life and death. As Proverbs 18:21 puts it, "Death and life are in the power of the tongue," or as Sirach 28:12 has it,

> If you blow on a spark, it will glow;
> if you spit on it, it will be put out;
> yet both come out of your mouth.

Testament of Benjamin also says it well: "The good set of mind does not talk from both sides of the mouth: praises and curses, abuse and honor, calm and strife, hypocrisy and truth, poverty and wealth, but it has one disposition, uncontaminated and pure, toward all men" (6:5). Philo, in speaking of a person about to take an oath, makes a similar observation: "it would be a sacrilege to employ the mouth by which one pronounces the holiest of all names, to utter any words of shame" (*Decalogue* 93).

James first observes that (we) teachers use the tongue to *bless* God.[114] The Qumran Thanksgiving Hymns (1QH[a] 9:27-31) speak of God designing the lip to give praise:

> You created breath for the tongue, and You know its words. You determined the fruit of the lips before they came about. You appoint words by a measuring line and the utterance of the breath of the lips by calculation. You bring forth the measuring lines in respect to their mysteries, and the utterances of spirits in accordance with their plan in order to make known Your glory and recount Your wonders in all Your works of truth and Your righteous jud[gments] and to praise Your name openly, so that all who know You might bless You according to their insight for ever [and ever.]

By the time of the first century, God was frequently referred to (in a form of reverence that created periphrasis) as "The Blessed One," as in Mark 14:61 and Romans 1:25 and 9:5. While James's language cannot be restricted ex-

---

113. See Ng, "Father-God Language," 50-52.

114. On εὐλογέω, etc., see BDAG, 407-9; *EDNT* 2.79-80. Once again, James uses the present tense to sketch a vivid scene before his readers' eyes.

clusively to the liturgical words of blessing in formal prayers, we would be on track to connect teachers, blessings, and public prayers.[115] The standard Jewish prayer, the *Amidah,* over and over blesses God. James, though, is less concerned with specific liturgical words than with the incongruity of appropriate use of the tongue to bless God and simultaneous inappropriate use of the tongue to curse those made in God's image.

James calls God "Lord and Father." This varies from the standard Jewish blessing, which rarely refers to God as Father. A typical Jewish prayer can be seen in 1 Chronicles 29:10: "Blessed are you, O LORD, the God of our ancestor Israel, forever and ever." It has been customary for many (preachers included) to exaggerate the significance of Jesus' use of "Father" for God and to suggest even that Jesus was the first to do so in the Jewish world. But this is against the evidence. To begin with, there are signs of the use of Father for the God of Israel in the Bible. Thus, Isaiah 63:16:

> For you are our father,
>> though Abraham does not know us
>> and Israel does not acknowledge us;
> you, O LORD, are our father;
>> our Redeemer from of old is your name.

Or Sirach 23:1, 4-5:

> O Lord, Father and Master of my life . . .
> O Lord, Father and God of my life,
>> do not give me haughty eyes,
>> and remove evil desire from me.

Josephus, a contemporary of James, uses "Father" for God as well: "Seeing that God, the Father and Lord of the Hebrew race, has given to us to win this land and, being won, has promised to preserve it to us for ever . . ." (*Ant.* 5.93; cf. also LXX 1 Chron 29:10). There is, then, nothing *uniquely or exclusively* Christian about James calling God "Father." But, there is something *distinctive* about the Christian constant and consistent use of the word "Father" for God. It is distinctive because it was what those who followed Jesus called God.[116] In light, then, of James 1:1; 2:1; and 5:7, it is most likely that the word "Father" here reflects an early Christian understanding of God that involves God as creator and redeemer.[117]

---

115. Davids, 146.
116. See McKnight, *A New Vision for Israel,* 49-65; Dunn, *Jesus Remembered,* 548-55, 708-24.
117. So Ng, "Father-God Language," 50-52.

The first point James makes is that we (teachers) use the tongue to bless our God and Father. Second, (we) teachers use the same tongue to *curse* humans.[118] To set out the alternatives in terms of blessing and cursing[119] is not only rhetorical exaggeration but is also effective and affective. To use an imprecatory *curse* on someone, stemming as it did from an ancient perlocutionary understanding of how language works,[120] both labels a person socially but also renders that person's standing before God as one condemned. The two classic texts are Leviticus 26–27 and Deuteronomy 28. James does not call into doubt the legitimacy of the use of a curse, for ch. 4 will indulge in strong language. Instead, he finds incongruity among the teachers in rendering the same person both blessed and cursed or, perhaps more likely, a teacher using his or her tongue so indiscriminately that contradiction emerges. James probably has in mind a person who uses the tongue both to bless God's people and, carelessly and inexcusably, turns around to use the tongue inappropriately in ways that label persons. It is not impossible that James still has in mind the way the poor have been labeled (2:2-4). In light of teachings like Luke 6:28 and Romans 12:14, it is also possible that James has in mind a more gracious form of speech patterns, though 4:1-12 would challenge a sentimental approach to gracious speech patterns.

James grounds his critique of the teachers' misuse of language in the image of God in humans.[121] Two things happen here: not only does James connect humans to God, who in 3:9a is to be blessed, but James elevates all humans to the condition of being made in God's image — that is, they are God-like (and therefore indirectly "blessable").[122] Thus *2 Enoch* 44:2: "And

---

118. The choice to shift from the present active (εὐλογοῦμεν) to the present middle (καταρώμεθα) is not without possible import here. The subject/object has a cleaner distinction in the present active, while the subject's direct involvement in the middle voice is more pronounced. Thus, James makes the curser more culpable.

119. See BDAG, 525.

120. On this, see K. Vanhoozer, *Is There a Meaning in This Text?* (Grand Rapids: Zondervan, 1998), 201-80; R. S. Briggs, in *DTIB,* 763-66. For the biblical context, see *DOTP,* 83-87.

121. τοὺς ἀνθρώπους τοὺς καθ' ὁμοίωσιν θεοῦ γεγονότας. James uses the perfect active participle of γίνομαι, but the word (see BDAG, 197) is a near equivalent to γεννάω, which appears as a variant in the manuscript tradition. James uses the perfect here to depict completed, or perfected, action. Image of God, then, is the condition of humans.

122. See L. Stevenson and D. L. Haberman, *Ten Theories of Human Nature* (4th ed.; New York: Oxford University Press, 2004); for theological studies, see G. Carey, *I Believe in Man* (Grand Rapids: Eerdmans, 1977); P. E. Hughes, *The True Image* (Grand Rapids: Eerdmans, 1989); F. LeRon Shults, *Reforming Theological Anthropology* (Grand Rapids: Eerdmans, 2003); R. W. Jenson, *On Thinking the Human* (Grand Rapids: Eerdmans, 2003); J. Richard Middleton, *The Liberating Image* (Grand Rapids: Brazos, 2005); McKnight, *A Community Called Atonement,* 17-22.

whoever insults a person's face, insults the face of a king, and treats the face of the LORD with repugnance." In saying "those who are made in the likeness of God," James uses *homoiōsis,* the Septuagint translation of Hebrew *demut* in Genesis 1:26.[123] Though this term would take on special meaning among later theologians and is not the more common term used in Paul's writings *(eikōn),*[124] what James has in mind is human *God-likeness,* and hence all humans are to be treated with utter dignity and respect.[125] The use then of this expression for humans, especially those in the messianic community, sheds light on what James means by the word "curse." Does it not suggest that the God-likeness of some humans was being called into question by the language the teachers in the messianic community were using?

3:10   Again James restates the problem he finds among the teachers: "From the same mouth come blessing and cursing."[126] The emphasis here is on the word "same": the incongruity is that words that bless and words that curse come from the same source. James here probably borrows an image from Jesus (Matt 15:10-11, 16-20):

> Listen and understand: it is not what goes into the mouth that defiles a person, but it is what comes out of the mouth that defiles. . . . Are you also still without understanding? Do you not see that whatever goes into the mouth enters the stomach, and goes out into the sewer? But what comes out of the mouth proceeds from the heart, and this is what defiles. For out of the heart come evil intentions, murder, adultery, fornication, theft, false witness, slander. These are what defile a person, but to eat with unwashed hands does not defile.

James now offers his negative evaluation. His language interrupts the flow and is strong: "My brothers and sisters,[127] this ought not to be so." The Greek grammar, literally and for emphasis, reads like this: "Not necessary,

123. See also Gen 9:6; Sir 17:3; Wis 2:23. ὁμοίωσις is often rendered "likeness" in translations of the LXX. A most notable instance can be found in Ezek 28:12, where the king of Tyre is told that he was the "signet of *homoiōsis.*" Jas 3:9 is the only instance of the term in the New Testament.

124. See 1 Cor 11:7; 2 Cor 3:18; 4:4. See also Irenaeus, *Against Heresies* 5.16.2.

125. It is impossible to resist a reference to C. S. Lewis, *The Weight of Glory* (San Francisco: HarperSanFrancisco, 2000), 25-46.

126. The use of present tense ἔρχεται does not indicate that one or more teachers are both blessing and cursing as James writes; instead, the present is used to depict action that is not complete. Here James's use of the present tense is almost timeless and creates a sense of vividness for the listener and reader.

127. As with other instances of inclusive translation, the Greek has only ἀδελφοί μου. If James is addressing here only the teachers, and if the teachers are males, then "brothers" would be the preferred translation. See above at 3:1.

my brothers, for such things to happen."[128] Yet again: the God-like are not to be cursed.

6.1.2.3.2. The Problem Illustrated (3:11-12)

The problem is that the same source, a teacher, uses words that both bless and curse someone who is God-like. To exhort the teachers to change, James uses four images. Each image leads the reader to think of a source producing something inappropriate: a spring producing both fresh and brackish water (3:11), a fig tree producing olives (3:12a), a grapevine producing figs (3:12b), and salt water producing fresh water (3:12c). The fourth image comes back to the first, though with slight variations.

3:11 The first question, "does a spring pour forth[129] from the same opening both fresh and brackish water?" begins with *mēti*, a word that invites a negative response. In fact, the term is a little more emphatic than *mē* (2:14; 3:12), and the question could be rendered, "Surely, no spring produces both fresh and brackish water, does it?" James assumes that the teachers will answer his questions accurately, and if they do they will connect the images to the incongruity of being a God-blesser and a human-curser.

The concrete language of a spring or a crack in a rock where water bubbles forth, which was often enough to establish a village, and both fresh and brackish[130] water finds its focal point in "the same opening."[131] Davids is confident that James is referring to a natural phenomenon in the Jordan valley and observes that the sometimes absence of fresh water is a "sad fact of life in Palestine."[132] Similarity of language leads us back to 3:10: "from the same mouth." Here the focus is on the source or perhaps on the connection of source and what is produced. Again, the analogy is to the tongue of a teacher whose responsibility it is to love others and speak in a way that emerges from that love. That sort of source should produce God-blessing language but not human-cursing language.

3:12 As geological observations create images for the congruity of nature, so do plants: "Can a fig tree, my brothers and sisters, yield olives?" (3:12a). Anyone who has traveled the Mediterranean knows of the ubiquity

---

128. The impersonal verb χρή is used here only in the New Testament (BDAG, 1089). It is used with the accusative and an infinitive. See Davids, 147.

129. The Greek word βρύω suggests bubbling, gushing, overflowing, and even the budding of the flower; BDAG, 184.

130. James uses τὸ γλυκὺ καὶ τὸ πικρόν, both "sweet" and "sour" water. Perhaps James uses "sour" or "brackish" instead of "salty," found in 3:12, because of Ps 64:3; Prov 5:4; and Sir 29:25.

131. ἐκ τῆς αὐτῆς ὀπῆς. See BDAG, 715; Justin, *Dialogue* 114.4.

132. Davids, 147-48.

of olives, grapes, and figs. A good example is Jotham's fable in Judges 9:7-15. James, whose style is to absorb rather than quote his sources, could be rooted in a saying of Jesus (Matt 7:16). Again, though using now *mē* instead of *mēti,* a negative answer is expected by James. Inasmuch as fig trees do not produce both figs *and* olives, so a teacher should not be a God-blesser *and* a human-curser. To be both is incongruous.

"[Can] a grapevine [produce] figs?" (3:12b) This question is tied to the second since the *mē* carries over and the verbal construction, "is able to produce," is implied. Again, inasmuch as grapevines do not produce both grapes *and* figs, so the teachers ought not to be both God-blessers *and* human-cursers. It would do little good to explore the variety of grapes and grapevines and the care of the same since that would detract from the analogy being made: namely, the impossibility of one kind of plant, a grapevine, producing another kind of fruit, a fig.

James's fourth image moves from a question to a "neither does" observation.[133] Since this marks the end of the paragraph, we are led also to think that this image brings closure to James's point. But he closes abruptly with a final analogy that makes the same point about the incongruity of a source bringing forth wildly different produce. Thus: "No more can salt water yield fresh." This image trades back on the first image in v. 11, but in this instance the source ("the same opening") is not the focus. Instead, the concern is solely with the congruity (or incongruity) of a source and its produce: salt water does not produce[134] fresh, or sweet, water. And, in contrast to the first image, this fourth image uses "salt"[135] instead of "brackish" (or "bitter"). Perhaps more significantly, it is reasonable to think "spring" is implied instead of "water": thus, "no more can a salty *spring* produce fresh water."[136] With this analogy about the rightful congruity of source and produce, James finishes our section. To return now to the supposed incongruity of how James ends this paragraph: perhaps it is our own form of writing and Bible translation with paragraph formatting that creates the problem we discover here in the lack of closure. 3:13 continues to address the teachers, even if there is a subtle sideways skip to a slightly different subject.

We need to keep the context in mind: James is concerned about the teachers in the messianic community, and his concern is with their tongue —

---

133. Not a few commentators, because of the lack of compelling closure, wonder if the text is corrupt; see Dibelius, 181, 205-6; Laws, 157-58, who calls this a "lame conclusion." Popkes, on the other hand, contends as confidently that it is not at all a corruption but instead a good transition to 3:13-18; Popkes, 237.

134. The sentence implies the reuse of the verb δύναται, as seen at the beginning of 3:12.

135. ἁλυκόν. See BDAG, 48.

136. So Moo, 166.

he advises them not to pursue teaching and to guard their tongues. Why? Because the tongue's impact is disproportionate to its size. In fact, the tongue demands attention to tame. As if crying out to his teachers, James pleads with them to realize the incongruity of being one who blesses God and at the same time one who curses humans who are made in God's likeness. By appealing to an assortment of analogies, James claims that this incongruity makes no sense; it is at odds with what everyone sees in nature. A better way is the way of wisdom, and the proper goal of the teacher is neither control nor curse but wisdom.

6.2. TEACHERS AND WISDOM (3:13-18)

13Who[137] is wise and understanding among you? Show by[a] your good life that your works are done with gentleness born of wisdom.[b] 14But[138] if you have[c] bitter envy and selfish ambition in your hearts, do not be boastful[139] and false to the truth.[d] 15Such wisdom[e] does not come down from above,[f] but is earthly, unspiritual, devilish.[g] 16For where there is envy and selfish ambition, there will also be disorder and wickedness of every kind.[h] 17But the wisdom from above[f] is first pure, then peaceable,[i] gentle, willing to yield, full of mercy and good fruits,[140] without a trace of partiality or hypocrisy.[j] 18And a harvest of righteousness is sown in peace for those who make peace.[k]

a. TNIV: Let them show it by

b. TNIV: in the humility that comes from wisdom

c. TNIV: harbor

d. TNIV: do not boast about it or deny the truth

137. Some manuscripts have ει τις (180*, 436, 621, some lectionaries, and Nilus Ancyranus); this not only converts v. 13 into a conditional sentence but also forms a tidy parallel with v. 14. The preponderance of evidence, along with most text-critical arguments, however, favors the absence of εἰ. As Davids points out (p. 150), the word τις can function as a virtual condition (see Judg 7:3; Isa 50:10; Pss 106:2; 107:43).

138. A number of early and good manuscripts add the inferential αρα in order to clarify the connection of v. 13 to v. 14. Added in A, P, Y, 33, 81, etc., including a lectionary and some Georgian and Slavonic manuscripts. The shorter, and more difficult or less clarified, reading is here preferred.

139. Instead of κατακαυχᾶσθε, many manuscripts have the less intensive καυχασθε; see BDAG, 517, 536.

140. Some manuscripts add εργων between καρπῶν and ἀγαθῶν. Thus, C, 252, 322, 323, 424Z, a lectionary (596), Didymus Alexandrinus, and the Georgian tradition. Its redundancy and obviousness notwithstanding, the addition is more difficult. The external evidence clearly favors its omission.

e. TNIV: "wisdom" in quotation marks

f. TNIV: heaven

g. TNIV: demonic

h. TNIV: and every evil practice

i. TNIV: peace-loving

j. TNIV: considerate, submissive, full of mercy and good fruit, impartial and sincere

k. TNIV: Peacemakers who sow in peace reap a harvest of righteousness.

The reader of James today asks how 3:13 is connected to what precedes,[141] but our interpretation of 3:1–4:12 as a section primarily (if not solely) directed toward teachers both clarifies the relationship and is supported by what we find in 3:13. To begin with, "who is wise and understanding among you?" makes most sense if addressed to the teachers of 3:1-2.[142] Furthermore, "boastful" and "disorder" tie back to similar terms in 3:5 and 3:8. Thus, if 3:13-18 is addressed to teachers, then the virtues and sins it mentions clarify the problems mentioned directly and indirectly in 3:1-12. The speech patterns that most concerned James, speech that like a spark sets the messianic community on fire with destructive forces, are about envy, ambition, and boasting (3:14-16). The rhetoric of 3:1-12 implicitly, then, also was leading James toward the exhortation to the moral virtues one finds in 3:17-18. These arguments lead us to conclude that 3:13-18 demonstrates that all of 3:1-12 was directed toward the teachers in the messianic community.

This section begins with a question (3:13a), which prompts an answer that reveals what the question was designed to answer (3:13b). The question prompts James to claim that what he is seeking among the teachers is *wisdom*. But he also knows of problems in the messianic community. James thus inserts into the teachers' situation in the community an exposition of two kinds of wisdom: the so-called wisdom some teachers are pursuing in their envy and ambition (3:14-16) and the true wisdom on the part of those who teach and use their tongues for peace (3:17-18). Structurally, "wisdom" *(sophia)* and its cognates tie the entire section together ("wise" and "wisdom" in 3:13, "such wisdom" in 3:15, and "wisdom" in 3:17). The question

141. Dibelius, 207, sees no connection to what precedes; Laws, 158-59, finds a new theme in our section; Davids, 149, agrees with us that 3:13-18 addresses the teachers of 3:1-2. Johnson expounds 3:13–4:10 through the lens of "envy"; see Johnson, *Brother of Jesus, Friend of God,* 182-201.

142. The indirect rhetoric of metaphors in 3:3-12 amplifies what is said in 3:1-2; 3:1-12 never leaves concern with the teachers. Hence, one is pressed by the form of rhetoric, direct — indirect — direct, to tie together the two sections of direct communication, namely 3:1-2 and 3:13-18.

seeks wisdom, the answer is wisdom, and the situation in the messianic community is sketched through the alternative forms of wisdom.[143]

6.2.1. Question (3:13a)

The question "Who is wise and understanding among you?" is more than a quest for information. James's rhetorical intent is not so much to identify *who* are such persons as to *describe* such persons, as both the answer in 3:13b and the expositions in 3:14-18 will reveal. James's description will not permit the teacher to think his or her mastery of theology or exegesis is sufficient to pass muster. What passes muster for James is behavior shaped by humble wisdom.

The combination of "wise and understanding"[144] is found often enough in the Hebrew Bible that we can take it as shorthand for "teaching" in 3:1. Thus, Deuteronomy 1:13, 15:

> Choose for each of your tribes individuals who are wise, discerning, and reputable to be your leaders. . . . So I took the leaders of your tribes, wise and reputable individuals, and installed them as leaders over you (see also 4:6; Job 28:28).

The wording is Solomonic:

> God gave Solomon very great wisdom, discernment, and breadth of understanding as vast as the sand on the seashore (1 Kgs 4:29).

And Danielic:

> There is a man in your kingdom who is endowed with a spirit of the holy gods. In the days of your father he was found to have enlightenment, understanding, and wisdom like the wisdom of the gods. Your father, King Nebuchadnezzar, made him chief of the magicians, enchanters, Chaldeans, and diviners, because an excellent spirit, knowledge, and understanding to interpret dreams, explain riddles, and solve problems were found in this Daniel, whom the king named Bel-

---

143. A similar and longer contrast of true and false wisdom is seen in 1QS 4:2-17. See the excellent sketch of the themes in Jas 3:13-18 in Hoppe, *Der theologische Hintergrund,* 44-71; Martin, 136-38; Cheung, *Genre, Composition,* 138-47. One can find good exposition in Doriani, 116-27.

144. σοφὸς καὶ ἐπιστήμων. The reputation of some kinds of wisdom was checked by early Christians; see 1 Cor 1:20. For similar uses of the term σοφός, see Prov 9:8-12; Wis 7:15; Sir 1:8; 9:17; 21:13; for the term among early Christians, see Matt 23:34; 1 Cor 3:10; Eph 5:15.

teshazzar. Now let Daniel be called, and he will give the interpretation (Dan 5:11-12).

And common in the Dead Sea Scrolls:

> Upon earth their operations are these: one enlightens a man's mind, making straight before him the paths of true righteousness and causing his heart to fear the laws of God. This spirit engenders humility, patience, abundant compassion, perpetual goodness, insight, understanding, and powerful wisdom resonating to each of God's deeds, sustained by His constant faithfulness. It engenders a spirit knowledgeable in every plan of action, zealous for the laws of righteousness, holy in its thoughts and steadfast in purpose. This spirit encourages plenteous compassion upon all who hold fast to truth, and glorious purity combined with visceral hatred of impurity in its every guise. It results in humble deportment allied with a general discernment, concealing the truth, that is, the mysteries of knowledge. To these ends is the earthly counsel of the spirit to those whose nature yearns for truth (1QS 4:2-6; also 11:6; 1QS20 19:25).

Once again, we need to turn to the audience of these verses. James's concern is with leaders in the messianic community,[145] and they were identified as teachers in 3:1.[146] Moo contends the terms in 3:13a are not regular titles for teachers,[147] but I have to wonder if we have enough evidence of "titles" and whether this sort of observation is not imposing a modern way of referring to functions/gifts on the ancient world. Moo admits that in the Old Testament these expressions refer in all but one instance to leaders, and that concession is not without significance for understanding James 3:13. Furthermore, what needs to be observed is that the wisdom tradition, from Proverbs to Sirach, was shaped for sages. It might be wiser to say that teaching is a characteristic behavior of the sage than to say that sagacity is a characteristic of teachers.[148] It would also be wise to observe that "sage" is a charisma more than it is a title or an office.[149]

145. Hence ἐν ὑμῖν.
146. This will become clearer in 3:14-18 below. Popkes sees the language evoking the elite (p. 245).
147. Moo, 169.
148. A very good source on this is Blenkinsopp, *Sage, Priest, Prophet,* especially 9-65; see also A. R. Millard, "Sages, Schools, Education," in *DOTWPW,* 704-10. *DOTWPW* has many fine articles on wisdom, especially those found on pp. 842-912. See also J. J. Collins, *Jewish Wisdom in the Hellenistic Age* (Louisville: Westminster John Knox, 1997), 42-61.
149. A good example of a man functioning as a sage in contemporary Judaism

6.2.2. Answer (3:13b)

James's answer is "Show by your good life that your works are done with gentleness born of wisdom." This sentence sounds as if James is once again appealing to the significance of works for genuine believers (1:22-27; 2:14-26). But what he says here is different. It is not so much that a person's faith must reveal works, but more that a genuinely wise teacher's works are done in ways that manifest meekness and wisdom. Thus, the order is not quite the same as we find in Jesus: "Yet wisdom is vindicated by her deeds" (Matt 11:19).

The wise teacher, or sage, will "show" "works" in his or her "good life."[150] The word "show" evokes the sense of manifest and exhibit.[151] By "works" James no doubt has in mind good human behavior, but one cannot fail to observe that it involves compassion for the poor (1:9-11, 26-27; 2:2-4; 5:1-6) and loving speech patterns (1:19-21; 3:1-12; 4:1-12). "Works" flow from "the good life," the pattern of one's life, a term *(anastrophē)* common in Paul's letters (Gal 1:13; Eph 4:22; 1 Tim 4:12) and 1 Peter (1:15; 2:12; 3:1-2, 16; also 2 Pet 2:7; 3:11) but not found elsewhere in James. James's concern here is a pattern of life that routinely and habitually manifests good works.

James now brings up the word "wisdom," the central concern of the paragraph (and some say the entire letter).[152] To remind ourselves of a point made above, he does not tell the good teacher to be wise, but to manifest good works in wisdom. A grammatical question arises here: Does "with gentleness born of wisdom" modify the verb "show," thus creating two prepositional modifiers of the verb? That is, "Show works, first, on the basis of a good life and, second, in the meekness of wisdom." Or does it modify the "works," thus connecting works to wisdom more tightly? That is, "Show works born of a gentle wisdom." Grammatically, the second option has in its favor the proximity of the prepositional phrase *(en praütēti sophias,* "in meekness of wisdom"), while the former view has in its favor a grammatical balancing of the verb by two prepositional phrases. However, this may be too fine analysis for James. By the time one gets to "in the meekness of wisdom," one has already heard "works." Thus, if one proposes a second modifier of

---

can be seen in the story of Rabbi Menahem Mendel Schneersohn; see the story in Sue Fishkoff, *The Rebbe's Army* (New York: Schocken, 2005).

150. The aorist imperative δειξάτω is categorical and sums up all the actions in one word: "Show." It does not speak to the inception of showing. One thinks here of 2:18, where the same verb is used.

151. BDAG, 214-15.

152. It is much easier to *explain* James through the lens of wisdom than to *demonstrate* that James was taking wisdom as his central theme.

the verb (first option) one has to admit that the second prepositional phrase, because it comes after "works," already includes the notion of works. Thus, the rhetoric is more consecutive and cumulative (second option) than the syntax is technically analytical. James builds from "show" to "on the basis of the good life" to "works" and then, after this, to "in the meekness of wisdom."

James, in solid Jewish tradition,[153] informs the teachers that they are to show their good works "with gentleness born of wisdom."[154] As in 1:21, where the messianic community was urged to receive the word with vulnerable receptivity, so here: the teacher is to do good works with a vulnerability, a non-aggressiveness, a non-boastful approach to life. The oddity of humility as a virtue among early Christians in the context of the Roman world, especially emphatic in Paul's letters, has been observed by many.[155] But, 'anavâ, the Hebrew term for this moral virtue, was also important to the rabbis.[156] It goes back to the classic line about Moses, who, when being criticized — and nothing could be more appropriate to the teachers in James's audience — was described in these words: "Now the man Moses was very humble, more so than anyone else on the face of the earth" (Num 12:3). And Jesus, too, was humble (Matt 11:29; 21:5; 2 Cor 10:1). The implication of this evidence is that humility or gentleness is non-retaliation in the face of criticism. Wise teachers are non-retaliatory, and teachers know full well the temptation to respond with harshness. Wisdom, then, for James has to do with both a grasp of God's will and a life that conforms to that will, and that life will not be noted

153. See Sir 3:17: τέκνον ἐν πραΰτητι τὰ ἔργα σου διέξαγε; "My child, perform your tasks with humility."

154. ἐν πραΰτητι σοφίας. On πραΰτης, see BDAG, 861; EDNT 3.146-47; TDOT 4.364-85; TLOT 1.418-24; and the many articles in DOTWPW. Also W. Bindemann, "Weisheit versus Weisheit. Der Jakobusbrief als innerkirchlichen Diskurs," ZNW (1995) 189-217; E. Borghi, "La sagesse de la vie selon l'épître de Jacques. Lignes de Lecture," NTS 52 (2006) 123-41; R. F. Chaffin Jr., "The Theme of Wisdom in the Epistle of James," ATJ 29 (1997) 23-49.

See 1 Cor 4:21; 2 Cor 10:1; Gal 5:23; 6:1; Eph 4:2; Col 3:12; 2 Tim 2:25; 1 Pet 3:16. Moo, for one, sees the genitive as a genitive of source; hence, a wisdom that produces humility (p. 170). I am more inclined to think here of something less defined, namely, a humility characteristic of wisdom (so Popkes, 246). While wisdom might produce humility, it seems more likely that wise people are humble, whether or not it is the wisdom that produces that humility. Humility, or meekness or gentleness, is the environment in which the deeds are done, and that environment is characteristic of wisdom.

155. See E. F. Osborn, Ethical Patterns in Early Christian Thought (New York: Cambridge University Press, 1978), 31-32. See The Rule of St. Benedict 7.

156. See E. B. Borowitz and F. W. Schwartz, The Jewish Moral Virtues (Philadelphia: JPS, 1999), 137-48. The theme of humility resonates throughout the study of M. Fishbane, Sacred Attunement: A Jewish Theology (Chicago: University of Chicago Press, 2008).

by the things we are about to find in 3:14-18. And it is there that we will be able to find a full understanding of what James means by "wisdom." But for now we need to observe that wisdom, as can be seen in Proverbs 1:1-7, produces in sages and leaders the following attributes: receptivity toward instruction, the moral virtues of righteousness, justice, and equity, cognitive prudence and instruction, and what can best be translated as "skill" (*tahbulot*, Prov 1:5; see also 9:7-12).

The question James asks in 3:13a is intended to open up the opportunity for him to clarify how the teachers of the messianic community are to behave. We are left with the suggestion that that wisdom and understanding are for James not simply cognitive mastery but behavioral. The climactic behavior James has in mind, as 3:18 will make abundantly clear, is a community marked by peaceableness. A simple summary of what James teaches in 3:13-18 to teachers is: a wise teacher is the one who creates godly, loving peace in the community.

6.2.3. The Problem of False Wisdom (3:14-16)

James has now asked "Who is wise?" and has, in effect, pointed to its answer ("Show by your good life . . ."). But James plays his game in the real world and knows that the messianic community is anything but a mirror of perfection. It needs concrete teaching. So he provides now an exposition of two kinds of wisdom, one from below (3:14-16) and one from above (3:17-18). James sketches the false wisdom from below first in a conditional sentence that reveals the impact it yields (3:14). Then he describes its source (3:15) and its communal impact (3:16). In short compass James unmasks much that goes wrong in churches before he expounds the "wisdom from above" (3:17).

6.2.3.1. The Impact on Truth of False Wisdom (3:14)

James may have included himself with the teachers at 3:9, but he clearly has now distanced himself from them: "But if *you*." This distance is only slightly lessened in 3:18 when, still using third person plural, James says, "for those who make peace." James uses a conditional sentence in 3:14, but it is abnormal in form since the second half (the apodosis) does not draw an inference.[157] Nonetheless, James's point is clear.

---

157. The protasis assumes that the teachers harbor bitter envy, and the implication and the apodosis find expression in these two prohibitions: "do not be boastful" and "do not be false to the truth." One might have expected the apodosis to have used the indicative mood. Thus: "If you harbor bitter envy, you then become boastful and deny the truth."

The condition James assumes, for the sake of his argument and probably also because it is the reality of the teachers in the messianic community,[158] is this: "But if you have bitter envy and selfish ambition in your hearts." The dominant words are "envy" or, what I prefer for a translation, "zeal" *(zēlos)*, and "ambition" *(eritheia)*. These two vices are rooted so deeply that James places them "in your heart." Zeal, as one knows from the ongoing development of zealotism in Judaism contemporary with James, not to mention its ongoing presence in the religious world today (and not just among radical Muslims), was prized as a form of extreme fidelity that could resort to violence and bloodshed. The term is often used to describe those who are willing to muster the courage to root out the unfaithful and cowardly. Thus, one thinks of Phinehas (Num 25:1-13; Ps 106:30), Elijah (1 Kgs 19:10, 14; Sir 48:1-2), and the Maccabees (1 Macc 2:54, 58; *4 Maccabees* 18:12).[159] That James describes "zeal" as "bitter" suggests that the teachers — at least as he portrays them — were ferocious, emotively expressive, harsh, and angry.[160] Paul applies the same term to speech in Romans 3:14: "Their mouths are full of cursing and bitterness." What the proponents here may see as fidelity and unrelenting commitment is seen by James as verbal fanaticism and ferocity with negative ends, including a domineering partisanship. However foreign it might be to the Western Christian world, we should not ignore the possible physical violence involved in this language (cf. 4:2; see also 1:20).

Their zeal is flanked by "ambition."[161] "Ambition" shows up in lists addressed to churches that are failing due to communal disruption (Gal 5:20; 2 Cor 12:20), but Paul also finds it in leaders and teachers who are bent on personal gain (Phil 1:17; 2:3). In two verses James will reveal that the leader marked by "ambition" creates disorder in the community (3:16). Laws has a notable definition of the term: "unscrupulous determination to gain one's own ends."[162] James's concern is that the teachers will anchor these two vices of zeal and ambition in the very core of their being; hence, "in your hearts" (1:26; 4:8; 5:5, 8).

And if they do anchor zeal and ambition in the core of their being, two

---

158. The present tense ἔχετε does not indicate that "having" is ongoing but that James wants to depict the having as "imperfective," that is, incomplete and ongoing.

159. M. Hengel's book remains unsurpassed; see *The Zealots* (trans. D. Smith; Edinburgh: Clark, 1989); see also W. Heard and C. A. Evans, "Revolutionary Movements, Jewish," in *DNTB*, 936-47.

160. See BDAG, 812-13, for this term and its cognates.

161. BDAG, 392. For a modern study of ambition, of much use to a preacher, see J. Epstein, *Ambition* (Chicago: Dee, 1980). One of its cousins is snobbery, on which see Epstein's *Snobbery: The American Version* (Boston: Houghton Mifflin, 2002).

162. Laws, 160.

results are inevitable. To make his point even more powerful, James turns what would have been an indicative apodosis into two prohibitions: "do not be boastful and (do not be) false to the truth."[163] That is, since zeal and ambition lead to boasting and denial of truth, James jumps ahead and simply prohibits the actions that zeal and ambition produce. Zealous, ambitious teachers, because they are concerned with their own reputation and the power that comes to those with cognitive skills, both boast (cf. Jer 9:23-24) and deny the truth. James uses a less intense form of "boast" in 4:16, but the wording reminds us of the potential these teachers could produce: "As it is, you boast in your arrogance; all such boasting is evil." It is reasonable to think that the intensive verb form at 3:14 *(kata + kauchaomai)* reveals the ambitious desire on the part of some teachers to boast over the claims of others.

James frequently ties together the cognitive and the behavioral. 3:13b was a perfect example. So also here: zealous, ambitious teachers, in their ferocity and fanaticism, deny the truth of the gospel by their behavior, reminding us that the gospel is both proclaimed and performed (see Matt 7:15-27). Proclamation without performance, which is clearly on James's mind (2:18-19), severs the truthfulness and fidelity of the gospel from its own anchors.[164] Sophie Laws suggests a narrowed meaning of "truth," namely that humility is characteristic of wisdom, which is true enough.[165] However, James uses this term two other times, and both of them are broad enough to think more in terms of the truth of the gospel (1:18; 5:19).[166]

6.2.3.2. The Source of False Wisdom (3:15)

With little preparation, James traces wisdom and its false alternative to their sources: one comes from above and one does not. The "wisdom" (so TNIV), or what Doug Moo calls "phantom wisdom,"[167] that emerges from zeal and ambition and that boasts and denies the truth "does not come down from above, but is earthly, unspiritual, devilish."[168] It might surprise that James would even call what he has just unmasked in 3:14 "wisdom," but the demonstrative "such" guides the reader/listener back to v. 14, and this leads the reader to think of the term "wisdom" in v. 15 as false wisdom, a so-called wisdom. James describes false wisdom in a classic dichotomous and rhetori-

163. Present tenses make both imperatives more vivid and graphic.
164. The prepositional phrase κατὰ τῆς ἀληθείας could modify only ψεύδεσθε, or it could modify both imperatives. One can only intuit a resolution.
165. Laws, 160.
166. See Popkes, 248.
167. Moo, 172. Popkes, 248-49: "ihr habt gar nicht begriffen, was Weisheit ist" ("you have simply not grasped what wisdom is").
168. The present tenses function well for definitions and attributions.

cally effective "not this but this" mode.[169] The first element is by way of negation: literally, "such wisdom does not come down from above." The second element attributes negative qualities to false wisdom: it "is earthly, unspiritual, devilish." False wisdom, thus, has four characteristics.

First, "does not come down from above." "Above" *(anōthen)*[170] can be a common, ordinary description of that which is above something else, as in Matthew 27:51, where the Temple's curtain is torn from "top [*anōthen*] to bottom" (also John 19:23). It can be temporal, as when Luke claims that he examined everything "from the very first [*anōthen*]" (Luke 1:3; cf. Acts 26:5). And it can mean "again" as in Galatians 4:9, "to be enslaved to them again." But James uses it three times of the heavenly or divine world (1:17; 3:15, 17). Which is to say that wisdom comes (down to earthlings) from God (Wis 7:7; 8:21; 9:4; Sir 1:1, 9; 39:6). This usage is quite like that found in John's Gospel: "no one can see the kingdom of God without being born from above" (3:3; see also 3:7) and "The one who comes from above is above all; the one who is of the earth belongs to the earth and speaks about earthly things. The one who comes from heaven is above all" (3:31).[171] There is an obvious moral dualism here: the above versus the below, the heavenly versus the earthly, the spiritual versus the unspiritual, and the divine versus the devilish. Such moral dualism make moral injunctions more forceful.

The three terms James uses next could form a crescendo.[172] But there is not that much difference among them, especially the first and the second, and a crescendo view requires fine distinctions that are beyond the evidence. The terms, as our exegesis will hope to demonstrate, describe in differing ways a life that is shaped by something other than God and God's Spirit.

Second, false wisdom is "earthly" *(epigeios)*. This word forms the negative pole of a number of early Christian binary oppositions. Thus, Jesus can ask, "If I have told you about *earthly* things and you do not believe, how can you believe if I tell you about *heavenly* things?" (John 3:12). Paul contrasts heavenly (raised) bodies and earthly bodies (1 Cor 15:40), and he clarifies that point in 2 Cor 5:1: "For we know that if the earthly tent we live in is destroyed, we have a building from God, a house not made with hands, eternal in the heavens." Earth, he also says, will be subject to Christ when he finally reigns (Phil 2:10). More like James is Phil 3:19: "Their end is destruction; their god is the belly; and their glory is in their shame; their minds are

169. There is a possible connection to the Two Ways tradition here. See especially K. Niederwimmer, *The Didache* (trans. L. M. Maloney; ed. H. W. Attridge; Hermeneia; Minneapolis: Fortress, 1998), 59-63.

170. BDAG, 92.

171. For Hebrew *lamin*, see, e.g., 1QH[a] 15:24; 1Q22 frag. 1 2:10; 4Q254 frag. 7:4; 4Q377 frag. 2 2:7; 4Q393 frag. 3:6; 4Q403 frag. 1 1:33, 44; 4Q404 frag. 5:2.

172. Dibelius, 210; similarly, Johnson, 272; Popkes, 249.

set on earthly things." James's term fits in, though not exactly, with Paul's potent contrast of spirit and flesh (e.g., Gal 3:3; 4:13, 21-31; 5:13-26). While an element of the physical inheres to this term, it evokes a *moral* category more than a physical, astronomic category.

Third, false wisdom is "unspiritual" *(psychikē).*[173] Here the similarity to Paul is even stronger. This term, a favorite in the earliest churches, is contrasted with *pneumatikos,* "spiritual." The *psychikos* person is one who is devoid of God's Spirit (e.g., 1 Cor 2:14; 15:44, 46; Jude 19). In the Greco-Roman world this term is connected to and contrasted with the body as its animating life, its soul (e.g., *4 Maccabees* 1:32). And Philo sees two sorts of humans, those who are characterized by *logos* and those characterized by *psychē (Creation* 134-35).[174] While "unspiritual" often takes on metaphysical connotations in the Greco-Roman world[175] and finds special connotations in the Platonic movement, which leads eventually to full-blown Gnosticism, we do well here to stick to the connotations James gives it. And James's issues are overwhelmingly shaped by moral and wisdom traditions and not metaphysical traditions.[176] It is important to see that James 3:13-18 is fundamentally concerned with behavioral and not speculative metaphysical categories, and vv. 16-18 will make the point clear.

Fourth, false wisdom is "devilish." That is, false wisdom *derives from* the infernal, lower spirit-world or is *like* that world.[177] The language is strong because the rhetoric is necessary: the divisiveness of the teachers who misuse the tongue for zeal and ambition destroys the fabric of God's messianic community, and that can only come from that which is not God. We need to connect this term back to 3:6, where James tied the teacher's misuse of the tongue to Gehenna. We might also connect it to 4:7: "Submit yourselves therefore to God. Resist the devil, and he will flee from you." Some trade in simplicities and connect everything — flat tires and missed appointments — to either God's will or the kingdom of darkness. James, however, is neck-deep in a pastoral problem of immense proportions. Those who are designed to follow Jesus, to live a life of loving God and others, and to live out the will of God are being fractured into bits by teachers who abuse their authority, seek to establish their reputations, and frame everything so as to enlarge their own borders, and James knows that the messianic community is at a crossroads. Either it gets back on track or it will disintegrate into ineffective witness and missed

173. BDAG, 1100; *EDNT* 3.500-503.
174. See Popkes, 249-50.
175. See Dibelius, 211-12.
176. Popkes, 250.
177. The word is unusual enough to prevent confidence in either option, though the emphasis in the text on "from above" suggests origins.

opportunity. The options are two: either the teachers pursue a wisdom that comes from God (see 3:17-18), or they continue on their reckless, destructive path, which comes from Gehenna and the evil spirit-world.[178] Such a spirit-world distorts human community and institutionalizes injustices.

False wisdom, in short, does not come from God; that is, instead of deriving from the heavenly, it derives from the earth; instead of abounding in God's Spirit, it is unspiritual; and instead of coming from God's Spirit, it derives from evil spirits. Assigning people and their motives and actions to either God or the evil one is sometimes called "attribution theory,"[179] and some no doubt are far more confident than accurate in their judgments. Nonetheless, James's attributions here are rooted in concrete, observable behaviors in the community on the part of teachers, and his judgment is on target. The next verse opens the lid onto the cauldron of sin stoked by the teachers, which James has now successfully labeled.

6.2.3.3. The Communal Impact of False Wisdom (3:16)

With explicative *gar* James ties false wisdom even more tightly now to the zeal and ambition of the teachers, and he focuses his attention on the communal impact of the teachers' false wisdom. He begins with "For where there is envy and selfish ambition" (3:16) and then unveils what happens when zeal and ambition are set loose in a community: "there will also be disorder and wickedness of every kind."

The "envy," or "zeal," and "ambition" on the part of the teachers recalls 3:14, but the concrete manifestations of that zeal and ambition are not named until 4:1: "Those conflicts and disputes among you, where do they come from? Do they not come from your cravings that are at war within you?"[180] We perhaps need a reminder: paragraph and chapter divisions might prevent contemporary readers from keeping all of 3:1–4:12 in mind as one

178. On the cosmology, see the exceptional studies of G. Twelftree, *Jesus the Exorcist* (Peabody: Hendrickson, n.d. [= 1993]); *Jesus the Miracle Worker* (Downers Grove: InterVarsity, 1999), 281-92; *In the Name of Jesus* (Grand Rapids: Baker, 2007). The exploration of the cosmology of demons and the spirit world as socio-political is not without merit in this case; see W. Wink, *Naming the Powers* (Philadelphia: Fortress, 1984); *Unmasking the Powers* (Philadelphia: Fortress, 1986); *Engaging the Powers* (Minneapolis: Fortress, 1992).

179. See W. Proudfoot and P. Shaver, "Attribution Theory and the Psychology of Religion," *JSSR* 14 (1975) 317-30; B. Spilka, P. Shaver, and L. A. Kirkpatrick, "A General Attribution Theory for the Psychology of Religion," *JSSR* 24 (1985) 1-20.

180. Jesus' language in Luke 21:9 connects wars (cf. Jas 4:1) and chaos (3:16). 2 Cor 12:20's listing of communal divisiveness shows a parallel phenomenon in the Pauline churches.

explores each term and line within this section. 4:1 may begin a new chapter in our Bibles, but it did not begin a new section in the mind of James. Once again, the zeal and ambition of community leaders produce two problems: "disorder" and "wickedness." Disorder, a community problem in 3:16, can be an individual's problem (1:8) or the result of misuse of the tongue (3:8). James still has the teachers in focus:[181] their abusive language turns the community into *chaos*. God, Paul writes (and James would agree), is not the author of chaos (1 Cor 14:33). Not only do zeal and ambition crack the infrastructures of a community, but they also produce "wickedness of every kind."[182] The word for "wickedness" *(phaulon)* is used in John 5:29 to designate those who will go to the "resurrection of condemnation" (see 3:20), and that same term forms a contrast for Paul with what is "good" (see Rom 9:11; 2 Cor 5:10).[183] It can identify both what we "do" and what we "say" (John 3:20; Tit 2:8). Here in James there is a deliberate generalization of moral wickedness, and it is unwise to narrow "wickedness" to one specific sin, say, unjust treatment of the poor, public speaking, or lawsuits against one another.[184] Rather, those are specific instances of a more general "wickedness." Zeal and ambition break loose moral anchors, on the part of teachers, their followers, and their opponents, so that control and dominance become the guiding lights.

6.2.4. The Potential of True Wisdom (3:17-18)

James now offers a positive sketch of wisdom or its manifestations. This is the kind of wisdom the teachers need to possess or be characterized by. Like Jesus' beatitudes (Luke 6:20-26), which are also split into positive and negative groups, and Paul's listing of deeds of the flesh and works of the Spirit (Gal 5:19-23) or traits of the kingdom of God (Rom 14:17), so James has a list of seven attributes of wisdom "from above" (James 3:17). Paul emphasizes Spirit-produced virtues while James focuses on Wisdom-produced virtues.[185] He closes this section off with a potent observation about peace, in which community peace is uppermost in his mind (3:18).

James's list varies from but reminds one of the list of wisdom's attributes in Wisdom 7:22-23:

181. A point made in Moo, 174.
182. πᾶν φαῦλον πρᾶγμα, or "every kind of foul deed."
183. BDAG, 1050-51.
184. Johnson, 273, only suggests lawsuits by connecting πρᾶγμα here with the lawsuits in 1 Cor 6:1 and Jas 2:6. See Davids, 153; Popkes, 252.
185. See J. A. Kirk, "The Meaning of Wisdom in James: Examination of a Hypothesis," *NTS* 16 (1970) 24-38; see also the sketch in J. D. G. Dunn, *Christology in the Making* (2d ed.; London: SCM, 1989), 168-76.

309

[W]isdom, the fashioner of all things, taught me. There is in her a spirit that is intelligent, holy, unique, manifold, subtle, mobile, clear, unpolluted, distinct, invulnerable, loving the good, keen, irresistible, beneficent, humane, steadfast, sure, free from anxiety, all-powerful, overseeing all, and penetrating through all spirits that are intelligent, pure, and altogether subtle.

Wisdom transcends cognitive mastery of facts and information. It is skill in living according to God's moral order, and the wise learn that skill through special scriptural revelation, personal experience of God, natural revelation, the traditions of their ancestors, and observation of both humans and nature. Furthermore, the wise person is skilled in discernment and judgment, rendering not only intelligent but godly decisions.[186] The wise person lives in God's world in God's way with God's people and so enjoys the blessing of the only wise God.[187] The true wisdom about which James speaks is from "above," that is, from God. Thus, "For the LORD gives wisdom" (Prov 2:6) or, when Wisdom is personified, it is emphasized that God created her (see also Sir 1:4), even if her wisdom helped to shape creation (Prov 8:22-31; Wis 9:9-18). Surely one of the more graphic and memorable scenes in the Bible can be found in Proverbs 8:30-31, where Wisdom is depicted as God's loving and loved companion when God created:

I [Wisdom] was beside him, like a master worker;
and I was daily his delight, rejoicing before him always,
rejoicing in his inhabited world and delighting in the human race.

There is more to this story of the history of wisdom. Wisdom, Sirach tells us, "sought a resting place."

Then the Creator of all things gave me a command,
and my Creator chose the place for my tent.
He said, "Make your dwelling in Jacob,
and in Israel receive your inheritance" (Sir 24:7-8).

Students of Jewish history know that for many wisdom must be connected to Torah so that Torah observance is wisdom.[188] So, when James says that wis-

186. See notes at 1:5-8 and 3:13 above. Also, cf. E. C. Lucas, "Wisdom Theology," in *DOTWPW,* 901-12.
187. The principal texts include Prov 8; Wis 7; 1QS 4; Luke 6:20-26; Gal 5:16-24; 1 Cor 13:4-6; and Col 3:12-17.
188. An older discussion can be found in S. Schechter, *Aspects of Rabbinic Theology* (Woodstock: Jewish Lights, 1993), 127-37; Collins, *Jewish Wisdom in the Hellenistic Age,* 42-61 (see note 148 above).

dom is "from above" he means more than "in the heavens" as if he were simply describing the heavenly origin of true wisdom. And it is more than a *place* the individual goes to in order to meet his or her needs. Instead, there is here in James 3:17 an almost certain allusion to the personification of Wisdom who, once created and then consulted in God's creation of the universe, was sent to dwell among humans.

While it might be instinctual for Christian theologians to wonder if James might also be alluding to Christ,[189] it is far more likely that James would have Torah and Spirit allusions in mind.[190] Judaism connected Spirit to wisdom in well-known charismatic individuals. In Genesis 41:38-39 Pharaoh observes the profundity of Joseph's wisdom and the presence of God's Spirit in him. The same connection is found in Bezalel, who combines wisdom and the presence of the Spirit in his capacity to make vessels for the tabernacle (Exod 31:1-11). Joshua is filled with the "spirit of wisdom" (Deut 34:9). Wisdom says, "Therefore I prayed, and understanding was given me; I called on God, and the spirit of wisdom came to me" (7:7), and one cannot help connecting this to James 1:5. Finally, in Jesus we find wisdom and Spirit connected, both as anticipated in Isaiah's prophecy (Isa 11:2) and in Jesus' straightforward statements (Luke 4:18-19). We might be tempted to ask why James does not speak of a more Pentecost-shaped Spirit theology, as we find in Luke-Acts, or a more ecclesial-shaped Spirit theology, as found in Paul's writings, but we should remember that James was himself working out both a christology and a pneumatology in his own *sophia*-shaped terms. Whether he is responding to Paul is unclear. In light of the evidence sketched above, the wisdom theology of James 3:17-18 is also a Spirit theology.

3:17   James proceeds to give seven attributes of wisdom.[191] Many observe — and it should not go unmentioned — that this is not a simple list

---

189. Christological overtones to wisdom abound in early Christian literature, but almost certainly not here. In general, see Hurtado, *Lord Jesus Christ;* Dunn, *Christology in the Making,* 163-212 (see note 185 above).

190. See Davids, 152; further at J. R. Levison, *The Spirit in First-Century Judaism* (Boston: Brill, 2002).

191. James begins with μὲν, but there is no corresponding δέ; see BDF, §447.2, 3; see also the German edition, F. Rehkopf, *Grammatik des neutestamentlichen Griechisch* (15th ed.; Göttingen: Vandenhoeck und Ruprecht, 1979), §447.2. James has both πρῶτον and ἔπειτα, and he uses some alliteration. After ἁγνή, which itself does not fit any pattern, the next four attributes of true wisdom begin with ε, and the last two begin with α. The first two end with η, the next two with -ης, and the last two with -ος. But ἐλέους does not fit any patterns and makes one wonder if the many observations about alliteration and symmetry are the result of chance instead of intention. Seeing the positive characteristics as strict antonyms to the attributes of false wisdom usually reveals more of the ingenuity of the commentator than the evidence permits.

of virtues but also a rhetoric that is shaped by James to form an alternative community.[192]

True wisdom is "first pure."[193] That is, it has no defects, like a pure sacrifice or a pure virgin (2 Cor 11:2) or a sinless person (1 Tim 5:22) who, through the witness of living, speaks the gospel (1 Pet 3:2). Ultimately, purity is a mark of Christ and of those in union with him (1 John 3:3) because God and his words and promises are pure (Ps 12:6). One text in Proverbs could suggest that "pure" is also connected to the kinds of words the teachers are to use: "gracious words are pure" (Prov 15:26). In this context, one thinks also of Wisdom 7:24-27:

> For wisdom is more mobile than any motion;
> because of her pureness she pervades and penetrates all things.
> For she is a breath of the power of God,
> and a pure emanation of the glory of the Almighty;
> therefore nothing defiled gains entrance into her.
> For she is a reflection of eternal light,
> a spotless mirror of the working of God,
> and an image of his goodness.
> Although she is but one, she can do all things,
> and while remaining in herself, she renews all things;
> in every generation she passes into holy souls
> and makes them friends of God, and prophets.

Thus, Lockett's definition summarizes the evidence well: "'wisdom from above' is free from moral pollution and, therefore, entails total sincerity and devotion."[194]

Second, true wisdom is "peaceable."[195] This term dare not be reduced

192. See here Aymer, *First Pure, Then Peaceable,* 30-52, who expounds the use Frederick Douglass made of this text as a way to "build a home."

193. ἀγνή; BDAG, 13; see also *GEL,* §88, especially §88.24-35, where the various words for holy and pure are mapped. A full study can be seen in Lockett, *Purity and Worldview;* see here pp. 126-30. It is difficult to know what to make of πρῶτον, since it would be easy to make too much — as if one must begin here in a chain of connections. Inasmuch as James will let the passage focus on peacemaking and he lists that attribute of wisdom only second, it is wise to see "first" as "first in this list I am about to give" instead of "first in importance" or "first logically" or "first theologically." A similar use of a ranking term is found at 5:12. But see Moo, 175; Popkes, 253; Lockett, *Purity and Worldview,* 128.

194. Lockett, *Purity and Worldview,* 128. He classifies the use here as figurative, trading in the concepts of social and ideological location.

195. ἔπειτα εἰρηνική; BDAG, 288. The term evokes the marvelous Israelite tradition of shalom; on which, see *TDOT* 15.13-49; *TLOT* 2.1337-48; P. B. Yoder, *Shalom: The Bible's Word for Salvation, Justice, and Peace* (Newton: Faith and Life, 1987). A recent

to the feeling of peace one has with God; instead, it must be expanded to biblical proportions: *shalom* describes God's designs for the relationship of humans with God, self, others, and the world. The "peaceable" person, then, is not simply the tranquil person at rest with himself or herself, but the person who, unlike the zealous and ambitious teachers who create chaos and every kind of wickedness and who foment wars within the community, uses the tongue and gifts and behaviors to foster peace with God, self, others, and the world. Some leaders and teachers are obstreperous and slashing in their pursuits, but James proposes another model: those who both live peaceably and create peace. Thus, James's use of this term bears striking resemblance to Jesus' beatitude (Matt 5:9) and, in effect, to the community exhortations in Paul's and Peter's letters. Again, Proverbs provides the source for the kind of statement made by James: Wisdom's "ways are ways of pleasantness, and all her paths are peace" (Prov 3:17). For James, the wisdom of peace not only forms the focal conclusion to these two verses but is at the heart of everything he has in mind for Christian living (James 1:19-27), for treatment of others (2:1-12), for how teachers are to use their tongues (3:13–4:12), for how the community is to live (4:1-2), for how the rich are to relate to the poor and to others (4:13–5:6), and how believers are to care for one another (5:13-20).

Third, true wisdom is "gentle."[196] Ceslas Spicq renders this word *(epieikēs)* as "friendly equilibrium" since the sense of the word in the New Testament moves through these ideas: goodness, courtesy, mildness, benevolence, generosity, and each in view of the need to render judgment with equity. The use of this Greek term in translating the Old Testament or in texts traditionally associated with the Old Testament suggests the act of judgment (Wis 12:18) and, in that judgment, mercy, moderation, clemency, and leniency (Dan 3:42; see also Acts 24:4).[197] A good example of how this attribute arises from moral testing can be found in Wisdom 2:19: "Let us test him with insult and torture, so that we may find out how gentle he is." Plutarch shows that this term speaks to a moderation of passions in the formation of virtue: "so in the soul moral virtue is produced when equity [*epieikeia*] and moderation [*metriotētos*] are engendered by reason in the emotional faculties and activities."[198] Hence, this term brings to expression what was said earlier in James 2:13: "mercy triumphs over judgment." This wise attribute of gen-

---

study puts together biblical theology through this theme: W. M. Swartley, *Covenant of Peace: The Missing Peace in New Testament Theology and Ethics* (Grand Rapids: Eerdmans, 2006). Popkes, drawing on scholarship on the ideal ruler of the ancient world, connects these attributes to the ideal ruler and sees a Christian alternative (p. 254).

196. ἐπιεικής; BDAG, 371; Spicq, 2.34-38, whose collection of texts here I have explored and used.

197. It reminds one of μετριοπαθεῖν in Heb 5:2.

198. *On Moral Virtue* 12 (451).

tleness also evoked for Paul the example of Christ (2 Cor 10:1) and became a virtue of Christ to be imitated (Phil 4:5). Like James, Paul thought gentleness was among the top virtues for a teacher and leader in the church (1 Tim 3:3; Tit 3:2). The zealous and ambitious teacher no doubt remembers moments when his or her honor has been assaulted or called into question, and the "gentle" person will not only drop the moment from memory, learn from the situation, and strive to improve, but will also work to create peace in the community in a non-combative manner. Both zeal and ambition are tempered by this wise attribute.

Fourth, true wisdom is "willing to yield,"[199] an inelegant translation of the compound *eupeithēs* (*eu,* "good, well," + *peithō,* "persuade"). I prefer "compliant," "persuadable," "conciliatory," or even "obedient" and "willingly conforming." James still has the teachers in mind: they must be teachable and persuadable and capable of letting evidence and arguments carry the day; they must know when to hold firm and when to adjust. One gains the impression from 3:1–4:12 that teachers in the messianic community were hotheads who generated more heat than light, more partisanship than harmony, more debate than conversation.[200] The wise teacher, because he or she knows mental and moral limitations, nurtures a willingness to listen and to change. For this reason, pastors and teachers do well to have someone to whom they are accountable, whether it be another pastor, an administrative leader, or a spiritual director.

Fifth, true wisdom is "full of mercy and good fruits."[201] James combines two attributes to form one idea. As Jesus said the Pharisees were "full of hypocrisy and lawlessness" (Matt 23:28), as Paul can say idolaters were "filled with every kind of wickedness" (Rom 1:29), and as James can say the tongue is "full of poison" (3:8), so James urges the teachers to be "full of mercy and good fruits" (3:17) and Paul wants the Roman Christians to be "full of goodness" (Rom 15:14). It is likely that "mercy" (Jas 1:8, 22, 27; 2:13, 15, 16) and "good fruits" are pointing at the same thing: the good works James speaks of are shown to those in need (1:26-27; 2:2-4, 14-17; 5:1-6).

---

199. εὐπειθής; BDAG, 410; Spicq, 2.129-30; *New Docs* 4.152. Josephus uses the term for obedient soldiers; cf. *War* 2.577. Its antonym is rebelliousness and not listening; see Acts 26:19; Rom 1:30. Popkes prefers, instead of the passive sense of being persuadable, a more active sense of being properly persuasive (p. 255). The evidence, some of which has been cited, is nearly all in the favor of a passive sense.

200. Ideals in history remain the famous academies of Greece and Rome; also, for a secular but highly suggestive example, one thinks of the (often idealized) French salon; on which, see Benedetta Craveri, *The Age of Conversation* (trans. T. Waugh; New York: New York Review Books, 2005).

201. μεστὴ ἐλέους καὶ καρπῶν ἀγαθῶν. The adjective μεστός, -ή, -όν is used with the genitive of that which is full.

Both "mercy" and "good fruits" are shaped by the Jesus Creed's "love your neighbor as yourself" (2:8-13).

Sixth, true wisdom is "without a trace of partiality,"[202] which is a fulsome translation of a single Greek word: *adiakritos,* "impartial" or "non-judgmental." In 3:1–4:12 partisanship appears as that which the zeal and ambition of loose-tongued teachers have generated. Furthermore, partiality toward the rich and against the poor and marginalized has evidently given some shape to the messianic community (1:19-21, 26-27; 2:1-13, 14-17; 5:1-6). "Impartiality" also needs to be connected to 2:12-13 and 4:11-12, where a rampant verbal partisanship and judgmentalism seem to have been set loose.[203] James does not say this, but it is worth suggesting that the partiality of the teachers creates an environment in which the community becomes characterized by the vices of its leaders.

Seventh, true wisdom is "without hypocrisy."[204] In the New Testament this term *(anypokritos)* characterizes love (Rom 12:9; 2 Cor 6:6; 1 Pet 1:22) and faith (1 Tim 1:5; 2 Tim 1:5). But, it is unwise to transport these connotations to James without evidence, and the evidence in James 3:1–4:12 does not explicitly or directly deal with love or faith. Standing on its own, the virtue of being unhypocritical recalls Jesus' potent vituperations toward the Pharisees and scribes, leaders of Israel, in Matthew 23. There "hypocrite" cannot be reduced to the contradiction between one's claims and one's behavior. Jesus excoriates the leaders not only for their behaviors but also for their false leadership.[205] The similarities to James 3 are worth exploring, and the following jump from the surface: a contradiction of teaching and practice (Matt 23:2-5), desire for honor, power, and reputation (23:6-12), zeal to gain personal disciples (23:13, 15), casuistic teaching (23:16-22), neglect of macro-ethics in pursuit of micro-ethics (23:23-24), neglect of interior virtue (23:25-28), and proud dissociation from corporate guilt (23:29-33). Furthermore, some noteworthy themes can be connected from Matthew 23 to James: the desire to be called "teacher" (Jas 3:1-2; Matt 23:6-10), the need for humility before God (Jas 4:6-7; Matt 23:11-12), swearing (Jas 5:12; Matt 23:16-22), neglect of justice and mercy (Jas 1:26-27; 2:1-17; 5:1-6; Matt 23:23-24), and (possibly) the use of violence (Jas 1:19-21; 4:2; Matt 23:29-36). We conclude that with the

---

202. ἀδιάκριτος. See BDAG, 19. A similar word, with the α-privitive, is used in Jas 1:6, where it means doubting or wavering. Davids, 154-55, lists four possible meanings: impartial, unwavering, non-partisan, or simple. Impartial and non-partisan are virtual synonyms, while the more moral "unwavering" and "simple" struggle to find a context in 3:1–4:12. But see Johnson, 274-75.

203. See Popkes, 256.

204. ἀνυπόκριτος; BDAG, 91.

205. On this, see D. E. Garland, *The Intention of Matthew 23* (NovTSup 52; Leiden: Brill, 1979), especially 91-123.

term "without hypocrisy" James may have in mind more than conscious pretense; instead, he may see in this term a charge of a zeal and ambition that lead to false teaching, inappropriate behaviors, and partisanship.

3:18 In contrast[206] to the negative side of the attributes of true wisdom, James now turns to his desired end for teachers who are characterized by true wisdom: they pursue peace in peaceful ways.[207] James could have quoted Jesus and the effect would have been the same: "Blessed are the peacemakers" (Matt 5:9). Even if James does not use "peace" often, a careful reading of his letter shows that peace in the community is a primary aim of the whole letter. This verse, because its opening words ("a harvest of righteousness") are the least clear in the sentence,[208] might best be interpreted by proceeding from its end back to its beginning.

James is concerned with those who characteristically (so the present tense) "make peace."[209] He has his doubts about whether the teachers and leaders of the messianic community really do seek peace, but his rhetoric assumes that this is the goal of one who is committed to true wisdom. In fact, the language James uses suggests that the teachers are *not* seeking peace: they are creating "conflicts and disputes" (4:1). As observed above in our comments on 3:17, "peace" (Hebrew *shalom*) is God's design for humans

206. Taking δὲ as an adversative. Many see here a detached logion; thus Dibelius, 214; Martin, 135; Moo, 177. This may be an accurate historical guess, but one methodological factor deserves consideration: the reason scholars infer detachment is that the line does not appear to fit the context as well as one might expect. It might also be considered that our judgment of what fits the context might not be what James thought fit. After all, that someone (like James) thought it "fit" here might be a clue that it does fit here.

207. See Baker, *Personal Speech-Ethics,* 139-76 (for background and a brief exegesis of 3:18); Swartley, *Covenant of Peace,* 259-62 (see note 195 above). See also the sketch by N. Wolterstorff, which can be applied in a variety of contexts, "Teaching for Shalom: On the Goal of Christian Collegiate Education," in *Educating for Shalom* (Grand Rapids: Eerdmans, 2004), 10-26.

208. The verb σπείρεται is passive, which renders the subject into the object of the action of the verb; further, the dative of agency or means (τοῖς ποιοῦσιν εἰρήνην) becomes the subject of the action. Some see the dative as a dative of advantage; Martin, 135. The TNIV's "Peacemakers" as the translation for the entire dative phrase seems to assume a "by" instead of "for." What strengthens the dative of means here is that James is laying responsibility on the leaders and teachers to use their tongues and gifts to produce peace. This seems to be acknowledged in all commentaries. The duplication of "peace" in 3:18 makes confidence in this matter difficult. Had James skipped from "harvest of righteousness" to "for those who make peace," the dative of advantage would be obvious. It is the addition of "is sown in peace," which mostly likely refers to the teachers themselves and those who "make peace," that makes the dative of means more likely. So Johnson, 275; see Popkes, 257-58.

209. James uses the term εἰρήνη only here and, less directly, in 2:16. A cognate is found, importantly, at 3:17 in "peaceable."

and this world as humans relate to God, self, others, and the world around them. In this instance, James's primary focus is on relationships among members of the messianic community, relationships now in jeopardy because of the zeal and ambition of its teachers and the unjust practices of the community (2:2-4; 5:1-6).

The emphasis of James is found in the heart of this verse and in the words "is sown[210] in peace." Those who "make peace" "sow in peace"; that is, they do everything in a way that is peaceable (3:17) and that creates peace in the community. They know that "anger does not produce God's righteousness" (1:20). What they sow is a "harvest of righteousness."[211] "Harvest" translates Greek *karpos,* which is normally translated "fruit," as in 3:17. While "harvest" and "fruit" are both the "yield" of a seed's maturation, the latter term is our preference. Proverbs 11:30 has a near parallel: "The fruit of the righteous is a tree of life." Proverbs uses "fruit" for words and speech (Prov 13:2; 18:20). Closer to James, however, is Isaiah 27:9:

> Therefore by this the guilt of Jacob will be expiated,
>   and this will be *the full fruit of* the removal of his sin:
> when he makes all the stones of the altars
>   like chalkstones crushed to pieces,
>   no sacred poles or incense altars will remain standing.

And Amos 6:12:

> Do horses run on rocks?
>   Does one plow the sea with oxen?
> But you have turned justice into poison
>   and the fruit of righteousness into wormwood.

In Amos "fruit of *righteousness*" is parallel to "justice." Finally, Hebrews 12:11 informs us that discipline "yields the peaceful fruit of righteousness."

---

210. The present tense is not used to describe someone or something going on as James writes, but to sketch before the reader's eyes a vivid image of action that is not yet completed.

211. καρπὸς δὲ δικαιοσύνης. The anarthrous state of each noun serves to emphasize quality rather than specificity, as if one fruit is in mind. The genitive δικαιοσύνης is most likely epexegetical ("the fruit that is righteousness") instead of source ("the fruit that emerges from righteousness"). Source can be seen in such expressions as "fruit of" the trees (Gen 3:2), the ground (4:3), the womb (30:2), labor (Exod 23:16; Ps 104:13), and the vine (Mark 14:25). A thick example is Deut 28:11. A more metaphorical example can be found at Prov 1:31 in "the fruit of their way" or at Eph 5:9 where we read "the fruit of the light." Furthermore, righteousness and peace are sometimes connected, as in Ps 85:10. See Davids, 155.

It is far too easy to think of "righteousness" in Pauline terms or to make it a matter of personal morality and holiness. For James and his Jewish world of thought, "righteous" described the person whose behaviors and life were in conformity with Torah. What James has in mind in this metaphorical expression is the yield of acting rightly, namely, concrete acts of justice. Also, even the need for leaders to render judgment in the community must be done peacefully and peaceably by those who pursue peace. James has turned his attention on the teachers' words, verbal judgments, and behaviors. His point is that such acts must be done, as 2:13 clearly stated, with mercy and gentleness and with a view to creating peace in the messianic community. Isaiah 32:17 said it well, and James 3:18 could be taken as a midrash on this verse:

> The effect of righteousness will be peace,
>   and the result of righteousness, quietness and trust forever.

6.3. TEACHERS AND DISSENSIONS (4:1-10)

1*Those conflicts and disputes among you, where*[212] *do they come from?*[a] *Do they not come from your cravings*[b] *that are at war*[c] *within you?* 2*You want something and do not have it; so you commit murder.*[d] *And you covet something and cannot obtain it;*[e] *so you engage in disputes and conflicts.*[f] *You*[213] *do not have, because you do not ask*[g].[214] 3*You ask and do not receive, because you ask wrongly,*[h] *in order to spend what you get on your pleasures.*

4*Adulterers!*[i][215] *Do you not know that friendship with the world*

212. With no difference in meaning discernible, many manuscripts and versions omit the second use of πόθεν in 4:1 (88, 218, 322, 323, etc.).

213. The majority of manuscripts add καί to this clause. This addition is part of the segmentation issue discussed in note 214 below.

214. The segmentation of 4:2 is difficult. It can be rendered, roughly, in one of two ways:

1. Tandem: "You want something and do not have it — so you commit murder. You covet something and cannot obtain it — so you engage in disputes and conflicts." So NRSV and TNIV, though with variations in wording.

2. Triple: "You want something and do not have it. You murder and you covet something and cannot obtain it. You engage in disputes and conflicts." So NIV.

215. Most manuscripts changed μοιχαλίδες to μοιχοι και μοιχαλίδες, and most think the addition occurred because the biblical image for Israel's unfaithfulness was not perceived; see Omanson, 475. The text of Nestle-Aland[27] is supported in P100 (see Elliott, "Five New Papyri"; P100 = P. Oxy. 4449) as well as ℵ, A, B, 33, etc. A copyist of ℵ added

is enmity[216] with God? Therefore whoever wishes to be a friend of the world[217] becomes an enemy of God. 5Or do you suppose that it is for nothing[j] that the scripture says, "God yearns jealously for the spirit that he has made to dwell[218] in us"? 6But he gives all the more grace; therefore it says,[k] "God[219] opposes the proud, but gives grace to the humble.[l]"

7Submit yourselves therefore[220] to God. Resist the devil, and he will flee from you. 8Draw[m] near to God, and he will draw[m] near to you. Cleanse[n] your hands, you sinners, and purify your hearts, you double-minded. 9Lament and mourn and weep.[o] Let your laughter be turned[p][221] into mourning and your joy into dejection.[q] 10Humble yourselves before the Lord,[222] and he will exalt you.[r]

a. TNIV: What causes fights and quarrels among you?

b. TNIV: desires

c. TNIV: battle

d. TNIV: kill

e. TNIV: cannot get what you want

f. TNIV: so you quarrel and fight

---

two words, and manuscript after manuscript followed suit (e.g., P, Y, 5, etc., including some Syriac, Georgian, and Slavonic manuscripts). Nestle-Aland[27] prints the shorter and more original reading.

216. Some manuscripts (104, 181, 307, 424, etc.) read the adjective (ἐχθρά) instead of the noun (ἔχθρα), but Ropes is right in suggesting that the noun is required for grammatical balance (p. 261).

217. The manuscript tradition is all over the map, with no clear consensus on ἐὰν (Nestle-Aland[27]) or αν, but the meaning is unchanged.

218. The manuscripts are divided: either κατῴκισεν (from κατοικίζειν; Nestle-Aland[27]; cf. P74, ℵ, B, Y, and many others) or κατῴκησεν (from κατοικεῖν; P, 5, 33, 69, 88, 322, 323, and many more). The former, meaning "to cause to dwell," being more unusual, is probably original; the meaning is slightly affected — shifting from "dwell" to "placed to dwell."

219. In conformity with the Old Testament text itself (Prov 3:34), some manuscripts change "God" to "Lord."

220. Whether the inferential οὖν is original (Nestle-Aland[27]) or not (some manuscripts), the inference is nonetheless drawn and at least implicit; the same can be said of the adversative δὲ with the sentence beginning with "Resist" (ἀντίστητε δὲ), for some manuscripts omit the adversative.

221. The verb μετατρέπω, found in many good manuscripts, which is more unusual and more difficult (Nestle-Aland[27]; P100, B, etc.), is changed to μεταστραφητω in many manuscripts, including ℵ, A, Y, 5, 33, etc.).

222. Some manuscripts add the article (του κυριου, including P100, 5, 69, etc.), while others turn "Lord" to "God" (945, 999, etc.). The more original reading is the widespread anarthrous κυρίου.

g. TNIV: adds "God"

h. TNIV: wrong motives

i. TNIV: You adulterous people

j. TNIV: without reason

k. TNIV: That is why Scripture says

l. TNIV: but shows favor to the humble and oppressed

m. TNIV: come

n. TNIV: Wash

o. TNIV: Grieve, mourn and wail.

p. TNIV: Change your laughter to

q. TNIV: gloom

r. TNIV: lift you up

James has not changed the focus of his attention since 3:1; he is concerned with teachers, their tongues, and the communal destructiveness they are generating.[223] If 3:1-2 was direct and most of 3:3-12 indirect and metaphorical, and if 3:13-18 explored the problems the teachers were creating by comparing false and true wisdom, then 4:1-10 is doubly so: the language is direct and the accusations are direct. To make it clear, he changes from third person to second person.

The connection with 3:1-12 and 13-18, is material and substantive rather than logical or progressive; that is, James keeps hammering away at the same issue: the problem with the teacher's loose tongue and its destructive powers. But now he makes one of the destructive features more explicit: we have not yet been told there were "conflicts and disputes" at work in the messianic community, though we could have inferred it from 1:19-21; 2:1-12; and 3:1-18. The teachers' loose tongues were fomenting communal chaos.[224]

This section is structured loosely, and the rhetoric mimics the tongues and their impact on the community. 4:1-10 moves forward sometimes with question-answer connections and other times with catchword connections. James begins by asking a question about the origin of the divisions at work in the community (4:1), and he answers that question with a question that assumes the answer: the origins are found in human desires (4:2), which leads James to a short exploration of desire, which leads back to the disputes and conflicts (4:2b), and this leads even further into more reflections on desires (4:3).

223. Martin, 141-44, has a good discussion of possible connections of 4:1-6 with 3:13-18 and 4:7-10.

224. Hence Johnson's contention that 4:1 follows from the word "peace" in 3:18 is not quite as simple as he suggests; see Johnson, 275. Yes, in fact, 4:1 follows out of 3:18, but also out of 3:1-12 and 3:13-18, so that 4:1-12 bears a more substantive than explicitly logical relation to what precedes.

James then suddenly turns toward the teachers and accuses them of spiritual adultery (4:4a). Their dabbling in political machinations leads him to reflect on what it means to be a true friend of God: such a person cannot be a friend of the world, which is code language for the machinations now at work in the community (4:4b). James then explores their friendship with God, seen as an intimacy now broken, by appealing to God's jealous love for friendship (4:5) and to God's open grace for those who will repent by becoming humble enough to be reunited in God's intimate friendship (4:6). Then James simply gives a series of ten commands and prohibitions (4:7-10).

6.3.1. The Origin of Division (4:1-3)

6.3.1.1. The Question (4:1a)

James opens ch. 4 as he did 3:13, with a question loaded with rhetorical force: "Those conflicts and disputes among you, where do they come from?" He will answer that question with another question, "Do they not come from your cravings that are at war within you?" This question assumes an answer of yes. The NRSV's rendering of 4:1a, while justifiable, both adds information with "those"[225] and gathers up the nouns and the questions into two separable corners.[226]

A pressing question, and one not asked often enough in the Western world, is whether James's terms "conflicts and disputes" refer to physical or verbal fights.[227] A more graphic, if less elegant, translation brings out word connections: "warring and swording." The word translated "conflicts" *(polemoi)*[228] could refer to a state of hostility or to an outright war or battle, which is the common meaning in early Christian literature (Matt 24:6; Luke 14:31; 1 Cor 14:8; Heb 11:34; Rev 9:7, 9).[229] But *polemoi* can also be meta-

---

225. There is nothing in the Greek text to indicate "those," but it does imply a backward glance at 3:13-18, or perhaps all of 3:1-18, where we encountered an implied presence of conflict.

226. James attaches the question to each noun: Πόθεν πόλεμοι καὶ πόθεν μάχαι ἐν ὑμῖν. The interrogative adverb πόθεν asks about source, origin, and place: hence the older English "whence?" or the German "Woher?"

227. Johnson explains all of 4:1-3 out of the rhetorical context, especially from the topos on envy. This is fine if James wants to trade in generalities. What is not examined sufficiently is how often "envy" (whether *zēlos* or *phthonos*) is tied also to committing murder. See Johnson, 276. See also M. J. Townsend, "James 4:1-4: A Warning against Zealotry?" *Expository Times* 87 (1976) 211-13.

228. πόλεμοι. See BDAG, 844.

229. Luke 21:9 connects *polemos* with a word found in Jas 3:16: "disorder" *(akatastasia)*.

phorical.[230] Furthermore, the second word, "disputes" *(machai)*,[231] can have the same flexible meaning: either physical or metaphorical battles. The New Testament evidence supports a metaphorical meaning (2 Cor 7:5; 2 Tim 2:23; Tit 3:9). Even if some might think "among you" would point toward a metaphorical meaning, that is not the case: there can be as much a physical as a metaphorical battle among those who claim attachment to Jesus. At a minimum, the expressions refer to rivalrous factions gathering around the teachers, even if we cannot be sure what they were fighting about or how they were fighting.[232] It is not at all impossible that "among you" could refer to the wider Jewish world.[233]

Religious violence, anchored as it was in both Old Testament and ancient ways, was more common to that society than most of us care to admit, and a good example is Paul's own example (Acts 8:3; 9:1-2, 21; 22:4, 19; 26:10-11; Gal 1:23). Nor has the church failed to keep the pace with ancient violence — one needs to think of the bloody battles around Nicea, Constantine, the Crusades, the Reformation, the Inquisition, and beyond.[234] I am not completely convinced that "conflicts and disputes" refers directly to physical violence, but that should remain as an open option, and v. 2 may well decide the issue. Ralph Martin speaks for this view: "Since James and his community were situated in a Zealot-infested society and since it is quite conceivable that (at least) some of the Jewish Christians were former Zealots (cf. Luke 6:15; Acts 1:13), the taking of another's life is not out of the realm of possibility for church members as a response to disagreement."[235] Physical or not, even to this day the words of James should embarrass those who are committed to a Lord who taught the way of love, the way of peace, and whose cross brought into graphic reality a new (cross) way of life.[236]

The question of 4:1a is directed at the teachers. The answer will probe deeply into their hearts.

230. See *Testament of Simeon* 4:8; *Testament of Gad* 5:1; *Pss Sol* 12:3; *1 Clement* 3:2.

231. μάχαι. See BDAG, 622.

232. Davids, 156; Popkes, 262; but see Mussner, 169, 188-89.

233. Thus, "among you" in the sense of "in the world"; see on this Laws, 172. But the second person is harder to explain in this interpretation.

234. See J. Riley-Smith, *The Crusades: A Short History* (New Haven: Yale University Press, 1987). On the first-century context, see D. Mendels, *The Rise and Fall of Jewish Nationalism* (ABRL; New York: Doubleday, 1992); M. Goodman, *The Ruling Class of Judaea* (Cambridge: Cambridge University Press, 1993).

235. Martin, 144.

236. Jesus' own words in Mark 8:31–9:1 form the foundation for that theology, but one cannot forget Paul's former zealotry that was miraculously transformed into a cruciform existence and theology; on which see especially M. J. Gorman, *Cruciformity* (Grand Rapids: Eerdmans, 2001).

6.3.1.2. The Question Answered with a Question (4:1b)

James answers this first question with a second one that implies the answer: "Do they not come from your cravings that are at war within you?" The implication is this: "Yes, in fact, the conflicts and disputes do come from our cravings."[237] James anchors the zeal and ambition that lead to conflicts and disputes in the teachers' "cravings."[238] While it is popular to utilize the etymology of "cravings" *(hēdonai)* and leap into a diatribe against hedonism in our culture, James's use needs to be seen for what it is, and there is no evidence of a hedonism in what James is addressing.[239] The teachers' "cravings" uppermost in his mind are for power, control, and partisanship. It is wise to connect James's use of *hēdonai* here with 1:14-15 and with Peter's (1 Pet 1:14; 2:11; 4:2-3) and Paul's use of the word "desires" *(epithymiai,* Rom 1:24; 6:12; 7:7-8; 13:14),[240] but there is little reason to expand the desires in random directions. James has the teachers in mind, and their problem was loose tongues used to abuse individuals and divide the community. The use of the verb "You want something" *(epithymeō)* in 4:2 secures the importance of connecting the terms "cravings" and "desires."

The "cravings" are "at war within you." Does this mean that the cravings fight for control within each person/teacher (as in Romans 7) or create war among the members of the messianic community? There is evidence on both sides, and it would exceed the evidence to render a judgment too firmly for either view. To begin with, "within you" translates *en tois melesin hymōn,* which literally would be "among your members." Inasmuch as "members" *(melos)*[241] was used in the early church for church members, and inasmuch as James clearly speaks of division among the members (2:4-7), the term could be ecclesial.[242] But an anthropological point could also be possible. After all,

237. οὐκ ἐντεῦθεν, ἐκ τῶν ἡδονῶν ὑμῶν τῶν στρατευομένων ἐν τοῖς μέλεσιν ὑμῶν. The negative οὐκ in a sentence understood to be an interrogative (there was no punctuation to tip this off) indicates an affirmation of the question asked: "Are they not from here? Yes, indeed, they are." The question οὐκ ἐντεῦθεν uses an adverb to describe an extension of something from a source (BDAG, 339), and it is entirely possible that an oral situation gave rise to this question. Thus, "Do they not come from here [gesturing toward his heart or belly]?" Grammatically, ἐκ serves to define: "Do they not come from here, *that is, from* your cravings . . . ?" The use of ἐν in the compound with ἐκ in Koine Greek of the New Testament is a difference without distinction. See MHT, 3.249-51; M. J. Harris, "Prepositions and Theology in the Greek New Testament," *NIDNTT* 3.1171-78.

238. τῶν ἡδονῶν ὑμῶν. See BDAG, 434-35.

239. In the New Testament, see Luke 8:14, where the general pursuit of a comfortable existence is in view; both Tit 3:3 and 2 Pet 2:13 could refer to baser passions.

240. See Dibelius, 215-16, nn. 40-41; Davids, 156; *contra* Laws, 168.

241. BDAG, 628.

242. Rom 12:4-5; 1 Cor 12:12-26; *1 Clement* 46:7. Perhaps Ropes, 253-54.

James knows of the divided soul (1:6-8) and the potency of human desires to overwhelm a Christian's intent to do what is right (1:13-15); furthermore, Greeks, Romans, Jews, and Christians knew of various parts of the person and fashioned various dualisms: heart, soul, mind, conscience, flesh, and body.[243] Inasmuch as James, at least in the immediate context, is less concerned with anthropology than with ecclesial division, I lean toward the ecclesial understanding of these terms.

Regardless, James's language is violent: "that are at war."[244] Nothing comments on this quite like the struggle described in Romans 7, which, even if it is the story of Israel's own experience in history under the Torah (as many today believe), still personifies or "corporatizes" the inner moral struggle to do what is good. Thus, Romans 7:21-23:

> So I find it to be a law that when I want to do what is good, evil lies close at hand. For I delight in the law of God in my inmost self, but I see in my members another law at war with the law of my mind, making me captive to the law of sin that dwells in my members.

The standard evidence for the war among us or within us favors a more individualistic, anthropological reading of these verses. Thus, Galatians 5:17: "For what the flesh desires is opposed to the Spirit, and what the Spirit desires is opposed to the flesh; for these are opposed to each other, to prevent you from doing what you want." When Peter turns to exhort his churches in his first epistle, he is on the same page as Paul: "Beloved, I urge you as aliens and exiles to abstain from the desires of the flesh that wage war against the soul" (2:11). Indeed, this is clearly an image for the individual's moral struggle, but, because of recent discussions, we should also observe that it cannot be argued that this must be Greek, even if Plato's famous lines in *Phaedo* 66c or Philo's own borrowings (*On the Decalogue* 151-53) might suggest that James is now on Greek soil. One need look no further than the Dead Sea Scrolls to find something altogether similar (1QS 3:21–4:3):

> The authority of the Angel of Darkness further extends to the corruption of all the righteous. All their sins, iniquities, shameful and rebellious deeds are at his prompting, a situation God in His mysteries allows to continue until His era dawns. Moreover, all the afflictions of the righteous, and every trial in its season, occur because of this Angel's diabolic rule. All the spirits allied with him share but a single resolve: to

---

243. On which see U. Schnelle, *The Human Condition* (trans. O. C. Dean Jr.; Minneapolis: Fortress, 1996); thus, Popkes, 263-64. A good parallel is 1 Pet 2:11.

244. τῶν στρατευομένων. The present tense (imperfective aspect) makes the battle vivid.

cause the Sons of Light to stumble. Yet the God of Israel (and the Angel of His Truth) assist all the Sons of Light. It is actually He who created the spirits of light and darkness, making them the cornerstone of every deed, their impulses the premise of every action. God's love for one spirit lasts forever. He will be pleased with its actions for always. The counsel of the other, however, He abhors, hating its every impulse for all time. Upon earth their operations are these: one enlightens a man's mind, making straight before him the paths of true righteousness and causing his heart to fear the laws of God.[245]

6.3.1.3. The Answer Explored (4:2-3)

4:2 The punctuation of 4:2 has its share of problems. As described in the note to the translation above, there are two basic options.[246] One can read this verse as containing either two parallel sentences or three separable sentences:[247]

You want something	and do not have it	so you commit murder.
You covet something	and cannot obtain it	so you engage in disputes and conflicts.

You want something and do not have it.
You murder and you covet something and cannot obtain it.
You engage in disputes and conflicts.

---

245. See also *Testament of Simeon* 3, where envy seeks to dominate.

246. The majority today interpret the text as tandem sentences; see Moo, 182-83. The piling up of present tenses here is dramatic and serves to sketch before the eyes and ears of his readers actions that are visible and palpable. While the use of presents does not necessitate an oral, homiletical background to this letter, it could indicate such.

247. Laws, who seems to find more independent paths than most, finds two sentences here: "You desire . . . you murder" and "You are jealous . . . you battle." See Laws, 172, following a lengthy discussion on 169-72. Not to be outdone, Peter Davids has cleverly discovered a possible chiastic structure (Davids, 157-58):

A. ἐπιθυμεῖτε καὶ οὐκ ἔχετε,
  B. φονεύετε καὶ ζηλοῦτε καὶ οὐ δύνασθε ἐπιτυχεῖν.
  B'. μάχεσθε καὶ πολεμεῖτε, οὐκ ἔχετε διὰ τὸ μὴ αἰτεῖσθαι ὑμᾶς.
A'. αἰτεῖτε καὶ οὐ λαμβάνετε διότι κακῶς αἰτεῖσθε, ἵνα . . .

The chiasm founders for me in "B" because I cannot see any connection of "murder" and "cannot obtain"; furthermore, the same logical disconnection occurs in B', where the opening verbs do not fit logically with the second half of the line. Furthermore, there is a natural closure in the opening verbs of B' that fits with 4:1, and this is not matched in this structural proposal. In its favor, A with A' is a nice connection.

If the Greek were clear, there would be no dispute. Still, the grammar favors the first interpretation, in which each sentence contains a positive clause and a negative clause followed by a statement of the action consequent of frustrated desire. This interpretation also makes better sense of the "commit murder" clause. The direct object "something" with both "want" and "covet" is added by the translators, and we could render the two sentences (of the first interpretation) without it: "You desire and do not have, so you commit murder. You covet and cannot obtain, so you engage in disputes."[248]

"Desire," "want" in the NRSV, is sometimes understood as referring to little more than broad urges and desires. But the logical sequence of 4:2a goes against this view. That is, the desire these teachers have is desire to put their enemies and rivals away: "so you commit murder." Many think it unthinkable that Christians could murder.[249] And the tones of 1:2-3 and 5:7-8 suggest to many that "commit murder" is metaphorical. Moo speaks for many: "Giving a word its normal meaning is a sound exegetical procedure. But sometimes the context makes the normal meaning difficult, if not impossible. We think this is the case here."[250] History, however, reminds us otherwise. We ought then to consider the evidence of 1 Peter 4:15; Acts 23:12-13 (where it is possible that some zealous Jewish Christians were involved in the plot; cf. 21:20-21); James 2:11; 5:6.[251] There is very little to suggest that these texts speak of anything but actual murder. One of the more illuminating texts in this regard is *1 Clement* 5–6, where the constant refrain is that "jealousy" (or "zeal," as in Jas 3:14, 16) on the part of some (it is not clear whether they were non-Christians or Christians) led to the martyrdom of some in the church. In my judgment, the connection of "zeal" to murder here and in James 3:14[252] deserves careful attention. *Didache* 3:2 reads "Do not become angry, for anger leads to murder" and then connects "zeal" once again to murder: "Do not be jealous or quarrelsome or hot-tempered, for all these things breed murders." Again, there is not the slightest clue that this text is speaking in metaphorical terms, for the next part is

248. The present tenses in 4:2-3 dramatize the action for the listeners; see Laws, 172.

249. This motive led to the emendation of the text from φονεύετε to φθονεύετε ("envy, jealousy"). It is found as a later emendation in 918, a sixteenth-century manuscript. Many have felt the charm of this emendation, including Erasmus, Luther, Moffatt, J. B. Phillips, J. B. Mayor, P. Chaine, and M. Dibelius. Indeed, "zeal" is often tied to "envy." Most disagree with the emendation; see Johnson, 277.

250. Moo, 183. See also Oecumenius in *ACC: James,* 45-46.

251. So Laws, 170.

252. Cf. *1 Clement* 3:4–4:13, which also connects zeal to murder in the case of Cain and Abel, and other biblical examples follow. *Testament of Gad* 4:6-7 is not altogether clear, but it appears to refer to physical death and murder.

about lust and roaming eyes leading to sexual sins.[253] Not a few commentators today are open to the possibility that murder was how some Christians "settled" disputes.[254]

On the other hand, it is not impossible that James could be using the language of Jesus, in which murder became a metaphor for hatred and abusive treatment of others (Matt 5:21-22). One can appeal to other texts, like 1 John 3:15: "All who hate a brother or sister are murderers, and you know that murderers do not have eternal life abiding in them."[255] One could read the treatment of the poor and marginalized as a form of metaphorical murder (see 1:26-27; 2:2-4).[256] This gives some a way of escaping the hook, and it seems to me that if one is looking for such an escape one can find it. However, the balance of the evidence, even if one lacks utter certitude in such matters, favors a physical reading of "commit murder." The zeal, ambition, and craving desires of the leaders of the messianic community evidently created "conflicts and disputes" (and our suggested translation above, "warring and swording," now becomes more suggestive) of such a magnitude that led them in desperation to put away their rivals. A shocking reality overcomes the reader of this text at this point. James presses on.

The second leg of this tandem, and absent of debate, reads "And you covet something and cannot obtain it; so you engage in disputes and conflicts" (4:2b). The word translated "covet" in the NRSV masks what is probably a stronger term: *zēloute* is connected to "zeal" and the ambition of 3:14, 16. A preferred translation might be "You are zealous and you cannot obtain it."[257]

---

253. See *Did* 3:1-6; the exhortations that follow in *Did* 3:7-10 resemble those of Jas 4:7-10.

254. So Martin, 146; Nystrom, 224-25.

255. Tongue is connected to death in Sir 28:17-21.

256. Moo seems to backtrack at this point: after stating that murder of one another is almost impossible and after observing that nothing in the context suggests a metaphorical rendering of "commit murder," Moo states: "Perhaps, then, the best alternative is to take 'you kill' in its normal, literal, sense, *but as a hypothetical eventuality rather than as an actual occurrence.* . . . James's readers are not yet killing each other" (p. 184, italics added). I do not see much distinction between potential real murder and actual murder, and the non-use of the subjunctive would favor actual murder having occurred. Here the use of the present would not, however, prove that murder is actually going on; what the present would show is that James wanted to *depict* murderous activity as going on before their very eyes, whether it was or not. Johnson, exploring everything here in terms of moral traditions about envy, sees murder as a logical extension in the topos of envy. His memorable line is this: "The logic of competition moves in the direction of elimination" (p. 277). It does not seem credible to me that James explored "murder" simply because the topos of envy led to it.

257. The present tenses make the actions more vivid because they are sketched as going on before the eyes of the readers and listeners.

"Zeal," as discussed already at 3:14, connotes not simply personal envy (desire for what others have) or jealousy (seeking to maintain what is one's own) but also the zeal connected to obedience of the God of the Torah, for whom nothing can be too extreme. Such zeal is often misdirected and leads to murderous attacks on others. A roughly contemporary text, *Testament of Simeon* 3, elucidates our term in a manner that might remind one of C. S. Lewis's capacity to enter into the heart of humans in *The Screwtape Letters:*

> And now, my children, pay heed to me. Beware of the spirit of deceit and *envy.* For envy dominates the whole of man's mind and does not permit him to eat or drink or to do anything good. Rather it keeps prodding him to destroy the one whom he envies. Whenever the one who is envied flourishes, the envious one languishes. . . . And I came to know that liberation from envy occurs through fear of the Lord. . . . From then on he has compassion on the one whom he envied and has sympathetic feelings with those who love him; thus his envy ceases.

So what do the teachers do? As James says to them, "you engage in disputes and conflicts." Here James repeats the very words he used in 4:1 in reverse order, thus bringing closure to his point. The problem the teachers have is "conflicts and disputes" or "warring and swording." James pushes them to consider the origins of their behaviors in their own craving desires for power and control. He pushes further and says, evidently, that their craving desires lead to murder and to the disputes and conflicts in the messianic community.

The beginning of v. 3 comes a sentence too late, leading some to think of "You do not have" (4:2c) as connected to what precedes, but it belongs with what follows it. Still, James brought up desires in 4:1b, he developed them to their darkest moments in 4:2ab, and now in 4:2c-3 he explores desires even further. Surprisingly he says, "You do not have, because you do not ask" (4:2c).[258] This then leads James to something more expected: "You ask and do not receive, because you ask wrongly, in order to spend what you get on your pleasures" (4:3).[259]

We begin with the more difficult expressions of 4:2c ("You do not have, because you do not ask"), which require both an adjustment to a new

---

258. οὐκ ἔχετε διὰ τὸ μὴ αἰτεῖσθαι ὑμᾶς. The middle of αἰτέω, so here, is probably indistinguishable from the active, found in 4:3a. See BDAG, 30; but cf. Mayor, 138, and Hort, 90-91. Mayor suggests the asking of 4:3 is uninvolved words, words without spirit, hence the active instead of the middle. Davids thinks James uses the active because the Gospels do (Davids, 160; so also Mussner, 179). Perhaps, but only perhaps. See Dibelius, 219; Moo, 185 n. 16.

259. Baker, *Personal Speech-Ethics,* 222-23.

idea on the part of James and to a new pastoral slant. We do not know what the teachers wanted, because in this context they could have it from God if they were to ask. Hence, we should not suppose that their desires were for power or for anything inappropriate. We are reminded immediately of the teaching of Jesus on prayer in Matthew 7:7: "Ask, and it will be given you" (par. Luke 11:9). James himself applies this teaching of Jesus in James 1:5-6: "If any of you is lacking in *wisdom,* ask God, who gives to all generously and ungrudgingly, and it will be given you. But ask in faith, never doubting. . . ." We should, then, think that inherent to James's point in 4:2c is the assumption that the teachers will be shamed by his words and led to a deeper desire to pursue *wisdom.* It is worth pondering why the teachers were not asking for wisdom, which is always the capacity to stop dead in one's tracks at a fork in the road and choose what is good, honorable, true, and in line with the sacred tradition. The evidence of 3:1–4:12 leads to one conclusion: they did not go to God for wisdom because they wanted what they wanted and not what God wanted. They had no capacity even to pause to consider what might be the good and honorable path. As the next verse will show, these leaders were praying. Zeal, ambition, cravings, and desires ruled their hearts and prevented them from having the very thing required of the one who grows into godly wisdom: humility. It is no surprise, then, that James will soon turn to an exhortation for the teachers to pursue humility (4:7-10).

4:3 James now turns his rhetoric around full circle:[260] "You ask and do not receive, because you ask wrongly, in order to spend what you get on your pleasures."[261] Now James assumes that they are in fact praying to God and bringing their petitions before him, but, instead of getting what they want (4:2c), they do not get what they want. The secure promise spoken by Jesus (Matt 7:7) and applied by James to wisdom (1:5-6) is now undone by the corrupt motives of the teachers.

Unanswered prayer is caused by doubt (1:6-8; cf. 5:14-15), not asking (4:2), and asking for the wrong reasons (4:3). Broadening out our scope, John will state that unanswered prayer can be laid at times at the door of disobedience (1 John 3:21-22) and the *Shepherd* will later explore the theme through the lens of double-mindedness, learned from James 1:6-8 (*Mandates*

---

260. I am not so sure that Jas 4:3 is a qualification of 4:2c, as seen in Laws, 172, and Popkes, 266, so much as a change of topics in the matter of the teachers and prayer. To see 4:3 as a modification of 4:2c is to see 4:3 erasing 4:2c, as if James were saying, "you do not ask, well, yes, you do but you ask amiss." Instead, it is more likely that we see a change in topics. In 4:2c they were not asking for wisdom, so they were not getting it; in 4:3a they are asking, but their prayer was wasted because of what they were asking for. Nor is it likely that James is addressing two different groups; see Popkes, 265 n. 288.

261. The vividness of the present tense verbs is brought to an abrupt halt in, or aims at, the aorist "spend."

9). These early Christian reflections on the reasons for unanswered prayer emerge from Old Testament reflections. Thus, Psalm 34:15-17 implies that obedience leads to answered prayer (cf. Prov 10:24); Psalm 145:18 implies that faithfulness is something that secures one's requests.[262]

The teachers' prayer request was asked "wrongly."[263] This word draws its meaning entirely from context and James virtually defines what he means by "wrongly" in the next clause. The teachers do not get what they ask because they asked "in order to spend what you get on your pleasures" (4:3b). Prayer is depicted here as capital or currency, and the teachers have spent all their requests, even if unaware of what they were doing, on the wrong thing. As L. T. Johnson puts it: "The gift-giving God is here manipulated as a kind of vending machine precisely for purposes of self-gratification."[264] The word "spend"[265] is graphic: the sick woman had "spent all she had" on doctors (Mark 5:26), the prodigal son has spent all his money (Luke 15:14), and Paul expresses the depth of his devotion and how far he will go for the Corinthians with "I will most gladly spend and be spent for you. If I love you more, am I to be loved less?" (2 Cor 12:15). The teachers have put all they had, spilled all their coins, into prayers for the wrong thing. To use James's words, they have spent their prayers *in the realm of exploring and increasing their pleasures* (dative of sphere). The preposition "in" reveals that their capital spent in prayer was "in the realm of" their cravings, pleasures, desires, zeal, and ambition. This was the world they inhabited; this was the world they sought to increase; this was the world that shaped their every thought and prayer.

Not only does "pleasure" recall the same word in 4:1, where it is translated "cravings," but it doubles the concentration on this as the problem at work in the teachers: their zeal, ambition, cravings, and desires shaped everything they taught and did. They wanted self-glory and power, not wisdom. Again, we should not expand the meaning of "pleasures" *(hēdonais)* to hedonism and all kinds of pleasure: the teachers' desires were singularly focused on control and partisanship. Their prayers, instead of being directed at gain-

262. The Mishnah has a reflection on "vain" prayers at *m Berakoth* 9:3. See the statements by Didymus the Blind, Augustine, Andreas, Pseudo-Dionysius, and Bede in *ACC: James,* 46.

263. κακῶς. BDAG, 502. It is better to translate this word generically, as in the NRSV with "wrongly," and then let 4:3b define it — which is what James does — than to articulate the meaning of the term too narrowly. Martin, 147, for instance, has "in the wrong spirit." Yes, of course, this is part of it, but James chooses a general term and then narrows it in his own definition in 4:3b.

264. Johnson, 278.

265. δαπανήσητε; see BDAG, 212. The aorist is constative: we are to see the action of spending in its totality.

ing wisdom, explored and sought to increase their own consuming zeal and ambition for power. Wise church leaders know the fine line between wanting what God wants and wanting what they want; the teachers in James's community had erased that line and were now well beyond it.

6.3.2. Accusations against the Divisive (4:4-6)

6.3.2.1. Friendship (4:4)

James now turns toward the teachers and accuses them of adultery (4:4a), and the NRSV's "Adulterers!" is not only a strong translation, but true to the original intent. The teachers' dabbling in political machinations leads James to reflect on what it means to be a true friend of God, which is that one cannot be both a friend of God and simultaneously a friend of the world (4:4b). His point seems to be that intimacy with God, which surely has a strong connection with wisdom, has been broken by this world-friendliness. James then draws in the human yearning of envy (4:5), which can be overcome by God's grace to those who are humble (4:6).[266]

In contrast to his routine use of "brothers [and sisters],"[267] James's decision to turn to the rhetorical and attention-grabbing "Adulterers!"[268] is also a labeling and shaming device,[269] not to mention something that an unbiased reader might see as in strange, contradictory conflict with the emphasis James gives to a gentle and well-behaved tongue (3:1-12). His language can be justified: he has an established relationship of trust with the messianic community; that community respects him; his language is accurate and theologically necessary. In the mouth of the wrong person, like the teachers he warns, this kind of labeling is destructive of community; in the mouth of James it is intended to preserve and build community.[270]

---

266. L. J. Prockter, "James 4.4-6: Midrash on Noah," *NTS* 35 (1989) 625-27, proposes that the verses emerge from Gen 6–9 and the desire is the evil *yetzer;* cf. LXX Gen 6:5.

267. See 1:2, 16; 2:1, 5, 14; 3:1, 10, 12; 4:11; 5:7, 9, 10, 12, 19.

268. μοιχαλίδες, a feminine vocative plural; see BDAG, 656; *EDNT* 2.436-39; J. J. Schmitt, "You Adulteresses! The Image in James 4:4," *NovT* 28 (1986) 327-37. Few have suggested that the term is literal; see Hort, 91-92, who postulates that James has broadened the audience to nonbelievers. The use of friendship and the Spirit's jealous yearning in 4:4-6 make the literal reading extremely unlikely.

269. Peter Davids perceives the tone of the shift at 4:4 well, even if the concrete suggestion he makes is harder to substantiate: "he has broken off analysis and is now preaching repentance" (Davids, 160). On labeling, see B. J. Malina and J. H. Neyrey, *Calling Jesus Names* (Sonoma: Polebridge, 1988), 8-67.

270. See M. Sawicki, "Person or Practice? Judging in James and in Paul," in Chilton and Evans, *Missions,* 385-408.

The term "adulterers" in this context has a rich and noble, if also highly evocative, history.[271] But, the rhetorically compelling nature of this theme makes it easy to overemphasize in James. Hosea was the first to speak of the covenant relationship of Israel with YHWH in terms of marital intimacy and marital infidelity (Hos 1–3; 9:1). His language was then picked up, like variations on a theme, by Isaiah (54:1-6; 57:3), Jeremiah (2:2; 3:6-14, 20), and Ezekiel (16:23-26, 38; 23:45). Both Jesus (Matt 12:39; 16:4; Mark 8:38) and the early Christians (1 Cor 6:15; 2 Cor 11:2; Eph 5:22-32; Rev 19:7; 21:9) carried on this tradition by using marital imagery for God's people and referring to disobedience as relational, covenantal infidelity. We need to be careful not to import more than James intends. Had he wanted to speak of his readers' situation as one of infidelity more than he does, he might have spoken in terms of marriage rather than friendship in 4:4-6.

The shaming continues with a rhetorical question that assumes its own answer: "Do you not know that friendship with the world is enmity with God?"[272] Early Christian writers, not the least James, formed connections with their readers by using "do you not know?" as a rhetorical device. The term can be found like this in 3:1 and seems evident in 1:19 and 4:17.[273] What the readers can be assumed to know is that "friendship with the world[274] is enmity with God." For James the "world" *(kosmos)* is something from which the messianic community is to keep itself unstained (1:27) and a place where the wealthy dwell (2:5). James's *kosmos* theology evidently shares the perspective of 1 John 2:15-17, which may well be the best commentary one might have on James's "friendship with the world":

> Do not love the world or the things in the world. The love of the Father is not in those who love the world; for all that is in the world — the desire of the flesh, the desire of the eyes, the pride in riches — comes not

271. Schmitt, "You Adulteresses!" (see note 268 above) sees an appeal to the adulterous woman in Proverbs. A debate into which we cannot enter here regards the social implication of a female label like this; see R. J. Weems, *Battered Love: Marriage, Sex, and Violence in the Hebrew Prophets* (Minneapolis: Fortress, 1995), for a strong warning.

272. The verb οἴδατε, "you know," is a perfect of the εἰδ- stem but has by the time of the New Testament become a virtual present and should be rendered along the lines of the other presents in James. The emphasis of this verb in this context is more cognitive than it is personal, that is, experiential and existential knowing. On the theme of friendship with the world versus God, see especially Johnson, *Brother of Jesus, Friend of God*, 202-20, who expounds discipleship in James through this set of categories. See also W. Popkes, "Two Interpretations of 'Justification' in the New Testament: Reflections on Galatians 2:15-21 and James 2:21-25," *ST* 59 (2005) 129-46, here pp. 135-36.

273. See also Rom 6:16; 1 Cor 3:16; 5:6; 1 Thess 3:3-4; 2 Thess 2:6.

274. Taking τοῦ κόσμου as an objective genitive. The friendship James here denounces is with the world.

from the Father but from the world. And the world and its desire are passing away, but those who do the will of God live forever.

At any rate, the thinking is the typical either-or of ethical dualism, as one finds in 2 Timothy 3:4 and in the Dead Sea Scrolls, say, in 1QS.[275]

Friendship, a value greatly discussed in the ancient world — and one cannot find a better study than that of Aristotle in *Nicomachean Ethics* 8–9 — comes into play indirectly in this text.[276] James's interest is not so much in an abstract theory of "friendship" as in that toward which the teachers' friendship is directed, namely the "world" or God. From his own world context James would have learned that friendship is much more than casual acquaintance and that genuine friends are both sought after and restricted in number. Friendship involves commitment to one another, fidelity, and the expectation of mutual instruction for mutual moral development. This is why James forms a simple binary opposition:

Friendship with God = enmity with the world,[277]
and
friendship with the world = enmity with God.

Thus friendship stands in opposition to enmity, and world to God. In each case, the active noun — friendship or enmity — is a disposition of the human, that is, of the teachers James addresses. It is possible for one to see friendship with the world as a human disposition but the enmity of God to be God's response to human infidelity. However, the emphasis in the text is on the responsibility of humans.[278]

275. See Ladd, *A Theology of the New Testament,* 259-72; W. Meeks, *The Origins of Christian Morality* (New Haven: Yale University Press, 1993), 52-65.

276. See also Plato, *Lysis;* Cicero, *On Friendship;* Seneca, *Letters.* For studies, see *OCD,* 611-13; David Konstan, *Friendship in the Classical World* (Cambridge: Cambridge University Press, 1997); J. Fitzgerald, ed., *Greco-Roman Perspectives on Friendship* (Atlanta: Society of Biblical Literature, 1997); for a wider discussion, see Neera Kapur Badhwar, ed., *Friendship: A Philosophical Reader* (Ithaca: Cornell University Press, 1993); for a quotatious modern essay on friendship, see J. Epstein, *Friendship: An Exposé* (Boston: Houghton Mifflin, 2006); and the fine anthology edited by D. J. Enright and D. Rawlinson, *The Oxford Book of Friendship* (New York: Oxford University Press, 1991).

277. James does not, however, explicitly speak of friendship with God in James 4. But Abraham is a friend of God (see 2:23). The word "friendship" (φιλία) is found only here in the New Testament, but the word "friend" (φίλος) is found often; see especially Luke 12:4; John 3:29; 11:11; 15:13-15; 3 John 15.

278. See Ropes, 260-61; Johnson, 279. Davids seems to think the enmity is God's enmity; see Davids, 161. Moo, 187, understands the enmity to be both on the part of hu-

James does not so much define friendship with the world (as enmity with God) with "is" as say that enmity with God is characteristic of and correlated with friendship with the world.[279] The rhetoric trades in exclusive oppositions, and this use of friend versus enemy is common among early Christians. Herod and Pilate had been enemies, but during the trial of Jesus became friends (Luke 23:12). Paul sees the flesh as an enemy of God (Rom 8:7) and the cross as that which dissolved Gentile-Jewish animosity into friendship (Eph 2:14, 16). Not out of the picture of James is that the Evil One is sometimes called the Enemy in the New Testament (Matt 13:25, 28, 39; Luke 10:19), and we find the same term used for those who oppose God's people, Jesus and his followers (Luke 1:71, 74; Acts 13:10; Rom 11:28; Phil 3:18), and the term is used by Paul for humans by nature (Rom 5:10; Col 1:21). God's enemies will eventually be defeated (1 Cor 15:25-26; Rev 11:12). To be called an "enemy of God," then, is just as evocative as "adulteresses" because the teachers are hereby placed with the Evil One and the enemies of God's people.

It is worth asking what James has in mind, so far as we can reconstruct it from the text, when he speaks of "friendship with the world," and one can presume that he is not discussing morality in the abstract. Something particular is no doubt on his mind. Suggestions would have to include the zeal, ambition, craving, and desires for power and control in the messianic community. Perhaps murder is in mind as well (4:2). Warring and swording (4:1, 2) manifest those negative moral qualities, as do inappropriate and demeaning words on the part of the teachers (3:1-12). The immediate context then would suggest a variation on what Jesus said to his disciples about wanting to lord it over others as the Gentiles do (Mark 10:35-45). Lording it over others was not something that went away among the early followers of Jesus; it is the teacher's temptation. In context, then, James's focus is on accusations against the teachers and leaders for creating chaos in the community by

---

mans toward God and on the part of God toward humans. I see little reason to muddy the waters by reading the genitive as subjective (or both objective and subjective): James is warning the teachers that their friendship with the world establishes them as enemies of God instead of friends with God; his concern is their disposition, not God's. As we will see below, 4:4b focuses on human choice.

279. Again, τοῦ θεοῦ is an objective genitive and not a subjective genitive, as if James were describing God's active hostility; the enmity of Jas 4:4 is directed at God. The word εχθρα could be accented to form a noun (Nestle-Aland[27]: ἔχθρα) or an adjective (ἐχθρά). Some manuscripts accent it as an adjective (104, 181, 307, 424, 453, etc., Byzantine and Latin manuscripts, Coptic manuscripts, Syriac manuscripts). The majority and earliest manuscripts read it as a noun (B [copyist], P, Y, 5, 33, and many more). The substantive meaning does not change, though the translation would: instead of reading "enmity with God" one might translate "hostile with God."

yearning for lordship. What might surprise the modern reader of James is how blatantly sinful and violent the leaders and teachers of the messianic community were.

James now repeats himself but does so by stepping up the pressure in that he focuses on choice and consequences: "Therefore whoever wishes to be a friend of the world becomes an enemy of God."[280] James sweeps anyone and everyone who chooses to be a friend of the world into the same category in his apodosis: they are established[281] as enemies of God. The emphasis in the verb "becomes"[282] is less on the person's involvement and more on the divinely-assigned or appointed consequences or effects of a dallying friendship with the world.

6.3.2.2. Scriptural Exploration (4:5-6)

6.3.2.2.1. Paraphrase (4:5-6a)

4:5 James continues his rhetorical angle into the teachers' weaknesses with a question: "do you think *it is for nothing . . . ?*"[283] The logical connection of v. 5 with v. 4 is not obvious, but it works something like this, as we will seek to show in what follows: James has interpreted the actions of the teachers as infidelity (4:4a: "Adulteresses!") and has expounded the theme of the intimate relationship with God through the idea of choosing friendship or enmity. The "Or" of v. 5 attends to that theme by exploring the theme of human envy and God's provision against it.[284] I offer this explanation as a general orientation, but it only opens the gate for an assortment of debates, in which some disagree sharply with the sketch just offered.[285]

---

280. The assumption in the protasis is found in the subjunctive verb βουληθῇ (see BDAG, 182), an aorist passive, and the action here is depicted without reference to its progress or completion. This verb works with εἶναι to emphasize the state of the person: the person has chosen "to be" in the condition and state of a friend with the world, and this amounts to choosing to be an enemy of God.

281. The Greek verb is καθίσταται, a third person singular present passive of καθίστημι; see BDAG, 492 (3). This verb often has a sense of appointment to a task (e.g., Luke 12:14, 42, 44; Acts 6:3; 7:10, 27, 35; Rom 5:19; Heb 5:1; 7:28; 8:3).

282. Also used at Jas 3:6: "The tongue is placed among our members. . . ."

283. "Nothing" = κενῶς. BDAG, 540. This term reiterates from a different angle the promise of Isa 55:11: "so shall my word be that goes out from my mouth; it shall not return to me empty, but it shall accomplish that which I purpose, and succeed in the thing for which I sent it." The question of the truthfulness of Scripture must be connected to the intent of God in the communicative event. On this, see K. Vanhoozer, *First Theology* (Downers Grove: InterVarsity, 2002), especially 159-203.

284. For a similar view, see Johnson, 281-82.

285. Almost as if he throws up his arms in despair, Popkes, 266, 269-71, finds

There are several nagging ambiguities behind the NRSV's "God yearns jealously for the spirit that he has made to dwell in us." Some — and I would include myself in this group — interpret the verse in a significantly different sense, so I offer three translations that illustrate the complexity and connectedness of the issues and problems. This translation, that of the NIV, represents what I will argue for in what follows:[286]

> Or do you think Scripture says without reason that the spirit he caused to live in us envies intensely? But he gives us more grace.

The TNIV sides here with the NRSV:

> Or do you suppose that it is for nothing that the scripture says, "God yearns jealously for the spirit that he has made to dwell in us"? But he gives all the more grace. . . .

Ralph Martin, in his commentary, translates the verse thus:

> the Spirit God made to dwell in us opposes envy.[287]

First, what Old Testament text is referred to with "Scripture says"? There are three basic options here:

1. James is referring to Proverbs 3:34, which he will cite in the next verse but suspends from view until he has clarified himself so that the text will make more sense: "Or do you suppose that it is for nothing that Scripture says . . . 'God opposes the proud but gives grace to the humble'?"

2. "Scripture" refers to the general theme of God's jealous love (or perhaps human jealousy) in Scripture. One would then think of texts like

---

enough problems here that he brackets Jas 4:5b-6a. See also J. Michl, "Der Spruch Jakobusbrief 4,5," in *Neutestamentliche Aufsätze. Festschrift für Prof. Josef Schmid zum 70. Geburtstag* (ed. J. Blinzer, O. Kuss, and F. Mussner; Regensburg: Pustet, 1963), 167-74; Burchard, 171-74.

286. Laws, 167, with 174-79, has suggested that there are two questions: "Or do you think that scripture speaks to no effect? Does the spirit which he made to dwell in us long enviously?" The Greek grammar does not suggest a second question and lacks the customary μή for a question expecting a negative answer. Furthermore, the verb of this second question is dependent on the implied repetition of the ὅτι in the opening part of the verse, without "and" or "or."

287. Martin, 149-50. But the verb ἐπιποθέω cannot mean "oppose," and I find no evidence in Martin's discussion that supports such a rendering. Though φθόνον is not used of God and is always negative, that alone is not as decisive a factor as he suggests. See further Mussner, 183.

Exodus 20:5 and 34:14. Or perhaps James is referring to the single word "desire" in texts like Numbers 11:25-30 or Psalms 42:2; 84:2; 119:20.[288]

3. James appeals here to an undetectable scriptural allusion.[289]

The answer to this problem awaits the investigation of the various terms in the verse, but we indicate now that we prefer the first option above: Proverbs 3:34 is in fact the only text cited and the word "Scripture" leads us to look for a specific citation.[290]

Several issues overlap in regard to "the S/spirit," and it might be simplest to begin by asking what the subject of the verb *epipotheo*, "yearns," is. There are three alternatives:

1. "the Spirit," understood to be the Holy Spirit: "The Spirit, which dwells in you, yearns with jealousy."
2. "the spirit," understood to be the human spirit: "The spirit that dwells in you yearns with jealousy."
3. an understood "God," with "the spirit" as the object of the verb: "[God] yearns with jealousy for the spirit which dwells in you."

The second view has the advantage of picking up the theme of human zeal, ambition, and envy/jealousy from 3:14, 16; 4:2, though different words are used here, *epipotheo* and the noun *phthonos*, both of which appear only here in James. We will argue below that 4:5b-6a is a paraphrase of the text cited in 4:6b.

But the third view also has evidence in its favor, particularly the theme of infidelity and friendship in 4:4-6. "Adulteresses!" and the broken friendship with God combine with the two strong words "yearns" and "jealously" to suggest that "the spirit" is the object of (God's) yearning.[291] The teachers' infidelity is causing division in the messianic community, but God yearns jealously for the spirit he has placed in his people — and this yearning, we are led to infer, is for a spirit that will be set loose to create peace,

288. "Spirit" (πνεῦμα) is not used in the LXX of these verses; ψυχή is used. For Laws's explanation, see 179. An imaginative study can be seen in R. Bauckham, "The Spirit of God in Us Loathes Envy: James 4:5," in *The Holy Spirit and Christian Origins* (ed. G. N. Stanton et al.; Grand Rapids: Eerdmans, 2004), 270-81. If James prospectively refers to Prov 3:34, this complicated set of connections is simply not necessary.

289. So Davids, 162, who correctly notes that γραφή should refer to a specific text. This point alone establishes either the first option or the third and eliminates the second. I think the first option is most natural.

290. See Martin, 149.

291. See Davids, 164.

love, and good works. The psalmists sometimes expressed their own yearning for God with the same term that James uses (Pss 42:1; 84:2; 119:20, 131, 174), and, on this view, James applies this language of human longing for intimacy to a characteristic theme of the Old Testament, *God's* jealous love (Exod 20:5; 34:14; Deut 4:24).[292] James 4:5 thus speaks of God's jealous love working to protect the spirit he has placed in us.

But, as we have seen, it seems likely that James has a specific Old Testament text in mind. Furthermore, and in our view decisive, *phthonos,* "jealousy," is uniformly negative and is not used of God's jealousy in the Septuagint.[293] Therefore, it most likely refers to human envy and thus continues a theme going back to 3:14.[294]

"Spirit," *pneuma,* appears only one other time in James, in 2:26, where it refers to the principle that animates the body into life. Since James does not mention the Holy Spirit elsewhere, some argue quite reasonably that he does not do so here. But two other verses might touch on this very issue of the presence of God's Spirit, 1:18[295] and 1:21. I have suggested above that those two verses, one speaking of new birth by the word and the other of the implanted word, are early indicators of the development of a pneumatology in James. While neither mentions the Spirit, that 4:5 brings up the same sense of the internal work of God (if it does) means that they may mutually interpret one another as an early Jewish sense of the presence of God's Spirit in the soul of the believer.

Furthermore, the use of the plural "in us" is not without import here. That is, the S/spirit dwells "among us" and not just in the teachers James addresses.[296] It is something that permits him, rhetorically, to connect once

292. See J. E. Hartley, "Holy and Holiness, Clean and Unclean," *DOTP,* 429-30, on the jealousy of God. Because of the number of texts that speak this way of God, I cannot agree with Davids that, because James uses "Scripture" only for a specific text and since no specific text is named, he must be referring to some text to which we now do not have access. To be sure, James's usage here is abnormal, but "jealous" is perhaps enough reason to consider identifying the "Scripture" as the term or the theme. See Davids, 162.

293. See Johnson, 281-82, for an important listing and elucidation of the evidence.

294. The verb ἐπιποθέω could be either negative, "yearns toward envy" (NIV), or positive, "yearns jealously" (NRSV). In the latter case πρὸς φθόνον is adverbial. See J. Jeremias, "Jac 4:5: ἐπιποθεῖ," *ZNW* 50 (1959) 137-38. But it is not the verb but φθόνος that is decisive for the former view.

295. Laws, 176-77, makes much of this as a creation theme and points to Gen 2:7; 6:3; Job 27:3; 32:8; 1QH 4:31. Others see more of a Pentecostal theme and point to Acts 2. With the difficulty of discerning the meaning of "spirit," it is unwise to speculate any further.

296. κατῴκισεν is causative (BDAG, 535): "[he] caused to dwell." The aorist verb indicates action conceived without reference to progress or completion; simply put, the spirit "dwells" in persons. One thinks here of Gen 2:7 and 6:3.

again with them. This stands in notable contrast with "among *you*" and the constant battering use of "you" in 4:1-3.[297]

But we should use caution here. Any kind of inference drawn from 1:18, 21 is at best suggestive if not speculative. Perhaps we should turn, with other commentators, to the *Shepherd* of Hermas, where we find a text so closely connected to James 4:5 that it may well tip the balance in favor of "the spirit" being the divinely granted *human spirit:*

> Love the truth and let all truth come from your mouth, so that *the spirit that God made to live in this flesh*[298] may be recognized as true by everyone; in this way the Lord who dwells in you will be glorified. . . . And so, those who lie reject the Lord and defraud him, not handing over to him the deposit [the spirit] they received. For they received from a spirit that does not lie; if they return it to him as a liar, they defile the commandment of the Lord and become defrauders. (*Mandates 3:1-2*)

Many argue that Hermas used James and understood James, in what might be the earliest commentary on this passage, to be speaking not of the Holy Spirit but of the human spirit given to us by God. That spirit is given to us and can be used improperly. This is an important if not decisive clue for interpreting James 4:5: "the spirit" is the life-animating principle, as in 2:26, which God gives to us and summons us to use for his glory. This spirit has another desire: it yearns for what it ought not yearn for.

So the subject of *epipotheō* is most likely "the spirit," understood as the human spirit given by God to be used for God's glory. The teachers addressed by James were using God's bestowal of the spirit not for God's glory but for their own glory; they were letting the spirit of envy rule their hearts. This text sounds, then, very much like the two desires theology of Judaism and the sort of thing one finds in Romans 7.[299]

To anticipate what follows, this reading of 4:5 sets up the most compelling contrast with what we find in 4:6: the "but" of 4:6 marks a direct contrast with the teachers' zeal, ambition, cravings, and desires and especially with the envious yearning mentioned in 4:5. The Scripture reference James

---

297. I am not convinced that this is simply and exclusively a corporate indwelling; instead, it is a distributive indwelling in that the spirit/Spirit indwells each of them and not just all of them as a body.

298. ἵνα τὸ πνεῦμα, ὃ ὁ θεὸς κατῴκισεν ἐν τῇ σαρκί.

299. See W. D. Davies, *Paul and Rabbinic Judaism* (Philadelphia: Fortress, 1980), 17-57. Johnson lays out important parallels in the *Testaments of the Twelve Patriarchs* and at Qumran (Johnson, 281). The problem with these parallels is that they refer to two spirits. For James it is one spirit — given by God — that is yearning toward envy, and the resolution is not the good *yetzer* or a different spirit but God's conquering grace. The difference is not without significance for understanding this text.

refers to in 4:5 is found in 4:6 (Prov 3:34), and the point he makes before getting to that citation is that the teachers have within them a divinely-planted spirit that (un)naturally craves for envy and that the good news is that God is there to supplant those cravings with his grace.[300]

4:6a It was indicated above that James delayed the citation of Prov 3:34 until he had laid the groundwork. To make sense of this Old Testament text from Proverbs James had to show that the teachers were given a spirit that could be used in one of two ways: they could either let that spirit yearn toward envy or let that spirit yearn toward what is godly. In fact, James states this once again in a contrastive manner: 4:5 states that the human spirit has a natural desire toward envy, and 4:6 forms the contrast for the person who wants to overcome that envy, that is, rely on God's grace. 4:4-6, taken as a whole, is an accusation against the divisiveness of the teachers. V. 4 sets out the alternative in terms of friendship and enmity. V. 5 explains friendship of the world as the natural yearning of the human spirit, a spirit that God in his freedom placed in humans to use in their freedom. V. 6 forms the contrast with v. 5 and, at the same time, provides the alternative to divisiveness: God's grace.

The grammar, however, is not that smooth, so a map of that grammar will both clarify the meaning of "Scripture says" in v. 5 and spell out how v. 6 is related to v. 5:

> Or do you think it is for nothing that the Scripture says (v. 5a):
> Paraphrase of Proverbs 3:34:
> 1. The human spirit yearns toward envy (v. 5b).
> 2. God gives grace (v. 6a).
> Quotation of Proverbs 3:34 (v. 6b):
> "God opposes the proud,
> but gives grace to the humble."

The grammar of 4:5b-6 is often said to be difficult, and for that reason Wiard Popkes brackets it out of the text![301] Since "Scripture says" most likely refers to a specific text, and since neither "God yearns jealously . . ." nor "the human spirit yearns toward envy" is such a text, we conclude that 4:6b contains that text. Which means that 4:5b-6a is an "interruption" that sets up and anticipates the actual Scripture quotation. More importantly, on closer inspection it is actually not an interruption but an anticipatory paraphrase of the text

---

300. After I had worked this solution out I discovered the article by Craig B. Carpenter, "James 4.5 Reconsidered," *NTS* 47 (2000) 189-205, which confirms in some ways my line of thinking, though his focus is on the indirect speech of the construction. For the alternative see S. Laws, "Does Scripture Speak in Vain? A Reconsideration of James IV.5," *NTS* 20 (1974) 210-15.

301. Popkes, 266, where his translation makes this clear.

to be quoted. The verses are not as difficult as they might appear at first, but the verse divisions have prevented us from seeing a connection. Comparing 4:5b-6a with the Scripture quotation in 4:6b opens up the interpretation and explains the rhetorical moves James is making.

If one compares the two units one finds a kind of Hebrew climactic parallel:

> A   v. 5b   Humans yearn toward envy
>   B   v. 6a   God gives grace
> A′   v. 6b1   God resists the proud
>   B′   v. 6b2   God gives grace to the humble

The B lines are nearly synonymous, though the second takes us one more step: God not only gives grace, but he gives it to the humble. The suspension of the condition needed to obtain God's grace, namely humility, is rhetorically clever and leads to everything we find in 4:7-10. If we take the two A lines as addressing the same issue, namely envy prompted by pride, then 4:5b-6a (A-B) states what the Scripture (A′-B′) states with only slight adjustments in a rhetorically compelling manner. In particular, A is the human counterpart/ground for A′, where we find the divine response to that human envy. When James wrote "Scripture says" in v. 5, instead of providing the quotation immediately he paraphrased Proverbs 3:34, realized that he might as well quote the text itself, and did so in 4:6b, which is why he writes the resumptive "therefore it says."[302]

But since not all read v. 5 as we have, not all see v. 6 as a simple contrast with v. 5.[303] Peter Davids sees a contrast in God's relationship: God is jealous *but* God's grace is deeper than his jealousy.[304] This sounds a bit like

302. διὸ λέγει. The διὸ is resumptive in that it sums up what is found in 4:5b-6a. Perhaps one could render it, "That is, it says. . . ."

303. Thus, δὲ is adversative; those who read v. 5 as God's jealous yearning for the human spirit often need to read the particle as inferential ("so") or as a simple addition ("and"), neither of which is as compelling as a simple adversative. See BDAG, 213, which provides a brief sketch of the particle. In addition, the comparative adjective μείζων also forms a contrast with something that precedes; *pace,* Laws, 180. It is true that the adjective was losing some of its comparative force (BDAG, 623), but words are not just words; they are words in context, and if one connects 4:5 to 4:6 with an adversative particle, recognizes the need for grace in contrast to something in what precedes, and factors in the potent contrastive nature of Prov 3:34, one is left with confidence that the adjective is comparative. When James wants to make additive points, he uses καί, as we can see in 4:8 and 4:10; the adversative is found in 4:7. See also the intense study of Penner, *The Epistle of James and Eschatology,* 160-81, who sees the introduction to the concluding portion of James at 4:6.

304. Davids, 164.

2:13. The problem here is that, if we read 4:5 as speaking of God's jealous yearning, there is no indication that it is in need of the mollification that some suggest is needed. Some see the contrast signaled by the "but" of 4:6 to be with v. 4: God's grace stands over against friendship with the world. Which it does, but that is surely gasping for air in waters we need not enter. V. 6 makes reasonable sense in connection to v. 5, especially if we read "spirit" as the human spirit and as the subject of the verb "yearns."

James has unquestionably called into question the character and behavior of the teachers in 3:1–4:3, and vv. 4 and 5 turn up the heat, but James is a pastor who wants the teachers to repent, which will be his emphasis in vv. 7-10. Before he utters those commanding calls to repent, he promises God's grace: "But he gives all the more grace."[305] As seen in our map above, this line counters 4:5b, the human striving toward envy, as it paraphrases 4:6b2, the gift of God's grace. Inasmuch as James is in a Jewish world and has brought up the issue of human desire (*yetzer* in Hebrew), it is reasonable to connect God's grace to the good *yetzer*. But this pushes what James is saying: he does not see two desires at work. He sees one desire for envy and its counterpart in God's grace. The battle then is not between two *yetzers* but between humans and God, between the human natural desire for envy and the divine desire for humans to do the divine will.

Does the word "grace," used in James in this verse, refer to power for the teachers to overcome the yearning for envy, to the gift of the Holy Spirit, or to God's willingness to forgive if they repent?[306] The question must be answered in light of James's rhetorical intentions. If we read this term in the context of 3:1–4:12, the problem is clear: the teachers' tongues are the embodiment of their zeal, ambition, cravings, desires, and yearnings for envy. If that is the problem, James's goal is to get the teachers to repent. This is made abundantly clear in 4:7-10, where he will not go much farther than their need to repent and the promise that God will forgive. In context, then, the grace that God gives in 4:6ab is the grace of his gift of forgiveness to those who repent.[307] This grace, comparatively speaking, is "greater" than something. What might that something be? Again, "grace" and "greater" are tied together: God's grace is greater than the abusive power-mongering of the teachers, just as it is greater than their yearnings toward envy. God's grace

---

305. Nestle-Aland[27] includes this in the interrogative with v. 5. This makes for clumsy grammar. Rather, the opening clause of v. 6 continues the need for James to fill in information prior to using Prov 3:34. The present tense of the verb here is used to describe characteristic (incomplete aspect) behavior of God.

306. See Davids, 164. To read "grace" here as the gift of God's Spirit is to assume a conclusion I have found less likely in 4:5, namely that the "spirit" of 4:5 is God's Holy Spirit.

307. So Davids, 164.

can wipe the slate clean and restore the teachers so that they can become what God desires.

6.3.2.2.2. Citation of Scripture (4:6b)

4:6b resumes what was said in 4:5a. But this time, instead of paraphrasing Proverbs 3:34, James quotes it. This is the text James had in mind when he anticipated that the teachers might be thinking they were beyond the pale. No, he says, God's grace is enough to get them back on track. The word of God is not "for nothing"; it is, in fact, effective and powerful. And that power is the availability of God's grace, as Proverbs 3:34 indicates.[308]

Reading the Scripture quotation in light of the preceding paraphrase and vice versa, the human spirit yearning for envy (v. 5) is a divine denunciation of the desire of envy, and "the proud" (v. 6) are human spirits yearning toward envy.[309] The paraphrase in v. 6a is nearly identical to v. 6b2, but the latter takes one further step: the grace of God comes to those who are "humble." By offering grace and then specifying that to obtain that grace one must be humble before God, James's rhetoric becomes more potent.

"Proud" *(hyperēphanois)* describes "a person's exaggerated opinion of himself, which entails disdain for others, even scorn for the divinity."[310] This term was especially connected with those who had scornful speech patterns (Pss 17:10; 31:18; 119:51, 69, 78; Sir 23:8; 27:15, 28; 32:12), who revealed

---

308. The quotation comes from the LXX with only one difference: instead of the LXX's κύριος, James has θεός. A more literal rendering of the Hebrew text would be:

Toward the scorners [God] is scornful;
and/but to the humble [וְלַעֲנָיִים] [God] gives grace.

It is the use of "God opposes the proud" that demonstrates that James has opted for the Septuagintal translation of the Hebrew.

It is interesting how frequently early Christians cited Prov 3. A full listing can be found in Laws, 182-83. Prov 3:34 is found perhaps at Luke 1:51, but clearly also at 1 Pet 5:5; *1 Clement* 30:2; and Ignatius, *Ephesians* 5:3. Ignatius, not surprisingly, applies this to the humility needed before the bishop.

309. The verb ἀντιτάσσω, "oppose" (see BDAG, 90), is found elsewhere in the New Testament at Acts 18:6; Rom 13:2; Jas 5:6; and 1 Pet 5:5, where once again Prov 3:34 is cited. The text from 1 Pet 5:5, in context, deals with young leaders in the church, and it makes one wonder if James is not also speaking to young leaders/teachers who were facing similar problems. It would be speculative to suggest that a common text like this would indicate some kind of early Christian instruction for young teachers. The substantival adjective ὑπερήφανος is found in Luke 1:51; Rom 1:30; 2 Tim 3:2; and, once again, 1 Pet 5:5; cf. Mark 7:22 for the noun. See BDAG, 1033; Spicq, 3.390-95, for an excellent collection of evidence.

310. Spicq, 3.392.

343

proud behaviors (Deut 17:12; Ps 31:23), and who were not hesitant to use violence (Prov 8:13; Ps 10:2; Sir 27:15; 31:26). God, who is Sovereign and Lord of all, opposes those who strive for what belongs only to God. James speaks against the vaunted pride, zeal, ambition, cravings, desires, and yearning for envy of the teachers because God himself speaks against such behaviors.

The text is replete with exclusive alternatives: friendship of the world versus friendship with God, the proud over against the humble. Because James wants to assure the teachers of grace and forgiveness, he turns from God's opposition to God's approval with the second line of the quotation: "but [God] gives grace to the humble." This is a general statement brought to bear on the teachers' situation, so we should be cautious about connecting the teachers to the poor people implicit in the word "humble" (tapeinos). But that word has a rich history and we have already commented on its meaning (see above on 1:9). The context shapes the meanings of both "gives grace," as seen in our comments in 4:6a, and "humble," which in this context means realizing how wrong one's zeal and ambition are and turning to God in repentance. In particular, because tapeinos is so firmly connected with the pious poor (the Anawim) tradition and because James pushes hard on this theme (see 1:9-11, 26-27; 2:1-12, 14-17; 4:13–5:6), it is not out of bounds to see in his reuse of this term from Proverbs 3:34 an implicit expectation that the leaders/teachers will align themselves with the poor of the messianic community and come down from their collective high horse of thinking themselves above the general ruck of messianists.

6.3.3. Commands for the Divisive (4:7-10)

James has now discussed the origin of division (4:1-3) and has accused the teachers/leaders of the messianic community of divisiveness (4:4-6). But, within the accusation James begins now to shift forward to his appeal for the divisive to repent. His appeal begins with "therefore," which connects it most likely to the statement just made: God resists the proud and gives grace to the humble, therefore, be humble. The commands form, in effect, an exhortation based on Proverbs 3:34. If God gives grace to the humble, then it is incumbent on the teachers to become or be humble before God.[311] In some ways, 4:7-10 is the climax for the entire unit (3:1–4:10) on teachers and the tongue.

Are these commands set in just a flowing list, or is there a discernible order? Peter Davids organizes the commands around the topic of submission and a concluding command:[312]

311. The second line of Prov 3:34 uses the noun ταπεινοῖς, and the final command of Jas 4:10 uses the cognate in imperative form: ταπεινώθητε.
312. See Davids, 165.

Topic: submit (4:7a)

    A1. Resist (4:7b)
    A2. Draw near (4:8a)

    B1. Cleanse (4:8b)
    B2. Purify (4:8c)

    C1. Lament . . . (4:9a)
    C2. Let your laughter . . . (4:9b)

Conclusion: humble yourselves (4:10)

Davids points out that the topic and conclusion have imperatives that are "virtual synonyms" but he concedes that v. 9 "may be a parallel couplet only or perhaps two units." But it is not above question that "submit" and "humble yourselves" are virtual synonyms except at the most general of levels. Further, v. 9 shows that the structuring is not as clear as it could have been.

There are ten imperatives in this section:

1. *Submit* yourselves therefore to God.
2. *Resist* the devil, and he will flee from you.
3. *Draw near* to God, and he will draw near to you.
4. *Cleanse* your hands, you sinners,
5. and *purify* your hearts, you double-minded.
6. *Lament*
7. and *mourn*
8. and *weep.*
9. *Let* your laughter *be turned* into mourning and your joy into dejection.
10. *Humble* yourselves before the Lord, and he will exalt you.

The first, "submit yourselves," could name an overall topic but that is far from certain. The second, "resist," is a separable command with a promise, and the third, "draw near," has the same form. Clearly, the fourth and fifth, "cleanse" and "purify," are a tidy, balanced pair of commands that belong together. And the next three, "Lament and mourn and weep," are not only a unit but are separable from the third person imperative that comes next. Finally, "humble yourselves" is indeed similar to "submit yourselves," but different words are used and "humble yourselves" comes with a promise. These units are clearly discernible.[313]

This collection of separable units has some structure, but their order is

313. Moo, 192.

more random than logical.[314] Some connect the commands: one must first submit and then resist and then approach God and then be pure and then repent, etc. Such connections are not made by James and reveal more the ingenuity of a scholar or preacher than the realities of the text. Martin describes the section well when he describes it as "a staccato burst of rapid commands."[315] Our brief sketch here breaks down into six separable sections because they are at least discernible units.

6.3.3.1. Submission (4:7a)

"Submit"[316] is found in the early Christian household regulations[317] and describes the position of a person living within some established order. Here it is the order of God, the sovereign creator, covenant God, and redeemer in Christ. This is not simply a call to a general disposition of living under the lordship of God but also a summons to submit to God for the grace of forgiveness that is granted to those who repent. A question arises whether this text is connected to others like it in the early churches. Thus, consider 1 Peter 5:5-9 for a striking parallel:[318]

---

314. It is likely that James's language is connected to an early Christian set of exhortations, since 1 Pet 5:5-9 shows so many similarities. This suggestion might help explain why it is that the verbs James now uses are only unusual in James. See Popkes, 273-74.

315. Martin, 152.

316. ὑποτάγητε οὖν τῷ θεῷ. See BDAG, 1042; *EDNT* 3.408. The imperative is a second aorist, from ὑποτάσσω; the form is passive, and the NRSV and TNIV make it middle by adding "yourselves." Since the person who submits is involved in the action, this translation is not without merit. The aorist is used, not in order to speak either to the singularity of the action or the inception of the action, but in order to depict the action without reference to completion or incompletion of the action. A more literal rendering would be "You should be subject to God." The verb is used 31 times in the New Testament; see Luke 2:51; 10:17, 20; Rom 8:7, 20; 10:3; 13:1, 5; 1 Cor 14:32, 34; 15:27-28; 16:16; Eph 5:21, 24; 1 Pet 3:22.

317. The term, or category of living within a social structure, could be catechetical in origin. However, for a case to be made for Jas 4:7-10 to come from the catechesis of the early church requires more than this verb. Two factors suggest that James either antedates those traditions or is not dependent upon them: the word ὑποτάσσω describes in household regulations a relationship to humans; there is no sign of social hierarchy in Jas 4:7-10, which is the hallmark of the household regulations (see Johnson, 283). The literature on the subject of household regulations is vast; a research report can be found in J. Woyke, *Die neutestamentlichen Haustafeln. Ein kritischer und konstruktiver Forschungsüberblick* (Stuttgarter Bibelstudien 184; Stuttgart: Katholisches Bibelwerk, 2000).

318. A looser parallel is Eph 6:10-17.

In the same way, you who are younger must accept the authority of the elders. And all of you must clothe yourselves with *humility* in your dealings with one another, for

> "*God opposes the proud,*
>   *but gives grace to the humble.*"

Humble yourselves therefore under the mighty hand of God, so that he may exalt you in due time. Cast all your anxiety on him, because he cares for you. Discipline yourselves, keep alert. Like a roaring lion your adversary *the devil* prowls around, looking for someone to devour. *Resist him,* steadfast in your faith, for you know that your brothers and sisters in all the world are undergoing the same kinds of suffering.

The connections are noteworthy and even more tantalizing because Peter's instructions are also directed at leaders, though leaders who are "younger" (1 Pet 5:5). But, we see (1) humility, (2) citation of Proverbs 3:34, (3) the need to be humble before God, and (4) a call to resist the devil. One parallel does not a catechetical pattern make, but it is at least worthy of consideration to wonder if this language did not emerge from the catechetical tradition of the early churches for leaders, teachers, and those aspiring to be such.[319]

6.3.3.2. Resistance (4:7b)

"Resist the devil, and he will flee from you."[320] James here draws on military[321] words in reference to the cosmological battle between Satan[322] and his minions and God and his people happening in the world. The opponents of Stephen could not *resist* his wisdom and the Spirit (Acts 6:10), a verse that implies prior resistance. In Acts 13:8 the magician Elymas *resisted* the gospel (see also 2 Tim 3:8; 4:15). More important are two texts that, with James 4:7b, convey ethical maxims for the early churches:

---

319. See Laws, 181-82.

320. The aorist here (ἀντίστητε), like the one in 4:7a, is categorical. On ἀνθίστημι, see BDAG, 80; see also Matt 5:39; Luke 21:15; Acts 6:10; 13:8; Rom 9:19; 13:2; Gal 2:11; 2 Tim 3:8; 4:15. The future tense is "defective" in aspectual theory because it combines action that is apparently both incomplete and temporally bound to the future. But on this, see Porter, *Idioms,* 43-45, where Porter argues that verbal aspect is removed in the future tense and that it grammaticizes expectation. Hermas, *Mandates* 12.4, 5, reflects the use of the language of James.

321. So Johnson, 283.

322. On which, cf. the studies of G. Twelftree cited in note 178 above: *Jesus the Exorcist,* 1-52; *Jesus, the Miracle Worker,* 281-92; *In the Name of Jesus.* See also M. Borg, *Jesus: A New Vision* (San Francisco: Harper and Row, 1987), 23-75.

> Therefore take up the whole armor of God, so that you may be able to withstand on that evil day, and having done everything, to stand firm (Eph 6:13).

> Resist him, steadfast in your faith, for you know that your brothers and sisters in all the world are undergoing the same kinds of suffering (1 Pet 5:9).

Resisting the evil one was an important theme in Judaism and early Christian catechesis.[323] The constant presence of demons and unclean spirits in the life of Jesus (e.g, Mark 1:21-28), the cosmic battle into which Jesus entered (Matt 11:12-13; Luke 16:16), and the grander cosmic battle of the book of Revelation elucidate what lies behind the words of James. James does not say what Peter says about the roaring lion (1 Pet 5:8), but that sort of belief gives rise to the commandment James presents to the teachers. The grammar focuses on resisting, and one resists an opponent who attacks; therefore, we are probably to see James here urging a *defensive response* to devilish temptations, which connects this verse to 3:15 ("devilish") and the false wisdom of zeal and ambition. The teachers and their temptations have not left James's vision: he offers advice here on how to deal with the temptations that arise from zeal, ambition, cravings, desires, and yearnings for envy.

If the emphasis so far has led us to think in terms of anthropology, James now brings into the discussion a cosmic force at work in the divisiveness of the community leaders. The desires that yearn toward envy are animated, at least in part, by "the devil."[324] It is reasonable to think that the desires of 1:13-15 are also partly inspired by the devil. But it would be inaccurate to flip completely into seeing all of sin as nothing but the cosmic victory of the devil. James, perhaps less than only Jesus in the New Testament, emphasizes human responsibility.

In addition, he believes the messianic leaders can overcome the enemy. James speaks here as does Paul in 1 Corinthians 10:13: "No testing has overtaken you that is not common to everyone. God is faithful, and he will not let you be tested beyond your strength, but with the testing he will also provide the way out so that you may be able to endure it." The devil will flee if the messianist resists the devil. This point is thoroughly Jewish. Tobit 6 speaks of Tobias being told how to rid a person of demons: one must smoke a fish's gall, heart, and liver. When they are smoked, "every affliction will flee away" (Tob 6:8; see 8:1-3). Perhaps more germane to James is the simpler method in the *Testament of Simeon:* "If anyone flees to the Lord for refuge,

---

323. Cf. Job 1:6-12; 2:1-7; Wis 2:24.
324. On this term see Matt 4:1-11; 13:39; 25:41; John 8:44; 13:2, 27; Acts 10:38; Eph 6:11; 1 Tim 3:6-7; 2 Tim 2:26; Heb 2:14; 1 John 3:8, 10; Rev 12; 20.

the evil spirit will quickly depart from him, and his mind will be eased" (3:5).[325] And, *Testament of Dan* explains this a little more completely: "Draw near to God and to the angel who intercedes for you, because he is the mediator between God and men for the peace of Israel. He shall stand in opposition to the kingdom of the enemy" (6:2).

We might ask what it might have meant to "resist" the devil. Certainly it involved prayer and a steely commitment to do what God wanted. That prayer and obedience, perhaps better yet a prayerful obedience, were involved is made clear by the parallels in the *Testaments of the Twelve Patriarchs,* and the next few commands remind us that obedience is essential to putting the devil to flight.

6.3.3.3. Drawing Near to God (4:8a)

"Draw near to God, and he will draw near to you."[326] This command, like the previous one, brings in its wake a promise. Both *Testaments* texts cited above speak of drawing near to God in the context of the flight of the evil one, so it is likely that James is drawing upon a traditional idea. In context, this line stands in dramatic contrast with 4:6b. Opposition to the proud stands in contrast to God's drawing near to the one who draws near to God, which implies that drawing near is a dimension of humility, submission, and resisting the devil. The metaphor has several connections, not the least of which is to the prophetic summons for God's people to draw near to God to hear him, to establish covenant relationship, and to turn from sin:

> The spirit of God came upon Azariah son of Oded. He went out to meet Asa and said to him, "Hear me, Asa, and all Judah and Benjamin: The LORD is with you, while you are with him. If you seek him, he will be found by you, but if you abandon him, he will abandon you. For a long time Israel was without the true God, and without a teaching priest, and without law; but when in their distress they turned to the LORD, the God of Israel, and sought him, he was found by them (2 Chron 15:1-4).

> Therefore say to them, "Thus says the LORD of hosts: Return to me, says the LORD of hosts, and I will return to you, says the LORD of hosts" (Zech 1:3).

325. See also *Testament of Issachar* 7:7; *Testament of Naphtali* 8:4; *Testament of Dan* 5:1; *Testament of Benjamin* 5:2 — when a person does what is good, the evil one flees. It might be tempting to think these Jewish texts are too *mitzvoth*-shaped, but if one reads them with Jas 4:7-10, the language and thought world are not distant: drawing near to God and obeying God are not mutually exclusive.

326. Again, the aorist (ἐγγίσατε) is categorical, and the future indicates expectation. On the verb, see BDAG, 270.

> Ever since the days of your ancestors you have turned aside from my statutes and have not kept them. Return to me, and I will return to you, says the LORD of hosts (Mal 3:7).

Other connections, and less likely in my opinion, would be the cultic expression of drawing near to the God of the Temple cultus even though the connection of drawing near and consecration is clearly at work in our text (cf. 4:8b). Thus, Exodus 19:22: "Even the priests who approach the LORD must consecrate themselves or the LORD will break out against them" (see also 24:2; Deut 16:16). Drawing on the cultic experience but closer to what James has in mind is Hebrews 4:16: "Let us therefore approach the throne of grace with boldness, so that we may receive mercy and find grace to help in time of need" (cf. 7:19). Prayer, too, is sometimes described as confessional, elective drawing near to God and God being near to the one praying (Deut 4:7; Ps 145:18), but an important warning is that physical and verbal proximity is no substitute for inner vulnerability to God (Isa 29:13).

Drawing near to God, then, is about a person's inner repentant disposition of vulnerability to God's will (cf. Jas 1:21) and is combined with the attentive behaviors of doing God's will. In short, it is repentance leading to holiness, faith accompanied by works, and hearing and doing. However it is understood, the act of God drawing near is God's choice of restoring the relationship with those who have fractured the relationship. This language of drawing near to God and God drawing near to us reminds one of the powerful covenant formula of the Old Testament: "I will be your God and you will be my people" (e.g., Gen 17:2, 4, 6-8; Exod 6:2-8).[327] James is speaking to teachers who have fractured the messianic community and is calling them to repentance in terms of drawing near to God if they wish to have God draw near to them.[328] What that drawing near of God would look like is not clear, but surely James would be thinking of peace in the community and compassion for those in need — both emerging from a leadership that has been renewed through repentance.

6.3.3.4. Cleansing and Purification (4:8b)

The fourth set of categories James uses to summons the teachers to repentance, a classic example of synonymous parallelism,[329] is drawn from the cultic world of purity, and to each imperative is attached a vocative:

327. On which see R. Rendtorff, *The Covenant Formula* (trans. M. Kohl; Edinburgh: Clark, 1998).
328. Davids, 166, is right in connecting the future tense in Jas 4:8a to the Hebrew condition.
329. See the excellent discussion now in *DOTWPW,* 502-15; A. Berlin, "Parallel-

Cleanse your hands,   you sinners,
Purify your hearts,   you double-minded.[330]

The notable development in these two lines is the shift from "hands" to "hearts" to emphasize total purification, body and heart or outer and inner. It is possible, though hard to demonstrate, that "hands" speaks of behaviors and "hearts" of commitment. The more metaphorical and moral these images are, the less likely such a distinction can be sustained.[331] Hands were used to offer gifts and sacrifices (cf. Lev 4:4; 14:15) and were cleansed as a form of purity (cf. Mark 7:2-5).[332]

The first line is aimed at "you sinners."[333] Calling the teachers "sinners" is rhetorically strong and reminds one of 2:20 and 3:15 and especially of "adulteresses" in 4:4. The emotional intensity of this word, though, is matched by other verses in James, including 1:19-21; 2:4, 5-7, 14-17, 19, 20; 3:10, 15; 4:1-4, 12; and 5:1-6. James perceives the teachers in terms of faithlessness and falling short of God's design and defilement by their desires and behaviors. Again, we are to think of passages like 3:1-12, 14-16; 4:1-4; and perhaps 2:1-4 to clarify the kind of sin involved. The teachers have defiled their hands with sin and are therefore called to "cleanse your hands." This expression evokes the purification rituals of the priests (e.g., Exod 29:4; 30:19-21; 40:12; Ps 26:6), the people (Exod 19:10; Lev 15:5-8; 17:15-16), and the sacrifices themselves (Exod 29:17). The community at Qumran is a good example from the time of James (CD 10:11; 1QM 14:2; 4Q514 fragment 1 1:6). Furthermore, this language became metaphorical for moral purification (Isa 1:16; Jer 4:14), and that is the primary sense here. Surely also Psalm 24:3-4 is in the background to James's statement:[334]

---

ism," in *ABD* 5.135-62. Synonymous, though, does not mean identical. In Jas 4:8b, the second line advances the first by altering semantically similar vocabulary.

330. The imperatives of Jas 4:7-10 are all aorist because the emphasis is on conceptualizing the action in its totality; this gives them a sense of the categorical. See Porter, *Idioms,* 224-26; McKay, *New Syntax,* 77-81, who finds the aorist is used in the imperative when the verb is active rather than stative.

331. But see Davids, 167; Martin, 153; Moo, 194.

332. There is an entire tractate in the Mishnah called *Yadayim,* "Hands."

333. The other use of ἁμαρτωλός in James is at 5:20, where pastoral compassion leads to guiding a wandering sinner back into the community. See BDAG, 51-52; a good Old Testament passage is Ps 1:1-5. The word in this context is not theologically explored. One of the finest studies of sin I have seen is J. Goldingay, "Your Iniquities Have Made a Separation Between You and Your God," in *Atonement Today* (ed. J. Goldingay; London: SPCK, 1995), 39-53; see also his *Old Testament Theology: Israel's Faith* (vol. 2; Downers Grove: InterVarsity, 2006), 254-349.

334. Different words are used in the LXX: 24:4 — ἀθῷος χερσὶν καὶ καθαρὸς τῇ καρδίᾳ.

Who shall ascend the hill of the LORD?
  And who shall stand in his holy place?
Those who have clean hands and pure hearts,
  who do not lift up their souls to what is false,
  and do not swear deceitfully.

And the psalmist's doubts emerge in similar words in Psalm 73:13: "All in vain I have kept my heart clean and washed my hands in innocence." The second line is directed at the "double-minded," a word used elsewhere in James of the person whose confidence in God is shaken and whose faith is unstable (1:8). The issue here, however, is not a shaken faith. Instead, the teachers' zeal and ambition have compromised their moral integrity in desiring friendship with the world (4:4) while leading the messianic community. The particular accusations can be found throughout 3:1–4:12. This is the third strong term in this chapter James uses for the failures of the teachers: "adulteresses" speaks to their infidelities, "sinners" to their failure to accomplish God's designs, and "double-minded" to their lack of moral integrity. James urges the double-minded teachers to "purify your hearts."[335] The heart is for Judaism the core or center of a person with respect to behavior, faith, mind and emotion; it is, as it were, the core of one's being and the moral compass. Thus, in James 1:26 the person who thinks herself religious, but lacks control of the tongue, deceives the heart. Envy and ambition, the central moral failing of the teachers, embed themselves in the heart (3:14) and the rich person's luxury fattens the heart (5:5). Hence, another central moral exhortation in James is for the community to strengthen the heart in light of the Lord's coming (5:8). The teachers must get the very center of their being purified. The leading word in James's list of qualifiers of genuine wisdom is "pure" (*hagnē*, 3:17). Once again, we are led to the Jewish world of purification and the status of purity — that is, of being in right order before God so that one can enter the Temple. Thus, Moses and Joshua consecrated the people (Exod 19:10; Josh 3:5), the Nazirites were to purify themselves from wine and strong drink (Num 6:3) and the Levites purified themselves from sin and washed their clothes (8:21). Purification was made for sacred tasks (1 Chron 15:12, 14; 2 Chron 29:5, 15-19; 2 Macc 12:38). We find the same ideas in the New Testament (John 11:55; Acts 21:24, 26; 24:18). But this term, like "cleanse" in the previous line, became a metaphor for moral purity (1 Pet 1:22; 1 John 3:3).[336]

It is easy to get lost in the variety of images James spills onto the

---

335. ἁγνίσατε καρδίας. See BDAG, 12. On "heart," see H. W. Wolff, *Anthropology of the Old Testament* (Philadelphia: Fortress, 1974), 40-59; *TDOT*, 7.399-437.

336. Again, see Lockett, *Purity and Worldview*, 130-37, who sees here a *"figurative label for social/ideological location"* and *"cleansing"* (p. 137).

page, and it is also easy to lose contact with James's intent: to summon the teachers from their zeal, ambition, cravings, desires, and yearning toward envy to repentance. The next verse makes that intent clear.

6.3.3.5. Repentance (4:9)

James uses three words connected to the sorrowful side of repentance: "Lament and mourn and weep."[337] If that is not enough, he then urges the teachers to wipe the smiles off their faces and turn down the music: "Let your laughter be turned into mourning and your joy into dejection." Lamenting, mourning, weeping, mourning[338] and dejection are all metaphors for repentance. Repentance, as Esau learned (Heb 12:16-17), cannot be manufactured by strenuous effort. Furthermore, as the rebellious son learned, it involves both the inner and outer dimensions of life (Luke 15:14-21; cf. 2 Cor 7:9-10). It is a work in the heart by the Spirit of God as one is awakened to the goodness, mercy, and holiness of God (e.g., Phil 2:13; Eph 2:8-9).[339] Hence, these graphic terms in James 4:9 are concrete embodiments of genuine repentance.[340]

4:9a The word "lament" describes the experience of discovering that one's future prospect is awful and inescapable.[341] The noun form of this word appears in both Romans 3:16, "ruin and *misery* are in their paths," and in James for the future prospects of the rich: "Come now, you rich people, weep and wail for the *miseries* that are coming to you" (Jas 5:1; cf. Rev 3:17). The prospect of future misery leads to lamenting. Inasmuch as James 4:9 inculcates repentance over one's moral behaviors, the misery that would come to the non-lamenting or unrepentant person would be the full consequences of sin at the judgment. Romans 7:24 forms a substantive parallel: "Wretched man that I am! Who will rescue me from this body of death?" The Septuagint of Psalm 12:5 (LXX 11:6) speaks of God rising up over the laments of the poor, and the same prospect of God's mercy awaits the person who laments over one's sin and prospects of judgment.[342]

So, what does James have in mind? Does he have in mind simply moral repentance[343] or, as Mayor long ago suggested, voluntary abstinence as

337. The imperatives are all aorist to conceptualize the action in its totality.

338. The verb of 4:9a is cognate with the noun in 4:9b.

339. On which see P. Toon, *Born Again: A Biblical and Theological Study of Regeneration* (Grand Rapids: Baker, 1987).

340. For a sketch of the idea of repentance, see these studies of μετανοέω: *EDNT*, 2.415-19; Spicq, 2.471-77; Popkes, 280.

341. See BDAG, 988, where the verb and cognates appear.

342. Hermas, *Similitudes* 1:3 connects foolishness, double-mindedness, and misery/lamentation.

343. See Laws, 184-85; Davids, 167.

form of penitent hardship and response to near-death (moral or otherwise) as an expression of one's repentance?[344] The Septuagint might suggest this. Thus (and I refer to the English text verse numbers):

> from the wicked who *despoil me,*
>> my deadly enemies who surround me (Ps 17:9).

> I am *utterly bowed down* and prostrate;
>> all day long I go around mourning (Ps 38:6).

Perhaps Mayor's suggestion appears too mechanical. So we should consider the following text to be at least the sort of thing James has in mind. It connects with others that speak of captivity and the judgment of exile and how God's people responded in lamentation:

> On that day they shall take up a taunt song against you,
>> and wail with *bitter lamentation,*
> and say, "We are *utterly ruined;*
>> the LORD alters the inheritance of my people;
> how he removes it from me!
>> Among our captors he parcels out our fields" (Mic 2:4).[345]

Not only are the teachers to "lament" but they are also to "mourn" and "weep,"[346] two words that both accompany lamentations but also frequently and concretely embody genuine repentance. These actions inherent to lamentation can be feigned, and, while they are never absolute demonstrations of genuine repentance, they have been devalued in major segments of the church. No simple explanation can be given, but one must consider first the absorption of a Platonic thought-world from the second century onward that led to an elevation of the mind and spiritual life at the expense of the body and concrete embodiment in spiritual practices. Call it what one likes, it is a kind of dualism that prevents modern readers from seeing that James expected the teachers to

---

344. See Mayor, 147, who appeals to enough texts to give this view substance. Dibelius, 227-28, sees here an eschatological disaster, which is right in itself, but he then sees the lamenting "as a prophetic proclamation of disaster which was worded in the form of a command" (p. 227). In its present context in James, he concedes, it means repentance. Popkes, 277: "betrachtet euch als in jammervoller Lage" ("consider yourselves as in a miserable situation"). Fasting in the ancient Jewish world was a *response to a grievous situation or condition* rather than an instrument to get something. Once the responsive nature of fasting is grasped, a connection here from lamenting to abstinence and fasting is much easier to make. See my book *Fasting* (Nashville: Nelson, 2009).

345. See also Jer 4:13; 9:19; 10:20; 12:12.

346. καὶ πενθήσατε καὶ κλαύσατε. See BDAG, 795, 545.

repent in embodied forms.[347] Jacob provides an example of embodied sorrow when he hears the story of the death of Joseph: "Then Jacob tore his garments and put sackcloth on his loins, and mourned for his son many days" (Gen 37:34; cf. Num 14:39; 1 Chron 7:22). More pertinent is 1 Esdras 8:71-74, where we read of Ezra's response to mixed marriages:

> As soon as I heard these things I tore my garments and my holy mantle, and pulled out hair from my head and beard, and sat down in anxiety and grief. And all who were ever moved at the word of the Lord of Israel gathered around me, as I mourned over this iniquity, and I sat grief-stricken until the evening sacrifice. Then I rose from my fast, with my garments and my holy mantle torn, and kneeling down and stretching out my hands to the Lord I said,
>
> "O Lord, I am ashamed and confused before your face. . . ."

And Joel 2:12-13:

> Yet even now, says the LORD,
>   return to me with all your heart,
> with fasting, with weeping, and with mourning;
>   rend your hearts and not your clothing.
> Return to the LORD, your God,
>   for he is gracious and merciful,
> slow to anger, and abounding in steadfast love,
>   and relents from punishing.

This is the Israelite ideal form of repentance. Though the text lacks the *gravitas* of James's emotional words, Sirach 51:19 connects mourning to lack of wisdom: "My soul grappled with wisdom, and in my conduct I was strict; I spread out my hands to the heavens, and lamented my ignorance of her."[348] James's words are also not unlike Jesus' warning: "Woe to you who are laughing now, for you will mourn and weep" (Luke 6:25).

4:9b James turns to another set of images for repentance: "Let your laughter be turned into mourning[349] and your joy into dejection."[350] The lan-

---

347. The field is complex, but one could begin with P. Brown, *Body and Society* (New York: Columbia University Press, 1988); and T. M. Shaw, *The Burden of the Flesh* (Minneapolis: Fortress, 1998). One who has drawn this out into the issue of how Christians conceive of heaven as disembodied is N. T. Wright, *Surprised by Hope* (San Francisco: HarperOne, 2008).

348. See also Ps 69:10-11; Isa 24:4, 7; Jer 4:28; 12:4; Joel 1:8-9; Amos 5:16; Rev 18:11, 15, 19.

349. The noun here (πένθος) is cognate with the verb in the previous sentence.

350. Here James uses a third person aorist passive imperative: μετατραπήτω. See BDAG, 642. God is perhaps the ultimate actor in this passive construction, though the em-

guage reminds one of the reversal theme of 1:9-11 and the potent warnings in 4:13–5:6, and it probably derives in part from Jesus' words, just cited: "Woe to you who are laughing now, for you will mourn and weep" (Luke 6:25; cf. v. 21). Furthermore, the language is similar to what we find in Amos 8:10, where God threatens the same reversal:

> I will turn your feasts into mourning,
>   and all your songs into lamentation;
> I will bring sackcloth on all loins,
>   and baldness on every head;
> I will make it like the mourning for an only son,
>   and the end of it like a bitter day.[351]

But here James calls the teachers and leaders to "let" their laughter[352] and their joy be turned around. He has not mentioned either laughter or joy, and one is led to think he is using Jewish tropes and traditional language.[353] In context, the teachers' laughter and joy need to be connected to their zeal, ambition, cravings, desires, and yearnings toward envy (3:13–4:6). In other words, the language here is either sarcastic or ironic and recalls the rich person "rejoicing" in his humiliation in 1:10. "Dejection," *katēpheia*,[354] is unusual, but what evidence we have suggests that it speaks of depression and sadness, even self-pity. James's intent is to form binary oppositions, laughter over against mourning and joy over against dejection, instead of relying on the subtle nuances of the words.[355]

---

phasis here is on the responsibility of the teachers to transform their laughter and joy into mourning and dejection.

351. See also Tob 2:6 and 1 Macc 9:41, where we hear the report of vengeance by Simon Maccabeus against Jambri on behalf of his captured brother Jonathan: "So the wedding was turned into mourning and the voice of their musicians into a funeral dirge."

352. Thus, Eccl 10:19: "Feasts are made for laughter." See also Sir 19:30; 21:20; 27:13.

353. But see Moo, 195, and especially Martin, 154, who delineates a "festive" and a "foolish" kind of laughter. I see no evidence, especially in 3:1–4:12, of either festive partying or foolish banter. The sort of evidence one finds in Petronius, *Satyricon,* or in Athenaeus, *The Learned Banqueters,* is not to be found in James. So, while the term "laughter" can be connected to that sort of partying, to see it in James requires evidence that the teachers or the intended readers were doing such. It is wiser to leave the language as a trope and focus on what James focuses on: repentance from zeal, ambition, etc., which are destroying the fabric of the messianic community. Finally, the noun χαρά is most likely not connected to this party spirit; see Popkes, 277-78.

354. BDAG, 533; see Wis 17:4; Josephus, *Ant* 2.55, 108; 11.164; 16.122, 258; 19.260; *War* 2.649; 6.98; Hermas, *Visions* 1.2.3.

355. But see Davids, 167-68, in depending on Rengstorf, who suggests that the laughter and joy can be connected to feasting.

6.3.3.6. Humility and Its Promise (4:10)

James now turns to a final summons, and it brings to focus the theme of the entire section from 4:7-9: repentance. As in 4:7b and 4:8a, this last commandment entails a promise: "Humble yourselves before the Lord, and he will exalt you." The language evokes once again the reversal theme of 1:9-11. But instead of talking so directly to the poor as James did there, in the word "humble"[356] he summons the teachers to align themselves with those who are needy and dependent on God. His summons probably owes at least some of its origin to Jesus' teaching in Matthew 23:12: "All who exalt themselves will be humbled, and all who humble themselves will be exalted" (cf. Luke 14:11; 18:14). Paul, too, echoed the same saying of Jesus in 2 Cor 11:7 (cf. 12:21). It is possible, also, that the song behind Philippians 2:5-11 was already at work in the messianic community; there Jesus is the example of the one who humbled himself (2:8). Peter also echoes the saying of Jesus (1 Pet 5:6). James 4:10 brings to final expression, not so much as the culmination but as the final way of calling the teachers to repentance, what we have already encountered in 4:6 and 4:7-9.

The humbling is not just about what the teachers have done or what has now been exposed; nor is this the dishonor they may experience. It refers, rather, to an existential disposition "before the Lord," one that expresses accountability before God.[357] It is not James they have offended with their selfish ambitions; it is not the community; the teachers have offended the Lord in their proud behaviors and attitudes. As Paul states it, no one can boast in God's presence (1 Cor 1:29). Genuine humility is profoundly theological because it is a proper recognition of one's place in this world before the creator, the holy, loving God.

James speaks against the pride of the teachers, as Jesus so graphically did as well (cf. Luke 18:14), and James's promise that God will exalt them follows from the grace God gives to those who are humble (4:6ab). The promise of exaltation captures the reversal theme, but only if the zealous, ambitious, proud teachers will enter into a state of humility before God.[358] Thus, Job 5:11: "he sets on high those who are lowly, and those who mourn are lifted to safety." The exaltation James has in mind does not appeal to the teachers' zeal, ambition, and pride but takes them from their sinful condition into the realm of humble repentance and through that humiliation before God into the world of God's blessing. The exalted place into which God will elevate them is nothing more than living before God properly, loving one's

---

356. ταπεινώθητε. The passive could be middle; see Popkes, 279.

357. ἐνώπιον κυρίου. See, e.g., Luke 1:75; 12:9; 15:10, 18, 21; Acts 7:46. The expression is found more than five hundred times in the LXX. See *EDNT*, 1.462.

358. See Job 22:29; Ps 149:4; Ezek 17:24; Sir 2:17; 3:18; 1QH 15:16; *1 Clement* 18:8; 59:3.

neighbor as oneself, showing compassion for those in need, controlling the tongue, generating peace in the messianic community, and exercising gifts of teaching and leadership in the way God intended. Perhaps that state is best defined by 3:13: "Who is wise and understanding among you? Show by your good life that your works are done with gentleness born of wisdom."

Repentance takes on its genius in this passage, not the least reason being that James never uses the typical word *metanoia* ("repentance").[359] First, repentance is about a person's relationship, mind, and behaviors before God: it is profoundly theological. This is why this section begins and ends with the face of God (4:7, 8a, 10). Second, repentance leads to forgiveness that can be described in terms of purification (4:8b). Third, repentance is both embodied and emotive — as 4:9 makes clear. And, fourth, repentance leads to grace that elevates a person not into envy but into peacemaking, love, and compassionate deeds (4:10).

6.4. TEACHERS, THE COMMUNITY, AND THE TONGUE (4:11-12)

> 11Do not speak[360] evil[a] against one another, brothers and sisters. Whoever[361] speaks evil[a] against another or[362] judges another, speaks evil[a] against the law and judges the law; but if[b] you judge the law, you are not[363] a doer of the law[c] but a judge.[d] 12There is one lawgiver[364] and judge[e][365] who is able to save and to destroy. So who, then,[366] are you[367] to judge your neighbor[368]?[f]

359. See Popkes, 280, on whose observations I base this paragraph.

360. The present imperative is changed to aorist (καταλαλητε) in a number of manuscripts, but this is almost certainly a mistake in hearing. See the correct manuscripts 1, 33, 38, 323 (but not 322), and a number of lectionaries. On the other hand, James is fond of aorist imperatives.

361. Many manuscripts add γαρ, including 18, 35, and 206; also Antiochus Monachus, a Latin manuscript, Coptic Bohairic, Syriac Peshitta, Harklensis, Slavonic, and Ethiopic translations. Original or not, the text is read as providing a reason for 4:11a.

362. Some manuscripts have και instead of ἤ; see 5, 69, 88, 322, 323, Vulgate, some Coptic texts, Syriac Peshitta, and Harklensis.

363. A number of manuscripts have ουκετι instead of οὐκ εἶ (P, Y, 69, 252, etc.). This reading softens the blow.

364. The printed Nestle-Aland[27] is articular (ὁ νομοθέτης), but some early and good manuscripts omit the article (P74, P100, B, and P).

365. Some manuscripts omit καὶ κριτὴς (P74, K, L, 049, 1, 6, etc.).

366. An adversative or inferential particle is assumed, whether original or not. Some sources omit δὲ (206, 429, Pseudo-Oecumenius, Coptic, Armenian, and Georgian).

367. A few manuscripts change ὁ κρίνων to ος κρινεις.

368. πλησίον is altered in some manuscripts to ετερον (69, 88, etc.).

a. TNIV: slander
b. TNIV: When
c. TNIV: not keeping it
d. TNIV: but sitting in judgment on it
e. TNIV: Lawgiver and Judge
f. TNIV: But you — who are you to judge your neighbor?

4:11-12 forms an inclusio with 3:1-2 in that both are preoccupied with speech ethics. This connection provides solid support for the view that the entire section from 3:1 to 4:12 is concerned with teachers, how they speak publicly, and how their poor leadership is destroying the fabric of the messianic community. Not all, however, agree with this summary explanation of the connection of 4:11-12 to what precedes.[369] To be sure, James moves from disparate teachings about divisiveness in 4:1-6 to the summons to repent in 4:7-10, which could have been a climax to the whole section, and then to the theme of judgmental words in 4:11-12. The change in substance and theme at 4:11 is noticeable. But a cohesive reading of 3:1–4:12 leads one to think that verbal sins in the context of the messianic community have been the concern all along. One feature suggesting that 4:11-12 forms the final word on the topic of teachers, leadership, and speech patterns is the shift from distancing words ("adulteresses" in 4:4, "sinners" and "double-minded" in 4:8) to the reuse (from 3:1) of James's favorite pastoral word of inclusion ("brothers [and sisters]") in 4:11. 4:7-10 would have been too harsh an ending but 4:11-12 is not. Nonetheless, the shift from 4:10 to 4:11 is distinct.[370] Davids's suggestion, deriving as it does from his complicated but sophisticated source-critical approach to the letter, that 4:11-12 is a redactional conclusion, is possible. Methodologically I would counter with this observation: if a redactor could have thought of 4:11-12 as suitable to close 3:1–4:10, so also could have the author. Rather than seeing a more or less random exhortation in 4:11-12, it makes more sense to see here the completion of the exhortation about speech patterns, with the addition of a new idea — vaunting oneself as a lawgiver — that carries the polemic of 3:1–4:10 to an accusation at a new level, that of idolatry.

4:11-12 is organized as follows:

1. Prohibition (4:11a): "Do not speak evil against one another, brothers and sisters."

369. Popkes, 280-81, points out all the pressing questions.
370. See Laws, 186. More in line with my thinking, see Moo, 197; also Davids, 168-69. In response to Davids, the term ἀδελφοί is not always indicative of a new section in James but can be found within sections (see 2:5; 3:10, 12; 5:9). In fact, the rhetorical turning within a section with this pastoral term is noticeable in James.

2. Explanation of prohibition (4:11b-12a):
Statement (4:11b): "Whoever speaks evil against another or judges another, speaks evil against the law and judges the law."
Clarification (4:11c): "but if you judge the law, you are not a doer of the law but a judge."
Foundation (4:12a): "There is one lawgiver and judge who is able to save and to destroy."
3. Concluding question (4:12b): "So who, then, are you to judge your neighbor?"

The implicit answer to the concluding question is something like "You are not God; therefore, you should not be judging." The question is damning because its answer is clear, and James has used this technique of argument by way of implied answer to questions before in 3:1–4:12, most notably at 3:11-12; 4:4a, 5. The same was found in the potent ch. 2 (2:7, 14-16, 20-21).

6.4.1. Prohibition (4:11a)

With "do not speak evil against one another" James gives living legs to the general words in 3:1: "Not many of you should become teachers." It is because the teachers are using the tongue to speak evil against one another that that they should not be striving to teach. One of the more notable features of James's rhetoric is his alternation between pastoral inclusiveness, whether with first person plural (3:2, 9) or with "brothers [and sisters]" (3:1, 10), and a rhetorical distancing from his audience with the use of the second person (3:1, 13-16; 4:1-3) and harsh accusations (3:10, 14; 4:1, 4a, 7-10). He makes such a shift in 4:11-12: from harsh distancing language in 4:1-10, culminating in "adulteresses!" and "sinners" and "double-minded" (4:4a, 8b), to the pastoral "brothers and sisters"[371] in 4:11. If James has been forced to throw pointed accusations at the teachers, his intent has not been to accuse or destroy but to warn and lead to repentance and restoration.

The first two Greek words of 4:11 establishes the theme of vv. 11 and 12: "do not speak evil."[372] The verb, *katalaleō*, could indicate a more general speech problem — speaking carelessly, foolishly, or the like — or a more particular problem — slanderous or libelous verbal assaults. There is good evidence for both views.

First, the term can be general: "slander." Thus, Paul could speak of

371. ἀδελφοί. See the notes at 3:1.
372. See BDAG, 519. The present tense prohibition is used to prohibit evil speaking from having a life among them, from becoming a practice. The present tense does not mean that this is already going on (though the context reveals that it is) and that it needs to desist. See Porter, *Idioms,* 224-26.

those who rebel against God as "slanderers, God-haters, insolent . . ." (Rom 1:30) and he feared that among the Corinthians there would be "slanderers" (2 Cor 12:20). Peter, too, lumped "slander" into a batch of sins (1 Pet 2:1). We also find it in lists in *1 Clement* 30; 31; and 35:5; Ignatius, *Philippians* 2:2; 4:3; *Barnabas* 20:2; Hermas, *Mandates* 38.3 and *Similitudes* 92:3; 100:2. And it would be a rough equivalent for what we find in 1QS 4:9-11.[373]

Second, the term can be more particular, but this particularity moves only slightly, from "slander" to "libel." One thinks here of Miriam and Aaron speaking against Moses (Num 12:1-8). The wilderness generation spoke against God (Ps 78:19). A crystal-clear example is Psalm 50:20 (see also 101:5):

> You sit and speak against your kin;
> > you slander your own mother's child.

Jesus knows his followers will experience what he has experienced, namely, opponents speaking falsely against them (Matt 5:11-12). Gentiles, Peter says, speak against those who follow Jesus (1 Pet 2:12; 3:16). The wisdom tradition warns of this sin: "Beware then of useless grumbling, and keep your tongue from slander; because no secret word is without result, and a lying mouth destroys the soul" (Wis 1:11). The sense of the term here is speaking accusingly, falsely, degradingly, dishonorably, and with libelous or slanderous intent in order to label a person as dangerous or unworthy. This sense of "evil speaking" involves an act of judgment against or over another person, and this will become clear when James connects "evil speaking" in 4:11b with "judges."[374]

This sketch of the term is of value to understanding both 4:11-12 and 3:1–4:12 as a whole because it clarifies what has been implicit from the beginning: the particular speech problem the teachers of the messianic community had was slander, libel, and denunciation of others. This fits with the passions that were at work among these leaders: zeal, ambition, cravings, desires, and yearnings toward envy.

It remains to ask who James might have in mind when he says "against one another," and two options are open to us: he could be referring to slander of fellow teachers or of anyone in the messianic community. In context, the former makes the most sense.[375]

---

373. That is, for רָגַב with בְ.

374. See Johnson, 292-93, who discovers a potential connection to Lev 19:16 in theme.

375. It might be argued that James's language of 4:11-12 becomes general in the word ἀδελφός, the clearly gnomic tone of 4:11, and the use of the word πλησίον in 4:12. But it is just as reasonable, in context, to assume that James has applied general legal categories and scriptural allusions (Lev 19:18 is at work in πλησίον) to specify the problems of teachers.

6.4.2. Explanation of Prohibition (4:11b-12a)

6.4.2.1. Statement (4:11b)

James now explains[376] why they should not slander one another. He proceeds by repeating his words ("speaks evil") and clarifying those words with "or judges."[377] He enters into a three-step explanation, and perhaps seeing where he is headed will help us understand. He connects "speaks evil" *(katalalein)* to "judges" *(krinein)* and then connects *krinein* to speaking evil *(katalalein)* against the Torah itself; in fact, the one who speaks against the Torah actually exalts himself[378] to sit in judgment *(krinein)* on the Torah. The one who judges the Law is not under it as a doer but over it as a judge (4:11c). James identifies this as hubris of the highest order: God is the Lawgiver (4:12a), and this leads to James's final accusing question (4:12b): "So who, then, are you?" or, we might say, "Who do you think you are?"

To judge a brother (or sister) is to usurp God's role. Judging, and this is not recognized often enough, is different from discerning.[379] To judge is to condemn and thus to take on a role that is reserved only for God. A good example is the Parable of the Wheat and Weeds, where the desire to uproot weeds is the desire to act in judgment. Jesus meets this with words of patient coexistence until God does the judging (Matt 13:24-30, 36-43). That parable turns what Jesus teaches in Matthew 7:1-5 into a graphic story. Luke 6:37 shows the important connection of "judge" with "condemn": "Do not judge, and you will not be judged; do not condemn, and you will not be condemned." One common argument against judging in the sense of condemning is pragmatic: it turns back on the judging person (Matt 7:1-5; Rom 2:1). A more theological reason is given by Jesus (John 8:15-16), Paul (Rom 14:4; 1 Cor 4:5), and by James (2:12-13; 3:1; 5:9, 12): humans finally answer only to God and not to one another.

But this anticipates what is to come in 4:12. First James lays down the claim that the person who slanders or judges another person "speaks evil against the law and judges the law." The logic of this statement is not obvious, nor does it follow that sitting in judgment on a brother or sister legitimately or appropriately is to slander or condemn the Torah. In order to make sense of this we must consider both the grammar of 4:11b and the substance of 4:11c-12a. The subject of "speaks evil against the law and judges the law" is a complex clause:

376. Many manuscripts, functioning here at least as an early commentary, add explanatory γαρ.

377. ἢ κρίνων τὸν ἀδελφὸν αὐτοῦ. Both substantival participles are present tense because they are suited to sketch a scene. See BDAG, 567-69, 516. Johnson, 293, rightly observes clarification by adding *krinein* here.

378. See ὑπερηφάνοις in the use of Prov 3:34 at Jas 4:6.

379. See the valuable pastoral note in Moo, 199-200.

subject clause	verb and object
Whoever speaks evil against another	speaks evil against the law
or	and
judges another	judges the law.

It is thus the *slandering damner* who runs afoul of James's words. Such a person is actually slandering and judging the Torah because he has usurped the role of God in the act of condemnation and has chosen to defy what God has said not to do.[380] In this way, the slandering damner defies God and transfers authority from God's Torah to himself.[381] So, 4:11b's words make sense only by assuming what is about to be said in 4:11c and 4:12a: that judgment belongs to God alone.

But one question about 4:11b remains: is "the law" the Torah in general, or is James thinking of one particular *mitzvah,* one command? The language could be general, but "neighbor" at the end of 4:12 might indicate that James has Leviticus 19:18 in mind.[382] James has used this term already (2:8), and there are other indicators that Jesus' reformulated version of the *Shema* was central to the ethics of James (1:12, 25a; 2:8-10). If one factors into this the ubiquitous importance of liturgical recitations of the *Shema* among Jews of the period, the evidence is sufficient for us to think that James has Leviticus 19:18 in mind, or at least the combination of Deuteronomy 6:4-5 and Leviticus 19:18. The one who judges another puts himself or herself in the position of God and violates not only love of God but also love of one's neighbor, which is the core of the Torah.[383]

6.4.2.2. Clarification (4:11c)

The rhetorical move from 4:11a to 4:11b assumed the substance of both 4:11c and 4:12a. What James has in mind with "if you judge the law" becomes clear with "you are not a doer of the law but a judge." The fundamental imperative for Israel with respect to God's Torah was to "do" (*'aśâ, poiein*) what God said.[384] This was also what Jesus expected of his followers (Matt 7:21-28; 28:20). James walks the same path (1:22-25). We might call

380. See Johnson, 293.
381. See Martin, 164.
382. Johnson, 293, connects this to Lev 19:16 LXX, which I include for the reader's own inspection: οὐ πορεύσῃ δόλῳ ἐν τῷ ἔθνει σου. οὐκ ἐπισυστήσῃ ἐφ᾽ αἷμα τοῦ πλησίον σου. ἐγώ εἰμι κύριος ὁ θεὸς ὑμῶν. If James is thinking of this verse with the word *katalalia*, he has chosen deliberately to avoid any obvious connection. Moo affirms potential in this suggestion of Johnson, but in Moo's own exposition of Jas 4:11 he quickly, and rightly I think, moves to Lev 19:18 (Moo, 198).
383. See Laws, 187; Davids, 170; Popkes, 283.
384. See *TLOT,* 2.944-51.

this fundamental stance one of being "*under* the Torah." The teacher, however, who moves out from under the law and begins to see himself or herself "*over* the Torah" thus expresses hubris at the highest level. James's conclusion is that "if you judge the law . . . you are a judge." Whatever one thinks of his logic, the intent is clear and doubly expressed.

When James says such a person is a "judge" we must think not in terms of verbal slander of the Torah but, as 4:12a will make clear, sitting in the judge's seat instead of among the Torah-observant citizenship. James's point is where such a person — the slandering damner — locates himself with respect to others, and he will reveal that such a move is idolatrous. God, he says, is the Lawgiver and Judge; humans are "doers" of the Law, not makers of the Law.[385]

6.4.2.3. Foundation (4:12a)

Without punctuation James simply states his point: "There is one lawgiver and judge who is able to save and to destroy." This element of Israel's story, that God is the lawgiver, is the theological foundation of everything James has said in 4:11. His logic is almost like moving forward by walking backward: as he progresses in his argument he has to keep backing up to provide the logical elements he is assuming. Thus, speaking evil entails judging; judging entails sitting over the Torah in judgment; sitting over the Torah entails no longer being a doer. Underneath all these entailments, each of which undergirds why it is wrong to sit in judgment on another, is the obvious but all-important point: God alone is the Lawgiver and Judge. To sit in judgment, then, is to be outside the Torah and above and beyond it. But that is space occupied by God and God alone.

A literal translation of 4:12a reminds one of the *Shema:* "One is the Lawgiver and Judge."[386] There is a reason why "one" is here and it deserves emphasis: in a world where humans were deified and other gods enthroned, Israel heard from on high that there was in fact only one God (Exod 3:14-15; 20:3; Deut 5:6-7; 6:4-9; Zech 14:9). What is expressed here is the uniqueness, unity, and exclusivity of Israel's God.[387] James's words are potent: he has now pushed the teachers to the point where they are to see that their denunciatory rhetoric and their zeal, ambition, and envy have led them not to

---

385. Popkes, 282.

386. Behind εἷς, "one," is Hebrew אֶחָד, the unapproachable and incomprehensible and indivisible oneness of God. See *TLOT,* 1.78-80. Str-B 2.30 offers much later rabbinic evidence that God could be called "The One."

387. See especially R. Bauckham, "Biblical Theology and the Problems of Monotheism," in *Out of Egypt: Biblical Theology and Biblical Interpretation* (ed. C. Bartholomew, et al.; Grand Rapids: Zondervan, 2004), 187-232.

the top of the heap but to the gates of God's throne room, where they are now hubristically demanding a seat on the throne. This One is both Lawgiver and Judge.[388] The only use of the noun "Lawgiver" *(nomothetēs)* in the LXX subliminally works to defeat the zeal and ambition of the teachers in the book of James: Psalm 9:21 (9:20 in English versions) in the LXX reads "Put down, Lord, the *legislator* on them" with the implication that God is to activate the reality that he is the lawgiver and that the Gentiles are only human.[389] Because God is creator, redeemer, lawgiver, and judge of all creation, God alone is the one who can "judge the law."

James's point has been made with the statement that the one God is Lawgiver and Judge, but the rhetoric of the passage must move from the theological indicative to the ecclesial, practical imperative and so James adds a rhetorical warning: "who is able to save and to destroy."[390] This statement, even though so general it hardly needs a fixed origin, could be from Jesus: "Do not fear those who kill the body but cannot kill the soul; rather fear him who can destroy both soul and body in hell" (Matt 10:28).[391] The saying could also come from Deuteronomy 32:39:

> See now that I, even I, am he;
>> there is no god beside me.
> I kill and I make alive;
>> I wound and I heal;
>> and no one can deliver from my hand.[392]

Whether it comes from Jesus or from Moses the rhetorical function is the same: James hereby threatens the teachers with final judgment at the hand of the one God, who determines life and death.

388. There is (most likely) one article that joins the two nouns together: "the Lawgiver-and-Judge": [ὁ] νομοθέτης καὶ κριτὴς. On νομοθέτης, cf. BDAG, 676; the word is often translated "legislator."

389. The Hebrew has two lines: "Put them in fear, YHWH; let the nations know that they are only human." The "fear" in mind probably has to do with the Exodus. See also in the LXX translations of Exod 24:12; Deut 17:10; Pss 25:8, 12; 27:11; 119:33, 102, 104; 2 Macc 3:15; *4 Maccabees* 5:25; see also at Heb 7:11; 8:6. The word is used for Moses often; e.g., Philo, *Moses* 2:9; Josephus, *Against Apion* 1:284-85; *Ant* 1.19.

390. God, characteristically (hence present tense), has the capacity and ability both to save and to destroy — both aorists in order to conceptualize the acts of saving and destroying in their totality. These are acts *that* God can do (and does do).

391. Hermas, *Mandates* 12.6.3 and *Similitudes* 9.23.4, sound like Jas 4:12.

392. See also 1 Sam 2:6-7; 2 Kgs 5:7.

6.4.3. Concluding Question (4:12b)

One is tempted to translate the last question of this verse with "Who in the world do you think you are?" The "you," which is emphatic here,[393] is defined: "you" is the one who judges, the one who stands over his neighbor in the way that God stands over all creation.[394] Here James draws us into the Jesus Creed, the use of Deuteronomy 6:4-5 and Leviticus 19:18 as the foundational ethical directive for each follower of Jesus (Mark 12:28-32). Instead of standing next to the neighbor in love, the teachers had assumed the position of God and were over the neighbor. This, I am suggesting, is where James has driven the teachers: their zeal, ambition, cravings, desires, and yearnings toward envy have driven them up the ladder to the point where they are now assuming the prerogative of the one God who is Lawgiver and Judge. Such is their hubris; such is their idolatry.

James abruptly finishes the theme of the teachers and the tongue. He moves on and we will follow him.

7. THE MESSIANIC COMMUNITY AND THE WEALTHY (4:13–5:11)

7.1. THE SIN OF PRESUMPTION (4:13-17)

13*Come now,*[a] *you who say, "Today or*[1] *tomorrow we will go*[2] *to such*

---

393. "But you, who . . ." translates σὺ δὲ τίς. We should be careful to avoid suggesting that this δέ is equivalent to ἀλλά. It is not. The enclitic slides into the personal pronoun and the interrogative to give the force of "but you who do you think . . ." instead of a "but you, in contrast to God, who. . . ." The use of the singular can be given several explanations, including a charged focus on one person (which seems unlikely to me) or a highly personalized application (which seems more likely), but it remains unusual for James to move all the way through 3:1–4:11 with plurals and suddenly turn to a singular.

394. As stated above, the use of "neighbor" probably derives from Lev 19:18 and Jas 2:8-10.

1. Some manuscripts have καί instead of ἤ. The disjunctive is found in P74, א, B, Y, 5, 322, 323, etc., as well as in Latin, Coptic, Syriac, and Ethiopic versions. The support for καί, however, apart from the valuable witnesses for the disjunctive, includes A, P, 69, Byzantine, Cyril of Alexander, Gregorius Agrigentinus, Pseudo-Oecumenius, and Coptic, Syriac, and Armenian evidence.

2. The NRSV translates a text that has the future πορευσόμεθα, but a number of early and valuable manuscripts have the subjunctive πορευσώμεθα. The same occurs with the next three verbs in v. 13. The details can be overwhelming, and, since this is not a text-critical commentary on James, I shall stick to the major uncials for a brief sketch of the issues. (The four verbs, in future tense form, are πορευσόμεθα, ποιήσομεν, ἐμπορευσόμεθα,

and such[b] a town and spend a[3] year there, doing business and making money." 14*Yet you do not even know what[4] tomorrow will bring.[c5] What is your life? For you are[6] a mist that appears for a little while and then vanishes.* 15*Instead you ought to say, "If the Lord wishes,[d7] we will live and do[8] this or that."* 16*As it is, you boast in[9] your arrogance;[e10] all such boasting is evil.* 17*Anyone, then, who knows the right thing to do and fails to do it, commits sin.[f]*

a. TNIV: Now listen

b. TNIV: this or that

c. TNIV: Why, you do not even know what will happen tomorrow.

d. TNIV: If it is the Lord's will

e. TNIV: in your arrogant schemes

f. TNIV, *using second person:* if you know the good you ought to do and don't do it, you sin

The structure of James perplexes each of its serious readers.[11] Without warning, but with undeniable indicators of interest in similar themes, James launches into strong words for merchants. We consider 4:13–5:6 (or 4:13–

and κερδήσομεν, which are referred to as A, B, C, and D.) The future indicative of verb A is supported by ℵ, B, K, and P, and the subjunctive is found at A and Y. As for verb B, the future indicative is found at B and P, while the subjunctive is found at ℵ, A, and Y. Next, verb C: the future indicative is found at ℵ, A, B, and P, while the subjunctive can be seen in only Y. Finally, verb D is future in ℵ, A, B, and P, while again only Y has the subjunctive. It is more likely that a future indicative was shifted to an aorist subjunctive than the reverse, and the balance of the earliest evidence favors the indicatives against the Byzantine "correction."

3. Some manuscripts add "one" (ἕνα) to clarify how long.

4. Instead of the Nestle-Aland[27] τό, many manuscripts have the plural τα (A, P, 33, 81, etc.); B omits both articles.

5. Many manuscripts add γαρ: P74 and P100. ℵ has a second reading here; see A, P, Y, 5, 33, 322, 323, as well as the Byzantine tradition and Coptic, Syriac, Georgian, and Slavonic readings. The asyndeton may be more difficult, but it might also be seen as too difficult.

6. A number of manuscripts have the third singular future εσται (K, P, Y, 049, 1, 6, and many lectionaries) or the third singular present εστιν (e.g., L, 056, 0142, etc.) instead of ἐστε. Each of the readings makes sense, even if less personal than ἐστε, but the meaning is shifted only slightly. See Omanson, 477.

7. Some manuscripts alter the aorist subjunctive to a future indicative (049, 1*, 6, etc., and a few lectionaries), while a few others alter it to a present subjunctive (B, P, etc.).

8. Again, some later manuscripts alter both ζήσομεν and ποιήσομεν to the subjunctive.

9. Some manuscripts alter ἐν to επι (206, 429, etc.).

10. Later copyists added δε, ουν, or γαρ to clarify the relationship of the clauses.

11. See Taylor, "Recent Scholarship."

5:11) a new section in the letter,[12] not because it is clear this is a new section but because it is unclear how it fits with 3:1–4:12.[13] This next section connects to themes found in 1:9-11 and 2:5-7, but 2:5-7 did not appear to be addressed at all to business travelers, and to find the same in 1:9-11 is to import too much. Some have suggested that 4:13–5:6 develops friendship with the world, mentioned in 4:4, but we have already suggested that what James had in mind there was zeal and ambition for power with no thought there of wealth. Others, with more basis, connect 4:13-17 to the theme of arrogance in 4:1-6.[14] If we connect 4:13-17 with 5:1-6 and see in both the same targeted audience, since 5:1-6 brings up oppression, we could find connections back to 2:5-7 and perhaps even to where the zeal and ambitions of the leaders were taking them in 3:1–4:12. To anticipate some of our conclusions below, in 5:7-11 James tells the community how to respond to the wealthy, whom James has excoriated in 4:13–5:6.[15]

The passage flows from a description of the problem, namely the sin of presumption (4:13), into James's instruction (4:14-17). His instruction begins with the brevity of life (4:14), the alternative to presumption (4:15), the fundamental problem with presumption (4:16) and a final warning (4:17).[16]

7.1.1. Description of the Sin of Presumption (4:13)

James is fond of sudden, strong, attention-grabbing rhetoric. "Whenever you face trials of any kind, consider it nothing but joy" (1:2) and "Let the believer who is lowly boast in being raised up . . ." (1:9). "What good is it, my brothers and sisters, if you say you have faith but do not have works?" (2:14) or "Not many of you should become teachers" (3:1). So also in 4:13: "Come now, you who say, 'Today or tomorrow we will go to such and such a town and spend a year there, doing business and making money.'" Not only is the rhetoric arresting, but it is forceful enough to put his readers/listeners on their heels with his opening words: "Come now, you who say."[17]

---

12. See Moo, 200-201, though I cannot agree that 5:7-11 belongs with 4:13–5:6. The change of audience in 5:7 to ἀδελφοί is notable. As we will show below, it is quite likely that 5:7-11 is how the messianic community is to respond to the oppressive measures of the wealthy, who are accused of presumption and oppression in 4:13–5:6.

13. See Davids, 171. Martin, 159-62, explains 4:13–5:6 through the lens of verbal sins.

14. Laws, 189.

15. See Maynard-Reid, *Poverty and Wealth in James,* 68-98; B. Noack, "Jakobus wider die Reichen," *ST* 18 (1964) 10-25; Hartin, 231-40.

16. See J. Duncan M. Derrett, "The Epistle of James and the Dhammadapada Commentary," *STK* 82 (2006) 36-39, especially 37-39.

17. Ἄγε νῦν οἱ λέγοντες. The singular imperative of ἄγω has become an interjec-

A question immediately presents itself: Are the ones "who say" messianists or not?[18] In light of 1:10 (see the comments there), a case can be made that these traveling businesspersons are not messianists.[19] The language of James about the wealthy indicates that he uses the term "rich" the way other *Anawim* did: that term represents the ungodly oppressors (see also 2:6-7). Furthermore, if we connect 4:13-17 to 5:1-6 and see the same audience, then an even stronger case can be made for the businesspersons of 4:13 not being messianists.[20] Also, it is perhaps not without significance that James does not refer to his audience as "brothers and sisters" in 4:13–5:6.

But, the language of 4:13-17 convinces others that the travelers are messianists.[21] To begin with, and perhaps not observed carefully enough, James is a Christian (1:1; 2:1) and thinks these folks will and should listen to him. That assumption might indicate that his audience is the messianic community and that these business travelers are part of that community. Furthermore, 4:15's assumption that they should be consulting "the Lord," which in light of 1:1; 2:1; 5:7-8, 10-11, 14-15, where "Lord" refers to Jesus Christ, suggests they are messianists. (We will contest this reading of 4:15 below.) Also, 4:16-17 assumes that James's readers will agree with his understanding of both "arrogance" and "sin," and these may well be Christian perceptions of both. Even if 4:16-17 does not indicate a messianic orientation, 4:15 does for many.[22] In what follows we will suggest otherwise, but our commentary below will carry the responsibility for the argument.

The merchants' claims are fourfold, and James puts them into the fu-

---

tion in function, and this is visible in our verse because it is used with the plural οἱ λέγοντες; see BDAG, 9; BDF, §144; see also §364.2; see also the German edition, F. Rehkopf, *Grammatik des neutestamentlichen Griechisch* (15th ed.; Göttingen: Vandenhoeck und Ruprecht, 1979), §§107.2, 364.2. ἄγε is also found at 5:1, showing a subtle connection between 4:13-17 and 5:1-6. Johnson, 294-95, finds parallels in many sources, including two LXX references: Judg 19:6 and Isa 43:6. The present tense of the substantival participle makes the quotation more vivid.

18. We need to be careful about a facile "in" versus "out" mentality in this question. James is writing to messianic followers of Jesus, but they are most likely Jews. The distinction in this book between a non-messianic Jew and a messianic Jew is not as radical as between a messianic Roman and a non-messianic (pagan) Roman who offers a sacrifice on any one of the many altars at, say, Pompeii.

19. See Martin, 159, even though he calls it a "moot question." See also the discussion in Guthrie, 260-61.

20. See Laws, 190. See the discussion in Maynard-Reid, *Poverty and Wealth in James,* 69.

21. So Moo, 201; Blomberg and Kamell, 206-11.

22. So Davids, 171. The Christian teachings of Rom 2:14-15; 13:3-4; 1 Pet 2:12; 3:13, however, suggest that the leaders of the earliest messianic groups expected moral perceptions on the part of Gentiles and non-believers. See Laws, 190.

ture tense to give them vitality and conviction, even while he exposes the shameless, impious presumption of these people: (1) "we will go," (2) we will "spend a year," (3) we will be "doing business," and (4) we will be "making money." First, time is under their control: they will do these things "today or tomorrow."[23] Second, location is also under their control: "we will go to such and such a town."[24] Third, the duration of their business dealings is in their hands: "spend a year there."[25] Fourth, their labors and profits are under their control: "doing business and making money."[26] What kind of business dealing took place is not specified, but it might have involved selling local products elsewhere — say grain, figs, wine, olives, or shoes — purchasing items elsewhere to import — say incense, spices, silk, rare woods, livestock, pottery, or baskets — establishing a business in another location, or hiring oneself out to such a business. Regardless, the Hellenization of the land of Israel led to increasing opportunities for business. The last term, "making money," is the goal of James's rhetoric: the merchants have it all mapped out, and the goal is financial profit. Gain is the goal of business (cf. Matt 25:16-17, 20, 22). But just as James is not against planning, so also he is not against profits. He uses this language of planning and profit to construct a scenario of arrogant presumption, not to cut into the very nature of human existence. In other words, 4:13 is not fully clear until 4:15-17.

A similar castigation of presumption can be seen in Jesus' words: "what it will profit them if they *gain* the whole world but forfeit their life?" (Matt 16:26). Paul, agreeing with both Jesus and James, turns the language on its head in Philippians 3:8: "More than that, I regard everything as loss because of the surpassing value of knowing Christ Jesus my Lord. For his sake I have suffered the loss of all things, and I regard them as rubbish, in order that I may *gain* Christ" (see also 1:21; 3:7; Tit 1:11). James 4:16's fo-

---

23. σήμερον ἢ αὔριον. On αὔριον in tropes, see Matt 6:30, 34; 1 Cor 15:32.

24. εἰς τήνδε τὴν πόλιν. The word τήνδε, according to BDF, §289 (see also Rehkopf, *Grammatik* §289, n. 4), does not stem from ὅδε but from combining τὴν καὶ τὴν. But see BDAG, 689-90. The use of τοῦτο ἢ ἐκεῖνο in Jas 4:15 is a near synonym. On travel, see L. Casson, *Travel in the Ancient World* (Baltimore: Johns Hopkins University Press, 1994); a sketch can be found in Maynard-Reid, *Poverty and Wealth in James,* 71-73; on trade for Palestine, see Z. Safrai, *The Economy of Roman Palestine* (New York: Routledge, 1994), 269-304; S. Appelbaum, "Economic Life in Palestine," in Safrai, *JPFC,* 1.2. 631-700; Jeremias, *Jerusalem,* 25-57. See also Martin, 162.

25. The verb ποιεῖν with ἐνιαυτόν, literally "do a year," means spend a year (BDAG, 336-37). See other time expressions of duration at Acts 15:33; 18:23; 20:3.

26. καὶ ἐμπορευσόμεθα καὶ κερδήσομεν. There is nothing in the Greek to indicate a change in verbal form as we see in the NRSV when it moves from simple verbs to "doing business and making money." The staccato effect of one thing after another is a chain of confidence. On ἐμπορεύομαι, see BDAG, 324 (also at 2 Pet 2:3); Popkes, 188-289; on κερδαίνω, see BDAG, 541; Spicq, 2.159-60.

cus on pride clarifies the meaning of "today or tomorrow" as an expression of presumption.

These words and the disposition of merchants stand diametrically opposed to the stance of Jesus regarding time (Matt 6:11, 25-34). They also are against the wisdom tradition's theme: "The human mind plans the way, but the Lord directs the steps" (Prov 16:9) or "All our steps are ordered by the Lord; how then can we understand our own ways?" (20:24). The prophets, too, warn of presumption: "I know, O LORD, that the way of human beings is not in their control, that mortals as they walk cannot direct their steps" (Jer 10:23).[27]

7.1.2. James's Instruction (4:14-17)

Now that he has sketched the sin of presumption on the part of merchants, James begins his instruction (4:14-17). First, the span of life is not in our control (4:14); second, instead of the merchant living under the providence and guidance of the Lord (4:15), he is living in arrogance (4:16). Finally, James offers a dual conclusion that simultaneously warns and exhorts (4:17).

7.1.2.1. The Brevity of Life (4:14)

The merchants presume upon God for travel, safety, business, and profits. James counters their presumption with a stern reminder of the brevity of life, a reminder that evokes what he said in 1:9-11. Rhetorically James opens up with a word that leads to a suddenly incomplete thought, but the translations struggle to make it clear and readable English. The NRSV reads "Yet" and the TNIV "Why." The Greek sentence, however, begins with the indefinite personal pronoun (masculine) "whoever."[28] But a verb does not follow — instead, James moves to "you do not even know what tomorrow will bring." One might translate, "I don't care who you are" or "Whoever you might be, it doesn't matter . . ." because "you do not even know. . . ." C. F. D. Moule suggested the "whoever" functions here as a mild adversative: "whereas actually."[29]

The merchants, in spite of their presumption, "do not even know what tomorrow will bring." This translation is clear and is probably an accurate rendering of the Greek, but the Greek itself is messy. It begins with "you do

27. See also Pss 37:23; 119:133. Behind their presumption could be avarice as well: Prov 20:23; Mic 6:11; Amos 8:4-6; Sir 26:29–27:2.
28. οἵτινες. BDAG, 729-30. It forms an anacolouthon in Jas 4:14a, though it could be part of an ellipsis: "Those who say [4:13] . . . you are those [who say and] who do not even know. . . ." See Martin, 165.
29. Moule, *Idiom Book,* 124. I have been inclined in my career to trust Moule's suggestions.

not even know," and this is the clear part. The verb is one of mental apprehension (*epistamai*, related to our word "epistemology").[30] Abraham trusted God "not knowing where he was going" (Heb 11:8), but the presumptuous merchants were not trusting God and still thought they knew where they were going, what they would do, and that they would profit. The grammar next becomes elliptical, and it is even possible that we are to read two clauses together: "You do not even know what your life will be tomorrow." But, because so many early manuscripts add a "for" between "will bring" and "What is your life?" and because this early instinctual reading of the text functions at least as commentary, it is most likely that "What is your life?" is a separate sentence. That means we have to deal with "You do not even know what tomorrow will bring." And the problem here is the Greek:

> to   tēs   aurion
> that   of   tomorrow

The "that" is an article that appears to be the object of "know,"[31] but the "of" (*tēs*, the feminine genitive article) sends us looking for a feminine noun, and one is not to be found. So, we are left to infer the word "day" (*hēmeras*), leaving us with "you do not even know that, or what [will occur] on the day on the morrow." The ambiguity of this English translation matches the ambiguity of the Greek. The wisdom tradition routinely reflected on the transitoriness of life in terms not unlike James (cf. Wis 2:1-9).[32] James's saying is rooted in Proverbs 27:1, which in some ways clears up our verse: "Do not boast about tomorrow, for you do not know what a day may bring."[33] Jesus, too, made a similar statement (Matt 6:34). It seems safe to conclude that James asserts the brevity of life by asserting the merchants' ignorance even of what will happen tomorrow, let alone what they think will happen in their business accomplishments over the next year.

James now restates his point, perhaps knowing that some of his readers will have been confused by his ellipsis: "What is your life? For you are a mist that appears for a little while and then vanishes." The question deals with the merchants' ignorance of what kind[34] of life they may have: is it a

---

30. See BDAG, 380. Good examples in the New Testament include Mark 14:68; Acts 10:28; 15:7; 18:25; 19:15; 22:19; Jude 10.

31. As noted above, some manuscripts have the plural τὰ because they read it with ποία, but this is unlikely to be original.

32. See Seneca's essay *On the Shortness of Life*.

33. LXX: μὴ καυχῶ τὰ εἰς αὔριον οὐ γὰρ γινώσκεις τί τέξεται ἡ ἐπιοῦσα. See also Prov 3:6-8.

34. ποία, from ποῖος (BDAG, 843-44), but it could be equivalent to τίς and be rendered not "what kind of life is your life?" but "what is your life?"

long life? a profitable life? They do not know. Why? Because the life of a human being is "a mist that appears for a little while and then vanishes."[35] Once again, James's focus is the transitoriness of life and he draws on a stock image — a mist or vapor[36] in the sky that under the heat of the day dissipates and disappears.[37] When Abraham looked down the plain toward Sodom he saw a dense smoke, like "smoke [LXX *atmis*] from a furnace" (Gen 19:28). The sacrificial incense gave off a "smoke [*atmis*]" (Lev 16:13). But we are closer to James's sense of transitoriness with Hosea 13:3:

> Therefore they will be like the morning mist,
>> like the early dew that disappears,
>> like chaff swirling from a threshing floor,
>> like smoke escaping through a window.

And Wisdom 2:4-5:

> Our name will be forgotten in time,
> and no one will remember our works;
> our life will pass away like the traces of a cloud,
> and be scattered like mist
> that is chased by the rays of the sun
> and overcome by its heat.
> For our allotted time is the passing of a shadow,
> and there is no return from our death,
> because it is sealed up and no one turns back.

Acts 2:19 refers to portents in the sky, one of which is "smoky mist."[38] Agrarian cultures watch the weather, and few things are as noticeable as vaporous clouds that bring no rain. These puffs of mist appear for awhile and then disappear.

---

35. James again uses descriptive presents.

36. See BDAG, 149.

37. Grammatically, this is a simple predicate sentence: [ὑμεῖς] ἐστε ἀτμίς. Everything else modifies adjectivally the word ἀτμίς. Both φαινομένη and ἀφανιζομένη are adjectival participles, and the two adverbs (πρὸς ὀλίγον, ἔπειτα) work with the verbal element of the participles.

38. See also Job 7:7, 9, 16; Ps 39:5-6; Wis 5:13; Sir 11:19; *4 Ezra* 4:24 ("our life is like a mist"); 7:61 ("for it is now they who are like a mist, and are similar to a flame and smoke — they are set on fire and burn hotly, and are extinguished"); 1QM 15:10; 1Q27 fragment 1 1:5-6; *1 Clement* 17:5-6.

7.1.2.2. Providence or Presumption (4:15-16)

4:15 Even more than the pragmatic argument that life is short (4:14) is the argument that God is sovereign, that all of life is in God's hands, and that genuine piety looks to God's guidance even for business pursuits.[39] In direct contrast[40] to the merchants' presumptuous planning, James has an alternative plan: "Instead you ought to say, 'If the Lord wishes, we will live and do this or that.'" This is the standard interpretation, and I am unpersuaded that it is accurate, though one would be rash to think any solution will be compelling. To begin with, the Greek text — literally rendered — omits "ought" and simply has "Instead of your saying." It makes a significant difference if 4:15 is construed as direct, positive instruction — "you ought to be saying, 'If the Lord wills . . .'" — or as counter-instruction — "instead of your saying 'If the Lord wills. . . .'"

Once one renders the opening clause "instead of your saying," I suggest one can convert 4:15 and 4:16 into two legs of a tandem statement:

> Instead of your saying, "If the Lord wills, we will live and . . . ,"
> *you are now boasting. . . .*

In this rendering James is relentlessly critical: he describes the sin of presumption in 4:13, he criticizes that presumption by reminding his readers of the brevity of life in 4:14, and the impact of 4:15-16 then is that they are filled with arrogant boasts. While not impossible, the suggestion that 4:15 is a momentary reprieve from the critique is less likely than a consistent listing of the problems James has with the merchants that this alternate reading sug-

---

39. See K. Backhaus, "Condicio Jacobaea. Jüdische Weisheitstradition und christliche Alltagsethik nach Jak 4, 13-17," in *Schrift und Tradition* (ed. K. Backhaus and F. G. Untergassmair; Paderborn: Schöningh, 1996), 135-58.

40. Again without a conjunction, James begins his next thought with ἀντὶ plus the infinitive with its accusative subject (τοῦ λέγειν ὑμᾶς). Nearly everyone assumes that "ought" is implicit in this expression: "Instead you *ought* to say. . . ." E.g., Davids, 172, connects ἀντὶ τοῦ λέγειν ὑμᾶς to οἱ λέγοντες in v. 13, which makes sense but is even more difficult grammatically. Thus, "You say, 'today or tomorrow . . . ,' *instead of your saying*, 'if the Lord wishes. . . .'" And there seems to be an implicit understanding that the content of the saying expressed in λέγειν is found in v. 13. Thus, "Instead of saying what we read in v. 13, *you ought to be saying* what we read in v. 15." So also Johnson, 296. Not only does this mean one has to leave 4:15 as a suspended sentence, fill in lots of unexpressed words and — rhetorically and grammatically difficult — skip over v. 14, but it strains the participle of v. 13a into a verb and asks v. 15 to complete v. 13. I am not sure this is accurate. The Greek should be rendered, "Instead of your saying" (Moule, *Idiom Book*, 128) and not "instead you ought to be saying." When working on this verse I had some private correspondence with Denny Burk, and I am grateful to him for helping me to clarify my thinking.

gests. What I have observed is that most commentators, after suggesting that 4:15 completes 4:13 and therefore leaving 4:16 as a point on its own, interpret 4:15 with 4:16.[41]

That God is sovereign characterizes Israel's faith even if, as Josephus's famous passages on the differences among the Jewish parties, there was the common struggle to make sense of both human choice and divine providence.[42] Perhaps the later rabbinic statement represents most of Judaism: "Everything is foreseen, and free choice is given" (*m Avot* 3.15). James's aim, however, is not to speculate about how choice and providence are to be explained. His point is the attitude, disposition, and presumption of the merchants. The merchants were presumptuous when they should have been more reverential and humble about their plans. Thus, these words express what was not in fact their orientation: "If the Lord[43] wishes, we will live and do this or that."[44] This reminds one of Proverbs 19:21: "The human mind may devise many plans, but it is the purpose of the Lord that will be established." But this wisdom saying contrasts God with humans while James goes beyond the contrast to dependency. James is closer to 1QS 11:10-11:

> Surely a man's way is not his own; neither can any person firm his own step. Surely justification is of God; by His power is the way made perfect. All that shall be, He foreknows, all that is, His plans establish; apart from Him is nothing done.

Even if Jews did not knock on wood and utter *deo volente*[45] as the Romans did or speak of God's will as the Greeks did,[46] it boggles the mind that Sophie Laws can conclude that James's line is the "commendation of a

---

41. But see Popkes, 286, 289, who sees 2:14 as a parenthesis.

42. Josephus, *War* 2.119-66; *Ant* 13.171 and especially 18.11-25. For a robust discussion with a focus on the rabbis, see Urbach, *The Sages,* 255-85.

43. The evidence in James is not clear; this term can refer to Christ (1:1; 2:1) or to the Father (3:9; 4:10; 5:4). Some references are simply not clear (1:7-8; 5:7-8, 10-11, 14-15). I intuit that 4:15 refers to the Father; so Popkes, 291.

44. ἐὰν ὁ κύριος θελήσῃ καὶ ζήσομεν καὶ ποιήσομεν τοῦτο ἢ ἐκεῖνο. The potentiality of the aorist subjunctive, which depicts summative action, slides the apodosis into the future tense in the second and third verbs to increase the sense of deliberation in dependence on God. See Porter, *Idioms,* 45. The double καὶ could mean "both live and do"; see Davids, 172. (Some manuscripts have the subjunctive ζήσωμεν, giving the protasis two verbs.)

45. Dibelius, 233-34.

46. Thus, "You and the state, if you act wisely and justly, will act according to the will of God," from Plato's *Alcibiades* 135d (in the mouth of Socrates to Alcibiades); see also *Phaedrus* 80d; Epictetus, *Discourses* 1.1.17; 3.21.12, 22.2; Seneca, *Epistles* 101.

pious phrase of undeniably heathen origins."[47] Furthermore, James here advocates what is patently an early Christian theme and disposition, whether the terms are present or not. There ought to be contingency in all plans. It begins with the Lord's prayer (Matt 6:10), and Paul famously expresses himself in these terms, especially when speaking of travel plans: "But I will come to you soon, if the Lord wills, and I will find out not the talk of these arrogant people but their power" (1 Cor 4:19) and "I do not want to see you now just in passing, for I hope to spend some time with you, if the Lord permits" (16:7; cf. Rom 1:10; Phil 2:19, 24). The author of Acts depicted Paul in similar terms: "but on taking leave of them, he said, 'I will return to you, if God wills.' Then he set sail from Ephesus" (Acts 18:21).[48] That James moves from the summative dependence on the Lord's will to "will live" points to God as creator and sustainer of all of life. Even the indeterminacy of "do this or that" evokes dependence on the Lord's will.

4:16 Instead of an orientation in life that looks to God and depends on God, the merchants are presumptuous; their sin is hubris. In fact, James says to them directly, "As it is, you boast in your arrogance."[49] The contrast[50] here is between what their orientation should be and what in fact it is. The fundamental problem here is their "arrogance" *(alazoneia)*.[51] A sterling example of arrogance was Antiochus Epiphanes, of whom 2 Maccabees 9:8 says, "Thus he who only a little while before had thought in his superhuman *arrogance* that he could command the waves of the sea, and had imagined that he could weigh the high mountains in a balance, was brought down to earth and carried in a litter, making the power of God manifest to all."[52] There are even more resemblances in Wisdom 5:1-10, which not only suggests that the merchants are not messianists but that also contrasts the unrighteous with the righteous. On that day, the unrighteous oppressors will say of the righteous,

47. Laws, 192.
48. Cf. Heb 6:3; Ignatius, *Ephesians* 20:1. See Davids, 173.
49. νῦν δὲ καυχᾶσθε ἐν ταῖς ἀλαζονείαις ὑμῶν. Again, James prefers the present tense to describe something vividly. The prepositional phrase ἐν ταῖς ἀλαζονείαις is most likely the object of their boasting or perhaps the sphere in which the merchants live and out of which the boasting emerges. It is hard to imagine boasting about one's arrogance, for in admitting one's arrogance one has already condemned oneself. Laws takes the prepositional phrase adverbially (Laws, 192). But see Moo, 206-7, who observes that καυχάομαι with ἐν often indicates that in which one is boasting (see Rom 2:17; 5:3, 11; 1 Cor 1:31; 3:21, etc.). On ἀλαζονεία, see BDAG, 40.
50. νῦν δὲ, which may recall 4:13.
51. See also at 1 John 2:16: "for all that is in the world — the desire of the flesh, the desire of the eyes, the pride [ἀλαζονεία] in riches [τοῦ βίου] — comes not from the Father but from the world."
52. So also of Nicanor (2 Macc 15:6); contrasting reason with the passions, *4 Maccabees* 1:26 speaks of "arrogance" as a disease of the soul (see 2:15; 8:19).

We took our fill of the paths of lawlessness and destruction,
and we journeyed through trackless deserts,
but the way of the Lord we have not known.
What has our *arrogance* profited us?
And what good has our boasted wealth brought us?

(Wis 5:7-8; cf. 17:7)

The merchants are arrogant in that they think their time, the locations to which they can go, their business activities, and their profits are all under their control. None of this occurs out of respect for the providence of God and the need to depend on God for life and direction.

Emerging from the merchants' arrogance is boasting.[53] James shares the radical upside-down world of Paul, who boasts in the cross of Christ (Gal 6:13-14), in that the poor, humble believer is to boast in his or her own impoverishment (Jas 1:9). But this is not the pattern of the merchants, who, like the rich person of 1:10, needs to learn to boast, not in his or her own accomplishments or plans but about being connected to the Lord of glory, who suffered and identified with the poor and suffering. The merchants' boasting was both verbal (cf. 3:5) and behavioral (4:13).[54]

James says such boasting is "evil"[55] but he will quickly combine this sentence to another in which the word "sin" *(hamartia)* will be used. It is wise to interpret them together. It is easier to move from the heart of all sins in pride, as so many moralists and theologians have done and continue to do,[56] than it is to read James from the bottom up. For James, the sin involved here is a merchants' sin, the sin of presumptuous planning and arrogant confidence that they can control life and profits. Simultaneously, this arrogance ignores the all-too-common reminder that life is short and that God is in control of all.

53. Cognates behind our word "boast" are found twice in Jas 4:16: καυχάομαι and καύχησις; see BDAG, 536, 537; Popkes, 293. Paul likes to use this word for those who can establish themselves before God (Rom 2:17, 23), and Paul turns this around to boast in what God does for us (Rom 5:2, 11; 1 Cor 1:29, 31; 4:7; 2 Cor 11:30; 12:5, 9; Gal 6:13-14; Eph 2:9; Phil 3:3). The special use of "boasting" in 2 Cor 10–11 is not germane here.

54. *1 Clement* 21:5: "Let us offend foolish and senseless men who exalt themselves and boast in the arrogance of their words, rather than God." See also Prov 21:24.

55. πονηρά; see BDAG, 851-52. Used only here and at 2:4 in James. The word is found 72 times in the New Testament, including Matt 5:45; 7:11; 9:4; 12:34-35, 39, 45; 13:49; 15:19; 18:32; 22:10; Luke 3:19; John 3:19; 7:7; Acts 17:5; Rom 12:9; 1 Cor 5:13; Gal 1:4; Eph 5:16; 6:13, 16; Col 1:21; 1 Thess 5:22; 2 Thess 3:2-3; 2 Tim 3:13; Heb 3:12; 10:22; 2 John 11.

56. C. S. Lewis, *Mere Christianity* (New York: Macmillan, 1956), 94-99, where he discusses pride as the great sin.

7.1.2.3. Conclusion (4:17)

As was the case at the end of 3:1–4:12, this conclusion lacks potent closure. James has, however, made his point: he has accused the merchants of presumption and arrogance. He now reminds them of something they already know but are not following: "Anyone, then, who knows the right thing to do and fails to do it, commits sin" (4:17).[57] A logical inference is drawn with the word "then" *(oun)*. If the logical inference is retrospective, it is drawn from what James said at the end of 4:16: "such boasting is evil." In this case the logical move looks like this: "since boasting is sin, therefore, anyone who knows that and does it anyway is a sinner." If the inference is prospective, it is drawn from the substance of 4:17. In that case, James would be pointing to the truthfulness of some proverb[58] or to his own formulation of a truth.[59] James has already clinched his point with an apparent maxim (2:13; 3:18), and often enough it has become a line that Christians memorize. Some would argue that *oun* here assumes a connection between James and his audience that can only be explained if the audience is messianic. But, a close look at either 4:16 or 4:17 does not reveal anything specifically messianic or Christian. In fact, 4:17 operates at the level of a universal human conscience.

There are three parts to this conclusion: the person, the action, and the consequences. The person is "Anyone[60] who knows the right thing to do." The emphasis in this verse is on the person who *knows* what is right.[61] One thinks of this in many connections, but one that might come to mind is Luke 12:47: "That slave who knew what his master wanted, but did not prepare himself or do what was wanted, will receive a severe beating." Something similar, but hardly the same, is in Romans 14:23: "for whatever does not proceed from faith is sin." And the LXX of Deuteronomy 23:22 also comes to mind: "But if you

---

57. One is reminded of the prayer in *The Book of Common Prayer* that moves from knowledge to a petition for grace to live out what we know: "O Lord, mercifully receive the prayers of your servant who calls upon you, and grant that I may know and understand what things I ought to do, and that I also may have the grace and power faithfully to accomplish them; through Jesus Christ our Lord, who lives and reigns with you and the Holy Spirit, one God, for ever and ever. Amen."

58. E.g., Martin, 168. It is not difficult to assert the existence of a saying for which there is no direct evidence.

59. Laws, 193-94, sees here an afterthought rooted in Prov 3 and 27:1.

60. The Greek does not have this word. It has only εἰδότι, "to the one who knows." "Anyone" could be implicit, but the translation leads some readers to think more about "anyone" than "to the one who knows."

61. Which gives rise to the issue of sins of omission and sins of commission. On this see the short valuable note of Tasker, 106-8. Following *The Book of Common Prayer,* Anglicans confess weekly, "Most merciful God, we confess that we have sinned against thee in thought, word, and deed, by what we have done, and by what we have left undone."

refrain from vowing, you will not incur guilt" or "it will not be sin to you."[62] If James's language is thoroughly Jewish, he nevertheless has his own take: "who knows *the right thing to do.*" In thinking about "the right thing" (Greek, *kalos*) in the book of James[63] one could return to passages like 1:21-27, where we become aware of those who hear and those who do, or to 2:14-17 where one becomes aware of needs and does not properly respond; one could also appeal to the verbal sins of 3:1–4:12. Or one could also think of Paul's line in Galatians 6:9: "So let us not grow weary in doing what is right [*kalos*]." Or of Peter's use of "doing good" (1 Pet 2:15, 20; 3:6, 17). Wide nets have their place, especially moral ones, but this is not that place. James is fishing here for one kind of person and one kind of sin: his concern is the merchant and the sin is arrogant presumption. The opposite is trust in God and humility before God, especially with regard to one's orientation to business planning. That is the "good" on James's mind, and this good the merchants know.

The supposed action of the merchants, inferred as it is from their behaviors in 4:13, comes next: "and fails to do it."[64] More narrowly, then, James is speaking of the merchant who knows God's providence and care, his own finitude, and his need to trust in God, but does not act on the basis of that knowledge. For such a person, that disregard of God in financial planning is sinful. James speaks of sin emerging from desire (1:15), of sin as partiality (2:9), and of sins being confessed and forgiven (5:15-16, 20). But here he envisions the sin of presumption and of knowledgeable and culpable disregard of God in business pursuits.

7.2. THE SIN OF OPPRESSION (5:1-6)

> 1*Come now,*[a] *you rich people, weep and wail for the miseries*[b] *that are coming to*[c] *you.*[65] 2*Your riches*[d] *have rotted,*[66] *and your clothes are*

62. LXX Deut 23:23: ἐὰν δὲ μὴ θέλῃς εὔξασθαι οὐκ ἔστιν ἐν σοὶ ἁμαρτία. See also 24:15.

63. See Popkes, 296. See Jas 2:7-8; 3:13.

64. καὶ μὴ ποιοῦντι. The grammar of James is more complex than the NRSV: the entire clause beginning with εἰδότι and ending with ποιοῦντι modifies or defines the dative of reference (αὐτῷ) in the last clause. Thus, "It is sin for the person [who knows the good and does not do it]." The present tenses of ποιέω are again vivid descriptors rather than descriptions of what is going on at the present moment in the messianic community.

65. The Greek text has a personal pronoun with ταλαιπωρίαις, leaving ταῖς ἐπερχομέναις intransitive; but some manuscripts (ℵ, 5, 104, 459, 623, 629, 1838, as well as Armenian and Slavonic versions) add ὑμῖν as it makes sense with ἐπ- in the adjectival participle, as we see in both the NRSV and TNIV.

66. The evidence for the third singular second perfect active σέσηπεν (P74, ℵ, A,

moth-eaten.[e] *3Your gold and silver have rusted,*[f] *and their rust will be evidence against you, and it*[67] *will eat your flesh like fire. You have laid up treasure*[g] *for*[h] *the*[68] *last days. 4Listen!*[i] *The wages of the laborers who mowed your fields, which you kept back by fraud,*[j] *cry out,*[k] *and the cries of the harvesters have reached*[69] *the ears of the Lord of hosts.*[l] *5You have lived on the earth in luxury and*[70] *in pleasure;*[m] *you have fattened your hearts*[n] *in*[71] *a day of slaughter. 6You have condemned and murdered the righteous*[o] *one, who does not resist you.*[p]

a. TNIV: Now listen (cf. 4:13)

b. TNIV: misery (for a Greek plural)

c. TNIV: on

d. TNIV: wealth

e. TNIV: and moths have eaten your clothes

f. TNIV: are corroded

g. TNIV: hoarded wealth

h. TNIV: in

i. TNIV: Look!

j. TNIV: The wages you failed to pay the workers who mowed your fields

k. TNIV: are crying out against you

l. TNIV: Lord Almighty

m. TNIV: self-indulgence

n. TNIV: yourselves

o. TNIV: innocent

p. TNIV: who was not opposing you

B, P, Y, and many others, including 322 and 323) or first perfect passive σέσηπται (0142, 43, 94, and 181) favors the perfect active, which is used in a passive sense (LSJ, 1594), explaining why some cleared the air by making it a passive.

67. A number of manuscripts repeat ὁ ἰός, adding it between ὑμῶν and ὡς πῦρ (copyist of א, A, P, Y, 5, 33, etc., including Coptic, Syriac, and Ethiopic manuscripts). The insertion is easier to explain as a later addition, and, when it comes to interpretation, the insertion only makes clear what is otherwise obvious.

68. Whether the article is original or not (most manuscripts do not have ταῖς, but it is found in a few late manuscripts, including 643, 676, and a few others), the language is technical for "the last days."

69. Several editors put their hand on the verb εἰσέρχομαι, including third person plural perfect and third person pluperfect. The evidence is overwhelmingly in favor of the perfect active.

70. Some manuscripts omit καὶ, including A and Y.

71. Many manuscripts (including the second corrector of א, Y, probably 048, 5, 69, 322, 323, the Byzantine tradition, Syriac Peshitta, and Harclean, Armenian, Georgian, and Slavonic witnesses) add ως. Though probably not original, this addition clarifies the text.

The opening "Come now" is identical to the opening of 4:13, drawing these two paragraphs into a formal connection. Both passages also follow with a subject: "You who say" in 4:13 and "You rich people" in 5:1. Formal similarities end there, but all commentators on this text recognize the thematic connection of wealth. The prevailing question is whether the audience of 4:13-17 is drawn from the same pool of people as 5:1-6, even if one of them is a group of rich traveling merchants and the other a group of rich farmers.[72] One cannot know with certainty, but we will attempt to make a case that they are the same audience, the wealthy, in our note on 5:1, and that case will entail the conclusion that neither passage is directed to the messianic community. If it has not been obvious already in this letter, it becomes obvious in 4:13–5:6 that James's stance toward his audience, a Jewish audience, borders on that of a prophet of old. We emphasize that we cannot be certain, but the evidence strikes us as the words of an apostolic-like prophet who is concerned with the community, messianist or not, as much as with the local ecclesia. A structural question, which we cannot answer in full until our comments on 5:7-11, is how 4:13–5:6 fits with that passage. To anticipate a conclusion below, 5:7-11 makes most sense understood as relating how James thinks the messianic community ought to respond to the presumptuous arrogance and oppressive actions of the wealthy.

A word about the tone of these verses, and this also speaks to the tone of 4:13-17. In brief, it is *relentless accusation and warning,* and reminds one not only of the prophets' warnings against powerful, abusive Israelites as well as against the nations (Amos 7:10-17; Isa 3:11–4:1; 5; 13–27; 33–35; Jer 20:1-6; and Amos 4:1-3; 6:1-7; Hos 2:5-7; Isa 8:6-8; 30:12-14; Mic 3:1-4)[73] but also of variations on those prophetic oracles of doom in texts like *1 Enoch* 94–97; Luke 6:24-26; and Matthew 23. For example, from *1 Enoch:*

> Woe unto you, O rich people!
> For you have put your trust in your wealth. . . .
> In the days of your affluence, you committed oppression,
> you have become ready for death, and for the day of darkness and the
>   day of great judgment (94:8, 9).

> Judgment will catch up with you, sinners.
> You righteous ones, fear not the sinners! (95:2-3)

> Woe unto you, sinners, for you persecute the righteous (95:7).

72. See the lengthy discussions in Frankemölle, 630-35; Popkes, 297-302, 312-13; see also Maynard-Reid, *Poverty and Wealth in James,* 81-98.
73. On which, cf. C. Westermann, *Basic Forms of Prophetic Speech* (trans. H. C. White; Philadelphia: Westminster, 1967).

> Be hopeful, you righteous ones, for the sinners shall soon perish from
> before your presence (96:1).
>
> Woe unto you who eat the best bread!
> And drink wine in large bowls,
> trampling upon the weak people with your might (96:5).
>
> What do you intend to do, you sinners,
> whither will you flee on that day of judgment,
> when you hear the sound of the prayer of the righteous ones? (97:3)
>
> In those days, the prayers of the righteous ones shall reach unto the
> Lord (97:5).
>
> Woe unto you who gain silver and gold by unjust means . . .
> For your wealth shall not endure
> but it shall take off from you quickly
> for you have acquired it all unjustly,
> and you shall be given over to a great curse (97:8, 10).

James's approach is strikingly similar. We find the address in second person, as if the prophet or apocalyptist is talking directly to the rich; a concern with unjust wealth accumulation; a clear, known boundary between the wicked and the righteous; and a threat of judgment on the sinners and vindication for the righteous. James does not dwell in the apocalyptic world as much as *1 Enoch,* but he feeds at the wells of the prophetic-apocalyptic milieu of Judaism.[74] His tone is, then, both prophetic and apocalyptic, but probably more the former than the latter.[75]

The prophetic rhetoric of 5:1-6 unfolds as follows:[76] First we have an opening warning (5:1) that is followed by a staccato-like series of statements that describe the accumulative lifestyle and its impermanence (5:2-3). Sec-

---

74. On the *Sitz im Leben* of James, and the particular exigencies that give rise to this book, see the Introduction. My contention is that this kind of language, regardless of how stock its imagery, reflects the particularities affecting the messianic community. Thus, 4:13–5:6 are some particulars about the people who carry out the injustices of 2:1-7, and who are probably behind the language of 1:19-27 and 2:14-17.

75. There have been intense discussions on the meanings of both "prophetic" and "apocalyptic" for three or four decades, including S. L. Cook, *Prophecy and Apocalypticism* (Minneapolis: Fortress, 1995); J. C. VanderKam and W. Adler, eds., *The Jewish Apocalyptic Heritage in Early Christianity* (Compendia Rerum Iudaicarum ad Novum Testamentum 3/4; Minneapolis: Fortress, 1996).

76. See S. E. Wheeler, *Wealth as Peril and Obligation* (Grand Rapids: Eerdmans, 1995), 91-106, who, in her study of how to use the New Testament morally, examines this text and illustrates how important it is to read it concretely.

ond, v. 4 is almost parenthetical and rhetorically functions as sidebar revelation that the oppression of the poor by the rich has been registered with the Lord of hosts. Third, James adds to the descriptions of vv. 2-3 two more images of the lifestyle of the rich (5:5) and lets rise to the surface the undercurrent of what he has been saying: they are oppressors (5:6).

7.2.1. The Opening Warning (5:1)

James begins with a prophet's attention-grabbing "Come now."[77] It is arresting, even if not as jarring as the first usage of the expression in 4:13. There James addressed those who were making claims about their business ventures; here he broadens the audience to "you rich people."[78] The expression, at some levels so central to James, carries a heavy load in the debate about James's audience here and whether or not they are messianists. Some of this I have already discussed in the Introduction and at 1:9-11, and indirectly elsewhere, but one thing is clear: if one is suspicious that 4:13-17 might not be addressed to the believing messianic community, then 5:1-6 raises the suspicions much higher.[79] There is nothing in this passage that indicates that the "rich people" are messianists. We recall our observation that the tendency to read letters written by Christians as addressing only Christians is an unnecessary entailment of how Christians have learned to read the Bible canonically and for applications in life. If James picked a model for his letter, it was not Paul; instead, his letter, especially 4:13–5:6, sounds more like a prophetic remonstrance with a variety of groups than like a pastoral letter to pious Christians huddled into a corner waiting for the coming of the Lord. Once we shed this unnecessary burden of thinking the audience must be entirely Christian, we become more open to weighing here and there the audience in a different set of scales. James uses the language "rich people" very much the way Jesus did: it is "code" for the oppressors of the messianic community, and the letter speaks not only to the messianists but also to those who oppress them.[80]

---

77. Ἄγε νῦν. To repeat what was said at 4:13, the singular imperative of ἄγω has become an interjection in function, and this is visible in our verse because it is used with the plural οἱ πλούσιοι; see BDAG, 9; BDF, §144; see also §364.2; Rehkopf, *Grammatik,* §107.2; see also §364.2.

78. οἱ πλούσιοι. BDAG, 831. See also at Jas 1:10-11; 2:5-6. The word is used uniformly for the "bad guys" in James, and this fits in with a standard prophetic trope (Matt 19:23; Mark 12:41; Luke 6:24; 14:12; 16:1, 19, 21-22; 18:23; 19:2; 1 Tim 6:17; Rev 2:9; 3:17; 6:15; 13:16). But this term does not indicate simply the rich, but a kind of the rich, namely, powerful, abusive, ungodly rich who use their riches and power to oppress the people of God.

79. See the arguments in Laws, 195-96; also Nystrom, 267-68.

80. See Moo, 210, for sound pastoral wisdom.

383

Whether or not the oppressors were paying attention is of minimal concern, for that is the way Jews of that time wrote.[81] In sociological terms, for James and the messianic community "you rich people" are effectively labeled here as "the other."[82]

James summons "you rich people" to hear these words: "weep and wail for the miseries that are coming to you."[83] The language is dramatic, if not overcooked, because he is calling them to something they cannot manufacture apart from an act of God's grace. The wealthy, who are called to humiliate themselves in 1:9-11, are here called to intense misery and violent grief, something they cannot attain until they come to the end of their ways — and there is precious little in 5:1-6 to indicate that they will. Rhetorically, then, the language is designed to mark the rich farmers off as oppressors and under the imminent judgment of God, at which time they will "weep and wail." The language of weeping emerges in the New Testament frequently *after* and in response to (most often earthly) disaster (Matt 2:18; 26:75; Mark 5:38-39; Luke 6:21, 25; John 11:33; 20:11, 13, 15; Rev 18:9, 11, 15, 19). Wailing occurs sometimes in the context of repentance (Luke 7:38) and at the prospect of judgment, as when Jesus wept over the prospects of what would happen to Jerusalem (Luke 19:41; cf. Luke 23:28; Acts 21:13). Pertinent here is James 4:9: "Lament and mourn and *weep*. Let your laughter be turned into mourning and your joy into dejection." Here we should think of James summoning the rich to weep violently over what was yet to happen to them, as the next phrase indicates: "for the miseries that are coming to you."

"Wail" evokes the language of the prophets, as in Isaiah 13:6; Zechariah 11:2; Amos 8:3; and Lamentations 1:1-2 (see also Isa 14:31; 15:1-3; 16:7; 65:14; Jer 9:1; 13:17; Ezek 21:12). Before James even uses the word

---

81. This enters into the sticky wicket of so-called Jewish apologetic literature, sometimes called propaganda; on this, cf. my *A Light among the Gentiles* (Minneapolis: Fortress, 1991), 57-62, 75-76, where in the notes one can find other literature. It is doubtful that Jewish apologetic literature was written for Gentiles; it was most likely written for Jews to bolster their faith and arguments. I consider this germane to James's rhetoric and attention to the rich in 1:9-11 and 4:13–5:6. In other words, whether they read or heard this text read, the messianic community did receive the message and were accordingly armed in their faith, their commitments, and their arguments.

82. See J. M. Lieu, *Christian Identity in the Jewish and Graeco-Roman World* (Oxford: Oxford University Press, 2004), especially 269-97.

83. κλαύσατε ὀλολύζοντες ἐπὶ ταῖς ταλαιπωρίαις ὑμῶν ταῖς ἐπερχομέναις. The aorist imperative is constative, a summary action. The participle, again a descriptive and vivid present, is adverbial and defines what James means in κλαίω (see BDAG, 545; on the onomatopoeic ὀλολύζω, see BDAG, 704). Most translations, instead of translating "wailing" as an adverbial expression, make it an attendant verb. Thus, "weep and wail" as in the NRSV and TNIV. The second participle is adjectival, but again the present makes the action immanent in perception.

"day," as he will in 5:3, his readers recognize that he is warning of the Day of the Lord.[84] Before he gets to that word he simply speaks of "the miseries that are coming to you."[85] In 4:9 James used the verb cognate for "miseries" (*talaipōria*), addressing the teachers as part of his variegated summons to repentance.[86] Coming as he does out of a Jewish prophetic world, now with "miseries" James would have in mind at least something on the order of the destruction of Jerusalem. Thus, associations with passages like Joel 1:5-11 would come to mind for those who knew the history of Jewish prophecy.

The judgment about to come upon the people is imminent, and evidence suggests this. First, James uses the verb *erchomai* ("come")[87] and uses it in the present tense, which makes the scene vivid. Second, 5:7-8 will indicate that "the coming of the Lord is near." That verb was commonly used of judgment "coming upon" sinners from the hand of God, especially where the "Day of the Lord" was mentioned (Luke 21:26; Acts 13:40).[88] The words of Zophar in the Septuagint of Job 20:28 illustrate the use of this term: "The possessions of his house will be taken away completely when the day of wrath *comes* to him."[89]

7.2.2. The Lifestyle of the Rich Farmers (5:2-3)

5:2 Instead of a direct warning, which James rhetorically suspends until the end of v. 3 (and even then states somewhat indirectly), James simply brings to mind that the riches of the rich are impermanent. He lists three kinds of possessions that do not last: riches and clothes and money (gold and silver). Three terms for consumption accompany the possessions: rotted, moth-eaten, and rusted. The last term is used to shift from the impermanence of

---

84. See G. von Rad, *The Message of the Prophets* (New York: Harper and Row, 1965), 95-99; see also R. E. Clements, *Old Testament Prophecy* (Louisville: Westminster John Knox, 1996); J. Blenkinsopp, *A History of Prophecy in Israel* (rev. ed.; Louisville: Westminster John Knox, 1996); Elmer Martens, "Day of the Lord, God, Christ," *Evangelical Dictionary of Biblical Theology* (ed. W. A. Elwell; Grand Rapids: Baker, 1996), 146-49.

85. ἐπὶ ταῖς ταλαιπωρίαις ὑμῶν ταῖς ἐπερχομέναις. The present tense dative plural participle describes the action; it does not convey that these things are coming upon them right now as James speaks, but it is used in order to make the action vivid.

86. See the notes at 4:9, where it is suggested that "lament" (cognate of "miseries" in 5:1) involved embodied actions of contrition and repentance.

87. Found only here in James; see BDAG, 361-62.

88. The verb occurs 103 times in the LXX. A sampling of pertinent texts includes Josh 24:20; Judg 9:57; 1 Sam 11:7; 2 Sam 17:2; 19:7; 2 Chron 20:9; 32:26; 2 Macc 1:7; Prov 3:25 (from a text that figures in James at 4:6); Job 1:19; 2:11; 20:22; 20:28; 21:17; Wis 12:27; 19:13; Zeph 2:2; Isa 13:13; Bar 4:9, 25; Dan 9:11, 13. Of course, good things can come with the coming of God as well: Isa 48:3; 63:4; 65:17; Bar 4:24.

89. ἑλκύσαι τὸν οἶκον αὐτοῦ ἀπώλεια εἰς τέλος, ἡμέρα ὀργῆς ἐπέλθοι αὐτῷ.

possessions to the use of the rusted remains as evidence against the rich on the Day of the Lord. That, James says with sarcasm, is their "treasure."

"Your riches have rotted"[90] involves a verb in the perfect tense, indicating that the author depicts the act of rotting as complete and as having brought into being a state of affairs.[91] One might easily infer that this rotting has not yet happened and therefore question why the rhetoric finds such strong semantic expression in the perfect tense. Most, therefore, would call this a "prophetic" perfect, and the future tenses at the end of 5:3, which parallel the perfect tenses of 5:2, support such a view.[92] But there is a difference between a perfect and a future tense, with the former emphasizing a state of affairs and the latter expectation. In James's mind, therefore, the rotting of riches is a condition he assumes, not the least because they have not been used compassionately, and this is the condition to which he speaks.[93] The "riches"[94] are most likely not distinguished from clothes and gold and silver but are instead the encompassing category of which the clothing and money are but examples. As in 5:1, "riches" signifies not simply possessions but also how one has acquired them, what one does with them, and what one does to those in need (2:1-4, 5-7, 14-17; 5:4-6).

The first concrete instantiation of the rotting of their riches is that "your clothes are moth-eaten."[95] The statement evokes a similar saying of Jesus in Matthew 6:19: "Do not store up for yourselves treasures on earth, where moth and rust consume and where thieves break in and steal," and these lines from Job 13:28: "One wastes away like a rotten thing, like a garment that is moth-eaten."[96] Moth-eaten clothing is an image of impermanence and, in this context, of the impermanence of the focused investment of

90. ὁ πλοῦτος ὑμῶν σέσηπεν. On σήπω, see BDAG, 921-22. The verb is flexible and graphic: cf. LXX Ps 38:5 (37:6); Job 16:7; 33:21; Sir 14:19; Bar 6:72; Ezek 17:9.

91. See the excellent summary in Porter, *Idioms*, 39-40, with a brief explanation of the perfects in Jas 5:2-3 on p. 41.

92. E.g., Mayor, 154; Dibelius, 236. But see also Laws, 198, who thinks the perfects refer to the present (state of) the worthlessness of riches when it comes to spiritual hope. One needs to observe not only the move from two perfects to two futures but also the final verb of 4:3 being aorist.

93. See more at M. Mayordomo-Marin, "Jak 5, 2.3a. Zukünftiges Gericht oder gegenwärtiger Zustand?" *ZNW* 83 (1992) 132-37.

94. Here πλοῦτος. The term is found only here in James, but it needs to be connected to πλούσιος (1:10-11; 2:5-6; 5:1). See BDAG, 832. See also T. E. Schmidt, "Hostility to Wealth in Philo of Alexandria," *JSNT* 19 (1983) 85-97; Maynard-Reid, *Poverty and Wealth in James*, 81-98; Wheeler, *Wealth as Peril and Obligation* (see note 76 above); C. L. Blomberg, *Neither Poverty nor Riches* (Downers Grove: InterVarsity, 2001). See also R. Sider, *Rich Christians in an Age of Hunger* (5th ed.; Nashville: W, 1997).

95. καὶ τὰ ἱμάτια ὑμῶν σητόβρωτα γέγονεν. See BDAG, 922.

96. See also Prov 25:20; Sir 42:13; Isa 50:9.

the rich and their attention to their appearance. Extravagant, status-expressing dress marked the rich (Jas 2:2-3). It is possible that the warning of Isaiah 51:8 lurks behind the words of James:

> For the moth will eat them up like a garment,
>   and the worm will eat them like wool;
> but my deliverance will be forever,
>   and my salvation to all generations.

5:3   The second instantiation of the rotting of riches concerns money: "Your gold and silver have rusted."[97] A common Jewish monotheistic critique of idols was that they waste away, and Baruch 6:11 uses similar language to James 5:2-3 for the idols of Babylon: "They deck their gods out with garments like human beings — these gods of silver and gold and wood that cannot save themselves from rust and corrosion." The word translated "rust," Greek *ios*,[98] sometimes means poison (e.g., Ps 140:3) but here it refers to decay of metals, including the partial oxidation of gold and silver (Bar 6:24; Ezek 24:6, 11, 12), especially as a disclosure of false metals. James has in mind, then, the false claims of the rich, which will be exposed in the judgment. The theme is typical of Jesus as well: cf. Matt 6:19-34.

The concrete instantiations are now complete; James next deconstructs the farmers' obsession with riches: "their rust will be evidence against you, and it will eat your flesh like fire. You have laid up treasure for the last days." The very thing they focused on, riches like clothing and gold and silver, will turn against the rich in a final act of cosmic betrayal. The rust on them will become a witness to the idolatrous commitment to mammon on the part of the rich. How it will do so is not clear, but perhaps it is because the rich hold these possessions in abundance instead of using them compassionately for those in need that James can say that they will become evidence.[99] The Greek expression *eis martyrion* at face value means "unto a witness," but context often clarifies the witness as either negative or positive. Thus, after healing a leper Jesus told the man to go to the priestly authority, show him his

---

97. ὁ χρυσὸς ὑμῶν καὶ ὁ ἄργυρος κατίωται. The passive perfect of κατίωται continues the theme of describing a state of affairs in light of the Day of the Lord. See BDAG, 534. See Sir 12:11, where it refers to tarnishing a mirror (cf. Jas 1:23-24).

98. See BDAG, 477; W. Weiser, "Durch Grünspan verdorbenes Edelmetall? Zur Deutung des Wortes 'IOS' im Brief des Jakobus," *BZ* 43 (1999) 220-23, who examines the evidence for decay and oxidation of false metals or gold- or silver-plating that demonstrate the inauthenticity of coins and metals. See also C. Böttrich, "Vom Gold das rostet (Jak 5.3)," *NTS* 47 (2001) 519-36, who also draws attention to the contrast between pursuit of the material and pursuit of the kingdom of God.

99. See Moo, 213-14.

body, and make the appropriate sacrificial offerings "as a testimony *to* them [the priests]" that he was now clean (Mark 1:44). But frequently the context is negative. Thus, the twelve apostles were to shake the local dust off their feet where they were not welcomed "as a testimony *against* them" (Mark 6:11). James has this latter sense in mind when he thinks of the rust witnessing on the Day of the Lord.[100]

James now asks rust to do what it does not do except in the world of apocalyptic imagination: "and it will eat your flesh like fire."[101] Rust does not eat, and it does not eat like fire, since fire consumes quickly, but James's evocative imagery is spoiled by thinking of it with such narrow literalism. If rust can corrode precious metals like gold and silver, which were sometimes considered non-corrodible, it will also corrode the very flesh of the rich.[102] And if it can corrode, it can be extended to consuming things the way fire does. The language again is graphic and designed to evoke a response of repentance. Flesh eaten away images death, perhaps even eternal death (cf. 1:14-15). Perhaps by "flesh" James simply means the body (cf. 3:6); it is possible he has in mind something on the order of Paul's use of "flesh" for the unspiritual and unredeemed human in his or her bodily existence. By adding "like fire"[103] James intends an image of total destruction: all to be found after a fire is only charred remains. In 3:5-6 fire was not only destructive but its source was hell. It is a stretch to think that that is on James's mind here, though it could be. Instead, the focus here is the fact of destruction: the rich themselves will be destroyed the way fire destroys what it burns. Once again, the language emerges from a strong biblical tradition that connects God's judgment with fire (Isa 30:27, 30; Jer 5:14; Ezek 15:7; Amos 1:12, 14; Jdth 16:17). We find a similar use of "fire" with Jesus (Mark 9:47-48; Matt 13:42). The Apocalypse, where "fire" is used no fewer than twenty-five times, cannot be forgotten in this context either (e.g., Rev 8:5; 14:10; 18:8).

Before his appeal to the rich, James clarifies what he is saying: "You have laid up treasure for the last days."[104] James seems at times to be in direct

100. So Laws, 199; Davids, 176.

101. καὶ φάγεται τὰς σάρκας ὑμῶν ὡς πῦρ. Again, the future indicative of ἐσθίω clarifies the perfects of 4:2. See BDAG, 396.

102. The imagery gives rise to notable imaginative treatments, not the least of which is Dante's *Inferno* in his *The Divine Comedy*.

103. Ropes, 288, thinks ὡς πῦρ works with ἐθησαυρίσατε in 5:3 since that verb expects an object, but this creates the need to fill in even more ellipses. James uses ὡς both with what precedes (2:8, 9) and with what follows (1:10; 2:12).

104. ἐθησαυρίσατε ἐν ἐσχάταις ἡμέραις. The choice of the aorist is to sum up the act of storing up treasures, without reference to when or how the storing up was done. "You *have stored up* . . ." is appropriate here, and this aorist stands proudly alongside the perfects of 4:3.

dialogue with Jesus, even offering midrashes rooted in the teachings of Jesus. Here one thinks again of Matthew 6:19-20: "Do not store up for yourselves treasures on earth, where moth and rust consume and where thieves break in and steal; but store up for yourselves treasures in heaven, where neither moth nor rust consumes and where thieves do not break in and steal." James extends this subtly: instead of doing what Jesus commanded, the rich are doing what Jesus prohibited. They are storing up treasures, false ones to be sure, for the Day of the Lord. The focus here is less on the leisurely, devil-may-care approach to life that one finds, for instance, in the parable of the rich man and Lazarus (Luke 16:19-31) and more on the object of the affections of the rich: riches.[105] James's language is ironic if not sarcastic: what is being treasured up is not a treasure that will survive divine scrutiny in the judgment; instead it is a treasure that will, like Satan, be their accusers.

Peter Davids, though, wonders if this interpretation of "last days" is too specific. He judges rightly that New Testament eschatology is best described as inaugurated, as in texts like Mark 1:15; Acts 2:17; or Hebrews 1:2, and concludes that by "last days" James means "the NT conviction that the end times, the age of consummation, had already broken in upon the world." Therefore, he says, "*These* people had treasured up as if they would live and the world would go on forever, but the end times, in which they have a last chance to repent and put their goods to righteous uses, are already upon them."[106] Davids is correct with regard to inaugurated eschatology, and his sense of imminence in James is properly accounted for, but he lays too much stress on the realized dimensions of the kingdom and not enough on the apocalyptic and catastrophic experience of the yet-future judgment, the Day of the Lord, that finds expression in the images of James 5:1-6. A closer look at the early Christian evidence for this expression helps.[107] Indeed, there is a

---

105. *Pace* Davids, 177.

106. See Davids, 177; he appeals here to O. Cullmann, *Christ and Time* (rev. ed.; trans. F. V. Filson; Philadelphia: Westminster, 1964).

107. The literature here continues to grow. A good place to begin is with G. K. Beale, "Eschatology," in *DLNTD,* 330-45, which has an exceptional bibliography. The discussion of New Testament eschatology has encountered some deep shifts as a result of the use of Caird, *Language and Imagery,* by scholars like Wright, *Jesus and the Victory of God;* see also B. Witherington, *Jesus, Paul and the End of the World* (Downers Grove: InterVarsity, 1992). Amazingly, in the fine volume *DTIB,* there is no entry for eschatology. The following are worthy of consultation in framing a Christian eschatology: S. Holmes and R. Rook, eds., *What Are We Waiting For?* (Milton Keynes: Paternoster, 2008); R. Bauckham and T. Hart, *Hope against Hope* (Grand Rapids: Eerdmans, 1999); H. Schwarz, *Eschatology* (Grand Rapids: Eerdmans, 2000); K. E. Brower and M. W. Elliott, eds., *Eschatology in the Bible and Theology* (Downers Grove: InterVarsity, 1997); R. C. Doyle, *Eschatology and the Shape of Christian Belief* (Carlisle: Paternoster, 1999); C. C. Hill, *In God's Time* (Grand Rapids: Eerdmans, 2002); B. E. Daley, *The Hope of the*

sense in which the advent of Jesus as Messiah is the dawning of the last days (Acts 2:16-17; 1 Cor 10:11; Heb 1:2; 9:26). But the early Christian vision entailed not only an inauguration but a "now but not yet" sense that the (final) end was yet to come (2 Tim 3:1; 1 John 2:18; 2 Pet 3:1-4; Jude 18). The emphasis of James in 5:1-6 is not on the realization of the kingdom in the here and now but on the prospect — observe the future tenses of 5:3 — of an imminent judgment that will undo injustice and judge the unjust but also establish justice.

7.2.3. A Revelation (5:4)

By now a reader of James may be forgiven for being as weary as the commentator in having to explain the logical movements of the book. From the substance of 5:4 one can infer that James now informs the rich, even if they are not listening, that their oppressive behaviors against the poor have now entered the ears of the God of hosts. The substance, in other words, provides what we need to know about the logical movement: from descriptions of the impermanence of riches, to the implication of the sustained affections of those who pursue riches, to a revelation in v. 4. This revelation is designed rhetorically to awaken the rich from their immoral slumbering by appealing to an Old Testament trope — the unjust actions of the powerful rich, the oppression of the poor, the prayers of the poor to God for justice, the ears of God hearing the prayers, and God acting to judge oppressors and liberate the oppressed.[108] The language roots us in Moses' choice of violence as well as the exodus event and all its many variations throughout Israel's history, not the least of which are Acts 7:23-29, 35 and Hebrews 11:24-28.[109] Thus, after Moses slays the Egyptian (Exod 2:11-14), we read Exodus 2:23b-25:

> The Israelites groaned under their slavery, and cried out. Out of the slavery their cry for help rose up to God. God heard their groaning, and God remembered his covenant with Abraham, Isaac, and Jacob. God looked upon the Israelites, and God took notice of them.

Early Church (Peabody: Hendrickson, 1991); C. E. Hill, *Regnum Caelorum* (2d ed.; Grand Rapids: Eerdmans, 2001); A. Perriman, *The Coming of the Son of Man* (Milton Keynes: Paternoster, 2005).

108. Martin rightly observes that, in contrast to 4:13-17, there is no direct call to repentance in 5:1-6 (Martin, 175; also Moo, 210). However, the revelatory nature of 5:4 may have functioned as a call to repentance.

109. See T. E. Fretheim's brief sketch, "Exodus, Book of," in *DOTP*, 256-58; P. Enns, "Exodus/New Exodus," in *DTIB*, 216-18; M. Daniel Carroll (Rodas), "Exodus," in *DMT*, 119-21; Goldingay, *Old Testament Theology*, 1.288-368. See also B. S. Childs, *The Book of Exodus* (Louisville: Westminster, 1976), 42-46.

One suspects that such a contrast, the violence of Pharaoh and the people's cry to God for liberation, forms some of the backdrop to James's warnings about the need to resist the attractiveness of violence and his confidence that God will hear the cries of the oppressed.

5:4a The alarm James rings in the ears of the rich opens up with a loud imperative: "Listen!" or possibly "Remember!"[110] The tenses used open a window on the rhetoric of James: "The wages of the laborers who mowed your fields, which you kept back by fraud, cry out [*present*], and the cries of the harvesters have reached [*perfect*] the ears of the Lord of hosts." The present tense, now frequently called the imperfective aspect, is used to depict action that is not complete, while the perfect tense (perfective or stative aspect) is used to depict action that is complete and has led to an existing state of affairs.[111] The state of affairs is that God has heard; the cries of the oppressed, however, are not yet completed — they are going on as the readers listen.

The oppressed, who may well be the poor of 1:9-11, have labored to earn wages: "the wages of the laborers."[112] The graphic realities of day laborers appear in the parables of Jesus, as do the themes of injustice, generosity, and final vindication (e.g., Matt 20:1-16). The labor involved is mowing fields, that is, harvesting grain.[113]

But the rich farmers have defrauded the workers of their rightful wages: "which you kept back by fraud."[114] Here we encounter a typical accusation against the rich because, and our society is no different, it is a typical behavior. Laws were written to protect the poor from such behavior. Hence, Leviticus 19:13: "You shall not defraud your neighbor; you shall not steal; and you shall not keep for yourself the wages of a laborer until morning." Or Deuteronomy 24:15: "You shall pay them their wages daily before sunset, because they are poor and their livelihood depends on them; otherwise they might cry to the LORD against you, and you would incur guilt."[115] One of Je-

110. ἰδού. The TNIV translates "Look!" The Greek word reflects the Hebrew הִנֵּה. See BDAG, 468 (1c), where the translation "Remember" is suggested.

111. See Porter, *Idioms,* 39-40. The words here are κράζει and εἰσεληλύθασιν.

112. ὁ μισθὸς τῶν ἐργατῶν. BDAG, 653, 390-91.

113. τῶν ἀμησάντων τὰς χώρας ὑμῶν. The aorist sums up the action of the workers and therefore the fraud and rich farmers' culpability; see BDAG, 52. The personal pronoun ὑμῶν throws even more emphasis on the farmers. Again, see Safrai, *Economy* (note 24 above).

114. ὁ ἀπεστερημένος. BDAG, 121. The action in the perfect passive participle is performed by the rich (ἀφ᾽ ὑμῶν).

115. See also Tob 4:14: "Do not keep over until the next day the wages of those who work for you, but pay them at once." Pseudo-Phocylides 19: "Give the laborer his pay, do not afflict the poor." Mark's Gospel uses this word to translate one of the commandments (Mark 10:19), though this term is not found in either Exod 20:12-16 or Deut 5:16-20. See also 1 Cor 6:7-8 and Paul's expansion of the meaning of the term at 7:5 and 1 Tim 6:5.

sus' parables describes the norm: "When evening came, the owner of the vineyard said to his manager, 'Call the laborers and give them their pay'" (Matt 20:8). So, there were prophetic warnings against the oppression of withholding wages. Thus, Jeremiah 22:13:

> Woe to him who builds his house by unrighteousness,
>   and his upper rooms by injustice;
> who makes his neighbors work for nothing,
>   and does not give them their wages.[116]

Sirach's language is strong: "To take away a neighbor's living is to commit murder" (Sir 34:26 [LXX 34:22]). And the wealthy could examine their hearts on this matter, as we find in *Testament of Job* 12:4: "Nor did I allow the wage earner's pay to remain at home with me in my house." So the poor, or their wages, are crying out to God.[117]

The theme of the oppressed crying out, which, as indicated above, evokes the children of Israel in Egypt, appears first in the primeval story of Cain and Abel, whose blood cried out to God for justice (Gen 4:10),[118] and then later in the account of Sodom and Gomorrah (18:20; 19:13). Injustice leads to a cry for help and justice as the oppressed appeal to God (1 Sam 9:16; Isa 5:7; Sir 21:5; 35:17; 1QH 13:12; 4Q381 fragment 24ab 8).

5:4b If the cry of the oppressed forms the first part of this revelation, the second is that God hears these cries, as James both repeats what he has said and extends his thoughts into the heavenly court: "and the cries of the harvesters have reached the ears of the Lord of hosts." The verb "cry" *(krazō)* in the first part of the revelation is replaced now by the noun "cry," *boē*, conforming this text to the formative words of Exodus 2:23, where the Septuagint uses cognates of *boē*.[119] Instead of "laborers" in this substantive repeat of 4:a, James uses "harvesters."[120] Most importantly, the cries of the oppressed harvesters "have reached the ears of the Lord of hosts."[121]

Just why James speaks here of "the Lord of hosts" is not entirely clear. The language evokes the Warrior God tradition of ancient Israel, and

116. See also Mal 3:5.

117. κράζει. The subject of this verb is ὁ μισθός, a personification of the oppressed laborers. See *TDOT*, 14.532-36.

118. See John Byron, "Living in the Shadow of Cain: Echoes of a Developing Tradition in James 5:1-6," *NovT* 48 (2006) 261-74.

119. See BDAG, 180. See also 1 Sam 4:14; 9:16; 2 Chron 33:13; Jdth 14:16, 19; *3 Maccabees* 1:28; 4:2; 5:7; Isa 15:8.

120. Thus, instead of ἐργάται he has θερισταί; cf. BDAG, 454. This, in part, may clarify the kind of work envisioned in 5:4a. See Dan 14:33 (LXX); Matt 13:30, 39.

121. εἰς τὰ ὦτα κυρίου σαβαὼθ εἰσεληλύθασιν. Or, "have entered into the ears. . . ." See Ps 17:6.

one thinks first of a text like David's words to Goliath in 1 Samuel 17:45: "You come to me with sword and spear and javelin; but I come to you in the name of the YHWH of hosts, the God of the armies of Israel, whom you have defied." Here in James the hosts are probably the heavenly retinue (Ps 103:21). As the covenant formula promises that YHWH will be Israel's God, so YHWH of hosts has chosen Israel as his vineyard (Isa 5:5, 7). Even more pertinent to our text, and this language evokes the great and fulfilled prophecies of Isaiah, is that YHWH of hosts brings justice (Isa 5:16, 24, and see Rom 9:29). James's use of "Lord of hosts" most likely draws on this theme of the God of justice who, along with the heavenly retinue, enacts justice for the oppressed in judgment. The oppressed cry out (Pss 17:1-6; 18:6; 31:2), and the Lord of hosts brings justice — in this context, justice against rich, defrauding employers. Vv. 7-11, where James will counsel the messianic community on what to do in the face of this oppression, make it clear that James uses "Lord of hosts" because he has in mind an imminent act of judgment against the oppressors.

Some have disputed whether his language is real or simply biblical imagery, a fashionable trope that carries meaning without necessarily referring to real fraud.[122] In light of 1:9-11, the concrete descriptions in 2:1-7, 14-17, and the business pursuits of 4:13-17, it is hard to think of anything other than a plain reality when James accuses the rich of fraud, even if he uses stock language from the Old Testament. The same texts in the letter inform us of the likely protest on the part of the poor as they implore God out of their helplessness to intervene to establish justice. Simple reality might also best explain why James speaks against violence (1:20) and murder (4:2). The theme of patience that quickly follows in 5:7-11 is a logical corollary of learning to wait on God to establish justice instead of relying on one's own violent measures.

7.2.4. The Description of the Rich Resumed (5:5-6)

James opened the window to the divine perspective on what was happening in v. 4, but now he will resume the description of the rich oppressors that occupied his attention in vv. 2-3. The end of 5:3, in the heated if not sarcastic words "You have laid up treasure for the last days," is heightened in 5:5-6, and I here give an edited version of the NRSV:

> You have lived on the earth in luxury,
> and you have indulged yourselves;
> you have fattened your hearts in a day of slaughter.

122. See the nuance in Laws, 201-2.

You have condemned and
You have murdered the righteous one
(who does not resist you).

Seeing this visibly in lines preserves the staccato form of the words: five accusing descriptions in the second person plural; five constative aorists, designed solely to keep the whole action in front of the reader's eyes. The first three are substantively similar but the fourth and fifth develop something new, that is, we encounter here luxury (5:5) and violence (5:6).

7.2.4.1. Luxury (5:5)

James gives three descriptions of luxury: "you have lived in luxury" (tryphaō), "you indulged yourselves" (spatalaō), and "you have fattened" (trephō). One is reminded of Petronius's *Satyricon,* with its famous opulent and debauched feast of Trimalchio, or one can find any number of descriptions of opulent lifestyles or events in the ancient Mediterranean. There is nothing distinctively Greek, Roman, Jewish, or Alexandrian about this description, and we read it most accurately if we leave it as a general description. There is a subtle deconstructive commentary in this piling up of verbs in the phrase "on the earth."[123] This fits with other expressions for this life in the letter, not the least of which are "body" (2:16, 26; 3:2, 3, 6) and "flesh" (5:3). It is not clear that James has in mind here a vertical dualism of earth versus heaven, and it is at least as likely, if not probable, that he has in mind a temporal dualism of this earth/now versus the age to come (cf. 5:7-11).

During their "now" the rich, opulent, and violent have reveled in luxury, luxuriated in opulence, and fattened their hearts.[124] Bounty is not necessarily bad; the deuteronomic theology of blessing finds itself in words like these (cf. Neh 9:25; Isa 66:11). But in this context the words, because the actions occur on the backs of the defrauded poor, denote the accumulation of good and pleasures as a result of unloving, sinful pursuits (cf. Ezek 16:49; Josephus, *Ant.* 2:201; 1 Tim 5:6; *Barnabas* 10:3). In the next century, Hermas will tell a parable to this effect (*Similitude* 64.1.4). Perhaps Hermas's explanations of luxury had the same impact as C. S. Lewis's *Screwtape Letters* do in our day:

"The one who lives in luxury and deception for one day and does what he wants has clothed himself in much foolishness and does not understand what he is doing, for on the next day he forgets what he did the

123. ἐπὶ τῆς γῆς is an adverbial prepositional phrase of time, "while you are on earth."
124. See BDAG, 1018 (τρυφάω), 936 (σπαταλάω), and 1014-15 (τρέφω). On "hearts," cf. 1:26; 3:14; 4:8; 5:8.

day before. For luxury and deception have no memories, because of the foolishness with which they are clothed. But when punishment and torment cling to a man for a single day, he is punished and tormented for a year, for punishment and torment have long memories. So, being punished and tormented for a whole year, he then remembers the luxury and deceit and realizes that he is suffering these evils because of them. Every man, therefore, who lives in luxury and deception is tormented in this way, because even though they have life, they have handed themselves over to death." "Sir," I said, "what kinds of luxuries are harmful?" "Everything a man enjoys doing," he said, "is a luxury for him. For even the ill-tempered man indulges himself when he gives free rein to his passion. And the adulterer and the drunkard and the slanderer and the liar and the anxious and the robber and the one who does things such as these each gives free rein to his own sickness; he indulges himself, therefore, by his action" (*Similitude* 65:3-5).

"You have fattened your hearts in a day of slaughter" recalls 5:3's "You have laid up treasure for the last days." 5:1-6 is laced up with the theme of the threat of judgment: "miseries that are coming to you" (5:1), the perfect tenses of 5:2 and futures of 5:3, the certain threat of judgment at the end of 5:3, the cries of the defrauded heard by the Lord of hosts in 5:4, and now the "day of slaughter." Both judgment and especially the Day of the Lord are sometimes called a "slaughter" by the prophets (Obad 10; Zech 11:4, 7; Isa 30:25; 34:2, 6; 53:7;[125] 65:12; Jer 12:3; 15:3; 19:6; 25:34; 48:15; 50:27; 51:40; Ezek 7:14-23; 21:15; cf. Rev 19:17-21).[126] And the Jewish apocalypses often combine warnings about riches and the final judgment.[127] For example,

Now therefore, my children, live in patience and meekness for the number of your days, so that you may inherit the endless age that is coming. And every assault and every wound and burn and every evil word, if they happen to you on account of the LORD, endure them. . . . Let each one of you put up with the loss of his gold and silver on account of a brother, so that he may receive a full treasury in that age. Widows and orphans and foreigners do not distress, so that God's anger does not come upon you (*2 Enoch* 50:2-6).

In light of what will be said below, it is more likely that James is referring here to the destruction of Jerusalem in 70 AD than to the final assize,

125. Cf. *1 Clement* 16:7; *Barnabas* 5:2; 8:2 for commentary on Isa 53:7.
126. See Laws, 203-4; Davids, 178.
127. See also *1 Enoch* 94:8-9; 97:8-10; 98:10; 99:15-16; *2 Enoch* 50:1-6; *Jubilees* 36:9-11; and one needs to consult 1QM for envisioning the future as involving a battle of destruction and slaughter.

though the former is a foretaste of the latter. His language traffics in the all-too-typical warnings to Israel and her corrupt leaders that Jerusalem will be sacked if they do not turn from corruption. James warns the rich and opulent, and violent in the next verse, that they will experience the rough side of God's tongue on the Day of the Lord.[128]

7.2.4.2. Violence (5:6)

The first verb of this verse, "You have condemned,"[129] recalls 2:6-7, where it is said that the rich haul poor messianists into court and deal them injustice. The language is from the courtroom; it describes abuse of power against the powerless with the intent to increase wealth and power. But the image of the powerful oppressing the powerless is so common that we should not assume that it refers to a literal courtroom. Perhaps the general descriptions of wicked injustices, as in Psalm 10 or Wisdom 2:10-20, describe the context of James's "condemned" the best.[130] Thus, Psalm 10 has lines like these:

> They sit in ambush in the villages;
>> in hiding places they murder the innocent.
> Their eyes stealthily watch for the helpless;
>> they lurk in secret like a lion in its covert;
>> they lurk that they may seize the poor;
>> they seize the poor and drag them off in their net.
> They stoop, they crouch,
>> and the helpless fall by their might (vv. 8-10).

1 Enoch 96:8 has a striking parallel to our passage:

> Woe unto you, O powerful people!
> You who coerce the righteous with your power,
> the day of your destruction is coming!
> In those days, at the time of your condemnation,
> many and good days shall come for the righteous ones.

The first verb of this verse ("condemn") describes legal violence and the second physical violence. It is highly likely, though, that they are used together

---

128. See Mussner, 197 n. 5. But see Popkes, 309-10, who finds a more generic meaning to the notion of judgment in this verse.

129. κατεδικάσατε. See BDAG, 516. The use of this term in Matt 12:7, 37 and Luke 6:37 is more general, while our text is more legal.

130. See also Ps 37:14, 32; Prov 1:11; Amos 2:6; 5:12; *1 Enoch* 96:5; 98:12; 99:15-16; 103:15.

of legal abuse that leads to physical violence, even murder.[131] This first *(katadikazō)* describes justice deconstructed, such as corrupt policemen and conniving lawyers.[132] It not only unleashes more injustices but sets the balance of society on edge. The second verb is "and [you have] murdered."[133] Three times James brings up murder (2:11; 4:2 and here), and in each instance the tendency has been for interpreters to minimize its meaning. These texts, combined as they need to be with 1:20 and 2:1-7, lead me to think that actual murders were occurring among those to whom James wrote.

But this brings us once again face to face with the intended audience of the letter. The best explanation, one that has unfolded in this commentary, is that James writes to messianic communities that are embedded in Jewish communities, with boundary lines that are simply not clear. Some in the crosshairs of James, so we think the evidence suggests, are violent. It also appears that they are leaders at some level, for they have enough influence to shape who sits where in the synagogue and can dominate the courtroom. I lean toward the view that these violent people are not messianists, though that is far from clear. Injustices and violence have been part and parcel of Israel's history, and it is found in all the circles of power in the world, as described in Amos 5:11-12; Isaiah 3:14-15; and Micah 2:1-2.[134] What we deplore today we cannot dismiss from yesterday. The evidence at least suggests that murderous violence emerged in the messianic community. Perhaps our memory of murderous events among God's people has been tainted by our good intentions, current situations, and resolute hopes.

The second verb of this verse, and the last in the series of five descriptive accusations against the rich, opens up a series of debates, particularly concerning the identity of "the righteous one." The most common view, the *representative view,* thinks the "righteous one" stands for anyone who is righteous, that is, anyone who does God's will. One can appeal to well-known descriptions like those in Psalm 1 or Psalm 37.[135] That the label "righteous one" could apply to the obedient and compassionate in the messianic community is established by the attention James gives to the importance of righteousness (1:20; 3:18) and to a true understanding of justification (2:21, 23, 24-25) as well as by his use of this label in 5:16 for messianists.

131. Martin, 181.
132. See Ps 94:21.
133. ἐφονεύσατε, but without a conjunction. Jas 5:6 has three verbs and no conjunctions. On φονεύω, see BDAG, 1063. Moo sees an indirect sense of murder in that the judicial decisions deprive the poor of life; Moo, 219. Popkes, 311, sees both indirect and direct brutality of the rich.
134. See also Amos 8:4; Isa 3:10-15; 5:23.
135. So Laws, 204-5; Davids, 179-80; Popkes, 311. Other texts include Wis 2:20; 4QpPs37.

THE LETTER OF JAMES

A second view is that "the righteous one" is *James*, the Christian leader who is behind this book and who was later called "the righteous [one]."[136] The reason for this suggestion emerges from considering the near titular or semi-official expression "the righteous one." This view is tied into the question of the letter's authorship, though one could maintain that it came indirectly from the brother of Jesus and was composed after his death on the basis of notes from his sermons and addresses. In that case "the righteous one" would be a subtle allusion to James that only the author(s) and readers would recognize. What gives this view support, besides the tricky matter of confidence in one's dating of the letter, are the words of Hegesippus and Eusebius. This evidence, explained more completely in the Introduction, establishes that "the righteous one" could refer to James the Just if one also concludes that the text (or at least this verse) was composed after the death of James.[137] In describing the various accounts and traditions about the death of James the brother of Jesus, Eusebius says things like this: ". . . since he was by all men believed to be the most righteous . . ." and "He was called the 'Just' [or 'Righteous'] by all men from the Lord's time to ours . . ." and "So from his excessive righteousness he was called the Just."

Others, however, go further to point out that the noun is not only singular but also *messianic* and refers to Jesus Christ, who is on three occasions in the New Testament called "the Righteous One" (Acts 3:14; 7:52; 22:14).[138] In addition, other texts describe Jesus as righteous (Matt 27:24; Luke 23:47; 1 Pet 3:18; 1 John 2:1, 29; 3:7). *1 Enoch* 38:2 (see also 53:6) calls the Messiah "the Righteous One":

> . . . and when the Righteous One shall appear before the face of the righteous, those elect ones, . . . he shall reveal light to the righteous and the elect who dwell upon the earth, where will the dwelling of the sinners be, and where the resting place of those who denied the name of the Lord of the Spirits?

Qumran seems to run in the same circles:

> You alone have [creat]ed the righteous one, and from the womb You established him to give heed to Your covenant . . . (1QH^a 7:14-15).[139]

---

136. Martin, 182.

137. See Eusebius, *Eccl Hist* 2.23, where Eusebius gives his own view and quotes Hegesippus.

138. See R. N. Longenecker, *The Christology of Early Jewish Christianity* (SBTS 2.17; Naperville: Allenson, 1970), 46-47. Other pertinent texts include Jer 23:5-6; 33:15; Zech 9:9; *Pss Sol* 17:23-51; 18:8-9.

139. Wise, Abegg, and Cook, *Dead Sea Scrolls,* 89. See also 4Q511 frag. 44 47:6; frag. 63 3:4.

Some early Christian texts give support to the messianic reading of James 5:6. Thus, relying on the Septuagint of Isaiah 3:9-10, *Barnabas* says, "Let us bind the righteous one, because he is troublesome to us" (6:7).[140] What most impresses about this evidence, and that in the notes, is the unjust death of the "righteous one." Other New Testament texts also come to mind when one interprets this text as referring to Jesus, not the least of which is the statement of Peter in Acts 2:36: "God has made him both Lord and Messiah, this Jesus whom you crucified."[141]

There is, then, evidence for each view, and "You have condemned and murdered" can be accounted for by each. If one sees here martyrs for following Jesus, one can support the *representative* view. The evidence for the hideous murder of James, however much disputed in details, could give rise to the language of James 5:6, and the appropriateness of the same verse for describing Jesus is obvious. Is any of the options more probable than the others?

Perhaps the last clause of the sentence can help. The NRSV smoothes out terseness of the grammar with "who does not resist you" and takes a stand for the syntax being a simple indicative statement when it could be an interrogative that anticipates an affirmation: "Does he not oppose you? Yes, in fact he does."[142] It is here, so I think, that we find the clue that eliminates both the second and the third view of "the righteous one." The sudden shift from aorists to a present tense reminds the careful reader of 5:1-6 of the similar shift to a present tense in 5:4: "cry out."[143] There those who are crying out are the poor oppressed, those who are following Jesus and doing the will of God, in other words the righteous. Thus, the tense shift connects the actor/subject of "does not resist" to those crying out in 5:4 and supports the *representative* view. James is speaking here of the one or the ones who have died for their faith and are now interceding with God for justice on earth. While this evidence is hardly the kind that produces certitude, it is my belief that

140. See also Justin, *Dialogue* 17.1; 133.1; 136.1-2; Melito of Sardis, *Passover Homily*, 72.

141. See also Acts 2:23; 3:15; 4:10; 5:30.

142. οὐκ ἀντιτάσσεται ὑμῖν. Notably, the aorists have ended, and James here uses a present, making the resistance all the more vivid. This is a middle (Mayor, 160). It is unlikely that the subject is God (see Martin, 172), though that would fit with 4:6 and with the cries of the poor in 5:4 to the Lord of hosts. If one opts for God as the subject (Johnson, 305), it would be more likely that this verb formed an interrogative than a statement. Otherwise, one would have to have the cries being heard by the Lord of hosts in 5:4 and then in 5:6 that same God not resisting the injustices. ἀντιτάσσεται means "he opposes" (BDAG, 90), and οὐκ would make it a negated question that expects an affirmation.

143. Moo, 219-20, thinks the interrogative reading of this sentence should have had a future tense if the cries of the righteous are in view, but this seems to miss that the cries of the righteous in 5:4 are in the present.

THE LETTER OF JAMES

James has sketched a scene in 5:1-6 in which all kinds of actions are seen in their totality (aorists) or as describing a state of affairs (perfects) or as incomplete but certain (futures), but only one that is, as it were, occurring now (presents). It is the action of the poor, the Anawim, who are crying out before the Lord of Hosts and who are "resisting" the rich by that very action. But this view assumes that the clause is interrogative.

It is not impossible that James is a pacifist[144] and that he suggests here that those who were condemned and murdered by the rich did not resist them because, as 2:1-7 implies, they were powerless. One thinks then of formative texts like Isaiah 53:7-8 or Matthew 5:39 or even 1 Peter 2:20. But it is just as likely that the alteration to a present tense is not only a signal of a connection back to "cry out" in 5:4 but also one that points to a rhetorical twist to the end of this otherwise brutal set of words, a twist that leads to a question with the assumption that the poor *are* resisting injustice with protests.[145] The scene in Revelation 6:9-11 describes the very point James seems to be making, again with an interrogative as the oppressed cry out to God "How long?" This supports the view that James 5:6 ends not with an indicative but with an interrogative: "Does not that righteous person resist you [as proof that what you are doing is unjust]?"

We have no idea how the rich responded to this series of accusations by James. And, while we also do not know how the messianic community responded, we can assume that the poor heard these words as good news. What we do know is that James now turns to the messianic community and counsels them on how to deal with the oppressions they are experiencing.

7.3. The Messianic Community's Response to the Wealthy (5:7-11)

7*Be patient, therefore,*[146] *beloved,*[a] *until the coming of the Lord. The*[b] *farmer waits for the precious*[c] *crop from the earth,*[d] *being patient with it*[147] *until it receives*[148] *the early and the late rains.*[e][149] 8*You also must*

144. Jas 1:20 and 4:6 could be appealed to.

145. See Davids's excellent defense, 180.

146. A few manuscripts (Y, 631, and versions) omit οὖν, while a few others add μου (94, 252, 945, etc.).

147. Some manuscripts mistakenly change ἐπ' αὐτῷ to ἐπ' αυτον (K, L, 049, 322, 323, 400, 996, Byzantine), as if James is speaking of being patient for the Lord's coming.

148. A number of good, early manuscripts (e.g., ℵ, P, and Y) add the particle αν after ἕως; it has a good chance of being original but does not affect the meaning since the element of contingency can be inferred from the temporal conjunction. It is more likely that the particle was added than omitted.

149. Most manuscripts insert υετον ("rains") (A, P, Y, etc., Byzantine, Latin, Syriac, Georgian, and Slavonic). Clearly the word is added to clarify what is implicit, and the

*be patient. Strengthen your hearts[f] for the coming of the Lord is near.
9Beloved,[a][150] do not grumble against one another, so that you may not
be judged.[g] See,[h] the Judge is standing at the doors![i] 10As an example
of suffering and patience,[j][151] beloved,[a] take the prophets who spoke in
the name of the Lord.[152] 11Indeed[k] we call[l] blessed[153] those who
showed[154] endurance.[m] You have heard of the endurance[n] of Job, and
you have seen[155] the purpose[156] of the Lord,[o] how the Lord is compassionate and merciful.[p]*

a. TNIV: brothers and sisters

b. TNIV: See how the

c. TNIV: valuable

d. TNIV: the change of word order in: for the land to yield its valuable crop

e. TNIV: patiently waiting for the autumn and spring rains

---

only decision would be whether the omission is too difficult to have been the origin of the addition.

150. Some manuscripts add μου (e.g., A, 33, 81, etc.).

151. There are approximately twenty-five separable variations in the manu-script tradition of the opening clause in Jas 5:10. For a display, see *ECM*, 90-91. The Nestle-Aland[27] text behind the NRSV publishes the only variant with any chance of be-ing original.

152. The variants on this prepositional phrase are also numerous, almost as if scribes each tried their hand at saying the same thing in a different way. See again *ECM*, 91.

153. Some manuscripts use the subjunctive μακαριζωμεν (38, 181, 1241, 1563, 1838, 2242, 2464, L60, and L1440), but the evidence is overwhelmingly in favor of the in-dicative.

154. The past tense here is inferred from an aorist participle; some manuscripts have the present (69, 218, 322, 323, etc., and Byzantine), but the evidence for the aorist is widespread and early.

155. The evidence is split over εἴδετε and the imperative ἴδετε, but the external evidence (ℵ, B, and K) is against the imperative and the grammar becomes more diffi-cult. That is, the imperative would open up a new sentence with ὅτι, which makes sense, but then the object of ἠκούσατε would become both the patience of Job and the "end of the Lord," and one cannot be sure why one would add "end of the Lord" to the aorist verb. As it is, the last clause of 5:11 (NRSV: "how . . .") forms a brief clarification of the meaning of "the purpose of the Lord." See Davids, 187-88; Dibelius, 247-48, has ques-tioned the indicative.

156. The Greek reads τὴν ὑπομονὴν Ἰὼβ ἠκούσατε καὶ τὸ τέλος κυρίου εἴδετε. But some manuscripts have ελεος instead of τελος; the evidence is overwhelmingly in fa-vor of the reading as printed, but 322, 323, 424A, 915Z, 945, 1175, 1241, 1739T, and L1440* have ελεος. This reading conforms to the immediate context, while the printed text connects the two central themes of the passage: both patience and the coming of the Lord.

f. TNIV: and stand firm

g. TNIV: or you will be judged

h. TNIV omits "See"

i. TNIV: door

j. TNIV: patience in the face of suffering

k. TNIV: As you know

l. TNIV: count as blessed

m. TNIV: those who have persevered

n. TNIV: perseverance

o. TNIV: have seen what the Lord finally brought about

p. TNIV: The Lord is full of compassion and mercy.

The tone of the rhetoric finds a new, pastoral level. From "you who say" and "you rich," the operative word is now "beloved" (NRSV) or "brothers and sisters" (TNIV). James shifts from rich merchants (4:13-17) and oppressive rich farmers (5:1-6) to the beloved community (5:7-11), who have been oppressed by the merchants and farmers. Instead of a singular focus on "you," we have in 5:7-11 also an inclusive "we" in 5:11. Furthermore, the tone shifts from "the Lord of hosts" to the "compassionate and merciful" Lord in 5:11. In that tone we find the clue both to the audience and to the intent: James has shifted his eyes from the rich oppressors in the community to the faithful followers of Jesus. 5:7-11 explains how James thinks the messianic community should respond to the oppressing rich, essentially that they should wait for the coming of the Lord, that is, for the Day of the Lord when God judges the oppressors and sets the world to rights.

There are extensive discussions of both the length of the ending of James and how 5:7-11 fits into the letter.[157] We take the latter as a third part of 4:13–5:11,[158] but not all agree. As an example, Luke Timothy Johnson sees these verses as a hinge between 4:11–5:6 and 5:12-20.[159] Hubert Frankemölle, on the other hand, argues that 5:7-20 is the epilogue *(peroratio)* that answers the prologue (1:2-18, the *exordium*) as James makes use of ancient classical rhetoric.[160] The fatal flaw here is that it is unclear that James has intentionally made use of this specific form of Greek or Roman rhetoric.

---

157. See Francis, "Form and Function"; I agree with Davids (p. 181) that 5:7-20 brings to the surface a number of themes from the whole book, but I think 5:7-11 concludes 4:13–5:6 alone and belongs with those verses. Laws, 207-8, represents many who see the beginning of a new theme here. What connects 4:13–5:6 (especially 5:1-6) to 5:7-11 is the imminent eschatology of judgment, with the negative side in 5:1-6 and the positive side in 5:7-11.

158. See Moo, 220-21.

159. Johnson, 311-12.

160. Frankemölle, 667-76.

That parallels in ancient rhetoric can be found is above reason; that James purposefully modeled his letter on a genre of ancient rhetoric is not yet proven. Ben Witherington, who has exploited his knowledge of ancient rhetoric in commentaries on every book of the New Testament, after discussing the various rhetorical models of van der Westhuizen, Watson, and Thurén, concludes that James "appears to be deliberative rhetoric."[161] It is the word "appears" that leaves me less than confident that we can know of a rhetorical genre at work in James.

More importantly, as we will seek to show below, 5:12-20 does not form as tidy a summing up of the letter as some argue, and many argue that it does by appealing to big picture themes, like eschatology and community. A closer look shows that what we have in those final verses is three new topics: swearing, healing, and restoring a wandering sinner. James has brought up speech patterns, but has not said a word about swearing; he has said nothing about healing; and the ending of the letter on the note of rescuing wandering sinners is a surprise. The tidiness of the models we find for the rhetorical structure of James might convince some at the level of hints of general themes, but closer inspection reveals that James — as we have seen elsewhere in this letter — is not as tidy as we might like.[162] Tidying up James for him by filling in the lines with rhetorical theory gets in the way of reading the text in the broken staccato-like method James himself uses. It at least imposes on James categories that this reader does not see.

James does not proceed in this letter in a steady neat line of logic, and 5:7 opens a section that is unified in theme but unpredictable in flow. A first exhortation to patience (5:7a) is followed by an illustrative example that defines the meaning of patience (5:7b). The second exhortation to patience (5:8a) is followed by an exhortation to be strengthened (5:8b) and a reason to be both patient and strong, namely, the imminent coming of the Lord (5:8c). An exhortation against grumbling (5:9a) is followed by a reason for not grumbling: the Judge is at the door (5:9b). Then James gives two examples of patience: the prophets (5:10-11a) and Job (5:11b). James breathes here the same air as Psalm 37 (see particularly vv. 5-13, 23-24, and 34), though what he says cannot be harnessed to the psalm as an exposition of it.

---

161. Witherington, 388-93.

162. I must admit that ever since H. D. Betz's commentary on Galatians, in which he proposed a dense and articulate rhetorical borrowing from classical models, I have been wary of the excitement surrounding rhetorical models. And Galatians is far more susceptible to rhetorical explanation than James. It must be immediately noted, though, that I do not dispute rhetorical techniques in James (or Galatians). I doubt the deliberate, intentional, and informed use of an existing classical model by James.

7.3.1. First Exhortation to Patience (5:7)

7.3.1.1. Exhortation (5:7a)

"Therefore" *(oun)* indicates that James has a basis for his first exhortation, and five possibilities have been suggested for that reason for patience: (1) the *eschatological* reason:[163] the Lord of hosts is about to act against the oppressors, *therefore* be patient; (2) the *judgment* reason narrows the eschatological reason:[164] the Lord is about to condemn the oppressors; or (3) the *intercessory* reason: the Lord has heard the resisting cries of the oppressed (v. 6). This third view could be altered by a view of "who does not resist you" not supported above (namely, it speaks of the inability to do anything about oppression), to (4) the *piety* reason: the pious/righteous do not resist with violence, *therefore* follow their steps and be patient. Finally, (5) James's rhetoric is more *general* in the word "therefore": his logical inference is drawn from the total picture of God having heard the cries (v. 4) and having decided to act in judgment imminently. Because the points made in 5:7-11 encompass each of these points, it seems preferable to opt for the fifth view and see here a general logical inference.

James commands the messianic community, here designated "beloved" or, as the TNIV translates it, "brothers and sisters."[165] This word is the first indicator of a change in tone. James shifts from the accusatory "you who say" (4:13) and "you rich" (5:1), which were themselves notable shifts from the accusatory but pastorally shaped warnings, commands, and promises in 4:1-12, to the common life of Christian fellowship and unity with "beloved." As if to make his change of tone clear, James repeats the term in both 5:9 and 5:10 (see also 5:12, 19).

The command to "be patient"[166] needs to be tied (vocabularically) to the word "endurance"[167] in 5:11. This term, taken in context of 5:1-11, denotes fortitude, steadfastness, and patience in the context of stress, trial, and suffering, as 5:10-11 will make clear (cf. Luke 21:19; Rom 5:3; 2 Cor 1:6; 6:4; 2 Thess 1:4; Heb 10:32-39). Luke Timothy Johnson has observed that "be patient" is a response of a superior to an inferior while "endurance" *(hypomonē)*

163. Laws, 208.

164. Davids, 181.

165. ἀδελφοί. See notes on 1:2 and 1:19; the word occurs in James 17 times. The instances where James uses the vocative almost always have the personal pronoun μου, except at 4:11 and the references in this paragraph (5:7, 9, 10).

166. Μακροθυμήσατε. The aorist is used to sum up the entire action of patient waiting; the choice of aorist is not to get the community to begin doing something they are not right now doing. BDAG, 612.

167. Found twice, once as a participle (ὑπομείναντας) and once as a noun (ὑπομονήν). See BDAG, 1039-40.

expresses the opposite relationship.[168] This may be so, and the evidence can be used to support it, but it is hardly a foolproof case. If it is correct, the idea here would of the (superior in divine perspective) poor oppressed putting up with the (inferior in divine perspective) oppressors until the coming of the Lord. The palpability of the theme of reversal would be obvious. There is one major weakness to this view: James seems to use the terms synonymously in our paragraph. Thus, he uses *makrothymeō* and *makrothymia* ("be patient," "patience") several times in vv. 7-10 and *hypomonē* ("endurance") twice in 5:11, where he seems to be alluding to the same thing.[169]

The simple moral virtue of patience (1 Cor 13:4; 1 Thess 5:14) is not in James's mind here, nor is the general notion of waiting for God's promise (Heb 6:15). His thinking is more specific and is shaped by eschatology. He has spoken of the opulence and violence of the rich, the oppression of the poor, the cries of the poor to the Lord of hosts, and confidence that God has heard their cries (4:13–5:6). When we turn to 5:7-11 we encounter an emphasis on patience and perseverance *in an eschatological framework:* that is, *because the Lord is coming soon as Judge,* the readers are to be patient. I have argued throughout this commentary that James knows that hotheads in the messianic community are tempted to strike back with violence (1:19-21; 2:11; 4:1-12; 5:6). Once we tie 5:7-11, where God is the Judge, to 5:1-6, where God is about to act in judgment, the meaning of both patience and perseverance is shaped eschatologically to mean the choice to wait for God's judgment instead of taking matters in one's own (bloody) hands.[170] In addition, it is probably more accurate here to say that James has God's act of judgment against the oppressors more in view than he does God's act of delivering the oppressed, as in Hebrews 10:32-39 or 1 Peter 4:12-19,[171] though the former would involve the latter. Our passage is in that way more like Romans 12:19-21.

This conclusion somewhat anticipates what we need to examine in the pregnant expression "until the coming of the Lord."[172] It is not possible here

168. Johnson, 312-13.

169. So also Moo, 221-22.

170. See Davids, 182.

171. It ought to be observed, though, that 1 Pet 4:15 urges the Christian not to suffer for being a "murderer." So also Rev 13:10.

172. ἕως τῆς παρουσίας τοῦ κυρίου. Some think τοῦ κυρίου here might refer to the Day of the Lord as the Day of God, but that is far from clear because James uses the term both for Father and for Christ. It does little good to examine this expression in early Jewish literature in order to see if the word means Father or Jesus Christ, because "Lord" could not possibly refer to Christ there; it soon became standard reference to Jesus Christ in the early Christian literature (see Hermas, *Visions* 58.3; Ignatius, *Philadelphians* 9.2). We need to stick to the evidence in James. I repeat there the note from above: the evidence

to resolve either the exegetical issues nor the endless speculations involved when one begins to discuss particulars about Christian eschatology. The "coming of the Lord" (Greek, *parousia tou kuriou*) is far too often understood as the "return" of Christ or even as the "rapture" of the church, but *parousia* means "presence" and "appearing." Other words would have been used, such as *katabasis,* if one wanted to describe a descent to earth in a more intentional manner. Because the issues are complex, it is worth our time to examine the use of *parousia* in the New Testament.

In the Olivet Discourse (Mark 13, Matthew 24, and Luke 21) only Matthew uses *parousia,* in vv. 3, 27, 37, and 39. All but the first of those speak of the *parousia* of "the Son of Man." In the Olivet Discourse the event looming on the horizon, the answer to the questions Jesus was asked about "When?" and "What will be the sign?" (v. 3), is the destruction of Jerusalem in 66-73 AD. The clinching evidence that these texts speak of something that occurred within one generation of their prediction by Jesus is Matthew 24:29: "Immediately after" can only mean very soon after, and "the suffering of *those* days" refers to the things Jesus has just described. Furthermore, 24:33-34 does not speak of just "some" things but "*all* these things" as what will occur *within one generation.* Therefore, Jesus taught that the *parousia* would occur within a generation of the moment he spoke and that it had to do with the sacking of Jerusalem as an act of God against the Jewish leaders for their complicity in violence and their rejection of Jesus as God's Son and message for the nation (cf. Matthew 21–23). The *parousia* also meant hope and deliverance for Jesus' followers. So, *parousia* here refers to the presence of God/Christ in the destruction of Jerusalem and the deliverance of the church from that destruction. To be sure, there are debates about every point mentioned and every verse in Jesus' apocalyptic discourse, but the reader deserves to know where I stand on these matters, without my turning this commentary into a lengthy commentary on Mark 13 and its parallels.

There is no reason to think that Paul's use of *parousia* (1 Cor 15:23; 1 Thess 2:19; 3:13; 4:15; 5:23; 2 Thess 2:1, 8-9) matches that of Jesus' translators. In these Pauline texts, the *parousia* takes its place in a sequence of events. In 1 Thessalonians Paul refers to the Lord's *parousia* as a descent *(katabainō)* for the resurrection of saints (4:16), following which living saints will be snatched into the air "to be with the Lord forever." Just when this would happen was not clear in Paul's churches, so he sought to clarify it: it will come suddenly and believers will be ready if they are faithful (5:2, 4). That day will be a day of salvation and wrath (5:9). 1 Corinthians 15:23 more clearly spells out an order of events: (1) the resurrection of Jesus, (2) the res-

---

in James is not clear; this term can refer to Christ (1:1; 2:1; 5:7-8) or to the Father (3:9; 4:10; 5:4, 10-11). Some references are simply not clear (1:7-8; 5:14-15).

urrection of those who "belong to Christ" at his "coming," (3) the destruction of the enemies of God and death, (4) the end, when the Son hands the kingdom over to the Father, and (5) the Father's reign, with the Son in subjection. The "coming" of Christ thus occurs between the resurrection of Christ and the destruction of the enemies. 2 Thessalonians 2 largely confirms these points but adds to them: the "coming" *(parousia)* is connected to "our being gathered to him" and to the "day of the Lord" (2:1-2). Some thought that this had already occurred and that they had missed it. Paul spells out some order here also: first, a rebellion led by the rebellious one that is now being restrained until, second, the day of the Lord, when the Lord will destroy the lawless one. The references to *parousia* in Peter and John (2 Pet 1:16; 3:4, 12; 1 John 2:28) confirm what we have seen: just when the *parousia* will happen has long disturbed Christians, but it will happen and will lead to judgment and deliverance.

What needs to be decided here is where James fits in this spectrum of thinking, and some have fruitfully compared James with these other early Christian voices.[173] James may be concerned with the delay of the *parousia* in his need to inculcate patient nonviolence, but this is far from clear. There is no sign that his readers want to know the time or hour (1 Thess 5:1) or that some have concluded that the *parousia* will not happen after all (cf. 1 Corinthians 15; 2 Pet 3:3, 4, 9). Instead, James's focus is on the certainty of the *parousia,* the hope that it can inculcate, and its apparent imminence.

More particularly, James knows nothing of the rapture-like act of God that we find in Paul, there is nothing in his context that indicates that the coming of the Lord is a descent to earth by Jesus, there is nothing about resurrection or the reign of the Father and Son. To think James means these things one has to assume that what Paul meant by *parousia* James had to mean — because that is what the supposed early Christian lexicon says. If we take James at his word and add nothing to his words, we discover that he is like Jesus, 2 Peter, and John: the *parousia* is the act of God on earth in judgment against the disobedient (oppressors) that entails, probably, vindication for the righteous, poor, and obedient. I infer this from the cries of the poor heard by the Lord of hosts (v. 4) who then acts in judgment to establish justice. In 5:8-9 we learn that the *parousia* of the Lord is "near" and that it is an act of judgment. James here stands closer to Jesus than to Paul on what *parousia* means. In other words, it most likely refers here to an imminent act of judgment, fulfilled to some degree (I assume) in the destruction of Jerusalem as the act of God (in part) to vindicate the poor messianic community and to judge the rich oppressors of that messianic community.

This interpretation entails rethinking the meaning of "Lord" in "the

173. See Martin, 188, for an insightful paragraph.

coming of the Lord." James sometimes uses "Lord" to refer to Jesus (1:1; 2:1), but he uses it more often for the Father/God (3:9; 4:10; 5:4, 10-11).[174] It is common to think that "Lord" in 5:7-8 refers to the coming of the Lord Jesus Christ because *parousia* is used with Christ in Matthew, Paul, Peter, and John. In other words, that is how it appears in what we think was an early Christian lexicon.[175] But, the immediate context of 5:4 and 5:10-11 might lead us to think that "Lord" in 5:7-8 means God/Father instead of Jesus Christ. I am inclined to think that the *parousia* here refers to the manifestation of God's (the Father's) righteous judgment and establishment of justice in the destruction of Jerusalem.[176] James's usage, then, is thoroughly Jewish, as in *Testament of Judah* 22:2: "My rule shall be terminated by men of alien race, until the salvation of Israel comes, until the coming of the God of righteousness, so that Jacob may enjoy tranquility and peace, as well as the nations."[177]

An eschatological reading of 5:7 leads to the conclusion that James, once again, is warning the community against violence. He urges them to wait for God to take vengeance (Gen 4:15; Lev 19:18; 26:25; Ps 94:1; Isa 34:8; 61:2), as memorialized in Deuteronomy 32:35:

> Vengeance is mine, and recompense,
> for the time when their foot shall slip;
> because the day of their calamity is at hand,
> their doom comes swiftly.

Paul, too, refers to this text (Rom 12:19), and so does Hebrews (10:30). One thinks also of Jesus' parable of the weeds and wheat, where he urges his hearers not to uproot the weeds lest they rip up the wheat (Matt 13:24-30, 36-43). In James we have already seen this counsel to moderate the temptation to vi-

---

174. At the general level, it is the difficulty in discerning which is which in the use of κύριος in the New Testament that should be a cause for wonder. How it was that the early theologians began to use the sacred name for Jesus is a profundity that was not resolved until, and then only in part, Nicea. That we cannot always discern which is which in the New Testament only reveals how closely the Father and Son were from the very beginning. And, as Richard Bauckham has shown, if we approach this from the angle of ancient Israel's understanding of monotheism, an entirely different perspective arises, namely, that the early Christians identified Jesus by the terms and categories used to identify YHWH; see his "Biblical Theology and the Problems of Monotheism," in *Out of Egypt: Biblical Theology and Biblical Interpretation* (ed. C. Bartholomew, et al.; Grand Rapids: Zondervan, 2004), 187-232.

175. A good example is Martin, 190; see also Popkes, 321-22; Wachob, "Apocalyptic Intertexture," 169-70.

176. This is another indicator of an early date for James.

177. See also *Testament of Levi* 8:11; *Testament of Moses* 10:12; *1 Enoch* 92–105; *Testament of Abraham* 13:4, 6 (recension A, but not in B).

olence (1:19-21; 3:13-18, especially v. 18; 4:1-6). The cries of the poor oppressed have been heard, so James urges the poor to wait patiently for the act of God that will vindicate them. His counsel then is precisely the opposite of the growing influence of the Zealots.[178]

7.3.1.2. Reason (5:7b)

The poor messianists are urged to be patient until the coming of the Lord for a reason: "The farmer waits for [or 'expects'] the precious crop from the earth, being patient with it[179] until it receives the early and the late rains."[180] James thinks the example he gives is worthy of their attention.[181] The farmer's patience is an analogy to the patience the messianic community needs, but one needs to avoid pressing the details of the analogy, as in parable interpretation,[182] beyond their overall intent. I doubt we should find anything special in "precious," "greatly valued,"[183] "crop" *(karpon),* "from the earth," or the "early and late rains."[184] Laws stretches the evidence in seeing the

178. So Martin, 191.

179. Or, "waiting patiently for it."

180. ἰδοὺ ὁ γεωργὸς ἐκδέχεται τὸν τίμιον καρπὸν τῆς γῆς μακροθυμῶν ἐπ' αὐτῷ ἕως λάβῃ πρόϊμον καὶ ὄψιμον. Again, an illustration functions well with present tenses (ἐκδέχεται, μακροθυμῶν) in order to make it vivid before the eyes of those listening. The aorist subjunctive λάβῃ sums up the action of a subordinate clause. The participle's action is that of the farmer, and the participle is adverbial, modifying the verb ἐκδέχομαι. The prepositional phrase ἐπ' αὐτῷ probably refers to the καρπόν, and the subject of the verb is the crop that receives the rain. The two actions are "expecting" (ἐκδέχομαι) and "waiting patiently" (μακροθυμέω), with the latter a virtuous characteristic of the former.

181. The NRSV ignores ἰδοῦ. But see 3:4, 5; 5:4, 9, 11.

182. On the methodology I am using here, find a similar approach to parables in K. Snodgrass, *Stories with Intent* (Grand Rapids: Eerdmans, 2007).

183. For the farmer, the crop is "precious" because it sustains his family, not because the farmer is growing expensive wine or rare produce. BDAG, 1005-6.

184. Debate arises over whether or not πρόϊμον καὶ ὄψιμον indicates a land of Israel agricultural context or not. On this, see D. Baly, "Rain," in *ISBE* 4.35-36; B. J. Beitzel, *The Moody Atlas of Bible Lands* (Chicago: Moody, 1985), 46-53. The best rains begin in October and continue until April, but the rain in the land is erratic. Sometimes no rains come until late December or even later; such rains, if abundant, can redeem the crops. See allusions to the rains in Deut 11:14; Jer 5:24; Hos 6:3; Joel 2:23; Zech 10:1; *m Taanith* 1.1-7; 3.1-3. Davids, 183-84, thinks this indicates a land of Israel setting, while Laws thinks it is a literary trope (Laws, 212). Her reasons are that as 5:1-6 and 5:10-11 are loaded with Old Testament language, one should not be surprised to find it here. Furthermore, she observes that Deut 11:14 is perhaps part of the daily recitation of the *Shema,* making the language a commonplace if not boilerplate, but it is hard to know when that text became part of the daily recitation. That this language is not used in later Christian literature tips the balance in favor of the view that this language reflects the land of Israel's agrarian

farmer not experiencing suffering due to his patient farming as an analogy to the ordinary pressures the community experiences at the hand of the oppressing rich.[185] This ignores the clear evidence of persecution in 2:5-7 and 5:1-6, though one cannot be sure if there is any kind of sudden outburst. But this is not to say there is not a core analogy: as the farmer (see 5:4) expects crops but waits patiently for the rains, so the poor are to expect God's judgment but wait patiently for God to bring that about; as the farmer waits for a "precious crop," so the poor are to await their reward for obedience; and as the farmer must await the faithfulness of God[186] to provide both the early and the late rains, so they are to wait until the coming of the Lord. None of this is fanciful and each element is central to the point James makes in light of 5:1-6.

7.3.2. Second Exhortation to Patience (5:8)

7.3.2.1. Exhortation (5:8a)

James now repeats his exhortation to patience, but this time with some emphasis[187] and in light of his analogy: "You must also be patient." To this James adds a new idea before he gives his second reason for patient endurance: "Strengthen your hearts."[188] The word "strengthen" (Greek, *stērizō*) is used of fortifying oneself with food (Judg 19:5, 8), and by trusting in the strength of God one's heart can be fortified and the will made resolute (Ps 57:7; Sir 6:37; cf. 22:16-17). Paul wants to strengthen, or fortify, the Romans with some spiritual gift (1:11), he prays that God will fortify hearts in holiness (1 Thess 3:13), and he is confident that good works fortify the heart (2 Thess 2:17). Not surprisingly, strength of heart comes from grace not food observances (Heb 13:9). When James says he wants the messianists to be strengthened "in your hearts," he is thinking from the inside out, from the core of their being, both in resolution and confident faith (James 1:26; 3:14; 4:8; 5:5).

7.3.2.2. Reason (5:8b)

Why do they need to be patient and strengthen their hearts? As James puts it, "for the coming of the Lord is near."[189] We concluded above that "the coming

---

hopes. See also Ropes, 295-97. The language is vividly real, as any farmer dependent upon crops for sustenance would know. See again Safrai, *Economy* (note 24 above).

185. See Laws, 210.

186. A point made by Moo, 223.

187. In καὶ ὑμεῖς.

188. στηρίξατε τὰς καρδίας ὑμῶν. The command in the aorist is constative in that it sums up the whole action. See BDAG, 945.

189. ὅτι ἡ παρουσία τοῦ κυρίου ἤγγικεν. On the verb, see BDAG, 270. The verb is

of the Lord" refers to the act of God in judgment against the oppressors in the defeat of Jerusalem. But, again, some of this needs to be shown, and this verse and the next will clarify what remains to be demonstrated. Everything here hinges on the meaning of "is near" (Greek *ēngiken*). The word *(engizō)*, in short order, means "draw near." It speaks of something so near that its impact is beginning to be felt. The fear that somehow James, and therefore the Word of God, would be wrong if this word is given the meaning one expects it to have has led too many to less than obvious explanations.[190] The word is used forty-one times in the New Testament.[191] One of the more telling uses is in Mark 11:1 (par. Matt 21:1): "When they were approaching Jerusalem, at Bethphage and Bethany, near the Mount of Olives, he sent two of his disciples. . . ." The point is that they were close but not yet there; so close that Jesus sent two disciples on ahead to get things ready. Other uses, such as Matthew 21:34; 26:45-46; Luke 15:25; 18:35; 19:41; 21:8, 20; 22:1 confirm that *engizō* means to be near, very near, but not yet arrived — but close enough for things to start happening.

What matters in our context is that *ēngiken* is used for cataclysmic eschatological events in the time-plan of the early Christians. Hence, Jesus can say the kingdom of God has drawn near (Mark 1:15; Luke 10:9, 11). Of note are Luke 21:20: "When you see Jerusalem surrounded by armies, then know that its desolation has come near," and 21:28: "Now when these things begin to take place, stand up and raise your heads, because your redemption is drawing near." From Acts, we read in 7:17: "But as the time drew near for the fulfillment of the promise that God had made to Abraham, our people in Egypt increased and multiplied." Paul says in Romans 13:12: "the night is far gone, the day is near. Let us then lay aside the works of darkness and put on the armor of light." And Hebrews 10:25: "not neglecting to meet together, as is the habit of some, but encouraging one another, and all the more as you see

---

perfect and therefore speaks of a state of affairs, similar to the Lord of hosts' having heard the cries of the oppressed. The state in mind here is that God's appearing, or "coming," is in the state of having drawn near. I would emphasize that such a state of affairs could endure for millennia, for all the grammar requires is that one see the "drawing near" as the state of affairs. That language, however, intends to evoke imminence, and therefore the oppressed can wait it out. In other words, grammar needs to be tied to rhetorical intent.

190. Moo, 223-24, for instance, argues that the parousia is the next item on the divine calendar and the time is unknown, so the word "near" is appropriate. While this is perhaps true in a larger eschatological framework, it does not explain the ubiquity of the term "near" in so many New Testament references. One would have expected the term "next" or "certain," but *pace* Moo the word ἤγγικεν cannot be so easily dismissed, for it does have both spatial and temporal nearness in mind. I am suggesting that a more elastic sense of "parousia" might be the way forward.

191. The bibliography here, because Jesus uses this term in Mark 1:15, is immense. See McKnight, *New Vision,* 122-25, for a sketch.

the Day approaching." Peter too: "The end of all things is near; therefore be serious and discipline yourselves for the sake of your prayers" (1 Pet 4:7). In addition to these considerations we note that this term emerges at times in the context of oppression and serves to buttress the hope of the oppressed. Thus, Mark 13 speaks often of persecution and how the nearness of the Son of Man's coming brings hope (Mark 13:26-31). Peter's words about the end of all things being near immediately lead to encouragement about persecution (1 Pet 4:7-11, 12-19). The so-called roll-call of heroic faith in Hebrews 10 winds up its point in a combination of encouragement and promise that the Lord is coming (10:32-39).

One can read "the coming of the Lord is near" in James 5:8 in the context of Paul's statements about the coming of the Lord Jesus Christ, and, if *ēngiken* is understood as referring to something about to happen, then either Jesus did return somehow or James was wrong. Or one can read this text in light of the teachings of Jesus about the *parousia* in a Jewish context and see it as a prediction of the imminent judgment of God, and in this case one would have to think of the sacking of Jerusalem in 70 AD as told of so graphically by Josephus in his *Jewish War*.[192] The latter is far more probable, and

192. The following items are themes in Jesus' prophecies about the future that have parallels in Josephus, that suggest predictive prophecy, and that correspond to the theme of God acting in judgment against oppression:
- false prophetic/messianic claims: *War* 2.252-94 (John of Gischala); 4.529-44 (Simon ben Gioras);
- hideous persecution: 2.297-308, especially 306-8 (Florus); 2.457-80, 494-98 (50,000 Alexandrian Jews slaughtered in A.D. 66); 3.59-63 (Galilee a "scene of fire and blood"), 336-39, especially 336 (surrender of Jotapata), 414-27, especially 426-27 (Joppa exodus leads to sea of blood); 3.485-91 (Tarichaeae valley full of corpses), 522-31 (massacre on Sea of Galilee: blood, corpses, stench); 4.305-44 (bloody insurrection in Temple courts led by Zealots and Idumaeans, high priest Ananus killed); 5.446-59 (500 crucifixions per day), 512-26 (death everywhere); 6.351-55 (the city burns), 369 ("Not a spot in the city was left bare: every corner had its corpse, the victim of famine or sedition");
- defilement of the Temple: 4.377-88 (by Zealots); 5.11-38, especially 16-18 (lakes of blood in the Temple); 5.527-33 (high priestly murders); 6.1-8 (war ruined it all); 6.249-66 (Temple burned);
- horrors of famine: 5.429-38; 6.193-213 (a mother devours her own child);
- the ultimate in pain: 5.442-45;
- flights ending in horrific murders: 5.548-52 (2,000 Jewish refugees ripped open by Syrians and Arabs when it was discovered that one Jew had golden coins in his excrement); 6.366-73 (flights to caves and among rocks);
- constant observation that all this was the judgment of God (6.93-110);
- corresponding events connected with the last days of Jerusalem before its total destruction: 6.288-309 (star and comet [birth of Jesus?]; midnight light around the altar [birth of Jesus?]; cow gives birth to lamb; gates open of their own accord

the next verse tips the balance in its favor. There (5:9b) the *parousia* has to do with God appearing as Judge. Grammatically speaking, the perfect tense of *ēngiken* needs to be seen in context: the state of affairs that comes through the perfect tense is that God has heard the cries of the poor (5:4, perfect tense), so the flipside of that hearing is that the "coming near" of the Lord's *parousia* is a state of affairs. One might think of "being near" the way a plane might be put into a holding pattern just before it arrives. The Lord's *parousia* then mirrors the hearing of the cries of the oppressed as a state of affairs. The Judge's standing, or hovering, at the doors (5:9b) is another set of affairs sketched in the perfect tense. They need to be tied together: God having heard the cries, the coming near of the *parousia,* and the approach of God as Judge.

7.3.3. Exhortation about Speech (5:9)

Surprisingly, James turns to an exhortation about speech in 5:9, though it is connected to what precedes because the reason he gives is the imminence of God's judgment (5:9b). Some suggest that the theme is grounded in the ecclesiological interests of James and more particularly in his focus on the importance of proper speech patterns (1:19-21; 2:1-13; 3:1-12; 4:1-6, 11-12).[193] That suggestion, however, creates tension in the text because it would mean that James has interrupted his theme of perseverance (5:7-8) with a new theme (speech patterns, 5:9) only to settle down quickly into the theme of perseverance again (5:10-11). I find this interruption of the theme unlikely. Instead, it is more likely that 5:9's concern with words fits into the theme of perseverance, addressing a kind of grumbling connected to the readers' impatience.

7.3.3.1. Exhortation (5:9a)

James addresses the "beloved" or "brothers and sisters"[194] to bring them into the circle of fellowship. He commands them: "do not grumble against one another."[195] The verb James chooses, *stenazō,* is not the more common word used of Israel's grumbling in the wilderness against God *(gongyzō),* but the

[death of Jesus?]; chariots in the sky, with battalions; invisible voice saying, "We are departing hence"; a prophet named Jesus [not Jesus of Nazareth] announces judgment). I take this from my *New Vision,* 141 n. 52.

193. See Laws, 213. Dibelius, 241-42, understands Jas 5:9 as an independent logion that was attached to the letter at this point.

194. ἀδελφοί, again without a personal pronoun. See notes at 5:7.

195. μὴ στενάζετε κατ' ἀλλήλων. On στενάζω, see BDAG, 942. The preposition means "against."

LXX of Exodus 2:23-24 and 6:5 do use *stenazō*. Jesus *sighed* about a deaf man who also could not speak well when he prayed for that man's healing (Mark 7:34). Three Pauline texts use this term for human *yearnings* for final redemption (Rom 8:22; 2 Cor 5:2, 4). And Hebrews 13:17 exhorts leaders not to *sigh* over their congregation. What seems most relevant, though, is the use of this term in the Old Testament for the human response of grumbling against both God and fellow Israelites in the context of suffering, as in Job 24:12; Sirach 36:25; Ezek 21:6-7; and Lamentations 1:8, 21.[196]

One must imagine that the oppressive conditions led to the temptation not only to violence but also to turning against others (and God). Oppression leads to consternation and the yearning desire to find a way out. James knows this so he counsels the messianic community not to let their anger turn to grumbling, wrathful violence, yearning to climb over one another. Interpreters commonly connect "one another" to "brothers [and sisters]" as the messianic fellowship and see the grumbling as directed at others in the fellowship, not at the rich farmers and merchants of 4:13–5:6. This is reasonable, but one must at least leave open the possibility that James did not draw such a deep furrow and that "grumbling against one another" might be another form of violence against the oppressors.[197]

7.3.3.2. Reason (5:9b)

The reason James's addressees are not to turn against one another is now made clear: "so that you may not be judged. See, the Judge is standing at the doors!"[198] These two sentences need to be tied together as indicating the reality of judgment and the imminence of judgment. The reality of judgment is

---

196. See Johnson, *Brother of Jesus, Friend of God,* 129-31, for a possible allusion to Lev 19:18a.

197. Why does James change from aorist commands (5:7, 8) to a present prohibition in 5:9 and then back to an aorist in 5:10? Some would argue that the present indicates that they are to desist from something already going on, but this connects tense with reality too closely. We need to focus on the author's depiction of action in the present aspect, which is used for action that is not conceived of as completed. I would suggest that we connect this prohibition with the cries of the oppressed (5:4, present tense) and the prayerful resistance of the oppressed in 5:6 (present tense) as an indicator of how the author wants action to be perceived as he describes the scene. For him, the cries and resisting and not complaining are the actions that need to be emphasized with the "imperfective" aspect so they can be more vividly presented to the imagining eyes of his audience. Furthermore, the "not grumbling" stands out from the "be patient" and "take" of 5:7, 8, and 10.

198. ἵνα μὴ κριθῆτε· ἰδοὺ ὁ κριτὴς πρὸ τῶν θυρῶν ἔστηκεν. The aorist passive of κρίνω means "damned, condemned" by God (divine passive); see BDAG, 567-69. The perfect tense reminds one of the perfects in 5:4, where the cries have been heard by the Lord of hosts, and the having drawn near of 5:8.

not the reality of there being a judgment at all,[199] but the reality of that judgment being enacted against those who choose to grumble against one another. Judgment is both real and vivid for James (2:12; 4:11-12) and is the act of God (2:12-13; 4:11-12). We need to tie this act of God's judgment against the grumblers as divine vengeance with the human act of condemnation (*katadikazō*) and murder in 5:6, which we think is lurking in the shadows of what grumbling means in 5:9a. The possibility of judgment, made clear in the aorist subjunctive in "so that you may not be judged," shifts now to a different certainty in the state of affairs James now describes with the perfect tense. As the state of affairs was that God had heard the cries of the poor (5:4, perfect tense) and that the *parousia* had drawn near (5:8), so the flipside of that hearing is that God is now "standing at the doors." What is certain is that God is at the doors; what is potential is that the messianic community might experience the sword if they do not repent. If they choose to grumble against one another, the one standing at the doors will move that potentiality into the divine reality.

The one at the door is the "Judge,"[200] the one and only Judge (4:11-12), whose sole prerogative is usurped when humans seek to judge (2:4). Identification of this Judge follows who one thinks "the Lord" is in "the coming of the Lord." Hence, opinion is divided. Some think it refers to God/Father (4:12) while others think it refers to the Lord Jesus Christ (1 Cor 3:10-17; 2 Cor 5:10; Rev 3:20).[201] Two factors weigh in favor of God/Father in this context: in 4:12 the Lawgiver and Judge is God/Father, and our conclusion that "the coming *of the Lord*" more than likely referred to God/Father.

What is distinct here is the final expression: "at the doors."[202] The image, not unlike that in Revelation 3:20, is of physical proximity. This sense of imminence or proximity was inherited from Jesus, as seen in Mark 13:29 par. Luke 21:31; Mark 9:1; 13:30; Matthew 10:23, which show that from Jesus onward there was a sense of imminent expectation. But it is the *what* that creates problems for both theology and faith. Physical proximity here is a trope for temporal imminence. We appeal to the perfect tenses, tie them together, and form a clear image: God *has heard* the cries, the parousia *has drawn near,* and the Judge *is standing* at the doors. The image is one of an imminent act of God that will establish justice and send off the message that the oppressed have been vindicated. I see no reason here to make any of these ex-

199. See S. H. Travis, *Christ and the Judgment of God* (London: Marshall Pickering, 1986), though unfortunately he is almost entirely silent on James.

200. ὁ κριτής. See BDAG, 570. See also Acts 10:42; 2 Tim 4:8; Heb 12:23.

201. For the former, see Laws, 213; for the latter, Davids, 185.

202. Why the plural πρὸ τῶν θυρῶν? Perhaps for two reasons: first, because that is the image Jesus used at Mark 13:29, and, second, because gates at the cities had more than one opening.

pressions refer to anything more than an act of God on the plane of history (AD 70) in which the injustices are dealt a fatal blow. The Lord "came" to Jerusalem in judgment in the Roman army. James had in mind the sort of thing the prophets had in mind when the Assyrians and Babylonians entered the city and took it captive (2 Kings 17). Israel experiences this *because* Israel is the people of God, not because Israel is no longer the people of God.

7.3.4. Third Reason for Patience (5:10-11)

What many take to be an interruption (5:9) in James's message of eschatological patience (5:7-8) is discovered not to be an interruption of the theme at all. The grumbling he focused on may well have been the temptation of the hotheaded leaders or persons in the messianic community who thought the way to resolve the oppressions of the rich was to pick up a sword and deal with them directly. James warned them that such action would lead to judgment and that the Judge was at the very door. That interpretation of 5:9 then leaves a seamless connection to 5:10-11, where James continues his theme of exhorting the poor messianic community to turn down the tempting invitation to use violence and to rest assured in the confident condition that God has heard their cries and is about to act in judgment. Such a confidence in God as Judge leads to eschatological patience. James now gives two examples of patience: the prophets and Job. Behind it all are the compassion and mercy of God.

7.3.4.1. The Prophets (5:10-11a)

5:10   Without a conjunction James states: "As an example."[203] The use of examples, or a model of orientation,[204] was and is rhetorically effective and affective. Jeremiah, to take an example, saw himself as a negative example, a laughingstock (Jer 20:7-9), and Ezekiel spoke of knowing the abominations of the ancestors (20:4). Enoch was an example of repentance (Sir 44:16). Eleazar was a ninety-year-old example of fidelity and a "noble example of how to die" (2 Macc 6:21-31). Jesus left an example in footwashing (John 13:15), and 2 Peter says that Sodom and Gomorrah were an example of what happens to the ungodly (2:6). And we have lengthy lists as in Sirach 44–50's list of important figures in Israel's history, 1 Maccabees 2:49-64's list of the

---

203. ὑπόδειγμα λάβετε. On the accusative object ὑπόδειγμα, see BDAG, 1037. James has already used "examples," but he has not used the term; see 2:20-25 and also 5:17-18. The phrase τοὺς προφήτας is a double accusative, here functioning as a predicate. Thus, "take as an example the prophets."

204. So Popkes, 326.

deeds of the ancestors, and Hebrews 11's list of those who lived the life of faith. A list of examples of *zeal and envy* as well as *nobility* can be found in *1 Clement* (chs. 4–6), which also urges Christians to "cling" to such examples (46:1; 63:1).

"The prophets" were examples of "suffering and patience."[205] The grammar is perhaps an example of hendiadys, or expressing one thought with two words, but this is not as clear as some suggest. It is wiser to translate: "an example of suffering *and* patience."[206] That distinction aside, James wants the two terms kept close together because he is speaking here of a patience in suffering or a suffering with patience inasmuch as the two words are virtually combined to form "endurance" *(hypomonē)* in 5:11.

To which prophets is James referring? He could simply be using the trope of connecting prophets to suffering and persecution (cf. Matt 5:12 and Luke 6:22-23; 11:49; Matt 23:33-39; Acts 7:52; 1 Thess 2:15). Or he could have in mind one or more prophets (Jeremiah, Isaiah, Daniel) who either suffered or were understood in tradition to have suffered. Jesus' words point to a custom of honoring dead and martyred prophets (Matt 23:29-32).[207] If a priest represented the people before God, the prophet represented God before the people, and such a calling was multilayered: it involved actions, *pathos,* speaking, and advising.[208] James defines the prophets as those "who spoke in the name of the Lord."[209] Their message brought them suffering, and in that suffering they patiently awaited God's vindication. Hence, prophets, who are everywhere esteemed and held out as God's special instruments, are exam-

---

205. τῆς κακοπαθίας καὶ τῆς μακροθυμίας. On the former term, see BDAG, 500-501. It need not mean martyrdom.

206. See BDF, §442 (16), and Moo, 226-27, who states that a hendiadys would be better expressed with a single article.

207. See J. Jeremias, *Heiligengräber in Jesu Umwelt* (Göttingen: Vandenhoeck und Ruprecht, 1958).

208. On prophets, see the excellent anthology of R. P. Gordon, ed., *The Place Is Too Small for Us* (SBTS 5; Winona Lake: Eisenbraun, 1995). See further at A. J. Heschel, *The Prophets* (2 vols.; New York: Harper, 1962); R. R. Wilson, *Prophecy and Society in Ancient Israel* (Philadelphia: Fortress, 1980); D. E. Aune, *Prophecy in Early Christianity and the Ancient Mediterranean World* (Grand Rapids: Eerdmans, 1983); W. D. Stacey, *Prophetic Drama in the Old Testament* (London: Epworth, 1990); R. Gray, *Prophetic Figures in Late Second Temple Jewish Palestine* (New York: Oxford University Press, 1993); T. W. Gillespie, *The First Theologians* (Grand Rapids: Eerdmans, 1994); J. Blenkinsopp, *A History of Prophecy in Israel* (2d ed.; Louisville: Westminster John Knox, 1996); R. E. Clements, *Old Testament Prophecy* (Louisville: Westminster John Knox, 1996).

209. οἳ ἐλάλησαν ἐν τῷ ὀνόματι κυρίου. The action of the prophet's speaking is conceived in its totality; the emphasis is not on the pastness of their speaking. On "in the name of the Lord," see Amos 1:3; Isa 1:2; Jer 2:4-5; Acts 21:11; Rev 2:1. In James, see also 2:7.

ples for the oppressed poor of the messianic community because, though much esteemed, they, too, suffered.

5:11a Our reading of v. 11a connects it with the prophets in v. 10 as "those who showed endurance" instead of with Job, who emerges in v. 11b, but the matter is far from clear. Three factors cloud the issue: first, James begins with "Indeed," *idou* ("behold"), and this word often serves to introduce a new topic or level of argument. In 3:4 it marked the shift from the bit in a horse's mouth to the rudder of a ship; in 5:4 it intensifies the argument by shifting it to a new level; in 5:7 it particularizes the argument by providing a fresh analogy; and in 5:9 it turns the argument to a new level of seriousness. Second, there is a tense change: 5:10 "take" *(labete)* is aorist; in 5:11a we have a present tense ("we call blessed") and in 5:11b we turn back to the aorist ("you have heard"). Third, the term "showed endurance" *(hypomeinantas),* while clearly overlapping in sense with "patience" *(makrothymia),* is picked up again in 5:11b with the "endurance" *(hypomonē)* of Job. For these reasons, then, v. 11a could be taken as a transitional statement that leads to 5:11b. On the other hand, it can also serve to summarize the practical particularities of the theology of 5:10: if one asks what it means to say "As an example . . . take the prophets . . . ," one could not find a better manifestation than "we call blessed" in 5:11a. The use of the present tense then would serve to make the practical significance vivid. Furthermore, "those who showed endurance" is a single-term summary of what "suffering and patience" means. The issue is far from clear, but we think 5:11a functions as a summary statement of 5:10 and, at the same time, prepares the ground for 5:11b.

The Jewish community at large, and we can infer also the messianic community in particular, blessed those who endured: "we call blessed those who showed endurance."[210] If we see the present tense in aspectual terms, that is in terms of depiction of action instead of correspondence to time and reality, and if that aspectual intent is to describe action that is incomplete or "imperfective," then what is incomplete is the claims of the merchants (4:13), the mist-like nature of their duration (4:14), the "instead of . . . but" actions of 4:15-16, the knowledge of good and not doing it (4:17), the wailing of the rich farmers and the coming of miseries (5:1), the cries of the harvesters (5:4), the prayerful resistance of the harvesters (5:6), the reception of precious/valuable crops (5:7), the patience of the farmer (5:7), the intended non-

---

210. μακαρίζομεν τοὺς ὑπομείναντας. On the verb μακαρίζω, see Luke 1:48; also BDAG, 610. On the (aorist) participle, see BDAG, 1039. The aorist does not mean those who endured did so in the past but instead that the action is summarily described. Did they endure in the past? Probably so, but James's point is not a historical one. *Contra* Martin, 193, who makes much of the aorist indicating past tense.

grumbling of the messianic community (5:9a), and the blessing of those who endured (5:11a). In James's mental world, these are the focal elements of his exhortations in 4:13–5:11. My suggestion is that the blessing corresponds to these elements and, in particular, it corresponds with the cries of the oppressed. As the oppressed cry to God, the messianic community blesses those poor who are living faithfully.

Inherent to 5:11a's "we call blessed" is the macarism in 1:12,[211] where the messianic community was promised that endurance, prompted as it is by the steadfast love of God, will lead to reward. Thus, "we call blessed," in the sense of being blessed by God, also implies "and you will be too if you endure in spite of this oppression." Matthew 5:11-12 is probably behind both James 1:12 and 5:10-11a, and the text shows substantive parallels:

> *Blessed* are you when people revile you and persecute you and utter all kinds of evil against you falsely on my account. *Rejoice and be glad,* for your *reward* is great in heaven, for in the same way they persecuted the *prophets who were before you.*

It is not at all stretching the text to think that James connects the messianic community to that line of prophets in using the prophets as examples for how the messianists are also to endure and show patience in suffering.

Perseverance, the grace and resolution to remain faithful under serious stress, is promised not only happiness but salvation (Dan 12:12; Matt 10:22; 24:13). James cares about perseverance, apparently not in ways that have fascinated theologians, but in the pastoral context of knowing messianists who were asked to run the gauntlet. Thus, James 1:3-4 teaches that tests of faith lead to endurance *(hypomonē)* and endurance builds maturity; 1:12 teaches that the one who endures *(hypomenō)* temptation/testing will receive the "crown of life"; and now in the context of severe trial (5:1-6), the messianists are exhorted to take suffering prophets and Job as their example — and to wait for God's timing in judgment (5:7-11).[212] For James perseverance has to do with human will, the building of Christian character, connection to the story of God's people, and final destiny.

---

211. See the more extensive discussion of blessing at 1:12.

212. Perseverance is far too often bundled too tightly into the issues of soteriology, like apostasy or election, instead of the reality of martyrdom. See Augustine, *On the Gift of Perseverance* (Nicene and Post-Nicene Fathers 1/5; Grand Rapids: Eerdmans, 1980), 521-52; I. H. Marshall, *Kept by the Power of God* (Minneapolis: Bethany, 1969). But one is closer to James's sense of perseverance reading, say, the biography of William Tyndale (cf. D. Daniell, *Willim Tyndale: A Biography* [New Haven: Yale University Press, 1994]), or W. H. C. Frend, *Martyrdom and Persecution in the Early Church* (Oxford: Blackwell, 1965), or, more in tune with his own time, 1–2 Maccabees.

7.3.4.2. Job (5:11b)

"You have heard of the endurance of Job."[213] James finds in Job the quintessential example of patience in suffering or endurance and his example forms a model of how the messianists are to conduct themselves under stress. But why Job? His example is *sui generis,* an assault by the Satan on God's playground, and has nothing to do with oppression by the rich. Furthermore, he was not all that patient: "He was anything but an example of a godly person who was patient in the midst of adversity."[214] "The canonical book rather pictures Job as a bit self-righteous, overly insistent on getting an explanation for his unjust sufferings from the Lord."[215] Nor does the standard paradigm, "the patience of Job," help us. Nor does it help that such a stereotype has led to a complacent theory of patience. Indeed, Job's story tells us in no uncertain terms that he complained. But any reading of Job reveals a character who stuck it out, who trusted in God, and who did so fully aware of the fundamental injustice he had experienced. Maybe, then, Job is the perfect example for the oppressed poor. Patience here need not be understood as quietude or passivity; perhaps genuine patience involves realities like protesting to God,[216] yet without surrendering one's integrity or one's faith in God or losing the path of following Jesus.

Some suggest that James brings in Job because Job was seen by some as a prophet. Thus, Sirach 49:9 says "God also mentioned Job who held fast to all the ways of justice" and sandwiches Job between Ezekiel and the Twelve Prophets. Not only is this slender evidence but it is also not the focus of James, who is less concerned with who is a prophet and more with the need to endure.[217] Oddly enough, the word "endurance" *(hypomonē)* only appears once in the Septuagint of Job and then not of Job himself (14:19).[218] Perhaps we are to think of a general stereotype of Job as someone who was patient in suffering and who endured. Job is chosen because the story of Job was connected to suffering, patience, and endurance.

It may be that the canonical text of Job does not fit the stereotype James calls on, but perhaps the evidence of the Jewish world suggests that it

---

213. τὴν ὑπομονὴν Ἰὼβ ἠκούσατε. The aorist focuses attention on the reality of "hearing," not on the time when someone heard; nor does it focus attention on the perfective nature of that hearing as some translate ("you *have* heard"). One might translate: "You have all heard of the example of Job."

214. Martin, 194.

215. Moo, 228; also Popkes, 328.

216. See H. A. Fine, "The Tradition of a Patient Job," *JBL* 74 (1955) 28-32, who finds that patience of Job in the prologue, epilogue, and chs. 27–28. See the pastoral warning in Byron, 469-70.

217. So Laws, 215-16.

218. But see LXX at Job 7:3; 22:21; 33:5.

is the *interpreted* Job who is an example for James.[219] This is a central theme in the *Testament of Job,* and there are strong parallels between that book (especially 33) and James.[220] Thus, in *Testament of Job* 27:3-7 Satan admits defeat and his words tell the story: "So you also, Job, were the one below and in a plague, but you conquered my wrestling tactics which I brought on you." And then Job says to his children: "Now then, my children, you also must be patient in everything that happens to you. For patience is better than anything." That text is almost certainly later than the book of James, but it does reveal that the theme of perseverance was central to the perception of Job in the Jewish and Christian worlds.[221]

But we should not fall for this generality about patience so easily. Indeed, Job is cast in the *Testament of Job* in altogether patient terms, but that is not James's point. He has more in mind with Job; he has in mind the poor oppressed who cry out to God (like Job), who are not to resort to violence, and who will retain their faith and integrity without always falling from their commitments. It is then the combination of Job's (impatient!) protests along with his steady resolve to stick to what he believes to be true, even if God does not (!), that makes Job the most suitable character in the Bible for what James has to say.

"The purpose of the Lord"[222] not only continues the example of Job but provides for James a platform for what he has to say to the oppressed poor in the messianic community. The NRSV might lead some to think James has become abstract when he says "and you have seen[223] the purpose of the Lord," but the term translated "purpose" is *telos.*[224] Patience has been

219. Thus, see D. H. Gard, "The Concept of Job's Character according to the Greek Translator of the Hebrew Text," *JBL* 72 (1953) 182-86, where the "G" text is shown to have improved on the character of Job. Further studies have been done by C. Haas, "Job's Perseverance in the Testament of Job," in *Studies on the Testament of Job* (ed. M. A. Knibb and P. W. van der Horst; Cambridge: Cambridge University Press, 1989), 117-54; C. R. Seitz, "The Patience of Job in the Epistle of James," in *Konsequente Traditionsgeschichte* (ed. R. Bartelmus, et al.; Göttingen: Vandenhoeck und Ruprecht, 1999), 373-82.

220. See especially P. Gray, "Points and Lines: Thematic Parallelism in the Letter of James and the *Testament of Job,*" *NTS* 50 (2004) 406-24.

221. The realities of Job, though, remind us that his patience and endurance were not without some bitter struggle: cf. Job 7:11-16; 10:18; 30:20-23. See also *1 Clement* 17:3; 26:3; *m Sota* 5:5.

222. καὶ τὸ τέλος κυρίου εἴδετε. The genitive is agency or subjective (Popkes, 330); the word κυρίου refers here to God, the Father, and not to Jesus. See especially Mussner, 206-7; Moo, 229-30.

223. The verb εἴδετε could refer to "have seen [in Scripture]." See Martin, 194, who points to Job 42:5; see also Johnson, 320-21.

224. It is highly unlikely that James returns here in τέλος κυρίου to the eschatol-

connected to God's sovereign purposes in 1:2-4, but here *telos* seems to reflect the "end" of the book of Job, where "the Lord" forgives Job's friends through Job's prayers, that is, "the Lord's end" refers to the merciful resolution of the story of Job and his friends.[225] God not only forgives the friends but then also shows mercy to Job by restoring his fortunes. This best explains why James then says "how the Lord is compassionate and merciful."[226]

While Job 42:7-17 brings these themes to the fore, they are emphasized even more in the targum of Job from the Dead Sea Scrolls. Thus *11Q10* [*Tg Job*] 38:1-9:

> [(So Eliphaz the Temanite and Bildad) the Shuhite and Zophar the Naamathite went and] did [what they had been told by] God. And G[o]d listened to the voice of Job and forgave them their sins because of him. Then God turned back to Job in compassion and gave him twice what he once had possessed. There came to Job all his friends, brethren and those who had known him, and they ate bread with him in his house. They consoled him for all the evil that God had brought upon him, and each man gave him one sheep and one gold ring. So God blessed J[ob's] latt[er days, and h]e [had] [fourteen thousand] sh[eep . . .]

James here moves in the world of wisdom, as can also be seen in Wisdom 2:16-17 and 3:19.[227] But James goes beyond this wisdom conviction that we ought to live now in light of the end, to seeing "the Lord's end" as days of mercy, restoration, and blessing. Furthermore it is not just the *telos* of life that James has in mind but the *telos* of the Lord.

James appeals to the compassion and mercy of God, as he often does

---

ogy of 5:7-9 so that this expression is a functional equivalent to παρουσία τοῦ κυρίου. It is even more unlikely that James means "the death of Jesus" or the end of his life in τέλος κυρίου. A focus of this expression on "purpose," as if God planned this event for Job's life, however much it might agree with our theology, is not the focus of the canonical Job, in which Satan draws God into smiting Job and through which Job learns about God's majesty and providence and inscrutability. See Laws, 217-18.

225. The discussion concerns whether the term τέλος is the intended goal or the result; see Davids, 188; Johnson, 321. But see R. P. Gordon, "ΚΑΙ ΤΟ ΤΕΛΟΣ ΚΥΡΙΟΥ ΕΙΔΕΤΕ (JAS. V.11)," *JTS* 26 (1975) 91-95, who offers evidence from Jewish sources that at least a future reference could be connected to a reference back to the end of the book of Job.

226. ὅτι πολύσπλαγχνός ἐστιν ὁ κύριος καὶ οἰκτίρμων. It is hard to press the present tense ἐστιν, but it may fit with the rest of the presents in 4:13–5:11 as God's response to the cries of the poor and their cries being a form of resistance, as well as the messianists blessing those who suffer patiently in the history of Israel.

227. See *Testament of Gad* 7:4; *Testament of Asher* 6:4; *Testament of Benjamin* 4:1; *4 Maccabees* 12:3 for other references to the end of life shaping life now.

(1:5, 17-18, 27; 2:5, 11, 13; 5:4, 6), but he does so again not in the abstract nor casually but to assure the poor oppressed of the community that God can remake all things. As Job lost it all at the hands of the Enemy, and God restored it all in duplicate, so the oppressed poor can count on God's mercy and God's goodness that maybe they, too, will find "the Lord's end" better than the beginning. Surely the appeal to God's compassion and mercy evoke texts like Exodus 34:6-7, where we find not only mercy for God's good people but also the warning of judgment on those living in iniquity.

8. CONCLUDING EXHORTATIONS (5:12-20)

The attentive reader of James is in for a struggle when it comes to this letter's logical flow and structural design, and the commentaries on James 5, whether they begin the last section at 5:7 or 5:12, reveal the diversity of opinion. I have concluded that the last section begins at 5:12 and that its three parts, on oaths (5:12), on prayer and healing in the community (5:13-18), and on communal restoration (5:19-20), are largely unconnected to what precedes. Furthermore, there is no clear logical connection between these three units and, as if to flaunt everything we know about letters, there is nothing resembling a typical letter closing. The letter simply ends. Those who find ties between these three units and the beginning of the letter are capable of seeing finer lines than I. In what follows I will mention some of these proposals.

8.1. OATHS (5:12)

> 12*Above all, my beloved,*[a] *do not swear, either by heaven or by earth or by any other oath,*[b] *but let your "Yes" be yes and your "No" be no,*[c] *so that you may not fall under condemnation.*[d][1]

a. TNIV: my brothers and sisters
b. TNIV: by anything else
c. TNIV: All you need to say is a simple "Yes" or "No."
d. TNIV: Otherwise you will be condemned.

1. Instead of ὑπὸ κρίσιν πέσητε, some manuscripts have a slightly different idea in εἰς ὑποκρισιν πεσητε (P and the Alexandrian Ψ with a number of other manuscripts, including some Byzantine lectionaries and PsOec). The former reading is widespread at an earlier date.

There are two major questions to be answered about this verse: First, what is its relation to what precedes and what follows? Second, was there an oral tradition that showed up in Matthean (Matt 5:33-37; 23:16-22) and Jacobite forms, or is this a quotation of Jesus, or is James earlier than the form we find in Matthew — in other words, what is the tradition history behind James 5:12?[2]

To begin with the first question: there is an obvious connection to an important theme in James, namely, the speech patterns of the leaders (3:1–4:12) and of the whole community (1:19-21, 26).[3] But this general connection does not help much when subjected to a more careful analysis. The speech patterns mentioned earlier are not the issue in 5:12. Instead, this verse speaks of (legal?) oaths, for the first time in the letter. Too many have connected 5:12 thematically to the earlier speech passages and then stretch 5:13-20 to make those verses address speech patterns as well.[4] We need not try to give organization to James where he has not. The instructions of 3:1–4:12 and 5:12 are substantively different. In 5:12 James is not addressing teachers and how their speech has a potent impact; instead, James here addresses the inappropriateness of oaths as he draws on the early Christian emphasis on honesty.[5] Furthermore, this is hardly a concluding word about speech patterns in James because it neither summarizes what has been said nor concludes what has been taught. It introduces a distinct and narrow topic. Davids represents the more accurate view: there is no obvious connection of 5:12 to what precedes.[6]

Perhaps what confuses most is how James begins: "Above all." How can legal oaths take such significant importance in the concluding section to a letter that did not once raise the issue? J. H. Ropes long ago suggested that those who were enduring stresses might be tempted to use oaths and accuse God.[7] What is in the favor of this suggestion is that 1:12-18 moves in the direction of blaming God. But it is at best a stretch to connect these two pas-

2. On which see P. S. Minear, "Yes or No: The Demand for Honesty in the Early Church," *NovT* 13 (1971) 1-13.

3. On which see Baker, *Personal Speech-Ethics,* 249-82.

4. So Johnson, 326-27, who sees in 5:7-20 speech patterns about plain talk, prayer, confession, and correction. Indeed, each of these is something done with words, but the focus of James is on oath-taking, healing and prayer, confession of sin, and restoring the wandering, and it stretches the evidence to make it fit speech patterns. I don't know anyone who would classify "prayer" as a form of "speech" in ancient Judaism. Even more, Jas 5:19-20 must be disfigured to be connected to speech patterns. Instead of stretching the evidence into the skin of the fox, let the words be what they are — three important but random matters that end the letter.

5. See G. Stählin, "Zum Gebrach von Beteuerungsformeln im Neuen Testament," *NovT* 5 (1962) 115-43.

6. Davids, 188-89.

7. Ropes, 300.

sages, and it is probable that "above all" is a non-comparative, introductory expression with very little logical power.[8] Franz Mussner translates: "Above all, before I forget. . . ."[9] A similar use of this expression can be found in 1 Peter 4:8. It is an "epistolary cliché,"[10] perhaps synonymous with Paul's "finally" (2 Cor 13:11).[11] It strains logic to see it any other way.

The pastoral tone of 5:7-20 is notable, not the least of which evidence is the use of "my beloved."[12] This is the language of identification and motivation, and James's concern is this: "do not swear."[13] This leads back to our question about the origin of James 5:12.[14] The evidence in the Jesus tradition is found only in Matthew 23:16-22 and 5:33-37.[15] Matthew 23:16-22 shows no recognizable literary connection. It does not prohibit oaths or contrast oaths to simple, honest words. It is concerned, rather, to distinguish carefully between the sanctuary and its gold, between the altar and the offering. We can exclude Matthew 23:16-22 from having anything substantial to do with James 5:12.

The connection between James 5:12 and Matthew 5:33-37 is, however, substantial. Both prohibit oaths, specifically by heaven or earth, and include words to indicate that swearing by any object is prohibited. Both use the noun *horkos,* "oath," as well as the verb *omnyō,* "swear" (only the latter appears in Matthew 23). And both contrast swearing oaths to a simple "Yes" or "No," Matthew adding that "anything more than this comes from the evil one" and James "so that you may not fall under condemnation." When we look for the substantive words (and avoid commonplace words like "and") and for common word order, these two texts come up smelling like shrimp from the same gumbo. Furthermore, what they have in common is unusual and cannot be ascribed to commonplaces.

The texts are related, but that raises questions rather than answering them.[16] First, which is earlier? The little differences between the two texts

8. Cf. Laws, 220; Davids, 189; Popkes, 332. It is wiser not to stretch "do not swear" into a thematic conclusion to speech patterns than to diminish somewhat "Above all." The more one stretches the power of "Above all" the less one can explain why oaths become suddenly so important to the letter.

9. Mussner, 211 ("Vor allem darf ich nicht vergessen . . .").

10. White, *Light,* 326.

11. So Moo, 232; also Nystrom, 300-301.

12. ἀδελφοί μου: see on 1:2, 9, 16, 19; 2:1, 5, 14-15; 3:1, 10, 12; 4:11; 5:7, 9-10, 12, 19.

13. μὴ ὀμνύετε. The present tense prohibition is designed to prohibit the *practice* of swearing. One can connect this present with στενάζετε in Jas 5:9; see the notes on the present tenses in 5:11. The accusatives are adverbial.

14. See the sketch in Popkes, 334-35.

15. Many assign these two texts to the "M" traditions.

16. An excellent discussion of how to determine relationships, though in a different context, is found in D. C. Allison, *The Intertextual Jesus: Scripture in Q* (Harrisburg:

demonstrate beyond doubt that neither is copied from the other in the way, for example, that Matthew and Luke copy Q and Mark.[17] Matthew's text is more fulsome and even in the "Yes, yes . . . No, no" James differs from Matthew by setting them off with the article.[18] Finally, the two end differently even if their points are similar. Matthew ends with "anything more than this comes from the evil one" and James ends with "so that you may not fall under condemnation." The two texts are not literarily dependent.[19] Or, to be more nuanced, if they are literarily dependent the second author either has taken many liberties with the work of the first or has worked hard to avoid detection. Our conclusion is that they are not dependent at the literary level. But, because the texts are so substantially related we would argue that the text of James is a literary deposit of an oral tradition that goes back to Jesus. In other words, James has made the words of Jesus his own. He gives us a virtual quotation.

Matthew's fuller text suggests that James is the more primitive account of the words of Jesus, but the evidence is not clear enough to give the historian confidence. One could easily speculate on what is redaction in Matthew 5:33-37 and find the core behind the redaction, compare that core to James 5:12, and then make historical judgments on priority.[20] What ought to surprise us more is that James feels no compulsion to say that he is quoting Jesus.[21]

Trinity, 2000), 9-13. Recall the Introduction where we concluded that James's relationship to Jesus' words was in general a matter of James having absorbed Jesus' words and made them his own.

17. Assuming the Markan (or Oxford) hypothesis that Mark and Q were both used independently by Matthew and Luke. Thus, Matthew uses for his "imperative" the aorist infinitive (μὴ ὀμόσαι) with datives (μήτε ἐν τῷ οὐρανῷ), while James uses a present imperative (ὀμνύετε) with accusatives (μήτε τὸν οὐρανόν).

18. Thus cf. τὸ ναὶ ναὶ καὶ τὸ οὒ οὒ with ναὶ ναί, οὒ οὒ. The articular formula is found in Paul (2 Cor 1:17) and throughout the early church: Justin, *1 Apology* 16.5; Clement of Alexandria, *Stromateis* 5.99.1; 7.67.5; Eusebius, *Praeparatio Evangelica* 3.3.

19. See Laws, 224; Davids, 190.

20. In fact, the ending of James sounds more tailored to the context of James 5 (judgment, condemnation; cf. 5:9) and could be seen as "redaction" by James of the saying of Jesus. What is more, the ending of Matthew could have fit, at a more remote distance (cf. Jas 3:15; 4:7), into James. On the tradition-history of Matt 5:33-37, see Allison, *Matthew* 1.533, who sees the original core at Matt 5: (33a) + 34a + 37, which is not far from what we find in James. These sorts of conclusions, which at one time were of much more interest to me than they are now, lead to diminishing confidence and not increasing confidence in one's conclusions. See Johnson, *Brother of Jesus, Friend of God,* 137-43, who argues for the greater primitivity of the Jacobite form.

21. One might ask if it is a remote citation of Jesus that gives rise to James's expression πρὸ πάντων.

The words perhaps surprise: James is not drawing lines of halakah often drawn in his Jewish world, nor is he even permitting the legitimate oath found in the Old Testament. Instead, he prohibits any kind of oath-taking.[22] What is required of the follower of Jesus, according to Matthew 5:33-37 and James 5:12, is simple honesty. The command is to drop the buttressing of words with more words that demonstrate the levels of commitment to one's words. This runs counter to explicit Old Testament commands. Thus, it was wrong to swear falsely (Lev 19:12)[23] or to make use of God's name (Deut 5:11; but cf. 6:13; Jer 12:16), but it was not wrong to use oaths properly (Exod 20:7; 22:10-11; Num 30:3-15; Ps 50:14).[24] To be sure, oaths were held at bay by some, and the Essenes notoriously did not take oaths. Thus, according to Josephus,

> They dispense their anger after a just manner, and restrain their passion. They are eminent for fidelity, and are the ministers of peace; whatsoever they say also is firmer than an oath; but swearing is avoided by them, and they esteem it worse than perjury; for they say, that he who cannot be believed without [swearing by] God, is already condemned (*War* 2.135; cf. *Ant* 15:371).

But they took "tremendous oaths" upon joining the sect (*War* 2.139-42). Thus those who were described as never taking oaths apparently took oaths in some contexts,[25] and it might be wise to recognize that Jesus and James might not have intended absolute prohibition of oath-taking (but cf. Matt 26:63-64). On the other hand, many have taken Jesus' words as law.[26] But the New Testament does not show any awareness elsewhere that oath-taking is absolutely prohibited (Rom 1:9; 2 Cor 1:23; Gal 1:20; Phil 1:8; Heb 6:13-20; Rev 10:6). Philo, too, thought it wise not to get entrapped in oaths, expressing himself in ways also similar to Jesus and James:

> To swear not at all is the best course and most profitable to life . . . which has been taught to speak the truth so well on each occasion that its words are regarded as oaths; to swear truly is only, as some people

---

22. This is a point made by Allison, *Matthew* 1.532-33. But see also the discussion in G. Dautzenberg, "Ist das Schwurverbot Mt 5, 33-37; Jak 5, 12 ein Beispiel für die Torakritik Jesu?" *BZ* 25 (1981) 47-66, who connects the prohibition of oaths to Jewish Christianity.

23. For the allusion to Lev 19:12, see Johnson, *Brother of Jesus, Friend of God*, 131.

24. See also Judg 11:30-39; 1 Kgs 8:31-32; 17:1; CD 9:9-10; Acts 23:12.

25. And other oath-taking is seen: see Mussner, 214; Popkes, 333-34.

26. See Justin, *1 Apology* 16.5; Irenaeus, *Against Heresies* 2.32.1; Origen, *Principles* 4.3.4.

say, a "second-best voyage," for the mere fact of his swearing casts sus-
picion on the trustworthiness of the man.[27]

What Jesus and James say, then, is neither peculiar to them nor un-Jewish;
instead, their words represent a kind of Judaism with which many would
have been familiar, not the least of whom would have been the messianic
community.

James provides a bit of a laundry list of what Jews of his day used to
buttress their words: "by heaven or by earth or by any other oath." These
words extend the prohibition of using the name of God (YHWH) lightly,
which led to not pronouncing the name of God at all, and that led to substitut-
ing various circumlocutions for God's Name. This is why in Matthew 5:34-
35 each form of the oath is connected back to God: "either by heaven, *for it is
the throne of God,* or by the earth, *for it is his footstool,* or by Jerusalem, *for it
is the city of the great King.*" Thus, "heaven" and "earth" represent various
extensions of God. Jeremias may be accurate, though, when he observes that
these words are not legal oaths but everyday slogans: "the oaths with which
the oriental constantly underlines the truthfulness of his remarks in everyday
speech." Which would then mean that Jesus (and James following in his
wake) is advocating truthfulness more than prohibiting legal oath-taking:
"Each word is to be unconditionally reliable, without needing any confirma-
tion through an appeal to God."[28] One would have to ask, however, what
words would be used in a legal setting if not these? One could not by the time
of the first century use the name YHWH in an oath, so one must consider
these words as both normal and perhaps also legal ways of buttressing one's
words. A good example of how these words were used in oaths can be found
in the much later *Mishnah,* for example, *m Shevuot* 4:13:

A. (1) "I impose an oath on you," (2) "I command you," (3) "I bind you,"
— lo, these are liable.
B. "By heaven and earth," lo, these are exempt.
C. (1) "By [the name of] Alef-dalet [Adonai]" or (2) "Yud-he [Yahweh],"
(3) "By the Almighty," (4) "By Hosts," (5) "By him who is merciful
and gracious," (6) "By him who is long-suffering and abundant in
mercy," or by any other euphemism —
D. lo, these are liable.
E. "He who curses making use of any one of these is liable," the words of
R. Meir.

27. *De Decalogo* 84.
28. J. Jeremias, *New Testament Theology,* 1: *The Proclamation of Jesus* (trans.
J. Bowden: New York: Scribner, 1971), 220.

F. And sages exempt.

G. "He who curses his father or his mother with any one of them is liable," the words of R. Meir.

H. And sages exempt.

 I. He who curses himself and his friend with any one of them transgresses a negative commandment.

J. [If he said,] (1) "May God smite you," (2) "So may God smite you," this is [language for] an adjuration [conforming to] what is written in the Torah (Lev. 5:1).

K. (3) "May he not smite you," (4) "may he bless you," (5) "may he do good to you" —

L. R. Meir declares liable [for a false oath taken with such a formula].

M. And sages exempt.

What was prohibited by Jesus and carried on by James was connecting casuistry to the integrity of one's words: swearing by the earth is no less severe than swearing by heaven, so one ought to say what one means and no more. This is the meaning of "but let[29] your 'Yes' be yes and your 'No' be no." What we find in Greek is a doubling of the words "yes" and "no" *(nai nai, ou ou)*, and most recognize this as a Semitic expression "let your yes be a yes and your no be a no" (see 2 Cor 1:17-18). Reiteration of a word is designed to lead to distribution of the idea, and we see the same in Mark 6:7: "two by two" *(dyo dyo)*.

Verse James prohibits oath-taking "so that you may not fall under condemnation."[30] This is an interesting variant on Jesus' "anything more than this comes from the evil one." Wherever James got his wording, the two come at the same point from different angles: insincere or dishonest words reflect a character that is not in tune with God and is, therefore, liable to condemnation. James is given to what appears to many to be exaggeration: people can be condemned for not showing mercy (2:13), for grumbling (5:9), and for the inappropriate use of oaths (5:12). Each of these, on closer inspection, emerges from the depth of his theology: from a loving life, from a nonviolent approach to resolving one's economic situation, and from a heart that tells true words. These are not the concerns of austere severity but of one who thinks messianists ought to follow Jesus and be transformed in the community.

---

29. ἤτω, the third singular present imperative of εἰμί. The adversative could be translated "instead."

30. ἵνα μὴ ὑπὸ κρίσιν πέσητε. The aorist is constative and construes the action as a whole. See also 2:12-13; 4:11-12; 5:9. To fall under means to become liable for, accountable to, and thus to fall under the condemnation of God.

8.2. PRAYER AND HEALING IN THE COMMUNITY (5:13-18)

13*Are any among you suffering?*[a] *They should*[b] *pray. Are any cheerful?*[c] *They should*[b] *sing songs of praise.* 14*Are any among you sick?*[d] *They should*[b] *call for the elders of the church and have them pray over them, anointing*[e] *them with oil in the name of the Lord.*[31] 15*The prayer of faith will save the sick,*[f] *and the Lord will raise*[32] *them up; and anyone who has committed sins*[g] *will be forgiven.*[33] 16*Therefore*[34] *confess your*[35] *sins*[36] *to one another,*[h] *and pray*[37] *for one another,*[h] *so that you may be healed. The prayer of the righteous*[i] *is powerful and effective.* 17*Elijah was a human being like us,*[j] *and he prayed fervently*[k] *that it might*[l] *not rain,*[38] *and for three years and six months*[m] *it did not rain on the earth.* 18*Then he prayed again, and the heaven gave rain*[39] *and the earth yielded its harvest.*[n]

a. TNIV, singular: Is anyone among you in trouble?

b. TNIV: Let them

c. TNIV, singular: Is anyone happy?

d. TNIV, singular: Is anyone among you sick?

e. TNIV: to pray over them and anoint

f. TNIV: And the prayer offered in faith will make them well.

g. TNIV, plural: If they have sinned

h. TNIV: to each other

i. TNIV: a righteous person

31. Some manuscripts omit one or more of the articles, including the Alexandrian A and Y.

32. Some manuscripts use the present tense εγειρει (P, 35, 38, 81, 1175, 1838, etc.).

33. Some sources change the third person singular future passive ἀφεθήσεται to third person plural αφεθησονται (P, 69, 436, 643, Chrysostom, Syriac manuscripts, and Armenian manuscripts).

34. Many sources omit οὖν, including Y, 69, 322, 323, Byzantine, Anastasius Sinaita, John of Damascus, Didymus Alexandrinus, Eusebius, Photius, Pseudo-Oecumenius, some Latin manuscripts, Syriac, Armenian, Georgian, and Ethiopic. The evidence, though, is in favor of the inclusion and, for interpretation, is implicit.

35. Nestle-Aland[27] does not include ὑμῶν after τὰς ἁμαρτίας, though many manuscripts do (206, 429, etc.). It is omitted in ℵ, A, B, P, Y, 048V, etc.

36. A number of manuscripts read τα παραπτωματα [υμων]; see L, 69, 88, 322, and 323.

37. Three uncials have προσευχεσθε (A, B, and 048V).

38. A number of insubstantial variants emerge with τοῦ μὴ βρέξαι, the most interesting of which is the addition of υετον in 5, 252*, 322, 323, etc.

39. The word order is reversed in ℵ, A, Y, 5, 33, etc.

430

j. TNIV: even as we are

k. TNIV: earnestly

l. TNIV: would

m. TNIV: and a half years

n. TNIV: produced its crops

More than even v. 12, these verses demonstrate that James closes this letter with random themes. Nothing central to 5:13-18 has emerged earlier in the letter: we have not heard about healing, anointing, confessing sins to one another, or elders.[40] Only by a clever stretching of the evidence can the confession or prayer of this passage be fit into the speech ethics of James. Nor does it stand comfortably next to the prayer sections that end other New Testament letters (Rom 15:30-32; Eph 6:18-20; Col 4:2-4, 12; 1 Thess 5:16-18, 25; 2 Thess 3:1-5; Phlm 22; Heb 13:18-19; Jude 20). In those passages the prayer is general and requests for prayer are made. But here the prayer is tailored to a situation in the messianic community. It is best to let this passage be what it is: a paragraph on sickness, prayer, healing, and confession.[41] Furthermore, it does not genuinely fit with what follows in 5:19-20. Hence, we give this text permission to stand on its own.

It meanders pastorally within a topic. This schematic attempts to make that meandering clear, and the numbers will be used for organization in the comments that follow.

1. Communal responses to three ecclesial conditions: suffering, cheerfulness, and sickness (vv. 13-14).
2. Prayer to save from sickness leads to a comment on the need for faith (v. 15 through "the Lord will raise them up").
3. Since sickness and sin are connected, forgiveness also comes up (the rest of v. 15).
4. Sin triggers the need for confessing sins to promote healing (v. 16 through "so that you may be healed").
5. Prayer for healing leads to a comment on the need for righteous people praying, of whom Elijah is a premier example (the rest of v. 16 through v. 18).

40. Laws, 219, connects the suffering of 5:13 back to the general theme of the marginalized of 1:26-27. Davids, 191, draws attention to the customary ending of letters with prayer.

41. For an ecclesial approach, see the excellent study of K. Warrington, "James 5:14-18: Healing Then and Now," *International Review of Mission* 93 (2004) 346-67. For an exacting analysis see S. Kaiser, *Krankenheilung. Untersuchungen zu Form, Sprache, traditionsgeschichtlichen Hintergrund and Aussage zu Jak 5,13-18* (Neukirchen-Vluyn: Neukirchener, 2006).

8.3. THREE ECCLESIAL CONDITIONS AND THREE RESPONSES (5:13-14)

James brings up three ecclesial conditions, suffering, cheerfulness, and sickness, and provides three imperatives concerning how to respond to these conditions: pray, sing praise, and summon the elders to pray.[42] In spite of the best of intentions in the NRSV and the TNIV, James addresses a singular "you" and focuses on individual responsibility.

8.3.1. Suffering and Prayer (5:13a)

One condition James perceives in the messianic community is suffering: "Are any among you suffering?" As noted above, the singular subject and verb, even if applicable to anyone (and therefore to more than one person), leads more naturally to a translation like "Is anyone suffering among you?"[43] Just what kind of suffering James has in mind is not immediately clear. The verb *kakopatheō*[44] appears twice in 2 Timothy (2:9; 4:5), where it appears to describe physical persecution. But the word is broader than that meaning and often describes hardship in war as well as ordinary hardships in life. It could be synonymous with "is sick" in James 5:14.[45] Josephus, a contemporary of James, says "the soul, by being united to the body, is subject to miseries *(kakopathei)*, and is not freed therefrom again but by death" (*Apion* 2.203). If one looks into James for concrete evidence for suffering, one would have to think of the various trials of 1:2-4, the implication of oppression in 1:9-11, the need for perseverance in 1:12-14, and the suffering of the marginalized in 1:26-27; 2:1-4, 14-17; and 5:1-6. And the appearance of the cognate noun in

42. Structurally, the condition is shaped by a question with τις, and ἐν ὑμῖν is either stated (first, third condition) or implied (second condition) and then followed by a third person singular imperative ("let that person . . ."). In vv. 13-14 there is an emphasis on the responsibility of the individual that is mitigated by the NRSV's use of plurals. The TNIV makes the question part singular but then turns to the plural in the imperative part.

43. Κακοπαθεῖ τις ἐν ὑμῖν. The present tense makes the suffering more vivid to the audience; it does not mean that someone in particular is suffering at the moment James writes, however true that may have been. James has in mind the messianic community in ἐν ὑμῖν, and the summoning of elders in 5:14 and the confession of sins to one another in 5:16 make this clear. There is discussion on the function of τις in 5:13-14a. It could be an interrogative (NRSV), it could be no more than an indefinite that creates a subject clause ("Anyone who suffers, let that person pray"), or it could be a mild conditional construction ("If anyone . . ."). Many see it deriving from the diatribe tradition. See Popkes, 339; Martin, 205.

44. See BDAG, 500.

45. Josephus, *Ant* 6.172; 10.220; 12.3, 130, 336; 18.301 (simple troubles); *War* 4.135.

5:10 ("suffering and patience") suggests a connection with the marginalized who were enduring oppression at the hands of the rich farmers. Thus, "suffering" in 5:13a most likely refers to the suffering of the poor at the hand of the abusively powerful, and it would also describe the suffering inherent to persevering patience.

James calls the suffering person to pray.[46] The prayer of the suffering, and one could take any number of passages from the prayerbook of Israel, might look like Psalm 30, and a prototypical experience with suffering and prayer is seen in Psalm 77. *Psalms of Solomon* 15:1 expresses the intent of James 5:13a: "When I was persecuted I called on the Lord's name; I expected the help of Jacob's God and I was saved. For you, O God, are the hope and refuge of the poor."

8.3.2. Cheerfulness and Songs of Praise (5:13b)

The second condition, at the other end of the spectrum, is cheerfulness: "Are any cheerful?" Once again, the singular should perhaps be given more attention: "Is anyone cheerful?"[47] We should avoid thinking of "is cheerful" *(euthymeō)* in terms of a happy, smiley face because life is good. This term evokes enthusiasm, courage, and a confident faith and these often in the context of stress. Thus, in a storm at sea and after experiencing hunger, the apostle Paul urges the sailors to "keep up your courage [*euthymein*]" (Acts 27:22, 25). And when Antiochus recognizes the persistence of the Jews in the face of attempts to Hellenize them, he publicizes his decision to allow them to continue the temple worship "so that they may know our policy and *be of good cheer* and go on happily in the conduct of their own affairs" (2 Macc 11:24-26). Later, Ignatius can say that he has "become more *encouraged* in a God-given freedom from anxiety" (*Polycarp* 7.1).[48] The contrast here is not between suffering and the good life[49] but within a group where everyone is undergoing persecution or suffering, some of whom are struggling and others who have taken courage.

James exhorts this person to "sing songs of praise."[50] This translates

46. προσευχέσθω. The present indicates characteristic behavior and practice for the one who suffers. Terms connected to praying include προσεύχομαι (5:13, 14, 17, 18), εὔχομαι (5:16), αἰτέω (1:5, 6; 4:2, 3), εὐχή (5:15), and δέησις (5:16); in general, see *GEL*, §33.161-79.

47. εὐθυμεῖ τις. See BDAG, 406.

48. See also Josephus, *War* 1.272; 3.382; 6.184; Hermas, *Mandates* 38.10.

49. In which case James might have had in mind the rich merchants of 4:13-17.

50. ψαλλέτω. See BDAG, 1096; Johnson, 329-30. In general, see R. P. Martin, *Worship in the Early Church* (Grand Rapids: Eerdmans, 1975); L. T. Johnson, *Religious Experience in Earliest Christianity* (Minneapolis: Fortress, 1988); Hurtado, *At the Origins of Christian Worship*.

433

one word, *psallō* (the imperative *psalletō*), a cognate with the word "psalm," which appears twice in 1 Corinthians 14:15.[51] Most often it is used of direct praise to the name of God (e.g., Pss 7:17; 18:49). Those who suffer are to pray to God; those who are encouraged in the conditions of the messianic community are to sing praise to God, and we are probably to think that James intends for the "cheerful" (or "encouraged") to give credit to God for the strength they find to carry on faithfully. If we are accurate in thinking of a single condition — oppression — giving rise to two sorts of response, suffering and cheerfulness, then we should perhaps notice the connection to the "testing" or "tempting" *(peirasmos)* in 1:12-15, where the same condition *(peirasmos)* is perceived as either a "test" or a "temptation," depending in part on how a person responds to "desire" *(epithymia)*. And we could consider how the teachers use the tongue — either to bless God or to denounce those made in God's image (3:9). The letter thus repeatedly forces on the audience a fork-in-the-road kind of decision, but here the rhetoric is shaped less for decision and more to how different people respond to the same conditions.

8.3.3. Sickness — Summon the Elders (5:14)

James now moves into a new theme, that of sickness, sin and healing, which will occupy his attention through v. 18. But, as we indicated in the schematic above, he will meander from one subtopic to another within this theme. James describes the third condition of the community with "Are any among you sick?" or (preserving the singular) "Is anyone among you sick?"[52] and will unfold it in the following verses. If the suffering should pray and the encouraged should praise, the sick, one would think, should also pray for healing. But James lets this third condition open an entire theology and cultural perception and unfold a series of observations and implications for the messianic community.

The word translated "sick" is a general term denoting physical, spiritual, or mental[53] weakness and can even describe someone on the verge of death (e.g., John 4:46; 11:1-3; Acts 9:37; Phil 2:26-27). Jesus healed the sick (Matt 10:8; Luke 4:40), and exhorted his followers to tend to the sick (Matt 25:36). John 5:3 shows how general and encompassing this term can be: "In these lay many invalids — blind, lame, and paralyzed." In this text, while "in-

---

51. In Eph 5:19 the term is connected to ᾄδω, also suggesting singing in praise to God. See also Rom 15:9. The term is frequently used in the LXX; it is found 41 times in the Psalms.

52. ἀσθενεῖ τις ἐν ὑμῖν. See BDAG, 142.

53. See D. R. Hayden, "Calling the Elders to Pray," *BibSac* 138 (1981) 258-66.

valids" might be too strong of a term, we see that "blind, lame, and para-lyzed" are specifications of being "sick" (Greek *astheneō*).[54] Furthermore, it can describe those who are frail and needy (Acts 20:35) or aging (Rom 4:19).[55] Furthermore, this term is connected to the strength of one's faith and courage to persevere in the New Testament (1 Cor 8:11-12; 2 Cor 11:21, 29). So one is entitled to ask what kind of weakness is in view and just how sick James thinks this person might be. These factors deserve consideration: first, the situation is serious enough to summon the elders; the sick person will be anointed with oil; and the words "save the sick" and "raise them up" describe the effects of the healing.[56] Furthermore, this third condition provokes James to mention not only elders and anointing but also the need for strong faith and righteous people praying for the person. This evidence suggests this person is seriously and physically ill, perhaps near death, though the terms are expansive enough that they might include a number of issues.[57]

The ill person, who seems to be bedridden, is given this command: "They should call for the elders of the church," or as we prefer, "That person should call for the elders of the church."[58] James uses only one other term for a leader; in 3:1 he uses the word "teacher." This is not the place to sketch the rise of church offices nor the intricacies of church leadership where we find a

---

54. One could see τῶν ἀσθενούντων as the first in a list of terms that modify πλῆθος. At any rate, in the ancient world each of those could be described as a form of ἀσθένεια.

55. Rom 4:19 correlates Abraham's faith, which did not "weaken" (μὴ ἀσθενήσας τῇῇ πίστει), with his aging.

56. See Davids, 192.

57. Popkes, 341; Warrington, "Healing," 347-51 (see note 41 above); J. Wilkinson, "Healing in the Epistle of James," *Scottish Journal of Theology* 24 (1971) 326-43; M. C. Albl, "'Are Any among You Sick?' The Health Care System in the Letter of James," *JBL* 121 (2002) 123-43, who expounds the symbolic, integrated, communal worldview at work in this passage. It is possible that this deathly ill person is deathly or spiritually ill because of sin, explaining why the issue of sin comes up so forcefully, and that Jas 5:19-20 is a response to that sort of person and situation. The evidence weighs against this, not the least of which are that there are no strong indicators that a spiritual sickness is in view and that James exhorts them to confess their sins to one another instead of asking for the near-apostate to confess his or her sins to the faithful community (or its elders). See Moo, 236-37.

58. προσκαλεσάσθω τοὺς πρεσβυτέρους τῆς ἐκκλησίας. The switch from present commands to an aorist does not mean this person needs to do something he or she has been resisting until now, but that James wants to conceive of the act of summoning in its totality. The genitive could be either partitive ("elders who are part of the church") or possessive ("church's elders"). See J. C. Thomas, "The Devil, Disease and Deliverance: James 5:14-16," *JPT* 2 (1993) 25-50; and his newer study, *The Devil, Disease and Deliverance: Origins of Illness in New Testament Thought* (JPTSS 13; Sheffield: Sheffield Academic, 1998).

variety of terms, including bishop, pastor, deacon, and elder, but we can sketch briefly what it meant to call someone an "elder" in the early church.[59] To begin with, we are almost certainly dealing with males and with established males who operated in a structured society of respect and honor (Josh 9:11; Judg 11:5-11; 2 Sam 2:17; Jer 29:1; Ezek 8:1; Ezra 5:5; 6:7). One needs to think of patriarchs (Genesis 12–50), the grey-bearded wisdom of Proverbs, and a patriarchal, hierarchical, and honor-shaped culture where the elders were in the middle of what was most important (1 Macc 1:26; 14:28; Josephus, *War* 2.570). But the honor given to the elders in this culture is not so much formal as it is unofficial custom and collective wisdom. There is no evidence that "elder" was an "office." Campbell draws the right conclusion: elders "does not so much denote an office as connote prestige."[60]

This leads to an important observation: while it is true that "elder" *(presbyteros)* appears to be a little more of an official designation in the Pastorals (cf. 1 Tim 5:17, 19; Tit 1:5; cf. 1 Pet 5:5), it is a general term for senior wise, honored, respected males in the community who were household leaders. We find the term used this way in the New Testament. Thus, it refers to the "elders" who were leaders in the community (Luke 7:3), who safeguarded the oral, sacred tradition (Matt 15:2) and who seemed to be at the center of power in Jerusalem (Matt 16:21; 21:23; 26:3, 47; 27:20; 28:12; John 8:9; Acts 4:5, 23). Soon there were "elders" among the Christians (Acts 11:30; 14:23; 15:2, 4, 6, 22; 20:17, et al.). In Acts, we are probably to think of the senior wise, established leaders whether or not they were officially entitled "elders." The evidence, in other words, suggests an easy transfer of the term into the messianic communities. Hebrews 11:2 might express this transfer well: "Indeed, by faith our ancestors [*presbyteroi*] received approval." One finds at Qumran, for another example, a hierarchy: "This is the rule for the session of the general membership, each man being in his proper place. The priests shall sit in the first row, the elders in the second, then the rest of the people, each in his proper place" (1QS 6:8-9).

Where does James fit into all this? It is easy for us once again to pull out our imagined early Christian lexicon and impute to James 5:14 the meaning we think might be found in the Pastorals, but we should be cautious. It is the *absence* of the term "elders" in James 3:1–4:12 and the rather *casual appearance* of the term here in 5:14 that leads me to suspect that James does not have an office in mind with the word "elder" but a traditional Jewish reference to the senior wise, respected, and honorable — and probably male — leaders of the (messianic) community. It may be that James reflects the usage

---

59. See R. A. Campbell, *The Elders: Seniority within Earliest Christianity* (Edinburgh: Clark, 1994).

60. Campbell, *The Elders,* 65; *pace* Moo, 237.

of the term we find in the Pastorals, but even there the term is not as official as "bishop" or "deacon," and there is no evidence that James used the term that way. We are not left standing on firm ground: the balance of evidence favors an informal term designating the senior males in a community to whom honor and respect were given because of wisdom and prestige, but it is possible that James has gone from the informal to a more formal use.[61]

If James's use of "elders" surprises, so also does "of the church."[62] There are only two other references in James that expresses anything like a collective term for the messianic community: "the twelve tribes" in 1:1 and the "synagogue" of 2:2. James has not yet used the word "church" and will not use it again. Like "twelve tribes" and "synagogue," the word comes out of nowhere. Once again, we need to remind ourselves of our tendency to pull out our imaginary early church lexicon, pull the meaning of *ecclesia* ("church") from other places in the New Testament, and impute this meaning to the term in James 5:14. One of the more frustrating elements of interpreting James is that the author did not write a bundle of letters, as did Paul, that we can gather together for mutual interpretation. All we have is this one use of the word. But in light of the messianic theme of this entire letter, made most visible in texts like 1:1 and 2:1, we are on firm ground in assuming that "church" here refers to the local messianic community and not to a gathered body of community leaders drawn from the local civic "assembly" (e.g., Acts 19:32, 39-40).

Thus James urges the sick person to summon the elders to pray "over" the sick person for healing.[63] Besides the rather common Jewish practice of

61. See again Campbell, *The Elders,* 206, where proper caution is used regarding the evidence in James. That James had in mind "males" does not settle once and for all whether females can be "elders" in contemporary churches; that decision, resting as it does with denominational or local church leadership and congregations, is a hermeneutical decision. See W. Webb, *Slaves, Women, and Homosexuals* (Downers Grove: InterVarsity, 2001); J. Stackhouse, *Finally Feminist* (Grand Rapids: Baker, 2005); R. W. Pierce and R. M. Groothuis, eds., *Discovering Biblical Equality* (Downers Grove: InterVarsity, 2005). For an example of women exploring leadership themes, see N. A. Toyama, T. Gee, K. Khang, C. H. de Leon, and A. Dean, *More Than Serving Tea* (Downers Grove: InterVarsity, 2006).

62. τῆς ἐκκλησίας. See BDAG, 303-4, where the evidence is cited for the term referring both to the local community and to the catholic community. This word was used for the gathered people rather than the place where a group gathered. See Johnson, 330-31.

63. Once again, aorists are used because James chooses to depict the actions of praying and anointing without regard to completion or incompletion, but constatively. The aorist participle coordinates with the aorist imperative as an attending circumstance or *a* means of the prayer. On the issue of time with participles, see Porter, *Idioms,* 187-93; the general principle is that participles occurring before the main verb tend to refer to antecedent action, and participles occurring after the main verb tend to refer to subsequent action or simultaneous action; the latter best explains ἀλείψαντες. *Contra* Johnson, 331.

visiting the sick as an act of compassion and solidarity (Ps 35:13-14; Sir 7:35), a similar piece of advice for summoning the wise is found in the much later Babylonian Talmud, at *Baba Bathra* 116: "R. Phinehas b. Hama gave the following exposition: Whosoever has a sick person in his house should go to a Sage who will invoke [heavenly] mercy for him; as it is said: *The wrath of a king is as messengers of death; but a wise man will pacify it* [Prov 16:14]."[64] But both James and the later Talmudic line counter what is found in Sir 38:9: there the person makes petition himself or herself: "My child, when you are ill, do not delay, but pray to the Lord, and he will heal you." One might assume for James that the sick person has already prayed and not found healing and therefore was urged to seek the remedy of the spiritually gifted. James does not seem to be aware of the gift of healing (1 Cor 12:9, 28, 30),[65] though the prepositional phrase "over him" may well indicate laying on of hands (cf. Gen 48:14 with Num 8:10; Deut 34:9),[66] or it could simply indicate standing next to and over a sick person on a bed.

It was also customary in the ancient world to anoint someone with *oil*.[67] Such an act could be more medicinal, procedural, and connected to the natural healing process, as in Isaiah 1:6: the wounds "have not been drained, or bound up, or softened with oil." The same is found in the parable of the Good Samaritan: "He went to him and bandaged his wounds, having poured oil and wine on them" (Luke 10:34).[68] A text in Josephus about Herod makes this most clear:

Yet, struggling as he was with numerous sufferings, he clung to life, hoped for recovery, and devised one remedy after another. Thus he

64. In this text the editor of the Talmud points out that "king" is understood as "God's visitation" of wrath. Hence, the sickness was understood as God's judgment.

65. R. Haninah b. Dosa was famous for his sense of the outcome of his prayers, as recorded in *m Berakoth* 5:5:

D. They said concerning R. Haninah b. Dosa, "When he would pray for the sick he would say 'This one shall live' or 'This one shall die.'"
E. They said to him, "How do you know?"
F. He said to them, "If my prayer is fluent, then I know that it is accepted [and the person will live].
G. "But if not, I know that it is rejected [and the person will die]."

66. On which, see D. Daube, *The New Testament and Rabbinic Judaism* (Peabody: Hendrickson, n.d. [= 1956]), 224-46. Daube argues that Hebrew *samakh* means to "lean" while *sîm* and *shîth* mean "the employment of a special, supernatural faculty of one's hands" (p. 229). The latter would be meant here if laying on of hands was involved.

67. On ἀλείφω, see BDAG, 41. See the excellent sorting out of options in Moo, 238-42; G. Shogren, "Will God Heal Us — A Re-Examination of James 5:14-16," *Evangelical Quarterly* 61 (1989) 99-108.

68. See also Josephus, *Ant* 17.172.

crossed the Jordan to take warm baths as Callirrhoe. . . . There, the physicians deciding to raise the temperature of his whole body with hot oil, he was lowered into a bath full of that liquid, whereupon he fainted and turned up his eyes as though he were dead. His attendants raising an uproar, their cries brought him to himself . . . (*War* 1.657-58).[69]

But anointing with oil was also used for supernatural healing through the power and grace made available in Christ and through the Spirit.[70] Thus, Mark 6:13: "They cast out many demons, and anointed with oil many who were sick and cured them." In James's words the oil could symbolize consecration of the person to God (e.g., Exod 28:41; Acts 4:27; 10:38; 2 Cor 1:21) or could be sacramental, something that mediates God's healing grace. The latter developed through the history of the church into the Euchelaion, extreme unction, and the anointing of the sick.[71]

Anointing (the verb is *aleiphō*)[72] was sometimes done as an action of consecrating, dedicating, or purifying — it is not always clear which — an object, as when Jacob anointed a pillar (Gen 31:13), Ezekiel anointed a wall (Ezek 13:10-12), Ruth washed her body (Ruth 3:3; cf. Esth 2:12; Jdth 16:7), or David did the same to his body (2 Sam 12:20; cf. also 2 Chron 28:15; Matt 6:17). It was also done in consecrating a person to service (Exod 40:15; Num 3:3) and could express extravagant devotion (Luke 7:38, 46; John 11:2; 12:3). The absence of oil indicates mourning or abstinence (2 Sam 14:2; Dan 10:3). And dead bodies were anointed (Mark 16:1). This evidence suggests, to begin with, that the anointing James speaks of is not a medical procedure: not only is "anoint" not used this way, but elders would not be necessary for such a procedure.[73] Nor is there any indication that exorcism is in mind.[74] Thus, this evidence leads us to think that the elders were to anoint the sick person's body to consecrate and purify it as an act of devoting it to God for God's work of healing.[75]

---

69. See also Galen, *De simplicitate medicamentum temperatum* 2.10.

70. See also the effulgent nature of anointing in *2 Enoch* 22:8-9, where the transition to glory is accompanied by anointing.

71. See *Catechism of the Catholic Church*, §§1499-1532. See C. Pickar, "Is Anyone Sick Among You?" *CBQ* 7 (1945) 165-74, who anchors the dogma of extreme unction in Jas 5:14-15; see also D. J. Harrington, "'Is Anyone Among You Sick?' New Testament Foundations for the Anointing of the Sick," *Emmanuel* 101 (1995) 412-17. However this text might be connected to extreme unction, James's concern is with healing in this life and not simply the (older) notion of purgation prior to death.

72. The verb χρίω is not used in the New Testament for the physical act of anointing (see Luke 4:18; Acts 4:27; 10:30; 2 Cor 1:21; Heb 1:9).

73. See Moo, 241-42.

74. So Popkes, 344; cf. Dibelius, 252-54.

75. See Martin, 208-9.

This anointing was to be done "in the name of the Lord" (5:14). Once again, we are led to ask if "Lord" means God/Father or the Lord Jesus Christ. The evidence in Acts for the earliest Jewish communities of faith would suggest, rather one-sidedly, that "in the name of the Lord" would be "in the name of the Lord Jesus" (Acts 3:6; 4:30; 16:18; 19:13) and Gospel evidence supports the same (Mark 9:38; Matt 7:22). To pray and anoint in the name of the Lord Jesus involves invoking Jesus Christ to act in the power of the resurrection. In liturgical terms, it is epiclesis, or the calling upon the Lord Jesus Christ to become present in power for healing.[76]

We should be careful not to turn what we read here into an established rite to be followed on all occasions. James instructs the elders on what to do, but we cannot know if this is what he would say always, nor is it clear that he is laying down a law for all Christians of all times. This is what James said at that time to that group of messianic Christians. He instructs them to attend pastorally to the sick in prayer, and we need to recognize that intercessory prayer is the first thing he commands and is the main verb. The anointing accompanies the prayer.

James might here be seen as straddling the charismatic (healing, anointing) and the institutional (summoning elders) by bringing in a little of both, but I suspect that this happy compromise is not demonstrable. It is not clear that "the elders" is an institution, and once we admit that "elders" could be the informal senior, wise leaders of the messianic community, the quest to walk with both a charismatic leg and a more formal institutional leg loses its legs. The fact is that the earliest Christians believed God could and did heal, and they prayed for healing in a number of ways, not the least of which was the summoning of elders to anoint the sick person.[77] Spirit-endowment leads the way to gifts of all sorts among the earliest Christians rather than institutional order. One can have the latter without the former, but the New Testament emphasis is on the former, giving rise to both informal and more formal manifestations of the latter.

8.4. THE NEED FOR THE PRAYER OF FAITH (5:15A)

Casual, ritual, or routine pastoral prayers for healing are not effective, as most pastors know from experience. James speaks of the need for a special kind of prayer in this situation: "The prayer of faith will save the sick." What comes to mind immediately is 1:6-8, where James urged the community to ask for wisdom in faith for, apart from faith, they "must not expect to receive

---

76. See G. Twelftree, *In the Name of Jesus* (Grand Rapids: Baker, 2007), 180-82.
77. Laws, 230-31.

anything from the Lord." If faith is needed to acquire wisdom, so also for healing. One also thinks of 4:3, where the teachers were asking "wrongly." Here then are three specifics about how to pray properly: asking for wisdom in faith, asking for the right thing in the right way, and asking for healing with faith. Faith is particularly connected to healing (Mark 2:5; 5:34, 36; 9:23; 10:52; Acts 14:9), and without faith one does not obtain healing (Mark 6:6). Prayer by "faith" cannot be mustered; instead, it is the Spirit-empowered and trusting vulnerability and loving trust that characterize the genuine I-Thou relationship with God and that, in God's goodness, may or may not lead to healing.[78] Inasmuch as the ones being exhorted to pray are the elders, we are to think that the "faith" is theirs.

"The prayer of faith will save the sick."[79] The word translated "sick" (a participle of *kamnō*) covers a variety of symptoms, from weariness and fatigue (Heb 12:3) to death (Wis 4:16; 15:9). In this context the person is ill (5:14a) with the implication of exhaustion (cf. Job 10:1; *4 Maccabees* 7:13).[80] A text from Philo illustrates the meaning well: "for our Saviour God holds out, we may be sure, the most all-healing remedy, His gracious Power, and commits it to His suppliant and worshipper to use for the deliverance of those who are sickly . . ." (*On the Migration of Abraham* 124).[81] Philo uses the word commonly translated "salvation" (*sōtēria*) for healing and so does James — this was a common word for liberation and deliverance from bodily illnesses. Healing is a symptom of the kingdom's presence, and it would be unwise to separate physical salvation from spiritual salvation. Thus, Mark 5:23: "My little daughter is at the point of death. Come and lay your hands on

---

78. καὶ ἡ εὐχὴ τῆς πίστεως σώσει τὸν κάμνοντα. The adjectival genitive describes the kind of prayer, and the future is used because of potentiality. On εὐχή, a variant of προσευχή, see BDAG, 416; elsewhere in the New Testament the word means "vow" (Acts 18:18; 21:23); on κάμνω, see BDAG, 506-7.

79. I use the language here of M. Buber, *I and Thou* (New York: Scribner, 1958); see Moo, 244-45, for sound pastoral advice. On faith, see the sketch of G. Theissen, *The Miracle Stories of the Early Christian Tradition* (trans. F. McDonagh; Philadelphia: Fortress, 1983), 129-40. On miracles, see C. Brown, *Miracles and the Critical Mind* (Grand Rapids: Eerdmans, 1984); H. C. Kee, *Miracle in the Early Christian World* (New Haven: Yale University Press, 1983); *Medicine, Miracle and Magic in New Testament Times* (SNTSMS 55; New York: Cambridge University Press, 1986); P. Davids, "Healing, Illness," in *DLNTD*, 436-39; N. C. Croy, "Religion, Personal," in *DNTB*, 926-31. In addition, see H. D. Curtis, *Faith in the Great Physician: Suffering and Divine Healing in American Culture, 1860-1900* (Baltimore: Johns Hopkins University Press, 2007); A. Porterfield, *Healing in the History of Christianity* (New York: Oxford University Press, 2005).

80. Spicq, 2.251-53, with illustrative examples in Philo and Josephus and classical authors. See also *Martyrdom of Polycarp* 22.3.

81. The appropriate words are πρὸς τὴν τῶν καμνόντων σωτηρίαν ἐπιτρέπει.

her, so that she may be made well [*sōthē*], and live" (cf. 5:28, 34; 10:52; John 11:12). New Testament authors (Luke 19:10; Rom 10:13; 1 Cor 1:21; 1 Pet 4:18), including James (1:21; 2:14; 4:12; 5:20), use the same term for eschatological redemption, but the context here clearly favors the customary use of this term for healing from physical illnesses.

This salvation (healing) is restated: "and the Lord will raise them up."[82] Once again, the word "raise" *(egeirō)* commonly appears in healing scenes. Jesus took Simon Peter's mother-in-law by the hand "and lifted her up" (Mark 1:31; cf. 9:27; Matt 9:5-7; Luke 6:8; John 5:8). Acts describes Peter's healing of the lame beggar in similar terms: "And he took him by the right hand and raised him up" (Acts 3:7; cf. 9:41). Though the word could be used of the final resurrection, that would make no sense in this context where a sick person has called the elders for healing. It is tempting for some to connect "save" and "raise" and arrive at the conclusion that James is speaking here of spiritual salvation, but the words are too commonly used for healing and the context is about healing.[83] James informs the community that it will be the "Lord" who raises the sick person up. Because the elders have been instructed to anoint the sick person "in the name of *the Lord*," that is, the Lord Jesus Christ, it is more than likely that the raising from the sickbed is done by Jesus Christ.[84]

As we have indicated above, we should read James 5:13-18 as a pastoral meandering. Perhaps the multivalence of the words provokes James's next idea: that "faith," "save," "sick," and "raise" can also refer to spiritual redemption might have suggested to James that forgiveness might also be needed. But there is a further complexity: in the ancient world sickness was connected to sinfulness.

8.5. THE PROMISE OF FORGIVENESS (5:15B)

Sickness in a world far more primitive than ours was a mystery, and one way of resolving that mystery was to connect sickness and illnesses to sin. James seems to make that connection when he says "and anyone who has committed sins will be forgiven."[85] Why he moves in this direction is not altogether

82. Again, the future tense indicates potentiality.
83. Moo, 243.
84. But cf. Laws, 228.
85. The conditional particle ἐάν should not be downgraded to a simple indefinite as in the NRSV: "anyone who." It should be given its conditional force, as in the TNIV: "If they have sinned." The periphrastic construction with the perfect participle (see also John 3:27; 2 Cor 1:9) is used to emphasize the state or condition: "and if that person be a person who is in the state of having sinned. . . ." See Porter, *Verbal Aspect,* 466-86. Again, the fu-

clear, and some think he is preparing for the backslider of 5:19-20, but those verses are marked off by "my brothers and sisters," they deal with a person who has wandered from the faith, and they do not mention healing.

What is clear is that James 5:15b reveals a very common connection made in the ancient world: sickness derives from sinfulness.[86] Standing tall to the point of dominating the deuteronomic history are Deuteronomy 28, Leviticus 26–27, and 2 Kings 17. The correlation of sickness with sin and health with covenant faithfulness shapes the core of the Old Testament and of Israel's identity and consciousness. It worked its way into the mind of the entire nation and of each person (e.g., Deut 28:21-22, 27-29; Ps 38:3; Sir 18:19-21; 38:15). "Health, fertility, and long life are promised as blessings for covenantal obedience, while disease, plagues, incurable illnesses, infertility, and premature death are threatened as curses for breaches of covenant."[87]

The theme emerges, for instance, in the *Testaments of the Twelve Patriarchs*. Thus, at his death bed Reuben tells his brothers:

See here, I call the God of heaven to bear witness to you this day, so that you will not behave yourselves in the ignorant ways of youth and sexual promiscuity in which I indulged myself and defiled the marriage bed of my father, Jacob. But I tell you he struck me with a severe wound in my loins for seven months, and if my father, Jacob, had not prayed to the Lord in my behalf, the Lord would have destroyed me (*Testament of Reuben* 1:6-7).

Zebulon, for his part, knows that his own innocence preserved him from the sin-shaped illness that fell upon each of his brothers (*Testament of Zebulon* 5). And Gad offers this confession:

For God brought on me a disease of the liver [the seat of anger], and if it had not been for the prayers of Jacob, my father, he would shortly have summoned me from my spirit. For by whatever human capacity anyone transgresses, by that he is also chastised. Since my anger was merciless in opposition to Joseph, through this anger of mine I suffered mercilessly, and was brought under judgment for eleven months, as long as I had it in for Joseph, until he was sold (*Testament of Gad* 5:9-11).

---

ture indicates potentiality: if that person be in a state of having sinned, that person's sin will be forgiven (not be reckoned to him as sin). On ἀφίημι, BDAG, 156-57.

86. On which see J. Hempel, "Heilung als Symbol und Wirklichkeit im biblischen Schrifttum," *Nachrichten von der Gesellschaft der Wissenschaften zu Göttingen. Philosophisch-historische Klasse* 3 (1958) 237-314; M. Brown, *Israel's Divine Healer* (Grand Rapids: Zondervan, 1995).

87. Brown, *Israel's Divine Healer*, 237.

A rabbinic text expresses the same theology:

> A. On account of three transgressions do women die in childbirth:
>   B. because they are not meticulous in the laws of (1) menstrual separa-
> tion, (2) in [those covering] the dough offering, and (3) in [those cover-
> ing] the kindling of a lamp [for the Sabbath] (*m Shabbat* 2.6).

This text is unfolded in the Talmud from many angles, including why children die in childbirth. One statement there illustrates the same theology for
males: "Our Rabbis taught: If one falls sick and his life is in danger, he is
told, Make confession, for all who are sentenced to death make confession."[88] Another text is even closer to James: "R. Alexandri said in the name
of R. Hihha b. Abba: A sick man does not recover from his sickness until all
his sins are forgiven him, as it is written, *Who forgiveth all thine iniquities;
who healeth all thy diseases* [Ps 103:3]."

The same connection is found in the New Testament. Jesus said as he
healed a paralyzed man, "Son, your sins are forgiven," and this implies that
the paralysis was the result of sin (Mark 2:5; cf. John 5:14). Paul knows that
some are sick at Corinth because of sin (1 Cor 11:30). And John 9:2-3 asks
the question behind all this and offers an alternative: "Neither this man nor
his parents sinned; he was born blind so that God's works might be revealed
in him." Job at some level deconstructs a superficial deuteronomic theology,
as does John 9:2-3 from a different angle. The instinct was there, and the
principle was in place: sickness correlates with sin, health with faithfulness.
But not always. Sometimes there is another explanation, not the least of
which in James is oppression (see Matt 25:36; Jas 2:1-4, 14-17; 5:1-6). But
this does not prevent the instinct nor eliminate the principle.

This instinct and principle then prompt James to make the connection
between the sick person's illness and possible sin. James is not certain that
the sickness is from sin, or he would have used the indicative; instead, he
uses the subjunctive in a periphrastic construction. I would translate: "And if
he be a person who is in the state of having sinned." It is possible that the illness is sin-induced; it is possible that it is not. What James says is that if the
sickness is from sin, the sin "will be forgiven." James combines the sick person's requesting the elders — a sign in and of itself of need and faith in
Christ — the elders' prayer and anointing, the prayer of faith, and, as the next
verse will clarify, confession of sin. This leads to the sick person's forgiveness, itself sometimes a trigger of healing (Mark 2:5; Matt 8:16-17), and
healing, itself an indication of forgiveness.[89]

---

88. See *b Shabbat* 31b-32b, where commentary is found.
89. See Davids, 195; Laws, 232-33.

8.6. THE EXHORTATION TO CONFESSION (5:16A)

This person's possible sin-shaped sickness leads James to meander to a related topic: the need for all to confess their sins, presumably to avoid what has happened to the sick person. James thus shifts from a particular case to a more general situation. Or perhaps 5:16 is the conclusion to 5:14-15: the prayer ultimately had to do with sin and the need for routine communal confession and prayer.

"Therefore confess your sins to one another, and pray for one another."[90] The command to "confess," so foreign to much of the church today, characterized the life of ancient Israel. Such an act of communal confession is described in Leviticus 5:5-6 (also Lev 16:21; 26:40; Ezra 10; Judith 9; Tobit 3). The institutionalization of confession led to a community much both more in tune with its sins and peccadilloes and more comfortable, if one can ever be that, with confession. But Israel instituted not only public confession through public ritual, but also restitution procedures, as in Numbers 5:5-10. Israelites made peace with God privately as well, as can be seen in some of the Psalms' greatest lines (e.g., Pss 32:5; 51:3-4). Confession was a commonplace: "No one who conceals transgressions will prosper, but one who confesses and forsakes them will obtain mercy" (Prov 28:13). "To whom will you be good, O God," the author of *The Psalms of Solomon* asks,

> except to those who call upon the Lord? He will cleanse from sins the soul in confessing, in restoring, so that for all these things the shame is on us, and (it shows) on our faces. And whose sins will he forgive except those who have sinned? You bless the righteous, and do not accuse them for what they sinned. And your goodness is upon those that sin, when they repent (*Pss Sol* 9:6-7).[91]

There are signs of mutual or public confession of sins in the early churches. One thinks of Matthew 3:6, 18:15, Luke 17:3-4, Acts 19:18 and 1 John 1:8-9. *Didache* 4:14 calls for such confession: "In church you shall confess your transgressions, and you shall not approach your prayer with an evil conscience. This is the way of life." And mutual confession may be in mind at 14:1: "On the Lord's own day gather together and break bread and

---

90. The present imperatives are appropriate: James wants confession and intercession to be characteristic of the community. The potential healing is found in ὅπως ἰαθῆτε. On ἐξομολογέω, see BDAG, 351; the term often means "profession" instead of "confession," but the meaning here is the latter. On εὔχομαι, see BDAG, 417; on ἰάομαι, BDAG, 465.

91. See further R. A. Werline, *Penitential Prayers in Second Temple Judaism* (Early Judaism and Its Literature 13; Atlanta: Scholars, 1998).

give thanks, having first confessed your sins so that your sacrifice [of worship?] may be pure." Finally, *Barnabas* 19:12 says "You shall not cause division, but shall make peace between those who quarrel by bringing them together. You shall confess your sins. You shall not come to prayer with an evil conscience. This is the way of light." The liturgical use of the Psalms, another spiritual custom of Israel and the messianic communities, made confession even more common.

James's words then are not a new instruction; they speak of an old practice of admitting one's guilt before God and others and now urge the same on the messianic community. This confession of sins to one another was not a substitute for confession to God. What sins James had in mind might be discerned from the letter. Surely it would involve mistreatment of the poor (2:1-17), verbal sins prompted by ambition (3:1–4:12), violence against one another (1:19-21; 4:1-4; 5:7-11), judgmentalism (4:11-12), and sins prompted by greed (4:13–5:6). No doubt one could multiply the sorts of things the messianists did, but at least these were in mind.

Church praxis has evolved out of this command by James: for some, it involves the discipline of regular confession to a priest and is often called the sacrament of penance or reconciliation.[92] For others it is followed in a general sense as the gathered church publicly confesses its sins weekly through the liturgical recitation of a prayer of confession, a request for forgiveness, and the public pastoral assurance of absolution. The Augsburg Confession (XI) clarifies the importance of confession for Lutherans. In the Eastern Church one of the more common forms of confession is the rite of Mutual Forgiveness on Forgiveness Sunday.

For others, particularly those who emphasize the authority of Scripture in a low church context today, there has been a noticeable discomfort with this text in James, which may be precipitated by both the obvious meaning of the text and the obvious absence of confession in churches. One is forced either to begin the discipline of confession or, not meaning this disrespectfully, to find a way out of it. The most obvious way out is to understand James as referring to confession to a person one has offended or to restrict his concern to sickness caused by sin. Only in the last century or two has confession been completely abandoned. This is not the place and I am not the person for a full study of confession, but "to one another" provides an early insight into the priesthood of all believers, the significance of *koinōnia* in the messianic community, and the clear non-need of a priest for confession to be what it is intended to be. The biblical pattern is for believ-

---

92. See *Catechism of the Catholic Church,* §§1422-98. Even if I do not agree with the framing of confession in the catechism, particularly in the acts of the penitent, the wisdom of this text is palpable.

ers to confess their sins both to God and to one another, but I see nothing institutionalized about it.[93]

A second command here is to "pray for one another." This is the pastoral response to confession: one who confesses sins to another will be met with both absolution, whether formal or not, and a prayer of forgiveness and restoration. It is slightly possible that this imperative represents a more general idea. Just as the messianists confess sins to one another, so also they practice intercession for one another's needs. But the context favors narrowing the meaning of "pray" to the need for healing as a result of sin. It is not entirely clear if we are to think of public gatherings or of individuals praying for others in the privacy of their homes, but "to one another" and "for one another" suggest the former.[94]

The promise is good news: "so that you may be healed." This clause ties us back to 5:13, to the summoning of the elders, the prayer of faith, and the Lord Jesus healing the person. In effect, we have come back where we started, another indicator of the meandering nature of 5:13-18. One could say that 5:16 generalizes what we find for a particular sick person in 5:13-15. But it goes farther to include mutual confession as a preventive measure against the development of sickness. Of what will these folks be healed? If we stayed with 5:13-15, we would be led to think that they are healed of sicknesses. If 5:16 is more general than 5:13-15, and I think it is, then they are "healed" of their sins and the word becomes synonymous with "forgiven" in 5:15, but in a way that includes physical healing.[95] What makes this more likely is the role Isaiah 6:9-10, especially v. 10, played in shaping the meaning of the word "healed." Isaiah 6:10 reads:

> Make the mind of this people dull,
>   and stop their ears,
>   and shut their eyes,
> so that they may not look with their eyes,
>   and listen with their ears,
> and comprehend with their minds,
>   and turn and be *healed*."

This verse is picked up in Matthew 13:15; John 12:40; and Acts 28:27 as a warning to those who sluggishly persist in their sins, and James turns that

---

93. See the little-known study by John Stott, *Confess Your Sins* (London: Hodder and Stoughton, 1964), which weighs in against habitual auricular confession to a priest. Also, R. J. Foster, *Celebration of Discipline* (rev. ed.; San Francisco: Harper and Row, 1988), 143-57; D. Tippens, *Pilgrim Heart* (Abilene: Leafwood, 2006), 99-111.

94. Davids, 196.

95. See Popkes, 349.

text around to say to his community that they are the ones who will instead experience the mercy and forgiving healing of God.[96] It is likely that James thought, as did Peter, that this healing occurs through the cross (cf. Isa 53:5; 1 Pet 2:24), and clearly Matthew 8:16-17 thinks along these lines.[97]

8.7. THE NEED FOR RIGHTEOUS PERSONS TO PRAY (5:16B-18)

5:16b Almost backing up to the "prayer of faith" in 5:15a, James now promises healing if the righteous are the ones praying for the sick: "The prayer of the righteous is powerful and effective."[98] This translation is in need of some repairs. A more literal rendering would look like this: "The working prayer of a righteous [person] accomplishes much." This inelegant translation recognizes that "working" *(energoumenē)* is an adjectival participle modifying the word "prayer." This participle denotes that which is at work or that which is effectively operating. It represents not so much the (divine) source of a righteous person's prayers, as in "God's work at work in the prayer," but the fact that a righteous person's prayers are alive, at work, energized and energizing, and ongoing.[99] One thinks of Mark 6:14, where King Herod thinks John the Baptist's powers are at work in Jesus, of Romans 7:5, where the passions of sin are energized in our members to lead toward death, or of the Spirit's energizing of gifts in 1 Corinthians 12:6, 11. Paul uses this term for the working of miracles (Gal 3:5), for faith working through love (5:6), and for God's power at work in raising Jesus (Eph 1:20) and energizing God's people (3:20; Phil 2:13). Instead, however, of focusing on God at work in the prayer, James sees the working-ness of the prayer because righteous people can prevail with God.

The language here is general and axiomatic:[100] the righteous person's

---

96. See Laws, 233-34.

97. See also Hermas, *Visions* 1.1.9; *Similitudes* 9.28.5.

98. The grammar is not as simple as the NRSV's "The prayer of the righteous is powerful and effective." The subject is δέησις, and that word is modified by δικαίου. So the "prayer [of the righteous one]" is the subject, and the verb is ἰσχύει, which is directed at a neuter adjective functioning as an adverb (πολύ). The anarthrous active participle is feminine and can be adjectival with δέησις ("the working prayer of the righteous is very strong") or predicative/adverbial ("the prayer of the righteous is very strong and effective"). The participle, though possibly passive in the sense of "having been energized by God" or "made actual through the efforts of the righteous person" (Mayor, 177-79), is most likely middle in the sense of "when it is exercised" (Ropes, 309-10).

99. See Popkes, 350-51.

100. Note the anarthrous and poetic nature of δέησις δικαίου.

prayer accomplishes much. Who then is the righteous person? The word is found like this only one other time, in James 5:6, and we argued there that it refers to the poor oppressed person. But here it is anarthrous, which suggests a broader meaning. This term, as we have indicated at 1:19-21 and 2:21, 24, refers to the person whose behaviors conform to God's will, in a Christian context, God's will as taught by Jesus. But here, since James is using an axiom and will shortly illustrate his point with the Old Testament prophet Elijah, we must think of "righteous" in the more general sense of the person who does God's will. Although one might appeal to Proverbs 15:29 to argue that "righteous" is any person who does God's will,[101] it is entirely possible that James is "elitist" here. He could be thinking of the sort of person whose life is dedicated to God and whom God has anointed for something special, so that James appeals to Elijah and has already appealed to the elders (5:14). James could be thinking of what the rabbis called the *hasid* or holy man.[102] But most today see here a term for anyone who does God's will, particularly (in James's context) the messianist.[103] In my estimation, one piece of evidence overwhelms all other evidence to support this view: the expression "a human being like us" in 5:17 suggests that we are dealing with any saintly human.

This kind of person's prayer accomplishes much or "is powerful." This translates two Greek words: *ischyō* ("have power, act with power, be able to prevail")[104] and *poly* ("much"). It could be rendered "can prevail for much." Just what James means has been made clear in 5:13-16a, namely, the capacity to petition God for healing of those who are sick and to see that person healed. James will now provide a perfect example of a person who both was a righteous person and prevailed for much when it came to praying.

5:17-18   James takes Elijah for his example.[105] The Bible has a few stories of Elijah's power, not only in his role in bringing drought and then bringing back the rain in his contest on Mount Carmel (1 Kgs 17:1–18:46; see especially 17:1; 18:1), but also in healing the widow's son (17:17-24). 1 Kings 17:1 does not really say Elijah prayed, though it can easily be assumed, nor does 18:1 say Elijah prayed. For some this is enough: the biblical narrative does not say Elijah prayed. But, 18:42 says Elijah "bent down to the ground and put his face between his knees," a customary posture for prayer.

---

101. Or to Pss 1:5-6; 2:12, etc.

102. See G. Vermes, *Jesus the Jew* (New York: Macmillan, 1973), 58-82.

103. See Davids, 196; Moo, 247; Johnson, 335. Popkes, 350, points especially to 1:20 and 3:18 for the person James has in mind.

104. See Matt 5:13; Mark 5:4; Luke 8:43; John 21:6; Phil 4:13.

105. On Elijah, see J. T. Walsh, "Elijah," in *ABD* 2.463-66; J. K. Mead, *DOTHB*, 249-54; see also the portrayal in L. J. Wood, *Elijah: Prophet of God* (Des Plaines: Regular Baptist, 1973).

Furthermore in the middle of all this is the story of the widow's son over whom Elijah uttered these words: "O LORD my God, let this child's life come into him again" (17:21). The tradition of Elijah as a man of great prayer, in other words, is grounded in the text. In addition, even if many find little reference to prayer in 1 Kings 17–18, in Judaism Elijah's reputation for prayer was frequently mentioned and enhanced over time and became a prototype for intercessory prayer (2 Esdr 7:109; Josephus, *Ant* 14.22; *m Taanith* 2.4; 3.8).[106]

Rather than the drought-rain miracle, the healing of the widow's son might seem the more suitable illustration for James. Some find the connection of the prophet to this text in James in the analogy of drought (as sickness and death of the land) and illness, but this stretches the analogy. Instead, it seems preferable to see in the appeal to Elijah a reference to Elijah's power (in prayer), and that James mentions the drought and rain as the concrete illustration of Elijah's power in prayer. Pressing the drought-rain element into service for the immediate context is unnecessary. In addition, Elijah is normally depicted in heroic terms (Sir 48:1-12), listed as he was with such folks as Abraham, Moses, and Samuel, but James's focus is at the other end: James says of the great prophet that he was a "mere mortal like all of us," *homoiopathēs*.[107] When Paul healed a man in Lystra, the locals thought gods had come down to dwell among them, so they prepared a sacrifice. Paul and Barnabas's response was "We are mortals just like you [*homoiopatheis*]." It may be tempting to etymologize this term into "humans with similar *passions*," but the meaning is closer to "mortals like you."[108] What should strike the reader is that James uses the example of a prophet, one of the greatest of prophets, and then says that the prophet was in fact a mortal like everyone else. Though James does not put it this way, he is referring again to humans as *eikons* of God (cf. 3:9). As he used Job, so he can use Elijah as examples for ordinary messianists.

This mortal Elijah "prayed" for it not to rain, and it did not rain; then he prayed that it would rain, and it rained.[109] Like other Jewish writers James

---

106. His return, stated in Mal 4:5-6, is developed in the Gospels (Matt 11:14; 16:14; 17:10-12; 27:47; Luke 1:17; John 1:21, 25).

107. On ὁμοιοπαθής, see BDAG, 706; Wis 7:3-4; *4 Maccabees* 12:13.

108. Martin, 212, finds a suggestion of "suffering" in the πάθος of the noun, but a reading of 1 Kgs 17–18 does not suggest that Elijah was suffering from the drought, for the Lord provided for him. The connection James makes, then, is not about similar desires or suffering, but about similar human make-up.

109. Johnson, 336, gives καί a concessive sense ("yet"), but this would require an emphasis on the heroic elements of Elijah. On the cognate dative, see the next note. The infinitive object includes a constative aorist, "not to rain," and ἔβρεξεν does largely the same: the focus is not on the past but on the action of not raining. The accusatives

focuses on Elijah's power in prayer. Elijah "prayed fervently"[110] and we need to connect this expression back to "effective" *(energoumenē)* in 5:16. In other words, a more literal rendering, "he prayed in praying" or "prayed and prayed," reveals the duplication, which is an intensification of the normal meaning and brings out what it means to have a "working" prayer life. Similar duplications like this can be found in Joshua 24:10 ("therefore he blessed you" = "he blessed you with a blessing"); Isaiah 30:19 ("you shall weep no more" = "you shall weep with weeping no more"); Luke 22:15 ("I have eagerly desired" = "I desire with desire"); and Galatians 5:1 ("For freedom Christ has set us free" = "Christ set us free in freedom").

James 5:17 and 18 essentially summarize 1 Kings 17:1 (where Elijah declares that it will not rain) and 18:1 (where Elijah learns that he will be used to bring back the rains). Neither text focuses on Elijah's prayer, but it can be assumed (as mentioned above). James's language is neatly balanced and brings out that assumption of prayer:

> A. 1. Elijah prayed fervently that it might not rain,
> 2. and for three years and six months it did not rain on the earth.
> B. 1. Then he prayed again,
> 2. and the heaven gave rain and the earth yielded its harvest.

The prayer life of Elijah became important in the early Christian tradition, including the three and one half years (Luke 4:25). Because the same number is used elsewhere for a period of judgment (Dan 7:25; 12:7; Rev 11:2-3; 12:14), some say these numbers are less literal and more symbolic.[111] The Elijah narrative does not specify the duration of the drought. 1 Kings 17:1 says "nor rain these years," and 18:1 says "in the third year of the drought." The careful reader, then, realizes that the Bible James read was an interpreted Bible.[112]

The rhetorical function of this example is not to make Elijah a hero but to encourage the messianic community that they too can pray for miracles and that God hears their voice as he did in the days of Elijah. In fact,

---

ἐνιαυτούς and μῆνας are adverbial accusatives of duration. The aorists are constative, suited for summing up what Elijah did without reference to how the action occurred.

110. προσευχῇ προσηύξατο is a cognitive dative, a virtual equivalent to the Hebrew infinitive absolute with a cognate; cf. Moule, *Idiom Book,* 177-78. But this is also found in the Greek world; cf. Popkes, 352.

111. See Dibelius, 256-57; Davids, 197.

112. The scholarship on the ubiquitous presence of the Old Testament and interpretive traditions in the New Testament writings is enormous. See M. Fishbane, *Biblical Interpretation in Ancient Israel* (Oxford: Clarendon, 1985); R. Hays, *The Conversion of the Imagination* (Grand Rapids: Eerdmans, 2005); J. D. Charles, "Old Testament in General Epistles," in *DLNTD,* 834-41; B. N. Fisk, "Rewritten Bible in Pseudepigrapha and Qumran," in *DNTB,* 947-53; and *CNTOT,* 997-1013.

James's point is bigger: those who do God's will are exhorted to pray as Elijah did, with fervency, and they too can bring healing, both physical and spiritual, to the community.

8.8. COMMUNAL RESTORATION (5:19-20)

19My[113] *brothers and sisters, if anyone among you wanders from the[114] truth and is brought back by another,[a]* 20*you should know[b] that whoever brings back a sinner from wandering[c] will save the sinner's soul[115] from death[d] and will cover[e] a multitude of sins.[116]*

a. TNIV: and someone should bring them back
b. TNIV: remember this:
c. TNIV: Whoever turns a sinner from the way of error
d. TNIV: will save them from death
e. TNIV: cover over

We have made the case that James 5:12-20 is randomly arranged and, as a whole, mostly unconnected to what precedes in the letter. Nothing illustrates this more than 5:19-20. These two verses are about pastoral care for those who have wandered from the faith. We might find causes of wandering in James, not the least of which would be oppression and violent reaction, but

113. Even though at minimum implied, μου is omitted in the Alexandrian manuscripts 322 and 323 as well in Byzantine, *Didache,* etc.
114. Many manuscripts add της οδου, including P47, ℵ, 33, 81, 218, and 2464, some lectionaries, Andreas Cretensis, and Armenian and Georgian witnesses.
115. The manuscripts vary notably here, with the following readings:

1. σωσει ψυχην αυτου εκ θανατου
2. σωσει την ψυχην αυτου εκ θανατου
3. σωσει ψυχην εκ θανατου αυτου
4. σωσει την ψυχην εκ θανατου αυτου
5. σωσει ψυχην εκ θανατου
6. σωσει την ψυχην εκ θανατου.

1. and 5. have the most witnesses, 1.'s personal pronoun having earlier Alexandrian witnesses (ℵ, 048), along with general support from readings 2.-4., and 5.'s absence of the personal pronoun reading having Y, 322, 323, Byzantine, and Coptic, Armenian, Georgian, and Slavonic witnesses.
116. The addition of αμην is late, but various manuscripts found a way to end the letter more elegantly or with a firmer sense of closure. Thus, some have "amen," and another set has "Because to him be glory forever. Amen." Another set has "To our God be glory always now and forever and ever. Amen." Furthermore, see *ECM,* 102, for the variant *subscriptia* to the letter.

452

nothing in these suggests why a person might be wandering. The logic typi-fies the entire letter. Of all the suggested connections, this has the most going for it: the sin-induced sick person of 5:14-15 could be someone who has wandered from the faith, and the elders being summoned to the bedside could have restoration to the faith as one of their primary hopes. The sugges-tion is contextual and clever and too clever by half because most of the con-text has to be read into the text. Instead, James has simply added this theme to the end of the letter because he is compelled to say what he says.

James 5:19-20 is one sentence, a conditional sentence with a protasis (5:19) describing the pastoral task of restoring and an apodosis (5:20) de-scribing the results of the restoration.

8.8.1. The Restorer's Task (5:19)

Once again, James's approach to this problem is pastoral and communal in his use of "brothers [and sisters]." This sense of family and community glues the audience together in 5:7-20 (*adelphoi* in vv. 7, 9, 10, 12, and 19). The pastoral concern is with someone "among you," that is, a person in the messi-anic community, who "wanders from the truth."[117]

James uses "wander" *(planaō)* only one other time, in 1:16, where it had a softer meaning: "do not be deceived [into thinking less of God]."[118] But here the word broaches what the church has consistently called apostasy.[119] It is used, in one of the most instructive parallels to our text, of a sheep who wanders from the fold and is parabolic for those who are supposed to be re-maining with Jesus in the fold (Matt 18:12-13). Jesus also warned against be-ing led astray by claims of false messiahs and prophets (24:4, 11, 24). Some accused Jesus of leading Israel astray (John 7:12, 47). Deception and wan-dering away were connected to the end times (2 Tim 3:3), and the term was also used of the condition of humans prior to conversion (Tit 3:3; 1 Pet 2:25; 1 John 1:8). A prototypical example of wandering was found in Israel's moral failure in the wilderness (Heb 3:10). Priests, since they are human, are able to empathize with the temptation to wander (Heb 5:2). But the word has a special place in the warnings against apostasy (2 Pet 2:15; 1 John 2:26; 3:7; Rev 2:20; 12:9; 13:14; 18:23; 19:20; 20:3, 8, 10).[120]

117. On the aorist passive subjunctive of πλανάω, "wander," see BDAG, 821-22. On ἀλήθεια, "truth," see BDAG, 42-43. On ἐν ὑμῖν, "among you," see 3:13; 4:1; 5:13, 14.

118. See 1 Cor 6:9; 15:33; Gal 6:7.

119. Martin, 218-19. See also my "Apostasy," in *DTIB,* 58-60; cf. R. Ortlund, "Apostasy," in *NDBT,* 383-86. Byron, 471, connects "wandering" to "Diaspora" of 1:1.

120. As also in the Septuagint and other Jewish sources, where the root issues are the stubborn heart, idolatry, anger, hatred, sexual seduction, avarice, and abuse of wine, all of these at times tied to the devil (Deut 4:19; 11:28; 2 Kgs 21:9; Ps 95:10; Prov 12:26; Tob

It is possible that James has in mind the sorts of sins one finds throughout the letter, including lack of trust, temptations to violence, lack of compassion on the poor and marginalized, speech sins, and temptations to avarice[121] — but James has not even suggested that such persons have "wandered" into apostasy. While such a reading of "wandering" is possible and contextual, it seems preferable to leave this image of wandering both general and as something new to the letter. It is both useful and useless to dissect "wander" into backsliders who return and apostates who do not return. There is a difference, so the distinction is useful for theology and pastoral care. But for our text it is well-nigh useless because one does not know if the people so described were actually restored. For James, this person has wandered, whether apostate or backslider. Put more succinctly, there is no evidence he knew of such distinctions.

James frames the wandering neither in ecclesial terms (as wandering from the community) nor in terms of one's faith (from believing, from the faith), but places it in a category so typical of the biblical world: "from the truth." The addition of "*the way of* truth" in the later manuscripts,[122] while not an indicator of the earliest recoverable texts, does provide a commentary and a clue on how to read "the truth." For James and his Jewish world, "the truth" is both *what* one knows and *how* one lives; truth is the wedding of theology/gospel and praxis.[123] We catch a glimmer of the depth and breadth of this term already in 1:18, where it is said that we are born anew by the "word of truth," and 3:14, where it is said that the ambitious zeal of the teachers leads them to be "boastful and false to the truth."

The Old Testament Hebrew word *'emet* combines the notions of "truth" and "faithfulness" or "reliability." It is a truth upon which God's people rely and in which they trust because the God who stands behind that truth tells the truth, does not deceive, and is reliable (Gen 24:27; Exod 18:21; 34:6; Deut 1:32; Ps 25:10; Prov 8:7; Isa 43:9).[124] In the New Testament, which can

---

5:13; 2 Macc 6:25; Wis 5:6; Sir 31:5; *Testament of Simeon* 2:7; *Testament of Levi* 16:1; *Testament of Judah* 14:1, 8; 19:4; 23:1; *Testament of Dan* 2:4; *Testament of Gad* 3:1; CD 3:1-12; 4Q169 frags. 3-4 2:8; 4Q213a frag. 1:18; 4Q266 frag. 2 1:18; see also 4Q394-99 [4QMMT]). See Davids, 198, for further references.

121. Martin, 218.

122. See above.

123. See Martin, 219. I do not see how Johnson, 337, can say that truth "in this context does not mean theoretical correctness, but rather the proper 'way' of behaving." I can see the latter, but the former denies one of the central dimensions of ἀλήθεια among early Christians.

124. See *TDOT* 1.292-323; *TLOT* 1.134-57. The word "amen" means "indeed, so it is" in the sense that one agrees that what is said or seen is what is supposed to be said or seen.

be sketched more completely, there is "biblical or divine truth" in the sense that something corresponds to what God says in the Bible (Mark 12:14; cf. John 4:23-24; 17:17; Rom 2:20; 15:8; 2 Cor 4:2; 2 Tim 2:15) or to life's questions (John 18:38). There is christological, gospel truth in that in Jesus Christ we see "glory . . . full of grace and truth" (John 1:14; cf. 1:17; 5:33; 14:6; Gal 2:5; Eph 1:13; Col 1:5-6; 1 Pet 1:22) and Jesus is the one who tells the truth about God (John 8:40, 44-46). There is "existential, personal truth" in that humans who come to the light are living in truth (3:21; Eph 4:25; 1 Tim 3:15; 1 John 1:8), and it sets them free (John 8:32; cf. 1 Tim 4:3); those who oppose that truth are suppressing it (Rom 1:18, 25; 2 Thess 2:10). One finds truth through the Spirit, and the Spirit leads to truth (John 14:17; 15:26; 16:13) as that truth unfolds (Acts 10:34).

Some of the more pertinent texts are 2 Timothy 4:4 ("and will turn away from listening to the truth and wander away to myths"); Hebrews 10:26 ("if we willfully persist in sin after having received the knowledge of the truth, there no longer remains a sacrifice for sins"); and 1 John 2:21 ("I write to you, not because you do not know the truth, but because you know it, and you know that no lie comes from the truth"). By speaking of someone who "wanders from the truth," then, James refers to one who has veered away from the truth of the gospel found in Jesus Christ, the way of life rooted in Jesus Christ, and the community that embodies that way of life.[125] Truth, here, is that which corresponds to reality and coheres with the Spirit-shaped gospel understanding of that reality.

The second half of the protasis moves from the wandering one to the restorer's task: "and is brought back by another."[126] Restoring lapsed believers was already a concern in Jesus' teaching, where there was a strong emphasis on forgiveness (Matt 18:21-35; Luke 17:3-4). But it became a bigger concern in the earliest churches and is accompanied by proper pastoral discipline and care in the New Testament texts (Gal 6:1-2; Rom 14:1–15:7; 1 Cor 5; 8:7-13; 10:23–11:1; 1 Thess 5:14; 2 Thess 3:14-15; Heb 4:1; 1 Pet 4:8; 1 John 5:16-17; Jude 22-23). James's text belongs with concerns for forgiveness and pastoral sensitivity, but he further emphasizes in 5:20 the results of restoring the wandering. We find the same emphasis in *2 Clement* 17:1-3:

> Let us repent, therefore, with our whole heart, lest any of us should perish needlessly. For if we have orders that we should make it our busi-

125. See the excellent studies of A. C. Thiselton, "Truth," in *NIDNTT* 3.874-902, and K. Vanhoozer, "Truth," in *DTIB*, 818-22.

126. καὶ ἐπιστρέψῃ τις αὐτόν, or "and if someone restores that person." Both aorists in the protasis are constative, throwing the action into simplicity and into the background so the apodosis can be given emphasis with its present tense imperative and the future indicatives.

ness to tear men away from idols and to instruct them, how much more wrong is it that a soul which already knows God should perish? Therefore let us help one another to restore those who are weak with respect to goodness, so that we may all be saved, and let us admonish and turn back one another. And let us think about paying attention and believing not only now, while we are being admonished by the elders, but also when we have returned home let us remember the Lord's commands and not allow ourselves to be dragged off the other way by worldly desires, but let us come here more frequently and strive to advance in the commandments of the Lord, in order that all of us, being of one mind, may be gathered together into life.

The church has not always done well with those who have lapsed, and one thinks of the Donatist controversy, but at other times it has done well, and one thinks here of the Confessing Church in Germany and the acts of reconciliation in South Africa. But from the beginning there has been a double duty: to warn with clarity those who lapse and to forgive those who come back.[127]

Restoring *(epistrephō)* involves pastoral attention to a person that enables repentance (Mark 4:12; Luke 1:16-17) even more than once (Luke 17:4), pastoral prayer, and the restoration of that person — sometimes — to their previous ministry (Luke 22:32). But James's emphasis is on leading the wandering to repentance: "restore" is frequently connected to repentance (e.g., Acts 9:35; 11:21; 15:19; 26:18; 2 Cor 3:16; 1 Thess 1:9).

8.8.2. The Results of Restoration (5:20)

The NRSV's "you should know" masks a subtle grammatical issue. The subject of the verb is third person singular and could be literally rendered "let the person know."[128] The question is "Which person?" Is James addressing the one who has wandered, the one who restores, or the community? The nearest antecedent would be the restorer, and asking the subject of the verb to refer back to the wanderer (as direct address) creates tension with "brings a sinner back," for it should then have been "brings you back." The singular would be harder to explain if this were addressed to the community, so it seems preferable to take this as addressed to the restorer. The almost distant and clinical words here of James are shifted by the NRSV into direct address ("you should know"), but it seems preferable and more in keeping with James's tone to translate more clinically: "let that person know."

127. See Hermas, *Mandates* 8.10. A similar stance is found at Qumran: cf. 1QS 5:24–6:1.
128. γινωσκέτω, third person singular imperative.

What James wants the restorer to know is that he or she has accomplished two things: the sinner is saved from death, and this restoration covers a multitude of sins. The use here of "sinner" and "sin" *(hamartolos, hamartia)* does not mean that the focus has shifted to sin in general. The concern is still wandering from the truth. Hence, "brings back a sinner from wandering."

First, then, the restorer[129] "will save the sinner's soul from death."[130] James has used "save" in 1:21 ("the implanted word . . . has the power to save your souls") and 2:14 (faith without works is not faith that can save). Behind all this is that God is the one who saves (4:12). But in 5:15 James used the term for physical healing, and it is not impossible that "save the sinner's soul from death" here could refer to the kind of prayer that leads to healing. But, because James uses "soul" in this context and we have a similar expression in 1:21, it is far more likely that the salvation here is spiritual, eternal salvation and not simply physical healing, even if one would not want to separate the two too much.

Immediate death appears to have been the penalty for eating fruit from the forbidden tree (Gen 2:17; 3:3), but this was not carried out. Adam and Eve did experience shame (3:7), fearful hiding from God's presence (3:9), blaming of each other (3:11-13), conflict over control (3:16b), pain (3:16a), laborious efforts to get the earth to yield its fruits (3:17-19), and being thrown out of Eden (3:22-24). They were either set on a course of life that would lead to death, or, and I think this is more probable, they were destined for eternal death. This is one of the emphases of the Old Testament. As Adam and Eve were given a choice, so was Israel: "I call heaven and earth to witness against you today that I have set before you life and death, blessings and curses. Choose life" (Deut 30:19).[131] Or Proverbs 12:28: "In the path of righteousness there is life, in walking its path there is no death."

The same can be found in the New Testament. Thus, Jesus' appearance in Galilee brought life where there had been death (Luke 1:79; Matt 4:16). John's Gospel sees life apart from Christ now as death (5:24), and those who believe in the Son will never taste death, even if they die physically (8:51-52; cf. 1 Cor 15:54-56). Paul thinks similarly (Rom 6:3-4, 9). There is death, and there is (eternal) death (Acts 2:24; 2 Cor 3:7). Christ re-

---

129. ὁ ἐπιστρέψας ἁμαρτωλὸν ἐκ πλάνης ὁδοῦ αὐτοῦ. The aorist substantival participle recaptures the verb from 5:19. The "object" of ἐκ is ὁδοῦ, leaving both πλάνης and αὐτοῦ as adjectives modifying ὁδοῦ. Thus, "from his way of wandering."

130. σώσει ψυχὴν αὐτοῦ ἐκ θανάτου. The future tense, along with καλύψει, emphasizes potentiality in James's depiction of what happens when someone is restored to the truth. σῴζω with ἐκ refers to that from which one is liberated or that from which one escapes. See BDAG, 982-83.

131. See also Job 8:13; Pss 1:6; 2:12; Prov 2:18; 14:12.

leases, or saves, people from the cycle of sin that leads to death (Rom 8:2). Nothing says this like Romans 5:12-21, but James 1:15 can be taken as another version of the same thing. Since it makes no sense to think James thought believers would never die physically, since it seems unlikely that he is referring in 5:19-20 simply to being healed and saved from physical death, and since life and death in an ultimate sense were the options (*Didache* 1), it is probable that James sees "save the sinner's soul from death" as referring to eternal death.

The Greek text does not say "the sinner's soul" but "his life" *(psychēn autou)* and one can conceivably think the "his" is the restorer: that is, by his action of caring for the wanderer the restorer saves his own soul. In fact, there is evidence to support this suggestion, even if it goes against Reformation instincts — something we have seen James do already. God tells Ezekiel that if he does not warn the wicked, both they and he will die; if he warns the wicked, they will not repent but he will save himself (3:16-21; cf. 33:9). Daniel 4:27 can speak of atoning for sins with deeds of righteousness, and 12:3 can say those who lead many to righteousness will be like the stars. Tobit 4:10 and 12:9 say almsgiving saves one from death (see Sir 3:30). In fact, Tobit 12:9-10 is so similar to James 5:20 that many think they have to be read together: "For almsgiving saves from death and purges away every sin. Those who give alms will enjoy a full life, but those who commit sin and do wrong are their own worst enemies."[132] Sirach 3:3 finds atonement in honoring one's father.

Some early Christian texts contain similar ideas. Thus, *2 Clement* 16:4 mixes ideas that will later be separated:

> Charitable giving, therefore, is good, as is repentance from sin. Fasting is better than prayer, while charitable giving is better than both, and "love covers a multitude of sins," while prayer arising from a good conscience delivers one from death. Blessed is everyone who is found full of these, for charitable giving relieves the burden of sin.

Didache 4:6 approaches the same issue: "If you earned something by working with your hands, you will give a ransom for your sins." Perhaps *Barnabas* 19:10 puts James 5:20 in its context: "Remember the day of judgment night and day, and you shall seek out on a daily basis the presence of the saints, either laboring in word and going out to encourage, and endeavoring to save a soul by the word, or with your hands, *working for a ransom for your sins.*" It might be easy to assign these texts to sub-apostolic, and therefore inferior,

---

132. ἐλεημοσύνη γὰρ ἐκ θανάτου ῥύεται καὶ αὐτὴ ἀποκαθαριεῖ πᾶσαν ἁμαρτίαν. οἱ ποιοῦντες ἐλεημοσύνας καὶ δικαιοσύνας πλησθήσονται ζωῆς. οἱ δὲ ἁμαρτάνοντες πολέμιοί εἰσιν τῆς ἑαυτῶν ζωῆς.

days and thoughts, but the line of continuity from Daniel to Barnabas must be given its fair hearing. And a similar idea is found in what Paul tells Timothy: "Pay close attention to yourself and to your teaching; continue in these things, for in doing this you will save both yourself and your hearers" (1 Tim 4:16).

The decision on the referent of "his" alters everything that follows: if it is the restorer, then it is the restorer's soul that is saved from eternal death and the restorer's sins that are covered. If it is the wanderer, then the wanderer's soul is saved and the wanderer's sins are covered. Sophie Laws sees the wanderer as the one saved and the restorer whose sins are forgiven.[133] Such subtlety on the part of James would try his readers, which it still does! Two facts may lead us toward the view that James has the benefits to the restorer in mind in 5:20. The first is the evidence cited above, which clearly connects redemption with such efforts — not that such efforts earn the person his or her redemption but that they are connected. The second is grammar: James is concerned in 5:19a with the wanderer but shifts in 5:19b and the shift, difficult as it is grammatically, is never reversed. The simplest grammatical reading of 5:19b-20 is:

> [And if] a person restores the wanderer, let the restorer know that the one who restores a sinner saves himself from death, and covers a multitude of his own sins.

But one could read it thus:

> [And if] a person restores the wanderer, let the restorer know that the one who restores a sinner restores the wanderer from death and covers a multitude of the wanderer's sins.

But another grammatical consideration may finally yield the light we need. James uses the word "his" *(autou)* twice in 5:20, and it is grammatically likely that they refer to the same person since there are only two words separating them. So, while we cannot extricate ourselves from the difficulty of this grammar, the evidence leans toward the second reading above.[134] The restorer's pastoral actions lead toward two results: he saves a wanderer from death and leads the wanderer toward forgiveness of sins.[135]

The second result of pastoral care for a wanderer is expressed with a

---

133. Support from this is drawn from early Christian citations of 1 Pet 4:8, where the expression refers to the restorer's sins. See Laws, 241.

134. So Davids, 201; Martin, 220; Johnson, 339; Moo, 250-51; Popkes, 356.

135. Laws, 238-39, accurately observes an order issue: "restore" as forgiveness (5:19-20a), save (5:20b), and cover (5:20c). She suggests that since "restore" implies forgiveness, then it is unnecessary to bring up forgiveness again at the end of the verse.

common idiom, probably circulating freely in oral form in the world of James: "and will cover a multitude of sins" (5:20).[136] The expression comes from Proverbs 10:12:

> Hatred stirs up strife,
> but love covers all offenses.[137]

What Proverbs has in mind can be seen by comparing the two verbs "stirs" and "covers." Hatred stirs things up, love seeks to calm things down; hatred wants the fight to occur in the open, love wants the parties to meet in private. Hatred alienates; love conciliates.[138] Peter quotes this passage in 1 Peter 4:8: "Above all, maintain constant love for one another, for love covers a multitude of sins." He knows that loving one another conciliates and creates community. James is moving in the same direction, but, though he takes the line from Proverbs, does not have the word "love," and he narrows the saying's scope. He would have conciliation in mind, but more particularly he has the impact of restoring a wanderer on the wanderer's own moral life and on the community, where fewer sins will occur. So James has in mind the specifics of conciliation: forgiveness promotes personal and community holiness. The word "cover" is used often enough of "covering sin" that it becomes an alternate form for forgiveness. Thus, "Happy are those whose transgression is forgiven, whose sin is covered" (Ps 32:1).[139]

Some suggest James, in "multitude," has in mind the abject state of the sinner or the numerical list of things he or she might have done, but others suggest that he has in mind rather the extent of grace in God's forgiveness.[140] But Psalm 5:10 speaks of "many transgressions," and Ezekiel 28:18, which adds an expression like what we find in James 5:20, does the same.[141] Indeed, God's gracious forgiveness abounds but it abounds over the many, many sins that would have been committed had not the restorer taken up the task.

Like 1 John, the letter ends abruptly, and we can only guess why. My intuition is that it is less an official letter and more a letter-shaped collection

---

136. καὶ καλύψει πλῆθος ἁμαρτιῶν. The accusative πλῆθος is modified by ἁμαρτιῶν, with the latter a genitive of content.

137. μῖσος ἐγείρει νεῖκος, πάντας δὲ τοὺς μὴ φιλονεικοῦντας καλύπτει φιλία in the Septuagint.

138. See Ellen F. Davis, *Proverbs, Ecclesiastes, and the Song of Songs* (Westminster Bible Companion; Louisville: Westminster John Knox, 2000), 76-77.

139. See also Ps 85:2; Sir 5:6. See also BDAG, 505. In the LXX, καλύπτω does not translate "atone" *(kipper)* but "cover" *(kasah);* on which, see *TDOT* 7.259-64. For early Christian texts citing 1 Pet 4:8, see Laws, 240-41.

140. Davids, 200.

141. See also Sir 5:6; 1QH 4.19 speaks of "my deeds and the perverseness of my heart."

of the teachings of James, three of which are added to the end in 5:12-20. One can suggest that James ends on this note because he wants his readers to repent and be restored, which makes sense for the last few verses, but it is a stretch to think 5:19-20 represents the purpose of James. Better yet, it is one of James's purposes to exhort sinners to repent and to encourage elders, teachers, and others to work for the restoration of the wandering. He does not finish up with greetings or benedictions, but this may indicate that he has not yet become aware of the Pauline and Petrine patterns.

INDEX OF AUTHORS

Adamson, J. B., 25, 37, 42, 60, 104, 120, 143, 236, 237, 243, 262
Adler, W., 382
Ådna, J., 24
Alana, O. E., 95
Aland, K., 281
Albl, M. C., 435
Allert, C. D., 29
Allison, D. C., Jr., 23, 38, 65, 75, 108, 115, 126, 127, 141, 171, 185, 286, 425, 426, 427
Amphoux, C. B., 125, 134, 175, 281
Andria, S., 195
Appelbaum, S., 370
Arterbury, A., 257
Augustine of Hippo, 224, 264, 289, 330, 419
Aune, D., 10, 237, 417
Avemarie, F., 227, 261
Aymer, M. P., 4, 39, 312

Baasland, E., 47
Backhaus, K., 374
Badhwar, N. K., 333
Baird, W., 245
Baker, W. R., 10, 35, 40, 42, 43, 136, 137, 138, 141, 146, 162, 164, 267, 316, 328, 424
Baltzer, K., 103
Baly, D., 409
Balz, H. R., 115, 137
Bammel, E., 62

Banks, R., 78, 257, 257
Barnett, P. W., 38
Barrett, C. K., 31
Bartholomew, C., 364
Batten, A., 3, 42, 98, 109, 173
Bauckham, R. A., 3, 5, 9, 13, 14, 16, 18, 19, 21, 22, 23, 24, 27, 32, 35, 43, 44, 54, 55, 62, 64, 65, 109, 136, 178, 183, 259, 262, 263, 280, 285, 286, 337, 364, 389, 408
Beale, G. K., 389
Beasley-Murray, G. R., 195
Becker, J., 62
Beitzel, B. J., 409
Berger, K., 10
Berger, P., 69, 259
Berlin, A., 350
Bernheim, P.-A., 12, 14, 15, 16, 17
Betz, H. D., 403
Biddle, M., 210
Bindemann, W., 8, 42, 302
Bird, M., 246
Black, C., 235
Black, M., 167
Blenkinsopp, J., 84, 269, 300, 385, 417
Blomberg, C. L., 4, 49, 72, 85, 88, 95, 97, 98, 104, 122, 126, 132, 157, 179, 182, 185, 195, 217, 235, 242, 244, 268, 369, 386
Blount, B., 4
Boccaccini, G., 8, 262
Bock, D., 200

462

Bockmuehl, M., 18, 19
Bonhoeffer, D., 225
Borg, M., 347
Borghi, E., 6, 302
Borowitz, E. B., 302
Botha, J. E., 7, 35
Böttrich, C., 387
Boyarin, D., 62, 64
Boyle, M. O'Rourke, 215
Braaten, C. E., 129
Brandon, S. G. F., 17
Bray, G., 282
Brettler, M. Z., 5
Briggs, R. S., 293
Brosend, W. F., II, 27, 138, 179
Brower, K. E., 389
Brown, C., 62, 84, 441
Brown, J. K., 192
Brown, M., 443
Brown, P., 355
Brown, R. E., 62, 75, 96, 116
Brown, R. E., with Meier, J. P., 8
Brown, W. P., 84
Bruce, F. F., 29, 62, 149
Bruckner, J. K., 222
Buber, M., 441
Bultmann, R., 9
Burchard, C., 6, 40, 43, 70, 75, 77, 78,
   92, 95, 98, 108, 120, 126, 128, 163,
   178, 183, 205, 206, 336
Burge, G. M., 225
Byron, G. L., 4, 68, 267, 290, 420, 453
Byron, J., 392

Caird, G. B., 66, 219, 229, 389
Caird, G. B., with L. D. Hurst, 10
Callan, T., 18
Calvin, J., 3, 110, 158, 233, 240, 244
Campbell, C. R., 71, 161
Campbell, D. A., 246
Campbell, R. A., 269, 436, 437
Cantinat, J., 236, 238
Capper, B., 41
Caragounis, C., 195
Cargal, T. B., 2, 39, 42, 48, 49, 65
Carpenter, C., 340
Carroll, M. D., 390

Carson, D. A., 15, 27, 28, 64, 259
Carter, J. C., 4
Carter, P., 256
Casson, L., 279, 370
Catto, S. K., 182
Chaffin, R. F., Jr., 6, 302
Chaine, P., 326
Charles, J. D., 451
Charry, E., 258
Chester, A., 10
Cheung, L. L., 3, 40, 47, 48, 53, 54, 81,
   91, 95, 113, 131, 143, 155, 158, 206,
   259, 299
Childs, B. S., 23, 390
Chilton, B. D., 2, 6, 9, 14, 19, 62, 167,
   248, 259, 269, 331
Cladder, H., 49
Clements, R. E., 385, 417
Coenen, L., 62
Cohen, S. J. D., 32, 112
Cohick, L. H., 182
Coker, J., 259
Collins, J. J., 300, 310
Conzelmann, H., 126
Cook, S. L., 382
Cranfield, C. E. B., 40
Craveri, B., 314
Crenshaw, J. L., 32, 269
Crossan, J. D., 10, 62
Crotty, R., 4, 95
Croy, N. C., 441
Cullmann, O., 389
Curtis, H. D., 441

Daley, B. E., 109, 389
Daniel, D., 419
Dante Alighieri, 388
Daube, D., 438
Dautzenberg, G., 427
Davids, P. H., 2, 15, 19, 33, 37, 42, 46,
   48, 50, 51, 60, 67, 72, 75, 77, 78, 80,
   82, 84, 86, 87, 91, 94, 95, 97, 99, 102,
   103, 105, 109, 110, 111, 112, 114,
   115, 118, 119, 120, 121, 122, 123,
   126, 127, 128, 129, 130, 131, 132,
   135, 136, 140, 141, 142, 143, 149,
   150, 151, 152, 155, 164, 166, 172,

175, 178, 179, 180, 181, 182, 183,
184, 185, 195, 197, 205, 208, 210,
215, 216, 217, 219, 220, 221, 227,
228, 231, 237, 241, 243, 247, 250,
253, 259, 263, 275, 279, 286, 287,
289, 292, 295, 297, 298, 309, 311,
315, 317, 322, 323, 325, 328, 331,
333, 337, 338, 341, 342, 344, 345,
350, 351, 353, 356, 359, 363, 368,
369, 374, 375, 376, 389, 395, 397,
400, 401, 402, 404, 405, 409, 415,
422, 424, 425, 426, 431, 435, 441,
444, 447, 449, 451, 454, 459, 460

Davies, P. R., 15, 248

Davies, W. D., 92, 108, 119, 339

Davis, C. J., 64

Davis, E. F., 460

Deissmann, A., 69, 70

Delling, G., 81

Denyer, N., 152

Derrett, J. D. M., 280, 368

Dibelius, M., 9, 13, 48, 49, 50, 54, 55,
62, 63, 67, 72, 75, 77, 84, 93, 99, 115,
123, 131, 135, 137, 138, 140, 141,
142, 143, 146, 155, 164, 178, 180,
181, 195, 206, 215, 221, 233, 236,
237, 238, 254, 274, 281, 285, 296,
298, 306, 307, 316, 323, 326, 328,
354, 375, 386, 401, 413, 439, 451

Dodd, C. H., 64, 106, 108

Donker, C. E., 235

Doriani, D., 272, 299

Dorsett, L., 172

Doty, W. G., 34

Dowd, S., 263

Doyle, R. C., 389

Dunn, J. D. G., 8, 9, 10, 15, 20, 35, 62,
127, 136, 139, 151, 202, 219, 227,
246, 250, 269, 271, 292, 309, 311

Dyrness, W., 223, 263

Edgar, D. H., 6, 24, 37, 39, 63, 65, 92,
95, 113, 196, 240, 269

Eisenman, R. H., 15

Elliott, J. H., 40, 41, 49, 53, 67, 141,
161, 167

Elliott, J. K., 318

Elliott, M. W., 389

Elliott-Binns, L. E., 130, 280

Ellis, E. E., 64

Enis, L. L., 4

Enns, P., 5, 390

Enright, D. J., 333

Epstein, J., 304, 333

Erasmus, D., 326

Esser, H.-H., 62

Evans, C. A., 2, 12, 13, 15, 22, 167,
259, 262, 268, 304, 331

Evans, M. J., 117, 130

Fanning, B., 71

Farmer, W. R., 18

Feldman, L., 19

Fine, H. A., 420

Fishbane, M., 5, 64, 245, 253, 302, 451

Fishkoff, Sue, 301

Fisk, B., 248, 251, 451

Fitzgerald, J., 333

Fitzmyer, J. A., 33, 248

Flusser, D., 95

Foster, R. J., 447

France, R. T., 268

Francis, F. O., 50, 51, 402

Frankemölle, H., 6, 14, 28, 43, 49, 52,
53, 67, 68, 78, 85, 95, 157, 201, 227,
259, 381, 402

Fredriksen, P., 18

Freeborn, J., 178

Frend, W. H. C., 72, 199, 419

Fretheim, T. E., 390

Freyne, S., 31

Fung, R. Y. K., 259, 263

Furfey, P. H., 97

Gard, D. H., 421

Garland, D. E., 149, 315

Gehring, R. W., 182

Gillespie, T. W., 417

Gnilka, J., 10

Goetzmann, J., 84

Goldingay, J., 5, 192, 193, 351, 390

Gonzalez, J. L., 199

Goodman, M., 19, 322

Goppelt, L., 64

Gordis, R., 96
Gordon, R. P., 417, 422
Gorman, M. J., 322
Gray, P., 421
Gray, R., 417
Green, J. B., 96, 258
Grenz, S., 78, 131
Groothius, R. M., 268, 437
Gruen, E. S., 112
Grünzweig, F., 60
Gundry Volf, J. M., 110
Guthrie, G. H., 54, 75, 262, 262, 266, 289, 369

Haacker, K., 261
Haas, C., 421
Haberman, D. L., 151, 258, 293
Hagner, D. A., 125, 246
Hahn, F., 2, 37, 42
Hamann, H. P., 261
Hamilton, A., 74, 116
Hanson, A. T., 257
Hanson, P. D., 230
Harland, P. A., 62, 182
Harrington, D. J., 439
Harris, M. J., 323
Harris, W. V., 34, 154, 269
Hart, T., 109, 389
Hartin, P. J., 6, 7, 8, 14, 15, 16, 17, 20, 25, 26, 37, 40, 42, 43, 44, 65, 68, 81, 98, 155, 173, 177, 206, 259, 368
Hartley, J. E., 167, 338
Hartman, L., 202
Hasel, G. F., 112
Hayden, D. R., 434
Hays, R. D., 27, 451
Hayward, R., 248
Heard, W., 142, 304
Heine, R. E., 5
Hellerman, J. H., 230
Hempel, J., 443
Hengel, M., 7, 15, 17, 23, 29, 31, 32, 37, 62, 68, 94, 97, 142, 182, 259, 262, 269, 304
Heschel, A. J., 417
Hill, C. C., 68, 389
Hill, C. E., 390

Hill, C. F., 109
Hoekema, A. A., 219
Hoffman, L. A., 113, 196
Hoffmann, E., 112
Hogan, M., 40, 155
Holmén, T., 12, 228
Holmes, S., 389
Hoppe, R., 6, 40, 41, 44, 81, 95, 173, 224, 299
Horsley, R. A., 31, 32
Hort, F. J. A., 130, 179, 236, 237, 238, 279, 280, 281, 328, 331
Howard, G. F., 17
Howard, W. F., 243
Hübner, H., 81
Hughes, P. E., 151, 258, 293
Hurtado, L. W., 43, 64, 126, 201, 202, 311, 433
Huther, J. E., 236

Ilan, T., 257
Isaacs, M. E., 77

Jackson-McCabe, M., 10, 35, 43, 143
Jacobs, I., 245
Jenson, R. W., 129, 293
Jeremias, J., 182, 259, 263, 269, 338, 370, 417, 428
Jervis, L. A., 199
Johanson, B. C., 167
Johnson, E. A., 96
Johnson, L. T., 6, 9, 14, 22, 27, 28, 29, 30, 37, 42, 44, 46, 51, 52, 60, 70, 72, 86, 87, 88, 96, 120, 121, 126, 127, 132, 135, 138, 146, 147, 152, 155, 162, 164, 165, 166, 167, 171, 174, 176, 182, 185, 192, 199, 207, 217, 221, 226, 237, 242, 246, 250, 255, 259, 262, 275, 278, 279, 285, 298, 306, 309, 315, 316, 320, 321, 326, 327, 330, 332, 333, 335, 338, 339, 346, 347, 361, 362, 363, 369, 374, 399, 402, 404, 405, 414, 421, 422, 424, 426, 427, 433, 437, 449, 450, 454, 459
Johnson, T. M., 199
Juel, D., 64

Kaiser, S., 431

Kamell, M. J., 49, 72, 85, 88, 95, 98, 104, 122, 126, 132, 157, 179, 182, 185, 195, 217, 235, 241, 244, 268, 369

Keck, L. E., 95

Kee, H. C., 182, 441

Keener, C. S., 257

Kilpatrick, G. D., 203

Kim, S., 246

Kirk, J. A., 85, 309

Kirkpatrick, L. A., 74, 308

Klauck, H.-J., 34

Klawaans, J., 141

Klein, M., 2, 7, 40, 50, 52, 81, 118, 131, 143

Klijn, A. F. J., 35

Kloppenborg, J. (also Kloppenborg Verbin), 25, 27, 47, 48, 175, 176, 184

Kloppenborg, J. S., 2, 3, 17, 25, 27, 39, 49, 98, 109, 167, 237, 259, 260

Konradt, M., 2, 7, 26, 40, 41, 42, 43, 48, 81, 113, 235, 236, 247, 259, 261

Konstan, D., 333

Kort, W. A., 5

Kraabel, A. T., 185

Kraemer, R. S., 268

Kraus, T. J., 31

Kugel, J., 5, 91, 141

Laato, T., 246

Ladd, G. E., 333

Lambers-Petry, D., 17

Laws, S., 28, 63, 67, 75, 80, 82, 87, 91, 93, 95, 99, 101, 102, 103, 105, 110, 111, 112, 114, 118, 122, 124, 126, 129, 130, 137, 140, 141, 142, 143, 148, 151, 154, 171, 172, 178, 180, 181, 182, 188, 195, 197, 200, 212, 216, 220, 221, 230, 231, 236, 241, 242, 245, 253, 270, 275, 286, 288, 289, 296, 298, 304, 305, 322, 323, 325, 326, 329, 336, 337, 338, 340, 341, 343, 347, 353, 359, 363, 368, 369, 375, 376, 378, 383, 386, 388, 393, 395, 397, 402, 404, 409, 410,

413, 415, 420, 422, 425, 426, 431, 440, 442, 444, 448, 459

Levenson, J. D., 248, 250

Levine, A.-J., 96, 256

Levine, L. I., 31, 182

Levinskaya, I., 19

Levison, J. R., 311

Lewis, C. S., 294, 328, 377, 394

Lieu, J. M., 61, 62, 112, 384

Limberis, V., 262

Lindars, B., 64

Llewelyn, S. R., 59

Lockett, D., 7, 141, 167, 284, 312, 352

Lodge, J. G., 225

Longenecker, R., 64, 201, 202, 245, 263, 398

Lorenzen., T., 223, 224, 263

Loughlin, G., 5

Lowe, B. A., 177

Lucas, E. C., 310

Luck, U., 71

Luckmann, T., 69

Ludwig, M., 6, 131

Luedemann, G., 29

Lund, N., 135

Luomanen, P., 35, 36

Luther, M., 30, 47, 215, 223, 224, 326

Magness, J., 16

Malherbe, A. J., 48, 60, 61

Malina, B. J., 200, 331

Marcus, J., 119

Marshall, I. H., 110, 419

Martens, E., 112, 385

Martin, R. P., 8, 10, 14, 15, 20, 28, 29, 37, 38, 42, 51, 63, 67, 68, 75, 77, 80, 82, 86, 87, 88, 92, 94, 95, 96, 97, 99, 101, 102, 109, 110, 111, 118, 119, 120, 121, 126, 127, 128, 129, 131, 134, 138, 140, 142, 150, 151, 154, 158, 162, 164, 168, 171, 172, 174, 178, 180, 181, 185, 189, 193, 195, 206, 207, 208, 216, 218, 219, 221, 223, 236, 253, 255, 259, 268, 271, 274, 275, 276, 279, 281, 283, 284, 288, 289, 299, 316, 320, 322, 327, 330, 336, 337, 346, 351, 356, 363,

368, 369, 370, 371, 378, 390, 397,
398, 399, 407, 408, 409, 418, 420,
421, 432, 433, 439, 450, 453, 454,
459
Martyn, J. L., 20
Maynard-Reid, P. U., 4, 46, 94, 95, 99,
173, 185, 368, 369, 370, 381, 386
Mayor, J. B., 25, 30, 49, 64, 70, 72, 75,
77, 80, 82, 84, 86, 87, 89, 91, 95, 97,
98, 100, 102, 103, 135, 138, 139, 140,
141, 146, 148, 150, 152, 153, 154,
162, 178, 236, 238, 254, 279, 326,
328, 353, 354, 386, 399, 448
Mayordomo-Marin, M., 386
McCormack, B. L., 246
McDonald, L. M., 29
McHugh, J., 96
McKay, K. L., 199, 209, 268, 351
McKnight, S., 2, 16, 17, 18, 66, 71, 74,
78, 96, 103, 110, 126, 143, 151, 155,
167, 168, 170, 195, 200, 210, 219,
235, 237, 268, 292, 293, 354, 384,
411
Meeks, W., 333
Meier, J. P., 16
Mendels, D., 322
Metzger, B. M., 29, 127, 234, 281
Meyers, E. M., 32
Michaelis, W., 74
Michl, J., 336
Middleton, J. R., 151, 293
Millard, A., 34, 154, 269, 300
Miller, J. D., 105, 130
Miller, P., 2, 37, 42
Miller, P. D., 87
Minear, P. S., 230, 424
Mitchell, M. M., 1, 259, 260, 262
Mitton, C. L., 237
Modica, J. B., 200
Mohrlang, R., 111
Montefiore, H., 24, 92, 196, 207
Moo, D. J., xii, 41, 42, 51, 52, 88, 89,
93, 97, 98, 100, 110, 118, 120, 127,
139, 155, 184, 205, 223, 227, 239,
247, 252, 254, 262, 263, 267, 271,
278, 280, 283, 286, 288, 289, 296,
300, 302, 305, 309, 312, 316, 325,

326, 327, 328, 333, 345, 351, 356,
359, 362, 363, 368, 369, 376, 383,
387, 390, 397, 399, 402, 405, 410,
411, 417, 420, 421, 425, 435, 436,
438, 439, 441, 442, 449, 459
Morrice, W. G., 72
Morris, L. L., 113
Motyer, J. A., 219
Moule, C. F. D., 77, 102, 124, 150, 153,
189, 371, 374, 451
Moulton, J. H., 243
Mounce, W. D., 63, 178
Mussner, F., 2, 3, 30, 37, 40, 42, 70, 74,
82, 88, 95, 118, 157, 174, 181, 184,
205, 236, 263, 268, 274, 283, 322,
328, 336, 396, 421, 425, 427
Myllykoski, M., 2, 15, 19, 20

Naselli, A. D., 71
Neusner, J., 2, 6, 12, 19, 62, 258
Neyrey, J. H., 183, 187, 200, 331
Ng, E. Y. L., 42, 70, 127, 168
Nicol, 260
Niebuhr, K.-W., 13
Niederwimmer, K., 306
Noack, B., 40, 368
Noort, E., 248
Novak, D., 129, 193
Nystrom, D. P., xii, 40, 42, 52, 79, 98,
263, 277, 327, 383, 425

O'Connor, F., 181
Oden, A. G., 257
O'Fearghail, F., 48, 51
Ollenburger, B. C., 112
Omanson, R. L., 234, 264, 265, 318, 367
Ortlund, R., 453
Osborn, E. F., 302

Pachuau, L., 5
Paget, J. C., 19
Painter, J., 5, 9, 14, 15, 16, 17, 18, 20,
39, 62
Palmer, D. V., 223
Palmer, F. H., 131
Patzia, A. G., 7, 78
Penner, T. C., 2, 3, 7, 8, 14, 25, 26, 28,

29, 34, 41, 47, 48, 49, 53, 67, 73, 105, 109, 259, 262, 263, 341
Perdue, L., 13, 48
Perkins, P., 6
Perriman, A., 390
Perry, T., 96
Peters, T., 210
Peterson, D. G., 172, 252
Pfleiderer, O., 237
Phillips, J. B., 326
Pickar, C., 439
Pierce, R. W., 268, 437
Piper, J., 246
Pitre, B., 67
Plantinga, C., Jr., 120, 210
Pohl, C. D., 257
Poirier, J. C., 125
Popkes, W., xx, 2, 5, 13, 14, 27, 28, 39, 49, 52, 53, 67, 72, 75, 81, 88, 91, 98, 103, 118, 119, 122, 125, 130, 132, 135, 137, 142, 143, 163, 166, 169, 174, 178, 179, 181, 182, 183, 185, 194, 201, 205, 209, 219, 220, 227, 229, 230, 231, 235, 239, 241, 242, 244, 246, 259, 261, 262, 263, 275, 279, 283, 286, 289, 296, 300, 302, 305, 306, 307, 309, 312, 313, 314, 315, 316, 322, 324, 329, 332, 335, 340, 346, 353, 354, 356, 357, 358, 359, 363, 364, 370, 375, 377, 379, 381, 396, 397, 408, 416, 420, 421, 425, 427, 432, 435, 439, 447, 448, 449, 451, 459
Porter, S. E., 33, 71, 77, 91, 124, 141, 153, 209, 347, 351, 360, 375, 386, 391, 437, 442
Porter, V. V., Jr., 26
Porterfield, A., 441
Pratscher, W., 8, 14, 15, 16, 17, 20
Price, J. L., 20
Pritz, R. A., 35, 62
Prockter, L. J., 331
Proctor, M., 260
Proudfoot, W., 74, 308
Przybylski, B., 140, 246

Rad, G. von, 385

Rainbow, P., 64
Rapinchuk, M., 32
Rapske, B. M., 279
Rawlinson, D., 333
Rehkopf, F., 311, 369, 370, 383
Reicke, B., 138, 180, 181
Reinink, G. J., 35
Reiser, M., 103, 219
Rendtorff, R., 350
Rese, J. M., 49
Reumann, J., 43, 139
Richards, E. R., 34
Richardson, P., 182
Ridderbos, H. R., 151
Riesner, R., 183, 268
Riley-Smith, J., 322
Robbins, V. K., 35
Roberts, D. J., 167
Robinson, J. A. T., 25
Robinson, J. M., 20
Rolland, P., 38, 261
Rook, R., 389
Ropes, J. H., 49, 60, 63, 67, 70, 71, 72, 75, 77, 80, 84, 86, 87, 91, 92, 93, 95, 96, 97, 98, 100, 102, 103, 112, 115, 127, 137, 140, 142, 143, 146, 152, 153, 154, 161, 162, 164, 168, 171, 172, 174, 178, 187, 236, 237, 238, 241, 247, 254, 280, 281, 319, 323, 333, 388, 410, 424, 448

Safrai, S., 270
Safrai, Z., 370, 391, 410
Sanders, E. P., 140, 147, 148, 160, 199, 207, 212, 246
Sanders, J. A., 262
Sanders, J. T., 253
Sawicki, M., 331
Schechter, S., 310
Schippers, R., 81
Schlatter, A., 237
Schmidt, T. E., 386
Schmitt, J. J., 331, 332
Schnabel, E., 7
Schneider, G., 236, 237
Schnelle, U., 258, 324
Schrage, W., 115, 137

Schwartz, F. W., 302
Schwarz, H., 109, 389
Schweizer, E., 269
Seebass, H., 144
Segal, A. F., 248
Seitz, C. R., 421
Selwyn, E. G., 141
Setzer, C., 7, 62
Sevenster, J. N., 33
Shaver, P., 74, 308
Shaw, T. M., 355
Shepherd, M., 26
Shogren, G., 438
Shults, F. L., 114, 258, 293
Shultz, C. E., 268
Sider, R. A., 3, 146, 386
Sigal, P., 38, 40, 155
Siker, J. S., 242, 245, 250, 263
Skarsaune, O. (with R. Hvalvik), 8, 10, 35, 62
Smith, J., 278
Snodgrass, K., 192, 263, 409
Soards, M. L., 245
Sohn, S. T., 193
Soulen, R. K., 129
Spicq, C., 63, 74, 75, 82, 95, 108, 109, 111, 113, 131, 132, 163, 178, 313, 314, 343, 353, 370, 441
Spilka, B., 74, 308
Shaver, P., 308
Spitta, F., 281
Stacey, W. D., 417
Stackhouse, J., 268, 287, 437
Stählin, G., 424
Stark, R., 199
Stauffer, E., 155
Steer, S., 287
Stegemann, E. W., 7, 35, 62, 78
Stegemann, W., 7, 35, 62, 78
Stevenson, L., 151, 258, 293
Stott, J., 447
Stowers, S. K., 60, 237
Strecker, G., 10, 13, 26, 31, 39, 42, 259, 263
Stuhlmacher, P., 9, 246
Swartley, W. M., 231, 313, 316
Swindell, A. C., 248

Syreeni, K., 38, 259

Tabor, J. D., 17
Tamez, E., 3, 4, 13, 42, 46, 73, 80, 81, 95, 99
Tasker, R. V. G., 30, 378
Taylor, J., 18
Taylor, M. E., 48, 49, 53, 54, 266, 367
Taylor, S. S., 233
Theissen, G., 40, 441
Thiselton, A. C., 4, 171, 226, 258, 455
Thomas, J. C., 435
Thurén, L., 53
Tiessen, T., 116
Tigchelaar, E., 248
Tiller, P. A., 46, 195
Tippens, D., 447
Tollefson, K. D., 39, 49
Toon, P., 130, 353
Townsend, M. J., 321
Travis, S. H., 415
Treier, D., 9, 233
Trudinger, L. P., 17
Tsuji, M., 13, 262
Turner, N. (also MHT 3, 4), 28, 31, 68, 79, 81, 90, 91, 102, 137, 153, 172, 174, 178, 181, 215, 287
Twelftree, G., 308, 347, 440

Unnik, W. C. van, 166
Urbach, E. E., 222, 375

Vagany, L., 281
Van Landingham, C., 246, 247
VanderKam, J. C., 382
Vanhoozer, K., 4, 192, 293, 335, 455
Verene, D. P., 269
Vermes, G., 31, 248, 449
Verseput, D. J., xi, xiii, 6, 7, 13, 41, 47, 66, 123, 124, 247, 259, 260
Viviano, B. T., 157
Volf, M., 78
Vouga, F., 43, 51, 71

Wachob, W. H., 7, 14, 23, 25, 27, 39, 45, 173, 180, 191, 195, 207, 221, 408
Walker, P. W. L., 11

Wall, R., 4, 5, 6, 9, 13, 14, 37, 41, 99, 143, 155, 157, 178, 181, 217, 233, 250, 259
Wallis, J., 146
Walsh, J. T., 449
Waltke, B. K., 130
Ward, R. B., 175, 185, 245, 251
Warden, D., 4
Warrington, K., 431, 435
Watson, D. F., 17, 49, 236, 237, 246, 267, 270
Webb, W., 268, 437
Webb, R. L., 2, 3, 17, 25, 27, 39, 49, 98, 109, 167, 237, 259, 260
Webster, J., 172
Wedderburn, A. J. M., 18
Weems, R. J., 332
Wehnert, J., 18
Weigelt, H., 84
Weiser, W., 289, 387
Welzen, H., 40, 42
Wenell, K. J., 11
Wenham, J. W., 9
Werline, R. A., 445
Wesley, J., 81, 95
Westcott, B. F., 281
Westerholm, S., 246
Westermann, C., 381
Westhuizen, J. D. N., 225, 403
Wheeler, S. E., 98, 382, 386
White, J. L., 60, 425
Wilken, R. L., 11

Wilkinson, J., 435
Williams, H. H. D., III, 98
Williams, R. I., 95
Williams, R. H., 182
Williamson, H. G., 64
Wilson, R. R., 417
Wilson, S. G., 18
Wilson, W. T., 114, 119
Windisch, H., 236
Wink, W., 308
Wiseman, D. J., 256
Witherington, B., III, 16, 29, 49, 149, 183, 219, 235, 259, 389, 403
Wolff, H. W., 144, 258, 352
Wolmaran, J. L. P., 116
Wolterstorff, N., 316
Wolverton, W. I., 91
Wood, L. J., 449
Work, T., 5, 192
Woyke, J., 346
Wright, C. J. H., 5, 116, 130
Wright, D. F., 96
Wright, N. T., 4, 73, 139, 219, 246, 355, 389
Wuellner, W., 52

Yates, J., 30
Yoder, P. B., 312

Zahn, T., 236
Zimmerli, W., 108
Zimmermann, A. F., 268, 269, 271

INDEX OF SUBJECTS

Abraham, 244-56
Anawim, 62, 77, 94, 95, 96, 99, 142, 170, 171, 194, 195, 344, 369, 400
Aqedah, 244-45, 247-48, 250-56

Christology, 59-68, 175-80, 200-201, 206

Day of Atonement, 211

Eikon. See Image of God
Ethics, 43-47

Faith, 7, 40, 46, 75, 77-80, 83, 86, 88, 89, 90, 113, 121, 123, 143, 146, 160, 161, 164, 166, 167, 173, 175-80, 181, 185, 188, 189, 190, 191, 195, 198, 199, 218, 223, 224-63, 440-42
Favoritism, 174-203, 318-58
Friendship, 331-35

God, 42-43, 122-32; as Father, 122-28
Gospel, 132

Image of God, 5

James (author, apostle), 9-11; life of, 16-23; name of, 14; ossuary of, 15-16
James (book); authorship, 13-38; canon, 29-30; genre, 47-49, 59-60; introduction, 1-55; and Jesus, 25-28; land, 11-12; and Matthew, 26-28; and Paul, 259-63; and Q, 26-28; and Story, 4-13; structure, 47-55; style of, 28-34; theology, 34-47. *See also* Ethics; God
Jesus Creed. *See Shema*
Joy, 72-75
Judging, 188-90, 218-24, 271
Justification, 242-63

Love. *See Shema*

Magnificat, 62, 77, 94, 96, 98, 100, 108, 160, 189, 194
Mary, 16, 36, 62, 96, 99, 154, 161, 194. *See also Magnificat*
Maturity. *See* Perfection

Oppression, 174-203, 379-400

Partiality. *See* Favoritism
Paul, 3, 7
Perfection, 80-82, 123-28, 153-61
Poverty, 70-77, 93-104, 106-14, 174-90, 190-203, 226-33
Prayer, 83-93, 329-31, 430-52

Rahab, 244, 256-59
Reformation, 10, 11, 158, 211, 223

Shema, 6, 24, 29, 44, 46, 64, 65, 92, 113, 124, 136, 148, 155-58, 161, 170, 173, 176, 189, 192, 196, 203-24, 229, 234, 240, 241, 263, 363, 364, 409,

471

Sin, 118-22, 209-18
Speech, 134-44, 163-66, 264-97, 358-66

Teachers 264-366
Testing, 70-77, 106-22
Tongue. *See* Speech
Torah, 3, 5, 6, 8, 145-61. *See also*
  Shema
Trials. *See* Testing

Violence, 134-44

Wealth, 97-102, 181-90, 196-99, 366-
  423
Wisdom, 6, 7, 46, 47, 48, 49, 69, 82, 84-
  98, 108, 109, 123, 124, 125, 128, 133,
  136, 149, 154, 161, 166, 172, 179,
  218, 297-318
Women in Ministry, 268
Works, 145-61, 162-72, 224-63

INDEX OF SCRIPTURE REFERENCES

References in footnotes are not indexed unless the text is discussed.

OLD TESTAMENT

Genesis

1–2	5
1	132
1:26-27	151, 189, 287, 294
1:28	287
2:7	258, 338
2:17	457
3	5, 122
3:2	317
3:3	457
4:3	317
4:7	119
4:10	392
4:15	408
6–9	331
6:3	338
6:5	119, 331
6:9	81
6:17	258
8:20	168
8:21	119
9:2	287
9:6	294
12–50	436
12	5

15	253, 254, 262
15:6	234, 244, 245, 247, 253, 254, 255, 261, 262
15:16	254
17	5
17:1	81
17:2	350
17:4	350
17:5	234
17:6-8	350
18–22	253, 256
18	250
18:18	250
19	87
19:28	373
22	5, 115, 244, 249, 250, 253, 254
22:1-19	248
22:9	248
22:18	250
24:27	454
25	62
27:36	62
28	127
30:2	317
31:1	180
31:13	439

37:34	355
38:26	246
41:38-39	311
45:13	180
48:14	438

Exodus

2:2	256
2:11-14	390
2:23	392
2:23-25	390, 414
3:14-15	364
6:2-8	350
18:21	454
19–24	5
19:10	351, 352
19:22	350
20:1-17	216, 240
20:3	364
20:5	337, 338
20:6	113, 196
20:7	200, 427
20:12-16	391
22:10-11	427
22:22	168
23:16	317
23:20-21	200
28:36	103

28:41	439	25:46	70	10:17-18	179
29:4	351	26–27	209, 293, 443	10:17	176
29:17	351	26:25	408	10:18	168
30:19-21	351	26:40	445	11:14	409
31:1-11	311			14:2	193
34:6-7	423, 454	**Numbers**		15:3	70
34:14	337, 338	3:3	439	16:16	350
39:30	103	5:5-10	445	17:12	344
40:12	351	6:3	352	18:13	81
40:15	439	8:10	438	21:23	168
		11:25-30	337	22:5	183
Leviticus		12:1-8	361	23:22	378
4:4	351	12:3	302	23:23	379
4:12	168	14:39	355	24:15	391
5:1	429	15:37-41	240	26:7	194
5:5-6	445	18:22	289	26:13	159
7:19	168	25:1-13	304	27:6	82
8:9	103	30:3-15	427	27:9-10	107
14:15	351			27:15	106
15:5-8	351	**Deuteronomy**		27:26	155
16:13	373	1:13	299	28	41, 109, 209,
16:21	445	1:15	299		293, 443
17–18	18	1:32	454	28:4	106
17:15-16	351	4:7	350	28:10	200
18:24	168	4:17-18	287	28:11	317
19	6	4:23	159	28:21-22	443
19:12	6, 176, 427	4:24	338	28:27-29	443
19:12-18	6	4:37-38	193	30:1	143
19:13	6, 176, 391	5:6-7	364	30:11-14	143
19:15	6, 176, 189, 204,	5:6-21	216, 240	30:15-20	41
	205, 207, 208,	5:10	113, 196	30:19	457
	210, 214	5:11	427	32:35	408
19:16	6, 361, 363	5:16-20	391	32:39	365
19:17	6, 176	5:17	216	34:9	311, 438
19:18	6, 29, 45, 65,	6:3-5	192		
	113, 132, 148,	6:4-5	*see* 6:4-9	**Joshua**	
	173, 176, 189,	6:4-9	6, 45, 148, 173,	2	256
	196, 197, 203,		176, 229, 234,	3:5	352
	204, 205, 206,		240, 241, 363,	6:16-25	256
	207, 208, 209,		364, 366	9:11	436
	210, 214, 222,	6:12	159	19:5	410
	227, 241, 275,	6:13	427	19:8	410
	361, 363, 366,	6:16	118	24:10	451
	408, 414	7:7-8	193	24:20	385
22:27	250	7:25	274		
25	157	9:1	192		

Judges
5:20	127
9:4	243
9:7-15	296
11:5-11	436
18:6	231
19:5	410
19:6	369
19:8	410

Ruth
3:3	439

1 Samuel
1:17	231
2:6-7	365
4:2-3	274
4:10	274
7:10	274
9:16	392
17:45	393
20:42	231
29:7	231

2 Samuel
2:17	436
10:19	274
12:16-23	87
12:20	439
14:2	439
15:9	231

1 Kings
3:1-14	87
3:9	192
3:12	192
4:29	299
8:33	274
17–18	450, 449, 450
17:1	449, 451
18:1	449
18:26	148
19:10	304
19:14	304

2 Kings
17	416, 443
23:10	285

1 Chronicles
7:22	355
15:12	352
15:14	352
29:10	292
29:25	180

2 Chronicles
1:7-13	87
15:1-4	349
20:7	255
28:15	439
29:5	352
29:15-19	352

Ezra
5:5	436
9–10	109
10	445

Nehemiah
9:8	248
9:25	394

Esther
2:12	439

Job
4:17	272
5:11	357
7:3	420
7:11-16	421
10:1	441
10:18	421
13:28	386
20:28	385
22:21	420
24:12	414
27:3	338
28:28	299
30:20-23	421
33:5	420

38:7	127
38:39–39:12	287
42:7-17	422

Psalms
1	41, 397
1:1-5	351
1:2	156
1:5-6	449
2:12	449
5:10	460
7:17	434
9:18	194
9:21 [LXX]	365
10	396
10:2	344
10:14	194
12:5	353
12:6	312
17:1-6	393
17:6	392
17:9	354
17:10	343
18:6	393
18:27	194
18:49	434
19:7-11	156
19:12	272
24:3-4	351
25:10	454
26:6	351
26:8 [LXX]	103
30	433
31:2	393
31:5	258
31:18	343
31:23	344
32:1	460
32:5	445
34:15-17	330
35:13-14	438
37	397, 403
37:23	371
38:3	443
38:6	354

39:7	109	1:5	303	**Ecclesiastes**	
42:1	338	1:31	317	10:16-17	107
42:2	337	2:6	310	10:19	356
50:2 [LXX]	103	2:6-8	85		
50:14	427	3	378	**Isaiah**	
50:20	361	3:6-8	372	1:6	408
51	87	3:17	313	1:16	351
51:3-4	445	3:34	319, 336, 337,	1:17	169
57:7	410		340, 341, 342,	3:9-10	399
58:3-4	290		343, 344, 347,	3:10	22
64:3	295		362	3:11–4:1	381
71:5	109	4:10-27	41	3:14-15	397
73:13	352	5	121	5	381
77	433	5:4	295	5:5	393
78:19	361	7	121	5:7	392, 393
84:2	337, 338	8:7	454	5:16	393
85:2	460	8:13	344	5:24	393
85:10	317	8:22-31	310	6:9-10	447
90:3-6	101, 102	8:30-31	310	7:13	192
93:1 [LXX]	103	9:1-6	86	8:6-8	381
94:1	408	9:7-12	303	10:17	280
94:21	397	10:9	88	11:2	311
103:3	444	10:12	460	11:3-4	194
103:15-16	101, 102	10:24	330	13–27	381
103:21	393	11:30	317	13:6	384
104:13	317	12:18	273, 288	14:12	127
106:2	297	12:28	457	14:31	384
106:30	304	13:2	317	15:1-3	384
107:43	297	14:21	197	16:7	384
118	22	15:26	312	21:7	148
119:16	159	15:29	449	27:9	317
119:20	337, 338	16:9	371	29:13	350
119:45	157	16:14	438	30:19	451
119:51	343	16:27	282, 286	30:25	395
119:69	343	17:27	137	30:27	282, 388
119:78	343	18:5	176	30:30	388
119:131	338	18:20	317	32:15	143
119:133	371	18:21	291	32:17	318
119:174	338	19:21	375	33–35	381
136	127	20:9	272	34:2	395
140:3	290, 387	21:24	377	34:6	395
145:18	330, 350	22:22	197	34:8	408
		27:1	372, 378	34:16-17	143
Proverbs		28:13	445	40:2	101, 102
1:1-7	85, 303			40:6-8	101, 102

40:7	102, 103	20:7-9	416	10:3	439
41:8	254, 255	22:13	392	12:7	451
43:6	369	25:34	395	12:12	109, 419
43:7	200	29:1	436		
43:9	454	29:12-14	88	**Hosea**	
45:21	18	31	5, 143	1–3	332
46:13	139	31:31-34	143, 146, 158	2:5-7	381
51:8	387	31:33	143	3:5	18
53:5	448	48:15	395	9:1	332
53:7	395	50:27	395	13:3	373
53:7-8	400	51:40	395	14:3	169
54:1-6	332				
54:11-12	21	**Lamentations**		**Joel**	
55:11	335	1:1-2	384	1:2	192
57:3	332	1:8	414	1:5-11	385
58	189	1:21	414	2:12-13	355
59:21	143			2:28-32	143
61:2	408	**Ezekiel**			
63:16	292	7:14-23	395	**Amos**	
63:19	200	8:1	436	1:12	388
65:12	395	13:10-12	439	1:14	388
65:14	384	15:7	388	3:1-4	381
66:11	394	16:23-26	332	4:1-3	98, 381
		16:38	332	5:11-12	397
Jeremiah		16:49	394	6:1-7	381
2:2	332	21:6-7	414	6:12	317
3:6-14	332	21:12	384	7:10-17	381
3:20	332	21:15	395	8:3	384
4:13	354	22:7	169	8:10	356
4:14	351	23:45	332	9:11-12	18, 67
5:14	388	24:6	387		
7:31	285	24:11	387	**Obadiah**	
9:1	384	24:12	387	10	395
9:19	354	28:12	294		
9:23-24	96, 97, 98, 305	28:18	460	**Micah**	
10:20	354	36:22-38	143	1:2	192
10:23	371	37:8-10	258	2:1-2	397
12:3	395	47:15-17	19	2:4	354
12:12	354	48:1	19		
12:15	18			**Habakkuk**	
12:16	427	**Daniel**		1:4	198
15:3	395	3:42	313		
17:9	272	4:27	458	**Zechariah**	
19:6	395	5:11-12	300	1:3	349
20:1-6	381	7:25	451	11:2	384
				11:4	395

11:7	395	6:11	371	10:41	111
14:9	364	6:13	75, 115	11:1	206
		6:17	439	11:12-13	348
Malachi		6:19	386	11:19	301
3:5	198	6:19-20	389	11:29	302
3:6	128	6:19-34	102, 387	12:36	219
3:7	350	6:22	88	12:39	332, 332
4:5-6	450	6:22-23	125	13:15	447
		6:24	26	13:18	192
		6:25-34	26, 371	13:19	132
NEW TESTAMENT		6:34	372	13:24-30	362, 408
		7:1-5	26, 362	13:25	334, 334
Matthew		7:1-23	167	13:28	334, 334
1–2	5	7:7	85, 329, 329	13:36-43	362, 408
1:1-17	151	7:7-9	25	13:39	334
1:18	151	7:7-11	88, 125	13:42	388
2:17	254	7:11	273	13:48	253
2:18	384	7:12-27	146, 148	13:55	15
3:6	445	7:15-21	256	14:20	231
3:7-10	260	7:15-23	220	15:1-20	157
4:1-11	75	7:15-27	227, 305	15:2	436
4:16	457	7:16	296	15:10	192
5:3	107, 195	7:21-23	149	15:10-11	294
5:5	11, 25	7:21-28	363	15:16-20	294
5:6	231	7:22	440	15:19	189
5:7	25	7:23	138	15:37	231
5:9	25, 313, 316	7:24	132, 192	16:4	332
5:10-12	25, 72, 199	7:24-27	25	16:21	436
5:11	107	7:26	132	16:26	370
5:11-12	361, 419	7:28	206	16:27	219, 247
5:12	26, 111, 417	8–9	169	17:5	192
5:13-16	11	8:5-13	33	17:24	206
5:17	254	8:8	132	18:12-13	453
5:17-20	157, 158, 206,	8:16	132	18:15	445
	253	8:16-17	444, 448	18:21-35	455
5:17-48	220	9:5-7	442	19:21	25, 81, 82
5:19	25	9:32-34	200	19:28	67, 130
5:21-22	217, 273, 327	10:3	14	20:1-16	111, 391
5:22	25, 286	10:4	14	20:8	392
5:33-37	26, 424, 425,	10:8	434	21–23	406
	426, 427	10:16-25	199, 200	21:1	411
5:34-35	200, 428	10:19-20	199	21:5	302
5:39	400	10:22	109, 419	21:23	436
5:48	25, 81, 82, 158	10:23	219, 415	21:33	192
6:1	111	10:28	365	21:34	411
6:10	376				

23	271, 272, 315, 381, 425	**Mark**		12:13-17	33	
23:2-5	315	1:15	389, 411	12:14	455	
23:6	182	1:19	15	12:28-32	24, 113, 157, 158, 189, 196, 206, 207, 220, 241, 366	
23:6-7	187	1:21-28	348			
23:6-8	269	1:24	242			
23:6-10	315	1:31	442			
23:8	71	1:44	388	12:39	182	
23:11-12	315	2:5	441, 444	13	406, 412	
23:12	357	2:7	200	13:9-13	199	
23:16-22	315, 424, 425	2:13-14	33	13:13	109, 110	
23:23-24	315	3:11	242	13:26-31	412	
23:28	314	3:13-19	67	13:29	415	
23:29-32	417	3:17	15, 62	13:30	219	
23:29-36	315	3:18	14, 62	14:6	138	
23:33-39	417	4:12	456	14:12-26	5	
24	406	5:23	441	14:25	317	
24:6	321	5:26	330	14:61	200, 291	
24:13	419	5:34	231, 441	14:62	200	
24:29	406	5:36	441	15:2-5	33	
25:16-17	370	5:38-39	384	15:40	14	
25:20	370	6:3	15, 16, 62	16:1	14, 439	
25:22	370	6:6	441			
25:31-46	146, 219, 220, 230	6:7	429	**Luke**		
25:36	169, 230, 434, 444	6:11	388	1–2	99, 142	
		6:13	439	1:3	306	
		6:14	448	1:5	230	
25:38	230	7:2-5	351	1:8	230	
25:40	71	7:20-23	273	1:16-17	456	
25:43	169	7:21	118, 189	1:46-55	77, 94, 160, 189	
25:43-44	230	7:22	343	1:48	96, 187, 194	
26:3	436	7:25-30	33	1:51	343	
26:45-46	411	7:34	414	1:52-53	96, 194, 195	
26:47	436	8:27-30	33	1:68	169	
26:63-64	427	8:31–9:1	322	1:71	334	
26:75	384	8:34–9:1	109, 199	1:74	334	
27:20	436	8:38	332	1:78	169	
27:24	398	9:1	219, 415	1:79	457	
27:39	200	9:23	441	2:25-38	194	
27:51	306	9:27	442	2:35	189	
27:56	14	9:38	440	2:39	206	
28:12	436	9:47-48	388	3:7-14	227	
28:16-20	201	10:19	391	4:16-30	94	
28:20	363	10:35-45	100, 175, 334	4:18-19	311	
		10:52	441	4:25	451	
		11:1	411	4:40	434	

5:22	189	11:49	417	23:12	334
6:8	442	12:4	255	23:28	384
6:14	15	12:11-12	199	23:46	258
6:15	14, 322	12:13-21	103	23:47	398
6:16	14	12:22-31	26	24:10	14
6:20	195	12:47	378	24:38	189
6:20-26	77, 94, 106,	12:48	271		
	189, 194, 195,	12:49	280	**John**	
	309	12:50	206	1	5
6:21	384	12:56	103	1:1-14	132
6:22-23	25, 417	13:22	103	1:12-13	130
6:23	26	14:7-14	187	1:14	455
6:24	99	14:11	357	1:17	455
6:24-26	107, 381	14:15-24	103	3:3	130
6:25	355, 356	14:31	321	3:12	306
6:28	293	15:14	330	3:14	179
6:35	200	15:14-21	353	3:20	309
6:36	25	15:25	411	3:21	139
6:37	362	16:9	283	3:27	442
6:37-39	26	16:13	25, 26	3:29	255
6:41-42	26	16:16	348	4:4-26	33
6:47-49	25	16:19-21	184	4:23-24	455
7:3	436	16:19-31	94, 186, 389	4:36	111
7:18-23	94	17:3-4	445, 455	4:46	434
7:22	194	17:4	456	4:46-54	33
7:25	184	17:26-31	103	5:3	434
7:38	384, 439	18:6	192	5:8	442
7:46	439	18:14	246, 357	5:14	444
7:50	231	18:20	216	5:17	139
8:14	323	18:21	25	5:24	132
8:18	192	18:35	411	5:29	309
8:55	258	19:1-10	98	5:33	455
9:38	187	19:10	442	6:26	231
9:47	189	19:41	384, 411	6:28-29	139
10:5	231	21	406	7:3-5	15, 16
10:9	411	21:8	411	7:12	453
10:11	411	21:9	308, 321	7:47	453
10:19	334	21:19	404	8:9	436
10:30	74	21:20	411	8:15-16	362
10:34	438	21:26	385	8:28	179
11:4	115	21:31	415	8:31	154
11:9	329	22:1	411	8:32	455
11:9-11	25	22:15	451	8:40	455
11:13	85	22:28	75	8:44-46	455
11:34	88	22:32	456	9:2-3	444

9:4	139	3:16	82	13:40	385
11:1-3	434	3:13-21	130	13:45	200
11:2	439	3:14	398	13:50	199
11:12	442	4:1-4	199	14:9	441
11:33	384	4:5	436	14:15	166
11:55	352	4:12	202	14:23	436
12:3	253	4:13	31	15	12, 18, 22, 24,
12:32	179	4:23	436		26, 28, 260, 261
12:40	447	4:27	439	15:1-5	35, 261
13:15	416	4:30	440	15:2	18, 436
13:17	146	4:32-35	94, 194	15:4	436
13:34-35	158, 208	5:33-39	35	15:6	436
14:6	132, 455	5:41	72, 73	15:7	193
14:17	455	6:1	32, 230	15:13	15, 24, 192
15:12	189	6:9	182	15:13-21	18, 62, 67
15:26	455	6:10	347	15:13-35	18
16:13	455	7:22	219	15:14	24
17:11	189	7:23-29	390	15:14-21	24
17:17	455	7:35	390	15:16-18	67
17:21-23	189	7:52	398, 417	15:17	24
18:38	455	8:1	66, 68	15:19	24, 456
19	17	8:3	322	15:19-21	18
19:23	306	9:1-2	198, 322	15:21	18, 185
19:25-27	16	9:2	182	15:22	436
19:28	206	9:14	198	15:23	24, 68
19:30	206	9:15	201	15:23-29	61
21:7	230	9:21	322	15:25	24
		9:31	68	15:29	24
Acts		9:35	456	16:13	185
1	17	9:37	434	16:17	242
1:1	219	9:41	442	16:18	440
1:13	14, 15, 322	10:34	455	16:19	199
1:13-14	17	10:38	198, 439	16:36	231
2	5, 158, 338	11:19	68	18:6	200
2:16-17	390	11:19-30	2	18:18	441
2:17	389	11:21	456	18:21	376
2:19	373	11:27-30	126	18:26	275
2:24	457	11:29	68	19:13	440
2:29	70	11:30	436	19:15	242
2:36	399	12	22	19:18	445
2:38	202	12:2	15, 62	19:32	437
2:42-46	194	12:17	15, 17, 18	19:39-40	437
2:43-47	94	13:1	270	20:17	436
3:6	440	13:8	347	20:35	435
3:7	442	13:10	334	21	22

21:13	384	2:17	377	8:23	131
21:17-26	260	2:20	455	8:28	252
21:18	12, 15, 18, 19, 62	2:23	377	8:28-30	78-80
21:18-25	28	2:27	206	8:29	5
21:20	35	3:12	411	9:3	70
21:20-21	326	3:13	290	9:5	291
21:20-26	19	3:14	304	9:11	309
21:23	441	3:16	353	9:29	393
21:24	352	3:20	253	9:31-32	253
21:26	352	3:23-26	246	10:13	201, 442
21:30	199	3:28	253, 262	11:2	243
22:4	322	4:4-5	139	11:11	274
22:14	398	4:5	246	11:16	131
22:19	322	4:9-11	253	11:18	223
23:12-13	326	4:11-12	253	11:28	334
24:4	313	4:17	130	12:1-2	253
24:18	352	4:18	253	12:2	81
26:2	71	4:19	435	12:8	88
26:5	163, 306	4:22	253	12:9	315
26:10-11	322	5:2-3	97	12:12	110
26:18	456	5:2-5	73, 74	12:14	293
27:22	433	5:3	271, 404	12:19	206, 208, 408
27:25	433	5:3-5	78-80	12:19-21	405
27:41	74	5:10	334	13:9	206, 208, 216,
28:27	447	5:12-21	458		217
		6:1-12	261	13:10	139
Romans		6:3-4	457	13:11	271
1:5	227	6:9	271, 457	13:14	323
1:9	427	6:12	323	14:1	190
1:10	376	6:16	243	14:1–15:7	455
1:18	455	6:17-18	227	14:4	362
1:21	190	7	92, 119, 323,	14:17	309
1:24	323		324, 339	14:23	378
1:25	291, 455	7:5	448	15:8	455
1:29	314	7:7-8	323	15:9	434
1:30	361	7:7-13	122	15:14	314
2	148	7:8	233	15:30-32	431
2:1	362	7:19	118	16:5	131
2:6-8	227	7:21-23	324		
2:6-16	263	7:24	353	**1 Corinthians**	
2:7	110	8:2	158, 458	1:20	299
2:10	139	8:7	334	1:21	442
2:13	146, 246	8:11	130	1:27-29	194
2:14-15	369	8:19-24	130	1:29	357
2:14-16	147	8:22	414	2:6	81, 87

2:6-16	81	12:9-10	237	4:4	5
2:8	178, 179	12:28	270, 438	4:14	271
2:14	307	12:30	438	5:1	306
3:8	111	13:2	227, 256	5:1-10	219
3:10	299	13:4	405	5:2	414
3:10-15	219	13:10	81	5:4	414
3:10-17	415	13:12	152	5:10	247, 253, 309,
3:13	253	14:2	192		415
3:14	111	14:8	321	5:17	130
3:16	243	14:15	434	6:1	252
3:17	286	14:20	81, 82	6:4	404
3:18	163	14:23	184	6:4-7	132
3:20	166, 190	14:33	289, 309	6:6	315
4:5	362	15	407	7:5	322
4:19	376	15:7	17, 18, 62	7:8	251
4:21	302	15:17	166	7:9-10	353
5	455	15:20	131	8:1-9	73
5:6	243	15:22	130	8:2	88
6:2	199	15:23	406	8:9	179
6:2-3	243	15:25-26	334	9:8	256
6:4	199	15:26	130	9:11	88
6:7-8	391	15:32	227	9:13	88
6:9	243	15:40	306	10:1	302, 314
6:15	243, 332	15:44	307	10:5-6	227
6:16	243	15:45	130	11:2	312, 332
6:19	243	15:46	307	11:3	88
7:5	391	15:49	5	11:7	357
7:34	258	15:54-56	457	11:21	435
8:4-6	64	15:58	271	11:29	435
8:6	234	16:15	131	12:9	206
8:7-13	455	16:16	252	12:12	110
8:11-12	435			12:15	330
9:5	15	**2 Corinthians**		12:20	304, 308, 361
9:13	243	1:6	79, 404	13:11	425
9:24	243	1:9	442		
10:11	390	1:12	88	**Galatians**	
10:12	163	1:17	426	1:13	301
10:13	75, 116, 348	1:17-18	429	1:18-19	260
10:23–11:1	455	1:21	439	1:19	15, 17, 260
11:14-15	183	1:23	427	1:20	427
11:17-34	5	3:6	130	1:23	322
11:30	444	3:7	457	2	28, 261
12–14	189, 276	3:16	456	2:4-5	261
12:6	448	3:18	5	2:5	455
12:9	438	4:2	455	2:7	261

2:9	12, 15, 17, 62, 260, 261	**Ephesians**		**Colossians**	
		1:4	194	1:5-6	455
2:10	126, 261	1:13	455	1:11	110
2:11-14	2, 11, 29	1:20	448	1:15	5
2:12	15, 17, 19, 62, 260, 261	2:8-9	353	1:21	334
		2:14	334	1:24	74
2:15-21	246, 252, 332	2:16	334	1:28	81, 82, 87
2:16	255	4:1-5	189	2:18	163
3:3	307	4:6	234	3:22	88
3:5	448	4:11	270	4:2-4	431
3:6	253	4:13	81	4:12	81, 82
3:7-8	245	4:22	301		
3:7-9	253	4:25	455	**1 Thessalonians**	
3:10-11	253	5:9	317	1:3	110
3:11-12	246	5:19	434	1:9	456
3:15–4:7	245	5:22-32	332	2:15	417
3:16	253	6:5	88	2:19	406
3:21	130	6:10-17	346	3:3	72
4:9	306	6:13	348	3:5	75
4:13	307	6:14-17	183	3:13	406, 410
4:21-31	307	6:18-20	431	4:15	219, 406
5	45, 119			4:17	219
5:1	451	**Philippians**		5:1	407
5:3	211, 212	1:8	427	5:13	71
5:6	252, 256	1:17	304	5:14	405, 455
5:13-14	157, 158	2:3	71, 304	5:16-18	431
5:13-16	82	2:5-11	357	5:23	406
5:13-26	307	2:6	71	5:25	431
5:14	206, 208	2:9-11	201		
5:17	324	2:10	306	**2 Thessalonians**	
5:18	253	2:13	353, 448	1:4	404
5:19-21	85	2:14	190	2	407
5:19-23	309	2:19	376	2:1	406
5:20	304	2:24	376	2:8-9	406
5:22	253	2:26-27	434	2:10	455
5:22-23	79	3:6	140	2:13	131
6:1-2	455	3:7-8	71	2:17	410
6:3	163	3:8	370	3:1-5	431
6:4	256	3:10	252	3:14-15	455
6:4-6	227	3:15	81, 82		
6:6-10	126	3:18	334	**1 Timothy**	
6:9	379	3:19	306	1:5	315
6:10	230	4:5	314	1:7	271
6:13-14	377	4:12	231	2:8	190
		4:15	126	3:3	314

3:15	455	3:10	453	1:2	25, 70, 72, 73,
3:16	178	4:1	455		74, 76, 77, 94,
4:3	455	4:16	350		96, 108, 110,
4:12	301	5:2	313, 453		125, 192, 368,
4:16	459	5:11–6:8	227		404
5:3-20	230	5:14	82	1:2-4	45, 69, 70, 73,
5:6	394	6:3	376		74, 75, 76, 78,
5:17	271, 436	6:13-20	427		84, 86, 87, 89,
5:19	436	6:15	405		93, 94, 96, 97,
5:22	312	9:26	390		105, 106, 109,
6:3	270	10	412		110, 115, 121,
6:5	391	10:25	411		123, 133, 149,
6:11	79	10:26	455		154, 161, 162,
6:14	172	10:30	408		171, 422, 432
		10:32	110	1:2-11	94, 106
2 Timothy		10:32-39	404, 405	1:2-12	115, 121
1:5	315	11	417, 256	1:2-15	105, 123
2:9	432	11:2	436	1:2-18	68, 110, 113,
2:10, 12	110	11:8	372		115, 126, 129,
2:15	455	11:11	72		133, 402
2:23	322	11:17-19	249	1:2-27	68, 133
3:1	390	11:24-28	390	1:3	111, 113, 232
3:3	453	11:26	72	1:3-4	70, 161, 419
3:4	333	11:31	257	1:3-8	68
3:8	347	11:33	139	1:4	25, 40, 46, 81,
4:3	270	11:34	321		84, 86, 125, 149,
4:4	455	12:1-3	112		252, 275
4:5	432	12:2-3	109	1:4-5	84, 137
4:15	347	12:3	441	1:5	25, 42, 44, 82,
		12:7	110		84, 88, 123, 125,
Titus		12:11	317		128, 149, 311,
1:5	436	12:16-17	353		423, 433
1:9	271	13:9	410	1:5-6	329
1:11	370	13:17	414	1:5-8	76, 80, 83, 84,
2:8	309	13:18-19	431		85, 86, 89, 94,
3:2	314				105, 123, 128,
3:3	323, 453	**James**			133, 161
3:4-7	130	1–2	6	1:5-11	105
3:9	322	1:1	13, 23, 28, 37,	1:6	26, 232, 315, 433
			38, 39, 42, 44,	1:6-7	188
Philemon			59, 61, 70, 183,	1:6-8	84, 88, 323, 329,
22	431		292, 369, 375,		440
			408, 437	1:7	92
Hebrews		1:1-2	24	1:7-8	149, 375
1:2	389, 390	1:1-4	105	1:8	46, 289, 309,
2:10	252				314, 352

1:9   71, 76, 94, 96,
    97, 98, 112, 185,
    368, 377
1:9-10   96, 108
1:9-11   45, 46, 47, 69,
    73, 80, 84, 94,
    97, 98, 104, 105,
    110, 149, 154,
    161, 175, 180,
    184, 185, 194,
    195, 198, 301,
    344, 356, 357,
    368, 371, 383,
    384, 391, 393,
    432
1:10   98, 100, 131,
    356, 369, 377,
    388
1:10-11   120, 185, 383,
    386
1:11   23, 66, 99, 100,
    101, 102, 103
1:12   24, 44, 45, 46,
    65, 73, 97, 105,
    106, 108, 109,
    110, 111, 113,
    138, 148, 149,
    161, 166, 196,
    208, 209, 241,
    363, 419
1:12-14   110, 432
1:12-15   41, 434
1:12-18   69, 84, 110,
    116, 122, 134,
    424
1:13   42, 110, 117,
    123, 128
1:13-15   23, 44, 47, 66,
    75, 76, 80, 86,
    92, 116, 122,
    123, 137, 149,
    154, 161, 165,
    323, 348
1:13-18   105, 106, 110,
    114, 117
1:13-21   94
1:14   120

1:14-15   124, 209, 210,
    323, 388
1:15   73, 108, 121,
    130, 210, 252,
    379, 458
1:16   24, 71, 122, 123,
    129, 192
1:16-18   123, 154
1:17   40, 42, 44, 81,
    122, 123, 124,
    125, 126, 129,
    130, 176, 275,
    306
1:17-18   423
1:18   40, 43, 47, 69,
    70, 82, 100, 114,
    119, 122, 124,
    126, 129, 130,
    132, 144, 149,
    155, 161, 206,
    247, 305, 338,
    339, 454
1:19   24, 133, 134,
    135, 136, 138,
    140, 141, 142,
    145, 192, 219,
    267, 332, 404
1:19-20   46, 140, 142,
    161, 164, 166,
    175
1:19-21   45, 46, 75, 76,
    80, 81, 86, 92,
    100, 116, 133,
    134, 138, 145,
    149, 154, 189,
    206, 217, 276,
    284, 289, 301,
    315, 320, 351,
    405, 409, 413,
    424, 446, 449
1:19-27   133, 175, 221,
    223, 251, 258,
    313, 382
1:20   25, 42, 73, 76,
    86, 97, 108, 117,
    133, 137, 138,
    139, 149, 161,

    166, 209, 304,
    317, 393, 397,
    399
1:21   40, 44, 45, 46,
    47, 94, 133, 138,
    141, 142, 144,
    145, 146, 149,
    150, 152, 155,
    161, 206, 220,
    229, 274, 302,
    338, 339, 350,
    442, 457
1:21-27   379
1:22   33, 145, 146,
    147, 149, 150,
    153, 155, 158,
    162, 165, 243,
    314
1:22-23   152
1:22-25   25, 81, 133,
    144, 145, 146,
    161, 219, 363
1:22-27   46, 227, 258, 301
1:23   151, 152, 155,
    284
1:23-24   47, 146, 150,
    154, 158
1:24   153, 154
1:25   24, 40, 44, 45,
    86, 140, 144,
    146, 149, 152,
    153, 154, 158,
    160, 204, 205,
    206, 207, 209,
    220, 224, 228,
    275, 363
1:25-26   121
1:25-27   204, 205, 209,
    274
1:26   46, 47, 81, 163,
    164, 165, 219,
    233, 267, 304,
    352, 410, 424
1:26-27   16, 45, 46, 51,
    73, 133, 160,
    162, 172, 189,
    205, 206, 223,

	246, 301, 314, 315, 327, 344, 432		289, 293, 301, 314, 317, 327		138, 204, 205, 207, 209, 214, 218, 220, 222, 224, 379, 388
1:27	23, 24, 42, 46, 76, 163, 164, 165, 167, 175, 219, 283, 284, 314, 332, 423	2:2-7	205	2:10	25, 45, 214, 215, 218, 274, 284
		2:3	117, 186, 187		
		2:4	45, 175, 184, 186, 187, 188, 189, 351, 377, 415	2:10-11	204, 205, 211, 214, 217, 218
2	29, 194	2:4-7	323	2:11	121, 204, 210, 215, 217, 326, 397, 405, 423
2:1	6, 38, 39, 43, 44, 175, 177, 180, 185, 188, 189, 192, 195, 197, 201, 205, 218, 223, 224, 228, 229, 232, 237, 240, 243, 257, 260, 292, 369, 375, 408, 437	2:5	24, 42, 44, 73, 112, 172, 192, 193, 196, 208, 230, 232, 241, 283, 332, 423	2:12	44, 125, 158, 204, 205, 207, 214, 218, 220, 221, 222, 224, 267, 388, 415
		2:5-6	383, 386	2:12-13	45, 73, 121, 205, 211, 218, 315, 362, 415
		2:5-7	46, 76, 110, 173, 184, 185, 205, 258, 351, 368, 386, 410	2:13	25, 42, 46, 204, 205, 218, 221, 222, 223, 224, 313, 314, 318, 342, 378, 423, 429
2:1-4	46, 47, 76, 173, 175, 176, 185, 189, 224, 227, 251, 257, 258, 386, 432, 444	2:6	186, 196, 198, 199, 230		
		2:6-7	46, 76, 99, 100, 187, 196, 197, 198, 369, 396		
2:1-7	68, 137, 185, 204, 393, 397, 400	2:7	24, 76, 100, 187, 198, 205, 360, 417	2:14	46, 144, 160, 166, 192, 224, 225, 226, 228, 229, 231, 232, 233, 243, 247, 258, 295, 368, 442, 457
2:1-11	219	2:8	6, 26, 40, 43, 44, 144, 204, 205, 206, 207, 208, 209, 218, 220, 221, 241, 275, 363, 388		
2:1-12	65, 313, 320, 344				
2:1-13	49, 67, 73, 81, 98, 99, 133, 176, 218, 221, 223, 315, 413			2:14-16	185, 232, 241, 360
		2:8-9	121, 125, 189, 204, 205, 215	2:14-17	45, 46, 47, 73, 81, 175, 189, 206, 223, 224, 226, 227, 251, 253, 314, 315, 344, 351, 379, 382, 386, 393, 432, 444
2:1-17	256, 315, 446	2:8-10	23, 24, 363, 366		
2:1-26	219	2:8-11	24, 35, 44, 45, 47, 86, 97, 113, 136, 144, 148, 158, 170		
2:2	67, 98, 99, 100, 181, 183, 184, 187, 188, 437				
		2:8-12	158		
2:2-3	175, 188, 190, 196, 197, 387	2:8-13	173, 204, 209, 210, 228, 246, 255, 258, 274, 315	2:14-26	37, 46, 49, 133, 146, 224, 227, 228, 260, 261, 262, 265, 301
2:2-4	99, 181, 186, 187, 204, 205, 209, 214, 218, 221, 222, 223, 224, 228, 239,				
		2:9	6, 45, 46, 76,	2:15	82, 230, 314

487

2:15-16	76, 224, 226, 232, 239	2:25-26	45		279, 280, 298, 377
2:15-17	258	2:26	166, 225, 242, 256, 258, 338, 394	3:5-6	267, 276, 388
2:16	117, 225, 230, 231, 314, 316, 394			3:6	276, 280, 281, 283, 290, 307, 335, 388, 394
2:17	46, 160, 166, 225, 226, 232, 233, 243, 247, 258	3:1	26, 192, 266, 267, 271, 275, 299, 300, 320, 332, 359, 360, 362, 368, 435	3:7-8	267, 286, 288
				3:8	287, 290, 298, 309, 314
2:18	114, 117, 175, 225, 232, 233, 235, 236, 237, 238, 241, 244, 258	3:1-2	267, 275, 286, 290, 298, 320, 359	3:9	23, 42, 143, 151, 189, 293, 294, 303, 360, 408, 434, 450
		3:1-12	49, 75, 81, 137, 164, 166, 189, 206, 219, 223, 243, 265, 266, 267, 269, 290, 298, 301, 320, 331, 334, 351, 413	3:9-10	290
2:18-19	46, 225, 237, 305			3:9-11	286
2:18-26	223, 224, 225, 235			3:9-12	47, 267
				3:10	192, 290, 291, 351, 360
2:19	42, 44, 65, 177, 209, 229, 235, 236, 239, 243, 247, 256, 258, 351			3:11	290, 295
				3:11-12	360
		3:1-18	142, 320, 321	3:12	192, 290, 295, 296
		3:1–4:3	342		
		3:1–4:10	26, 344, 359	3:13	137, 142, 160, 172, 223, 266, 267, 268, 274, 275, 296, 298, 299, 300, 303, 305, 321, 358
2:20	166, 225, 232, 241, 242, 243, 252, 255, 258, 351	3:1–4:11	366		
		3:1–4:12	45, 46, 49, 51, 133, 265, 266, 267, 269, 274, 276, 298, 308, 314, 315, 329, 342, 352, 359, 360, 361, 368, 378, 379, 424, 436, 446		
2:20-21	360			3:13-16	360
2:20-23	255			3:13-18	46, 47, 73, 86, 175, 206, 266, 271, 276, 289, 298, 303, 307, 320, 321, 409
2:20-25	416				
2:20-26	23, 177, 225, 235, 242, 246				
2:21	239, 245, 247, 255, 397, 449	3:2	40, 46, 81, 86, 121, 267, 274, 275, 276, 277, 288, 360, 394	3:13–4:6	356
2:21-23	65			3:13–4:10	47
2:21-24	242, 246, 258			3:13–4:12	75, 86, 117, 137, 138, 279, 313
2:22	40, 166, 232, 244, 251, 254, 255, 275	3:2-3	26, 164, 276		
		3:2-12	273		
2:23	23, 29, 42, 46, 63, 177, 244, 247, 255, 397	3:3	267, 276, 277, 394	3:14	137, 172, 223, 303, 305, 308, 326, 327, 328, 337, 338, 352, 360, 410, 454
		3:3-6	286		
2:24	160, 232, 239, 262, 449	3:3-12	267, 274, 275, 320		
2:24-25	397	3:4	267, 276, 418	3:14-16	81, 189, 279, 298, 303, 351
2:25	65, 242, 258	3:5	275, 276, 278,		

3:14-18	299, 303	4:2-4	217		359, 360, 361,
3:15	85, 125, 126,	4:3	320, 328, 329,		413, 415, 446
	172, 290, 298,		330, 433, 441	4:11-16	219
	303, 305, 306,	4:4	42, 46, 47, 167,	4:11-17	81
	348, 351, 426		172, 243, 255,	4:11–5:6	402
3:15-17	47		283, 321, 331,	4:12	73, 144, 202,
3:16	289, 303, 304,		334, 351, 352,		229, 351, 359,
	308, 309, 326,		359, 360, 368		360, 362, 363,
	327, 337	4:4-6	340, 344		364, 442, 457
3:16-18	307	4:5	47, 72, 138, 321,	4:13	117, 184, 368,
3:17	85, 125, 126,		331, 338, 339,		369, 370, 374,
	221, 298, 303,		340, 342, 343,		375, 377, 379,
	306, 309, 311,		360		381, 383, 404,
	314, 316, 317,	4:5-6	336, 337, 340		418
	352	4:5-10	119	4:13-17	47, 68, 73, 98,
3:17-18	46, 298, 303,	4:6	23, 42, 47, 138,		99, 103, 197,
	308, 311		185, 320, 331,		206, 368, 369,
3:18	18, 25, 73, 76,		337, 339, 340,		381, 383, 393,
	85, 86, 94, 97,		341, 342, 343,		402
	108, 137, 139,		349, 357, 399	4:13–5:6	46, 47, 49,
	142, 161, 166,	4:6-7	315		103, 313, 344,
	189, 303, 309,	4:7	47, 307, 347,		356, 367, 368,
	318, 378, 397,		357, 358, 426		369, 381, 382,
	409	4:7-8	42		383, 384, 405,
4:1	47, 308, 309,	4:7-9	357		414, 446
	316, 320, 321,	4:7-10	23, 320, 329,	4:13–5:11	368, 402, 419
	322, 328, 330,		340, 342, 344,	4:14	103, 368, 371,
	334, 360		346, 349, 351,		374, 418
4:1-2	46, 76, 137, 138,		359, 360	4:14-17	371
	142, 217, 313	4:7-11	42, 73	4:15	42, 368, 369,
4:1-3	137, 165, 189,	4:8	304, 350, 351,		370, 371, 374,
	321, 339, 344,		357, 358, 359,		375
	360		360, 410	4:15-16	374, 418
4:1-4	206, 351, 446	4:9	25, 353, 358,	4:15-17	370
4:1-6	81, 279, 359,		384, 385	4:16	305, 368, 370,
	368, 409, 413	4:10	42, 142, 357,		371, 374, 375,
4:1-10	47, 175, 219,		358, 359, 408		377, 378
	266, 275, 276,	4:11	6, 42, 192, 243,	4:16-17	279, 369
	320, 360		266, 359, 360,	4:17	47, 209, 332,
4:1-12	80, 92, 117, 223,		361, 362, 363,		371, 378, 418
	289, 293, 301,		364, 404	5	3
	404, 405	4:11-12	7, 23, 24, 26,	5:1	353, 381, 382,
4:2	304, 315, 320,		43, 44, 45, 137,		385, 386, 404,
	323, 325, 327,		142, 188, 189,		418
	328, 329, 334,		190, 206, 266,	5:1-5	3
	337, 393, 397,		276, 279, 315,	5:1-6	45, 46, 47, 68,
	433				

	73, 76, 81, 98, 99, 110, 137, 142, 175, 185, 197, 198, 218, 219, 301, 314, 315, 317, 351, 368, 369, 381, 382, 383, 384, 389, 390, 395, 399, 400, 402, 405, 410, 419, 432, 444	5:8-9	189		453, 458, 459, 461
		5:9	26, 176, 192, 362, 403, 404, 413, 415, 416, 418, 419, 425, 426, 429	5:20	6, 73, 144, 176, 210, 229, 351, 379, 442, 453, 458, 459, 460
		5:10	26, 43, 65, 401, 403, 404, 414, 418, 433	**1 Peter**	
				1:3-5	130
		5:10-11	23, 42, 73, 76, 375, 403, 404, 408, 416, 419	1:6	75
5:1-11	404	5:11	40, 65, 79, 401, 402, 404, 405, 417, 418, 419, 425	1:6-7	73, 74, 78-80, 111
5:2	386, 395			1:14	323
5:2-3	382, 386, 387			1:15	301
5:2-6	26			1:18	166
5:3	385, 386, 390, 393, 394, 395	5:12	6, 26, 44, 176, 192, 219, 315, 362, 404, 423, 424, 425, 426, 427, 429	1:22	315, 352, 455
				1:23	130
5:4	6, 23, 42, 176, 388, 390, 399, 400, 408, 410, 413, 418, 423			2:1	361
				2:2-3	130
		5:12–20	402, 403, 452, 461	2:9	194
5:4-6	386			2:11	323, 324
5:5	23, 304, 352, 383, 394, 410	5:13	76, 433, 449	2:12	301, 361
		5:13-16	449	2:15	379
5:5-6	393	5:13-18	45, 423, 431, 442	2:20	110, 379, 400
5:6	214, 217, 326, 383, 394, 397, 399, 400, 405, 414, 415, 418, 423, 449			2:24	448
		5:13-20	214, 313, 424	2:25	453
		5:14	42, 67, 183, 271, 432, 433, 436, 437, 440	3:1-2	301
				3:2	312
				3:6	379
5:7	76, 80, 99, 180, 192, 292, 403, 404, 408, 414, 418, 423	5:14-15	329, 375, 445, 453	3:16	301, 361
				3:17	379
		5:15	42, 81, 210, 232, 443, 448, 457	3:18	398
5:7-8	42, 219, 375, 385, 408, 413, 416			4:2-3	323
		5:15-16	87, 379	4:7	412
		5:16	210, 432, 445	4:7-11	412
5:7-9	73, 190	5:17	23, 65, 433, 449, 451	4:8	206, 208, 425, 455, 459, 460
5:7-11	7, 45, 46, 116, 142, 368, 381, 381, 393, 394, 402, 404, 405, 419, 446			4:12-14	72
		5:17-18	416	4:12-19	405, 412
		5:18	433, 451	4:14-16	202
		5:19	192, 305, 404, 459	4:15	326, 405
				4:18	442
5:7-20	402, 425, 453	5:19-20	43, 45, 47, 233, 423, 424, 431, 435, 443, 452,	5:1	270
5:8	304, 352, 403, 414			5:5	343, 347, 436
				5:5-9	346
				5:6	357

5:9	348	2:29	398	8:5	388
		3:3	312, 352	9:7	321
2 Peter		3:7	398, 453	9:9	321
1:5-8	78-80	3:9	82	10:6	427
1:10	274	3:11	206, 208	11:2-3	451
1:16	407	3:15	327	11:12	334
2:1	271	3:18	219	11:18	111
2:3	370	3:21-22	329	12:4	127
2:6	416	3:23	206, 208	12:9	453
2:7	301	4:12	252	12:14	451
2:9	75	4:17	206, 208	13:6	200
2:13	323	4:18	81	13:10	405
2:15	453	5:16-17	455	13:14	453
3:1-4	390			14:10	388
3:3	407	**2 John**		16:15	230
3:4	407	8	111	17:16	230
3:9	407			18:1	127
3:10-13	130	**3 John**		18:8	388
3:11	301	15	255	18:9	384
3:12	407			18:11	384
3:14	172	**Jude**		18:11-13	184
3:15	72	1	15, 17	18:15	384
		18	390	18:19	384
1 John		19	307	18:23	453
1:5	127	20	431	19:7	332
1:5-7	82	22-23	455	19:17-21	395
1:6	227			19:20	453
1:8	274, 453, 455	**Revelation**		19:21	231
1:8-9	445	2:1	201	20:1	127
2:1	398	2:9	182	20:3	453
2:3-6	256	2:13	201	20:8	453
2:9-11	82	2:20	453	20:10	453
2:15-17	332	3:9	182	21–22	5
2:16	376	3:10	75	21:1-4	131
2:18	390	3:12	202	21:9	332
2:21	455	3:17	353	22:12	111
2:26	453	3:20	415		
2:28	407	6:9-11	400		

INDEX OF EXTRABIBLICAL
ANCIENT LITERATURE

References in footnotes are not indexed unless the text is discussed.

OLD TESTAMENT		2:4-5	373	13:13	243
APOCRYPHA		2:10	22	14:5	243
		2:10-20	396	14:27	163
Tobit		2:16-17	422	15:3	82
1:3-9	169	2:19	313	15:9	441
1:8	169	3:19	422	17:7	377
2:6	356	4:16	441		
3	445	5:1-10	376	**Sirach**	
4:10	458	5:7-8	377	1:1	306
4:14	391	6:12-14	86	1:9	306
6	348	7:5-6	151	1:22	138
6:8	348	7:7	306, 311	3:3	458
8:1-3	348	7:15	86	3:17	302
12:9-10	458	7:22-23	309	3:29	148
13:12	107	7:23-26	86	4:10	168
13:14	107	7:24-27	312	4:17	86
		7:26	151	5:11	136
Judith		7:27	255	6:37	410
9	445	7:29-30	128	7:35	438
12:18	151	8–9	86	10:3-31	179
16:7	439	8:21	86, 306	11:1	179
16:17	388	9:4	306	11:4	179
		9:6	87	11:12-13	179
Wisdom		9:9-18	310	11:27	158-59
1:1-2	88	10:5	249	12:11	387
1:11	361	12:10	143	15:11-20	117, 121
2:1-9	372	12:18	313	18:19-21	443

19:16	273	**1 Maccabees**		19	250	
20:14-15	88	1:26	436	19:9	255	
21:5	392	2:49-64	416			
22:16-17	410	2:51-52	249, 254	**1 Enoch**		
23:1	292	2:54	304	38:2	398	
23:4-5	292	2:58	304	53:6	398	
23:8	343	9:41	356	94–97	381	
24:7-8	310	14:28	436	94:8	381	
26:29–27:2	371			94:9	381	
27:11	128	**2 Maccabees**		95:2-3	381	
27:15	343, 344	4:12	183	95:7	381	
27:28	343	6:13	74	96:1	381	
28:1-9	222	6:16	74	96:5	381	
28:12	291	6:21-31	416	96:8	396	
28:13-14	282	8:15	200	97:3	381	
28:18-22	282	9:7	74	97:5	381	
28:22-23	286	9:8	376	97:8	381	
31:26	344	11:24-26	433	97:10	381	
32:12	343	12:38	352			
35:10-15	179	15:6	376	**2 Enoch**		
35:17	392			22:8-9	439	
36:25	414	**3 Maccabees**		44:2	293	
37:12	274	6:16-29	127	50:2-6	395	
38:9	438					
38:15	443	**4 Maccabees**	125	**Joseph and Aseneth**		
39:6	306	1:26	376	14:1-7	127	
44–50	416	1:32	307			
44:16	416	2:15	376	**Odes of Solomon**		
44:19-20	248	5:16-34	212	13:1	151	
48:1-2	304	7:13	441			
48:1-12	450	8:19	376	**Psalms of Solomon**		
49:9	420	12:3	422	9:6-7	445	
51:19	355	14:2	156	10:1-4	41	
		18:12	304	12:1-4	286	
				15:1	433	
Baruch						
6:11	387	**PSEUDEPIGRAPHA**		**Sibylline Oracles**		
6:24	387			2:87	285	
		2 Baruch		3:32-33	290	
1 Esdras		78:2	61			
8:71-74	355			**Testament of Benjamin**		
		Jubilees		5:2	349	
		11–12	252	6:5	291	
2 Esdras		17–18	249			
3:14	255	17:15-18	249	**Testament of Dan**		
7:109	450	18:13	249	6:2	349	

5:1	349	7:14-15	398	4QMMT	48
		9:27-31	291		
Testament of Gad		13:12	392	**11Q10**	
4:6-7	326	13:26-27	290	38:1-9	422
5:1	290	13:27	290		
5:9-11	443	15:10	273		
		15:16	357	**PHILO**	
Testament of Issachar					
7:7	349	**1QHa**		**De Abrahamo**	
		7:14-15	398	191-99	250
Testament of Judah				273	254, 255
22:2	408	**1QM**			
		14:2	351	**De Confusione**	
Testament of Naphtali				**Linguarum**	
8:4	349	**1QS**	333	181	252
		3:13-26	41		
Testament of Reuben		3:21–4:3	324	**De Decalogo**	
1:6-7	443	4:2-6	300	84	428
		4:2-17	299	93	291
Testament of Simeon		4:9-11	361	113	287
3	325, 328	6:8-9	436	151-53	324
3:5	348-49	8	213	173	280
		10	157		
Testament of Zebulun		10:1-3, 10	113	**De Fuga et Inventione**	
5	443	11:6	300	79-80	123
		11:10-11	375		
Testament of Job				**Legum Allegoriae**	
27:3-7	421	**1QS20**		3.224	277
		19:25	300	3.228	252
Sentences of Pseudo-				3.27	255
Phocylides	3, 6, 285, 391	**1Q26**	7		
				De Migratione Abrahami	
		4Q381	392	124	441
DEAD SEA SCROLLS					
		4Q415-418	7	**De Opificio Mundi**	
CD				83-86	276-77
3:2	255	**4Q423**	7	134-35	307
3:20	255				
10:11	351	**4Q470**	147	**Quod Omnis Probus**	
				Liber Sit	
1QH		**4Q504**	143	45-46	155
3:26	120			81	182
4:19	460	**4Q514**	351		
4:31	338			**De Sobrietate**	
5:8	120	**4Q525**	159, 273	56	255
5:26-27	290				

De Somniis	285	4.305-44	412	*m. Taanith*			
		4.377-88	412	2.4	450		
De Virtutibus	216	4.529-44	412	*m. Tamid*			
		5.429-38	412	5.1	113		
De Vita Mosis		5.442-45	412				
1.28	255	5.446-59	412	**Talmud**			
2.216	186	5.512-26	412	*b. Baba Bathra*			
		5.527-33	412	116	438		
		5.548-52	412	*b. Berakoth*			
JOSEPHUS		6.1-8	412	61b	107, 119		
		6.93-110	412				
Against Apion		6.193-213	412	*b. Horayot*			
1.50	32	6.249-66	412	8b	212		
2.171	147	6.288-309	412				
2.203	432	6.351-55	412	*b. Shabbat*			
		6.366-73	412	70b	212		
Antiquities		6.369	412	31b-32b	444		
1.54-57	252	7.44	182				
1.220-36	250			*b. Shevuot*			
2.201	394			30a	186		
2.271	163	**RABBINIC**		31a	186		
5.7-15	257	**LITERATURE**					
5.93	292			**Midrash**			
13.171	375	**Mishnah**		*Genesis Rabbah*			
14.22	450	*m. Avot*		9	119		
15.371	427	1:17	148				
17.172	438	3:8	159-60				
18.11-25	375	3:15	375	**EARLY CHRISTIAN**			
20.199-200	20	5:12	160	**LITERATURE**			
		5:14	148				
Jewish War		6:2	157	**Augustine**			
1.657-58	439			*Letters*			
2.119-66	375	*m. Bekhorot*	170	75	18		
2.135	427	*m. Berakot*					
2.139-42	427	5:5	438	*De Natura et Gratia*			
2.252-94	412	7:3	200	16	289		
2.285, 289	182	9:3	330				
2.297-308	412			**Letter of Barnabas**	3		
2.457-80	412	*m. Horayot*	147	1:2	143		
2.494-98	412	*m. Hullin*		2:6	158		
2.570	436	4.7-8	19	6:7	399		
2.577	314			9:9	143		
3.36-39	412	*m. Shabbat*		10:3	394		
3.414-27	412	2.6	444	19:10	458		
3.59-63	412			19:12	446		
3.522-31	412	*m. Shevuot*		20:2	361		
		4.13	428				

1 Clement 3
3:4–4:13 326
4–6 417
5–6 326
10:1 255
10:7 245
12 257
12:1 245
16:7 395
17:2 255
21:5 377
30 361
30:2 343
31 361
35:5 361
36:2 151
46:1 417
51:2 74
62:1 163
63:1 417

2 Clement
8:6 172
16:4 458
17:1-3 455

Didache 3
1 458
1:1-2 41
3:1-6 327
3:2 137, 326
3:7-10 327
4:6 458
4:14 445
13:1-2 270
15:1-2 270

Eusebius
Church History
2.1.5 20
2.23 20-22, 30, 157, 398
3.25 30
3.27.1 36
4.5.3 11
7.19.1 11

Gregory of Nyssa
Life of St. Macrina 72

Ignatius
Ephesians
5:3 343
20:1 376

Philadelphians
9:2 405

Philippians
2:2 361
4:3 361

Polycarp
7:1 433

Romans
10:3 80

Smyrnaeans
11:3 81

Irenaeus
Against Heresies
4.16.2 29

Jerome
Letters
112 18

Justin Martyr
Dialogue with Trypho
47 36

***Martyrdom of Perpetua
and Felicitas*** 72

Martyrdom of Polycarp
16.1-2 271
19.2 80

Origen
Commentary on John
19.6 29

Commentary on Romans
4.1 29

Homilies on Joshua
7.1 29

Homilies on Leviticus
2.4 29

De Viris Illustribus
2 30

**2 Apocalypse of
James** 20-22, 30

***Shepherd* of Hermas**
Mandates
3.1-2 339
9 329-30
9 [39] 84
12.1.1-2 288
12.4, 5 347
12.4.2-3 288
12.6.3 365
38.3 361

Similitudes
1.3 353
9.13.2-3 202
9.23.4 365
15.2 202
16.3-4 202
60.1 [5.7.1] 167
64.1.4 394
65.3-5 395
92.3 361
100.2 361

Visions
24.5 172
58.3 405

Teachings of Silvanus 3

Tertullian
Adversus Haereses
4.14.4 255
16.2 255

Adversus Judaeos
2:7 255

OTHER ANCIENT LITERATURE

Aristophanes
Lysistrata — 138

Aristotle
Nicomachean Ethics
8 — 255
8-9 — 333

Athenaeus
The Learned Banqueters — 356

Cicero
De Amicitia — 255

Epictetus
Discourses
1.1.17 — 375
1.21.2 — 243
2.16-17 — 243
3.21.12 — 375
4.1 — 156

22.2 — 375

Galen
De Simpliciter Medicamentum Temperatum
2.10 — 439

Petronius
Satyricon — 356, 394

Pindar
Odes — 112

Plato
Alcibiades
135d — 375

Phaedo
66 — 324
80d — 375

Plutarch
De Audiendis Poetis
12 — 277

De Garrulitate
10 — 276

De Virtute Morali
12 — 313

Essays — 152

Quomodo Adolescens Poetas Audire Debeat — 255

Moralia — 152

Seneca
Moral Epistles
75.1-2 — 61
101 — 375

On the Good Life
15:7 — 156

On the Shortness of Life — 372

Sextus
Sentences — 3